INTRODUCTION TO PERSONALITY

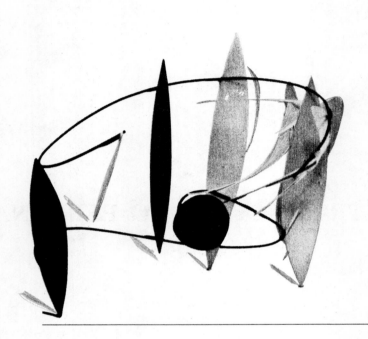

FOURTH EDITION
INTRODUCTION TO PERSONALITY
A New Look

Walter Mischel
Columbia University

Holt, Rinehart and Winston

New York   Chicago   San Francisco   Philadelphia
Montreal   Toronto   London   Sydney
Tokyo   Mexico City   Rio de Janeiro   Madrid

| Cover Art | From a poster by McRay Magleby, BYU Graphics, Provo, Utah. |
| Part Opening Art | *Sidewinder* (1984) by Robert Cronin. $13\frac{1}{2}''$ h. $\times$ $15\frac{1}{2}''$ w. $\times$ 20″ d. Courtesy of Gimpel & Weitzenhoffer Gallery, New York. |

Publisher	Bob Woodbury
Acquiring Editor	Susan Meyers
Senior Project Editor	Gordon Powell
Production Manager	Robin B. Besofsky
Art Director	Gloria Gentile
Photo Researcher	Nicolette Harlan
Text Designer	Arthur Ritter

Library of Congress Cataloging-in-Publication Data

Mischel, Walter.
   Introduction to personality.

   Bibliography: p.
   Includes index.
   1. Personality. I. Title.
BF698.M555   1986   155.2   85-8548
ISBN 0-03-005243-2

CBS COLLEGE PUBLISHING
Holt, Rinehart and Winston
The Dryden Press
Saunders College Publishing

Copyright Acknowledgments

The author is indebted to the following for permission to reprint from copyrighted material:

The American Psychological Association: Figure 1-2 (copyright 1976); Figure 4-3 (copyright 1983).

(continued on page 582)

Preface

THE FOURTH EDITION of *Introduction to Personality* provides a new overview meant to capture the excitement and vigor of the current field of personality while preserving its main historical roots. The text maintains the original objectives and basic perspective that characterized previous editions, but this edition contains substantial changes in organization, contents, and style that are intended to be responsive to major developments in the field and increasingly sensitive to the interests and needs of students. To realize these ambitious intentions, we sought extensive feedback both from students and from consultants, including classroom teachers in a wide range of schools and area experts. The revision attempts to be especially attentive to the advice and experiences that come from the classroom. The major innovations include:

1. Total reorganization of chapter sequence and text organization to give readers a coherent and complete treatment of each major approach to personality before they proceed to the next one.

2. The style was revised to engage student interest and reduce difficulty level in every chapter. The writing is more direct and more examples, more tables and visual features, and more topics of current interest to students are included. The text assumes little preparation, tries to increase the student's involvement, and is easy to understand and master even by the beginner.

3. The point-by-point summaries at the end of each chapter have been retained. They now are supplemented by a detailed outline at the start of each chapter that surveys the topics to be covered. Each chapter also contains *In Focus* boxes that highlight related items of special interest.

4. To enhance the student's sense of the basic contributions of the major theoretical alternatives in the field, the main strengths and weaknesses of each approach are evaluated and summarized simply at the end of each Part.

5. Much of the research previously condensed into the last half of the text is now integrated into the particular approach to which it is most relevant. This change enriches each approach and avoids confronting students with a mass of studies near the end. The final Part of the text is devoted to adaptation and the coping process. It draws heavily on the important applications of personality research that relate clearly to the earlier theoretical ideas as well as to problems that students care about.

6. For a less research-oriented or briefer course, instructors may wish to omit Chapters 4, 7, 10, and 14, which present the research most relevant to each approach. The brief Evaluation and Overview sections at the ends of each of those chapters may be retained even if the chapters themselves are not as-

signed. Likewise, chapters in Part Six may be freely omitted for a briefer course or if supplementary readings beyond the text are employed.

7. The publisher has introduced a new look visually that is designed to be more readable and appealing and that should make mastery of the text more enjoyable and efficient.

8. Instructors and their assistants should obtain from the publisher the greatly expanded Test Manual prepared for this edition by Harriet N. Mischel.

It is a pleasure to thank the many people who have helped to develop this revision. The list is long and includes many reviewers whose comments were of critical importance:

James Calhoun, University of Georgia
Bernardo Carducci, Indiana University
Bertram Cohler, University of Chicago
Amerigo Farina, University of Connecticut
John F. Kihlstrom, University of Wisconsin—Madison
Gerard Mendelsohn, University of California—Berkeley
Tom Randall, Rhode Island College
Jerry Venn, Mary Baldwin College
Brian Yates, American University

Special thanks also are due to Lauren Levine for helping to revise the material dealing with sex typing and sex roles, especially throughout Chapter 17. She provided the perspective and sensitivity that served to sharpen the issues and modernize the presentation of an intriguing but complex topic. Jan Eisenman was of invaluable help in readying the manuscript for composition and compiling the reference materials. Michael Susi contributed greatly both to the preparation of the reference lists and to completion of the glossary and indexes. As in previous editions, Harriet Nerlove Mischel remained deeply involved with the preparation of the revision as well as being responsible for the *Instructor's Test Manual* that accompanies it. Linda C. Mischel provided useful criticisms of manuscript drafts. Finally, Susan Meyers, Gordon Powell, Alison Podel, Robin B. Besofsky, Gloria Gentile, David de Campo, Nicolette Harlan, and the Holt staff made preparation of this edition a pleasure and added immeasurably to the quality of the final work.

Walter Mischel
New York City

Contents in Brief

vii

Contents in Brief
viii

Contents in Full

Contents in Full

Chapter 4
Psychodynamics: Defenses and Unconscious Processes 89

PART THREE
THE TRAIT APPROACH 113

Chapter 5
Trait Theories: Conceptions 115

Contents in Full

Contents in Full

Contents in Full

xiii

Contents in Full

PART FIVE
THE BEHAVIORAL APPROACH
271

Contents in Full

Contents in Full

Contents in Full

Contents in Full

Contents in Full

Contents in Full

INTRODUCTION TO PERSONALITY

PART ONE
INTRODUCTION

Chapter 1
Orientation to Personality

Chapter 1

Orientation to Personality

WHAT IS PERSONALITY?

Charles and Jane both are college freshmen taking an introductory course in economics. Their instructor returns the midterm examination in class, and both receive a D grade. Right after class, Charles goes up to the instructor and seems distressed and upset: He sweats as he talks, his hands tremble slightly, he speaks slowly and softly, almost whispering. His face is flushed and he appears to be on the edge of tears. He apologizes for his "poor performance," accusing himself bitterly: "I really have no good excuse—it was so stupid of me—I just don't know how I could have done such a sloppy job." He spends most of the rest of the day alone in his dormitory, cuts his classes, and writes a long entry in his diary.

Jane, on the other hand, rushes out of the lecture room at the end of class and quickly starts to joke loudly with her friend about the economics course. She makes fun of the course, comments acidly about the instructor's lecture, and seems to pay little attention to her grade as she strides briskly to her next class. In that class (English composition) Jane participates more actively than usual and, surprising her teacher, makes a few excellent comments.

This example illustrates a well-known fact: different people respond differently to similar events. Both students received a D, yet each reacted differently to the experience. Why? How consistent are these differences? Would Charles and Jane show similar differences in their response to a D in physical education? Would each respond similarly if they were fired from their part-time jobs? Would Charles also be apologetic and self-effacing if he received a personal rebuff from a close friend? Will Jane treat a poor grade the same way when she is a senior?

What do the observed differences in the reactions of the two students to their grade suggest about their other characteristics? That is, on the basis of what we know about them already, can we predict accurately other differences between them? For example, how do they also differ in their academic goals and in their past achievements and failures? Do they generally show different degrees of anxiety about tests? What might have caused such differences between them? How are such differences maintained, and how might they be changed? What else must we know about each to predict what he or she will do next? Personality psychologists ask questions of this sort as they try to understand personality. But what *is* personality? Many people have asked that question, but few agree on an answer. The term "personality" has many definitions, but no single meaning is accepted universally.

In popular usage, personality is often equated with social skill and effectiveness. In this usage, personality is the ability to elicit positive reactions from other people in one's typical dealings with them. For example, we may speak of someone as having "a lot of personality" or a "popular personality," and advertisements for glamour courses promise to give those who enroll "more personality."

Less superficially, personality may be taken to be an individual's most striking or dominant characteristic. In this sense a person may be said to be a "shy personality" or a "neurotic personality," meaning that his or her dominant attribute appears to be shyness or neurosis.

More formal definitions of personality by psychologists also show little agreement. Influential personality theorists tell us that personality is:

> . . . the dynamic organization within the individual of those psychophysical systems that determine his characteristic behavior and thought (Allport, 1961, p. 28).
> . . . a person's unique pattern of traits (Guilford, 1959, p. 5).
> . . . the most adequate conceptualization of a person's behavior in all its detail (McClelland, 1951, p. 69).

As these examples imply, there may be as many different meanings of the term "personality" as there are theorists who have tried to define it. Nevertheless, a common theme runs throughout most definitions of personality: "personality" usually refers to the distinctive patterns of behavior (including thoughts and emotions) that characterize each individual's adaptation to the situations of his or her life. Different theorists use the concepts and language of their theories to carve their preferred formulations of personality. These different views of personality will become increasingly clear throughout this book as we examine the concepts and findings of personality psychologists.

THE FIELD OF PERSONALITY PSYCHOLOGY

Within the discipline of psychology, personality is a field of study rather than a particular aspect of the individual. Although there are many different approaches to personality, there is some general agreement about what the study of personality must include. Traditionally, "Personality is that branch of psychology which is concerned with providing a systematic account of the ways in which individuals differ from one another" (Wiggins, 1979, p. 395). The traditional focus is on individual differences in basic tendencies, qualities, or dispositions.

Individual differences are always a core part of the definition of this field, but they are not necessarily the whole of it. Thus: " . . . the term 'personality psychology' does not need to be limited to the study of differences between individuals in their consistent attributes. . . . Personality psychology must also . . . study how people's [thoughts and actions] . . . interact with—and shape reciprocally—the conditions of their lives" (Mischel, 1980, p. 17).

This expanded view recognizes that human *tendencies* are a crucial part of personality. But it also asserts the need to study the basic *processes of adaptation* through which people interact with the conditions of their lives in their unique patterns of coping with and transforming their psychological environment. This view of personality focuses both on personal tendencies and on processes (such as learning and thinking) in the course of the individual's distinctive pattern of adaptation throughout the life span.

No other area of psychology covers as much territory as the field of personality does. Indeed personality study overlaps extensively with neighboring areas. The field of personality is at the crossroads of most areas of psychology: It is the meeting point between the study of human development and change, of abnormality and deviance, of competence and fulfillment, of emotions and thought, of learning, and of social relations. The breadth of the field is not surprising because for many psychologists the object of personality study has been nothing less than the total person. Given such an ambitious goal, the student cannot expect to find simple definitions of personality.

Although the boundaries between personality psychology and other parts of psychology are fuzzy, personality theories do tend to share certain distinctive goals; namely, they generally try to "integrate many aspects of human behavior into a single theoretical framework. Not satisfied with an inventory of psychological facts, personality theorists derive and explain these facts from a central theme" (Bavelas, 1978, p. 1).

What should that central theme be? What should a good theory of personality contain and exclude? How should such a theory be built? How can one best analyze and study human behavior? The answers to all these questions are controversial. In dealing with them, different theorists throughout this book will compete for your attention, interest, and even loyalty.

Personality theorists not only tend to cover large areas and seek broad integrations, they also tend to deal with questions of central personal, philosophical, and practical importance. It is personality theorists who typically have grappled with such questions as: What are the basic causes underlying everyday interpersonal behavior? What are the roots of, and best treatments for, psychological disorders? What is "healthy," adaptive, creative personal functioning and how can it be facilitated? What are the most fundamental, universal, enduring psychological qualities of human nature? How do they arise, change, or maintain themselves throughout the life cycle? Given the scope and personal implications of these questions, it is no wonder that personality theories (and theorists!) tend to provoke heated controversies. Sometimes the arguments are so heated that it becomes difficult to examine the questions objectively and to move beyond debate to research. Yet it is only through research that the psychological study of personality can make a scientific contribution.

Diverse Approaches to Personality

Most psychologists in the field of personality share certain basic interests but also favor and adapt one or more of a number of fundamentally different approaches. To understand some of the most crucial points of agreement and disagreement, let us briefly consider a concrete case: that of Jane, the college student whom we already met.

> Jane's test scores indicate that she is very bright, and yet she is having serious difficulties in college. She suffers severe anxiety about examinations and is plagued by an enduring tendency to be overweight. In spite of her chubbiness, there is wide agreement that she is a very attractive person. Her boyfriend describes her as a "knockout," her roommate says she is a very genuine person whose "inside is as beautiful as her outside." Jane's parents and sister see her as intelligent, sincere, and artistic. Her father thinks she may be experiencing an identity crisis but says, "She'll come through with flying colors." Jane says, "I remember being pretty lonely (as a very young child). I started turning into myself in seventh grade and often hated what I saw . . . what really excited me was painting and music." In college, she says, "I still don't have a major—I don't even have a meaning. I'm still searching. . . ."

Faced with a case such as Jane's, most psychologists try to understand and explain the basic causes of her behavior, including her thoughts and feelings. Many also would want to predict her future behavior as accurately and as fully as possible. With Jane, and everyone in general, they are interested in questions such as those listed in Table 1-1. Applying the issue of nature versus nurture to Jane, for example, raises some important questions. To what extent has inheritance produced her current problems and qualities, including her personal characteristics, her tendencies to be anxious, artistic, and overweight? If genes do play a significant role in determining such qualities, to what degree can Jane still change her own characteristics and behavior? What methods would be best to achieve this change? Most students of personality want to explain the causes of behavior, but they differ widely in the types of causes they emphasize, in the methods they use, and in the kinds of behavior on which they focus.

Table 1-1
Some Basic and Enduring Questions in Personality Psychology

1. What is given to the human being by inheritance (nature); what is acquired through experience with the environment (nurture)?
2. What are the best units for conceptualizing and studying people? Examples of the possible units include situations, physical responses, thoughts or cognitions, needs, conflicts, emotional states, inferred motives, and dispositions.
3. How stable and enduring are particular psychological qualities? How easily can they be changed? By what means? For what ends should such change be attempted?
4. Does behavior depend mostly on the individual or on the situation? How do the two interact? How can one best understand and study the important social interactions between organism and environment?
5. What basic, general principles emerge from the study of personality? How do these principles inform us about the causes of behavior and the ways to understand, to modify, and/or to predict behavior?

Personality Theories: Alternative Conceptions

Some personality psychologists are most concerned with theory and generate ideas about the causes and nature of "personality." Each theorist conceptualizes personality somewhat differently. Obviously, Sigmund Freud's view of personality, which emphasized unconscious motives, is very different from the formulations of early behaviorists who stressed learned habits. Indeed, the concepts employed by such widely differing theories may have almost nothing in common.

Some personality theorists believe that human behaviors have their roots in unconscious motives from one's distant past. Others focus on the individual's present relationships and current experiences. Although some theorists search for signs of character traits that are not directly observable, others attend to the person's overt actions—the things the individual does—and seek to sample them as directly and precisely as possible.

A few of the many theoretical alternatives for conceptualizing the same behavior are shown in Figure 1-1. The same behavior—Jane's becoming tense in response to an exam scheduled for tomorrow—is open to diverse interpretations about the reasons underlying her upset. Is Jane's reaction a sign of her more generalized fearfulness? Is it a symptom of an underlying problem provoked or symbolized in some complex way by the exam? Is it part of a learned pattern of exam fears and poor habits for studying? Is it related to more basic conflicts and insecurities about herself?

Conceptualizations about the meaning of behavior are more than idle games: they guide the ways we think about ourselves and the solutions we seek in efforts to better our lives. For example, if Jane's tension reflects unconscious conflicts about academic success and a fear that success would undermine her "femininity" (Horner, 1972), it might help her to seek better insights into her own motives. In contrast, if Jane's behavior reflects poor study skills, it might be better for her to

Figure 1-1
**Examples of Alternative Conceptualizations About the Mechanisms (Reasons)
Underlying the Same Behavior**

Situation	Conceptions about possible underlying mechanisms	Response
Jane is at her desk preparing for an exam tomorrow.	Jane is a generally fearful person with diffuse anxieties. Jane really fears "success" and unconsciously wants to fail. Jane has learned to fear exams and has poor study habits. Jane's upset reflects her identity crisis about herself as a person	Jane becomes increasingly tense and cannot study effectively.

learn ways of reducing exam-related tensions (e.g., by learning to relax) while also mastering more effective ways of studying.

Students are easily puzzled by a field in which different theorists may fail to agree even about the meaning of the same behavior. It may help, however, to recognize that lack of agreement in this instance merely means that the same events can be construed in many different ways. The events are tangible and real enough: Nature goes on "minding its own business;" the events of life keep on happening no matter how people understand them. People behave and act continuously, but the meaning of those actions and the reasons for them may be conceptualized from many vantage points and for many purposes by different theorists.

A Perspective

To the beginning student, the fact that there are so many different approaches to personality may seem bewildering. When entering a new field one may simply want to get The Truth without the complexities of considering different viewpoints. A little reflection, however, leads one to a basic conclusion: the individual is influenced by many determinants and human behavior reflects the continuous interaction of many forces both in the person and in the environment or situation.

Consider, for example, how a person chooses a career. The many influences on such a choice might include inherited and acquired abilities and skills, interests, and a wide range of specific experiences and circumstances. We can see this in the case of Barbara, a person whose decision to become a general practitioner of medicine in a poor rural area was affected by many factors throughout her life, as Figure 1-2 illustrates. If human behavior is determined by so many forces—both in the person and in the environment—it follows that a focus on any one of them is likely to have limited value.

Figure 1-2
**Many Factors, Both in Barbara and in Her Environment, Interacted and Combined to
Influence Her Progress Toward Her Present Occupation**
Adapted from Krumboltz et al. (1976).

Environmental, economic, social, and cultural events and conditions

		Time
	Barbara, white, female, no physical handicaps.	— 1944
War ends. Father returns home but parents have grown apart. Mother is embittered toward men.	Mother tells her men can't be trusted.	— 1946
New public library built near home with tax revenues.	At library reads book about Helen Keller.	— 1954
Charismatic Sunday School teacher emphasizes golden rule.	"I wish I could help other people."	
	Applies first aid to sister's burned hand. Hand heals without scar.	— 1962
High unemployment rate.	"I'd like to work in the medical field and I'd always have work."	
Careers for women become more the norm than the exception.	Decides to be a public health doctor.	— 1966
Rejected from medical school.	"Women are discriminated against. I must fight back.'"	
	Sues medical school; is admitted.	— 1967
Government cutbacks as part of anti-inflation economic policy mean no public health jobs.	Decides to seek alternatives	
	Searches for alternative rewarding openings.	— 1972
Current Occupational Activity	Working as general practitioner in poor rural area.	— 1977

Often our understanding improves when information from many perspectives and sources is taken into account. With Jane's anxiety about examinations, for example, it is both possible and informative to focus on her immediate fears and the conditions that currently evoke them. But it also may be worthwhile to examine the historical development of those fears, relating them to other aspects of her changing life. To use a historical focus, however, does not make it pointless to study the physiological mechanisms involved in Jane's anxiety, or to investigate the role of heredity in her tendency to be fearful, or to study how she processes information when she is emotionally upset.

Alternative approaches, then, can complement each other constructively, increasing our total understanding and knowledge of individual cases and of personality as a whole. At times, to be sure, they can also produce critical findings that contradict each other and generate real conflicts. But those are some of the most exciting moments in science and often set the stage for dramatic progress.

STUDYING PERSONALITY

To convert personality theories from speculations about people into ideas that can be studied scientifically, we must be able to put them into *testable* terms. It is basic to science that any conceptualization must be potentially testable. This is what makes science different from the simple assertion of opinions. Perhaps the most distinctive feature of modern personality psychology has been its concern with studying ideas about people by actually putting them to the test.

Resistance to a Science of Personality

Efforts to study personality scientifically face many problems. On the one hand, it seems fascinating to try to gain insight into the causes of one's own behavior and the roots of one's own personality. But at the same time we may resist actually achieving such an understanding and seeing ourselves objectively. Many scholars feel that it does violence to a person's complexity and "humanness" to study and "objectify" him or her in the framework of science. Instead, they suggest that perhaps the most perceptive and provoking studies of personality are found in great literary creations, such as the characters of a great novel.

People do not perceive themselves entirely objectively. Thus although it may be fashionable to say in public that human behavior, like that of other organisms, is "lawfully determined," privately the laws of nature may seem to be operating on everyone except oneself. Subjectively, while other people's behavior may be seen as controlled by "variables" or "conditions," one's own important thoughts, feelings, dreams, and actions may seem to defy such control and to resist scientific analysis.

Even within the field of personality psychology, there is some resistance to "objectifying" personality. For every personality psychologist who believes that people must be studied under carefully controlled experimental conditions, there is another who believes that individuals can be understood only by investigating them under "naturalistic," lifelike conditions. As one sensitive student of people noted, lives are "too human for science, too beautiful for numbers, too sad for diagnosis, and too immortal for bound journals" (Vaillant, 1977, p. 11).

Some personality psychologists commit themselves to quantitative, statistical techniques for gathering information from large groups. Others rely on intuition and subjective judgments based on lengthy personal experience with a few people. Some urge us to concentrate on "peak experiences"—moments of personal, spiritual, or religious climax and fulfillment. Others prefer to study simpler behaviors under conditions that permit a clearer analysis of causation. For example, they prefer to study the responses of a young child to specific instructions under the closely controlled conditions of a testing room at school. Different experts favor different techniques of investigation, but all of them generally share a conviction that ultimately theoretical ideas about personality and human behavior must be tested and applied.

Sources of Information About the Person

Psychologists guided by different approaches obtain information about people from many sources and through a number of strategies. Just as alternative approaches can and do complement each other, so do the different methods employed in personality psychology provide useful information for answering different questions. One of the most frequently used sources of information for the personality psychologist (sometimes called the *personologist*) is the *test*. A test is any standardized measure of behavior, including school achievement tests, mental ability tests, and measures of personal qualities, such as anxiety or friendliness. Table 1-2 shows an example of a test question used to measure self-reported anxiety. Some tests are *questionnaires* or *ratings* that may be answered directly by the subject or by others

Table 1-2
Typical Test Item from a Questionnaire Used to Measure Self-Reported Anxiety

Situation 1 of the S-R Inventory of General Trait Anxiousness
"You are in Situations Involving Interaction with Other People"

(We are primarily interested in your reactions *in general* to those situations that involve interacting *with other people*. This includes situations that involve friends, family, acquaintances, strangers, etc.)

Mark on the ANSWER SHEET one of the five alternative degrees of reaction or attitude for each of the following 9 items.

Seek experiences like this	Very much	1	2	3	4	5	Not at all
Perspire	Not at all	1	2	3	4	5	Perspire much
Have an "uneasy feeling"	Not at all	1	2	3	4	5	Very much
Feel exhilarated and thrilled	Very much	1	2	3	4	5	Not at all
Get fluttering feeling in stomach	Not at all	1	2	3	4	5	Very much
Feel tense	Not at all	1	2	3	4	5	Very tense
Enjoy these situations	Very much	1	2	3	4	5	Not at all
Heart beats faster	Not at all	1	2	3	4	5	Much faster
Feel anxious	Not at all	1	2	3	4	5	Very anxious

SOURCE: Endler & Okada, 1975, p. 321.

who have observed the subject. Other tests involve *performance measures* (such as tests of arithmetic ability or spatial skills).

Another valuable source of information is the *interview*—a verbal exchange between the subject and the examiner. Some interviews are tightly structured and formal: the examiner follows a fixed, prescribed format. For example, in research to survey peoples' sexual activities, the interviewer might follow a standard series of questions, starting with questions about the subject's earliest experiences and going on to inquiries about current practices. Table 1-3 shows some typical questions from such an interview.

Responses to paper-and-pencil tests and to interviews are widely used sources of information but by no means the only ones. Valuable information also comes from *nonverbal responses,* such as changes in facial expression. Psychologists also study performance in special situations in which they can systematically observe selected behaviors. For example, they might investigate the frequency and intensity with which subjects engage in physical aggression, as when children are given a chance to attack a large inflated doll or adults have an opportunity to punish another person. Similarly, they might study responses to a solicitor who asks for charitable donations or reactions to someone who needs help and appears to be in distress. *Physiological measures,* such as heart rate, types of brain waves, amount of sweating, and degree of sexual arousal, can also provide valuable information. For an ingenious combination of methods used to study the ways in which obese and nonobese people differ, see *In Focus 1.1.*

The data that psychologists who study personality collect, regardless of their source, are conceptualized as *variables.* A variable is an attribute, quality, or characteristic that can be given two or more values. For example, a psychological variable might be attitude toward premarital sex treated in terms of two values—positive or negative. Of course, the same variable could also be categorized into finer units such as seven points on a single scale in which 0 is neutral, +3 is extremely positive, and −3 is extremely negative (Figure 1-3).

Correlation: What Goes with What?

One way to study personality is to try to find relations among variables. Often, two or more variables seem to be associated—seem to "go together"—in such a way

Table 1-3
Typical History-Taking Questions from a Survey of Sexual Activities and Attitudes

In adolescence, to which parent did you feel closest? Why?

In your school years, did you have special friends? Mostly boys? Mostly girls? Were your schools coeducational?

When did you first find out how babies are conceived and "where they come from"? How did you learn this? How did you react?

When did you start to date? Did you date in groups or on single dates?

NOTE: These questions are similar to those used by Masters & Johnson, 1970.

Figure 1-3
Any Attribute That Can Be Assigned Two or More Values is Called a "Variable." Here is an Example of Attitude Toward Premarital Sex Treated as a Seven-Point Variable

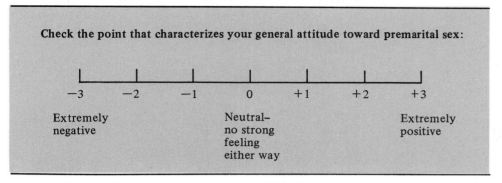

that when we know something about one variable, we can usually make a good guess about the other variables. For example, people who are taller generally tend to weigh more; when we know how tall someone is, we can roughly predict the person's weight. This "going together," this "co-relationship" or joint relationship between variables, is what psychologists mean by the term *correlation*. Correlations are discovered by searching for answers to specific questions such as: do attitudes toward premarital sex relate to subsequent marital adjustment? Is depression related to age? Do college grades relate to income in later life? A correlational study

---

In Focus 1.1
Individual Differences in Emotionality: Obese versus Normals

There are great individual differences in the intensity of emotional responses made to any situation. The sight of blood may cause one person to faint while another remains calm. The importance of individual differences in emotionality has been illustrated by studies that compare the reactions of obese people with those of normal-weight people (Schachter & Rodin, 1974). Obese and normal-weight male college students listened to one of two kinds of tape-recorded material: neutral or emotionally disturbing. The emotionally neutral tapes invited the listener to think about rain or about seashells. The emotionally disturbing tapes detailed horrible images of the bombing of Hiroshima (e.g., the skin of the victims coming off) or the listener's death as a result of leukemia (e.g., the incapacitating weakness and the terrible pain). Immediately after listening to the tape the

participants were asked the following five questions designed to measure emotionality:

1. Are you experiencing any palpitations?
2. Do you think your breathing rate is faster than usual?
3. Are you feeling generally upset?
4. Are you experiencing any anxiety?
5. Do you feel emotionally aroused?

Subjects responded to each of these questions by marking a scale numbered from zero to one hundred, with zero meaning "not at all" and one hundred meaning "extremely."

Comparisons show that the obese individuals were more disturbed by the emotional tapes than were the normal ones (see Figure 1-4). Note, however, that in their responses to neutral tapes the

Figure 1-4
Emotional Responses of Normal and Obese People After Listening to Neutral and Emotional Tapes

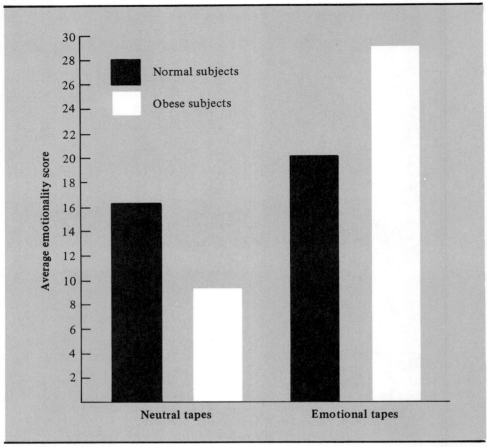

Adapted from Schachter & Rodin (1974).

obese were *less* emotional than the normals. In another study, when threatened with painful shock, obese individuals described themselves as more nervous than did normals (Schachter, Goldman, & Gordon, 1968). Although the differences in emotionality between obese and normals in both these studies were too large to be due to chance, there were great differences among the individuals in each group. Emotionality depends on many variables both in the person and in the situation, and body weight is only one relatively small influence.

seeks not only to answer such questions with "yes" or "no," but also to provide a quantitative estimate of the degree of relatedness.

Correlations are called *positive* when a high magnitude of one variable is associated with a high magnitude of the other variable. For example, there is a positive correlation between the number of years of schooling a person has had and that person's ultimate socioeconomic level: the more schooling, the higher the person's socioeconomic level, and vice versa. A *negative correlation,* on the other hand, occurs when high magnitude of one variable tends to be associated with a relatively low magnitude of the other variable. For example, there is a negative correlation between a person's intelligence and how satisfied she will be doing a dull job.

The degree of relationship or correlation may be expressed quantitatively by a number called a *correlation coefficient,* symbolized by the letter r. Theoretically, a correlation coefficient can go from no correlation whatsoever, expressed as 0, to a perfect positive correlation ($+1$) or a perfect negative correlation (-1). In fact, correlations that are even close to perfect are very rare in psychology, showing that although many psychological variables are, indeed, associated with each other, the association usually is not very strong. Correlations of about .30 to .50, either positive or negative, are fairly common in psychology. Such correlations may allow predictions that significantly exceed chance guesses, but they are still far from perfect. Statistical computations are used to evaluate the strength, or "statistical significance," of particular correlation coefficients and to determine how far a given association exceeds that which would be expected by chance.

Correlations are useful, but they do not indicate cause and effect. Suppose a positive correlation were found between the income level of parents and the IQ level of their children. You could not conclude from this that income causes intelligence; the correlation would only alert you to the many things that might make the two tend to occur together. For example, the correlation might partly reflect the enriched environment or special privileges that more affluent parents could provide. Correlations can, however, be used to make predictions. For instance, one study used correlational methods to try to predict which students would be among the 500 who drop out of American medical schools each year (Gough & Hall, 1975). Among the best predictors were poor scores on a quantitative ability test and poor premedical grades.

Experimentation: Trying to Control the Phenomenon

To study cause-and-effect relations systematically, most psychologists favor the *experiment*—the basic method of science. An experiment is an attempt to manipulate or alter one variable of interest so that its impact can be determined. To do that, one tries to control all other conditions so that their influences can be discounted, then the effects of the variable of interest can be measured. The main limitation of the experiment in psychology is that to achieve good control over extraneous conditions the experimenter may have to set up situations that are so artificial and simplified that they have no resemblance to real life. The challenge of good experimentation in psychology is to achieve a reasonable degree of control without distorting the phenomenon one wants to study.

Independent and Dependent Variables. The *independent variable* is the stimulus or condition that the experimenter systematically manipulates or varies in order to study its effects. It is called the "independent variable" because it does not depend on the subject's behavior; its presence or absence, increase or decrease occur regardless of what the subject does. For example, to study altruism, one might expose subjects to a confederate who solicits contributions for a charity. The confederate might dress well and present a high-status appearance when soliciting half of the subjects and dress in a sloppy, low-status fashion with the other half. This variable—the solicitor's appearance—would be independent of the subjects' behavior; it would be determined solely by the experimenter to see how it influences the subject's behavior.

The *dependent variable* is the aspect of a subject's behavior that is observed after the experimenter has manipulated the independent variable. It is a measure of the subject's response to the independent variable. In the altruism example it might be the amount of money that subjects promise to give the solicitor.

Control Groups. For many purposes *control groups* are essential in experimentation. Control groups are like the experimental group except for one crucial difference: they get no independent variable manipulation or treatment. They therefore provide comparisons for evaluating the effects of the experimental treatments that are given to the *experimental groups.* In the study of academic attitudes and course performance (see *In Focus 1.2*), for example, the inclusion of control groups made it possible to show that the measured improvement in grades and attitudes was not just due to taking tests, involvement in a prediction study, or the passage of time.

Random Assignment. Experimenters want to select groups of subjects who are comparable or matched in all respects, such as sex, age, intelligence, and general background so that these factors can be ruled out as the causes of any differences found in the dependent variable. All subjects receive the same treatment with the crucial exception of the one factor that the investigator varies. Because it is usually difficult or impossible to match subjects who are assigned to different conditions, assignments may be made by *randomization;* that is, on a purely chance basis, as by flipping a coin or picking names out of a hat. The psychologist recognizes that there will be great individual differences between the subjects in any one group but assumes that by using many subjects and assigning them to the groups at random, these differences will average out. For example, although there may be great differences in intelligence among the subjects who participate in a study, if they are all assigned to groups randomly, the number of bright and dull ones in each should be approximately equal so that the average level of intelligence for all groups will be similar and thus matched. In the study of course performance *(In Focus 1.2)* the assignment of subjects to groups in a strictly random fashion ruled out the possibility that the three groups differed in some way beyond the treatments they were given.

Blind Subjects and Blind Experimenters. Often a special control is required in psychological studies. Suppose, for example, an investigator wanted to test a drug intended to reduce anxiety. She would find some anxious subjects, administer specific dosages of the drug in the form of pills, and then test for reduced anxiety levels on such measures as self-reported tension or ability to cope with stress. But the subjects' improvement on these measures might reflect little more than their hopes and expectations that the drug would help them. Therefore,

In Focus 1.2
An Illustrative Experiment: Improving Course Performance

To illustrate some of the basic features of a psychological experiment, let us consider a study by Meichenbaum and Smart (1971). They investigated the academic performance and attitudes of freshman engineering students who were working at an academic level so low that it endangered their continuation in school. The researchers tested the hypothesis that these students could be helped to do better if they increased their expectations for academic success. For this experiment the investigators randomly assigned the students to serve as subjects in one of three groups after the end of the first semester.

The subjects in one group received the experimental treatment designed to increase their expectancies. They were informed by the counseling service that tests they had taken earlier showed they were "late bloomers" whose mental abilities would soon reach a fuller development. They were also told that their test results predicted a high likelihood of academic success for them by the end of their first year. In the second group subjects were told that their test results permitted no definite predictions for either better or worse performance. This group was called the "no-prediction control" group. The third group was called the "assessment control" group; its members had taken the same tests but were not given any expectation manipulation or prediction. The two control groups served as comparisons to see if the experimental treatment would produce more improvement than that which might result from the students' just knowing that they were participating in a special prediction study, or even from merely taking the tests.

Grades and measures of attitudes toward the school courses were obtained at the end of the year for all subjects. The results showed that in two out of four courses the students who had been told to expect success improved their grades more than did those in the two control groups. On the attitude measures the students who expected to succeed also reported greater interest in their course work and more confidence about schoolwork compared to both control groups. The study thus gave good evidence that by increasing their expectancy for academic success borderline students could be helped both to do better academic work and to feel more positive about it.

it is important to have at the same time another group, this one consisting of subjects who take an inactive substance, called a *placebo,* instead of the active drug. In the *single-blind method* the subjects do not know if they are receiving the active treatment or some control treatment such as a sugar pill that looks like the real drug but is inert (inactive).

Of course, experimenters, just like subjects, may also be biased by their own hopes and expectations. For example, the researcher who wants to prove the value of a new drug for reducing anxiety might be fooled into seeing improvement where there is none. To avoid this type of error, the experimenter must not know which subjects receive the real treatment and which ones serve as placebo controls. She might employ an independent third party to keep track of which subjects receive which treatment. The method of keeping the experimenter as well as the subject ignorant of the group to which each subject is assigned is called the *double-blind method.*

Significantly Beyond Chance?To assess the effect of an experimental treatment, the researcher compares the results obtained with the experimental group (the one that actually received the treatment) with the results obtained from the control group. Suppose there is a difference, and the average score in the experimental group is, say, five points higher than the average score in the control group. What may one conclude? Very little, unless one can be sure that this difference is greater than the difference that would be expected just on the basis of chance. For example, if you correctly predict how a tossed coin will land a few times, you could still not conclude that you have a special ability to predict heads or tails unless you could demonstrate your skill at a level that was clearly greater than chance. It is the same in experimentation: the differences found between experimental groups and controls must be shown to exceed chance. Statistics are used to calculate quantitative estimates of the degree to which a given finding or difference reflects more than a chance effect—in short, the degree to which it is *statistically significant.* Even if a finding is beyond chance, however, the psychologist needs to evaluate its strength or power. For example, given that a particular treatment decreases fear more than no treatment at all does, how powerful is it? Statistical analyses can help evaluate the impact of particular experimental variables and judge their relative strength as well as their occurrence at a level significantly beyond chance. Some of the main terms used in psychological research are summarized in Table 1-4.

Naturalistic Observation: Moving Out of the Lab

Often experimentation is not possible or not desirable. Just as astronomers cannot manipulate the actions of heavenly bodies, psychologists often cannot—or should not—manipulate certain aspects of human behavior. For example, one could not or would not create home environments in which children become delinquent or marital conflicts are provoked. Although such phenomena cannot be manipulated as independent variables, often they can be observed closely and systematically. Ethical considerations often prevent psychologists from trying to create powerful, life-like experimental treatments in the laboratories (see Consent Form, Figure 1-5).

Even when some variables can be manipulated, the investigator often prefers to observe behavior as it naturally occurs, without any scientific interference. Some of the most informative work using this method, called *naturalistic observation,* comes from students of animal behavior, who unobtrusively observe the moment-by-moment lives of such animals as chimpanzees in their natural environment. In a somewhat similar fashion, but usually on a smaller scale, unseen observers may study children from behind a one-way mirror in such settings as a playroom or a preschool class. Of course, observation is a commonplace method in everyday life; through observation we form impressions and learn about events and people. The distinguishing feature of observation as a scientific tool is that it is conducted as precisely, objectively, and systematically as possible.

Table 1-4
The Language of Personality Research

Term	Definition
Variable	Any attribute or quality that can be given two or more values, such as degree of friendliness
Correlation	The degree of relationship or association between two or more variables; for example, the degree to which people who are friendly in one situation are likely to be friendly in another situation
Independent variable	The event, condition, or treatment that is systematically varied by the experimenter
Dependent variable	A measure of the response to the independent variable
Control (control group)	The condition against which the effects of the experimental treatment are compared. For example, the control subjects might receive an inert substance while those in the experimental group get a drug.
Randomization	The distribution of subjects into different groups (experimental or control) on a purely chance or random basis
Single-blind technique	A method in which subjects are not informed of the group or treatment into which they have been placed. This is done so that subjects in different groups will have comparable expectations about the study.
Double-blind technique	In this method neither the subjects nor the experimenters know the group or treatment to which subjects are assigned. For example, neither the subjects nor the experimenters know who received the real drug or the inert substance until all the data have been collected and recorded.
Statistical significance	An effect, relationship, or difference that significantly exceeds that which might be expected by chance (as shown by a statistical test)

Figure 1-5
A Typical Consent Form for Participation in a Psychological Study. Ethical Standards Require That Participation in Research Comes Only After Volunteers Understand the Task and Freely Consent

CONSENT FORM

FOR PARTICIPATION IN AN EXPERIMENT IN _____

PSYCHOLOGY IN THE LABORATORY OF _____

1. In this experiment, you will be asked to

2. The benefit we hope to achieve from this work

3. The risks involved (if any)

CONSENT AGREEMENT

I have read the above statement and am consenting to participate in the experiment of my own volition. I understand that I am free to discontinue my participation at any time without suffering disadvantage. I understand that if I am dissatisfied with any aspect of this program at any time, I may report

grievances anonymously to _____

Signed: _____

Date: _____

Finally, in *case studies* the focus is on one individual only, assessed intensively. A variety of data sources may be used to study the person. For example, interviews, questionnaires, tests, and observations may be included. The study may deal with just one aspect of a person's life or may try to provide broad coverage of long periods or even an entire life.

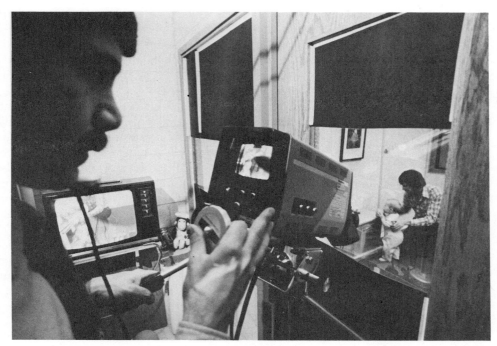

In naturalistic observation the observer records behavior without interfering with it.

OVERVIEW OF THIS BOOK

Methods like those described in the last section are essential for the scientific study of persons, but they are merely the tools, and they become useful only in the service of ideas. Personality psychology is rich in such ideas, and is filled with theories that try to further our understanding of human beings. In this book you will learn some of the major theoretical orientations toward personality. We will survey some of the main ideas developed to describe and understand psychological differences among people, and we will consider the concepts that are central to diverse views of human nature. The range of these concepts is great. Included are ideas about our most basic human characteristics; about the motives and attitudes that may underlie actions; about the chief crises of life; about the conditions of experience that mold human values, beliefs, and choices; and about the processes and concepts through which people try to understand themselves and make sense of their world.

When theorists develop their ideas, they often try to extend them as far as possible. They test the limits of the ideas by probing their relevance for diverse areas of life. Such a stretching of concepts can be extremely fruitful for builders of theories because it helps them to generalize and to see how widely their ideas apply. Thus the theorist may try to make his or her ideas about the "unconscious" or the "self" or "early experience" serve to explain many different human phenomena.

One or two favorite concepts may be used to deal with everything from love to hate, from birth trauma to fears about death, from deep disturbance to great achievement. While such an extension of ideas may help the theorist, the student should ask, "Does it fit? How does the theorist know? What would we have to do to discover whether he or she is right or wrong? What are the consequences of thinking about it that way?"

Such an analytical, skeptical attitude is the heart of the scientific approach. It is a necessary attitude if we want to go beyond learning what different theorists say about human nature and personality to testing their ideas so that we can discriminate between those that have no substance and those that are worthy of further study. To test theoretical ideas, it is necessary to turn from theories to methods, applications, and findings. Therefore, after discussing each theoretical approach we will consider those methods of personality study associated with that conception. We will describe the main methods of assessing persons favored by each approach and examine their relevance for understanding individuals. We also will consider some of the main research findings stimulated by each approach. It will become evident that personality assessment does not just supply assessments of persons: it also assesses the ideas and theory of the assessor. That is, efforts to measure and analyze behavior supply information not only about the people who are measured but also about the meaning of the tests and ideas used in the measurement process. What we learn about ten children from their answers to an intelligence test, for example, tells us something about the test and the concept of "intelligence," as well as something about the children.

Personality theories also may be *applied* to help improve the psychological qualities of our lives. Even people whose problems are not severe enough to seek help from professionals still search for ways to live their lives more fully and satisfyingly. But what constitutes a fuller, more satisfying life? Given the diversity and complexity of human strengths and problems, it seems evident that simple notions of psychological adequacy in terms of "good adjustment" or "sound personality" are naive. More adequate definitions of "adaptation" and "abnormality," of "mental health" and "deviance," hinge on the personality theory that is used as a guide. The theoretical conceptions discussed provide distinctive notions about the nature of psychological adequacy and deviance. Each also dictates the strategies chosen to try to change troublesome behaviors and to encourage better alternatives.

Many personality psychologists are concerned about practical questions. They tend to concentrate on searching for useful techniques to deal with human problems and to foster more advantageous patterns of growth. In addition to having enormous practical and social importance, attempts to understand and change behaviors provide one of the sharpest testing grounds for ideas about personality. These efforts include different forms of psychotherapy, drugs and physical treatments, various special learning programs, and changes in the psychological environment to permit people to develop to their full potential. Research on these topics informs us about the usefulness and implications of different ideas about personality change. The concepts, methods, and findings relevant to personality change and growth will be discussed at many points as they apply to each major approach. The final part of this book will consider personal coping and adaptation. There we will discuss research on the basic processes through which people deal with the conditions and problems of their lives.

SUMMARY

1. To psychologists, personality is a field of study rather than a particular aspect of people. Personality psychology is a field of great breadth. It overlaps with the neighboring areas of human development, creativity and abnormality, emotions, cognition, learning, and social relations. This book is an introduction to the field of personality. It surveys personality theories and their applications, as well as personal adaptation and basic coping processes.

2. Traditionally, much attention has been devoted to theories about human nature. Personality theories differ in their degree of emphasis on the past and the present, the conscious and the unconscious, the directly observable and the relatively unobservable. The essence of a scientific approach to personality is to test various ideas, to evaluate the evidence supporting them, and to seek better ones. It is this potential testability of personality theory that differentiates a science of personality from the simple assertion of opinions or beliefs.

3. Complex human behavior has many determinants. It is the result of the interaction between various qualities in the person and the situation, often over long periods of time. Information about various types of determinants from many alternative perspectives helps to improve our total understanding. Sometimes, however, different approaches to personality come into conflict, and it is from such conflict that progress in science is often stimulated.

4. Different approaches also favor different methods; each has distinct uses for getting particular types of information. Paper-and-pencil tests, interviews, performance in special situations, and physiological measures and other nonverbal responses are all among the sources of information used. Regardless of its source, any information may be treated as a variable, which is defined as a characteristic or quality that can be given two or more noticeably different values such as high and low.

5. Individual differences were illustrated in a study of how obese versus normal individuals react emotionally to the same situation. The obese individuals reported more emotionality than normal subjects when listening to emotionally disturbing material but less when listening to neutral material.

6. A correlation is an expression of the relationship between two variables (e.g., the association between people's height and their weight). When the correlation is zero, there is no relationship between the two variables. In a positive correlation the variables are related in such a way that a high value for one is associated with a high value for the other. In a negative correlation a high value for one variable is associated with a low value for the other.

7. Statistical techniques are needed to evaluate whether or not the relationship between two or more variables is statistically significant—that is, greater than would be expected by chance. If two variables are significantly related, then a prediction may be made about one on the basis of knowledge of the other. Correlations, however, cannot provide an answer to the question of cause and effect. Two variables may be associated even though neither one causes the other.

8. In the experiment, the basic method of science, the researcher systematically manipulates one treatment or variable while holding all other conditions constant. The group that receives the treatment or is exposed to this one variable is called the "experimental group" (treatment group). A "control group" does not receive the treatment so that it can serve as a comparison. The assignment of subjects to experimental or control groups is usually done at random to avoid bias (any difference between groups in any respect other than the experimental variable).

9. An independent variable is the variable or treatment that is administered systematically by the experimenter, independently of the subject's behavior. The dependent variable is the subject's response to the independent variable. A placebo is an inert substance that may be given to control group subjects in an experiment testing the efficacy of a drug. In the single-blind method, subjects do not know whether they are in the control or experimental group. In the double-blind method neither the experimenter nor the subjects know who is in the treatment or control groups.

10. Major personality theories have important applications for assessment and personality change. They provide strategies for seeking information about people and for changing maladaptive behavior in constructive ways. The successes achieved by these applications reflect the value (and limitations) of the personality theories that guide them. Contemporary personality research investigates the effects of experiences and events on personality and studies psychological differences among individuals.

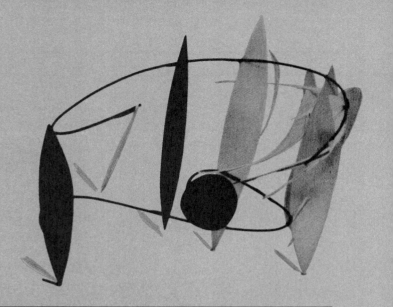

PART TWO
THE PSYCHODYNAMIC APPROACH

Psychodynamic Theories: Conceptions

The place is Vienna, the year 1905. The scene unfolds in a doctor's consulting room on a pleasant residential street. The physician is presented with a young girl who feels compelled to rinse out her wash basin over and over, dozens of times after each time she washes herself; she cannot stop, even though the basin is obviously clean. Her habit becomes so intense and upsetting that her whole life revolves around it. Why? Another woman appears to be physically well upon examination, yet she is able to sit in only one chair, clings to it for hours, and leaves it only with the greatest of difficulty. Why? A young boy becomes terrified of horses although he himself was never hurt by one. Why? Still another patient appears to be blind although tests of her vision show that her eyes and visual system are undamaged. Again, why? It was puzzles like these that intrigued a young genius—the Viennese physician Sigmund Freud (1856–1939)—who invented psychoanalysis, reshaped the field of psychology, and influenced many later developments in all the social sciences and in Western concepts of human nature.

From these puzzles Freud created a theory and a treatment method that changed our view of personality, health, and the mind itself. Working as a physician treating disturbed people in Vienna at the turn of the century, he formulated a theory that upset many cherished assumptions about human nature and startled the neo-Victorian world. Before Freud, peoples' behavior was believed to be under their conscious and rational control. Freud turned that conception upside down. Rather than seeing consciousness as the core of the mind, Freud compared personality to an iceberg: only the tip shows itself overtly, the rest lies below. Rather than viewing the person as a supremely rational being, he saw people as driven by impulses and

Sigmund Freud (1856–1939)

striving to satisfy deep and lasting sexual and aggressive urgings. Rather than relying on people's reports about themselves as accurate self-representations, he interpreted what they said and did as highly indirect, disguised, symbolic representations of unconscious underlying forces.

In the course of more than forty years of active writing and clinical research Freud developed a theory of personality, a method of treatment for personality disturbances, and a wealth of clinical observations based on his therapeutic experiences as well as on his analyses of himself. Freud based both his theory and his psychoanalytic treatment on his extensive clinical observation of disturbed persons. He first noted certain *sensory anesthesias,* which are losses of sensory ability, as in blindness, deafness, or loss of feeling in a body part. He also found patients with motor paralyses that seemed to have no neurological origin. He proposed that these symptoms expressed a way of defending against unacceptable unconscious wishes. For example, a soldier who cannot admit his fear of facing battle develops a motor paralysis without a neurological basis. Or a young bride, unable to admit her hostility to her husband, becomes confined to her chair, although she shows no physical disease. All these examples illustrate *hysteria.* The fundamental feature of hysteria, according to Freud, is the presence of massive repression and the development of a symptom pattern that indirectly or symbolically expresses the repressed needs and wishes. On the basis of careful clinical observations Freud gradually developed his theory of personality, continuously changing his ideas in the light of his growing clinical experiences and insights.

PSYCHIC STRUCTURE: LAYERS OF THE MIND

According to Freud (1933) personality has a three-part structure: id, ego, and superego. Although the three parts interact intimately, each has its own characteristics, which are summarized in Table 2-1.

The Id: At the Core; Sex and Aggression

The *id* is the mental agency that contains everything inherited, especially the instincts. It is the basis of personality, the energy source for the whole system, and the foundation from which the ego and superego later develop. The id, according to Freud, is the innermost core of personality, and it is closely linked to biological processes.

Increases in energy from internal or external stimulation produce tension and discomfort that the id cannot tolerate. The id seeks immediate tension reduction, regardless of the consequences. This tendency toward immediate tension reduction is called the *pleasure principle,* and the id obeys it, seeking immediate satisfaction of instinctual wishes and impulses, regardless of reason or logic.

Freud (1940) believed the impulses of the id to be chiefly sexual and aggressive instincts. He classified these impulses or instincts into the categories of "life" or sexual instincts and "death" or aggressive instincts. The psychological representations of these instincts are wishes, and they often are irrational and unconscious.

To discharge tension the id forms an internal image or hallucination of the

Table 2-1
The Freudian Conception of Mental Structure

Structure	Consciousness	Contents and Function
Id	Unconscious	Basic impulses (sex and aggression); seeks immediate gratification regardless of consequences; impervious to reason and logic; immediate, irrational, impulsive
Ego	Predominantly conscious	Executive mediating between id impulses and superego inhibitions; tests reality; seeks safety and survival; rational, logical taking account of space and time
Superego	Both conscious and unconscious	Ideals and morals; strives for perfection; incorporated (internalized) from parents; observes, dictates, criticizes, and prohibits; imposes limitations on satisfactions; becomes the conscience of the individual

desired object. The hungry infant, for example, may conjure up an internal representation of the mother's breast. The resulting image is considered a wish fulfillment, similar to the attempted wish fulfillment that Freud believed characterized normal dreams and the hallucinations of psychotics (see *In Focus 2.1*). "Primary process thinking" was Freud's term for such direct, reality-ignoring attempts to satisfy needs irrationally. Because mental images by themselves cannot reduce tension, the ego develops.

In Focus 2.1
Post-Freudian Dream Research

Beyond the clinical interpretation of dreams, the process of dreaming itself has become a major research topic in its own right in ways that would have surprised Freud.

REM and NREM

Sleep is not a constant state but one of changing physiological and mental activity. Just as in waking life, there are different activities that occur during sleep. Sleep may be divided into two types: *REM (rapid eye movement)* and *NREM (nonrapid eye movement)*. Periods of regularly occurring

eye movement during sleep were discovered quite by accident when a graduate student studying sleep patterns in infants observed that sometimes the sleeping infants' eyes continued to move under their closed lids (Aserinsky & Kleitman, 1953). Following up the hunch that these rapid eye movements during sleep were related to dreaming, researchers woke sleeping adults during REM periods and found that they generally reported dreaming (Aserinsky & Kleitman, 1955). Subjects awakened in other phases of sleep generally did not report dreaming. There may, however, be some mental activity during sleep not accompanied by REM (NREM sleep), probably consisting of vague and sporadic thoughts rather than dreams. Sleep talking, sleep walking, and intense nightmares also appear to occur more often during NREM sleep than during REM sleep.

REM Sleep and Dreaming

Activity During Dreaming. During REM sleep the brain is as active as it is in wakefulness, yet the external world is almost completely shut out. Nevertheless, sometimes dream content may be influenced by stimuli present in the environment of the dreamer. For example, a ringing telephone might be incorporated into a dream.

During dreaming, nerve impulses in the spinal cord are inhibited. There may be some slight muscle movement and occasional vocalization, but in general the dream state is one of virtual motor paralysis. Bodily movements are associated primarily with the termination of a dream period. Heart rate, blood pressure, and respiration show great variability during dreaming, but there is no clear evidence that these variations and changes are related to dream content. Eye movements may approximate the dreamer's visual activity. For example, the eye movement records of one sleeping subject showed alternating horizontal movements to the right and to the left. When awakened, the subject reported a dream in which he was watching a ping-pong game with a lengthy volley. In his dream he stood at the side of the table so that he had to look from side to side to follow the ball (Dement, 1967).

Studying the activity of brain waves during sleep at the Stanford University Sleep Disorders Clinic in Palo Alto, California.

Dream Time. Although some dreams seem subjectively to compress a long series of events into a moment, laboratory studies indicate that dream action may take about as much time as the same action would take in reality. For example, in one study a man who was in a period of rapid eye movement was sprayed on his back with cold water while sleeping on his stomach. Awakened exactly thirty seconds later, he recounted a dream that incorporated the water. He had been dreaming that he was acting in a play, and then

> I was walking behind the leading lady, when she suddenly collapsed and water was dripping on her. I ran over to her and felt water dripping on my back and head. The roof was leaking. I was very puzzled why she fell down and decided some plaster must have fallen on her. I looked up and there was a hole in the roof. I dragged her over to the side of the stage and began pulling the curtains. Just then I woke up (Dement & Wolpert, 1958, p. 550).

The amount of dream action between being sprayed with water and being awakened was about what could be expected to take place in reality during the same thirty seconds.

Daydreaming

Most people report that they do at least some daydreaming everyday—even when they are paid to be working or are trying hard to study. These reported daydreams vary greatly (as you probably know from your own introspection). Although strong sex differences have not been reported, women's fantasies, according to their own reports, tend "toward personal, passive and body-centered experiences" (Singer, 1974, p. 417). In contrast, men dwell more on active, heroic, and athletic achievements (for example, imagining winning the "Olympic Gold").

There may be some interesting—but still quite uncertain—connections between night dreaming and daydreaming. For instance, people who daydream a lot also may tend to show some peculiar thought processes and verbalizations after they have been deprived for several nights of Stage 1 REM sleep (Feldstein, 1972). Eye movements also have been studied during daydreaming. The results suggest that eye movement may be reduced during fantasy, as when subjects try to imagine their "secret wish coming true" (Klinger, Gregoire, & Barta, 1973; Singer, 1974). On the whole, ongoing fantasy does not seem strongly associated with physiological changes, although work on this problem is still at an early stage. The discoveries of physical changes during changing consciousness provide an exciting new window for the analysis of the fantasy process.

The Ego: Tester of Reality

The *ego* is a direct outgrowth of the id. Freud described its origin this way:

> Under the influence of the real external world around us, one portion of the id has undergone a special development. From what was originally a cortical layer, equipped with the organs for receiving stimuli and with arrangements for acting as a protective shield against stimuli, a special organization has arisen which henceforward acts as an intermediary between the id and the external world. To this region of our mind we have given the name of *ego* (Freud, 1933, p. 2).

The ego is in direct contact with the external world. It is governed by considerations of safety, and its task is preservation of the organism. The ego wages its battle for survival against both the external world and the internal instinctual demands of the id. In this task it has to continuously differentiate between the mental representations of wish-fulfilling images and the actual outer world of reality. In its search for food or sexual release, for example, it must find the appropriate tension-reducing objects in the environment so that tension reduction can actually occur. That is, it must go from image to object, and get satisfaction for id impulses while simultaneously preserving itself.

The ego's function is governed by the *reality principle,* which requires it to test reality and to delay discharge of tension until the appropriate object and environmental conditions are found. The ego operates by means of a "secondary process" that involves realistic, logical thinking and planning through the use of the higher or cognitive mental processes. That is, while the id seeks immediate tension reduction by such primary process means as wish-fulfilling imagery and direct gratification of sexual and aggressive impulses, the ego, like an executive, mediates between the id and the world, testing reality and making decisions about various courses of available action. For example, it delays impulses for immediate sexual gratification until the environmental conditions are appropriate.

The Superego: High Court in Pursuit of Perfection

Freud's third mental structure was the superego. He wrote:

> The long period of childhood, during which the growing human being lives in dependence on his parents, leaves behind it as a precipitate the formation in his ego of a special agency in which this parental influence is prolonged. It has received the name of *superego.* In so far as this superego is differentiated from the ego or is opposed to it, it constitutes a third power which the ego must take into account (Freud, 1933, p. 2).

Thus the *superego* is the agency that internalizes the influence of the parents. It represents the morals and standards of society that have become part of the internal world of the individual in the course of the development of personality. The superego is the conscience, the judge of right and wrong, of good and bad, in accord with the internalized standards of the parents and thus, indirectly, of society. It represents the ideal. Whereas the id seeks pleasure and the ego tests reality, the superego seeks perfection. The superego, for Freud, involved the internalization of parental control in the form of self-control. For example, the individual with a well-developed superego resists "bad" or "evil" temptations, such as stealing when hungry or killing when angry, even when there are no external constraints (in the form of police or other people) to stop him.

PERSONALITY DYNAMICS: THE INTERNAL BATTLE

According to Freud (1915), the three parts of the psychic structure—id, ego, and superego—are always in conflict. The term *dynamics* refers to a continuous interaction and clash between id impulses seeking release and inhibitions or restraining forces against them—an interplay between driving forces and forces that inhibit them. These forces and counterforces propel personality.

Conflict

The drive for immediate satisfaction of impulses reflects human nature: people are motivated to avoid pain and to achieve immediate tension reduction. This drive for immediate satisfaction of instinctual demands leads to a clash between the individual and the environment. Conflict develops to the degree that the environment and its representatives in the form of other persons, notably the parents in childhood, and later superego, punish or block immediate impulse expression.

The person in time comes to incorporate into the superego the values by which he is raised, largely by internalizing parental characteristics and morals. In Freud's view perpetual warfare and conflict exist between humans and environment. Insofar as societal values become "internalized" as part of the person, this warfare is waged internally between the id, ego, and superego, and it produces anxiety.

Anxiety

Freud (1933) distinguished three kinds of anxiety. In *neurotic anxiety* the person fears that his instincts will get out of control and cause him to behave in ways that will be punished. In *moral anxiety* the person feels conscience-stricken or guilty about unacceptable things that she feels she has done or even contemplates. Both neurotic and moral anxiety are derivatives of *reality anxiety,* the fear of real dangers in the external world.

The sequence of events in reality anxiety (or *objective anxiety*) is simple: a danger exists in the external world, the person perceives it, and this perception evokes anxiety. This sequence may be summarized as:

external danger → perception of danger → reality anxiety

Because anxiety is painful (tension producing), we try to reduce it as quickly as possible. Usually we try to cope with anxiety by anticipating and fighting dangers

In *neurotic anxiety* the person fears that his instincts will cause him to behave in ways that will be punished.

by realistic means: locking doors to keep out intruders, getting physical checkups to guard our health, cleansing wounds to prevent infection, seeking shelter against the elements. When realistic methods fail (or cannot be found), unrealistic *defense mechanisms* may be tried unconsciously. Defenses are used especially in the internal struggle, where the individual tries to cope with her own unacceptable wishes. These defenses serve as disguises through which people hide their motives and conflicts from themselves as well as from others.

In Self-Defense: Basic Mechanisms

Psychodynamic theorists emphasize that when a threat becomes especially serious it may lead to intense inhibitions. In the psychodynamic view, such defensive inhibition is desperate and primitive. It is a massive, generalized, inhibitory reaction rather than a specific response to the particular danger. This *denial* defense occurs when the person can neither escape nor attack the threat. If the panic is sufficient, the only possible alternative may be to deny it. Outright denial may be possible for the young child, who is not yet upset by violating the demands of reality testing. When the child becomes too mature to deny objective facts in the interests of defense, denial becomes a less plausible alternative and repression may occur.

In psychodynamic theory *repression* usually refers to a particular type of denial: "the forgetting, or ejection from consciousness, of memories of threat, and especially the ejection from awareness of impulses in oneself that might have objectionable consequences" (White, 1964, p. 214).

Repression was one of the initial concepts in Freud's theory and became one of its cornerstones. Freud (1920) believed that the mechanisms of denial and repression were the most fundamental or primitive defenses and played a part in other defenses. Indeed, he thought that other defenses started with a massive inhibition of an impulse, which was followed by various elaborations (see Table 2-2).

In *projection* the person's own unacceptable impulses are inhibited and the source of the anxiety is attributed to another person. For example, one's own temptations toward homosexuality are attributed to a friend. Projection presumably gives relief because it reduces anxiety.

Replacement in consciousness of an anxiety-producing impulse by its opposite is another defense termed *reaction formation*. For example, people frightened by their own sexual impulses may become actively involved in a "ban the filth" vigilante group. They use their energy to vigorously censor books and movies they consider obscene. Through projection and reaction formation the id impulse is expressed, but in a disguise that makes it acceptable to the ego.

Another defense mechanism is the *rationalization* of feelings by making excuses. Thus, a man who has unconscious, deeply hostile impulses toward his wife might invent elaborate excuses that serve to disrupt and even destroy their relations without admitting his true feelings. He might create many false reasons to stay away from home and persistently disappoint and hurt his wife. He might invoke "pressures at the office," "a hectic schedule," "worrying about inflation and politics," and "fatigue" as excuses for ignoring, avoiding, and frustrating his wife.

Sublimation, according to Freud, is an ego defense that is particularly significant in the development of culture. It consists of a displacement or redirection of

Table 2-2
Definitions and Examples of Some Defense Mechanisms

Mechanism	Definition	Example
Repression	Massive inhibition of a threatening impulse or event by rendering it unconscious (beyond awareness)	Guilt-producing sexual wishes are "forgotten"
Projection	Unacceptable aspects of oneself are attributed to someone else	Projecting one's own unacceptable sexual impulses by attributing them to one's boss
Reaction formation	Anxiety-producing impulse is replaced by its opposite in consciousness	Unacceptable feelings of hate are converted into "love"
Rationalization	Making something more acceptable by attributing it to more acceptable causes	Blaming an aggressive act on "being overworked" rather than on feeling angry
Sublimation	Expression of a socially unacceptable impulse in socially acceptable ways	Becoming a soldier to hurt others; becoming a plumber to indulge in anal desires

impulses from an object (or target) that is sexual to one that is social in character. Suppose, for example, that masturbation becomes too threatening to the young child. He or she may sublimate (or transform) these impulses into a socially acceptable form, such as horseback riding and other athletics.

Psychic Energy: The Many Faces of Libido

The essence of Freudian personality dynamics is the transformation of motives: the basic impulses persist and press for discharge, but the objects at which they are directed and the manner in which they are expressed are transformed (1917). Freud thought that these transformations involved a finite amount of energy that was contained in the person. This energy (called *libido*), is "cathected" (attached or fixed) on aspects of the internal and external environment. The energy available to the organism may be continuously transformed, fixed onto different "objects" (note that "objects" was a term that for Freud included people and not just inanimate things). However, the total amount of energy is conserved and stable. Freud's energy system thus was consistent with the hydraulic models of nineteenth-century physics. The id was seen as a kind of dynamo, and the total mind (or psyche) was viewed as a closed system motivated to maintain equilibrium: any forces that were built up required discharge. The discharge could be indirect. Instinctual impulses could be *displaced* from one object to another; for instance, from one's parents to other authority figures or more remotely, from the genitals, for example, to phallic symbols.

Some of these transformations or displacements are shown in Figure 2-1. For example, if sadistic aggressive impulses are too threatening to self-acceptance, they

Figure 2-1
The Psychodynamic Transformation of Motives: Examples of Displacement in the Form of Sublimation

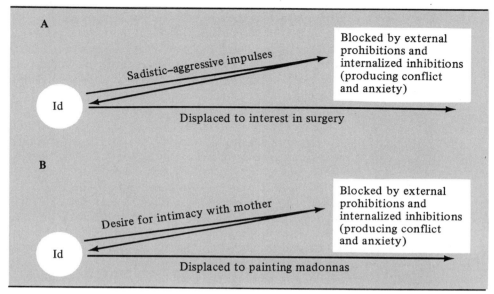

might be transformed into a more socially sanctioned form, such as an interest in surgery. Likewise, sexual wishes toward the mother might be displaced into a career of painting madonnas, as some Freudians think happened among certain Renaissance painters. Freud (1909) himself suggested such dynamics in the case of Leonardo Da Vinci.

In sum, psychodynamics involves a continuous conflict between id impulses seeking discharge and defenses designed to transform these wishes into an acceptable form for the person. In the course of these transformations, energy is exchanged and directed toward different objects.

When Defenses Fail: Neurotic Anxiety and Conflict

Sometimes the defenses that disguise basic motives may become inadequate, as in disturbed conditions. But even under the usual circumstances of everyday life the defenses are occasionally penetrated and the person betrays himself (Freud, 1901). Such betrayals of underlying motives are seen when defenses are relaxed, as in dream life during sleep or in jokes and slips of the tongue. The defense process involves distortion and displacement; private meanings develop as objects and events become symbols representing things quite different from themselves. It is believed that these meanings are partially revealed by behavioral "signs" or symptoms that may symbolize disguised wishes and unconscious conflicts. For example, phobias such as the fear of snakes may reflect basic sexual conflicts; in this case, the feared snake has symbolic meaning.

It is now possible to consider the Freudian conception of how neurotic anxiety may develop. The sequence here (depicted in Figure 2-2) begins with the child's aggressive or sexual impulses that seek direct release. These efforts at discharge may be strongly punished and blocked by dangers or threats (e.g., intense parental punishment such as withdrawal of love). Hence, they lead to objective anxiety. The child may become especially afraid that these impulses will lead to loss of parental love, and in time, therefore, may come to fear his or her own impulses. Because this state is painful, the child tries to repress these impulses. If the ego is weak, the repression is only partly successful and the instinctual impulses persist. Unless expressed in some acceptable form, these impulses become increasingly "pent up," gradually building up to the point where they become hard to repress. Consequently, there may be a partial breakdown of repression, and some of the impulses may break through, producing some neurotic anxiety. Anxiety, in this view, functions as a danger signal, a warning to the individual that repressed impulses are starting to break through the defenses. Rather than emerging directly, however, the unacceptable impulses express themselves indirectly in disguised and symbolic ways.

Freud felt that the symbolic meaning of behavior was clearest in neurotic acts. He cited the case of a girl who compulsively rinsed out her washbasin many times after washing. Freud thought that the significance of this ceremonial was expressed in the proverb, "Don't throw away dirty water until you have clean." He interpreted the girl's action as a warning to her sister, to whom she was very close, "not to separate from her unsatisfactory husband until she had established a relationship with a better man" (Freud, 1959, vol. 2, p. 28).

Another patient was able to sit only in a particular chair and could leave it only with much difficulty. In Freud's analysis of her problem, the chair symbolized the husband to whom she remained faithful. Freud saw the symbolic meaning of her compulsion in her sentence, "It is so hard to part from anything (chair or husband) in which one has once settled oneself" (Freud, 1959, vol. 2, p. 29). Thus the important object of conflict—the husband—was transformed into a trivial one—the chair. Freud cited these and many similar cases as evidence for the view that neurotic behaviors express unconscious motives and ideas symbolically. The clinician's task, then, is to decipher the unconscious meaning of the patient's behav-

Figure 2-2
Sequence in Freudian Conception of Neurotic Anxiety

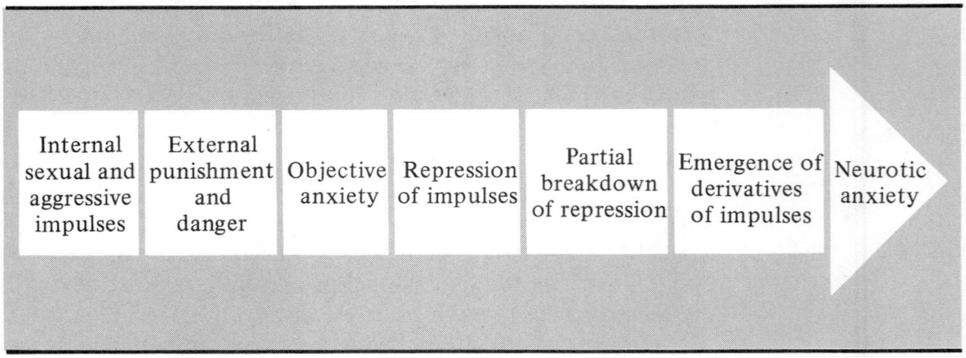

| Internal sexual and aggressive impulses | External punishment and danger | Objective anxiety | Repression of impulses | Partial breakdown of repression | Emergence of derivatives of impulses | Neurotic anxiety |

Table 2-3
Possible Meanings of Some Behavioral Signs According to Freudian Theory

Behavioral Sign	Possible Underlying Meaning
Fear of snakes	Sexual conflicts concerning genitals
Compulsive cleanliness	Reaction against anal impulses
Obsessive thought, "My mother is drowning,"	Imperfectly repressed hostility toward mother
Paranoid jealousy	Homosexual wishes
Preoccupation with money	Problems around toilet training
Crusading against obscenity	Reaction formation against own unacceptable wishes

ior, and to discover the conflicts and dynamics that might underlie seemingly irrational behavior patterns (see Table 2-3).

Traumatic Seeds: Origins of Neuroses

In Freud's view, serious problems, such as the neuroses, and the roots of the symptoms that characterize them begin in early childhood:

> . . . It seems that neuroses are acquired only in early childhood (up to the age of six), even though their symptoms may not make their appearance till much later. The childhood neurosis may become manifest for a short time or may even be overlooked. In every case the later neurotic illness links up with the prelude in childhood.
> . . . The neuroses are, as we know, disorders of the ego; and it is not to be wondered at if the ego, so long as it is feeble, immature and incapable of resistance, fails to deal with tasks which it could cope with later on with the utmost ease. In these circumstances instinctual demands from within, no less than excitations from the external world, operate as 'traumas', particularly if they are met halfway by certain innate dispositions (Freud, 1933, pp. 41–42).

As these quotations indicate, neuroses were seen as the products of early childhood traumas plus innate dispositions. But even the behavior of less disturbed persons was believed to reflect expressions of underlying unconscious motives and conflicts. These manifestations could be seen in the "psychopathology of everyday life"—the occurrence of meaningful but common unconscious expressions, as discussed next.

The Psychopathology of Everyday Life: "Mistakes" that Betray

Some of Freud's most fascinating—and controversial—ideas involved the elaboration of possible hidden meanings that might underlie such common occurrences

Table 2-4
Examples of Behaviors Motivated by Unconscious Wishes

Behavior	Unconscious Wish	Transformation Involved
Slip of tongue: May I "insert" (instead of escort) you.	to insult	condensation: (insult + escort = "insort")
Slip of tongue: "Gentlemen, I declare a quorum present and herewith declare the session *closed.*"	to close the meeting	association of opposites (open = closed)
Dream of disappointment in quality of theater tickets, as result of having gotten them too soon.	I married too soon; I could have gotten a better husband by waiting	symbolism (getting tickets too soon = marrying too soon)
Dream of breaking an arm	desire to break marriage vows	conversion into visual imagery (breaking vows = breaking an arm)

SOURCE: Freud, 1920.

as slips of the tongue, errors in writing, jokes, and dreams. In Freud's (1901, 1920) view, "mistakes" may be unconsciously motivated by impulses that the individual is afraid to express directly or openly. To show that mistakes may really be motivated by underlying wishes, Freud pointed out many instances in which even the attempt to "correct" the error appears to betray a hidden, unacceptable meaning. In one case, for example, an official introduced a general as "this battle-scared veteran" and tried to "correct" his mistake by saying "bottle-scarred veteran." Other examples are summarized in Table 2-4. Some common Freudian dream symbols are shown in Table 2-5.

Table 2-5
Some Freudian Dream Symbols and Their Meanings

Dream Symbol	Meaning
King, queen	Parents
Little animals, vermin	Siblings
Travel, journey	Dying
Clothes, uniforms	Nakedness
Flying	Sexual intercourse
Extraction of teeth	Castration

SOURCE: Based on Freud, 1920.

Motivational Determinism: Dynamic Causes

By now it should be clear that Freudian psychoanalytic theory offers the view that behavior is motivationally determined. The causal chain can be complex and indirect. Events in one area of the personality exert their effects on another, but every behavior, no matter how trivial, has its ultimate motivational cause. Suppose, for example, a man fights with his wife about money, is personally fussy about his appearance, and becomes very upset when he loses his umbrella. These seemingly different bits of behavior might actually be motivated by a common cause. Much of psychoanalytic assessment and therapy is a search for such underlying causes. A psychodynamic explanation of behavior consists of finding the motives that produced it. The focus is not on behavior but on the motivations that it serves and reflects.

Freudians tend to believe in *motivational* determinism: all behavior, even the seemingly most absurd or trivial (like losing an umbrella), is motivated and significant. They may view any behavior as a sign of basic, largely unconscious forces. This means that your most important motives are primarily unconscious. You may be victimized by these hidden motives and perceive them only through the distortions of defensive maneuvers used in ways only dimly known to you. The basic psychodynamics arise early in life during the stages of psychosexual development and they shape your future and how you will deal with the world.

PSYCHOSEXUAL STAGES AND PERSONALITY DEVELOPMENT

Freud believed that every person normally progresses through five *psychosexual stages.* During the first five years of life pleasure is successively focused on three zones of the body as the oral, anal, and phallic stages unfold. Then comes a quiet latency period of about five or six years. Finally, if progress through each stage has been successful, the person reaches the mature or genital stage after puberty. But special problems at any stage may retard or arrest (fixate) development and leave enduring marks on the person's character throughout life.

Freud's Stages

The *oral stage* occurs during the first year of life, when the baby is completely dependent on others for the satisfaction of all needs. In this stage body pleasure is focused on the mouth and on the satisfactions of sucking, eating, and biting in the course of feeding (but see *In Focus 2.2*).

The *anal stage,* in the second year of life, is marked by a shift in body pleasure to the anus and by a concern with the retention and expulsion of feces. According to Freud, during toilet training the child has his first experience with imposed control: the manner in which toilet training is handled may influence later personal qualities and conflicts. For example, extremely harsh, repressive training might produce a person characterized by obstinacy, stinginess, and a preoccupation with orderliness and cleanliness.

The *phallic stage* is the period in which the child observes the difference between male and female and experiences what Freud called the Oedipus complex. This

Although the feeding situation is a critical phase of early development, it is only one part of the total relationship between the growing organism and the world. Thus the baby is more than an "oral" creature. Babies respond to stimulation of the mouth, lips, and tongue, but in addition, they see, hear, and feel, obtaining stimulation visually, aurally, and from being handled.

Convinced that in spite of an abundance of theories, personality psychology has much too little real data, Professor Burton L. White of Harvard University began by carefully observing infants as they lay in their cribs. (The subjects were physically normal infants in an orphanage.) He and his colleagues recorded the quantity and quality of visual-motor activity to study the babies' attention. On the basis of these observations they plotted the development of the infants' tendency to explore the visual surroundings, as depicted in Figure 2-3. The findings surprised the investigators:

> One important revelation for me which resulted from these weekly observations was that, contrary to my academically bred expectations, infants weren't really very oral during the first months of life. In fact,

between two and six months, a far more appropriate description would be that they are visual-prehensory creatures. We observed subject after subject spend dozens of hours watching first his fists, then his fingers, and then the interactions between hands and fingers. Thumb-sucking and mouthing were rarely observed except for brief periods when the infant was either noticeably upset or unusually hungry (White, 1967, p. 207).

These observations point up how much more we need to know about the details of the infant's activities before we can reach conclusions about what events characterize early development. It may be, as this investigator's comments imply, that the "oral" infant will turn out to be much more attentive and active, and less oral and passive, then was believed in early formulations. Indeed, close observation of young children suggests a dramatic increase in the infant's competence by the second or third month. More wakefulness and alertness, greater receptivity to stimulation, more directed attention and less fussing begin to characterize the baby (Sroufe, 1977). Stimulation becomes less unsettling and may be sought out actively as the baby becomes more and more attentive, even to its own movements.

Figure 2-3
The Development of the Tendency to Explore the Surround (Control Group)

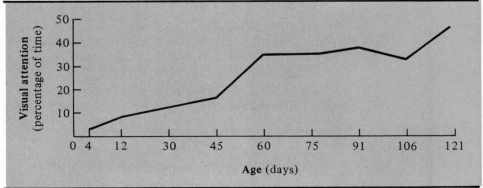

occurs at about age five. Freud thought that both boys and girls love their mother as the satisfier of their basic needs and resent their father as a rival for their mother's affections. In addition, the boy fears castration by the father as punishment for desiring his mother sexually. This fear of castration results in the repression of the boy's sexual desire for his mother and in hostility toward his father. To reduce the anxiety of possible castration by the father, the boy tries to become like him or to identify with him, gradually internalizing the father's standards and values as his own.

A *latency period* follows the phallic stage. Now there is less overt concern with sexuality; the child represses his memories of infantile sexuality and forbidden sexual activity.

The *genital stage* is the final, mature stage of psychosexual development. Now the person is capable of genuine love for other people and can achieve adult sexual satisfactions. No longer characterized by the selfishness and mixed, conflicting feelings that marked the earlier stages, he or she can relate to others in a mature, heterosexual fashion. But before he or she reaches this stage, excessive stress or overindulgence may cause the person to become fixated at earlier levels of psychosexual development.

Fixation and Regression

The concepts of *fixation* and *regression* are closely connected with Freud's conceptualization of psychosexual stages of development. Fixation means that a sexual impulse is arrested at an early stage. Regression is reversion to an earlier stage. Fixation occurs when conflict at a particular stage of psychosexual development is too great. Severe deprivation or overindulgence at a particular stage, or inconsistent alterations between indulgence and deprivation, may lead to fixation.

In sum, personality is intimately related to the individual's mode of coping with problems at each stage of psychosexual development. The result is reflected in the nature of character formation, symptoms, and relations with other people. When individuals' resolution of problems at any stage of development is inadequate, later stress may cause them to regress to that earlier stage. They then display behavior typical of that less mature period.

Freud's Theory of Identification

Parts of Freud's theory of psychosexual stages have been modified and even rejected in recent years. Some of his closely related concepts regarding identification, however, have continued to be influential.

Early personality development occurs in the setting of the family. In that context Freud strongly emphasized the child's attachment to the mother and the rivalry between son and father for her attentions. This triangle of relations is called the *Oedipus situation.* The relations between child and parent are the bases for identification with the standards of the parent. This identification process Freud attributed to two mechanisms that operate during psychosexual development.

Anaclitic identification is based on the intense dependency of a child on his mother, beginning early in the course of the infant's development. Because of the helplessness of the infant, his dependency upon his caretaker is profound. Identification for girls is based mainly on this early love or dependency relation with the mother. In anaclitic identification the child must first have developed a dependent love relationship with his caretaker (usually the mother). Later, when the mother begins to withdraw some of her nurturant attention, the child tries to recapture her by imitating and reproducing her in actions and fantasy.

For boys, dependency or "anaclitic" identification with the mother is followed later by *identification with the aggressor*. The "aggressor" is the father during the Oedipal phase of development. Identification with the aggressor is motivated by fear of harm and castration by the punitive father in retribution for the son's fantasies and his sexual wishes toward the mother. Freud described the situation vividly:

> . . . When a boy (from the age of two or three) has entered the phallic phase of his libidinal [sexual] development, is feeling pleasurable sensations in his sexual organ and has learnt to procure these at will by manual stimulation, he becomes his mother's lover. He wishes to possess her physically in such ways as he has divined from his observations and intuitions about sexual life, and he tries to seduce her by showing her the male organ which he is proud to own. In a word, his early awakened masculinity seeks to take his father's place with her; his father has hitherto in any case been an envied model to the boy, owing to the physical strength he perceives in him and the authority with which he finds him clothed. His father now becomes a rival who stands in his way and whom he would like to get rid of (Freud, 1933, p. 46).

The hostile feelings that the boy experiences in the Oedipal situation create great anxiety in him; he desires the mother but fears castration from the father. To defend against the anxiety he resolves the Oedipal conflict, repressing his aggressive wishes against his father and trying to become more like him. It is as though the boy believes that if he *"is"* the father he cannot be hurt by him. Identification with the aggressor requires that the boy have a strong (but ambivalent) relation with the father. In this relationship, love for the father is mixed with hostility because the father possesses the mother and interferes with the son's urges. Freud thought that through identification with the aggressor boys develop a stricter superego.

AFTER FREUD: NEO-FREUDIAN PSYCHOANALYTIC DEVELOPMENTS

Freud's Image of the Person

It is not simple—and probably impossible—to capture the essence of Freud's conceptions. Freud built a dramatic image of what a person might be, inventing a sweeping and novel theoretical system. Freud saw the person as struggling with himself and the world, blocked by anxieties, conflicted, and plagued by his own unacceptable wishes and unconscious secrets. This picture has captivated the imagination of many laymen as well as clinicians. Consequently, it has had an enormous impact on philosophical as well as psychological conceptions of human nature. In Freud's view humans are not the unemotional, rational beings that Victorian society thought they were. Instead, people are torn by unconscious conflicts and wishes that push them in seemingly puzzling ways.

Freud's emphasis on unconscious impulses as the most basic determinants of behavior is seen in an analogy in which the relation of the id and the ego is likened to that between a horse and its rider:

> . . . The horse provides the locomotive energy, and the rider has the prerogative of determining the goal and of guiding the movements of his powerful mount towards it. But all too often in the relations between the ego and the id we find a picture of the less ideal situation in which the rider is obliged to guide his horse in the direction in which it itself wants to go (Freud, 1933, p. 108).

Thus in Freud's psychology the id is stubborn and strong and often the ego cannot really control it effectively.

Freud believed that the environment is less important than inborn instincts in the dynamics of personality. He thought that external stimuli make fewer demands and, in any event, can always be avoided. In contrast, one's own impulses and needs cannot be escaped. Consequently, he made instinctual impulses the core of personality. In the years since Freud, many of his followers have gradually modified and extended his conception in new directions.

Common Themes: Toward Ego Psychology

Although each "neo-Freudian" writer has made a distinctive contribution, certain common themes emerge, especially in recent years. These themes suggest a gradual shift in focus, summarized in Table 2-6. Less attention seems to be paid to Freud's ideas about the basic sexual and aggressive instincts of the id and the id itself is given a less dominant role. This shift is accompanied by an expansion of the concept and functions of ego, and in the "self," to the point where the newer theoretical trends have been named "ego psychology."

With this growth of the role of ego, the person is viewed as a more competent, potentially creative problem solver, engaged in much more than the management of instincts that press for discharge. The neo-Freudians, as Table 2-6 suggests, also

Table 2-6
Post-Freudian Developments: Some Characteristics of the Neo-Freudians

Less Attention To	More Attention To
Id and instincts	Ego and self
Purely intrapsychic causes	Social, interpersonal causes
Earliest childhood	Later developments throughout the life span
Psychosexual stages	Social forces and positive strivings; the role of the culture and society

saw human development as a more continuous process that extends throughout the life span. More than the product of early psychosexual experiences, personality began to be viewed as a life-long development, rooted in social and interpersonal relations and in the context of culture and society. Much human striving began to be seen as motivated by social and personal goals as well as by the satisfaction of primitive instincts. Let us consider a few examples of these theoretical developments.

Carl Jung

Carl Jung began as an admirer and associate of Freud's but later became a dissenter and developed his own theory of psychoanalysis and his own method of psychotherapy. His approach became known as *analytical psychology.* Although it retains Freud's unconscious processes, it claims a *collective unconscious*—an inherited foundation of personality. The contents of the collective unconscious are *archetypes* or "primordial images." Unlike the personal unconscious, whose contents were once conscious but have been forgotten or repressed, the contents of the collective unconscious have never been in consciousness. Therefore the contents of the collective unconscious are not individually acquired; they are due to heredity. Examples of archetypes include God, the young potent hero, the wise old man, the Earth Mother, the Fairy Godmother, and the hostile brethren. They occur in myths, art, and dreams of all mankind.

In Jung's view, the psyche included not only a conscious side but also a covert or *shadow* aspect that is unconscious. Personal growth involves an unfolding of this

Carl Gustav Jung (1875–1961)

shadow and its gradual integration with the rest of the personality into a meaningful, coherent life pattern. The unconscious of every female includes a masculine, assertive element (the *animus*). The unconscious of every male includes a feminine, passive element (the *anima*). To be constructively masculine or feminine, individuals of each sex must recognize and integrate these opposite sex elements within themselves (see Table 2-7).

Jung described four basic ways of experiencing (contacting) the world: *sensing, intuition, feeling,* and *thinking,* summarized in Table 2-8. According to Jung, people differ consistently in the degree to which they emphasize each way of experiencing. One person, for example, might typically prefer intuitive leaps with little abstract thought. Another might know the world mostly through his or her senses with little use of either intuition or reason. In addition, Jung suggested *extraversion-introversion* (discussed further in Chapter 5). Like the four ways of experiencing, these two attitudes of extraversion-introversion are divided: one is dominant in the conscious life while the other influences the unconscious side of the personality.

Jung broadened the concept of psychic energy. He did not exclude the sexual instinct of Freudian theory but thought it was only one among many instincts. Jung placed great emphasis on the directed purposiveness of personality development. He believed that human behavior cannot be explained entirely by past history. For Jung the meaning of behavior became fully intelligible only in terms of its end products or final effects; we need to understand humans not only in terms of their past but also in the light of their purposes and goal strivings.

Jung, like Freud, emphasized symbolic meanings. He believed, for example, that "abnormal behaviors" are expressions of the unconscious mind. Some examples of these expressions are shown in Table 2-9, and they reveal clear overlap with Freud's thinking. Also like Freud, Jung thought that abnormal behaviors were merely one way in which the contents of the unconscious may reveal themselves. More often, he felt, they are expressed in dreams.

Jung went beyond Freud, however, in his increasing fascination with dreams as unconscious expressions of great interest in their own right. (He believed that this contrasts with their use merely as starting points for saying whatever comes to mind, i.e., "free associations," discussed in Chapter 3.) As Jung put it: " . . . I came increasingly to disagree with free association as Freud first employed it; I

Table 2-7
Examples of Jungian Concepts

The Collective Unconscious: Found in everyone and said to contain inherited memories and ancestral behavior patterns

Archetypes: Basic elements or primordial images forming the collective unconscious, manifested in dreams and myths (e.g., Earth Mother, the wise old man)

The Animus: The masculine, assertive element in the unconscious of every woman

The Anima: The feminine, soft, passive element in the unconscious of every man

The Mandala: Usually a circular shape, symbolizing the self, containing designs often divided into four parts

Table 2-8
Jung's Four Ways of Experiencing the World

Ways of Experiencing	Characteristics
Sensing	Knowing through sensory systems
Intuition	Quick guessing about what underlies sensory inputs
Feeling	Focus on the emotional aspects of experience—its beauty or ugliness, pleasantness or unpleasantness
Thinking	Abstract thought, reasoning

wanted to keep as close as possible to the dream itself, and to exclude all the irrelevant ideas and associations that it might evoke" (Jung, 1964, p. 28).

In the same direction, Jung became intrigued by the unconscious for its own sake. He viewed the unconscious not just as the source of instincts. For him it was a vital, rich part of everyone's life, more significant than the conscious world, full of symbols communicated through dreams. The focus of Jungian psychology became the study of people's relations to their unconscious. Jung's method taught individuals to become more receptive to their own dreams, and to let their unconscious serve as a guide for how to live.

Jung's conception of personality is complex, more a set of fascinating observations than a coherent theory. His observations often dwelled on the multiple, contradictory forces in life: "I see in all that happens the play of opposites" (1963, p. 235). Yet he also was one of the first to conceptualize a *self* that actively strives for oneness and unity. Jung saw the self (the striving for wholeness) as an archetype that is expressed in many ways. The expressions of the striving for wholeness include the *mandala* (a magic circle archetype shown in Figure 2-4), and various religious and transcendental experiences. He devoted much of his life to the study of these expressions in primitive societies, alchemy, mythology, dreams, and symbols. To achieve unity and wholeness the individual must become increasingly aware of the wisdom available in his or her personal and collective unconscious and must learn to live in harmony with it.

Table 2-9
Examples of Unconscious Symbolic Meanings Believed to Underlie Abnormal Behavior ("Symptoms") According to Jung

Behavior	Underlying Meaning
Asthma attack	"She can't breathe the atmosphere at home"
Vomiting	"He can't digest—(some unpleasant fact)"
Spasm and inability to swallow	"He can't swallow it"
Leg paralysis	"She can't go on any longer"

SOURCE: Jung, 1964.

**Figure 2-4
A Mandala**

Erich Fromm

Fromm (1941, 1947) helped to expand Freudian concepts to the individual as a member of society. Freud saw personality development as a reaction to satisfactions and frustrations of physiological drives. In contrast, for Fromm people are primarily social beings to be understood in terms of their relations to others. According to Fromm, individual psychology is fundamentally social psychology. People have psychological qualities, such as tendencies to grow, develop,and realize potentialities, that result in a desire for freedom and a striving for justice and truth. Thus human nature has a force of its own that influences social processes.

Fromm's explanation of character traits illustrates the difference between Freud's biological orientation and Fromm's social orientation. Fromm criticized Freud's idea that fixation at certain pleasure-giving stages is the cause of later character traits. According to Fromm, character traits develop from experiences with others. Psychosexual problems and attitudes are rooted in the whole of the character structure. They are expressions in the language of the body of an attitude toward the world that is socially conditioned. According to Freud, culture is the result of societal suppressions of instinctual drives. For Fromm, culture is molded

Erich Fromm (1900–1980)

by the mode of existence of a given society. In turn, the dominant character traits of the people in a society become forces shaping the social process and the culture itself.

Another major point of departure from Freud is Fromm's belief that ideals like truth, justice, and freedom can be genuine strivings and not simply rationalizations of biological motives. Freud's psychology is a psychology of instinctual drives that defines pleasure in terms of tension reduction. Fromm's psychology tries to make a place for positive attributes, such as tenderness and the human ability to love, and implies that these human needs have a force of their own. He believes that character is not the result of passive adaptation to social conditions. It is a dynamic adaptation on the basis of elements that are either biologically inherent in human nature or have become inherent as the result of historic evolution.

Erik Erikson

The psychoanalyst Erik Erikson (1963) has proposed stages of development that call attention to problems of social adaptation (Table 2-10). As children grow up they face a wider range of human relationships. The solution of the specific prob-

Table 2-10
Erikson's Stages of Psychosocial Development

Stage and Age	Psychosocial Crisis	Optimal Outcome
I. Oral-sensory (1st year of life)	Trust vs. Mistrust	Basic trust and optimism
II. Muscular-anal (2nd year)	Autonomy vs. Shame, doubt	Sense of control over oneself and the environment
III. Locomotor-genital (3rd through 5th year)	Initiative vs. Guilt	Goal-directedness and purpose
IV. Latency (6th year to start of puberty)	Industry vs. Inferiority	Competence
V. Puberty and Adolescence	Identity vs. Role Confusion	Reintegration of past with present and future goals, fidelity
VI. Early Adulthood	Intimacy vs. Isolation	Commitment, sharing, closeness, and love
VII. Young and Middle Adult	Generativity vs. Self-absorption	Production and concern with the world and future generations
VIII. Mature Adult	Integrity vs. Despair	Perspective, satisfaction with one's past life, wisdom

SOURCE: Based on Erikson, 1963, and modified from original.

lems at each of eight *psychosocial* stages (rather than psychosexual stages) determines how adequate they will become as adults. Erikson's focus on psychosocial development reflects the growing neo-Freudian emphasis on broad social and cultural forces, rather than instinctual drives alone.

At each stage of development Erikson hypothesizes a psychosocial "crisis." This crisis arises from the person's efforts to solve the problems at that stage. For example, in the first stage of life (the "oral sensory" stage of the first year) the crisis involves "trust versus mistrust." Erikson hypothesizes that at this stage the child's relation to its mother forms basic attitudes about "getting" and "giving." If the crisis is properly resolved, the experiences at this stage lay the foundation for later trust, drive, and hope.

Erikson's stages extend beyond infancy to include crises of adolescence and adulthood. He sees development as a process that extends throughout life, rather than being entirely determined in the early years. In this developmental process, "ego identity" is central:

> The integration . . . of ego identity is . . . more than the sum of the childhood identifications. It is the accrued experience of the ego's ability to integrate all identifications

Erik H. Erikson (b. 1902)

with the vicissitudes of the libido, with the aptitudes developed out of endowment, and with the opportunities offered in social roles (Erikson, 1963, p. 261).

The underlying assumptions of his view of development are:

(1) that the human personality in principle develops according to steps predetermined in the growing person's readiness to be driven toward, to be aware of, and to interact with, a widening social radius; and (2) that society, in principle, tends to be so constituted as to meet and invite this succession of potentialities for interaction and attempts to safeguard and to encourage the proper rate and the proper sequence of their enfolding (Erikson, 1963, p. 270).

Erikson's ideas have become popular in many parts of our culture. His thoughts concerning the "identity crises" of adolescence, for example, are discussed widely. Indeed the phrase "identity crisis" has become a part of everyday speech. Both provocative and literate, Erikson's ideas have influenced concepts of human nature and the general intellectual culture. Erikson believes that all young people must generate for themselves some "central perspective and direction" that gives them a meaningful sense of unity and purpose. This perspective integrates the remnants of their childhood with the expectations and hopes of adulthood (Erikson, 1968). This sense of identity involves a synthesis of how individuals have come to see themselves and their awareness of what the important other people in their lives expect them to be.

Erikson's stages go much beyond childhood and include the psychosocial crises of the adult.

Other Neo-Freudian Analysts

In many ways the formulations of Fromm and Erikson are representative of the contributions of numerous other "neo-Freudians," such as Alfred Adler, Harry Stack Sullivan, Karen Horney, and David Rapaport. Generally these neo-Freudians urged more concern with "ego-processes," "reality testing," and current interpersonal relationships. They paid less attention to the role of instincts and distinct psychosexual developmental stages.

For Freud the id and the instincts were the dominant aspects of the total personality. The ego was subservient to the id's instinctual wishes, even in healthy personalities. More recent theorists in the psychoanalytic tradition have put more emphasis on social variables shaping personality and less on the role of instincts. These neo-Freudians or "ego psychologists" assert a "conflict-free sphere" of the ego (Hartmann, Kris, & Loewenstein, 1947; Rapaport, 1951). In their view, the ego has its own sources of energy and follows a course of development independent of the id and the instincts. That is, some portion of ego functioning is not determined by the attempt to avoid conflict between the id and the demands of society.

Harry Stack Sullivan most explicitly emphasized the crucial importance of interpersonal processes and of human relations for the development of personality. He conceptualizes psychiatry as a form of *social* psychology. For Sullivan the individual can be understood only in his relations to the significant people in his life. A somewhat similar emphasis characterizes the writings of Alfred Adler. He focuses on the person's total "life style" and his "social interest," thus also viewing man as a social being. These theorists, just like Jung, Fromm, and Erikson, have influenced general views about man and personality and broad attitudes toward psychotherapy; they have not generated specific testable hypotheses for research. Most of them are or were practicing psychotherapists and writers rather than experimental researchers and scientists. Their contribution, therefore, may prove to have more impact on the history of ideas than on the field of psychology as a formal area of science.

**In Focus 2.3
Beyond Sex and Aggression: Competence Motivation**

In the years since Freud, psychodynamic theorists have paid attention to a variety of non-physiological motives that go beyond sex and aggression. Some of these so-called higher-order motives such as curiosity, the need for stimulation, and the desire for play and adventure may be seen as parts of a more basic motive: the desire for competence (White, 1959). Everyday activities such as a child's exploring, playing, talking, and even crawling and walking, according to Robert White, reflect the desire for mastery and effective functioning; they are satisfying for their own sake (intrinsically) and create in the person a feeling of efficacy. White argues the point in these words:

> If in our thinking about motives we do not include this overall tendency toward active dealing, we draw the picture of a creature that is helpless in the grip of its fears, drives, and passions; too helpless perhaps even to survive, certainly too helpless to have been the creator of civilization. It is in connection with strivings to attain competence that the activity inherent in living organisms is given

its clearest representation—the power of initiative and exertion that we experience as a sense of being an agent in the living of our lives. This experience may be called a *feeling of efficacy* (White, 1972, p. 209).

In sum, *competence motivation* is a desire for mastery of a task for its own sake and may apply to such diverse tasks as running, piano playing, juggling, chess, or the mastery of a new surgical procedure. According to White, the desire for mastery arises independently of other biological drives (such as hunger and sex) and is not derived from them. Moreover, people engage in activities that satisfy competence needs for the sake of the activity, not for the sake of any external reward such as the praise, attention, or money to which it may lead. The concept of competence motivation is valuable in emphasizing the enormous range of creative activities that humans pursue and appear to enjoy in their own right. It is only one of many newer directions explored by psychodynamic theorists.

This chapter has merely sketched the outline of psychodynamic conceptions. The applications of these ideas for the assessment and treatment of persons probably have been greater than those of any other psychological theory. Consequently an adequate view of the implications of psychodynamic theory, and of its current status, cannot be achieved until these applications are examined in the following chapters.

SUMMARY

1. The most influential psychodynamic theory has been that of Sigmund Freud. Freud's theory and method of treating personality disturbances were based on extensive clinical observation of neurotic persons and on self-analysis.

2. In Freud's view, the id, ego, and superego form the structure of the personality. The *id* is the primary, instinctual core. It obeys the "pleasure principle," seeking immediate gratification of impulses. The *ego* mediates between the instinctual demands of the id and the outer world of reality. Its energy is derived from the id, and it operates by means of "secondary processes": logical thinking and rational planning. The ego tests reality, localizing the appropriate objects for gratification in the environment so that tension reduction can occur. The *superego* represents the internalized moral standards of the society, achieved through the internalization of parental control and characteristics in the course of socialization.

3. Many years after Freud, the discovery that dreaming occurs during periods of sleep in which the sleeper's eyes move rapidly under closed lids led to the distinction between two kinds of sleep: REM (rapid eye movement) and NREM (non-rapid eye movement). During REM sleep the brain is fully active, yet the body is almost totally inactive with the exception of the characteristic eye movements and some visceral activity. These discoveries help open the way for studying the dream process itself and exploring its significance psychologically.

4. Personality dynamics involve a perpetual conflict between the id, ego, and superego. This conflict is accompanied by continuous transformations of the finite amount of energy or "libido" contained in the person. The basic conflict is between the person's instinctual impulses and learned inhibitions and anxieties regarding their expression. The major determinants of behavior are unconscious and irrational: Individuals are driven by persistent, illogical demands from within.

5. The desire for immediate gratification of sexual and aggressive instincts puts the person in conflict with the environment. The conflict becomes internal when the person has incorporated the prohibitions of the culture.

6. This struggle between impulse and inhibition produces anxiety. Defenses may be used by the ego when it is unable to handle anxiety effectively. Transformed by these defenses, the person's unacceptable impulses and unconscious motives express themselves indirectly or symbolically in disguised forms.

7. Freud's theory of personality development includes a series of psychosexual stages: oral, anal, phallic, and genital, so named for the erogenous zone which characterizes each. Later personality traits develop according to the individual's experience at each of these stages of maturation.

8. "Anaclitic identification" and "identification with the aggressor" are two Freudian identification mechanisms. The first is based on the intense dependency of a child on the mother. The second, identification with the aggressor, is based on the boy's fear of castration by his father as punishment for his incestuous desires for his mother.

9. In general, the psychoanalytic followers of Freud have deemphasized the role of instincts and psychosexual stages. They have concerned themselves more with the social milieu and the ego. Their conception of human nature has been less deterministic, less drive oriented, and more humanistic.

10. One especially striking departure from Freud is the psychology of Jung. Jung emphasized the unconscious and its symbolic and mystical expressions. He focused on dreams and on human beings' need to achieve unity through greater awareness of their collective and personal unconscious.

11. Freud saw sex and aggression as the basic human motives. Beginning with the neo-Freudians and continuing to the present, psychologists have expanded the list of human wishes by adding many higher-order motives. These motives, such as competence are purely psychological and have no specific physiological basis. A good example of a higher-order motive is competence motivation, which is the desire for mastery of a task for its own sake.

12. Freud's theory has many implications for our view of the human being. The impact and value of this theory cannot be judged fully until we examine its applications.

Chapter 3

Psychodynamic Assessment and Personality Change

GLOBAL PSYCHODYNAMIC ORIENTATION

Freudian psychology is especially exciting because it promises a way to understand and to treat each complex individual with the depth that he or she deserves. The last chapter gave you a sense of some of the main concepts that guide the psycho-dynamic approach to personality. Guided by these concepts, one tries to help the person to reveal unconscious motives, conflicts, and other dynamics. In this approach, the objective is to uncover disguises and defenses, to read the symbolic meanings of behaviors, and to find the unconscious motives that underlie action. In this way the clinician tries to find the distinctive qualities that characterize the individual.

The Core Beneath the Mask

Psychodynamic theorists recognized that a person's overt actions across seemingly similar situations often seem inconsistent. They felt, however, that these inconsis-tencies in behavior were merely superficial, because beneath them were underlying motives that actually drove the person consistently over the years. The basic motives persist across diverse settings, but their overt expressions are disguised. Therefore the task is to find the person's fundamental motives and dynamics under the defensive distortions of the overt behavior. The challenge is to discover the basic core hidden behind the mask, to find the truth beneath the surface. But how?

Minimizing the Situation: In Search of Underlying Dynamics

Psychodynamically oriented psychologists hoped that dynamic patterns would, under ambiguous conditions, penetrate the person's defenses and reveal them-selves. Therefore techniques were developed in which cues in the situation are kept vague and unclear. These beliefs about the importance of stimulus ambiguity guide assessment. If you experience such an assessment you will not be asked detailed and structured questions. Instead, psychodynamic inquiries tend to be "open-ended" probes that leave your task unclear so that underlying motives and dynam-ics can emerge.

Such assessment tries to reconstruct the person's history. These historical recon-structions deal with the ways in which the person handled sexual and aggressive impulses during childhood at each psychosexual stage. Clues are also sought about traumatic experiences, defenses, and basic character traits.

The Case of Gary W.

Approaches to personality become most meaningful when applied to an actual per-son. In this text, each of the major approaches will be applied to the same individ-ual. Gary W. is not an unusual person, except in the sense that everyone is unique. He is presented here as a case example of an essentially normal human being whose characteristics and history are neither dramatically bizarre nor especially exciting. Often case histories serve to illustrate rare and even esoteric qualities—the strange sex criminal, the twisted neurotic, the split personality. Our purpose in considering Gary, however, is not to display odd bits of abnormality, not to shock and titillate, but rather to make concrete the methods and ideas created to deal with personality. So that our concepts and techniques do not become too abstract, we must apply them to daily life and examine their relevance—and occasionally their irrelevance—for understanding the particular individual (and not just people in general). For this reason we have selected Gary as an ordinary person, one among hundreds of millions. Still, like all individuals, he is unique enough to surprise us occasionally, complex enough to defy pat explanations, troubled enough to encounter problems, and human enough to be confused about himself, at least some of the time, and even more often to confuse those who try to understand him.

As we proceed, you will get new information regarding Gary W. so that the contributions of different personality perspectives and data can be appreciated more fully. In later chapters Gary's case will be interpreted according to the different approaches available for studying personality. (As an exercise, you may find it interesting to apply each approach to yourself by writing down how you see yourself from that perspective.) Our first information about Gary will be limited to a few background facts that introduce him.

Gary W. was born in Boston twenty-five years ago. He comes from an old New England family of moderate means. His father is a businessman, his mother described herself as a homemaker. Both parents are alive and are currently divorcing. Gary has an older and now married brother who is a successful physician.

After attending a private boarding school as an adolescent, Gary went to Hilson College. His record was good but not outstanding. On tests of intellectual ability Gary's scores indicated he was of superior intelligence. On graduation he worked at various jobs for three years, part of that time abroad. He then returned to seek a Master's degree in business. Currently he is in graduate school and still unmarried.

We have already noted that psychodynamic assessors often begin by trying to reconstruct the person's history. How did Gary handle sexual and aggressive impulses during childhood? What were his struggles at each psychosexual stage? What are his defenses and basic character traits? The following excerpts are taken from a psychodynamic report about our Gary W., based on interviews and test situations that will be discussed later in this chapter.

Gary W.: The Psychodynamic View

Oedipal themes abound in the case of Gary W., although he has grown a long way toward resolving them. W. emotionally describes his feeling that his father was his "severest critic" and that he is his mother's favorite. He says that he no longer sees adults as all-knowing, and he refers to his father as mellowed and "out of it." He reports warmth and affection for his mother, although these feelings are mixed.

In his own sibling relationships, Gary seems to have displaced much of his rivalry with his father onto his older brother. W. describes great outbursts of anger vented on Charles with obvious intent to injure. He compares Charles with their father and says that the two are alike in many respects. He is on better terms with Charles since the latter was in a car crash in which he got pretty smashed up. (This in some respects parallels his present hostile condescension, rather than competitive hostility, toward the father since the latter has proved himself a failure in business.)

A recent revival of the Oedipal situation occurred when Gary's girl friend left him for his roommate. She may well have symbolized his mother to him more than is usual: She is older, was married before, and has a child from the previous marriage. After he had confessed his love to her, she told him that she had been seeing his roommate. W. felt humiliated and "wounded in my vanity" because these events went on "behind my back." His feelings are reminiscent of the chagrin felt by the little boy when he realizes his father's role vis-à-vis his mother. W. attempted to resolve his anger by recognizing that he was not in a position financially to marry her whereas his roommate was. His apparent satisfaction that his roommate after all has not married her, and that they may have broken up, also is consistent with the conceptualization that this relationship was filled with Oedipal themes.

The incomplete resolution of the Oedipal conflict is further evident in W.'s fear of injury and physical illness, in the depression that has followed a motorcycle accident (castration anxiety)—and in the distinction he makes between girl friends ("good girls") and sex objects ("fast girls"). Incomplete identification with his father, whether a cause or a result of this unresolved situation, is apparent. His search for a strong male figure is evident in his reactions to the headmaster and teacher at boarding school, described respectively as "a very definite, determined sort of person" and "not the sort of man you could push around." He is quite openly disparaging of his father, albeit on intellectual grounds. (This tends to be W.'s typical style.)

According to Gary, his mother sees sex as something bad and nasty. This report, as well as his suggestion that his mother has undermined his father's masculinity, may represent wishes that his mother may not be responsive to his father. He himself may regard sexuality ambivalently—his sexual experiences seem to involve much parental rebellion and he keeps his sex objects separate from his affections. When he speaks about sex he talks crudely of "making it."

Gary's anxiety in social situations in general, and his fear of public speaking in particular, are further indices of his basic insecurity and his brittle defenses. He is concerned that he will be found lacking. The underlying castration anxiety is expressed symbolically in his comment that when he stands up to speak in public, he is afraid "the audience is ready to chop my head off," and when there is a possibility of debate, that he will be "caught with my pants down."

Gary shows some concern about homosexuality. He mentions it spontaneously when talking about friendship, and his descriptions of living in close proximity with other males include tension, friction, and annoyance. This anxiety is illustrated in his uncomfortable relationship to his current roommate. His first two responses to cards on the Rorschach are also interesting in this connection. Laughter accompanies the statement that two figures are "grinding their bottoms." The perception of animals rather than human figures further serves as a defense to reduce his anxiety. Paranoid tendencies appear in both the fantasy and interview material (e.g., seeing "eyes" on the Rorschach) and suggest some projection of the homosexual conflict.

The battle being waged between impulses, reality, and conscience are evidenced by Gary's concern with control and his obsessive-compulsive traits. W. makes a tenuous distinction between passion and reason, rejecting the former and clinging to the latter. He extends this distinction to interpersonal relations, drawing a line between "companionship" and "love." He reports an inability to empathize and form good object-relations. An example of repression of affect is W.'s difficulty in expressing anger. In this area, as in others, he tends to intellectualize as a way to systematize and control anxiety. His problems in expressing anger may also be reflected in his speech difficulties and in his verbal blocks, especially in public and social situations.

Instinctual elements arise to disturb the tenuous control gained by secondary processes. He complains that he sometimes gets drunk when he should be accomplishing things. He says he admires people with enough self-discipline not to drink, smoke, and sleep late. He speaks of trying to force himself not to do the things that he knows are bad for him and that interfere with his long-range objectives.

The need to control is also apparent in his performance and behavior on many of the psychological tests, where his approach is analytic rather than imaginative, and his expressive movements tight and controlled. (His attention to detail and his constant intellectualization of real feeling on the Rorschach, his hobby of insect study, and his admission that often "trivialities" bother him for a long time add up to a picture of restriction and repression in the service of anxiety reduction.) There is an anal retentive aspect of this need to control, which comes out rather clearly in his interaction with the assessor when he says testily, "Didn't you show that to me already—are you trying to squeeze more out of me. . . ." A further compulsive trait is W.'s frequent counting, and the way he rigidly breaks his ability self-ratings down into component parts, and strives to ensure complete accuracy and coverage of whatever he is discussing about himself.

The need for control may circle back to castration anxiety. The two themes come together in W.'s fear of physical injury and in his fear of losing his brain capacity. The culmination of these two fears occurred when W.'s motorcycle failed him, and he is still preoccupied with this incident. He relates these fears more directly to the Oedipal conflict when, in the phrase association test, he links anger at his brother with fear of losing his "marbles."

Note that the focus in this report is on hypothesized underlying dynamics. It is implicitly assumed that sexual and aggressive motives and unconscious conflicts widely affect many behaviors. Statements about behavior tend to be relatively global and undifferentiated. The emphasis is on unacceptable impulses and defenses for coping with the anxiety they arouse. There is also an attempt to link current sexual and aggressive problems to relations with the parents and to Oedipal problems in early childhood.

This report provides a way of seeing meaning and unity throughout Gary's diverse behaviors. For example, his relations with his brother and with women became part of his larger efforts to cope with Oedipal problems. Indeed, a main attraction of psychodynamic theory is that it offers a systematic, unified view of the individual. It views him as an integrated, dynamic creature: When his underlying core personality is revealed, his seemingly diverse, discrepant behaviors become meaningful, and all fit into the total whole. It becomes easy to see why such an elegant conceptual system is attractive. But the key question for scientifically oriented students is: Do psychodynamic reports of the kind made about Gary provide accurate and useful insights?

Relying on the Clinician

Psychodynamic assessors make interpretations that depend more on intuitions than on tests. The rules for relating behavioral signs to unconscious meanings are not spelled out, and require clinicians to form their own judgments based on clinical experience and the "feel" of the case. The merit of such assessments depends on two things. First, it depends on the evidence supporting the techniques upon which the psychologist relies. Second, it depends on the value of clinical judgment itself. Because psychodynamic theories rest on the belief that the core of personality is revealed by highly indirect behavioral signs, evidence for the value of these indirect signs of personality is most important. This chapter reviews some of the main clinical methods that have been studied in the search for valuable signs of personality. Probably the most important of these methods are the projective techniques.

PROJECTIVE TECHNIQUES

Free association and the analysis of dreams are the methods of personality study that come most directly from Freud's work. In free association, you are instructed to give your thoughts complete freedom and to report daydreams, feelings, and images no matter how incoherent, illogical, or meaningless they might seem. This technique may be employed either with a little prompting or by offering brief phrases ("my mother . . ."; "I often . . .") as a stimulus to encourage associations (see *In Focus 3.1*).

Freud believed that dreams were similar to the patients' free associations. He thought the dream was an expression of the most primitive workings of the mind. Dreams were interpreted as fulfilling a wish or discharging tension by inducing an image of the desired goal. Freud felt that through the interpretation of dreams he was penetrating into the unconscious.

Beyond Dreams and Free Associations

Free association and dream analysis, while remaining the basic tools of orthodox psychoanalytic therapy, have had only indirect impacts for the personality assessments conducted by most psychologists. These techniques have been used for research purposes (Arkin, Antrobus, & Ellman, 1978; Klinger, 1977) and as parts of larger projects for the intensive assessment of individuals. They have not, how-

The following passages illustrate some typical instructions and responses in the process of encouraging free association during psychoanalytic interviews. The patient complains that she does not have any thoughts at the moment.

> *Therapist:* It may seem that way to you at first, but there are always some thoughts there. Just as your heart is always beating, there's always some thought or other going through your mind.
> *Patient:* Your mentioning the word "heart" reminds me that the doctor told my mother the other day she had a weak heart.

In a later interview the same woman became silent again and could not continue.

> *Therapist:* Just say what comes to you.
> *Patient:* Oh, odds and ends that aren't very important.
> *Therapist:* Say them anyway.
> *Patient:* I don't see how they could have much bearing. I was wondering what sort of books those are over there. But that hasn't anything to do with what I'm here for.
> *Therapist:* One never can tell, and actually you're in no position to judge what has bearing and what hasn't. Let me decide that. You just report what comes into your mind regardless of whether you think it's important or not (Colby, 1951).

ever, been widely adopted in personality study. They are considered too time consuming and are believed to require extensive contact with the subject to establish a comfortable atmosphere before they can be used profitably. Most personality psychologists currently believe it is uneconomical to devote much time to gathering dream data and free-association material. While intrigued by these methods, many personality psychologists have been influenced more by projective tests. Probably the two most influential and popular projective techniques have been the Rorschach and the Thematic Apperception Test.

The Rorschach

Developed by the psychiatrist Herman Rorschach in 1921, the Rorschach test consists of a series of inkblots on ten separate cards (Figure 3-1). Some of the blots are black and white, and some colored. The subject is instructed to look at the inkblots one at a time and to say everything that the inkblot could resemble or look like. The examiner then generally conducts an inquiry into the details of the subject's interpretation of the blot.

Responses may be scored for location (the place on the card that the response refers to) and such determinants as the physical aspects of the blot (e.g., shape, color, shading, or an expression of movement) that suggested the response. The originality of the responses, the content, and other characteristics also may be scored. The interpreter may try to relate these scores to aspects of personality, such as creative capacity, contact with reality, and anxiety.

The Thematic Apperception Test (TAT)

The Thematic Apperception Test or TAT was developed by Morgan and Murray in the Harvard Psychological Clinic research program during the 1930s and it is

Figure 3-1
Inkblot Similar to Those in the Rorschach Test

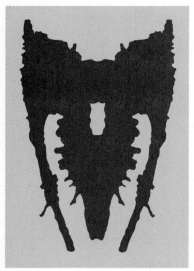

Figure 3-2
Picture Similar to Those on the TAT

Gary's Reactions to Two of the Rorschach Inkblot Cards

Response:

This looks like two dogs, head-to-foot (laughs), licking each other. That's about it, that's all.

Inquiry answers (to the question "What about the inkblot made you think of two dogs?"):

They're sort of fuzzy . . . kinda shapeless. It was the dark skin and the furry effect that made me think of it.

Response:

Didn't we have this one already?
This could be an ogre laughing—his head thrown back and he's laughing, his eyes and mouth wide open.
These over here look like insects, tsetse flies in fact, with tiny, tiny legs, and small, delicate and rather beautiful wings.
That's it, that's enough.

Inquiry answers:

It's the shaggyness and the hugeness, the massiveness of the shape. The wings over here, head here.

still popular in clinical work. The test consists of a series of pictures and one blank card (see Figure 3-2). The cards are presented one at a time.

If you take this test you will be told that it is a story-telling test and that you are to make up as dramatic or interesting a story as you can for each picture: "Tell what has led up to the event shown in the picture, describe what is happening at the moment, what the characters are feeling and thinking, and then give the outcome." You are encouraged to give free reign to your imagination and to say whatever comes to mind. Typically, the length of time before the subject begins telling the story and the total time for each story are recorded.

As the name of the test suggests, it is expected that people will interpret an ambiguous stimulus according to their individual readiness to perceive in a certain way ("apperception"). Furthermore, the themes that recur in these imaginative productions are thought to have basic significance. Special scoring keys have been designed for use with the TAT (e.g., McClelland et al., 1953; Mussen & Naylor, 1954), or the stories may be used "clinically," the clinician interpreting the themes intuitively in accord with his or her personality theory.

Characteristics of Projective Techniques

The main characteristic of projective techniques is the way in which the testing situation is usually structured so that the task is *ambiguous*. Typically, there are also attempts to *disguise the purpose* of the test (e.g., Bell, 1948), and the person is given *freedom to respond* in any way that he or she likes.

In projective testing assessors confront you with ambiguous stimuli and ask ambiguous questions. For example, they ask, "What might this be?" "What could

---

Two of Gary's Stories from the TAT

Card depicting two men: Two men have gone on a hunting trip. It is dawn now and the younger one is still sound asleep. The older one is watching over him. Thinking how much he reminds him of when he was young and could sleep no-matter-what. Also, seeing the boy sleeping there makes him long for the son he never had. He's raising his hand about to stroke him on the forehead. I think he'll be too embarrassed to go ahead with it. He'll start a fire and put on some coffee and wait for the younger man to wake up.

Card depicting young man and older woman: This depicts a mother-son relationship. The mother is a strong, stalwart person. Her son is hesitating at the doorway. He wants to ask her advice about something but isn't sure whether it's the right thing to do. Maybe he should make up his own mind. I think he'll just come in and have a chat with her. He won't ask her advice but will work things out for himself. Maybe it's a career choice, a girl friend . . . I don't know what, but whatever it is, he'll decide himself. He'll make his own plans, figure out what the consequences will be, and work it out from there.

this remind you of?" [while showing an inkblot] or say, "Create the most imaginative story that you can [showing a picture], including what the people are thinking and feeling, what led up to this situation, and how it all comes out." Or they read words and ask you to "say the first thing that comes to mind."

The same stimulus materials with different instructions could be used nonprojectively by asking you to trace the blots, count the pictures, or spell the words in the association list. Similarly, almost any test item can be used projectively with appropriate instructions. Some stimuli, of course, lend themselves more readily than others to projective use, primarily because they more easily evoke a wide range of responses. Therefore, fairly vague stimuli such as inkblots, unclear pictures, barely audible sounds, clay, plastic materials, and paint have been favorites. Some differences between projective techniques and more objective, structured performance tests (such as tests of achievement and ability) are shown in Figure 3-3.

Projective techniques have been favored by psychoanalytically oriented assessors because they assumed that the "unconscious inner life" is at least partially revealed in responses to the projective test situation. The assumptions underlying projective tests reflect the influences of psychoanalytic theory: the emphasis on the unconsciously motivated nature of behavior, the importance of unconscious material, and the conception that the person has a central, enduring "core" or basic personality organization. This core personality is reflected more or less pervasively in the person's behavior, according to psychodynamic theory. And this core is most readily revealed through free responses in an ambiguous, nonthreatening situation of the kind created by projective tests (MacFarlane & Tuddenham, 1951).

Figure 3-3
Some Differences Between an Objective Performance Test and a Projective Test

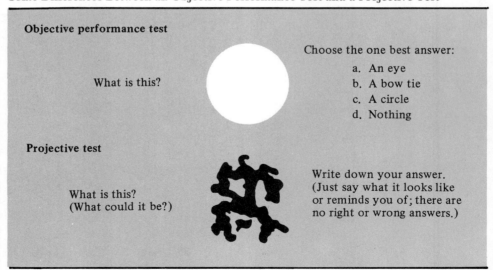

In objective performance tests the subject must choose between definite right or wrong answers. In projective tests the stimulus and instructions are ambiguous and the subject has greater freedom to respond in accord with his or her interpretation of the stimulus.

Traditionally, projective techniques are presented with special efforts to disguise their purposes. This practice reflects the belief that projective data reveal unacceptable unconscious aspects of the person. Presumably the person has erected defensive maneuvers that prevent the expression of these impulses unless the defenses are relaxed. But although the general characteristics and purposes of projective tests are widely agreed upon, there is much uncertainty about the actual nature of the "projection" that occurs in response to these tests.

Scoring and Interpretation

For many years the field was full of workers eagerly trying to invent projective devices. This search for stimulus materials that would elicit rich data about personality resulted in a flood of techniques, many of them lacking serious research support (e.g., Wiggins, 1973; Zubin, Eron, & Schumer, 1965).

While it has been relatively simple to invent projective devices, it has been extremely difficult to establish what they measure. The initial aim and hope was to create a "situationless" situation in which only the core or central aspects of personality would emerge (Frank, 1939). The data elicited by these techniques, however, instead of providing a royal road to the unconscious, seem to include a mixture of verbal responses, momentary states, bits of autobiography, and so on. Projective response, like most other behavior, is "subject to conscious control and distortion" and therefore does not necessarily provide a reflection of personality (Holmes, 1974, p. 328).

Just what is projected in response to the stimuli employed by projective devices is unclear and controversial (e.g., Murstein, 1963; Zubin, Eron, & Schumer, 1965). What the person's answers mean is open to diverse clinical interpretations and depends heavily on the theoretical preferences and subjective judgments of the interpreter.

Scores on projective techniques usually depend extensively on the clinician's judgments about the meaning of the responses as signs of underlying traits in the subject. *Interscorer consistency,* or interscorer agreement (called "interscorer reliability"), must be demonstrated whenever scoring involves subjective judgments, as often occurs with projective data. Interscorer reliability decreases to the extent that highly subjective interpretations are required by the judge. That is, reliability is likely to be low when judgments depend upon the intuitions of the interpreter. For example, "old man strangling boy on couch" in a TAT story might be categorized as reflecting underlying "psychopathic trends," "defense against repressed homosexuality," or "hostile acting-out," depending on the interpreter's subjective judgments. Such interpretation may be influenced by projection on the part of the interpreter. Manuals with explicit instructions for scoring help to increase agreement among judges. Agreement is also better when judges are trained with examples and sample scoring decisions so that they can learn to make similar judgments.

Research Application of the TAT: Need for Achievement

One especially important research application of projective techniques was developed by David C. McClelland and his colleagues (1953), who scored various fantasy indices on the TAT. Specifically, these researchers studied motives as expressed through TAT stories. The motive of greatest interest to them was the need to achieve ("*n* Ach"), defined as competition with a standard of excellence. (For other motives or needs, see *In Focus 3.2*)

The need to achieve has been studied extensively by scoring achievement imagery in stories to TAT cards (see Figure 3-4). If, for example, the person creates stories in which the hero is studying hard for a profession and strives to improve himself, to compete against standards of excellence, and to advance far in his career, the story gets high *n* Ach scores. This technique has become an important way of measuring the motive to achieve. It is not employed widely with individuals in clinical assessment, but it has been used often in research (Atkinson, 1958).

Although TAT and other projective themes and fantasies are interesting in their own right, their relations to other behaviors tend to be complex and indirect. Thoughts and fantasies as measured through projective and story-telling techniques

---

**In Focus 3.2
Inferring
Higher-Order
Motives: Henry
A. Murray's
Needs**

Even a casual look at our culture shows that sex and aggression remain dominant in human behavior: they make headlines in newspapers; are central themes in movies, television, and books; and play a significant part in each of our lives. It does not take a psychoanalyst to see how much human thought and effort are expended in the pursuit of sexual and aggressive activities. Love and hate, tenderness and hostility are basic ingredients of the human scene; how each person deals with them is a major part of his or her individuality.

Sex and aggression have therefore retained an important place among the human motivations recognized by Freud's successors, but other motives and wishes have been hypothesized as well. All these additional motives may be called *higher-order motives* in the sense that, unlike such basic biological needs as hunger and thirst, they do not involve specific physiological changes, such as increased salivation or stomach contraction. Instead, they are seen as psychological desires (wishes) for particular goals or outcomes that have value for the individual.

One can hypothesize many motives for which there are no specific physiological bases: infants appear to be motivated to

see and hear rattles shake; children seem motivated to play games; adolescents strive for recognition from each other but independence from their parents; playboys seem motivated by pleasure; businessmen by money and success; movie stars want fame and glamour; some politicians seek power, others work for reform; some students seem motivated by curiosity, others by grades or fear of failure.

Inferences about physiological motives can be made fairly reliably because one can identify specific physical changes and conditions that accompany the motive. For example, it is straightforward to infer that hunger motivation increases as the number of hours without food are increased. But what about higher-order motives? Obviously such inferences are much more difficult. Nevertheless many theorists have hypothesized a variety of higher-order motives, such as the organism's needs for competence, for achievement, and for stimulation. The great range of needs that may be inferred is illustrated by Henry Murray et al.'s (1938) classical listing which includes those shown in Table 3-1. Although not all of these motives have received serious attention, researchers have investigated

---

usually are correlated only marginally with measures of relevant overt behavior. For example, achievement concerns and ideation measured from TAT stories relate only in limited ways to other measures of achievement (such as grades or vocational achievements).

These conclusions emerge from an enormously extensive tabulation of the correlations obtained between many kinds of motivational imagery (TAT themes) and behavior ratings (Skolnick, 1966). Sometimes measures of fantasy and thought were found to be positively related to relevant actions, less often negatively, and most frequently not at all. McClelland (1966), reviewing this survey, noted that while the overall number of significant associations implied some degree of relationship, "the relationship is not close."

Nevertheless, about 25 percent of the predicted relationships were supported, and although they often tend to be small, many interesting associations have been found between n Ach and other measures, sometimes over long periods of time.

several of them. Probably the one studied most thoroughly, often by means of the TAT, has been the need for achievement, as discussed in the text.

Table 3-1
Some Hypothesized Nonphysiological Human Needs

Abasement (to comply and accept punishment)	Infavoidance (to avoid humiliation)
Achievement (to strive and reach goals quickly and well)	Nurturance (to aid or protect the helpless)
Affiliation (to form friendships)	Order (to achieve order and cleanliness)
Aggression (to hurt another)	Play (to relax)
Autonomy (to strive for independence)	Rejection (to reject disliked others)
Counteraction (to overcome defeat)	Seclusion (to be distant from others)
Deference (to serve gladly)	Sentience (to obtain sensual gratification)
Defendance (to defend and justify oneself)	Sex (to form an erotic relationship)
Dominance (to control or influence others)	Succorance (to ask for nourishment, love, aid)
Exhibition (to excite, shock, self-dramatize)	Superiority (to overcome obstacles)
Harmavoidance (to avoid pain and injury)	Understanding (to question and think)

SOURCE: Based on listing of needs by Murray et al., 1938.

Figure 3-4
A TAT Card Developed by David C. McClelland for Measuring the "Need to Achieve"

Such results are valuable for research and are of value in the study of group differences and broad trends. McClelland (1961), for example, has found intriguing relations between TAT achievement themes and many economic and social measures of achievement orientation in different cultures. His work suggests that careful measures of motives allow some impressive predictions of achievement performance and other important social behaviors (McClelland, 1985).

Applied to the individual case, however, we cannot assume that fantasy themes revealed on projective tests are reflected directly in the person's nontest behavior. Gary might show relatively little achievement striving on the stories he tells to the TAT; nevertheless, he might feel driven to achieve outstandingly in financial and business activities. Moreover, his achievement orientation in business might not be generalized to other areas. For example, he might show much less concern with achievement in intellectual pursuits and social relations.

Generally, predictions based on personality inferences from projective data tend to be less accurate than those more easily available from cheaper and simpler data

(Mischel, 1968; Peterson, 1968; Wiggins, 1973). Some researchers, while recognizing the practical limitations of projective testing, continue to be fascinated by the projective situation as a method for studying personality. They see such tests as the Rorschach as providing a kind of perceptual test or an interview setting. In these situations they seek to study persons clinically or to conduct research on the mechanisms of projection (e.g., Zubin, Eron, & Schumer, 1965). It is not clear just how most psychologists now use projective tests, but their popularity in everyday clinical practice remained strong when last surveyed (Wade & Baker, 1977).

Many psychologists insist that clinical assessments require individualized judgments of the meaning of the person's total pattern of behavior. Therefore they argue, properly, that the total personality configuration must be evaluated. This kind of global personality assessment involves intuitive judgments about the meaning of behavior patterns and their relations. Global assessment requires experienced clinicians guided by theory, as well as by intuition, and draws on many data sources rather than on just one or two tests.

CLINICAL JUDGMENT: A CONTROVERSIAL ISSUE

Most of Freudian psychology depends on the hypotheses and inferences generated by experienced clinicians. Consequently research into the efficacy of clinicians and their judgments is crucial. Some of the most sophisticated clinical studies were conducted by the "Harvard personologists," as discussed next.

The Harvard Personologists

Henry A. Murray, Robert W. White, and their many colleagues at the Harvard Psychological Clinic provided a rare model for the intensive clinical study of individual lives. Throughout the 1940s and early in the 1950s this group devoted itself to the portrayal of persons in depth. The Harvard "personologists" (as these students of personality called themselves) were influenced strongly by the dynamic motivational psychology of Freud. They also were influenced by "biosocial" organismic views that emphasized the wholeness, integration, and adaptiveness of personality. They synthesized these influences into a distinct assessment style that became widely respected although only rarely adopted by other psychologists.

The Harvard group focused on intensive studies of small samples of subjects. In one project (Murray et al., 1938) Harvard College undergraduates were studied over a period of many years and data were gathered on their personality development and maturation at many points in their lives. The techniques included administering projective and other tests of many kinds at different times. They also gathered extensive biographical data on each person, obtaining their autobiographical sketches, observing their behavior directly, and conducting elaborate interviews with them. These methods probed ingeniously and thoroughly into many topics and most facets of their lives (see Table 3-2). The results often provided rich narrative accounts of life histories, as in Robert White's *Lives in Progress* (1952), which traced several lives over many years.

The assessors in the Harvard clinical studies were experienced psychologists who interpreted their data clinically. Usually a group of several assessors studied

Table 3-2
Examples of Topics Included in the Study of Lives by the Harvard Personologists

Personal history (early development, school and college, major experiences)

Family relations and childhood memories (including school relations, reactions to authority)

Sexual development (earliest recollections, first experiences, masturbation)

Present dilemmas (discussion of current problems)

Abilities and interests (physical, mechanical, social, economic, erotic)

Aesthetic preferences (judgments, attitudes, tastes regarding art)

Level of aspiration (goal setting, reactions to success and failure)

Ethical standards (cheating to succeed, resistance to temptation)

Imaginal productivity (reactions to inkblots)

Musical reveries (report of images evoked by phonograph music)

Dramatic productions (constructing a dramatic scene with toys)

SOURCE: Based on Murray et al., 1938.

each subject. To share their insights they pooled their overall impressions at a staff conference or "diagnostic council." These councils became a model for clinical practice. In them a case conference was conducted in detail and in depth about each individual. On the basis of the council's discussions, inferences were generated about each subject's personality. They inferred basic needs, motives, conflicts, and dynamics; attitudes and values; main character strengths and liabilities. Each piece of information served as a sign of the individual's personality and was interpreted by the council of assessors.

This clinical strategy is illustrated in one of the important applied projects of the personologists—their effort to select officers for the supersensitive Office of Strategic Services (OSS) during World War II. OSS officers in World War II had to perform critical and difficult secret intelligence assignments, often behind enemy lines and under great stress. The personologists obviously could not devote the same lengthy time to studying OSS candidates that they had given to Harvard undergraduates in the relaxed prewar days in Cambridge. Nevertheless, they attempted to use the same general strategy of global clinical assessment. For this purpose, teams of assessors studied small groups of OSS candidates intensively, usually for a few days or a weekend, in special secret retreats or "stations" located in various parts of the country. Many different measures were obtained on each candidate.

One of the most interesting innovations was the situational test. In this procedure subjects were required to perform stressful, lifelike tasks under extremely difficult conditions. For example, "The Bridge" task required building a wooden bridge under simulated dangerous field conditions and under high stress and anxiety. But such situational tests were not used to obtain a sample of the subject's bridge-building skills. Instead, the clinicians made deep inferences, based on the behavior observed during the task, about each subject's underlying personality. It was these inferences of unobserved attributes or dispositions, rather than the behavior actually observed in the sampled situation, that entered into the assessment report and that became the bases for clinical predictions. In this fashion, behavior samples and situational tests were transformed into inferences about underlying dispositions.

To illustrate, in the *Assessment of Men* by the OSS staff (1948), the bridge-building situation was used to answer questions like these (p. 326):

> Who took the lead in finally crossing the chasm? And why did he do it? Was it to show his superiority? Why did each of the others fall back from the trip? Did they fear failure? It is obvious that the chief value of this situation was to raise questions about personality dynamics which required an explanation on the basis of the personality trends already explored. If these could not supply a reasonable explanation, then new information had to be sought, new deductions made.

In the situational test, just as on the projective test, behavior was interpreted as a clue revealing personality. Although behavior is sampled and observed, the observations serve mainly as signs from which to infer the motives that prompted the behaviors.

In the global clinical assessment strategy the assessors form their impressions of the person on the basis of many data sources: performance on various projective and objective tests, the autobiography and total personal history, and reactions to thorough interviews. Several assessors study the same person and each generates his or her own clinical impressions. Later, at a conference, the assessors discuss and share their interpretations and pool their judgments. Gradually they synthesize their impressions and achieve consensus, jointly arriving at a conceptualization of each subject's overall personality structure and dynamics (like the psychodynamic conceptualization of Gary given earlier in this chapter). To predict the person's behavior in a new situation (for example under attack behind enemy lines), they try to infer, from the personality they have hypothesized, how such an individual would probably react to the stresses of that situation. This global assessment model is schematized in Figure 3-5.

Assessing the Clinician

The explorations of the Harvard personologists made it plain that research on the clinical use of test data is inseparable from research on clinical judgment. That is because interpretations about the meaning of test responses as signs of underlying dynamics usually depend on the clinician's subjective inferences. Therefore, much attention has been devoted to investigations of clinical judgment.

Global judging ability has been evaluated by many different methods (Cline, 1964; Taft, 1955; Wiggins, 1973). Perception of emotional expression in photographs, pictures, and movies has sometimes been used in clinical skill research. Clinical judging skills also have been assessed by having judges rate and rank traits, write personality descriptions, match persons with data about them, and predict behavior. Predictions may be about specific behavior, like answers on a personality

Figure 3-5
Global Psychodynamic Assessment

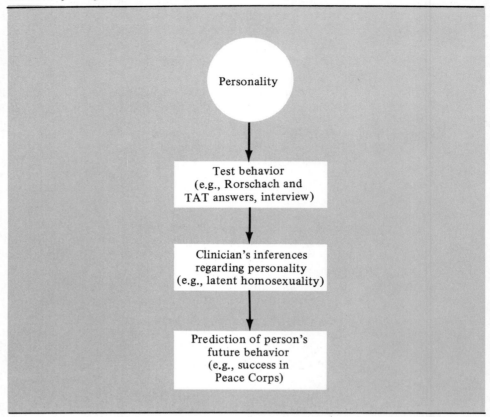

The clinician infers the subject's personality from his test behavior and predicts his future behavior by judging how a person with that personality would probably react to specific future situations.

questionnaire, or about behavior as general as the person's future occupational success and personality adjustment. Judges have been asked to predict the subject's own responses (e.g., self-ratings, test scores), as well as data about the subject obtained from observers (e.g., peers, experts). Some of the main results are reviewed next—and they have surprised many people.

Effects of Clinical Training

To study clinical ability researchers have compared the relative accuracy of judges who had varying degrees of clinical training with those who were untrained. Studies of this kind compare the judgmental accuracy of psychologists, psychiatrists, psychiatric social workers, or other trained clinicians with the judgments of clinically inexperienced groups (e.g., nurses, secretaries, college students). Some studies also investigate the effects of amount of training, usually by comparing the accuracy of judges who have different degrees of clinical experience. The effect of special training programs on subsequent judgmental skill has also been measured.

Crow (1957) studied the effects of clinical training upon judgmental skill. He placed some senior medical students in an experimental group that received extensive instruction on physician-patient relationships and obtained experience in such relationships through prolonged contacts with patients. Others were placed in a control group without any intensive interpersonal training. All students were given tests of interpersonal perception at the beginning, during, and at the conclusion of the training year. These tests measured how accurately the judges predicted the self-ratings and personality test responses of patients whose interview behavior they observed on films.

Unexpectedly, the clinically trained students tended to be *less* accurate than those in the control group. Training led these judges to become much more variable in their estimates (paying more attention to individual differences) than those in the control group. In addition, the trained judges expected less agreement than there was between the patients' self-ratings and their actual test responses. The more the judges tried to take account of individual differences between patients, the less accurate they became. In other words, because of their clinical training, judges became more sensitive and responsive to what they perceived to be individual differences. Consequently they also became less accurate than those who based their predictions on their stereotypes.

On the whole, studies show no clear advantage for trained judges. Psychologists do not score consistently better or worse than nonpsychologists (e.g., secretaries, college students, nurses), and clinical training and experience do not usually improve the accuracy of global judgments (e.g., Danet, 1965; Goldberg, 1959; Kremers, 1960; Luft, 1951). Clinical training and experience may even reduce judgmental accuracy, or at least introduce systematic biases, such as a greater emphasis on pathology and less favorable evaluation (e.g., Soskin, 1954, 1959; Taft, 1955). Surprisingly, giving judges accurate feedback information about their predictions does not seem to improve their accuracy (Sechrest, Gallimore, & Hersch, 1967).

It is possible to criticize much of the research on accuracy of global judgment because it uses artificial situations that do not represent the actual diagnostic problems faced by the practitioner. It may be argued that in practice clinicians are free to base their inferences on their favorite diagnostic technique and are not limited by the experimenter's techniques. Recognizing these objections, a number of investigators have studied the effects of training on accuracy in common diagnostic tasks typical of those used in the clinic (e.g., Goldberg, 1959). Again, the results tend to be negative and thus consistent with those found from the more artificial laboratory studies (Mischel, 1968; Nisbett & Ross, 1980; Wiggins, 1973).

Combining Clinical Judges and Tests

In their clinical practice, many judges tend to rely on a fairly standard battery of personality tests and techniques for the assessment of most problems. Perhaps to obtain good results the clinician has to draw on all these diagnostic aids. This set of procedures usually includes the Rorschach inkblots and often also the TAT and a standard personality questionnaire, the MMPI, discussed in Chapter 6. Many clinicians also ask the client to complete a series of unfinished sentences, to draw some pictures, and to participate in a short interview. Responses to all these tests then are interpreted clinically. Researchers have tried to analyze the relative contributions of the different parts of the total procedure as it is used in the clinic.

Kostlan (1954) studied which of the most common data sources and data combinations allow the clinician to make the best personality inferences. He selected four popular sources of clinical information: the social case history, the MMPI, the Rorschach, and an incomplete sentence test (on which the person must finish such sentence stems as "I feel . . ."). Twenty experienced clinical psychologists were the judges, and each was assigned data for five outpatients at a Veterans Administration Psychiatric Clinic. The clinicians worked under each of five conditions. In four conditions *one* of the data sources was missing. For example, the clinician obtained the Rorschach, the sentence completions, and the social history, but not the MMPI. In a fifth condition the clinician saw only a face sheet stating minimal identifying information (age, marital status, occupation, education, and referral source). The judges studied and used the diagnostic data as they would normally, and then indicated their inferences about the patient on a 283-item checklist. To assess the accuracy of these inferences they were compared with those made by a panel of judges who used all four sources of clinical information, and with progress reports from the patients' therapists.

The minimal identifying facts on the fact sheet (age, marital status, etc.) provided inferences that were not surpassed in accuracy by judgments based on any other data source or combination, unless the clinician also had the social case history. Thus only inferences from data that included the social history were more accurate than those from the identifying data alone.

Golden (1964) studied the gains when experienced clinicians combine the Rorschach, TAT, and MMPI tests as opposed to using them singly. He found that the accuracy of clinical inferences did not increase as a function of the number of tests used, nor were there any differences between tests or pairs of tests. In another study, information from none of the tests used improved predictions beyond the level attained from biographical data alone, and student nurses predicted as well as clinicians when both had only the basic biographical information (Soskin, 1959).

How well do experienced clinicians reach agreement with each other in the inferences that they derive from standard data sources? A classic study of clinical judgments examined the inferences made by expert clinicians from each of five sources (Little & Schneidman, 1959). The sources included the Rorschach, TAT, MMPI, and case histories. Agreement among judges about personality dynamics was only slight. On the whole, the investigators found their results "distressing" (p. 26). No matter how fascinating inferences about personality dynamics may seem intuitively, they cannot be useful when expert judges cannot agree about them (see *In Focus 3.3*).

In a sophisticated study of judgment (Goldberg & Werts, 1966), experienced clinical psychologists ranked psychiatric patients on one of four traits (such as adjustment and intelligence). These rankings were based on various standard data

The problems encountered by the human judge are open to different interpretations. In one interesting direction, Kahneman and Tversky (1973, 1984) have identified a number of rules or heuristics that guide—and often misguide—intuitive predictions (not just in professional clinicians but in all of us). One rule, called the *availability heuristic,* refers to the relative availability, salience, or accessibility of events in the judge's mind. This heuristic leads us to think that the greater the availability of an event cognitively (mentally), the more likely it will be to occur in reality. The more easily we think of something, the more frequent we believe it to be. As a result, people who major in music may overestimate the number of music majors; New Yorkers may believe that almost everyone comes from New York, and those who think and talk a lot about mental illness may tend to overestimate the frequency of its occurrence in the population. A number of other judgment mechanisms have been identified by Tversky (1977) and by Nisbett and Ross (1980) that make it easier to understand how clinicians may feel very confident even when they are objectively quite inaccurate.

But other psychologists continue to blame the shortcomings of the particular clinicians, judges, or research. They do not believe the findings necessarily undermine the general psychodynamic approach (Erdelyi & Goldberg, 1979; Silverman, 1976). Consequently, they still employ methods like the Rorschach and the TAT, rely on their intuitions, and continue to apply psychodynamic concepts to the analysis of individuals, hoping that better research in the future will provide better justification. In contrast, other psychologists, impressed by the negative evidence on clinical inferences about dispositions, are pursuing alternatives to the psychodynamic strategy, as discussed in Chapter 13, while still others have used different methods to search for different motives more objectively (e.g., McClelland, 1985).

sources (such as the Rorschach, or a vocational history). The results revealed that "the judgments of one experienced clinician working from one data source bear no relationship to the judgments of another clinician working from another data source" (p. 204), even when the different clinicians are all experienced and are diagnosing the same patient on what is supposed to be the same trait. Essentially similar results have come from numerous other investigations. For example, the average agreement was negligible for inferences from the Rorschach, TAT, and sentence completion protocols (Howard, 1962).

Are There Good Judges of Personality?

There are large individual differences in accuracy among judges for any judgment task. Is judgmental accuracy strongly consistent across diverse situations so that we can generalize confidently about relatively good or poor judges? One group of studies (Cline, 1964) found some generality in judgmental accuracy. Other studies, however, provided no support for any consistency in the accuracy of clinical judgments (e.g., Crow & Hammond, 1957; Krech, Crutchfield, & Ballachey, 1962).

In spite of the overall negative research findings on judgmental accuracy, many clinicians have faith in their judgments. Is confidence about inferences related to their accuracy? Oskamp (1965) found that judges became more confident of their judgments as they received more information about a case. However, although self-confidence increased with information, accuracy did not. Moreover, clinicians may confidently agree with each other about the meaning of cues, even when the cues are not accurate indicators (e.g., Chapman & Chapman, 1969 [see Table 3-3]; Mirels, 1976). On the other hand, some careful research does suggest that personality judgments are not mere illusions (Jackson, 1982). For example, judgments about how different personality attributes "go together" are related to independent information about the judged people, such as their own self-reports (Jackson, Chan, & Stricker, 1979).

In sum, studies of clinical inference generally have led to negative conclusions (e.g., Goldberg, 1959; Holtzman & Sells, 1954; Kelly & Fiske, 1951). Experienced clinicians tend to be no more accurate than inexperienced nonprofessionals like secretaries (Goldberg, 1959; Crow, 1957; Soskin, 1959). The accuracy of personality inferences is not improved by clinical training; when the judge departs from common stereotypes he or she may become less accurate (e.g., Crow, 1957). Moreover, these conclusions generally obtain regardless of the test data on which judges base their interpretations (e.g., Stelmachers & McHugh, 1964). Thus while clinical judgments are often better than random guesses, they usually provide poorer predictions than those available from cheaper and simpler sources like biographical and social case history information, or from the combination of facts by statistical rules (called "actuarial prediction"; see Meehl, 1954; Wiggins, 1973). But clinical judgments cannot be dismissed as merely illusory, since they some-

Table 3-3
Which of These Rorschach Responses Might Be Signs of Homosexuality?

Response	A Sign of Homosexuality? Answer Yes or No
1. Food	
2. Rectum and buttocks	
3. Figure—part man, part woman	
4. Figure—part animal, part human	
5. Feminine clothing	
6. Sexual organs	
7. Monsters	
8. Maps	

Both experienced clinicians and undergraduate students tend to believe that responses 2, 3, 5, and 6 might be signs of homosexuality. In fact, the only available research support is for an association (at a very modest level) of responses 4 and 7 with homosexuality. Responses 1 and 8 are irrelevant "filler" items. Thus the generally supposed signs of homosexuality tend to be invalid, while the more valid signs tend to be missed by both laypeople and clinicians (Chapman and Chapman, 1969).

times are linked to such independent information as the person's own self-reports (Jackson, Chan, & Striker, 1979).

Regardless of the research findings, many psychologists still use, and rely on, techniques like the Rorschach and the TAT, often employing them more like an interview than a standardized test. They point out that these devices simply provide a set of ambiguous stimuli to which the person reacts; the clinician then bases his assessments in part on his interpretations of the dynamic meanings revealed by the test behavior. Likewise, they continue to practice psychodynamically oriented therapy, although often in a less traditional, more eclectic fashion. Influenced by the neo-Freudians, they focus more on current problems and relations, and less on early history. And increasingly they incorporate into their work methods from other approaches.

Alternative Strategies

Many personality psychologists pursue a variety of directions vigorously. In one direction, the clinical judgment process itself is being analyzed (e.g., Jackson, 1982; Wiggins, 1973). Rather than studying the accuracy of the judge, researchers are examining *how* people judge personality and the mechanisms of inference they use. Other investigators have been studying the processes through which people form impressions of each other and of themselves (e.g., Anderson, 1965, 1974; Nisbett & Ross, 1980). Attention is thus turning to the "information processing" of the judge and of the clinician. These investigations reveal some of the complexities of the information processing that underlies social judgments in general, and clinical inferences in particular. Computers also may help to simulate human judgment processes and to analyze them.

Some researchers also have tried to analyze various types of person-clinician interactions and to discover the essential skills of effective therapists (e.g., Truax & Mitchell, 1971). These researchers suggest that the limitations of clinicians may reflect more on their lack of interpersonal skills than on the personality theory that guides them. Consequently they emphasize the therapist's personality more than his or her personality theory.

In still another direction, attention has turned to research on thought processes and emotions. Interest has tended to shift away from unconscious motives and impulses to the person's modes of dealing with information—to cognitive styles for handling problems. "Cognitive styles" refer to self-consistent ways of approaching and transforming information, especially through perception, memory, and thought. Influenced by the "ego psychologists," researchers have looked for consistent cognitive and emotional styles that people might employ in coping with the problems of their lives. These researchers are influenced by psychodynamic concepts. However, they follow a methodology that does not depend on the clinician and that takes account of developments in the study of information processing (e.g., Singer, 1981; Singer & Antrobus, 1972). For example, they use objective tests of perceptual and cognitive problem-solving, (e.g., the speed with which the subject can find a hidden figure embedded in a picture), as in the work of McKenna (1984) and Witkin (1965).

ADAPTATION, DEVIANCE, AND CHANGE

Psychodynamic theories have not only had a profound effect on personality assessment; they also have shaped ideas about adaptation, deviance, and personality change. And they have done this more than any other psychological approach.

The Healthy Personality: Freud's View

For Freud, a healthy personality showed itself in the ability to love and work and required a harmony among id, ego, and superego. Referring to the goal of psychotherapy, Freud wrote "Where id was, there shall ego be." He meant that for the healthy personality rational choice and control replace irrational, impulse-driven compulsion. A healthy personality also required mature (genital) psychosexual development. In the healthy person, for Freud, genital sexuality replaces earlier forms of psychosexuality. That is, the healthy individual is one who achieves psychosexual maturity, having progressed through the psychosexual stages of development (Chapter 2).

From the psychodynamic perspective, adequate adaptation requires insight into one's unconscious motives. Persons who can cope adequately are the ones who can face their impulses and conflicts without having to resort to massive unconscious defenses that sap psychic energy in the service of distorting either wishes or reality itself. Symptoms represent the return of unsuccessfully repressed materials, re-emerging to torture the person in disguised forms; breakdowns represent the inadequacy of defenses to deal with unconscious conflicts. If the ego fails to achieve sufficient strength to cope with the demands of external reality and the internal pressures of id and superego as they wage their warfare, the person becomes ill.

In Freud's words (1940, pp. 62–63):

. . . The ego has been weakened by the internal conflict; we must come to its aid. The position is like a civil war which can only be decided by the help of an ally from without. The analytical physician and the weakened ego of the patient, basing themselves upon the real external world, are to combine against the enemies, the instinctual demands of the id, and the moral demands of the superego. We form a pact with each other. The patient's sick ego promises us the most candor, promises, that is, to put at our disposal all of the material which his self-perception provides; we, on the other hand, assure him of the strictest discretion and put at his service our experience in interpreting material that has been influenced by the unconscious. Our knowledge shall compensate for his ignorance and shall give his ego once more mastery over the lost provinces of his mental life. This pact constitutes the analytic situation.

Behaviors as Symptoms

The psychodynamic approach views an individual's problematic behavior as symptomatic (rather than of main interest in its own right). It searches for the possible causes of these symptoms by making inferences about the underlying personality dynamics. For example, an individual who has a bad stutter might be viewed as repressing hostility, one with asthma as suffering from dependency conflicts, and one with snake fears as victimized by unconscious sexual problems. This focus on the meaning of behavior as a symptom (sign) guides the psychodynamic strategy for understanding both normal and abnormal behavior. Thus the psychodynamically oriented clinician seeks to infer unconscious conflicts, defense structure, problems in psychosexual development, and the symbolic meaning and functions of behavior.

Many features of the traditional psychodynamic approach to adaptation and deviance are illustrated in the Freudian conceptualization of Gary (pp. 59–61). The report refers to Gary's fear of injury, his anxiety in social situations and fear of public speaking, and his problems in forming close relations. Rather than conceptualizing these behaviors as problems in their own right, they are viewed as signs (symptoms) that reflect (often very indirectly) such hypothetical, inferred problems as his "castration anxiety," "need for control," "unresolved Oedipal themes," "brittle defenses," and "basic insecurity."

Psychoanalytic Treatment

The psychodynamic approach to treatment has had an enormous influence on American psychiatry and clinical psychology. Its major version is *psychoanalysis* or psychoanalytic therapy, a form of psychotherapy originally developed by Freud and practiced by psychoanalysts.

Traditionally, in psychoanalysis several weekly meetings, each about an hour long, are held between the therapist and client (or "patient"), often for a period of many years. The treatment is based on the premise that neurotic conflict and anxiety are the result of repressed (unconscious) impulses. The aim is to remove the repression and resolve the conflict by helping patients achieve insight into their unconscious impulses.

Free Association and Dream Interpretation. To uncover unconscious material (or lift the repression) the techniques of *free association* and *dream interpretation* are used in traditional psychoanalysis. As was noted in the context of assessment, in free association the patient, usually reclining on a couch, is instructed to report whatever comes to mind without screening or censoring his or her thoughts in any way. Here is a fragment of free association from a psychotherapy session as an example:

> I wonder how my mother is getting along. You know how she and I don't get along. Once when I was about twelve she and I were having an argument—I can't remember what it was about—argument 1001. Anyway, the phone rang and one of her darling friends offered her two tickets to the matinee performance of a ballet that day. What a day. She refused them to punish me. For a change! I don't think I even saw a ballet until I was grown up and married. Joe took me. I still get sad when I think about it. I could cry. All blue. It reminds me of all the times when I felt. . . .

Any difficulties or blocks in free association are considered as important as the material that is easily produced. These difficulties are interpreted as *resistances,* caused by unconscious defenses blocking access to material central to the patient's problems, and the person is encouraged to continue with the free association.

According to psychoanalytic theory, the ego's defense mechanisms are relaxed during sleep, making dreams an avenue to express repressed material. But the defenses still operate to distort the content of dreams, so interpretation is necessary to unravel their meaning. In treatment, the interpretation of blocks in association and of dreams is done carefully so that the patient continues to relax the defenses. When the patient's resistances to facing unconscious conflicts and true motives are fully overcome, the therapeutic goal of making the unconscious conscious is gradually realized.

The Transference Relationship and Working Through. The therapist in psychoanalysis is supposed to create an atmosphere of safety by remaining accepting and noncritical. Therapists deliberately reveal little about themselves and remain shadowy figures who often sit behind the patient and outside his view in order to facilitate a *transference* relationship. Transference is said to occur when the patient responds to the therapist as if he or she were the patient's father, mother, or some other important childhood figure. Feelings and problems initially experienced in childhood relations with these figures are transferred to the relationship with the therapist. Transference is regarded as inevitable and essential by most psychoanalysts. In the tranference the therapist demonstrates to patients the childhood origins of their conflicts and helps them to work through and face these problems. Here in the words of a distinguished psychoanalyst (Colby, 1951) is an example of how the transference is used and interpreted:

> The manner in which a patient acts and feels about his therapist is a bonanza of psychological information. In subtracting the inappropriate from appropriate responses the therapist has a first-hand, immediately observable illustration of the patient's psychodynamics in an interpersonal relationship. . . .
>
> A woman from an old Southern family broke away in late adolescence from family ties and values. She became a nomadic Bohemian vigorously opposed to all authority. She expressed her feelings by zealous work in Anarchist societies and other radical movements. In therapy she often told of fearlessly challenging policemen and openly sneering at successful businessmen.
>
> Yet her behavior toward the therapist was in marked contrast to this. She was very respectful, nonaggressive and acquiescent—all attitudes she faintly remembers having as a child toward her parents until adolescence. The therapist's concept was that the patient unconsciously saw him as a feared and loved parent who must not be antagonized. She really feared authority as a source of punishment (p. 113).

The insight to be achieved by the patient in psychoanalysis is not a detached, rational, intellectual understanding. People must work through their problems in the transference relationship. *Working through* involves repeated reexamination of basic problems in different contexts until one learns to handle them more appropriately and understands their emotional roots.

The Ego Analysts. As noted before, the neo-Freudians (Anna Freud, Erik Erikson, and many others) followed Freud in psychoanalysis but modified some of his ideas. Because they placed greater emphasis on the ego functions, they are sometimes referred to as *ego analysts*. As a group, they rejected Freud's emphasis on instinctual drives and paid more attention to a patient's current social interactions. These differences in emphasis resulted in a somewhat different focus in therapy, but they agreed with Freud that the therapeutic process is one in which the ego is strengthened and insight is achieved through the relationship formed between client and therapist.

Challenges and New Directions

Traditional psychodynamic psychotherapies in general (and psychoanalytic therapy in particular) have been criticized in recent years on at least three counts.

1. First, the meaning of the client's insights into his unconscious motives and "real underlying feelings" has been questioned. If experienced clinicians cannot reach agreement about the psychodynamic meaning of the client's behavior, and if they hold different conceptions of human motivation and personality dynamics, depending on their particular theory, then what do the client's "insights" and "awareness" really mean? Skeptics suggest that the patient's "cure" may largely consist of his conversion to the clinician's belief system (e.g., Bandura, 1969). Thus clients whose therapists are Freudians may acquire Freudian insights; those treated by Jungians gain Jungian insights; those treated by disciples of Fromm achieve insights consistent with his view; and so on. In other words, in treatment the client may learn to conceptualize himself in terms of his clinician's favored theoretical constructs (e.g., Grünbaum, 1984).

Even if this criticism was justified, it does not necessarily imply that these reconceptualizations have no value. Consider, for example, a man who has construed himself as "a failure, stupid and weak." He may benefit from reconceptualizing himself, in part, for example, as "neurotic, conflicted, victimized by a castrating mother, and driven by unconscious guilt." Regardless of their absolute truth value, such reinterpretations may provide the individual with a less painful and more convenient set of constructs about himself. It would be important, however, to show that these reconceptualizations also help the person to deal more effectively with life problems and with the troubles that led him to seek help in the first place.

2. Second, the value of traditional therapeutic activities has been persistently questioned by studies on the outcomes that they yield (e.g., Eysenck's, 1952, 1961). The negative conclusions are themselves open to severe criticism (e.g., Garfield & Bergin, 1978; Kiesler, 1966; Luborsky & Spence, 1978; Smith & Glass, 1977; Strupp, 1980). The methodological limitations of most research on treatment outcomes are great, and therefore firm conclusions have been hard to reach; the literature on the outcomes of psychotherapy is extremely difficult to interpret and the results on the whole are not as negative as was originally implied (Bergin, 1966, 1971; Kazdin & Wilson, 1978). Nor are they strongly supportive.

Some studies of outcomes indicate that psychotherapy (of various types) does help at least some people to a significant degree and that differences in effectiveness between the particular types are not large (e.g., Smith, Glass, & Miller, 1980; Landman & Dawes, 1982). Typical of outcome research of this sort is a study in which people who wanted treatment at a university clinic were assigned randomly to one of three groups. One group received short-term psychoanalytic therapy, another obtained more specific behavior therapy (of the sort discussed in Chapter 14). Those in a third group served as a "wait list control." (They were interviewed and asked for information and tested but received no treatment.) Both before and after participation, all participants were evaluated with a number of tests, ratings, and reports about them from other people who knew them. After four months, improvement on these measures was shown by all three groups. The percent of improvement was greater in the two treatment groups than in the wait-list controls, with a tendency for the behavior therapy group to improve somewhat more than the short-term psychoanalytic group (Sloane et al., 1975).

Many experienced clinicians are convinced that much of value exists in psychodynamically oriented therapy and are trying to identify its most promising components. Regardless of theoretical orientation, there is wide agreement that research must be more specific than it has been, and must be aimed at discovering "*what* treatment, by *whom,* is most effective for *this* individual with *that* specific problem, and under *which* set of circumstances" (Paul, 1967, p. 111). Even if traditional psychotherapy taken as a whole does not produce strong overall effects, some people seem to be significantly helped by it while others may be hurt by it. The potential gain or loss would depend on the particular person, problem, and therapist. And for people seeking to understand themselves better, it may provide a fruitful tool for personal exploration.

3. Finally, although traditional psychotherapies of a psychoanalytic type do help some people, they have only limited value for meeting the enormous psychological problems that our society faces. Indeed only a small percentage of people qualify for traditional psychotherapy. In regard to psychoanalysis, for example, Freud believed that good prospective patients should possess a reasonable degree of education and be fairly young; they should be sufficiently distressed by their problems

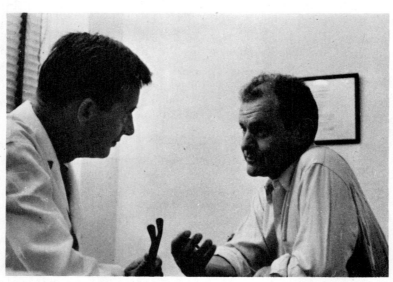

Psychotherapy research must discover "*what* treatment by *whom,* is most effective for *this* individual with *that* specific problem . . ."

to want to change, but not too distressed because psychoanalytic therapy cannot be conducted with severely confused, depressed, or debilitated persons (Freud, 1959, Vol. 1). Similarly, people with severe fears or obsessions were thought to be poor risks because they had given in to their symptoms completely, thus reducing anxiety and motivation for therapy (Freud, 1959, Vol. 2). Given these limitations and the costs and time required for psychoanalytic treatment, the method would be either inappropriate or unavailable for most troubled people even if it is valuable for some. As early as 1918 Freud said:

> You know that the therapeutic effects we can achieve are very inconsiderable in number. We are but a handful of people, and even by working hard each one of us can deal in a year with only a small number of persons. Against the vast amount of neurotic misery which is in the world, and perhaps need not be, the quantity we can do away with is almost negligible. Besides this, the necessities of our own existence limit our work to the well-to-do classes. . . . At present we can do nothing in the crowded ranks of the people, who suffer exceedingly from neuroses (1959, Vol. 2, p. 401).

Not surprisingly, people who benefit from psychotherapy "are those who experience acute discomfort because of their condition and are highly motivated to receive treatment and expect to be helped by it" (NIMH, 1975, p. 62). These people also tend to be relatively competent, intelligent, well educated, and "show a high degree of personal integration . . . have achieved some social success . . . and are able to experience and express emotion" (NIMH, 1975, p. 62). In other words, people who are already functioning at a high level and want help tend to benefit most from psychotherapy, while those whose functioning is least adequate are much less likely to profit from it.

Many clinicians have recognized the need for new forms of therapy and behavior change; numerous promising strategies have been developed to meet practical challenges in helping people. These efforts cover such diverse approaches as community mental health programs and preventive counseling in the schools (e.g., Cowen, Gardner, & Zax, 1967) and innovations stimulated by the concepts of existential psychology (e.g., Laing, 1965). Perhaps the most popular new developments are therapeutic groups (discussed in Chapter 9) and behavior therapies (Chapter 14). There also are attempts to integrate the best elements of psychodynamic therapy with the best features of behavior therapy (Wachtel, 1977), for example in the form of "family therapy," therapy conducted conjointly with the whole family rather than with the individual alone (Satir, 1967).

Family Therapy: Treating Interactions and Relationships

Family therapy is a promising approach to treatment, based in part on modern psychodynamic theory of the sort developed by the neo-Freudians. In family therapy the problem is seen as residing in the family's system of interactions rather than within the child. The goal of therapy is a transformation in the family system—allowing family members to relate to one another in more adaptive ways. This family therapy approach is illustrated nicely in efforts to treat anorexia nervosa (See *In Focus 3.4*), the psychophysiological problem of self-starvation (Minuchin, Roseman, & Baker, 1978). For example, the therapist may challenge the

Many people suffer from a mix of psychological and physical problems called *psychophysiological* (or psychosomatic) *disorders*. In psychophysiological disorders emotional or psychological problems are believed to be having negative effects on the "soma" or body, as in certain types of ulcers, skin disorders, cardiovascular problems, and backaches. One of the most intriguing— and potentially fatal—psychophysiological disorders occurs when people starve themselves virtually to death even in the midst of plenty and with no initial physical illness responsible for the starvation: this disorder is called *anorexia nervosa*. Consider the following case:

> Debby M. was 14 years old when she decided she wanted to be a fashion model and went on a diet. Gradually, she eliminated more and more foods until, one year later, she ate only cottage cheese, carrots, diet soda, and water. Her weight dropped from 115 to 81 pounds and her menstrual periods stopped. During this time Debby became excessively active physically. She would wake up at around 5 A.M. and jog two to three miles before getting ready for school, jogging another two to three miles in the afternoon when she returned home. Weekends were spent at the community swimming pool or practicing alone on the tennis court. She had always been a good student and continued to get excellent grades (often studying past midnight), but she withdrew from school activities and spent little or no time with friends. Her parents describe her as a good girl: they are proud of her grades and cannot explain why she will not eat. On her pediatrician's recommendation Debby has been hospitalized. After careful physical examination, no organic cause has been found for her refusal to eat. Debby is diagnosed as having anorexia nervosa (Minuchin, Roseman, & Baker, 1978).

As Debby's case illustrates, anorexia nervosa occurs most often in middle-class females and usually begins during adolescence. Symptoms include a loss of over 25 percent of total body weight, cessation of menstruation, excessive activity, below normal body temperature, denial of hunger, fear of gaining weight, and a distorted body image. From 10 to 15 percent of these cases die of self-inflicted starvation.

A group of psychologists working with people who have this disorder report similarities in the way the families of these patients function (Minuchin, Roseman, & Baker, 1978). There are some distinctive family characteristics which appear to encourage and maintain anorexia nervosa. For example, the family members are overinvolved (enmeshed) with one another. Changes within one member or between two members affect other members too much. In addition, the relationships between parents and children, brothers and sisters, and husband and wife become so intertwined that they may become ineffective and inappropriate. The enmeshed family's excessive togetherness and sharing intrude on individual autonomy, and family members have poorly differentiated perceptions of each other and often of themselves. The family's overprotectiveness retards the child's development of autonomy and competence. In turn, the "sick" child may use her symptoms to control and manipulate the family. While normal families are able to disagree, these families are characteristically unable to confront their differences to the extent of negotiating a resolution. They avoid conflict, deny the existence of problems, or diffuse the disagreements that do occur, ncluding the battles over the child's refusal to eat, sometimes to the point of death.

family's notion that the daughter is sick and the parents are helpless. The problem is recast for them as one in which both parents and daughter are involved in a fight for control. This reorientation mobilizes the parents to treat their daughter as a rebellious adolescent, not as an invalid. Specific therapeutic strategies are directed toward challenging maladaptive family characteristics. For example, all family members are encouraged to speak for themselves or not to speak if they so choose. The protectiveness valued by the family may be redefined to include the protection of each member's individuality. Overprotection may be challenged directly by pointing out, for instance, that the child can take her coat off herself or even by explicitly stating that excessive protection robs the individual of her right to try and fail, learning how to cope in the process. The tendency of the family to avoid conflict may be challenged by insisting that two family members who disagree discuss their disagreement without the possibility of intervention by other family members to diffuse the conflict. The therapist's role is to maintain or even increase the conflict and to prevent intrusion or escape. Thus, instead of simply treating the individual as having a problem, the entire family is seen as in need of learning new and healthier ways of relating to one another—an approach far different from the original strategies Freud favored. The focus has shifted from individual psychodynamics to the dynamics of the family as a social system.

Need for New Assumptions?

A final reaction to psychodynamic applications has questioned not merely psychodynamic methods but also the theoretical assumptions that guide them (e.g., Bandura, 1977, 1986; Grünbaum, 1984; Krasner & Ullmann, 1973). Thus not only the methods are being challenged but also the psychodynamic constructs that led to them and govern their use. These critics urge pursuing different routes. Rather than inferring unconscious motives, searching for insights, or seeking to clarify dynamics, they are trying to discover the specific conditions that cause important *change* in behavior (for example, as discussed in Chapter 14).

SUMMARY

1. Psychodynamically oriented psychologists attempt to study personality in depth and try to eliminate situational interferences. They hope to bypass defenses and reach basic dynamics and motives. Guided by psychoanalytic theory, the traditional focus has been on reconstructions of early history, particularly the early handling of sexual and aggressive impulses. Inferences are made regarding personality in global, dynamic terms.

2. In the psychodynamic approach, the Rorschach and the TAT (Thematic Apperception Test) are projective tests that have been especially popular. The Rorschach consists of a series of complex inkblots. The subject says what the inkblots resemble or look like to him or her. The TAT consists of a series of ambiguous pictures for which subjects are asked to make up a story.

3. The main characteristics of projective techniques are that they are presented as ambiguous tasks for the subject; the purpose of the test is disguised, and the person is free to respond as he or she wishes. Clinicians then may interpret the meaning of the answers in accord with their the-

ories and intuitions, trying to infer the person's psychodynamics and personality from his or her responses.

4. Several procedures have been devised to help interpret projective test responses. It is especially important to demonstrate interscorer consistency—the degree to which different judges arrive at the same interpretive statements from the same test data. Manuals with clear instructions, and practice training, help increase agreement among judges.

5. The study of achievement motives as expressed through TAT stories has been carefully developed. Research on the need for achievement as expressed in TAT themes has yielded an extensive network of correlations.

6. Research on the clinical uses of projective tests indicates that many methodological problems make it difficult to interpret the results clearly. Most important, the correlations that are found tend to be too low to permit more accurate predictions about individuals than could be made from simpler data.

7. The clinician is a central instrument in psychodynamic assessment. Harvard personologists have provided a model for the intensive clinical study of individuals. Trained assessors collected diverse data on each subject and, in council, made inferences about the individual's personality dynamics.

8. Surprisingly but consistently, studies on the effect of clinical training do not show a clear advantage for trained judges in making global judgments. Research also indicates that the information from various clinical tests does not enable the experienced clinician to make more accurate predictions than he or she could have made from biographical data. Experienced judges may not agree with each other in their inferences about personality dynamics even when they are using the same test data from the same individual.

9. The psychodynamic approach to adaptation and deviance distinguishes between symptom and underlying disorder. To understand the disorder the clinician seeks such hypothetical causes as internal conflicts, dynamics, and unconscious motives.

10. Influenced by Freud's theory, most traditional approaches to personality change have emphasized insight and awareness and acceptance of unconscious motives and feelings. There have been many variations in specific techniques and theory. The efficacy of these approaches to personality change has been questioned on both practical and theoretical grounds and there now is a search for useful innovations.

11. Reactions to criticisms regarding psychodynamic assessment and psychotherapy have been divided. On the one hand, the problems have been judged to reflect inadequacies in specific techniques and research methods. Consequently further attention is being focused on analyzing the person-clinician relationship. Influenced by the "ego psychologists" and new orientations in psychodynamic theory, other researchers have turned to the study of personality and "cognitive styles." Moreover, new forms of psychotherapy draw on psychodynamic concepts developed by the neo-Freudians. They focus more on current life problems and relationships, as in family therapy. Another reaction has been more radical: It has questioned the basic theoretical assumptions that guide psychodynamic applications and has found other ways of conceptualizing, assessing, and modifying behavior.

Chapter 4

Psychodynamics: Defenses and Unconscious Processes

The psychodynamic approach has stimulated a great deal of research. Especially important have been studies of unconscious processes and mechanisms of defense, and they are the subject of this chapter.

An outstanding characteristic of human beings is that they can create great anxiety in themselves even when they are not in any immediate external danger. A man may be seated comfortably in front of his hearth, adequately fed and luxuriously sheltered, seemingly safe from outside threats, and yet torture himself with anxiety-provoking memories of old events, with terrifying thoughts, or with expectations of imagined dangers in years to come. He also can, within his own mind, eliminate such internally cued anxiety without altering his external environment, simply by avoiding or changing his painful thoughts or memories.

"Defense mechanisms" are attempts to cope mentally (cognitively) with internal anxiety-arousing cues. Usually it has also been assumed, in line with Freudian theory, that these efforts are at least partly unconscious—that is, they occur without the person's awareness.

REPRESSION

Repression has received the greatest attention, probably because of its theoretical importance in Freudian psychology. Because most theoretical issues and research studies have focused on repression, it will be the defense that this chapter will emphasize. Rather than dealing with many defenses superficially, we will concentrate on this important one in depth.

The Concept of Unconscious Repression

Most people sometimes feel that they actively try to avoid painful memories and ideas and struggle to "put out of mind" thoughts that are aversive to them. Common examples are trying not to think about a forthcoming surgical operation, and trying to turn attention away from the unknown results of an important test. Psychologists often call such efforts to avoid painful thoughts "cognitive avoidance."

The existence of cognitive avoidance is widely recognized; few psychologists doubt that thoughts may be inhibited. However, the mechanisms underlying cognitive avoidance have been controversial. The basic controversy is whether or not cognitive avoidance includes an unconscious defense mechanism of "repression" that forces unacceptable material into an unconscious region without the person's awareness.

Repression versus Suppression

The psychoanalytic concept of repression as a defense mechanism is closely linked to the Freudian idea of an unconscious mind. The unconscious mind was seen by early Freudians as a supersensitive entity whose perceptual alertness and memory bank surpassed the same properties of the conscious mind (e.g., Blum, 1955). A chief function of the unconscious mind was to screen and monitor memories and perceptual inputs. This screening served to inhibit the breakthrough of anxiety-arousing stimuli from the unconscious mind to the conscious, or from the outside world to consciousness. Just as the conscious mind was believed capable of deliberately (consciously) inhibiting events by *suppression,* so the unconscious was considered capable of inhibition or cognitive avoidance at the unconscious level by *repression.*

Suppression occurs when one voluntarily and consciously withholds a response or turns attention away from it deliberately. Unconscious repression, in contrast, may function as an automatic guardian against anxiety, a safety mechanism that prevents threatening material from entering consciousness. Psychoanalysts offered clinical evidence for the existence of repression in the form of cases in which slips of the tongue ("parapraxes"), jokes, dreams, or free associations seemed to momentarily bypass the defenses and betray the person, revealing a brief glimpse of repressed unconscious impulses.

Hysteria

Recall that Freud based his ideas concerning repression and defense on his clinical observations of hysterical women at the turn of this century. He noted that some of these patients seemed to develop physical symptoms. These symptoms did not make sense neurologically. For example, in an hysterical difficulty called "glove anesthesia," the patient showed an inability to feel in the hands—a symptom that is impossible neurologically. In their 1895 studies of hysteria Freud and his associate Breuer hypnotized some of the patients and found, to their great surprise, that when the origins and meanings of hysterical symptoms were talked about under hypnosis, the symptoms tended to disappear. This finding proved beyond any doubt that the symptoms were not caused by organic damage or physical defects.

Partly to understand hysteria, Freud developed his theory of unconscious conflict and defense. In his view, such symptoms as hysterical blindness and hysterical anesthesias reflected defensive attempts to avoid painful thoughts and feelings by diversionary preoccupation with apparently physical symptoms. Freud thought that the key mechanism in this blocking was unconsciously motivated repression. Through repression the basic impulses that are unacceptable to the person are rendered unconscious and thereby less frightening. Because such diversionary measures are inherently ineffective ways of dealing with anxiety-provoking impulses, the impulses persist. The impulses continue to press for release in disguised and distorted forms that are called "symptoms."

Studying Repression

Repression has remained a cornerstone for most psychoanalysts (Erdelyi, 1985; Grünbaum, 1984) and it has been the subject of a great deal of research for many years. In general, many of the early efforts to assess whether or not particular findings demonstrated the truth of Freud's concepts created more controversy than clarity. In more recent years it has been recognized that well-designed experiments on the topic of cognitive avoidance can provide useful information about cognitive processes and personality regardless of their direct relevance to the Freudian theory of repression.

Early experimental research on repression studied the differential recall of pleasant and unpleasant experiences (e.g., Jersild, 1931; Meltzer, 1930). These investigators seemed to assume that repression showed itself in a tendency to selectively forget negative or unpleasant experiences rather than positive ones. It was soon pointed out, however, that the Freudian theory of repression does not imply that experiences associated with unpleasant affective tone are repressed (Rosenzweig & Mason, 1934; Sears, 1936). Freudian repression, instead, was believed to depend on the presence of an "ego threat" (for example, a basic threat to self-esteem) and not on mere unpleasantness.

Later it also was recognized that to study repression adequately one should be able to demonstrate that when the cause of the repression (the ego threat) is removed, the repressed material is restored to consciousness (Zeller, 1950). This assumption was consistent with the psychoanalytic belief that when the cause of a repression is discovered by insight in psychotherapy the repressed material rapidly emerges into the patient's consciousness. In other words, if the threat is eliminated it becomes safe for the repressed material to return to awareness. Reports by psychoanalysts often have cited cases in which a sudden insight supposedly lifted a long-standing amnesia (memory loss).

Experiments to demonstrate repression have been difficult to conduct and more difficult to interpret (Erdelyi, 1985). A good example is an experiment by D'Zurilla (1965) to see if stress produces defensive changes in memory. In this experiment, college students first were shown twenty words and tested for recall of the words (to establish that there were no preexperimental differences). Next they were exposed to a series of ten slides. Each slide contained one Holtzman inkblot (a modification of the Rorschach) and two of the words that had been shown to them previously. For each slide the subjects had to indicate the word that best described the inkblot. The experimental group was told that this was a test designed to detect latent homosexual tendencies. They were told that one of the two words on each slide was a response that homosexuals tend to give but the other word was given by heterosexuals. The control group was told only that it was taking part in the development of a new psychological inkblot test.

After responding to all of the cards the students in both groups were given another recall test. Again there were no group differences. Now threat was induced in the experimental subjects. They were told that they had picked nine of the 10 "homosexual" words. In contrast, the control group subjects were told that they had "done very well" on the test. After five minutes all the subjects took another recall test. The people in the control group improved from their prior recall performance, but, as expected, subjects in the experimental group did less well than they had before. The investigator then tried to remove the repression effect by revealing the deception to the subjects and explaining that the inkblot test did not measure homosexual tendencies. Finally, the last recall test was administered: On this test, as predicted, now that the threat had been removed, the two groups recalled equally well.

You might conclude that the concept of repression was supported by D'Zurilla's results. Some doubt is cast on this conclusion, however, by findings from interviews after the experiment. The students were asked to describe what they had thought about during the poststress retention interval. Contrary to expectations from repression theory, most of the experimental subjects had thought about things related to the threatening task; only a few control subjects had thought about the task at all. During the retention period the experimental subjects said they had thought about the inkblots, past memories, their "homosexual tendencies," and many other events. As the investigator noted, these cognitions could have reduced the efficiency of recall by competing with the responses to be recalled and interfering with them.

Repression or Response Competition?

Holmes and Schallow (1969) recognized that the threatened subjects may have spent the poststress retention interval thinking about their problems and that these competing cognitions could have disrupted their efforts to recall the words. Therefore they decided to study the role of response competition and interference. In their study, Holmes and Schallow included an ego-threatened group and a control group. They also added a group that was not ego-threatened but that was distracted during the retention interval by exposure to irrelevant neutral stimuli.

After the threat, the ego-threatened group recalled less well than the control group, replicating the effect previously attributed to repression. However, recall in the interference group was below that of the control group and quite similar to that of the ego-threatened group. The investigators therefore concluded that response interference, rather than repression, may have caused the differential performance of the threatened and control groups. Their interpretation is plausible, but it does not completely rule out the possibility of a repression effect. A more recent laboratory study (using recall for successes versus failures) found no support whatsoever for repression effects (Tudor & Holmes, 1973). Likewise, an extensive review of experimental research on repression, after surveying many studies, led the reviewer to conclude that "there is no evidence to support the predictions generated by the theory of repression" (Holmes, 1974, p. 651). In spite of the difficulties of demonstrating repression experimentally in a clearcut fashion, there is some evidence from other studies that emotionally charged topics and words (compared to neutral ones) tend to be associated more with memory lapses and are more difficult to remember (Luborsky & Spence, 1978). The exact mechanism underlying such findings, however, remains open to different interpretations.

PERCEPTUAL DEFENSE AND COGNITIVE SELECTIVITY

The studies described in the last section tried to investigate repression as a defense that blocks the memory for material connected with an ego threat. If unconscious repression is a mechanism that keeps painful material out of consciousness, one might also expect it to screen and block threatening perceptual inputs to the eyes and to monitor messages to the ears. Indeed, clinical reports from psychoanalysts suggest that in some cases of "hysteria" massive repression may prevent the individual from perceiving (consciously registering) threatening stimuli such as sexual scenes or symbols.

One very severe instance of this would be "hysterical blindness." In these cases the individual seems to lose his or her vision although no physical damage to the eyes or to the perceptual system can be detected. Case reports have suggested that such psychological failures to see might be linked to traumatic sexual experiences with resulting repression of stimuli that might unleash anxiety. Clinical case reports such as those on hysteria often may provide suggestive evidence, but they are never conclusive. To go beyond clinical impressions, researchers have tried to study possible anxiety-reducing distortions in perception. Since it was obviously both unfeasible and unethical to induce sexual traumas in human subjects, considerable ingenuity was needed to find even a rough experimental analog for perceptual defense.

Research Strategy

In the 1940s and 1950s a general research strategy was devised to explore perceptual defenses, guided by the then prevalent faith in projective devices as methods for revealing conflict. Specifically, it was believed that persons who did *not* give sexual or aggressive responses to ambiguous stimuli must be defending against this type of ideation, especially if the same stimuli generally elicited many such responses from most normal people. Consequently if a person fails to identify potentially threatening percepts, such as anxiety-arousing sexual words or threatening scenes, one may infer perceptual inhibition or defense.

To study this process, researchers present threatening perceptual stimuli in decreasing degrees of ambiguity. They began at a point at which subjects could reasonably interpret them in many ways to a point of definiteness that permitted only one clearly correct interpretation. A helpful device for this purpose was the *tachistoscope,* a machine through which potentially threatening words (e.g., "bitch," "penis," "whore") and neutral words (e.g., "house," "flowers") could be flashed at varying speeds. These stimulus words were presented on a screen very rapidly at first and then gradually exposed for increasingly long durations. The length of time required before each subject correctly recognized the stimulus served as the "defensiveness" score; the longer the time required to recognize threatening stimuli the greater the subject's defensive avoidance tendencies were assumed to be.

In one study college students viewed tachistoscopically presented words that were either emotional or neutral in meaning (McGinnies, 1949). Each student was asked what word had been seen after each exposure. If the answer was wrong the same word was presented again at a slightly longer exposure time, and the subject again tried to recognize it.

The emotional and neutral words used, and the mean recognition thresholds associated with them, are shown in Figure 4-1. It was predicted that such "taboo"

| *In Focus 4.1*
**Problems in
Perceptual
Defense** | An extremely serious methodological problem in perceptual defense research was pointed out by Howes and Solomon (1951). They called attention to the fact that the critical or "taboo" words used in perceptual defense experiments (e.g., McGinnies, 1949) were much less familiar to the subjects because they occurred much less frequently in the English language than did the "neutral" words. It therefore would not be surprising that people took longer to recognize them | when they were ambiguously presented by the tachistoscope! Longer recognition time for taboo words could easily reflect unfamiliarity with the words rather than unconscious defense against their threatening meanings. Their data demonstrated a direct relation between infrequency of use and recognition time, so that a subject would show "defense" against such unusual words as "flume," "chaise," or "rapt."

Howes and Solomon also noted that the |

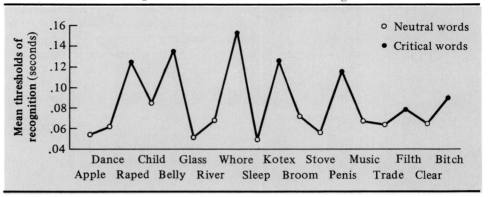

Figure 4-1
Mean Thresholds of Recognition of Neutral and Emotion-Charged Words

From McGinnies (1949).

words as "penis" or "raped" would be anxiety-laden and therefore more readily inhibited than neutral words such as "apple." As Figure 4-1 illustrates, the results confirmed this prediction, showing greater "perceptual defense" (longer recognition times) for taboo words than for neutral words. But as *In Focus 4.1* discusses, these results also can be interpreted quite differently.

Selective Perception

Under ambiguous conditions individuals may be somewhat more ready to interpret unclear events in accord with their expectations and momentary states. Consequently if people have just failed they more readily perceive failure words (tachistoscopically presented); if they have just succeeded they may perceive success words at shorter exposures (Postman & Brown, 1952). Stimuli that can satisfy strong needs also may be perceived somewhat more readily. The observer may even endow these need-relevant stimuli with more striking characteristics, such as greater size and brightness (e.g., Bruner & Goodman, 1947).

The tendency to interpret ambiguities in the environment in accord with one's

perceptual recognition situation placed the subject in an embarrassing predicament. In the typical procedure, an undergraduate was brought to the laboratory by a professor or an assistant and then exposed to brief and unclear stimulus presentations by the tachistoscope. The task is essentially a guessing game in which the subject tries to discern the correct word from fleeting fragments. On the first trial of a word, for example, something like an "r" and a "p"

may be seen and the subject may guess "rope." On the next trial, the subject may think "good grief, that looked like 'rape'!" But rather than make this guess to a professor or an assistant in the academic atmosphere of the scientific laboratory, the subject may deliberately suppress the response. Instead of saying "rape," "rope" is offered again and the taboo word is withheld until the subject is absolutely sure that this perception is correct.

momentary state has been studied extensively. For example, moderately hungry subjects tend to produce somewhat more food-related responses than satiated subjects when they try to identify briefly exposed ambiguous stimuli (e.g., Levine, Chein, & Murphy, 1942; McClelland & Atkinson, 1948). This tendency, however, seems weak and is not related to the degree of hunger induced in the subjects. Indeed, under conditions of more intense deprivation people may become *less* likely to ideate about drive-related themes (Lazarus, Yousem, & Arenberg, 1953; Murray, 1959).

There is no doubt that individuals interpret their environment subjectively. How we appraise or view any situation and potential source of stress influences how we cope with it (Lazarus, 1976). But the intrusion of subjective states and needs into actual *perceptions* of the environment is a far more complex matter. The possible distortions of perception by unconscious needs have been of special interest to Freudian psychologists. If the unconscious system is as powerful as Freud's theory assumed, then it should produce distortions of perceptual and learning processes without the individual's awareness. One approach to this critically important topic has taken the form of experiments on "subliminal perception" (unconscious perception).

Subliminal Perception and the Unconscious

Public interest in subliminal perception has been great because of its evident moral and social implications for subtly molding people's behavior without their awareness. What if stimuli—such as propaganda messages or advertisements presented below the threshold of perceptual awareness—could really shape people's beliefs and actions? During a movie, for example, if advertisements were secretly included and flashed too indistinctly for the victim's conscious awareness could his or her behavior be unconsciously influenced by the message? The potentialities—and the horrors—of "mind control" might be staggering; they are reminiscent of George Orwell's nightmarish *1984* and Huxley's *Brave New World*.

An experiment by Lazarus and McCleary (1951) attracted great attention because it seemed to demonstrate that subliminal perception does occur. In the first phase of their study, subjects watched as 10 nonsense syllables were projected on a screen supraliminally (above awareness thresholds) in random order. In the next phase the presentation of half the syllables was paired with electric shock to the subject, so that these "shock syllables" became the conditioned emotional stimuli eliciting the galvanic skin response (GSR). In the third phase of the study, the shock and nonshock syllables were again projected in random order, but now subliminally (at speeds too fast for clear awareness).

Two measures were obtained from the subject. One was their "conscious" recognition through verbal reports of the subliminal shock stimuli. The second was an "unconscious" index of recognition inferred from the emotional activity reflected in their GSR. It was assumed that if a subject does not report recognizing the shock-associated syllables, but the GSR measure shows that he is responding to them, then he must be recognizing them unconsciously. The investigators believed that they had found subliminal perception because when the self-report predicted the shock syllables poorly, the GSR predicted them relatively well. They interpreted these data as demonstrating that people can make unconscious discriminations of events that they cannot report recognizing consciously.

The foregoing conclusion is most exciting, but it has been seriously challenged. Some critics have interpreted the evidence for subliminal perception as reflecting nothing more than methodological problems (Eriksen, 1958, 1960). They imply that when these problems are removed, the phenomenon disappears. Others have argued seriously that there is enough evidence to support its reality and importance in spite of the difficulty of identifying the exact way it works (Dixon, 1971, 1981; Silverman, 1976).

Conscious Suppression or Unconscious Repression?

The conclusions that may be drawn from research on subliminal perception remain controversial. We are left with these fundamental questions: Do cognitive avoidance and selective perception merely involve suppression of responses so that they are less likely to become verbalized? Or are people driven by impulses whose meanings they unconsciously disguise beyond their own recognition? Can they thus be victimized unconsciously by their own minds? Or can the phenomena of cognitive avoidance and misperception be understood as learned inhibitions without requiring a special concept of the unconscious? Most critical, just what is the status of the unconscious as a force in mental functioning? The problem is a complicated one that resists easy answers because of the difficulties in defining and determining whether another person is or is not consciously aware of a given event.

The term "consciousness" may be confusing because it has many meanings. "Awareness" is the most common definition for consciousness in psychological usage. Conversely, the "unconscious" tends to be equated with lack of awareness. But how do you know whether or not another person is aware or unaware of something? A means of judging awareness that has been favored by many clinicians involves highly indirect inferences about people's insight into their motivations, internal states, feelings, and dynamics. Such a clinical strategy depends most heavily on the clinical judge and its limitations are serious, as we have seen (Chapter 3).

The more obvious and direct way to study awareness of an event is to ask people whether or not they recognized it. In research on perceptual defense, for example, as we have seen, subjects are exposed to various stimuli (such as taboo words) and asked to report their perceptions. But as was noted, such reports may not fully reflect private awareness. What people see and what they say about it are certainly not always the same.

There may be many reasons why a person's awareness and his verbalizations about it can be discrepant. One may not want to publicly acknowledge an event although aware of it (for example, because it is embarrassing or threatening). As pointed out before, students are unlikely to report seeing words like "penis" to their professor unless they are sure their perception is correct. Even when motivated to report accurately, words may not be capable of correctly describing subjective awareness. Consider, for instance, how difficult it would be to describe the image of a face with words. Even a detailed verbal description of a stranger's face might still not permit one to recognize the person in a crowd. The labels of language often are too gross to capture events, especially when the events keep changing rapidly.

The value of verbal self-reports about awareness depends on the adequacy of the questions. Techniques to help the subject verbalize the experience have to be thorough and ingenious. Otherwise we might conclude that someone is unaware of an event when, instead, we merely have not asked the right questions.

Discrimination Without Awareness?

Can people learn without awareness or consciousness? It would certainly be impressive evidence for the unconscious if important learning were shown to occur in people without their awareness. Eriksen (1960) undertook an extensive survey and analysis of research on human learning without awareness. The results led him to conclude that learning at levels not available to conscious awareness (equated with verbal report) has not been shown adequately. Although some simple responses may be learned without awareness, in most forms of human learning awareness seems to play a major role (e.g., Dulany, 1962; Spielberger & De Nike, 1966).

These findings cast doubt on the unconscious as a powerful force in human learning, and they have led some researchers to suggest abandoning the concept of the unconscious as a psychic entity:

> A science of personality is not furthered by the frequent tendency of psychologists to discuss the "unconscious" with all the ambiguity and reverence that religions accord to the soul. There is great need to spell out explicitly the assumed characteristics of the unconscious phenomena in terms of more commonplace psychological variables. To do so may destroy the titillating mystery that the unconscious seems to hold but then that is the business of science (Eriksen, 1960, p. 298).

Reviewing later developments, Eriksen (1966, p. 354) concluded that "the possibility must be seriously entertained that the concept of repression is only a very well-learned or overlearned response suppression."

Eriksen (1966) suggests that unpleasant or painful material may at first be consciously suppressed (rather than unconsciously repressed). Then after sufficient rehearsal, response suppression becomes automatic. It is also possible that even without a deliberate suppression mechanism, painful thoughts and memories are less likely to be evoked and covertly rehearsed because they are more aversive.

The foregoing does not imply that people are aware of everything they do. During new learning we usually feel aware and even "self-conscious," but once a behavior is mastered and over-learned it often seems to flow smoothly and automatically without any subjective awareness whatsoever. We usually stay safely clear of hot stoves, cross busy streets only when the traffic lights are appropriate, and drive our cars for miles without self-conscious awareness of every step and discrimination made along the route. Learning to park a car may at first require great awareness and self-conscious attention to subtle positional cues. Thousands of trials later one is likely to be unaware of the procedure (unless startled by a sudden bump). And it is certainly true that without being aware of it we very commonly bring our past knowledge to bear on how we act in the world. Consider, for example, how "automatically" we know what to expect and do in familiar situations, like birthday parties or restaurants (Schank & Abelson, 1977).

Relevance (or Irrelevance) for Clinical Problems

Understandably discouraged by experiments on unconscious processes, psychoanalytically oriented critics have been quite skeptical of the relevance of many of these experimental studies for their theory (Erdelyi & Goldberg, 1979). They argue that it is confusing and misleading to study single processes (such as repression) in isolation as lone variables outside the context of the person's total psychic functioning. Such critics believe that these experimental studies at best have value as independent and suggestive, but clinically irrelevant, analogs. They doubt that long-term psychodynamic processes can be studied under the artificial conditions of the typical laboratory experiment. The discouraging findings are dismissed as due to the artificiality of the measures typically used in such research and to the hazards of generalizing from college sophomores in a laboratory (or even from rats in a maze) to clinical populations and clinical problems. They assert that the mild anxiety induced by experimental threats to cognitively mature college students may have little relevance for understanding the traumas experienced by the young child trying to cope with Oedipal fantasies, or the severely disturbed patient in the clinic.

For example, experiments on repression usually provide only a remote analog of the motivational aspects of clinical repression in Freud's theory (Madison, 1960). Repression (or more broadly speaking, any defense) involves motives that were associated with traumatic childhood experiences for a particular individual. Thus, many psychoanalytically oriented critics believe that evidence obtained from controlled experimental research conducted outside the clinical setting (such as the studies reviewed in the preceding sections) is largely irrelevant. On the other hand, as we have seen (Chapter 3), the clinician's judgments and intuitive procedures for inferring unconscious dynamics cannot be relied upon either.

The two main ways of looking at the research results are well summarized by Erdelyi (1985, pp. 104–105):

> One may begin to understand why experimental psychology, in contrast to dynamic clinical psychology, has taken such a different stance on phenomena such as repression. Experimental psychology, in the service of simplification and control, has studied *manifest* events, specific memory episodes or percepts (as in perceptual defense). It is not typical, however, for a normal college subject to resort in the laboratory to such drastic defenses as to block out a clear memory episode or perceptual experience. Consequently, experimental psychology has had great difficulty in demonstrating repression in the laboratory and has understandably taken a skeptical attitude towards this phenomenon. Clinicians, on the other hand, deal continually with latent (hidden) contents, and in this realm the selective blocking or distortion of information through context manipulation is utterly commonplace. The clinician shakes his head in disbelief at the experimental psychologist, whose paltry methodology cannot even demonstrate a phenomenon as obvious and ubiquitous as repression. The experimentalist similarly shakes his head at the credulity of the psychodynamic clinician, who embraces notions unproven in the laboratory and which, moreover, rest on the presumed existence of nonconscious, indeed, physically non-existent, latent contents.

In sum, many clinicians remain convinced that evidence for the unconcious is almost everywhere; in contrast, most experimental researchers cannot find it anywhere.

Subconscious Information Processing: Selective Cognition

One promising new direction is suggested by reformulating the issue of "perceptual defense" in terms of modern approaches to how people think and deal mentally with information, called "cognition." Such a reformulation treats perceptual defense as just one instance of the selectivity that occurs throughout cognition. Selectivity (or bias) occurs in our choice of the things to which we attend, the manner in which we organize and rehearse the flood of information that enters the sense receptors and the response that we ultimately generate (Erdelyi, 1974). The information processing approach has already shown that the individual's mood state may lead to the recall of more mood-congruent materials. (e.g. Bower, 1981; Isen et al., 1978). People who feel sad, for example, are more likely to recall more negative material than do those in a happy mood. It is hoped that repression and perceptual defense can be studied more fruitfully when they are placed in the larger context of selective information processing (Broadbent, 1977; Erdelyi & Goldberg, 1979; Erdelyi, 1985; Silverman, 1976).

Consistent with this general formulation, there have been new, vigorous efforts to demonstrate experimentally instances in which people seem to make systematic errors without awareness (Dixon, 1981). In one direction, investigators began by carefully defining "self-deception" (Gur & Sackeim, 1979). In their view, to be self-deceived a person must simultaneously hold two contradictory beliefs, one of which "is not subject to awareness; and the nonawareness of this belief is motivated" (p. 147). In two clever experiments the researchers tried to demonstrate that self-deception, as they defined it, really exists. They confronted college students with tape recordings of their own voices mixed in with the voices of others. Measures included the subjects' reports of whether the voice was theirs or not and also their GSR (an index of electrical activity in the skin used to indicate emotional arousal). For example, when subjects were incorrect in their reports of whether or not the voice was theirs, they had made correct identifications at another, nonverbal level of processing (inferred from their GSR measures). The patterns of discrepancy found between these measures led the investigators to conclude that genuine self-deception had occurred at least for some subjects.

In a somewhat related vein, Nisbett and Wilson (1977) attempted to demonstrate that circumstances can be arranged so that people are unaware of their cognitions and misidentify the causes of their own behavior. In one experiment, for instance, people were asked to evaluate articles of clothing. The results clearly revealed that the clothing article in the right-hand position was evaluated more favorably. But when asked whether position had any effect on their choice, people vehemently and consistently denied it. The researchers concluded from their study that sometimes we seem to have little insight into our own thought processes. Others, however, have challenged this interpretation of the results (Smith & Miller, 1978).

In a similar direction, some studies also suggest that sometimes our behavior is so overlearned that we act more or less automatically, mindlessly ignoring relevant information in repeatedly encountered situations (Langer, 1978). Likewise, we may develop more positive feelings toward objects that were previously encountered without consciously knowing that the object is familiar to us. That is, exposure to objects led to enhanced feelings for them, even when there was no recognition that the objects had been seen before (Wilson, 1979). Hypnosis also provides relevant evidence, as discussed next.

HYPNOSIS

Beginning with Freud and his associates, psychologists have pursued hypnosis as a road into the unconscious. Although Freud himself moved away from hypnosis (Erdelyi, 1985), research into it has continued actively (Kihlstrom, 1980).

Consider subjects who are hypnotized and instructed to forget what happened during the hypnotic state. Afterward they may be influenced by their hypnotic experience (e.g., instructions that they were given) even though those experiences are outside their awareness. Later, at a prearranged time, the experiences may be recovered. Clearly studies of this sort are reviving interest (and belief) in the possibility of subconscious information processing. The final verdict is not in, but it is plain that the issues will continue to receive the intense attention that they merit (see *In Focus 4.2*).

In Focus 4.2
The Hypnotic State

Hypnosis, a highly controversial topic, excites much interest because of the dramatic effects it seems capable of producing, even under careful research conditions. In one study students trained through hypnosis have been able to vary the skin temperatures in each of their hands simultaneously but in the opposite direction (Maslach et al., 1972). One subject was instructed to make her left hand hotter and her right hand colder than normal. She raised the temperature of her left ring finger from just under 88 degrees to over 90 degrees while lowering the temperature of her right ring finger from just under 90 degrees to below 86 degrees. When she was instructed to return her hand temperature to normal, her right ring finger again became at least 1 degree warmer than her left. There were no systematic changes in the hand temperatures of unhypnotized control subjects (see Figure 4-2).

The hypnotic experience has been described often (see Table 4-1 for typical examples) and argued about even more. Historically, hypnosis was thought of as a form of sleep, but the EEG produced by a person in a hypnotic state is similar to that in the waking state. Although hypnotic induction typically occurs while the person is relaxed, it is possible to induce a hypnotic state in which the individual

Table 4-1
Elements of the Hypnotic Experience

1. A sense of mental and physical relaxation

2. A focusing or narrowing of attention

3. Vivid fantasy experiences

4. Heightened suggestibility

*Based on subjects' reports of their own hypnotic experiences.
SOURCE: Data from Hilgard & Hilgard, 1975.

Figure 4-2

Average Temperature Difference Between the Two Hands Produced by Hypnotized Subjects and Waking Controls

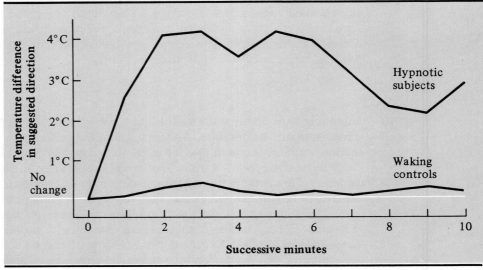

From Maslach et al. (1972)

experiences increased tenseness and alertness. No clear physiological indicators have been found that distinguish hypnosis from other states of consciousness.

In both the relaxed and the alert hypnotic states, subjects are responsive to suggestions. Suggestibility has become the hallmark of the hypnotic state, perhaps because it is so often demonstrated and easily seen by observers. But some researchers feel that suggestibility has been over-emphasized and that there is more to hypnosis than responsiveness to suggestion (Hilgard, 1973; Orne, 1972).

Explaining Hypnosis

There is considerable disagreement about how to conceptualize hypnosis. In one view, hypnotic phenomena are the result of strong demands and pressures toward taking a certain role and enacting particular behaviors rather than the reflections of a special state of consciousness (Barber, 1972; Sarbin & Coe, 1972). Support for this "role-playing" view comes from studies in which unhypnotized subjects, instructed briefly about how to perform as if they were hypnotized, acted like deeply hypnotized subjects. For example, awake subjects who were simply instructed to ignore red and green or to try to respond to certain test materials as if they were color-blind were compared to hypnotized subjects who had been given elaborate suggestions to induce color blindness. The awake and the hypnotized subjects did not differ appreciably in the number of color-blind responses they gave (Barber, 1970).

Other studies (Orne, 1972), however, have shown differences in the behavior of responsive hypnotic subjects ("reals") and unsusceptible subjects instructed to behave as though they were hypnotized (instructed simulators). The reals (in contrast to the instructed simulators) showed true reduction in pain inflicted from electric shock, performed a posthypnotic act outside the experimental setting, and came out of hypnosis more slowly when the hypnotist was away. These and other findings (see examples in Table 4-2) suggest that there may be something unique about the hypnotic state and that more is involved than merely suggestion, positive attitudes toward hypnosis, or wanting to please the hypnotist.

Individual Differences in Hypnotizability

While the explanation of hypnosis remains controversial, it is widely agreed that some people can be hypnotized more easily than others. One test designed to measure susceptibility to hypnosis is based on the subject's behavior following an attempt to induce hypnosis (Weitzenhoffer & Hilgard, 1959). The more the subject behaves in the way a successfully hypnotized person does, the higher his or her susceptibility rating. Scores on this test are quite stable, with strong links between a person's performance on tests taken ten years apart (Morgan et al., 1974). The scores of monozygotic (identical) twins are significantly more similar than those of dizygotic (fraternal) twins, suggesting that there may be a genetic component in hypnotizability (Morgan, 1973).

Hypnotizability scores tend to increase during childhood, peaking in preadolescence. Scores decline slightly with age, although some individuals may remain highly hypnotizable. Hypnotic susceptibility can be modified by instructions and information (Diamond, 1972) and by special experiences such as encounter groups (e.g., Tart, 1970).

The Uses of Hypnosis

Hypnosis has been used throughout its history as a therapeutic tool. Its clinical use has been increasing, ranging from helping individuals to stop smoking to the relief of pain in dentistry, obstetrics, surgery, and in diseases such as cancer. An important application of hypnosis is self-hypnosis (autohypnosis). Some people can hyp-

Table 4-2
Examples of Studies Supporting Unique Contributions of Hypnosis

Situation	Finding	Author
Pain (arterial blood flow in arm cut off by tourniquet)	Highly hypnotizable subjects, deeply hypnotized, were able to withstand pain significantly longer than when they were given a placebo.	McGlashin, Evans, & Orne, 1969
Eye movements	Hypnotized subjects instructed to see a rotating drum had eye movements as if they were actually watching such a drum, although they were unable to feign these movements in the waking state.	Brady & Levitt, 1969

Psychodynamics: Defenses and Unconscious Processes

notize themselves, bringing a variety of physiological processes and behaviors under their own control. For example, a cancer patient who experienced continuous pain often awakened at night or early in the morning and found it impossible to get back to sleep. She was taught through a method of self-hypnosis to imagine putting on a yellow pajama snowsuit. Her muscles would "go to sleep" as they were covered by the suit, and she would "turn off the switches" in her brain after the hood was on. Everything would grow dark and she would be asleep. The patient reported that she slept extremely well using this technique (Hilgard & Hilgard, 1975).

The powerful effects sometimes produced by hypnosis raise an important question: Do hypnotized people completely lose control of themselves? Will they do anything the hypnotist suggests? While there is some increase in suggestibility under hypnosis, subjects' descriptions of their experiences suggest that there may be a "hidden observer," a part of the hypnotized person that is monitoring and censoring what is going on (Hilgard & Hilgard, 1975), making unrealistic any fear that some power-mad hypnotist may turn his subjects into slaves.

PATTERNS OF DEFENSE: INDIVIDUAL DIFFERENCES IN COGNITIVE AVOIDANCE

Some people react to stimuli that arouse anxiety by avoiding them cognitively, but other people do not. For many years, individual differences in "defensive" patterns have been found (e.g., Bruner & Postman, 1947; Lazarus, 1976).

Repression-Sensitization

The dimension on which these differences seemed to fall was a continuum of behaviors ranging from avoiding the anxiety-arousing stimuli to approaching them more readily and being extravigilant or supersensitized to them. The former end of the continuum included behaviors similar to the defensive mechanisms that psychoanalysts called denial and repression; the latter pattern—vigilance or sensitization to anxiety-provoking cues—seemed more like obsessive worrying. This dimension now has become known as the *repression-sensitization* continuum. Repression-sensitization became the focus of much research both as a dynamic process and as a personality dimension on which individuals might show consistent patterns.

In general, individuals show some consistency in their cognitive avoidance of anxiety-provoking cues such as threatening words (e.g., Eriksen, 1952b; Eriksen & Kuethe, 1956). Consistency evidence usually has been strongest when extreme groups are preselected. In one study reaction time and other measures of avoidance were obtained in the auditory recognition of poorly audible sentences that had sexual and agressive content. People who were slow to recognize such sentences also tended to avoid sexual and aggressive materials in a sentence completion test (Lazarus, Eriksen, & Fonda, 1951). People who more readily recalled stimuli associated with a painful shock also tended to recall their failures; those who forgot one were more likely to forget the other (Lazarus & Longo, 1953).

**Some people cope with unpleasant events by mentally "blunting"
(distracting themselves).**

There also have been some failures to find consistency in cognitive avoidance patterns. In one study psychiatric patients were judged as using either predominantly repressive or sensitizing ("obsessive-compulsive") defense mechanisms for handling anxiety. The judgments were made by psychiatrists who saw the patients in intensive psychotherapy three times weekly. The defense mechanisms were unrelated to auditory recognition thresholds for emotional words (Kurland, 1954).

In sum, sometimes there is some significant consistency in approach versus avoidance responses to threatening stimuli of various kinds, but generally the degree of consistency is not very strong. A tendency for some consistency in cognitive avoidance may exist at least when extremely high and low groups are selected (Eriksen, 1966). Correlations between cognitive avoidance on experimental tasks and various other measures of repression-sensitization also imply some consistency (e.g., Byrne, 1964; Mischel, Zeiss, & Zeiss, 1974).

Blunting versus Monitoring

People differ considerably in their disposition to distract themselves or to monitor for (be alert to) danger signals. One promising scale tries to identify information-avoiders and information-seekers as two distinct coping styles. The Miller Behavioral Style Scale (MBSS) consists of four hypothetical stress-evoking scenes of an uncontrollable nature (Miller, 1981; Miller & Mangan, 1983). On this measure, people are asked to imagine vividly scenes like "you are afraid of the dentist and have to get some dental work done"; or "you are being held hostage by a group of armed terrorists in a public building"; or "you are on an airplane, 30 minutes from your destination, when the plane unexpectedly goes into a deep dive and then suddently levels off. After a short time, the pilot announces that nothing is wrong, although the rest of the ride may be rough. You, however, are not convinced that all is well."

Each scene is followed by statements that represent ways of coping with the situation, either by "monitoring" or by "blunting." Half of the statements accompanying each scene are of a monitoring variety. (For example, in the hostage situation: "If there was a radio present, I would stay near it and listen to the bulletins about what the police were doing"; or, in the airplane situation: "I would listen carefully to the engines for unusual noises and would watch the crew to see if their behavior was out of the ordinary." The other half of the statements are of the blunting type. For example, in the dental situation: "I would do mental puzzles in my head"; or, in the airplane situation: "I would watch the end of the movie, even if I had seen it before." The subject simply marks all the statements following each scene that might apply to him.

College students were threatened with a low probability shock and allowed to choose whether they wanted to monitor for information or distract themselves with music. As expected, the amount of time spent on information rather than on music was predicted reasonably well by an individual's MBSS score. In particular, the more blunting items endorsed on the scale, the less time the person spent listening to the information and the more to the music. Thus individuals differ in the extent to which they choose to monitor or distract themselves when faced with aversive events; and these differences in coping style were related to their questionnaire scores.

In a related study the scale was given to gynecologic patients about to undergo colposcopy, a diagnostic procedure to check for the presence of abnormal (cancerous) cells in the uterus. Based on scale scores, patients were first divided into monitors or blunters. Half the women in each group were then given extensive information about the forthcoming procedure, and half were given (the usual) minimal information. Psychophysiological reactions (like heart rate), subjective reports, and observer ratings of arousal and discomfort were taken before, during, and after the procedures. The results revealed, again as expected, that monitors showed more arousal overall than blunters (for example, see Figure 4-3 for the physician's rating of patient's tension during the exam). Most interesting, physiological arousal was reduced when the level of preparatory information was consistent with the patient's coping style. That is, physiological arousal was reduced for blunters who received minimal information and for monitors who received extensive information.

The total results clearly show strong individual differences in informational preferences during the coping process when people are faced with threats.

The Role of Control: When Don't You Want to Know?

Whether you react to potentially painful stimuli by trying to avoid them cognitively or by becoming vigilantly alert and monitoring them may depend in part on what

Figure 4-3
Doctor's Report—Tension During Exam

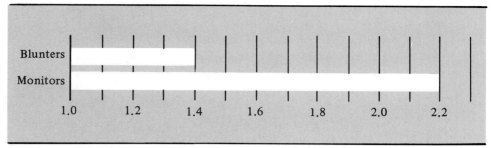

From Miller & Mangan (1983).

you can do to control the threat. Consider first the situation in which a person receives aversive stimulation but cannot control its occurrence. That is, the individual can do nothing to change the objective circumstances to render the aversive or negative stimuli less painful through his or her own problem-solving actions. Examples of this frustrating dilemma would include most experimentally induced stress experiments in which the researcher administers painful but unavoidable electric shocks to the subject, confronts him with embarrassing words or pictures, provides him with insoluble problems, or deprives him of food for long periods of time.

Under all these conditions the aversive stimulation is essentially inescapable (unless the subject terminates the situation altogether by abandoning the experiment). If the subject can have no control over the painful stimuli by means of his own instrumental actions such as problem-solving, it may be most adaptive for him to avoid them cognitively and thus not think about them or attend to them. On the other hand, if escape from the noxious or distressing stimulation is possible and depends on the person's ability to find a solution (cognitively or physically), then monitoring vigilance or sensitization to the anxiety-arousing cues would be adaptive and often even essential for survival.

The foregoing speculations have received some experimental support. Reece (1954) tested subjects' recognition thresholds for various nonsense syllables in the first phase of his experiment. Thereafter, the subjects underwent a training period during which some of the syllables were paired with electric shock. In the final phase of the study the subjects' recognition thresholds after training were assessed again. Post-training recognition thresholds for the syllables were longer if during training the syllable-shock combinations were inescapable (i.e., subjects could do nothing to prevent them). In contrast, if subjects could escape shock during training by verbalizing the syllable as soon as it was presented then the syllables were later recognized as rapidly as in a control group that received no shock. Similar evidence comes from a study by Rosen (1954), who controlled for the effect of the electric shock itself.

Thus whether or not persons react to negative stimuli by avoiding them "defensively" in their cognitions and perceptions may depend on whether or not they believe that they can somehow cope with them by problem-solving and action. If adaptive action seems impossible, cognitive suppressive attempts may be more

Table 4-3
Number of Subjects Who Seek Information (Warning Signal) or Distraction (Listen to Music) When Avoidance Is or Is Not Possible

	Information-Seeking	Distraction-Seeking
Avoidance Possible	24	10
Avoidance Not Possible	11	23

SOURCE: Based on Miller, 1979.

likely. But if the painful cues can be controlled by the person's actions then greater attention and vigilance to them may occur. This point is illustrated in a blunting-monitoring study that gave subjects a choice between stress-relevant information or distraction (Miller, 1979). The information was a warning signal for when an electric shock would come; the distraction was listening to music. Half the subjects were led to believe the shock was potentially avoidable; the rest believed it was unavoidable. As Table 4-3 shows, when subjects believed avoidance was possible, they preferred information; when they thought it was unavoidable, they preferred distraction. Other research has documented the many circumstances under which coping with problems is improved by the selective avoidance of threatening information (e.g., Janis, 1971; Lazarus, 1976; Lazarus & Folkman, 1984).

SUMMARY EVALUATION OF THE PSYCHODYNAMIC APPROACH

This section summarizes the most basic strengths and weaknesses of the psychodynamic approach and reviews its main features. Throughout Part II, as we presented the psychodynamic approach, these points were made or implied. As you review Part II, it helps to identify specific examples that illustrate each of the points in Table 4-4.

Table 4-4
Summary Evaluation of the Psychodynamic Approach

Strengths	Weaknesses
Stimulating, broad (comprehensive), systematic theory; revolutionary reconceptualization of human psyche and human condition	Concepts difficult to test scientifically
Extensive intellectual influence, including in other disciplines (e.g. history, literature); major impact on research	Limited research support: a. for key concepts (e.g. repression, unconscious) b. for key methods (e.g. clinical inference by clinical experts, projective methods)
Profound influence on clinical practice, especially treatment; pioneered twentieth century psychiatry	Efficacy of therapy remains in dispute

As a review exercise and learning experience, try to add to the table any other strengths or weaknesses you see. Illustrate each suggested strength or weakness with examples or reasons. At the conclusion of the presentation of each major theoretical approach in the text, there is a similar table that provides a summary evaluation of basic strengths and weaknesses. Each time you may want to conduct a similar exercise, providing examples from the text for the strengths and weaknesses of the approach in that part, and suggesting your own additions.

Strengths and Weaknesses

The impact of Freud's theory on society and on philosophy, as well as on the social sciences, is almost universally hailed as profound; its significance is frequently compared with that of Darwin. Freud's monumental contributions have been widely acknowledged. He opened the topic of childhood sexuality, revolutionized conceptions of the human psyche, provided strikingly powerful metaphors for the mind and human condition, and pioneered twentieth century psychiatry with his approach to the treatment of psychological problems. The evidence relevant to Freud's theory as a scientific psychological system, however, has been questioned persistently (e.g., Grünbaum, 1984).

Although Freud attempted to create a general psychology, his main work was with conflict-ridden persons caught up in personal crises. Moreover, Freud observed these tortured individuals only under extremely artificial conditions: lying on a couch during the psychotherapy hour in an environment deliberately made as nonsocial as possible. This drastically restricted observational base helped to foster a theory that originally was almost entirely a theory of anxiety and internal conflict. It paid little attention to the social environment and to the interpersonal context of behavior. We have already seen that many of Freud's own followers attempted to modify that initial emphasis and to devise a more ego-oriented and social approach. That trend is continuing.

This newer "ego psychology" is characterized by a greater focus on development beyond early childhood to include the entire life span. It attends more to the role of interpersonal relations and society, and to the nature and functions of the concept of ego rather than to the id and its impulses. Freud's ideas thus have been going through a considerable continuing revolution that extends beyond his own writings to the extensions introduced by his many followers over the years.

One of the main criticisms of Freud's theory is that it is hard to test. That is true in part because his constructs are ambiguous and hard to quantify. The terms often are loose and metaphoric and convey different meanings in different contexts. He rarely gives clear definitions for them. Just what observations are required to conclude, for example, that an individual is fixated at the anal stage? Under what conditions may we conclude that he or she *is not* fixated at that stage? How can the extent or amount of fixation be assessed? Likewise, is the college student who commits himself to fight the "establishment" really "intellectualizing" his emotional conflicts with "authority figures" (like his father) and his "Oedipal problems," or is he truly motivated to undo political evils? What would he have to do to show that he is motivated by his professed idealism rather than by unconscious conflicts? Often the answers to questions like these depend on the clinical judgments of

Table 4-5
Summary Overview of Psychodynamic Approach

Basic units:	Inferred motives and psychodynamics.
Causes of behavior:	Underlying stable motives and their unconscious transformations and conflicts.
Favored data:	Interpretations by expert judges (clinicians).
Observed responses used as:	Indirect signs.
Research focus:	Personality dynamics and psychopathology; unconscious processes; defense mechanisms.
Approach to personality change:	By insight into motives and conflicts underlying behavior.
Role of situation:	Deliberately minimized or ambiguous.

trained experts. It therefore becomes essential to study how closely experts really do agree with each other and how well they can support their opinions with evidence (Chapter 3). These results often have been disappointing.

Many critics view Freud's theory as providing little more than labels. Such labels (for example, the "death wish") cannot be tested by any methodology. Bluntly, some of these concepts do not offer the possibility of ever being disconfirmed by research. One danger here is that people may believe that these labels are useful when, instead, they merely lead to sweeping generalities and clichés.

In spite of these problems, many major attempts have been made to clarify Freudian constructs. Especially vigorous efforts have been made to deal with defense mechanisms and conflict, and to submit them to experimental study (e.g., Blum, 1953; Erdelyi, 1985; Holmes, 1974; Sears, 1943, 1944; Silverman 1976). You already saw some of the research that psychoanalytic ideas have influenced and you will see many more examples throughout the text. Although the research often has not clearly supported the original key Freudian concepts and methods, it almost always has led to useful insights and encouraging new directions.

Overview

Some of the essentials of the approach are summarized in Table 4-5, which provides a summary overview.

SUMMARY

1. People can cognitively avoid internal anxiety-generating cues such as threatening thoughts. While the phenomenon of "cognitive avoidance" is widely recognized, a controversial issue is whether or not it involves a mechanism of unconscious repression.

2. The Freudian concept of defense mechanisms refers to attempts to cope cognitively with internal anxiety-arousing cues without awareness—that is, unconsciously. Freud thought that the key mechanism of defense entailed unconsciously motivated repression of unacceptable (anxiety-arousing) material. According to this theory, repressed impulses are not eliminated but are only camouflaged; hence, they may ultimately return in disguised and distorted forms, such as "slips" of the tongue or symptoms.

3. The concept of repression has been the subject of extensive research for many years. Although several empirical studies have been interpreted as supporting the concept of repression, alternative interpretations are possible (such as poorer learning under conditions of emotional upset and response interference due to stress).

4. Repressive "perceptual defenses" might produce anxiety-reducing distortions and avoidance in perception. Some researchers reasoned that if certain stimuli generally elicited many sexual or aggressive responses, then the *failure* to give such responses meant that the person must be inhibiting or defending against this type of ideation. Often a tachistoscope was used to present stimuli briefly, and the length of time required to recognize threatening stimuli (such as taboo words) was the measure of defensive avoidance.

5. Methodological problems left the conclusions uncertain. For example, the threatening words used in perceptual defense experiments occur less frequently in the English language than the neutral words. Thus longer recognition time could result from unfamiliarity rather than from unconscious defense. Another difficulty lies in the problem of distinguishing between the subject's *report* and *perception.* The subject in a perceptual recognition situation may see the taboo stimulus but may deliberately suppress a response because of embarrassment about saying or admitting it. Other experiments on unconscious defense have been limited by many similar methodological dilemmas.

6. Evidence from controlled experimental research on unconscious defense and need-distorted perception is often negative. Many psychoanalytically oriented critics, however, maintain that most of this evidence is irrelevant. They point to the artificiality of the measures usually employed and to the hazards of generalizing from laboratory subjects to clinical populations and problems. Alternatively, the clinician's judgments and the intuitive procedures used for inferring the phenomena of unconscious dynamics have been questioned most seriously.

7. A major effort to assess the role of the unconscious has investigated learning to see if it can occur without awareness or consciousness. In general, while some simple conditioned responses may be learned without awareness, awareness plays a major role in most forms of human learning. Yet, although most learning may require awareness, once behavior is mastered it often seems to proceed without subjective awareness. Similarly, painful or unpleasant material at first may be deliberately suppressed and this response suppression may gradually become automatic. Thus the phenomenon of "repression" may reduce to overlearned response suppression.

8. But it is also likely that selectivity and "bias" may occur in the ways people process information, sometimes without their awareness. For example, people may engage in motivated self-deception, and they sometimes seem to have little insight into their own thought processes.

9. Suggestibility is a primary characteristic of a hypnotized individual. The ease with which a person can be hypnotized appears to be quite stable over time. There is considerable controversy about the best explanation of hypnosis.

10. Individual differences in coping with stress and anxiety-arousing cues seem to fall on a continuum from avoidance behaviors to supersensitive and vigilant ones. Repression-sensitization as well as blunting-monitoring are two concepts for studying such individual differences.

11. Whether one reacts to a painful stimulus by trying cognitively to avoid it or by becoming vigilantly alert to it may depend partly upon what one can do to control the threat. If adaptive action seems impossible, cognitive suppression may be more likely. If, however, the potentially painful events can be controlled by the person's actions, then greater attention and vigilance to them may be found.

12. The main strengths and weaknesses of the psychodynamic approach, and its basic features, were summarized.

PART THREE
THE TRAIT APPROACH

Chapter 5
Trait Theories: Conceptions

Chapter 6
Measuring Individual Differences

Chapter 7
Traits and Their Biological Bases

Trait Theories: Conceptions

"My father is a really great guy. He's absolutely dependable; I can always count on him."

"Nancy's very quiet and withdrawn. She never says hello to anybody. She's very unsure of herself."

"I've always wanted to succeed. Winning is everything. If you're not a winner you're nobody."

Descriptions like those above are the stuff of trait psychology. We see trait psychology in everyday life whenever people describe and group the differences among themselves into slots or categories. We all tend to classify each other readily on many dimensions: sex, race, religion, occupation, friendliness, and competitiveness are a few examples. Good-bad, strong-weak, friend-enemy, winner-loser—the ways of sorting and classifying human qualities seem virtually infinite.

A concern with classifying and naming things is also characteristic of most sciences in their early efforts to find order. Consider, for example, the classification system of biology, in which all life is sorted into genera and species. This effort to categorize also occurs in psychology, where, as the oldest and most enduring approach to individuality, it is known as the *trait approach.* This approach seeks to label, measure, and classify people with the trait terms of everyday language (e.g., friendly, aggressive, honest) in order to compare their psychological attributes.

TYPES AND TRAITS

Traditionally, the essence of the trait approach has been the assumption that behavior is primarily determined by generalized *traits*—basic qualities of the person that express themselves in many contexts. Guided by this assumption, many investigators have searched vigorously for these traits. Perhaps the chief goal of trait psychology has been to find the person's position on one or more trait dimensions (e.g., intelligence, introversion, anxiety) by comparing the individual with others under similar uniform conditions. Guided by the belief that positions on these dimensions tend to be stable across situations and over time, the focus in the study of individuality becomes the search to identify the person's basic traits.

Types: Sheldon and Jung

Some categorizations sort individuals into discrete categories or *types.* In the ancient theory of temperaments, for example, the Greek physician Hippocrates assigned persons to one of four types of temperament: *choleric* (irritable), *melancholic* (depressed), *sanguine* (optimistic), and *phlegmatic* (calm, listless). In accord with the biology of his time (about 400 B.C.), Hippocrates attributed each temperament to a predominance of one of the bodily humors; yellow bile, black bile, blood, and phlegm. A choleric temperament was caused by an excess of yellow bile; a depressive temperament reflected the predominance of black bile; the sanguine person had too much blood; and phlegmatic people suffered from an excess of phlegm.

Other typologies have searched for constitutional types, seeking associations between physique and indices of temperament. Such groupings in terms of body build have considerable popular appeal, as seen in the prevalence of stereotypes linking the body to the psyche: Fat people are "jolly" and "lazy," thin people are "morose" and "sensitive," and so on.

Formal classifications of the possible links between personality and body type were developed by the German psychiatrist Kretschmer and more recently by an American physician, William H. Sheldon. Sheldon's classification has received most attention. In 1942 he suggested three dimensions of physique and their corresponding temperaments. These are summarized in Figure 5-1.

As Figure 5-1 suggests, the endomorph is obese, the mesomorph has an athletic

Figure 5-1
Sheldon's Physique Dimensions and Their Associated Temperaments

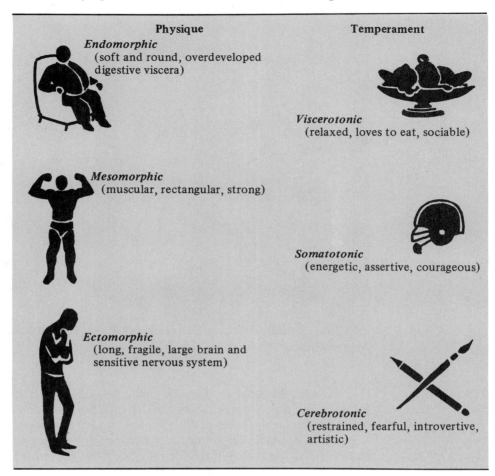

build, and the ectomorph is tall, thin, and stoop-shouldered. Rather than dividing people into three distinct types, Sheldon considered every individual's status on each dimension. He developed a seven-point rating system for measuring somatotypes. For example, a 7-3-1 would be high on endomorphy, moderate on mesomorphy, and low on ectomorphy, presumably with corresponding levels of the associated temperaments. Sheldon's typology thus was quite sophisticated,especially by comparison with earlier attempts.

Sheldon's ideas about the association between body build and temperament are supported to some extent when untrained people rate the personality characteristics of others. In part these findings may reflect the fact that stereotyped ideas about the characteristics of fat, athletic, and skinny people are shared by the raters. For example, if raters think most fat people are jolly and thin people are sensitive, they may base their judgments of the individuals they rate on these stereotypes rather

Are there links between physique and personality?

than on observed behavior. Thus they may rate a fat person as jolly, no matter how he or she behaves. Studies of behavior that avoid such stereotypes generally provide less evidence for the value of this system (e.g., Tyler, 1956).

Nevertheless, possible connections between body types and personality cannot be dismissed. On the contrary, they may be quite important. Physical appearance and physical characteristics certainly affect the ways in which others perceive us, what we can and cannot do, and ultimately even what we feel and experience about ourselves. Physical characteristics like strength, height, and muscularity affect the situations we select, the work and avocations we pursue, and the interests and values that develop. But the relations between physique and particular personality characteristics tend to be more complex and indirect than the early typologies suggested.

One of the most famous typologies was devised by the Swiss psychiatrist Carl Jung. He grouped all people into *introverts* or *extraverts.* According to this typology, the introvert withdraws into himself, especially when encountering stressful emotional conflict, prefers to be alone, tends to avoid others, and is shy. The extravert, in contrast, reacts to stress by trying to lose himself among people and social activity. He is drawn to an occupation that allows him to deal directly with many people, such as sales, and is apt to be conventional, sociable, and outgoing.

The very simplicity that makes such typologies appealing also reduces their

Jung described the introvert as consistently shy and withdrawn.

value. Because each person's behaviors are complex and variable, it is most difficult to assign an individual to a psychological slot. Such characteristics as blood or sex may be typed, but complex psychological qualities tend to defy categorization. Nevertheless, interesting and important typologies continue to be explored (see *In Focus 5.1*) and will be discussed later.

Individual Differences on Dimensions

While typologies assume discontinuous categories (like male or female), traits are continuous dimensions (see Figure 5-2). On such dimensions differences among individuals may be arranged quantitatively in terms of the degree of the quality the person has (like degrees of friendliness). Psychological measurements usually suggest a continuous dimension of individual differences in the degree of the measured quality: most people show intermediate amounts, and only a few are at each extreme, as Figure 5-2 shows. For example, on Jung's introversion—extraversion typology individuals differ in the extent to which they show either quality but usually do not belong totally to one category or the other. It is therefore better to think of a psychological continuum of individual differences for most qualities.

Many psychologists who use a trait approach investigate such personality dimensions as aggressiveness, dependency, and the striving to achieve high standards of excellence. An example of such a dimension is "repression-sensitization," as was discussed in the last chapter on defenses. Great differences have been found among people in the degree to which they show such dispositions.

In Focus 5.1
**Type A: A
Typology That
Predicts
Coronary
Disease**

In spite of recent significant declines in deaths due to coronary disease in American men, coronary disease remains the major cause of death in the United States. Many of the men killed by coronary disease are only thirty-five to fifty years old.

Recently psychologists and physicians have begun to look at the psychological variables that place individuals at higher risk of coronary heart disease. A coronary-prone behavior pattern was identified (Friedman & Roseman, 1974; Glass, 1977) and designated as *Type A*. This behavior pattern is characterized by:

1. Competitive Achievement Striving: Type As are likely to be involved in multiple activities, to have numerous community and social commitments, and to participate in competitive athletics. In laboratory studies they are persistent and behave as though they believe that with sufficient effort they can overcome a variety of obstacles or frustrations.

2. Exaggerated Sense of Time Urgency: Type As show great impatience and irritation at delay (for example, in a traffic jam, on a waiting line).

3. Aggressiveness and Hostility: Type As may not be generally more aggressive than other people, but they become more aggressive under circumstances which threaten their sense of task mastery, for example, when under criticism or high time pressure.

Individuals who manifest these behaviors to a great degree are called Type As; those who show the opposite patterns of relaxation, serenity, and lack of time urgency are designated as *Type B*.

A number of studies have suggested that Type A people may have at least twice the likelihood of coronary heart disease as Type B people. They also smoke more and have higher levels of cholesterol in their blood. Type A people also tend to describe themselves as more impulsive, self-confident, and higher in achievement and aggression. Both Type A men and women fail to report physical symptoms and fatigue (Carver et al., 1976; Weidner & Matthews, 1978). This tendency to ignore symptoms may result in a Type A individual failing to rest or to seek medical care in the early phases of heart disease and may be one reason why these people push themselves into greater risk of premature coronary death. Identifying individuals at high risk for heart disease and teaching them to pay more attention to physical symptoms may be an important part of programs aimed at reducing the toll of heart disease.

There may be a less strong relationship between the total pattern of Type A behavior and coronary disease than was suggested initially, especially among high-risk subjects (Matthews, 1984). Rather than looking at the relationship between the Type A pattern as a whole and coronary disease, it may be more useful to isolate such specific components of the pattern as anger and hostility. These components were found to be related to coronary disease even in the more recent studies. In sum, it now seems that specific behaviors, rather than the more global typology, are linked to a higher risk of coronary disease.

The trait approach begins with the common-sense observation that individuals often differ greatly and consistently in their responses to the same psychological situation or stimulus. That is, when different people are confronted with the same event—the same social encounter, the same test question, the same frightening experience—each individual tends to react in a somewhat different way. The basic idea that no two people react identically to the same stimulus is shown schemati-

Figure 5-2
Examples of Discontinuous Categories (Type) and Continuous Dimensions (Traits)

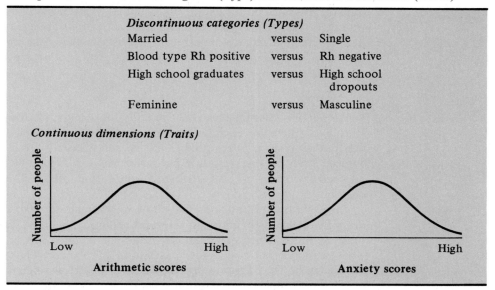

Discontinuous categories (Types)

Married	versus	Single
Blood type Rh positive	versus	Rh negative
High school graduates	versus	High school dropouts
Feminine	versus	Masculine

Continuous dimensions (Traits)

cally in Figure 5-3. Moreover, in everyday life most of us are impressed with the distinctive *consistency* of one individual's responses over a wide variety of stimulus situations: We expect an "aggressive" person to differ consistently from others in his or her responses to many stimuli.

In its simplest meaning, the term "trait" refers to consistent differences between the behavior or characteristics of two or more people. Thus, "a trait is any distinguishable, relatively enduring way in which one individual varies from another" (Guilford, 1959, p. 6.).

In addition to using trait labels to describe individual differences, some early theorists also invoked the trait as an explanation: in their view the trait was the

Figure 5-3
Individual Differences in Response to the Same Stimulus

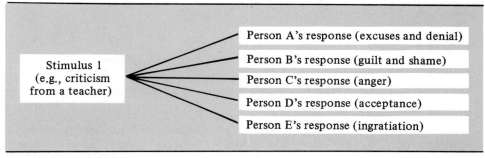

The trait approach emphasizes consistent differences among people in their response to the same stimulus.

property within the person that accounted for his or her unique but relatively stable reactions to stimuli. Thus the trait became a construct to explain behavior—a hypothesized reason for enduring individual differences. Before examining formal trait theories, however, we should consider how traits are used informally by people in daily life. Indeed we are all trait theorists in the sense that we generate ideas about our own dispositions and the characteristics of other people.

Trait Attributions

When people describe each other in daily life, they spontaneously use trait terms. We all characterize each other (and ourselves) with such terms as aggressive, dependent, fearful, introverted, anxious, submissive—the list is almost endless. We see a person behaving in a particular way—for example, sitting at a desk for an hour yawning—and we attribute a trait—"unmotivated" or "lazy" or "bored" or "dull."

These simple trait attributions are often adequate to "explain" events for many everyday purposes in common-sense psychology (Heider, 1958; Kelley, 1973). In these common-sense explanations, traits are invoked not just as descriptions of what people do but also as the causes of their behavior. Thus in everyday practice traits may be used first simply as adjectives describing behavior ("He behaves in a lazy way"), but the description is soon generalized from the behavior to the person ("He *is* lazy") and then abstracted to "He has a lazy disposition" or "He is unmotivated." These descriptions pose no problems as long as their basis is recalled—he is construed as behaving in a lazy way and no more. A hazard in trait attribution is that we easily forget that nothing is explained if the state *we* have attributed to the person from his behavior ("He has a trait of laziness") is now invoked as the *cause* of the behavior from which it was inferred. We then quickly emerge with the tautology, "He behaves in a lazy way because he has a lazy disposition," or because he is "unmotivated."

The trait approach to formal personality study begins with the common-sense conviction that personality can be described with trait terms. But it extends and refines those descriptions by arriving at them quantitatively and systematically. Efforts to explain individual differences by formal trait theories face some of the same problems that arise when traits are offered as causes by the layman. However, numerous safeguards have been developed to try to control some of these difficulties (see Chapter 6).

Gordon Allport

One of the most outstanding trait psychologists was Gordon Allport, whose conceptions of traits have had an important influence for more than thirty years. In Allport's theory, traits have a very real existence: They are the ultimate realities of psychological organization. Allport favored a biophysical conception that

> does not hold that every trait-name necessarily implies a trait; but rather that behind all confusion of terms, behind the disagreement of judges, and apart from errors and failures of empirical observation, there are none the less *bona fide* mental structures in each personality that account for the consistency of its behavior (1937, p. 289).

Gordon Allport (1897–1967)

According to Allport, traits are determining tendencies or predispositions to respond. These dispositions serve to integrate what would otherwise be dissimilar stimuli and responses. In other words, a trait is

> a generalized and focalized neuropsychic system (peculiar to the individual) with the capacity to render many stimuli functionally equivalent, and to initiate and guide consistent (equivalent) forms of adaptive and expressive behavior (1937, p. 295).

Allport implied that traits are not linked to a small number of specific stimuli or responses, but are relatively general and enduring: By uniting responses to numerous stimuli, they produce fairly broad consistencies in behavior, as schematized in Figure 5-4.

Allport was convinced that some people have dispositions that influence most aspects of their behavior. He called these highly generalized dispositions *cardinal* traits. For example, if a person's whole life seems to be organized around goal achievement and the attainment of excellence, then achievement might be his or her cardinal trait. Less pervasive but still quite generalized dispositions are *central* traits, and Allport thought that many people are broadly influenced by central traits. Finally, more specific, narrow traits are called *secondary* dispositions or "attitudes."

Allport believed that one's pattern of dispositions or "personality structure" determines one's behavior. This emphasis on structure rather than environment or stimulus conditions is seen in his colorful phrase, "The same fire that melts the

Figure 5-4
An Example of a Trait as the Unifier of Stimuli and Responses

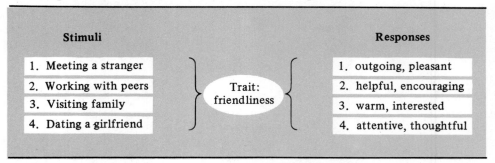

Stimuli		Responses
1. Meeting a stranger		1. outgoing, pleasant
2. Working with peers	Trait: friendliness	2. helpful, encouraging
3. Visiting family		3. warm, interested
4. Dating a girlfriend		4. attentive, thoughtful

butter hardens the egg'' (1937, p. 102). Allport was a pioneering spokesman for the importance of individual differences: No two people are completely alike, and hence no two people respond identically to the same event. Each person's behavior is determined by a particular trait structure.

According to Allport, traits never occur in any two people in exactly the same way: They operate in *unique* ways in each person. This conviction was consistent with his emphasis on the individuality and uniqueness of each personality. To the extent that any trait is unique within a person rather than common among many people, it cannot be studied by making comparisons among people. Consequently Allport urged the thorough study of individuals through intensive and long-term case studies. He also believed, however, that because of shared experiences and common cultural influences, most persons tend to develop some *roughly* common kinds of traits: They can be compared on these common dispositions.

Many of Allport's theories were most relevant to the in-depth study of lives and experience rather than to the quantitative study of groups. He contributed to trait theory, but he was critical of many of the statistical methods and quantitative research strategies favored by other trait theorists.

R. B. Cattell

Raymond B. Cattell (e.g., 1950, 1965) is another important trait theorist. For Cattell the trait is also the basic unit of study; it is a "mental structure," inferred from behavior, and a fundamental construct that accounts for behavioral regularity or consistency. Like Allport, Cattell distinguished between *common traits,* which are possessed by all people, and *unique traits,* which occur only in a particular person and cannot be found in another in exactly the same form.

Cattell also distinguished *surface traits* from *source traits* (see Table 5-1 for selected examples). Surface traits are clusters of overt or manifest trait elements (responses) that seem to go together. Source traits are the underlying variables that are the causal entities determining the surface manifestations. In research, trait elements (in the form of test responses or scores) are analyzed statistically until collections of elements that correlate positively in all possible combinations are discovered. This procedure, according to Cattell, yields surface traits.

For Cattell source traits can be found only by means of the mathematical tech-

Raymond B. Cattell (b. 1905)

nique of factor analysis (discussed further in Chapter 6). Using this technique, the investigator tries to estimate the factors or dimensions that appear to underlie surface variations in behavior. According to Cattell, the basic aim in research and assessment should be identification of source traits. In this view, these traits are divided between those that reflect environmental conditions *(environmental-mold traits)* and those that reflect constitutional factors *(constitutional traits)*. Moreover, source traits may either be *general* (those affecting behavior in many different sit-

Table 5-1
Surface Traits and Source Traits Studied by Cattell

Examples of Surface Traits (Cattell, 1950)	Integrity, altrusim—dishonesty, undependability
	Disciplined thoughtfulness—foolishness
	Thrift, tidiness, obstinacy—lability, curiosity, intuition
Examples of Source Traits (Cattell, 1965)	Ego strength—emotionality and neuroticism
	Dominance—submissiveness

NOTE: These are selected and abbreviated examples from much longer lists.

uations) or *specific*. Specific source traits are particularized sources of personality reaction that operate in one situation only, and Cattell pays little attention to them.

Cattell uses three kinds of data to discover general source traits: *life records,* in which everyday behavior situations are observed and rated; *self-ratings;* and *objective tests,* in which the person is observed in situations that are specifically designed to elicit responses from which behavior in other situations can be predicted. The data from all three sources are subjected to factor analysis. In his own work, Cattell shows a preference for factor analysis of life-record data based on many behavior ratings for large samples of persons. Some fourteen or fifteen source traits have been reported from such investigations, but only six have been found repeatedly (Vernon, 1964).

In Cattell's system, traits may also be grouped into classes on the basis of how they are expressed. Those that are relevant to the individual's being "set into action" with respect to some goal are called *dynamic traits.* Those concerned with effectiveness in gaining the goal are *ability traits.* Traits concerned with energy or emotional reactivity are named *temperament traits.* Cattell has speculated extensively about the relationships between various traits and the development of personality (1965).

H. J. Eysenck

The extensive researches of the English psychologist Hans Eysenck have complemented the work of the American trait theorists in many important ways. Eysenck (1961) has extended the search for personality dimensions to the area of abnormal behavior, studying such traits as *neuroticism.* He also has investigated *introversion-extraversion* as a dimensional trait (although Carl Jung originally proposed "introvert" and "extravert" as personality *types*). Eysenck and his associates have pursued an elaborate and sophisticated statistical methodology in their search for personality dimensions. In addition to providing a set of descriptive dimensions, Eysenck and his colleagues have studied the associations between people's status on these dimensions and their scores on a variety of other personality and intellectual measures.

Eysenck emphasized that his dimension of introversion-extraversion is based entirely on research and "must stand and fall by empirical confirmation" (Eysenck & Rachman, 1965, p. 19). In his words:

> The typical extravert is sociable, likes parties, has many friends, needs to have people to talk to, and does not like reading or studying by himself. He craves excitement, takes chances, often sticks his neck out, acts on the spur of the moment, and is generally an impulsive individual. He is fond of practical jokes, always has a ready answer, and generally likes change; he is carefree, easygoing, optimistic, and "likes to laugh and be merry." He prefers to keep moving and doing things, tends to be aggressive and loses his temper quickly; altogether his feelings are not kept under tight control, and he is not always a reliable person.
>
> The typical introvert is a quiet, retiring sort of person, introspective, fond of books rather than people; he is reserved and distant except to intimate friends. He tends to plan ahead, "looks before he leaps," and mistrusts the impulse of the moment. He does not like excitement, takes matters of everyday life with proper seriousness, and likes a well-

Hans J. Eysenck (b. 1916)

ordered mode of life. He keeps his feelings under close control, seldom behaves in an aggressive manner, and does not lose his temper easily. He is reliable, somewhat pessimistic and places great value on ethical standards.

Eysenck and his colleagues recognized that these descriptions may sound almost like caricatures because they portray "perfect" extraverts and introverts while in fact most people are mixtures who fall in the middle rather than at the extremes of the dimensions (see Figure 5-5). As Figure 5-5 shows, Eysenck suggested that the second major dimension of personality is *emotional stability* or *neuroticism.* This dimension describes at one end people who tend to be moody, touchy, anxious, restless, and so on. At the other extreme are people who are characterized by such terms as stable, calm, carefree, even-tempered, and reliable. As Eysenck stressed, the ultimate value of these dimensions will depend on the research support they receive.

To clarify the meaning of both dimensions, Eysenck and his associates have studied the relations between people's status on them and their scores on many other measures. An example of the results found is summarized in Table 5-2 which shows self-reported differences in the sexual activities of extraverts and introverts (reported in Eysenck, 1973). As expected, the extraverts generally reported earlier, more frequent, and more varied sexual experiences. While the groups differed on the average, there was still considerable overlap, making it difficult to predict any particular individual's behavior from his introversion-extraversion score alone.

Figure 5-5
Dimensions of Personality

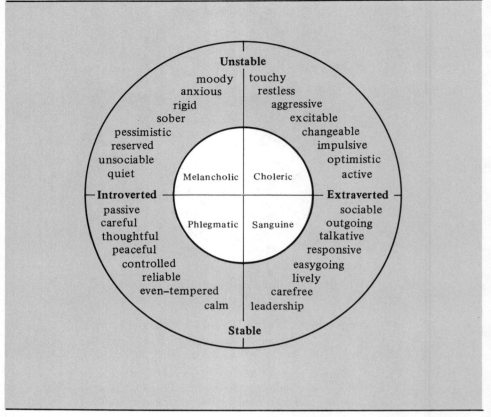

The inner ring shows the "four temperaments" of Hippocrates; the outer ring shows the results of modern factor analytic studies of the intercorrelations between traits by Eysenck and others (Eysenck & Rachman, 1965).

Moreover, one cannot be sure to what degree the differences between extraverts and introverts reflect their different sexual practices or only show that they give different self-reports, describing their activities in more or less venturesome ways. But the results of many studies of this type provide an increasingly comprehensive picture of Eysenck's dimensions.

COMMON FEATURES OF TRAIT THEORIES

Now consider the principal common characteristics of trait approaches.

Generality and Stability of Traits

Trait theorists often disagree about the specific content and structure of the basic traits needed to describe personality, but their general conceptions have much similarity. They all use the trait to account for consistencies in an individual's behavior

Table 5-2
Sexual Activities Reported by Introverted (I) and Extraverted (E) Students[a]

Activity		Males I	Males E	Females I	Females E
Masturbation at present		86	72	47	39
Petting: at seventeen		16	40	15	24
at nineteen		31	56	30	47
at present		57	78	62	76
Coitus (intercourse): at seventeen		5	21	4	8
at nineteen		15	45	12	29
at present		47	77	42	71
Median frequency of coitus per month (sexually active students only)		3.0	5.5	3.1	7.5
Coitus partners in the last twelve months (unmarried students only)	one	75	46	72	60
	two or three	18	30	25	23
	four or more	7	25	4	17

[a]The numbers are the frequencies of endorsements by each group.
SOURCE: Based on data from Giese & Schmidt, 1968, cited in Eysenck, 1973.

and to explain why persons respond differently to the same stimulus. They view traits as dispositions that determine such behaviors. Each differentiatesbetween relatively superficial traits (e.g., Cattell's surface traits) and more basic, underlying traits (e.g., Cattell's source traits). Each recognizes that traits vary in breadth or generality. Allport puts the strongest emphasis on the relative generality of traits across many situations. Each theorist also admits trait fluctuations, or changes in a person's position with respect to a disposition. At the same time, each is committed to a search for relatively broad, stable traits (see *In Focus 5.2*).

In Focus 5.2
Do the Beginnings Predict the Future?

How stable are a person's qualities? Do early characteristics predict later qualities? When parents say "Charlie was always so friendly, even as a little baby," are their comments justified? Can we predict the six-year-old's behavior from responses in the first year of life? Is there much continuity in the qualities and behaviors of the child throughout childhood?

A number of important connections have been found. For example, babies who make certain responses with lower intensity at birth tend to show some positive qualities later in life (see Figure 5-6). Such newborn behaviors as lower sensitivity to touch on the skin, for

example, in the newborn predicted more mature communication and coping at age two and one-half and at age seven and one-half. High touch sensitivity and high respiration rates at birth were related to low interest, low participation, lower assertiveness, and less communicativeness in later years (Bell et al., 1971; Halverson, 1971a, 1971b). But these links between newborn and later behaviors were exceptions. Most of the relations that were examined turned out to be nonexistent, and the associations that were found generally were not strong. So there are some connections between a newborn's qualities and characteristics later in life.

Figure 5-6
Examples of Relationships between Children's Behavior at Different Ages. The Relationship Holds for Both Sexes Unless Otherwise Indicated in the Chart

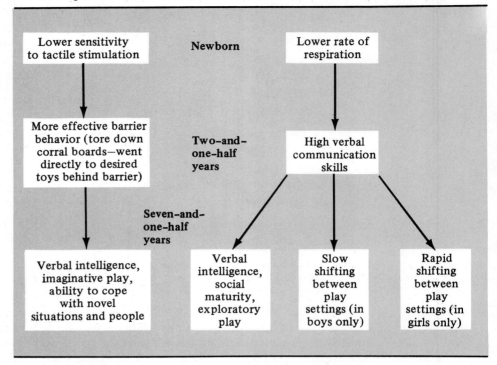

Based on data from Bell, et al. (1971); Halverson (1971a, b); Halverson & Waldrop (1974).

But in the individual case one could not predict confidently from responses at birth to later characteristics:

> To use an analogy, newborn behavior is more like a preface to a book than a table of its contents yet to be unfolded. Further, the preface is itself merely a rough draft undergoing rapid revision. There are some clues to the nature of the book in the preface, but these are in code form and taking them as literally prophetic is likely to lead to disappointment (Bell et al., 1971, p. 132).

As one progresses beyond the "preface of the book" to the first few chapters (to the early years of life) continuities in development do become increasingly evident (e.g., Block & Block, 1980; Mischel, 1984). Children who are seen as more active, assertive, aggressive, competitive, outgoing, and so on at age three years are also more likely to be described as having more of those qualities later in development, for example. In sum, the specific links between qualities of the child say in the fourth year and in the eighth year may be complex and indirect. But a thorough analysis of the patterns indicates that significant threads of continuity do emerge over time. Thus childhood characteristics may be connected coherently to later behavior and attributes at least to some degree (Arend, Gove, & Sroufe, 1979; Block, 1971). Experiences in the early pages of the book do affect what happens in the later pages, although these early experiences do not prevent the possibility of genuine changes later. The amount of stability or change over time varies for different types of characteristics and different types of experiences at different points in development.

Search for Basic Traits

Guided by the assumption that highly generalized dispositions exist, trait psychologists try to identify the individual's position on one or more dimensions (e.g., neuroticism, extraversion). They do this by comparing people tested under standardized conditions. They believe that positions on these dimensions are relatively stable across testing situations and over long time periods. Their main emphasis in the study of personality is the development of instruments that can accurately tap the person's underlying traits. Less attention has been paid to the effects of environmental conditions on traits and behavior.

Inferring Traits from Behavioral Signs

In the search for dispositions one always *infers* traits from behavior—for example, from what people say about themselves on a questionnaire. The person's responses or behaviors are taken as *indicators* of underlying traits. The trait approach to personality is a "sign" approach in the sense that there is no interest in the test behavior itself. That is, test responses are of value not in their own right but only as *signs* of the traits that underlie them; test behavior is always used as a sign of nontest behavior (Loevinger, 1957). The trait psychologist is not interested in answers on an inventory or IBM score sheet for their own sake, but only in a subject's responses to a test as cues or signs of dispositions. It is therefore essential to demonstrate the relation between test behaviors and the traits they supposedly represent. We will consider efforts of this sort later (Chapter 6).

Quantification

A main feature of the trait approach has been its methodology. This methodology is "psychometric" in the sense that it attempts to measure individual differences and to quantify them. Psychometricians study persons and groups on trait dimensions by comparing their scores on tests. To do this, they sample many subjects, compare large groups under uniform testing conditions, and devise statistical techniques to infer basic traits (Chapters 6 and 7).

Trait Dimensions and Individual Differences

After many years of searching, trait theorists still disagree as to which personality trait dimensions are the basic ones. Some suggest as many as sixteen basic traits; others as few as two or three. Table 5-3 gives the five trait dimensions that were studied in one research program. For each dimension, it shows the adjectives describing the two ends of each rating scale it includes. In spite of disagreement about basic dimensions, there is usually some overlap in the findings of different trait theorists. Probably the dimensions found most consistently involve extraversion-introversion, and adjustment and integration as opposed to disorganization and anxiety (e.g., Vernon, 1964).

Table 5-3
Some Trait Dimensions and Their Components

Trait Dimension	Descriptive Components[a]
I. Extraversion or Surgency	Talkative—Silent Frank, Open—Secretive Adventurous—Cautious Sociable—Reclusive
II. Agreeableness	Good-natured—Irritable Not Jealous—Jealous Mild, Gentle—Headstrong Cooperative—Negativistic
III. Conscientiousness	Fussy, Tidy—Careless Responsible—Undependable Scrupulous—Unscrupulous Persevering—Quitting, Fickle
IV. Emotional Stability	Poised—Nervous, Tense Calm—Anxious Composed—Excitable Not Hypochondriacal—Hypochondriacal
V. Culture	Artistically Sensitive—Artistically Insensitive Intellectual—Unreflective, Narrow Polished, Refined—Crude, Boorish Imaginative—Simple, Direct

[a]Adjectives describing the two ends of the scales that comprise the dimension.
SOURCE: Adapted from Norman, 1963.

Many trait researchers remain committed to identifying "the most important individual differences in mankind" (Goldberg, 1973, p. 1). They assume that the most significant individual differences—those that are most important in daily human relationships—enter into the natural language of the culture as single-word trait terms. Using a variety of methods (discussed in Chapters 6 and 7) they try to identify basic trait terms in the language and to categorize them into comprehensive groupings. This classification task is an enormous one, given that thousands of trait terms (over 18,000 in one count) are found in English. The researchers hope that an extensive, well-organized vocabulary for describing human attributes in trait terms will lead to better theories of personality and better methods of personality assessment.

Some highly sophisticated research is advancing this important goal. One of the most comprehensive efforts builds on the earlier work shown in Table 5-3. Eight scales of adjectives were developed for the domain of interpersonal behavior (Wiggins, 1979, 1980). Figure 5-7 presents the eight dimensions. Note that each dimension is "bipolar," i.e., has two opposite ends or poles. The dimensions are structured in a circular pattern like a pie. Each pole is made up of a set of adjectives

Figure 5-7
Wiggins' (1980) Taxonomy of the Interpersonal Domain

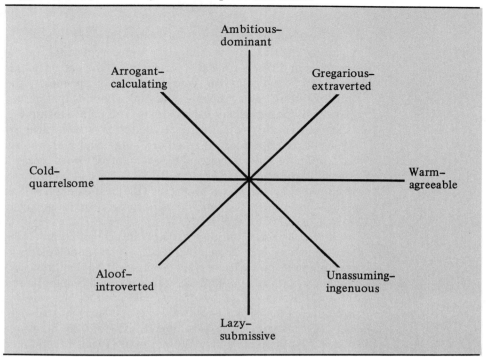

so that *Ambitious (Dominant),* for example, is defined with such terms as persevering, persistent, industrious. The opposite pole, *Lazy (Submissive),* includes such terms as unproductive, unthorough, unindustrious. Wiggins reports that these eight dimensions fit well the results of earlier descriptions of the interpersonal domain (e.g., Leary, 1957). They seem to be reasonably robust and useful when different samples of people are rated on them.

Research in the trait tradition does not only describe individual differences. It also examines the relationships between an individual's position on many personality dimensions and his or her behavior in other situations. For example, a group of school children may be tested for their intellectual abilities and also given questionnaires concerning beliefs and attitudes. In addition they may be asked to rate themselves on a set of characteristics and they may be rated by their teachers and their peers. The results are examined statistically to discover the associations (correlations) among all of the obtained measures. When very many associations emerge from this procedure it often helps to simplify them by means of further statistical techniques. The findings of trait research help to illuminate what kinds of behaviors are most likely to occur together. The results help us to answer questions like these: Do aggressive children become aggressive adults? Are adolescent boys who are aggressive at home likely to be aggressive at school?

NEW DIRECTIONS

Prototypes: "Typical" People

In a new direction that may allow a fresh approach to traits, psychologists have also begun to identify how we judge the "prototypicality" or "typicality" of different members of a category. Take, for example, the category "birds." To demonstrate the idea of "typicality" to yourself, think of the most typical, representative, or "birdlike" bird. You probably will think of a bird that is something like a robin or sparrow—not a chicken or an ostrich. The point is simply that some members of a category (in this case, birds) are better or more typical examples of a category: Some reds are "redder" than others, some chairs are more chairlike than others. This point has been elegantly documented for everyday categories of natural objects like furniture (Rosch et al., 1976). Thus natural categories may be organized around *prototypical* examples (the best examples of the concept), with less prototypical or less good members forming a continuum away from the central one (Rosch, 1975; Tversky, 1977).

The important point here is that trait categories, like other categories, may be best thought of *not* as well-defined, distinct, nonoverlapping categories in which each member of a category has all its defining features. (While many birds sing, not all do, and some nonbirds surely do.) Well-defined, nonoverlapping categories are built into artificial, logical systems, but they are rare in the real world. If we turn from the abstract world of logic and formal, artificial systems to common, everyday categories—to furniture, birds, and clothing—the categories become "fuzzy." As the philosopher Wittgenstein (1953) first pointed out, the members of common, everyday categories do not all share all of a set of single, essential features critical for category membership. If you closely examine a set of natural objects all labeled by one general term (like "birds") you will not find a single set of features that all members of the category share: Rather, a *pattern* of overlapping similarities—a *family resemblance* structure—seems to emerge.

Might "typicality" and "family resemblance" and "fuzziness" also characterize everyday judgments about categories of people? The answer seems to be that they do (Cantor & Mischel, 1979; Wiggins, 1980). When making these judgments while forming our everyday impressions of people we seem able to agree about who is a more or less typical or even "ideal" kind of personality, just as we agree that a robin is a more birdlike bird than a chicken. For instance, such qualities as "sociable" and "outgoing" are the characteristics of a "typical extravert."

The study of prototypicality rules and family resemblance principles in judgments of people is helping to show how consistency and coherence are perceived in spite of variations in behavior (Mischel, 1984). To illustrate, someone who really knows Rembrandt's work, who has seen dozens of his paintings, can easily identify whether a previously unseen painting is a real Rembrandt, an imitation, or a fake. The art expert seems able to extract a central distinctive gist from a wide range of variations. The same processes that permit such judgments must underlie how we identify personality coherence in the face of behavioral variability, and agree that someone is or is not a "real" introvert, or an anxious neurotic, or a sincere friendly person. This "prototypicality" approach to traits is still too young to evaluate firmly, but is promising. One of its attractive features is that it seems highly compatible with attempts to quantify interpersonal behavior into dimensions (e.g., Wiggins, 1979, 1980).

Act Trends: Traits as Summaries

In a related direction, Buss and Craik (1983) moved away from the traditional trait view of dispositions as underlying internal causes (or explanations) of cross-situational consistencies in behavior. Instead, they see dispositions as summary statements of "act trends," not explanations of those trends. Dispositions are natural categories made up of various acts. The acts within a category differ in the degree to which they are prototypical or ideal members. Perhaps most importantly, the new view of dispositions makes it evident that dispositions do not provide explanations of behavior; instead, they are summary statements of behavioral trends that must themselves be explained (Buss & Craik, 1983; Wiggins, 1980).

Interaction of Traits and Situations

In recent years it has been increasingly recognized that an adequate approach to the study of traits must deal seriously with how the qualities of the person and the situation influence each other—that is, their "interaction" (e.g., Bowers, 1973; Endler, 1973; Magnusson, 1980). The expressions of a person's traits depend on his or her psychological situation at the moment. For example, rather than exhibit anxiety everywhere, an individual may be anxious only under some set of relatively narrow circumstances, such as test-taking in math, but not under many other conditions (e.g., Endler, 1973). Moreover, this anxiety may be expressed in some ways (such as subjective feelings of fear and upset) but not in others (for example, there may be no physical changes, such as increased perspiration or heart rate). The implications of these specific interactions for contemporary trait theory are profound, as will become evident when the applications of trait approaches are discussed and when we consider the topic of interaction in detail.

SUMMARY

1. Since earliest times people have labeled and classified each other according to their psychological characteristics. *Typologies* classify people into discrete categories. Among others, Hippocrates, Sheldon, and Jung have proposed typologies of personality, but the very simplicity that makes these typologies appealing also limits their value. An individual personality cannot be fitted neatly into one category or another.

2. *Traits* are continuous dimensions on which individual differences may be arranged quantitatively in accord with the amount of an attribute that the individual has.

3. In everyday life people habitually use trait terms. They employ these terms not just to describe what people do but also to explain their behavior. We have not really explained anything,

however, if after attributing a trait to a person on the basis of behavior, we later invoke that trait as the cause of the very behavior from which we inferred it.

4. Trait theorists conceptualize traits as underlying properties, qualities, or processes that exist in persons. Traits also are constructs to account for observed behavioral consistencies within persons and for the enduring and stable behavioral differences among them in their responses to similar stimuli (situations).

5. For Allport, traits are the ultimate realities of psychological organization. They are the mental structures that account for consistency in behavior. In his view, traits are predispositions to respond, and they serve to integrate what would otherwise be dissimilar stimuli and responses. Traits are relatively general and enduring, although they may range in generality from highly generalized *cardinal* through *central* to *secondary* traits or more specific "attitudes." An individual's "personality structure" is his or her pattern of dispositions or traits. Allport emphasized this structure, rather than the environment or stimulus conditions, in his analysis of human behavior. He stressed individual differences and the uniqueness of each person. Although he recognized some roughly common traits on which individuals can be compared, he urged the intensive study of the individual. He disapproved of many of the statistical methods and quantitative research strategies favored by other trait theorists.

6. Cattell distinguished between *surface* traits and *source* traits. Surface traits are identified by statistical correlations; source traits, by factor analysis. Through factor analysis Cattell tried to estimate the basic dimensions or factors underlying surface variations in behavior. Extensions of trait theory have been provided by Eysenck, who emphasizes the dimensions of introversion-extraversion and emotional stability (neuroticism).

7. In spite of their many differences, most trait theorists share the following theoretical assumptions and strategies:

a. Traits are assumed to be general underlying dispositions that account for consistencies in behavior.
b. Some traits are considered to be relatively superficial and specific; others that are more basic and widely generalized are assumed to produce consistencies across many situations.
c. The predominant objective is the identification of underlying broad dispositions. Emphasis is on the measurement of an individual's position on one or more dimensions by means of objective instruments or tests administered under standard conditions.
d. People's tested or sampled behaviors (including what they say about themselves) are viewed as signs of their underlying traits.
e. To search for basic traits a psychometric strategy is used that samples and compares large groups of subjects quantitatively under uniform conditions.

8. In a new approach to traits, the focus is finding typical (prototypical or best) examples of particular categories about people. One tries to identify the pattern of overlapping similarities, "the family resemblance," shared by typical members of the category. For example, a typical extravert is sociable and outgoing. Traits may be seen as summaries of behavior or "act trends," not as explanations of behavior.

9. There is still disagreement about which traits are the basic units of personality, but the search continues. There is also increasing recognition that the qualities of the person interact with those of the situation(s) in which he or she functions.

Chapter 6

Measuring Individual Differences

In this chapter you will learn how trait theories are applied to measure important individual differences. We begin by looking at the history of the trait approach to measurement. Later you will see some of the main methods that have grown from these theoretical roots. Most important, the trait approach has contributed basic concepts and measures to assess how individuals differ and to test hypotheses about their personalities. It permits a quantitative, orderly study of individual differences in an area that before had defied measurement.

Late in the nineteenth century psychologists who pioneered the trait approach recognized the hazards of basing impressions of people on informal, subjective judgments about them. To avoid those dangers, they tried to go beyond casual impressions and to create more formal tests. Tests, they hoped, would measure important individual differences objectively and accurately. For these trait theorists any attempt to study personality without tests would be as naive as a biological science without microscopes. Since the end of the nineteenth century there have been continuous efforts to study personality traits quantitatively by means of tests. This movement, often called the *psychometric trait approach,* has been one of the main forces in the study of personality; its roots extend far into the past and its implications for an understanding of personality are profound. It has yielded results that are both important and controversial.

ROOTS OF THE PSYCHOMETRIC APPROACH: MEASURING INTELLIGENCE

Psychometric testing started in the psychological laboratories during the last decades of the nineteenth century. Sir Francis Galton was administering tests in his London laboratory as early as 1882, in an effort to establish an inventory of human abilities. He included measures of sensory acuity, reaction time, and strength of movement. His aim was to measure the resemblance between large numbers of related and unrelated persons to explore the role of inheritance. Galton also devised a questionnaire that was an important forerunner of those developed in later years.

James McKeen Cattell was an American psychologist who had a major role in the development of psychological testing. In 1890 Cattell suggested a standard series of tests for the study of mental processes. These tests were typical of the kind appearing at that time. They included measures of strength of grip, rate of arm movement, amount of pressure needed to produce pain on the forehead, reaction time for sound, and speed of color naming.

Tests of reading, judgment, and memory were also being used with some schoolchildren toward the end of the last century. A first attempt to evaluate test scores systematically is found in a study by T. L. Bolton that appeared in 1892. Bolton analyzed data from about 1500 schoolchildren, comparing their memory spans with their teachers' estimates of their "intellectual acuteness." He found little correspondence. A 1901 monograph likewise reported disappointing results: The relationships found between Cattell's various tests at Columbia College and students' academic standing were negligible (Wissler, 1901).

The simple, specific, sensorimotor measures popular in the laboratories at the end of the nineteenth century were important forerunners of later tests. But the tests favored during this period were laboratory-bound techniques for comparing individual differences on single measures rather than on organized scales. It was the development of intelligence testing in the early twentieth century that made "psychometrics" a special and prominent field in its own right (Watson, 1959).

Intelligence testing grew out of efforts to separate retarded children into special programs.

Intelligence Testing

Intelligence testing evolved in response to practical demands, mostly the need to separate the "uneducable" or severely retarded children into special schools that could give a simplified curriculum. In the 1890s, Alfred Binet, a Frenchman and a physician by training, began to try to measure intelligence. He wanted to discover how "bright" and "dull" children differ and started without any clear ideas about the nature of their difference. Binet and his associates believed that available tests lacked measures of complex processes and overemphasized sensory tasks. They hoped that individual differences in ability would be seen better in more complex tasks. Accordingly they proposed a series of tests including measures of aesthetic appreciation, attention, comprehension, imagination, memory, mental imagery, moral feelings, muscular force, force of will, motor ability, suggestibility, and visual discrimination.

Ultimately, Binet's scales successfully differentiated children with respect to scholastic standing. The Binet scales were enthusiastically received because they seemed to fill the urgent need for a practical way to study mental processes. The test supplied a single overall score that offered a general and simple summary of mental status. It permitted ready comparisons between individuals in terms of their level of mental development. The Binet scales were revised and extended several times, most notably by Lewis M. Terman of Stanford University in 1916. Terman's revision produced the now classic Stanford-Binet, which became a popular standard for all later work on mental ability testing (see Table 6-1).

Most of the developments in mental and personality testing have been influenced more or less directly by Binet's original work. Following his pioneering lead, an extremely influential series of intelligence scales that are still very popular was developed by David Wechsler. These scales assess the individual's standing in relation to many other people of the same age, and have considerable practical value. The person's general intelligence quotient or "IQ" score summarizes his "full-scale" or total test achievement. His standing on the main subcomponentsof the test also is computed. Items similar to those found on such IQ scales are presented in Figure 6-1.

Table 6-1
Examples of Items from the Stanford-Binet Test

Age	Sample Task
Two	Naming parts of the body. Child is shown a paper doll and asked to identify mouth, feet, etc.
Four	Opposite analogies. Can complete sentences like "Father is a man; mother is a _____."
Six	Number concepts. Is able to give the examiner nine blocks when instructed to do so.
Eight	Memory for stories. Listens to a story, then answers questions about it.
Ten	Abstract words. Able to define such words as "pity," "curiosity," "grief," and "surprise."
Twelve	Verbal absurdities. Finds what is foolish about statements such as the following: "Bill Jones's feet are so big that he has to put his trousers on over his head."
Fourteen	Inference. Examiner notches folded paper, repeatedly adding folds. Subject gives rule for determining how many holes there will be when paper is unfolded.
Average adult	Essential differences. Answers to the question, "What is the principal difference between an optimist and a pessimist?"
Superior adult	Digits reversed. Can repeat six digits backwards, that is, in reverse order.

SOURCE: Adapted from Terman and Merrill, 1960.

Figure 6-1
Items Similar to Those on Standard Intelligence Tests (such as the Wechsler Intelligence Scale)

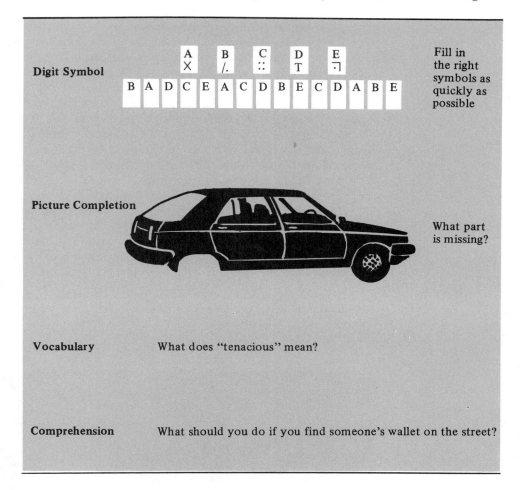

Intelligence, Heredity, and Race: A Controversial Issue

One of the most hotly debated topics in psychology concerns the relationships between intelligence, heredity, and race. First let us consider the links between intelligence and heredity.

Many studies have investigated the question of whether individuals' IQ scores are more nearly alike when the individuals are more closely related genetically. Erlenmeyer-Kimling and Jarvik (1963) have provided a summary of over fifty such studies. What is the conclusion of these studies? Are people who are more closely related also more alike in IQ? In general, the answer is clearly yes. For example, identical twins (who of course have identical genes) tend to have much more similar IQs than do fraternal twins. Even when identical twins are reared apart in different home environments, they tend to emerge with IQs more similar to each other than do fraternal twins who grow up together in the same home. Likewise, parents are much closer in IQ to their natural children than to their adopted ones.

Thus it is plain that genes do play an important part as determinants of intelligence. But genes and environment interact in their effects, and there is evidence that a stimulating early childhood environment enhances the child's cognitive growth while severe social deprivation may harm it (e.g., Honzik, 1972; Skeels, 1966). In sum, intelligence is importantly influenced by heredity and to a significant but probably lesser extent by environment: the two influences continually interact.

Let us consider the possible links between race and intelligence. This topic became explosive in 1969 when Arthur Jensen published his conclusion that blacks innately are below whites in certain mental abilities and that educational programs should heed these differences (Jensen, 1969, 1980). Moreover, in Jensen's view, the failure of earlier compensatory programs reflects the innate differences in intelligence between American black and white people.

The political as well as the scholarly response to Jensen came immediately, and it resulted in many stormy battles that went far beyond scientific issues and data. The passionate arguments against Jensen included criticisms (usually justified) of the research that he had used to support his conclusion. Reviewing those same studies, Kamin (1974, p. 175), for example, concluded the following:

> The data have repeatedly demonstrated profound environmental effects on IQ scores in circumstances where the genes cannot be implicated. The apparent genetic effects, upon analysis, have invariably been confounded with environmental factors that have been slighted or ignored.

The possible links between race and intelligence have become an explosive topic.

The specific arguments pro and con on this topic are practically endless. Too often they overlook what may be the most crucial point: for now, at least, there is no way to answer the question. Indeed, the question itself is meaningless as long as black and white people continue to live in a biased society and hence are exposed to different environments and experiences. In the absence of a fair society, there is no way to equate (or adequately compare) the environments of the different groups that live in that society because those groups experience unequal treatment.

Other problems also make the question of racial differences in intelligence unanswerable. For example, at present in the United States a great deal of overlap exists both in the genetic structure and in the environments of members of both groups; such overlap prevents precise analysis of genetic versus environmental contributions. The genetic differences within each group may be greater than they are between the two groups (e.g., Loehlin, Lindzey, & Spuhler, 1975). Indeed, Scarr and associates (1977) found there was no relationship between intellectual ability and degree of African ancestry. Moreover, scores on IQ tests are affected by many variables such as specific school learning, motivation, test-taking skills, and anxiety, all of which make these tests poor measures for determining intellectual differences between groups. The difficulty of estimating genetic versus environmental influences is further compounded by the fact that these two influences operate interdependently rather than separately through the course of the individual's development, mutually affecting each other as they interact (Scarr-Salapatek, 1971). Further, environmental influences, no less than hereditary influences, often operate in complex ways to affect intelligence (see *In Focus 6.1.*)

In sum, many considerations make the question of racial differences in intelligence an explosive rather than a scientific one and prevent a definitive answer. These same considerations suggest that it might be wise to abandon (or at least shelve) this question in favor of investing scientific energy in efforts to remove the very biases from society that make the question both unanswerable and inflammatory.

In Focus 6.1
Intelligence, Family Size, and the SAT

The Scholastic Aptitude Test (SAT), a measure of verbal and quantitative skills, is given routinely to high school seniors and is used by colleges in their admissions decisions. The average score of high school seniors in 1962 was 490, but it has declined steadily, falling to about 450 by 1975. What accounts for the decline? Speculations about the possible reasons include an erosion of interest in basic language skills and the negative effects of television, but there is no hard evidence to support either of these interpretations. A fascinating alternative has been developed recently (Zajonc, Markus, & Markus, 1979).

Robert Zajonc speculates that the intellectual growth of each child depends on the total intellectual environment of the whole family. In turn, the total intellectual environment of the family may be defined as the average of the intellectual level of all its members (including the newborn). Note that intellectual level here does not mean IQ but refers instead to the absolute level of mental growth, or to the "mental age," of the members. Suppose, for example, that the intellectual level of a newborn first child in a family is zero and the level of each parent has reached its maximum of 30 units. In that case, the child's intellectual environment will have an average value of 20. We arrive at that figure by simply adding the child's level (0) to that of each parent (30 + 30) and dividing by the total number in the family to obtain the average level (0 + 30 + 30 divided by 3 = 20).

Now consider what happens if a second child is born when the first child has reached a level of, let us say, 4 units. The intellectual environment entered by the secondborn will be:

$$\frac{0 + 4 + 30 + 30}{4} = 16$$

Suppose a third child is born when the first one has reached a level of 7 units and the second child is at a level of 3 units. The family's intellectual environment becomes a mere 14:

$$\frac{0 + 7 + 3 + 30 + 30}{5} = 14$$

The crucial point made by these examples is that each additional child depreciates the family's intellectual environment. It follows that intelligence declines with family size so that a family with fewer children is more likely to have brighter ones. Likewise, intelligence would decline with birth order, children who arrive later becoming less bright. Of greatest importance is the spacing between children. The shorter the spacing between siblings, the lower the intellectual environment will be that each addition to the family enters. A number of interesting predictions are made by the model, and they have received some promising support.

For example, the model predicts that twins should score lower on intelligence tests than nontwins because twins have the shortest possible gap in age of any siblings. Even if twins are the firstborn in the family used in our example, their intellectual environment at birth is only 15:

$$\frac{0 + 0 + 30 + 30}{4} = 15$$

Recall that in the same family, the intellectual environment of a firstborn child if he did not have a twin would be:

$$\frac{0 + 30 + 30}{3} = 20$$

No matter how young the firstborn nontwin would be at the birth of the second child, the intellectual level of his environment still would be greater than the environment of 15 into which the twins would be born.

In fact, twins do score consistently and significantly lower than singly born children on tests of intelligence such as the National Merit Scholarship Qualification Test (Breland, 1974). Moreover, twins whose co-twins were stillborn or died within the first four weeks score nearly as high on intelligence tests as singly born children (Record, McKeown, & Edwards, 1970). Might these effects be due to physiological differences that favor the surviving twin? That explanation seems unlikely because the birth weights (and general health) of twin pairs in which one twin dies early are lower than in pairs where both survive. Hence differences in the intellectual environments of the children seem to be a more reasonable explanation of the total findings.

The drop in SAT scores since 1962 noted at the start of this *In Focus* can be understood as reflecting the decline in the proportion of firstborns taking the test. As the number of firstborns decreased, so did the average SAT score. But now a new trend is beginning to appear. Families have been getting smaller and the proportion of firstborns is climbing. According to Zajonc's theory these trends should be reflected in higher SAT scores beginning in the mid-1980s. At the time of this writing, his theory seems to be getting support.

What Do Intelligence Tests Predict?

The question remains, What is intelligence? At first, some testers tried to avoid this question simply by defining intelligence circularly as "whatever intelligence tests measure." Beyond such circular reasoning there is considerable disagreement about the nature and meaning of intelligence.

Some theorists have argued that intelligence is a *generalized mental ability* (called *g*) that is important for success in many mental tasks; others propose that it is made up of a large number of distinct, more *specific mental abilities* that are specific to particular tasks or problems. In a compromise, Thurstone (1938) suggested seven *primary mental abilities,* including verbal, memory, reasoning, and spatial abilities. Thurstone thought of them as distinct basic abilities that combine to determine performance on groups of complex tasks. In another direction, an extremely elaborate theory has been developed that suggests as many as 120 subcategories of intelligence (Guilford, 1967). The 120 subcategories represent elements of knowledge, skill for operating on these elements, and knowledge of the products (outcomes) of operations. Theorizing and research on the skills involved in intelligence continue actively (e.g. Sternberg, 1982).

At a simple, practical level intelligence tests often predict later classroom achievements with reasonable accuracy (e.g., Ames & Walker, 1964). The practical value of intelligence tests for predictions and decisions beyond the classroom has often been assumed but with little proof (Cronbach, 1970). Consequently, one may legitimately criticize basing important nonschool decisions on such tests.

One large study investigated the meaning of intelligence test scores from the verbal and mathematical portions of the Scholastic Aptitude Test (SAT) that most high school students take routinely (Wallach & Wing, 1969); see *In Focus 6.1.* As expected, they found the usual connection between high intelligence and superior academic performance in the classroom (see Figure 6-2).

The same researchers also examined the relations between intelligence and tal-

Figure 6-2
Academic Achievement in High School and in College, for Groups of High and Low Intelligence

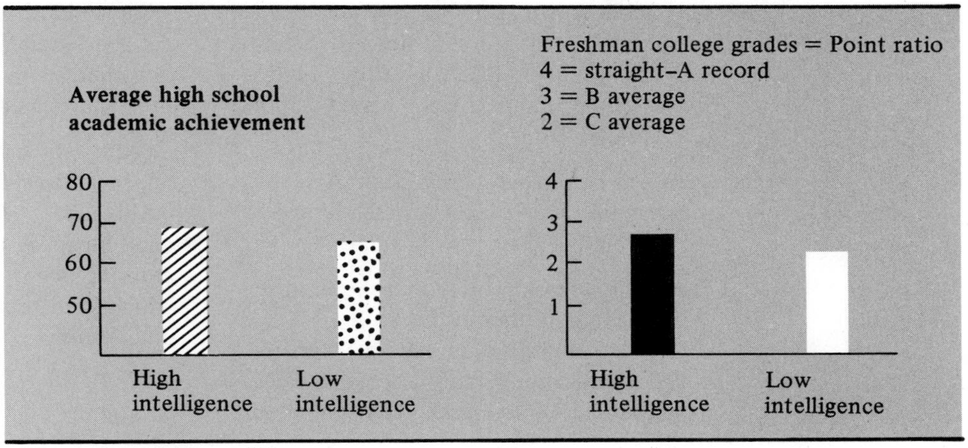

Data from Wallach & Wing (1969).

ented accomplishments outside the classroom in such areas as leadership, writing, science, and art. They found consistently that intelligence was unrelated to all measures of nonacademic accomplishment. In contrast, significant relations were found between nonclassroom achievements and simple measures of cognitive productivity or effort. (The productivity tests required subjects to generate ideas, for example, by naming as many uses as possible for everyday objects such as a chair, or by generating as many interpretations as possible of a series of abstract visual designs.) The authors concluded that the prediction of talent requires that we go beyond intelligence and include such considerations as the student's "cognitive vitality" or energy as one important ingredient of success beyond the classroom. A strongly motivated person, for example, might actually achieve more than a person whose test scores are ten points higher but who is poorly motivated. Character sketches of two students, both with average intelligence but one with extremely high cognitive productivity and the other scoring low in this trait, are given in Table 6-2.

Other studies support the results of Wallach and Wing (1969) in showing that measures of academic ability may fail to predict real-life achievements outside the classroom to a surprising degree (e.g., Gough, Hall, & Harris, 1963; Holland &

Table 6-2
Character Sketches of Students Differing in "Creativity" (Ideational Productivity) But Similar in Intelligence

John Ideational Productivity: Very High Intelligence: Average	Bob Ideational Productivity: Very Low Intelligence: Average
Involved in leadership roles in student government and other student organizations. Committed to activism and working with people.	Disappointed by high degree of liberalism on campus.
Political science major who gets good grades but is dispassionate toward the academic. Feels an urgent need to "do something," to be effective in the practical world rather than extending his education past college.	Studies hard and although he occasionally questions his own diligence and wonders if he would study so hard if not for his need to get good grades, he would not want any changes that would affect the prestige of his degree.
Wants to help teach others to find meaningful lives in society. "There are still people needed to teach values."	Desire for good grades is based on approval from family and others and on his career plans; getting into a good business school and then entering one of the many fields for which such preparation would qualify him.
Feels somewhat unsure about the future. Describes his former unthinking confidence having given way to a "crisis of self-identity" involving a sense of not realizing his full potential.	

SOURCE: Wallach & Wing, 1969.

Richards, 1965). Thus academic and nonacademic, artistic, scientific, and social achievements tend to be more independent than is often thought. An outstanding success in one field may be a painful failure in other endeavors, and school success may not generalize to success in life.

On the other hand, people who fail to complete schooling are less likely to succeed in the future; dropping out of high school is one of the best predictors of adjustment and occupational problems (Robbins, 1972). Poor classroom work or inadequate schooling are good ways to lock the door to many opportunities such as admission to professional and graduate schools and to the careers that they permit. Although children's scores on intelligence tests do not allow confident "long-term predictions for individual normal children," on the whole (for large groups), they do relate significantly to the ultimate level of education and occupation likely to be attained (McCall, 1977, p. 482).

Early Personality Measurement

Early questionnaires to measure individual differences in personality arose in the wake of the successful measurement of intelligence and flourished especially during the 1920s and 1930s. Interest in self-description or self-report as a method of personality assessment was stimulated by an inventory devised during World War I (Watson, 1959). This was Woodworth's *Personal Data Sheet,* later known as the *Psychoneurotic Inventory.* It was aimed at detecting soldiers who would be likely to break down under wartime stress. Because it was impractical to give individual psychiatric interviews to recruits, Woodworth listed the kinds of symptoms psychiatrists would probably ask about in interviews. He then condensed them into a paper-and-pencil questionnaire of more than one hundred items. Examples are: "Do you wet your bed at night?" "Do you daydream frequently?" The respondent must answer "yes" or "no" to each question. Soldiers who gave many affirmative responses were followed up with individual interviews. This method was valuable as a simplified and economic alternative to interviewing all subjects individually. Often questionnaires are still employed as substitutes for interviews.

The Woodworth questionnaire was not used widely, but it was a forerunner of the many other self-report devices that flourished in the next two decades. These self-reports compared people usually with respect to a single summary score. This total score served as an index of their "overall level of adjustment," just as single scores or mental quotients were developed to describe the level of "general intelligence." In addition to efforts to assess adjustment, attempts to measure individuals on various personality dimensions soon became extremely popular.

THE NATURE OF TRAIT TESTS

The psychometric approach to the study of personality relies on tests to tap personality traits. These traits or dispositions are assumed to be quantifiable and scalable. As J. P. Guilford, a leading spokesman for the psychometric trait position, said:

> By [scalability] we mean that a trait is a certain quality or attribute, and different individuals have different degrees of it. . . . If individuals differ in a trait by having higher or

lower degrees of it, we can represent the trait by means of a single straight line. . . . Individual trait positions may be represented by points on the line (Guilford, 1959, pp. 64–65).

Scoring: Allowing Comparisons

Thus traits like aggressiveness or introversion, or submissiveness or masculinity, for example, may be thought of as like physical dimensions. It is assumed that individuals differ from each other more or less enduringly in the degree (or amount) to which they possess each of these attributes. It is also assumed that at least some traits are *common* in the population. Measurement usually proceeds with respect to one trait at a time. On the basis of his test results, each individual is assigned a point position on a single trait scale. It is generally assumed that most traits are scalable in some way and can be described quantitatively.

Given these assumptions, the challenge is to find the appropriate measure for important personality traits (Guilford, 1959). To illustrate, Figure 6-3 depicts a hypothetical profile of test scores for one person on eight trait scales. The profile suggests that this person's scores were highest on the "submissiveness" test, lowest on the "aggressiveness" test, and intermediate on the other measures.

But what do these scores mean? Just how high or low is this person on each of these attributes? The scores have little meaning unless they can be compared with norms or with the scores of other people who took the same tests. Trait psychologists compare the scores of different people on one measure at a time, as Figure 6-4 illustrates. The figure shows a hypothetical distribution of scores for 230 people on a dependency scale.

Figure 6-3
One Person's Hypothetical Test Profile on Eight Trait Scales

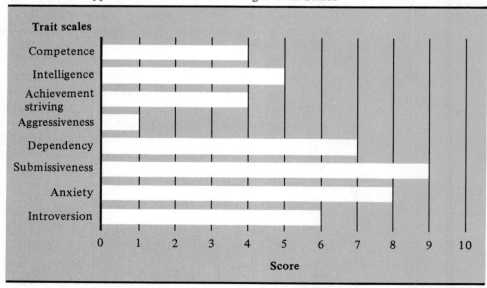

The subject's dependency score was 7 (as shown in Figure 6-3). A comparison of this dependency score with the data in Figure 6-4 suggests that the subject's score was the same as that of 40 of the 230 tested people. Only 60 people scored higher, and 130 scored lower than he did.

The meaning of these comparisons depends, of course, on many considerations, such as the appropriateness of the comparison sample. For example, how many of the 230 people were much older or younger than the subject? How many came from utterly different backgrounds, or were of the opposite sex? Most important, the meaning of the scores depends on the nature and quality of the test.

Self-Reports and Ratings

Data about persons can be obtained from three sources: people may report or rate (judge) aspects of themselves; other people may judge the person; or performance may be elicited and observed directly.

Psychometric inferences about traits usually have been based on self-reports. The term "self-report" refers to any statements people make about themselves, "structured" self-reports are statements in the form of restricted reactions to items. On structured self-report tests respondents must react to sets of questions or items with one of a limited number of prescribed choices (e.g., "yes," "no," "strongly agree," "frequently," "don't know"). Examples are shown in Figure 6-5. These items contrast with open-ended or unstructured tests (like the projective devices in Chapter 3), on which subjects may supply their own reactions freely. The distinction between "structured" and "unstructured" or "open-ended" tests is a matter of degree only. The extent to which a test is structured depends on the items and the instructions to the subjects: Less structured techniques allow greater variation in response.

Many formats have been devised for trait ratings (see Figure 6-5). On some scales, for example, subjects may be told that "7" indicates that the item is com-

Figure 6-4
Number of People at Each Score Level on a Dependency Test

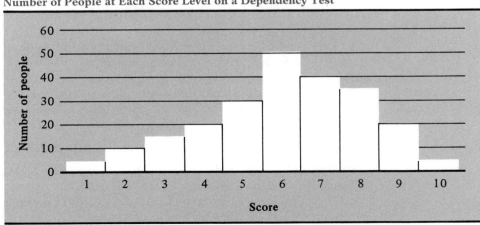

Figure 6-5
Examples of Different Types of Structured Test Items

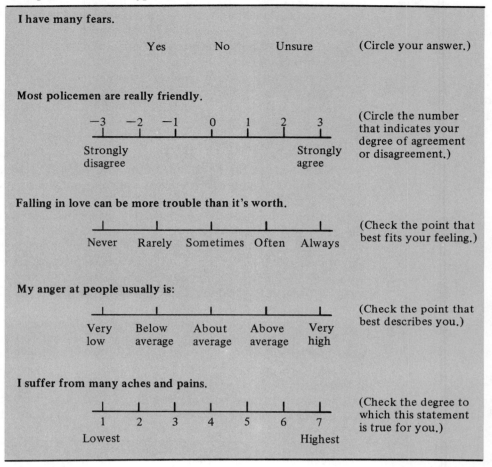

I have many fears.

          Yes   No   Unsure   (Circle your answer.)

Most policemen are really friendly.

-3 -2 -1 0 1 2 3 (Circle the number that indicates your degree of agreement or disagreement.)

Strongly   Strongly
disagree   agree

Falling in love can be more trouble than it's worth.

Never Rarely Sometimes Often Always   (Check the point that best fits your feeling.)

My anger at people usually is:

Very Below About Above Very
low average average average high   (Check the point that best describes you.)

I suffer from many aches and pains.

1 2 3 4 5 6 7 (Check the degree to which this statement is true for you.)

Lowest   Highest

pletely applicable to themselves and "1" indicates complete nonapplicability, and that they should check the point on the continuum that describes their own reactions. On scales like this, subjects are asked to express the extent of their agreement or disagreement with the particular item or to rate themselves with respect to the particular descriptions supplied. They may also be asked to judge the attributes of other people they know, for example, their peers at work or in school.

Objectivity: Are the Procedures Standardized?

"Objectivity" in the study of personality is the condition that exists when every observer (or "judge") who sees a particular sample of behavior (e.g., a test answer sheet) draws the same conclusions from it. Objectivity depends on the entire testing procedure. That includes the interaction between the examiner and subject, the instructions and test items, the available response choices, and the scoring and interpretation procedures. Anything that enhances the uniformity of the testing conditions to which different subjects are exposed increases the objectivity of a test. Objectivity is also furthered by standardized (uniform) test materials, instructions, answer sheets, and scoring procedures. Effective standardization requires uniformity in other conditions that could affect test performance. Depending on what is being measured, these conditions may include the time of administration, the physical conditions under which measurement occurs, the sex of the examiner, and so on. The psychometrician thus attempts to make the stimulus material as uniform as possible by giving every subject the same standardized test and directions.

A lack of objectivity increases the risk of bias. It certainly would be unfair to test some people with a "friendly" examiner in a comfortable, relaxed setting but others with a "cold" examiner in a noisy, crowded room. Likewise, objectivity is reduced, and fair comparisons among people are prevented, if the test questions are changed on different occasions or scored differently depending on the prejudices of the tester or other momentary whims.

No matter how careful the attempt to maintain objectivity may be, it is beset with problems. In practice it has become increasingly evident that scores on any personality trait test are affected by all sorts of variables that are irrelevant to the trait the test is trying to measure. For example, even such gross examiner and subject characteristics as sex, as well as such subtler attributes as friendliness, may affect scores (Masling, 1960; Mischel, 1968). Other irrelevant characteristics of the respondent, such as his or her manner, may significantly affect the examiner's evaluation of the test results. There are many possible sources for bias. More attractive or appealing persons, for example, may be scored more liberally, even when scoring is relatively objective and standardized, as it is on intelligence tests (Masling, 1959).

In spite of some early hopes to the contrary, no psychological test provides anything remotely like a mental X-ray. A test merely yields a sample of behavior under particular conditions. The observed behavior is always elicited in a context—in a psychological situation. No matter how carefully standardized, the test is never able to eliminate or "control out" all determinants other than the trait of interest. The consistency and meaning of what is being sampled therefore must be demonstrated and cannot be assumed no matter how uniform the conditions may be for all subjects.

Correlations: What Relates to What?

The specific techniques for assessing the consistency and meaning of test behavior are considered in later chapters. At this point, just note that most applications of trait psychology involve a search for *correlations* among tests (Chapter 1). Such correlations simply examine the degree of association (relation) between the scores achieved by a group of individuals on one set of measures with their scores on another set. For example, do people who score high on Test 1 also tend to score higher on Test 2, and do those who score low on Test 1 also score low on Test 2? To the degree that the relative position of individuals remains consistent across the measures, high correlations are obtained; conversely, when relative positions change easily, correlations decrease, indicating that responses to the two tests are not as closely related. When correlations among tests are high, responses on one test can be used to predict responses on the other; e.g., if you succeed on 1 you are likely to succeed on 2. When correlations are low, one cannot predict performance (relative position) on one test from knowing scores on the other test.

Moderator Variables

Wallach (1962) and Kogan and Wallach (1964) have noted that many "moderator variables" may influence the correlations found in trait research. That is, the relations between any two variables often depend on several other variables. For instance, correlations between measures of risk-taking and impulsivity may be found for males but not for females; they may even be negative for one sex but positive for the other. Similarly, relations between two measures might be positive for children with low IQ but negative for highly intelligent children, or they might occur under "relaxed" testing conditions but not under "anxious" conditions. The concept of moderator variables was introduced to trait theory to refer to the fact that the effects of any particular disposition generally are "moderated" by or dependent upon many other conditions and variables. Such variables as the person's age, sex, IQ, the experimenter's sex, and the characteristics of the situation all are common moderators of test behavior.

PERSONALITY SCALES: EXAMPLES

So far we have been considering tests in general, ignoring the individual person. It is time to apply those methods to individuals. Therefore we now turn again to "Gary W.," our case history, whom we glimpsed before from a psychodynamic perspective. Here is what one of his friends says about him:

Impressions of Gary W. by a Fellow Graduate Student

From the moment I first met Gary, one year ago, he seemed likable enough, but he always seemed preoccupied. His personality had a forced quality, as though he were trying to be something he wasn't. Central to his personality is his overconcern with himself. It's not conceit, but rather continual self-observation and self-criticism. In personal relationships he seems always to be trying to figure out what the other person expects of him and seems to have no personality of his own. He can be friendly and outgoing with a shy, self-conscious person. He often displays a cynical humor and arbitrary bossiness bordering on personal insult, which seems to be his only method of feeling at ease. Feeling at ease seems to mean dominating the relationship as completely as possible. If he encounters someone more capable than he is, Gary tends to draw back within himself, too afraid of being shown up by the other person to develop any kind of close relationship. Gary is something of a "loner." He has few close friends, since his relationships are based on domination (or fear of being dominated) rather than companionship. Gary is very conscious of social standards, grades, any measure of superiority. If he doesn't reach the mark, he feels he is a failure, but even if he does he seems not to be satisfied. An ironic feature of his personality is that though he seems to seek attention, he is uncomfortable once he gets it. When speaking to a group of people, he becomes extremely nervous, and, at times, so confused that he cannot continue, and starts falling apart. He wants to succeed. He is ambitious and able, and very persistent. He seems really driven to do well.

The impression Gary's friend gives us, while interesting, is of uncertain value: We know neither its accuracy nor its meaning. Then how can we find out more about Gary? From the viewpoint of trait theory, we want quantitative information that reveals Gary's status on important dispositions so that we can compare him with others. One major step in that direction is provided by Gary's scores on psychometric tests. So that these data can be properly understood, they will be introduced in the context of our discussion of some major trait measures.

The MMPI

The most thoroughly studied questionnaire is the Minnesota Multiphasic Personality Inventory (MMPI), and it has become the basis for investigating many personality traits and types. The MMPI best illustrates the psychometric approach. This widely used, influential test contains a set of self-report scales that initially were devised to classify mental patients into types on many psychiatric dimensions (Hathaway & McKinley, 1942, 1943). In format, the MMPI comprises 550 printed statements to which one may answer "true," "false," or "cannot say" (undecided). The items range over diverse topics and differ widely in style. They inquire into attitudes, emotional reactions, psychiatric symptoms, the subject's past, and other content, with items similar to these:

Sometimes I think I may kill myself.
My greatest troubles are inside myself.
I certainly have little self-assurance.
I wish I were not so awkward.
I am shy.

Self-report tests such as the MMPI are called "psychometric," "objective," and "standardized." These terms correctly describe the stimulus material, the scoring procedure, and the administration. The stimulus materials are objective and standardized or reproducible in the sense that they usually are presented as printed items on questionnaires, inventories, or rating scales. Likewise, the scoring procedure is objective because the respondent has to react to each question or item with one of a limited number of prescribed or "structured" choices by selecting, for example, from printed answers like "yes," "no," "strongly agree," "frequently," "don't know."

Both the questions and the instructions on psychometric tests, however, usually require the respondent to go far beyond direct behavior observation and to supply subjective inferences about the psychological meaning of behavior. While the questions are standardized, that is, printed and always the same on each occasion, they often are vague. For example, the test asks questions like "Are you shy?" or "Do you worry a lot?" or "Is it really wise to trust other people?" Such items are ambiguous. They require one to evaluate behavior, and generalize about it, rather than describe particular behaviors in particular contexts on clear dimensions.

People may not be willing or able to reveal themselves accurately in response to such items, especially when they are emotionally upset, or aware that their answers may be used to make important decisions about them. Recognizing these problems (e.g., Meehl, 1945), researchers have tried to establish the meaning of particular answer patterns on the test by research.

The investigator starts with a pool of items and administers them to a group known to differ on an external criterion or measure (for example, males versus females, or hospitalized versus nonhospitalized people). Ideally, the test scales are constructed so that ultimately only those items are retained that best discriminate among people who differ on the selected criterion. Suppose, for example, an item such as "I cry easily" tends to be answered affirmatively by people who have been hospitalized for psychiatric problems, but not by those who have no history of psychiatric hospitalization. That item would be retained on a "maladjustment" scale.

The MMPI scales are administered to many groups of subjects, such as college students, medical personnel, and nonpsychiatric patients , as well as psychiatric patients who have been independently diagnosed as having symptoms of some type of schizophrenia. The items then are examined to determine the ones on which there are significant differences between the answers of particular diagnostic groups as compared to "normals." In this manner it becomes possible gradually to devise scales that discriminate among different groups of people.

MMPI items have been sorted into ten basic scales named Hypochondriasis (Hs), Depression (D), Hysteria (Hy), Psychopathic deviate (Pd), Masculinity-femininity (Mf), Paranoia (Pa), Psychasthenia (Pt), Schizophrenia (Sc), Hypomania (Ma), and Social introversion (Si). It would be incorrect, however, to think that these scales tap what their names indicate. Instead, these labels serve as abbreviations for scales whose meanings are defined by their extensive correlations (associations) with other indices (e.g., psychiatrists' ratings of adjustment, scores on other personality questionnaires). These correlations have been amassed during decades of vigorous research with the scales.

In addition to the ten basic scales, three "control" scales have been devised. The L or Lie scale was intended to measure the tendency to falsify about oneself by "faking good." High scores on this scale indicate that the individual has endorsed many items that suggest he does unlikely things such as daily reading all the newspaper editorials or never telling a lie. The K scale, the second control, was intended to indicate defensiveness in the form of a tendency to present oneself in a more socially desirable way. The F scale, the third control, sought to tap the intrusive effects of answering the items carelessly and confusedly, as indicated by describing oneself as having rare and improbable characteristics.

The results of an individuals's MMPI answers (or the summary of a group's average responses) may be recorded in the form of a "profile." Such a profile for our case, Gary W., is illustrated in Figure 6-6. Gary's position on each scale is sum-

Figure 6-6
Gary's MMPI Profile

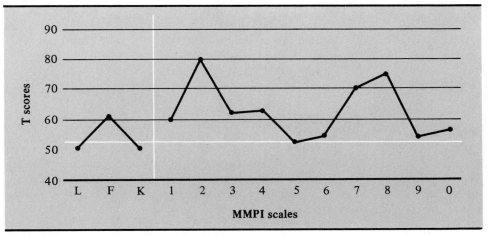

Similar to atlas code type 2-8/8-2, Marks & Seeman (1963).

marized in terms of converted or T scores. These scores readily provide quantitative comparisons against norms. A T score of 50 is the average score for the particular normative reference group. Procedures have been developed to discriminate people with extreme scores for many different diagnostic and selection purposes. Collections of MMPI profiles have been "coded" in different ways and catalogued in "handbooks" or "atlases." They may be used to compare a single individual's profile to similar profiles and information collected in many cases (Marks & Seeman, 1963; Gilberstadt & Duker, 1965).

Gary's MMPI profile fits most closely a 2-8/8-2 code in the atlas developed by Marks and Seeman (1963, p. 137). We can see what types of information the atlas provides for individuals whose average MMPI profiles are most similar to Gary's. The atlas tells us that people with this type of profile are most often described with characteristics like these:

> Keeps his distance and avoids close relations with people; tends to fear emotional involvement with others; manifests his psychic conflicts with somatic symptoms, tends to be resentful, shows obsessive thinking, feels tense, jumpy, and high-strung.

The atlas also gives much other information found previously on the average for people with Gary's profile. These data are a helpful first step. How well they really fit Gary and how closely they match other data about him is still a question. On first impression, some of the atlas statements seem at least somewhat consistent with the impressions given by Gary's fellow graduate student, who also judged him to be "shy" and a "loner." On the other hand, the same student rated Gary as high in ambition, aspiration level, and "drive." These ratings seem to contradict parts of the atlas information. Specifically, the 2-8/8-2 atlas code lists high aspirations and ambitiousness as characteristics that are *least* descriptive of people with his profile. Who is right? Is Gary's friend inaccurate, or does this part of the atlas simply not fit Gary? To understand Gary better, we would need much more information about him.

The MMPI has become the model for dozens of other personality questionnaires. Many investigators drew on the large pool of MMPI items to create special personality scales (e.g., dealing with anxiety), whose meaning they studied empirically. Popular descendants of the MMPI include the California Psychological Inventory (CPI), the Taylor Manifest Anxiety Scale (MAS), and the Jackson Personality Inventory (1976).

The California *F* Scale

MMPI scales and atlases have some practical value in personality assessment and clinical work. Many psychologists, however, are most interested in the search for theoretically important personality traits, and have tried to use a variety of personality questionnaires for that purpose. One of the most popular of these self-report measures is the California *F* Scale (Adorno et al., 1950). This measure was intended to assess authoritarian attitudes. It contains a set of items like these:

> The most important thing to teach children is absolute obedience to their parents.
>
> Any good leader should be strict with people under him in order to gain their respect.
>
> Prison is too good for sex criminals. They should be publicly whipped or worse.
>
> There are two kinds of people in the world: the weak and the strong.
>
> No decent man can respect a woman who has had sex relations before marriage.

Strong agreement with items like these results in a high *F* Scale, or "authoritarianism," score.

Gary's score on the *F* Scale was slightly below average when compared to other college students. What does that imply about him? As with all scales, the meaning of high or low scores on this measure depends on the network of associations that have been found for the test in research.

An enormous set of correlations has emerged from more than a hundred studies that have related *F* Scale scores to other variables. Correlations have been found, for example, with intelligence, family ideology, prejudice, anxiety, voting behavior, military reenlistment intent, and cooperation in psychological experiments (Titus & Hollander, 1957), and even reactions to the U.S.-Soviet space race (Mischel & Schopler, 1959).

In one study among college students with high scores on the California *F* Scale (suggesting strong ideological conservatism), 76 percent stated they preferred the Republican Party, whereas 65 percent of those low on the *F* Scale preferred the Democratic Party (Leventhal, Jacobs, & Kurdirka, 1964). The relationships between *F* Scale scores and stated voting behavior indicated that students with high *F* Scale scores tended to choose the more conservative political candidate. Results like these are typical.

The *F* Scale is most strongly correlated with other paper-and-pencil measures, but not as closely associated with nonquestionnaire measures of interpersonal behaviors (Titus & Hollander, 1957). Correlations between the *F* Scale and other questionnaires sampling attitudes (e.g., toward minority groups) sometimes are impressive. The relationships obtained between the *F* Scale and nonquestionnaire measures, on the other hand, tend to be much weaker. Scores on the *F* Scale also tend to be highly correlated with education; more highly educated people tend to respond in a much less authoritarian fashion.

The Q-Sort Technique

Another helpful way to study a person's traits is through a special rating technique. The Q-sort or Q technique consists of a large number of cards, each containing a printed statement (e.g., Block 1961). The cards may contain such statements as "I am a submissive person, " "I am likable," and "I am an impulsive person." Or the items might be "is a thoughtful person," "gets anxious easily," "works efficiently."

The Q-sort may be used for self-description, for describing how one would like to be (the ideal self), or even to describe a relationship. For a self-sort, clients would be instructed to sort the cards to describe themselves as they see themselves curently, placing cards in separate piles according to their applicability, ranging from those attributes that are least like them to those that are most like them. For example, the terms that Gary W. had indicated as most self-descriptive were: "haughty, determined, ambitious, critical, logical, moody, uncertain."

Or people might be instructed to use the cards to describe the person they would most like to be—their ideal person. To describe a relationship, they would sort the cards into piles ranging from those that are most characteristic of the relationship to those least characteristic. As these examples indicate, the method asks one to sort the cards into a distribution along a continuum from items that are least characteristic (or descriptive) to those that are most characteristic of what one is describing.

The items for a Q-sort may come from a variety of sources. They may stem from a particular theory of personality (Stephenson, 1953), from therapeutic protocols (Butler & Haigh, 1954), or from personality inventories (Block, 1961). It is also possible to use the Q-sort to describe the characteristics associated with successful performance in a given task. For example, one can find the profile of qualities "most characteristic" of people who succeed in a particular situation. One can then search for those individuals who best match that profile when trying to predict who will or will not do well in that type of situation (Bem & Funder, 1978).

Do the Measures Overlap?

Methods like those summarized in this section have many uses and often yield interesting correlations. But one must interpret the correlations found among tests carefully. For example, high correlations among paper-and-pencil inventories may partly reflect the fact that inventory constructors often borrow items from earlier inventories. Different tests actually may contain similar items presented in similar formats. Thus Eysenck's (1952) measure for inferring neuroticism and extraversion-introversion contains such questions as: Are your feelings easily hurt? Are you rather shy? Do you find it difficult to get into conversation with strangers? Are you troubled with feelings of inferiority? Very similar items occur on such tests as the MMPI. Even within the subscales of a single test, items may overlap considerably. Shure and Rogers (1965) noted that the basic scales of the MMPI consist of items that overlap 69 percent, on the average, with items on one or more other scales of the test.

Campbell and Fiske (1959) analyzed many of the correlations that have been obtained among personality measures. They found that much commonality was attributable to similarity or overlap between the methods employed to elicit responses. In other words, correlations among measures intended to tap different traits may reflect similarities between methods (Campbell, 1960; Campbell & Fiske, 1959). If, for example, three questionnaires are used to measure "dependency," the correlations obtained among them may be more due to similarity in the questionnaires than to the trait they intend to elicit. If different methods were employed (e.g., a questionnaire, a peer rating, and a Rorschach), the correlations would be substantially lower. On the basis of a review of relevant studies, Campbell and Fiske (1959) concluded that the effect of the method is usually greater than the effect of the trait measured. Applied to our case, this means that we have to be sure that the patterns of traits attributed to Gary do not merely reflect overlap among the questionnaires he has answered.

Moreover, we would want to know if Gary's trait would test out identically if it were measured by a technique that is not a questionnaire. To be most confident of his level of authoritarianism, for example, we would want to see what he *does* with authority figures behaviorally as well as what he *says* about authority on questionnaires. To have faith that he is a "loner," fears emotional involvement, and is anxious, we would want to measure each of these attributes in several ways, not just by questionnaires. Otherwise, how could we be sure that the impression we get of him reflects more than his manner of talking about himself on inventories?

Is It More Than Intelligence?

It is also important to examine the correlations found between personality tests and measures of intelligence. Consider, for example, the relations among measures of personality and performance in a small group. Mann (1959) reviewed and surveyed the voluminous research on this topic. The personality variables in his survey included adjustment, extraversion-introversion, dominance, masculinity-femininity, and interpersonal sensitivity. He also measured intelligence. The behavior of the people in groups served as the performance measure. These behaviors were scored on leadership, popularity, activity rate, conformity, and other dimensions. From the hundreds of correlations obtained it was concluded that "the best predictor of an individual's performance in groups is intelligence" (p. 264).

Such results are not atypical. Many personality measures are substantially correlated with tests of intelligence. Intelligence has been found to correlate negatively with authoritarianism and prejudice, and positively with certain measures of honesty and indices of impulse control, creativity, and so on. The magnitude of these correlations is quite variable, but not infrequently it is as large as the associations between the personality test and the other indicators that serve to define it (e.g., Getzels & Jackson, 1962). The correlations obtained among personality indices therefore may depend partly on relations between the personality measures and intelligence.

In light of these facts, Campbell and Fiske (1959) have rightly urged that investigations of all traits should include correlations between the trait and measures of intelligence. If a personality trait correlates largely with intelligence, to invoke it as a new disposition is of little value.

FROM TEST RESPONSES TO BASIC TRAITS

How can one go from test responses to the traits that they reflect? As noted before (Chapter 5), trait theorists are interested mainly in discovering basis traits, not just in comparing people's test scores. In their search for "underlying traits" they begin with test responses, usually in the form of self-ratings or ratings by others. But the range of possible trait ratings is as large as the number of trait names available in the language. A casual glance at any dictionary makes it plain that when people try to describe personality in trait terms, an almost endless set of names is available to them. A systematic search for all "trait names" in a standard English dictionary produced some 18,000 terms (Allport & Odbert, 1936). In a later effort Cattell (1947, 1957) selected from this list 4,504 terms that Allport (1937, p. 366) had characterized as real traits of personality.

Factor Analysis

Trait terms that number in the thousands—even the 550 responses of the MMPI—are unmanageable as descriptive units, especially in attempts to evaluate many people and to characterize the patternings of their behavior. Consider, for example, the mass of data yielded by the 550 MMPI responses from each of a hundred persons.

To extract order from such a stack of facts, investigators searching for underlying traits try to group responses into more basic clusters. For this purpose many trait psychologists (e.g., Cattell, 1965) have turned to factor analysis, a mathematical procedure that helps to sort test responses into relatively homogeneous clusters.

Factor analysis does not necessarily reveal the basic traits of persons. The results depend on the tests and the subjects selected by the researcher, and on the details of his or her procedures and decisions. Factor analysis is a very useful tool for reducing a large set of correlated measures to fewer unrelated dimensions. As such, it can be a powerful aid to psychological research by clarifying which response patterns go together. Suppose, for example, that fifty students have answered ten personality questionnaires, each of which contains one hundred questions. A factor analysis of this mass of information can show which parts of the test performances go together (i.e., are closely correlated with each other yet uncorrelated with other parts).

But as Overall (1964) has noted, factor analysis cannot establish which characteristics of persons or things being measured are "real" or "primary." The factors obtained are simply names given to the correlations found among the particular measures. In other words, factor analysis yields a greatly simplified patterning of the test data put into it; but it cannot go beyond the limitations of the original tests and it depends on many decisions by the investigator (e.g., in the type of factor analysis he or she conducts). Consequently, while the factor analytic search for underlying "source traits" (Chapter 5) favored by such trait theorists as Cattell (1965) may yield mathematically pure factors, their psychological meaningfulness and relevance for the person's actual behavior cannot be assumed or taken for granted; they must be demonstrated.

Both the approach and the problems of trying to discover traits through factor analysis of ratings are illustrated in a series of extensive and sophisticated factor-analytic studies (Norman, 1961, 1963; Tupes & Christal, 1958, 1961). These studies investigated the factors obtained for diverse samples of subjects rated by their peers on rating scales. The scales themselves came from a condensed version of the thousands of trait names originally identified by Allport and Odbert's search for trait names in the dictionary. After much research, twenty scales were selected and many judges were asked to rate other people on them. The results were carefully factor-analyzed.

The same set of five relatively independent factors appeared consistently across several studies. This exciting finding led to the conclusion that a "highly stable structure of personal characteristics has been identified" (Norman, 1963, p. 581). The five factors (summarized in Table 5-3) were extraversion, agreeableness, conscientiousness, emotional stability, and culture.

It seemed reasonable to conclude from these results that a stable, five-factor structure of personality exists. The findings came from many different samples of subjects and raters; the data included ratings based on interpersonal observations up to three years in length; and, most important, the agreement found between factors across samples was excellent (Norman, 1963). The conclusion that these data revealed a consistent, stable, generalized, five-factor personality structure rested on the basic assumption that the "obtained structure reflected the organization of these attributes in the ratees" (Passini & Norman, 1966, p. 44).

In fact, this assumption was not justified. Surprisingly, the factor structure that emerged when total strangers were rated was very similar to the five-factor structure obtained from ratings of people the raters knew well (Passini & Norman, 1966). In this study judges rated fellow college students whom they did not know. The judges' contacts with the ratees in the rating situation were made by being in the same room with them for less than fifteen minutes, and there was no opportunity for verbal communication. The rating task was made credible by asking the raters to judge the subjects as "you would imagine" them to be. The authors pointed out that the raters could not possibly have known the ratee's attributes on dimensions like "sociable-reclusive," "cooperative-negativistic," or "responsible-undependable." The results nevertheless yielded factors extremely similar to the five factors found from ratings by close acquaintances in the earlier studies. As the authors noted, the main information available to the raters "was whatever they carried in their heads"!

Trait Structures: In the Perceiver or in the Perceived? Or in Both?

Thus the factors identified by trait ratings may reflect the social stereotypes and concepts of the judges rather than the trait organization of the rated persons. Mulaik (1964), for example, conducted three separate factor-analytic studies, using many trait-rating scales, to determine the degree to which the method reveals the subject's personality factors as opposed to the rater's conceptual factors. The judges in one study rated real persons on the scales, including family members, close acquaintances, and themselves. In a second study they rated stereotypes like "Suburban Housewife," "Mental Patient," and "Air Force General." The raters in the third study rated the "meaning" of twenty trait words. An index of factor similarity revealed much similarity between the factors found for ratings of real persons and those found for ratings of stereotypes and words. On the basis of these and many similar results the investigator concluded that personality factors that emerge from ratings may reflect the raters' conceptual categories rather than the traits of the subjects being judged.

Different investigators may arrive at somewhat different views of trait organization. Nevertheless, a few basic trait dimensions seem to be found over and over again. Introversion-extraversion, adjustment, and some variation of potency ("strong-weak") and adequacy ("good-bad") are often included. And for interpersonal behavior reasonably similar dimensions continue to be found in a variety of samples (Wiggins, 1979). It is difficult to know the extent to which these dimensions reflect the concept shared by observers or the attributes of subjects. Probably they reflect both to some extent; perhaps the two are almost impossible to separate clearly. What perceivers know certainly influences their judgments: we expect certain qualities to go together and therefore may tend to see them as co-occuring. But it seems unlikely that our expectations are pure fictions, unrelated to actual regularities in the real world. Indeed, it is possible to show significant links between the specific acts people emit and the kinds of dispositions that are attributed to them by raters (Mischel, 1984): see *In Focus 6.2.*

The Debate about Personality Ratings

A debate has been raging about how to interpret the meaning of personality ratings. D'Andrade argued that the associations (correlations) found among such measures "are primarily an artifact of the rater's or the questionnaire taker's cognitive structure, and not a reflection of the real world" (1974, p. 181). He claims that personality ratings tell us about "what is like what" in the heads of the judge, not "what goes with what" in the behavior of the judged. His basic argument is that when rating or judging personality, judges are unwittingly biased. Consider items that "go together" semantically (i.e., in the language because they seem similar or related), like "sincere" and "kind" or "aggressive" and "masculine." Raters tend to believe that such items go together in the actual behavior of the same person even when they do not (Shweder, 1975).

You will not be surprised to learn that such a sweeping attack on personality

Do trait judgments reflect the constructs of perceivers rather than the behavior of the perceived? What are the links between perceiver's judgments of what people "are like" and the behaviors that those people actually display? Some theorists argue that personality structure exists "all in the head" of the perceiver (Shweder, 1975). Others believe it is "all in the person" perceived (Epstein, 1977); Still others favor the view that it depends both on the beliefs of observers and on the characteristics of the observed (e.g., Magnusson, 1977; Mischel, 1977; Cantor & Mischel, 1979). They believe that ratings may be influenced by the rater's expectations but have roots in the behavior of the perceived.

Until recently, researchers studied either the judgments of the perceiver, or the behavior of the perceived; they rarely considered the fit between the two.

One recent study tried to relate observers' overall judgments of childrens' aggressiveness (and other traits) to the childrens' independently coded actual behavior (Mischel, 1984; Wright, 1983). Specifically, their trait-related acts were recorded during repeated observation periods on fifteen separate occasions distributed across three camp situations during a summer. Examples of the behavior code for aggression are: "I'm gonna punch your face" or "Let's go beat up. . . . " are scored as *threat*; "your father is a sissy" or "you stink" are scored as *provoke*; lifting a dog by his collar and choking him is *destructive*.

The question was: Do raters' judgments of the child's overall aggression relate to the actual frequency of the child's agressive acts as coded by other independent observers? The results clearly answered the question: yes. Thus, children who are rated by independent observers as more aggressive, actually tend to be aggressive more frequently. For instance, they yell and provoke more. In sum, personality judgments seem to have links to the judged person's actual behavior.

---

measurement did not go unanswered for long (Block, Weiss, and Thorne, 1979; Romer & Revelle, 1984) and it is still debated. Some of the many issues raised by the debate will be explored further in later chapters. You should know, however, that the descriptions of people obtained from different raters in different contexts often do agree with each other. For example, ratings of a student by peers may match to a considerable degree independent behavior ratings by other observers. Thus, agreement was found between peer judgments on dimensions of aggressive and dependent behavior and separate behavior ratings of actual aggressive and dependent behavior (Winder & Wiggins, 1964). Subjects were first classified into high, intermediate, and low groups on aggression and dependency on the basis of their peer reputations. Separate behavior ratings made later indicated that the three groups differed from each other significantly in the amount of aggression and dependency they displayed in an experimental situation. Similarly, college students were preselected as extremely high or low in aggressiveness (on the basis of ratings by their peers). They tended to be rated in similar ways by independent judges who observed their interaction (Gormly & Edelberg, 1974).

In sum, people obviously do not perceive an empty world. There are linkages between a rater's trait constructs and the behavior of people he or she rates (e.g., Norman, 1966, 1969; Jackson & Paunonen, 1980; Mischel, 1984).

EVALUATING TRAIT TESTS

To evaluate trait approaches and their applications requires that we evaluate the trait tests on which they rely. In recent years there has been a loud public outcry against the widespread use of trait tests in schools, business, and government. Critics both inside and outside the psychological profession have raised grave questions about the ethics, as well as the value, of many personality assessment practices that are most central to the trait approach. Neither the questions nor the answers are simple.

You saw that trait-oriented research usually has assessed differences between people on paper-and-pencil inventories and questionnaires. Many problems arise in efforts to clarify the meaning of the answers. Notice that almost all the psychometric information we have about Gary is based on what he *says* about himself. His MMPI profile, his California *F* Scale, all rest on self-reports on questionnaires. Since we want to know more about Gary than how he answers questionnaires, it is crucial to establish what his scores do and do not imply about him. Here we will consider only problems relevant to the interpretation of objective personality trait tests. In later chapters, the discussion will extend to many other techniques for evaluating personality.

Ethical Concerns

There have been strong objections to judging people's personalities with tests. Much of the public outrage has centered on the fear that tests are invasions of privacy, that they force people to answer questions that may be used to discriminate against them. Understandably people are reluctant to have testers pry into their lives and extract information that may contribute to negative decisions about them.

Proper evaluation of the ethics of personality assessment and rational assessment of the testing procedures are matters of great social importance. The public and its legal representatives (in Congress, for example) have been handicapped by widespread ignorance of the tests and the techniques underlying their development. The ethical and social problems involved in the multimillion dollar personality-testing business are formidable indeed. The scope of the problem is indicated by the publication of literally thousands of personality tests, many of which are widely used throughout our society. Given the magnitude of the problem and the public's confusion about personality testing, it is especially important to consider in some depth the main problems that arise in attempts to interpret what personality tests really do and really don't permit us to say about individuals. We now have a considerable amount of data about Gary W., for example, but we are still very uncertain about how to evaluate it. How sure can we be of the impressions we have? How wise or hazardous would it be to base important decisions on this information?

Tests Can Deceive

In daily life people function like trait psychologists to the extent that they infer personality dispositions from behavioral cues. Often these impressions are formed quickly and are based on minimal information. The taxi driver who claims he can spot the main qualities of his rider's personality in ten minutes is a common example. Usually such snap diagnoses are not taken seriously and are dismissed easily as clichés. When a personality description is offered by a more creditable diagnostician it tends to be accepted much more readily even if it is equally wrong (see *In Focus 6.3*).

The ease with which students in the *In Focus 6.3* study were duped about their own personality is not at all atypical; it reflects less their gullibility than the hazards of personality impressions and everyday trait descriptions. When personality impressions are stated in broad terms they are difficult to disconfirm. The individual may readily add extra meaning to clichés and adopt them with great confidence even when they turn out to be untrue (or untestable). Thus the naive person may attribute profound significance to the vague comments provided by palmists and newspaper astrologers and may accept as personal revelations "insights" that could fit almost anyone.

It is therefore extremely important for psychologists to provide real support and evidence for their statements about personality and to make their statements in a

---

In Focus 6.3
Do Psychological Tests Dupe You?

Imagine that you have taken a large battery of psychological tests. A week later you receive a report based on the results that includes the following:

> You have a tendency to be critical of yourself. . . . You pride yourself on being an independent thinker and do not accept others' opinions without satisfactory proof. . . . At times you are extroverted, affable, sociable, while at other times you are introverted, wary, and reserved. Some of your aspirations tend to be pretty unrealistic (Ulrich et al., 1963, p. 832).

How well do these descriptions fit? Perhaps they do not seem very apt to you because you know they were not tailor-made for you individually and based on tests you actually took. However, in an actual study a paragraph containing these excerpts was given to college students who had taken a test battery earlier (Ulrich et al., 1963). All of the students received the same report, though each one believed it was unique and that it was based on his or her own test responses. Almost all of the students felt the report captured the essence of their

personalities, hailing it with such phrases as:

> For the first time things that I have been vaguely aware of have been put into concise and constructive statements which I would like to use as a plan for improving myself.

> I believe this interpretation applies to me individually, as there are too many facets which fit me too well to be a generalization.

> It appears to me that the results of this test are unbelievably close to the truth (Ulrich et al., 1963, p. 838).

People can be fooled easily into believing that psychological tests actually measure their personal qualities even when they are getting statements similar to those in fortune cookies, mass produced and therefore unrelated to the individuals they supposedly describe. What can psychological tests really tell us then? How can we evaluate their worth and their limitations? This chapter considers these questions and examines some of the problems and findings of efforts to study and compare individuals with tests. You will have to draw your own conclusions.

---

form that is testable. You should approach the matters of "reliability" and "validity" in personality study (defined and discussed next) not as mere textbook terms to be memorized and not used: instead, try to see these concepts as guides for establishing the value of psychologists' claims about the nature of personality.

Reliability: Are the Measurements Consistent?

A number of techniques are available for estimating the consistency or "reliability" of personality measures. When the same test is given to the same group of people on two occasions, a retest correlation or "coefficient of stability" is obtained. This measure provides an index of *temporal reliability*. Generally, the longer the time interval, the lower the coefficient of stability. If there is only a short interval between test and retest, the two occasions are not entirely independent. For example, if subjects remember some of their initial responses, the correlation is strengthened.

Other reliability estimates are more concerned with the consistency with which different parts or alternate forms of a test measure behavior. The correlation between parts of a single form gives an index of *internal consistency*. Consistency may also be measured by the intercorrelation of scores on *alternateforms* of a test administered to the same set of subjects. The alternate-form method is especially valuable for assessing the effects of an intervening procedure, such as psychotherapy or special training, on test performance, because it avoids the contaminating effects of administering the same form twice.

If subjective judgment enters into scoring decisions, a special kind of reliability check is needed. This check is called *interscorer agreement* or consistency. It is the degree to which different scorers or judges arrive at the same statements about the same test data. For example, if three judges try to infer personality traits from subjects' interview behavior and dream reports, it would be necessary to establish the degree to which the three assessors reach the same conclusions. As noted before, interscorer agreement is easiest to achieve when scoring is objective, as on highly structured tests (for example, when all answers are given as either "yes" or "no").

The reliability of a test increases when the number of items in the test is increased (Epstein, 1979). Measures that consist of single items ("Are you happy?") tend to have very low reliability and therefore do not allow any meaningful conclusions.

Validity: What Do the Measurements Mean?

A woman's self-report on a ten-item questionnaire provides her *stated* reactions to the items under the specific testing conditions. Thus if a person reports that she is "very friendly," that is what she *says* about herself on the test. To know more than that, one needs validity research to establish the meaning and implications of the test answers. Test results may seem valid even when they are not (e.g., *In Focus 6.3*).

Content or *face validity* is the demonstration that the items on a test adequately represent a defined broader *class* of behavior. For example, judges would have to agree that the different items on a "friendliness" questionnaire all in fact seem to deal with the class or topic of friendliness. In practice, content validity often is assumed rather than demonstrated. Even if the content validity of the items is shown acceptably, it cannot be assumed that the answers provide an index of the individual's "true" trait position. We do not know whether or not the person who says she is friendly, for example, is really friendly.

To obtain external validity one must relate scores on the measure to other measures. For example, one might relate test scores to psychiatrists' ratings about progress in therapy, teachers' ratings of school performance, and the subject's behavior on another test. Such relationships help to provide evidence for a claim of validity and provide information about what the person's test behavior does and does not allow one to predict.

Personality psychologists guided by trait theory ususally want to infer and describe a person's dispositions from his or her test responses. *Construct* or *trait validation* is the effort to elaborate the inferred traits determining test behavior (Campbell, 1960). Basically, it tries to answer the question: what does this test measure? The concept of "construct validity" was introduced by trait psychologists for problems in which the assessor accepts

> no existing measure as a definitive criterion of the quality with which he is concerned. Here the traits or qualities underlying test performance are of central importance (American Psychological Association, 1966, pp. 13–14.)

Investigators interested in the traits supposedly accounting for personality test responses must generate a concept or theory about the underlying traits that they believe determine responses on their test. They then can employ a variety of methods to establish a network of relationships to illuminate what is related to the trait and what is not.

Traditionally, construct validity involves the following steps. The investigator begins with a hunch about a dimension on which individuals can be compared, for example, "submissiveness." The researchers might regard submissiveness as a "tendency to yield to the will and suggestions of others" (Sarason, 1966, p. 127). To study this tendency they devise a measure of submissiveness. They have no one definite criterion, however, and instead may use diverse indices of the subject's underlying trait of submissiveness. Hypotheses then are tested about how submissiveness, as displayed on the tests, does and does not relate to the other indices of submissiveness. On the basis of their findings the construct is revised.

SUMMARY

1. Mental testing at the turn of the century was the forerunner of later developments in the psychometric approach to personality. The intelligence test developed by Binet early in the twentieth century profoundly influenced the history of psychometric mental and personality testing.

2. A person's intelligence is the result of heredity and environment inextricably intertwined. The question of racial differences in intelligence is inflammatory and can distract from work toward elimination of the very social injustices that make the question unanswerable. High

intelligence is usually related to better school grades (academic achievements). However, it is not sufficiently related to achievement outside the classroom to allow confident predictions about how well particular individuals will do beyond school.

3. In the psychometric approach to personality, the aim is to measure an individual with respect to one or more single traits, such as aggressiveness or introversion. In order to measure objectively, the psychometrician attempts to create *standardized* self-report questionnaires and rating scales that will yield results that can be *reproduced* easily by independent observers.

4. The trait approach was applied to the case of Gary W.

5. The MMPI is one of the most widely used personality tests. It contains a set of self-report scales whose meanings are defined by their correlations with other measures. MMPI "atlases" provide descriptive information for various average test profiles or code types.

6. One especially useful technique for obtaining a person's self-appraisal is the Q-sort. In this measure the person takes a large number of cards, each containing a descriptive statement, and sorts them into a number of categories. These Q-sorts may be used for self-description, to describe the ideal self, or to describe a relationship.

7. Similarity and overlap of measurement methods often contribute to the correlations found among traits. To demonstrate that a distinctive trait is being tapped, it is helpful to study it by at least two different methods.

8. It is also necessary to demonstrate that a new trait test measures a trait that is not already measured by another test. Intelligence measures are frequently substantially correlated with personality tests. Therefore it is important to demonstrate that any new personality test is not mainly redundant with IQ tests.

9. Factor analysis is a mathematical procedure that sorts test responses into homogeneous clusters. It is a useful procedure for simplifying data but it does not automatically reveal basic traits. For example, the personality factors identified from ratings of personalities may partly reflect the rater's conceptual categories.

10. Trait research tends to focus on correlations among what people say on paper-and-pencil inventories and questionnaires. The interpretation of these questionnaire findings poses some special problems, because what a person says about his attributes does not necessarily reflect accurately either his traits or the things that he does outside the test. Self-reports thus may or may not be closely related to other indices of the person's nontest behavior.

11. The consistency *(reliability)* and meaning *(validity)* of a personality test has to be demonstrated by research. *Construct validation* tries to elaborate the inferred traits determining test behavior.

Chapter 7

Traits and Their Biological Bases

We move now beyond specific tests generated by the trait approach. In this chapter we will consider issues and strategies that must be understood in order to achieve a perspective on trait theories, their applications, and their value.

PERSONALITY TRAITS: EXAMPLES

Ego-Control and Ego-Resiliency: Lives Through Time

Ego-control refers to the degree of impulse control in such functions as delay of gratification, inhibition of aggression, and planfulness. A related construct, *ego-*

resiliency, refers to the individual's ability to adapt to environmental demands by appropriately modifying his or her habitual level of ego-control. Ego-resiliency allows functioning with some "elasticity." Together, these two constructs represent the core qualities of "ego" from a broadly psychodynamic perspective (Block & Block, 1980).

A number of tasks have been developed to measure these two constructs. For example, individual differences were examined in children's patterns of ego-control. The adequacy and type of ego-control were inferred from ratings of the children's tendency to inhibit impulses. Their delay behavior in experimental situations was also observed (Block & Martin, 1955). The children were exposed to a frustration in which a barrier separated the child from desired and expected toys. The "undercontrolling" children (those who had been rated as not inhibiting their impulses) reacted more violently to the frustrating barrier than did "overcontrolling," inhibited children. The undercontrolling youngsters also became less constructive in their play.

Individual differences in ego-control also have been inferred from indirect measures such as responses to inkblots on the Rorschach test (e.g., Singer, 1955; Spivack, Levine, & Sprigle, 1959). Individuals who are high (rather than low) on such indices of ego-control tend to be somewhat more able to control and inhibit their motoric activity. For example, they may be able to sit still longer or draw a line more slowly without lifting their pencil. These are only a few examples from much larger, meaningful networks of correlations that have been obtained to support the ego-control construct for many years (Block & Block, 1980; Mischel, 1984).

In studies of the ego-resiliency construct, toddlers were evaluated for the degree to which they seemed secure and for their degree of competence (in a problem-solving task). The toddlers who were secure and competent also scored higher on measures of ego-resiliency when they reached the age of four to five years (Gove, et al., 1979; Matas, Arend, & Sroufe, 1978). As another example, ego-resilient children at age three years are also viewed as popular, interesting, and attractive a year later (Block & Block, 1980). A large network of associations like these, found with many measures over long periods of childhood, suggests that both the concepts of ego-control and ego-resiliency may offer useful characterizations of important individual differences. When ego-control behaviors are studied comprehensively, with enough good measures, coherent, meaningful patterns tend to emerge (Block & Block, 1980). These patterns suggest that there are significant threads of continuity in personality.

Perceived Locus of Control

Are your successes due to what you did, or just to good luck? Are peoples' troubles "their fault," or are they the victims of unfortunate life circumstances and accidents? How one answers such questions may tap an important set of beliefs about the world that is basic for personality. People differ in the degree to which they believe that they have self-control and feel personally responsible for what happens to them. According to Rotter (1966) such perceptions involve a dimension of "perceived locus of control" (also called "internal-external control of reinforcement"). *Internal control* refers to "the perception of positive and/or negative events as being a consequence of one's own actions and thereby under personal control" (Lefcourt, 1966, p. 207). Conversely, *external control* refers to the "perception of positive and/or negative events as being unrelated to one's own behaviors" (Lefcourt, 1966, p. 207) and hence beyond personal control (see Table 7-1). Individual differences on this internal-external control dimension have been measured by a questionnaire that has yielded many correlates (e.g., Phares, 1978; Phares, Ritchie, & Davis, 1968; Rotter, 1966, 1975). For example, more intelligent people tend to perceive more outcomes as under their own control, presumably because they in fact can control their fate better than can less competent individuals.

People often react quite differently to situations in which the pay-offs or outcomes seem to involve luck or chance and those that, instead, appear to depend on their own skill. Many variables may affect whether or not individuals will attribute responsibility to themselves for the outcomes that they encounter. For example, people attribute causality to internal sources more for success outcomes than for failure outcomes: they tend to credit success to themselves but to blame failure on external conditions (Fitch, 1970).

Internal-external control may not be a single dimension. For example, it is helpful to distinguish between perceived locus of control at the *personal* (self) and *ideological* (social system) levels (Lao, 1970). Thus among Black college students in the deep South, an "internal" belief in personal control (that is, attributing responsibility for personal outcomes to the self) was positively related to general competence. However, an "external" belief in social ideology (that is, blaming the "system" rather than the self for the Blacks' disadvantages in society) was related positively to creative, innovative behavior. As Lao noted, it is not always desirable and adaptive for individuals to believe in internal control and to blame themselves. She reports that Black students who can focus on "system obstacles" (societal barriers and racial discrimination) seem to be more realistic in their assessment of the situation, and they are more likely to select innovative occupational roles and social action.

Perceived locus of control may be of special theoretical importance because it seems to influence how people may react to many situations (Lefcourt, 1972, 1980; Phares, 1973, 1978). Especially reactions to stress seem to be affected by

Table 7-1
Items Like Those Used to Measure Internal-External Locus of Control

1.a. Usually when people lose things it's because they were careless.
   b. It's easy to lose things by sheer accident.

2.a. When good things happen it's because they are earned.
   b. The best things in life are matters of luck.

3.a. People mostly make their own fate.
   b. Circumstances often victimize people.

4.a. It's not really possible to influence what others believe.
   b. When you believe it yourself you can persuade others of it.

External control refers to the belief that events are unrelated to one's own behavior.

whether or not individuals believe they can control the particular stress (for example, prevent or terminate pain), as discussed in Chapter 15. That is why this dimension seems especially important to many personality psychologists concerned with how people deal with stress and cope with threat.

TRAITS, SITUATIONS, AND THEIR INTERACTIONS

The early trait psychologists tended to follow the example of simple physical measurement. They hoped that the measurement of traits would be basically similar to such measurements as table length with rulers, or temperature with thermometers. It was assumed that broad trait structures exist and lead people to behave consistently. Consequently, trait theorists did not pay much attention to environmental variables as determinants of behavior. Instead, they concentrated on standardization of measurement conditions in the hope that broad traits would emerge.

How Broad or Specific Are Traits?

Will a person who is conscientious about homework also be conscientious about keeping social appointments and honoring obligations and responsibilities to other people? Will an individual who is anxious about school also be anxious about meeting strangers or taking on a new job? How broad (general) or specific (narrow) are traits like conscientiousness and anxiety? How stable versus open to change? Do people have dispositions that reveal themselves consistently in a wide range of behaviors and over many situations? Perhaps no topic in personality psychology is more controversial—and more important—than the question of the relative specificity versus generality of traits (Epstein, 1983; Mischel, 1983).

A great deal of research has shown that performances on trait measures are affected by the context (Mischel & Peake, 1982) and can be modified by numerous environmental changes (Masling, 1960; Mischel, 1968; Peterson, 1968; Vernon, 1964). Normal people tend to show considerable variability in their behavior even across seemingly similar conditions. A person may be dependent with his wife, for example, but not with his boss, and even his dependency at home may be highly specific, varying as a result of slight situational alterations, such as subtle changes in his wife's reactions to him, or the presence of other family members. Thus behavior may be much more situation-specific and discriminative than early trait theorists had thought.

Studies of individual differences on trait dimensions have produced many networks of correlations. These associations tend to be large and enduring when people rate themselves or others with broad trait terms (e.g., Block, 1971; E. L. Kelly, 1955). Such ratings suggest some significant continuity and stability in how people are perceived over the years. For example, see Table 7-2.

When ongoing behavior in specific situations is sampled objectively by different, independent measures, however, the association generally tends to be modest. Thus while people often show consistency on questionnaires and ratings, these data may not predict their actual behavior in specific situations very accurately. Therefore we have to be cautious about generalizing from an individual's test behavior to his or her behavior outside the test. For example, we cannot safely conclude that Gary's lack of authoritarianism on the California *F* Scale precludes his behaving in highly arbitrary, "authoritarian" ways under certain life conditions. Perhaps, then, his friend was right when he noted that Gary could be "arbitrary" and "bossy," with an insulting cynical humor. The same friend also described Gary as "friendly and outgoing"—but only when he is "with a shy, self-conscious person." As these examples indicate, Gary's authoritarianism, his friendliness or hostility, and other key features of his behavior are not situation-free attributes: They depend on many modifying conditions.

Table 7-2
Examples of Significant Stability over Time in Ratings of Personality

	Correlations		
	From Junior to Senior High School	From Senior High School to Adulthood	Item Rated
Males	.57	.59	Tends toward undercontrol of needs and impulses; unable to delay gratification
	.58	.53	Is a genuinely dependable and responsible person
	.50	.42	Is self-defeating
Females	.50	.46	Basically submissive
	.48	.49	Tends to be rebellious, nonconforming
	.39	.43	Emphasizes being with others, gregarious

SOURCE: Based on Block, 1971.

The evaluation of all data on trait consistency also depends of course on the standards selected to evaluate them and the goals of the research. A modest consistency coefficient (of about .30, for example) can be taken as evidence either of the relative specificity of the particular behaviors or of the presence of some cross-situational generality (Burton, 1963; Epstein, 1983; Mischel, 1983). Furthermore, one has to infer dispositions from imperfect behavioral measurements that involve errors. Nevertheless, behavioral fluctuations reflect more than imperfections in measuring instruments (Loevinger, 1957). All individuals may be consistent in their own behavior on some traits (e.g., Bem & Allen, 1974). But on many traits most of us show only limited consistency from one specific situation to another situation (Mischel & Peake, 1982).

In Defense of Traits: Aggregation Helps

Although they acknowledge that the specific situation is important, many psychologists are convinced that past research has underestimated the personal constancies in behavior. They point out that if we want to test how well a disposition (trait) can be used to predict behavior we have to sample adequately not only the disposition but also the behavior that we want to predict (Ajzen & Fishbein, 1977; Block, 1977; Epstein, 1979, 1983; Jaccard, 1974; Weigel & Newman, 1976). Yet in the past, researchers often attempted to predict single acts (for example, physical aggression when insulted) from a dispositional measure (e.g., self-rated aggression). Generally such attempts did not succeed. But while measures of traits may not be able to predict such single acts they may do much better if one uses a "multiple act criterion": a pooled combination of many behaviors that are relevant to the trait.

The methods and results of this new line of research are illustrated in a study in which undergraduate women were given the "dominance scale" from two personality inventories (Jaccard, 1974). The women also were asked whether or not they had performed a set of forty dominance-related behaviors. For example, did they initiate a discussion in class, argue with a teacher, ask a male out on a date. The dominance scales from the personality inventories did not predict the individual behaviors well. But the researcher found that when the forty behavioral items were summed into one pooled measure they related substantially to the personality scores. Namely, women high on the dominance scales also tended to report performing more dominant behaviors, and the reverse was also true. Thus a longer, aggregated and therefore more reliable behavioral measure revealed associations to other measures (the self-reports on the personality tests) that would not otherwise have been seen.

This study provided a useful demonstration. But the results were limited by the fact that both the dispositional (personality) and the behavioral measures were based on self-reports. It is possible that the women might have been biased to describe themselves in consistent ways regardless of what they actually did. However, similar results are found when the behaviors are measured directly by observation (e.g., Weigel & Newman, 1976).

In much the same vein, there have been a number of demonstrations to show that reliability will increase when the number of items in a test sample are increased and combined. Making this point, Epstein (1979) demonstrated that temporal stability (of, for example, self-reported emotions and experiences recorded daily, and observer judgments) becomes much larger when it is based on averages over many days than when it is based on only single items on single days. Such demonstrations also indicate that even when one cannot safely predict the individual's specific behavior in a specific situation, one may be able to predict the person's overall standing relative to other people when the behaviors are aggregated (combined) across many situations (Epstein, 1983).

People do not start with a blank mind in every new situation; we have memories, we generalize from past to future, and our earlier experiences influence our present behavior. Overall "average" differences between individuals can be construed easily and used to discriminate among them for many purposes. Knowing how your friend behaved before can help you predict how he or she probably will act again in similar situations. The impact of any situation or stimulus depends on the person who experiences it, and different people differ greatly in how they cope with most stimulus conditions. It is a truism that one person's favorite "stimulus" may be the stuff of another's nightmares and that in the same "stimulus situation" one individual may react with aggression, another with love, a third with indifference. Different people act differently with some consistency in particular classes of situations, but the particular classes of conditions tend to be narrower than traditional trait theories have assumed. For purposes of important individual decision making one may need highly individualized assessments of what the specific situations mean to the person.

To apply these abstract points more concretely, think again about Gary. It is certainly possible to form some generalizations about his seemingly major qualities, strengths, and problems. Such generalizations help us to differentiate Gary from other people, and to compare him with them. We learned, for example, that the MMPI indicated Gary tended to be interpersonally distant, to avoid close relations with people, and to fear emotional involvement. Such characterizations may help one to gain a quick overall impression of Gary. But in order to predict what Gary will do in specific situations, or to make decisions about him (as in therapy or vocational counseling), it would be necessary to conduct a much more individually oriented study that considers the specific qualities of Gary as they relate to the specific situations of interest in his life. Just when does Gary become more—or less—"interpersonally distant"? Under what conditions does he *not* avoid close relations with people? When does his tendency to "fear emotional involvement" increase? When does it decrease? The analysis and prediction of specific behavior requires that we ask specific questions like these to link behavior to conditions rather than to paint personality portraits with more general characterizations (see *In Focus 7.1*).

The utility of inferring broad traits depends on the particular purpose for which the inference is made. Inferences about global traits may have limited value for the practical prediction of a person's specific future behavior in specific situations, or for the design of specific treatment programs to help him. But traits have other uses. Indeed they may have value for the person himself—for example, when he must abstract attributes to answer such everyday questions as: "Is your friend reli-

A comprehensive approach to traits must take account of the interaction of person and situation because the expressions of a person's traits hinge on the particular psychological situation at that time (e.g., Magnusson, 1980; Magnusson & Endler, 1977; Mischel, 1973). For instance, rather than display situation-free anxiety, Gary may be anxious only under some relatively limited conditions (such as when having to speak in public) but not under many other circumstances. His anxiety may manifest itself in some ways (a subjective sense of dread, for example) but not in others (there may be no alteration in heart rate).

To study how a person's anxiety reaction at any moment depends on the particular situation as well as on his or her disposition, questionnaires were developed (see sample item given in Table 7-3) that asked about reactions to many situations, ranging from everyday occurrences (you are undressing for bed) to highly anxiety-evoking situations (you are on a ledge high upon a mountainside). The modes of response to each situation were varied to sample many possible reactions, including the subject's perception of his physiological reaction, such as "perspire" or "heart beats faster," and self-reported anxious feelings, such as "become immobilized" (Endler & Hunt, 1969, p. 4). The questionnaires were administered to students in many schools in order to sample a broad range of individual differences.

Statistical analyses of the results gave separate estimates of the relative effects (power) of stimulus situations, response modes, and individual differences. The

Table 7-3
Sample Item from the Endler-Hunt (S-R) Inventory of Anxiousness

	"You are entering a contest before spectators."						
1. Heart beats faster	Not at all	1	2	3	4	5	Much faster
2. Get an uneasy feeling	None	1	2	3	4	5	Very strongly
3. Emotions disrupt action	Not at all	1	2	3	4	5	Very disruptive
4. Feel exhilarated and thrilled	Not at all	1	2	3	4	5	Very strongly
5. Want to avoid situation	Not at all	1	2	3	4	5	Very strongly
6. Perspire	Not at all	1	2	3	4	5	Perspire much
7. Need to urinate frequently	No	1	2	3	4	5	Very frequently
8. Enjoy the challenge	Not at all	1	2	3	4	5	Very much
9. Mouth gets dry	Not at all	1	2	3	4	5	Very dry
10. Become immobilized	Not at all	1	2	3	4	5	Very immobilized
11. Stomach feels full	Not at all	1	2	3	4	5	Very full
12. Seek such experiences	Not at all	1	2	3	4	5	Very much
13. Have loose bowels	Not at all	1	2	3	4	5	Very loose
14. Experience nausea	Not at all	1	2	3	4	5	Very nauseous

SOURCE: Endler, Hunt, & Rosenstein, 1962.

results showed that anxiety is not a stimulus-free characteristic of the person, nor is it a function of situation alone. Anxiety depends on the interaction of stimulus, person, and response mode. Thus the occurrence of anxiety is a joint function of the individual, the particular stimulus (e.g., undressing for bed), and the specific mode of response, such as "perspire" or "heart beats faster." The overall findings showed the unique patterning of anxiety in each person.

---

able?"; "What kind of person is my sister?"; "Might this person be a good roommate?"; or "What are *you* like?" Inferences about broad traits also have value for such purposes as gross initial screening decisions (as in personnel selection), studying average differences between groups of individuals in personality research (Block & Block, 1980), or the layman's everyday perception of persons (e.g., Mischel, Jeffery, & Patterson, 1974; Schneider, 1973). Especially when measures are combined or aggregated over a variety of situations, one can demonstrate stable differences among individuals in their relative overall standing on many dimensions of social behavior (e.g., Epstein, 1983).

Dispositions and Conditions Interact

Sophisticated trait research is taking situations into account seriously (e.g., Argyle & Little, 1972; Magnusson & Endler, 1977; Moos, 1974). Knowledge of individual differences alone often tells us little unless it is combined with information about the conditions and situational variables that influence the behavior of interest. Conversely, the effects of conditions depend on the individuals in them. Thus the interaction of individual differences and particular conditions tends to be most important (Bem & Funder, 1978; Magnusson, 1980; Magnusson & Allen, 1983).

Consider, for example, Moos's (1968) studies of the reactions reported by staff and psychiatric patients to various settings in the hospital. They rated nine settings with regard to a dimension of "sociable, friendly, peaceful" versus "unsociable, hostile, angry" behavior. The results revealed, first, that different individuals reacted differently to the settings. Second, a given person might be high on the dimension in the morning but not at lunch, high with another patient but not when with a nurse, low in small group therapy, moderate in industrial therapy, but high in individual therapy, etc. An entirely different pattern might characterize the next person.

We might be able to predict many of the things Gary will do simply by knowing something about the situation in which he will be: At school in an economics course Gary is likely to behave very differently than he does on a date with his girlfriend at a football game. On the other hand, our predictions in each case probably would be best if we considered Gary's relevant qualities as an individual—his academic interests and skills, his attitudes toward girls, his past behavior on dates at football games—as well as the situation when we try to predict his behavior in each setting. In other words, we may predict best if we know what each situation means to the individual, and consider the unique interaction of the person and the setting, rather than concentrating either on the situation itself or on the individual in an environment and social vacuum.

The Personality of Situations?

One seemingly promising approach to situations attempts to characterize their personality (Bem & Funder, 1978). It tries to do so by creating a portrait of the personality traits of people who function particularly well in a given situation. Consider, for example, a situation in which children have a chance to delay taking an immediate, smaller reward in order to obtain a more preferred reward later. Bem and Funder exposed children to such a situation, measured how long they waited, and also asked the children's parents to rate their traits on a version of the Q-sort (a rating measure described in Chapter 6). The Q-sort ratings were used to make profiles of the personality of the ideal "delaying" child by simply seeing what traits had been used to characterize the children who waited longest in that situation.

The authors also proposed that the same method could be applied to create portraits of the ideal personality in other situations that should tap the same basic disposition—in this case, the tendency to delay gratification. For example, one can create another situation in which the child has somewhat different opportunities to defer instant pleasure for the sake of better but delayed gratifications and again get the Q-sort portraits of the youngsters who wait longest. To the degree that the portraits in the two situations overlap, one may conclude that the two situations are really psychologically similar. But to the degree that the two portraits are different, the two situations may really be tapping different personal qualities although both situations may appear to be similar. Hopefully a search for situations that yield similar personality portraits would yield situations that are basically similar (rather than situations that merely look alike in superficial ways). After such psychologically similar situations have been identified through their common Q-sort portraits, it should be possible to demonstrate consistency in the behavior that people will display in them. That is the gist of the Bem and Funder thesis, and it has aroused much interest by suggesting a way to uncover equivalencies among situations by finding the overlapping personality characteristics that they tap.

The logic of the Bem-Funder approach is appealing. But it remains to be seen whether or not it will yield impressive cross-situational consistencies in behavior (across situations with similar Q-sort portraits). A first effort has been made to repeat the Bem-Funder study in the delay of gratification situation to see if similar results would be found again (Mischel & Peake, 1982). Although the same procedures were followed as closely as possible, the findings were quite different. That is, the distinctive Q-sort trait ratings that Bem and Funder found for children who showed the greatest delay were not found again when a new sample of children was exposed to the same situation in the same preschool. This failure to replicate the results suggests the need for more research before firm conclusions can be reached.

THE GENETIC AND BIOCHEMICAL APPROACH TO PERSONALITY

Trait theories emphasize the stability of human qualities, not their change and potential modification. A number of trait theorists believe that certain dispositions, like extraversion-introversion, have a biological basis (e.g., Eysenck, 1973). It is certainly possible that at least some stable personality patterns, both normal and abnormal, have biological roots and might ultimately be understood in genetic and biochemical terms.

Biological Bases of Personality

Humans are both biological and social organisms, and the effects of both heredity and environment are impressive and interact in their impact on the total organism. The role of genetic processes is seen most clearly when one examines embryological development and the structural features of human growth.

Beyond physical development, inheritance certainly contributes to intelligence. Research with twins raised in various environments (either together or apart) suggests that when environments are similar, measured intelligence tends to be increasingly similar to the degree that the individuals have an increasing proportion of genes in common (e.g., Cartwright, 1974; Vandenberg, 1971). Consistent with these results, it is often suggested that a person's genetic endowment sets an upper limit or ceiling on the degree to which his or her intelligence can be developed (e.g., Royce, 1973); the environment may help or hinder achievement of that ceiling.

Even some personality characteristics, such as emotional expressiveness (including sociability and extraversion measured on personality questionnaires like the MMPI) may involve a genetic component (e.g., Dworkin et al., 1977; Gottesman, 1963, 1966; Wilson, 1977). Anxiety is another example of the kinds of personal qualities in which genes may play a part (Dworkin et al., 1977). Some psychological disorders, most notably schizophrenia, also seem to involve at least some degree of heritability (e.g., Gottesman & Shields, 1969; Kety, 1979; Rosenthal, 1971), and certain kinds of mental deficiency reflect a specific genetic influence (Vandenberg, 1971). An increasing number of researchers believe that even social behaviors like altruism and aggression (Rushton et al., 1985), as well as crime (Hernstein & Wilson, 1985), are caused in part by genes.

People are physical creatures, and biology provides their basic foundations. Although at present neither the magnitude nor the mechanisms of the genetic and hormonal contribution to personality and social development are clear, they are receiving increasing attention in research, and it would be foolish to ignore them (see *In Focus 7.2*).

Biochemistry, Heredity, and Schizophrenia

Schizophrenia, a major form of psychosis, is a complex and severe emotional and thought disorder with diverse symptoms. It provides a great challenge for researchers who try to understand its biological causes, chemically and genetically. Research on the causes of schizophrenia gives important insights into both the promise and the problems of the biochemical approach applied to psychological problems and characteristics. Let us consider some highlights as illustrations.

It is difficult to interpret studies into the possible biochemical bases of schizophrenia. For example, even when distinctive chemicals are found, is schizophrenia caused by such chemicals or do schizophrenics simply produce them as part of the response to their disorder? Researchers in this area have become used to excited

The genes dictate whether a person will be male or female, blue eyed or brown eyed, curly haired or straight haired. To some extent they also influence height and weight. But what psychological traits are inherited? The developing field of behavior genetics studies the role of inheritance in behavior and personality.

Neither the extent nor the mechanisms of the genetic contribution to social development are certain at the present time, but these questions are the object of much current research. Genes have been found to play a crucial role in certain forms of mental retardation (examples are shown in Table 7-4).

Table 7-4
Effects of Some Genetic Abnormalities: Two Examples

Name of Disorder	Description	Cause
Down's Syndrome (sometimes called mongolism)	Severe mental retardation. Physical appearance: small skull, sparse hair, flat nose, fissured tongue, a fold over the eyelids, short neck.	A third extra chromosome in the twenty-first chromosome pair. Appears to be associated with advanced age in the mother.
PKU (phenylketonuria)	Results in mental retardation if not treated soon after birth.	A gene that produces a critical enzyme is missing.

Psychological characteristics such as intelligence are probably influenced by a great many genes and occur in gradations rather than in distinct types. While intelligence is influenced by numerous genes, a single pair of genes can disrupt the central nervous system in such a fashion as to produce mental deficiency; *PKU* is a case in point (see Table 7-4). PKU *(phenylketonuria)* disease is an inherited disorder in which a genetic abnormality results in the lack of an enzyme necessary for normal metabolism. Because of this enzyme deficiency, a toxic chemical accumulates in the body and results in central nervous system damage and mental retardation. Diagnosis of PKU disease is now possible immediately after birth, and highly successful treatment has been devised. The child is placed on a special diet that prevents the toxic substance from building up in the bloodstream. When the biological mechanisms underlying other forms of mental deficiency are known, equally effective cures may be possible.

Some psychological characteristics are determined by an individual's genetic structure but are not inherited. For example, when the twenty-first chromosome in the body cell of an individual has a third member instead of occurring as a pair, the individual will have *Down's Syndrome* (mongolism), a form of mental retardation. A technique for drawing amniotic fluid from the uterus of the pregnant mother enables doctors and prospective parents to know in advance if the developing fetus has this chromosome abnormality. This procedure is performed routinely for pregnant women forty years of age or older because women in this age group are more likely to give birth to children with Down's Syndrome. If the fetus is defective, the parents then have the option of abortion.

announcements of discoveries followed by failures to reproduce the findings. Often such "discoveries" have turned out to reflect methodological problems rather than real breakthroughs. For example, chemicals found in the urine of schizophrenics but not in control groups have sometimes turned out to be the result of the special drugs or diets given to schizophrenics in the hospital. In spite of these and related problems, many researchers are convinced that such biochemicals as dopamine in the brain will prove to have a crucial role in schizophrenia (e.g., Snyder et al., 1974). At present there are many promising leads, but further research is needed before firm conclusions can be reached. In the words of a National Institute of Mental Health report:

> To date, no anatomical or biochemical abnormalities have been associated consistently and exclusively with schizophrenia. The search continues, however, and a number of highly promising biochemical hypotheses are being actively explored (NIMH, 1975, p. 175).

Twin Studies of Schizophrenia. The search for hereditary roots of schizophrenia is complicated by the difficulty of finding evidence that supports an interpretation of genetic determination and does not at the same time support an interpretation of environmental determination. For example, it had been shown that, in general, parents and brothers and sisters of schizophrenics are more likely to be labeled schizophrenic than are those who are not so related. Moreover, the more closely one is related to a schizophrenic, the greater the likelihood of also being labeled schizophrenic.

Specifically, identical (monozygotic) twins have been compared to fraternal (dizygotic) twins and a *concordance rate*—the percent of pairs of twins in which the second twin is diagnosed as schizophrenic if the first twin has that diagnosis—has been computed. The concordance rate for monozygotic twins is higher than that for dizygotic twins and for siblings in all studies; the most careful investigations show that the concordance rate for monozygotic twins tends to range from about 25 to 40 percent (NIMH, 1975).

The monozygotic twin of a schizophrenic is not only more likely to be diagnosed as schizophrenic, but he is also more likely to show various other forms of psychopathology or abnormal behavior even if he is not diagnosed as schizophrenic (Heston, 1970). Distant relatives of schizophrenics, such as cousins, are no more likely to be schizophrenic (or otherwise disturbed) than anyone in the general population (Rosenthal, 1971).

These findings do not rule out an environmental or life-experience explanation. The closer the relationship between individuals, the more likely they are to interact to influence each other's environments, and to model deviant behavior. The study of identical twins reared apart could compare genetic and environmental factors. However, relatively little reliable information from such studies is available.

One well-known study (Kallman, 1953) has been criticized because the separation of the twins occurred late in life, after important early development had taken place. A possible solution is the study of children with schizophrenic parents who have been adopted or reared away from their parents. A study of 5,000 such children was conducted in Denmark (Kety et al., 1975). It was found that the biological relatives of schizophrenics were significantly more often schizophrenic than the biological relatives of a control group matched for age, sex, and social class. The adopted relatives of the schizophrenics showed no greater incidence of schizophrenia in spite of their close social interaction with these individuals. The findings thus support the influence of heredity in schizophrenia.

The Interaction of Factors. An extensive survey of research on schizophrenia has led to the conclusion that while schizophrenia "itself is not inherited, a predisposition to it, or perhaps to psychopathology in general, almost certainly is" (NIMH, 1975, p. 30). But even in the children of parents who were both diagnosed as schizophrenic, disturbance is not inevitable. The fact that concordance rates for identical twins are far below 100 percent also suppports the view that

> the explanation of schizophrenia lies in the interaction—the joint occurrence—of genetic predisposition, social stress, other conditions of life associated with social class position, and undoubtedly, other factors as well (NIMH, 1975, p. 131).

In sum, schizophrenia and related forms of severe abnormality, like most complex social behaviors, are likely to be caused by the interaction of many factors. Genetics is sure to play a significant but not exclusive role and so are biochemistry and the social environment, but the specific mix of ingredients in the interaction is still uncertain.

Genes, Twins, and Individual Differences

The provocative links found between genes and some disorders *(In Focus 7.2)* encourage a continuing search for the genetic roots of other patterns of behavior, including social traits, such as introversion-extraversion (e.g., Eysenck, 1973). As a result, the study of genetic influences on personality traits has become increasingly vigorous. A variety of methods are employed. It is particularly informative to compare the degree of similarity on personality measures found for genetically identical (monozygotic) twins as opposed to twins who are fraternal (dizygotic). A number of sophisticated methods have been devised to estimate the degree of heritability indicated by such investigations (e.g., Goldsmith & Campos, 1982).

A study of 850 sets of twins (Loehlin & Nichols, 1976) provides typical results: identical twin pairs tend to be more alike than fraternal twin pairs. The resemblance within identical twin pairs tends to be strongest for general ability and is less strong for special abilities. The resemblance is still somewhat lower for personality inventory scales, and lowest for interests, goals, and self-concepts (see Table 7-5).

On the whole, the identical twins are more alike, suggesting genetic influences on abilities and on some personality characteristics. The influence of the genes in these studies is complicated, however, by the fact that identical twins tend to have more similar early experiences than do fraternal twins. The authors conclude (1976, p. 94):

> Our data have thus not yielded any final and conclusive answer to the heredity-environment question for personality, abilities, and interests. The data are generally consistent with a substantial influence of the genes in accounting for individual differences in

Table 7-5
Resemblance of Identical and Fraternal Twin Pairs

Trait Area	Typical Correlations within Pairs	
	Identical Twins	Fraternal Twins
General ability	.86	.62
Special abilities	.74	.52
Personality scales	.50	.28
Ideals, goals, interests	.37	.20

SOURCE: Adapted from Loehlin & Nichols, 1976, p. 87, Table 7-1

these domains, but they imply a substantial influence of the environment as well—indeed, they do not altogether exclude a completely environmentalist position.

One careful review of a large number of studies of this type led to the following conclusion:

> With substantial confidence it can be asserted that theories of personality development ignore the action of genetic factors at some risk. Across ages, across traits, and across methods, moderate genetic influences on individual differences have been demonstrated. The genetic evidence is perhaps weakest in three areas: at young ages (the first half year of life in twin studies, childhood in adoption studies), for personality traits bordering on social attitudes and when variables are relatively "unprocessed" recordings of discrete behaviors. [Evidence is strongest for] . . . genetic effects on the broad dimension of sociability, followed by emotionality and activity . . . narrower constructs such as specific fears, certain components of sensation seeking and physical anxiety, anger, task persistence, and fidgeting are good candidates for psychobiological study (Goldsmith, 1983, p. 349).

In sum, although the influence of genes on individual differences in personality implicated to date appear to be "moderate," they certainly demand to continue to be pursued, and the results so far are quite provocative. Examples of particular personal characteristics in which genetic endowment may have some significant part are shown in Table 7-6. Similar evidence has been reported in a number of sources (e.g., Schaffer & Emerson, 1964; Thomas & Chess, 1977; Carey, Goldsmith, Tellegen, & Gottesman, 1978; Plomin & Foch, 1980).

Figure 7-1 illustrates these types of results more concretely. It shows that on the dimension of "emotionality" identical twins (monozygotic) are rated as much more similar by their mothers than are fraternal (dizygotic) twins. Although the results are impressive, they are not easy to interpret. Some of the greater similarity found may reflect that the mothers themselves may treat the identical twins more similarly, as might other people in the environment. The mothers also may have been influenced in their ratings not only by the twins' behavior but by their own expectations and preconceptions for identical versus fraternal twins. Nevertheless, results like these tend to be obtained so consistently that they suggest some support for a significant genetic role in personality.

Table 7-6

Examples of Personal Characteristics in Which Genetic Endowment May Have a Role

(Based on Maternal Ratings of Monozygotic Versus Dizygotic Twin Pairs)

Characteristic	Types of Items Rated
Emotionality (temperament, reactivity)	Cries easily Quick temper Easily frightened Gets upset quickly
Introversion-extraversion (e.g., anxious shyness versus sociability)	Makes friends easily Shy Is independent
Activity level (response output, e.g., hyperactive versus inactive)	Always on the go Cannot sit still long

SOURCE: Based on data from Buss, Plomin, and Willerman, 1973.

Identical Twins Reared Apart. To separate the role of genetics and environment more clearly, it is especially interesting to examine identical twins who have been reared apart, preferably in extremely different environments. A large scale project now underway at the University of Minnesota searched for and found such twins and is now beginning to provide much information (e.g., Bouchard et al.,

Figure 7-1
Similarity of Emotionality: Mother's Ratings of Monozygotic and Dizygotic Twin Pairs

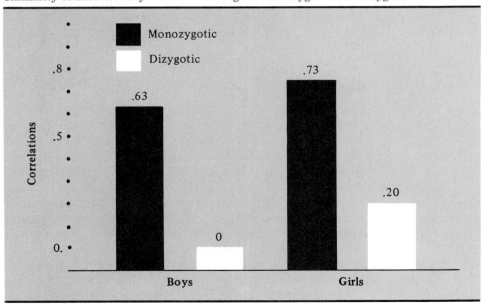

Correlation coefficients for degree of similarity from data in Buss, Plomin, & Willerman, 1973.

1981; Lykken, 1982). The subjects include thirty pairs of identical twins who had been separated on the average before the end of the second month of life, and thereafter were reared apart by different families. (Of course, the separations were caused by real-life events, not by the researchers.) The twins remained totally separated for many years and in some cases did not meet till the research project united them by seeking them out and bringing them together for testing. The twins have been tested extensively on many different measures, both physical and psychological.

Preliminary reports suggest instances of dramatic psychological similarities within the twin pairs, even for twins who grew up in radically different environments. In spite of their background differences, these twins seemed to share some quite distinctive mannerisms, postures, attitudes, and interests. For example, in some cases they posed alike for photos.

The instances of similarity in the reports are striking and remarkable. But even when identical twins are reared apart, their similarities are not necessarily due to their genes. For example, similar interests and values in identical twins may reflect their similar physiques, constitutions, and physical characteristics rather than any specific personality genes. These physical qualities may lead other people to treat them similarly even when the twins live in different environments. A shared interest in becoming a photography fashion model, for example, may say more about the inheritance of faces than of personality. Unquestionably one's physical endowment has extensive influences on one's life and personality development. The degree to which there are specific genes for particular psychological characteristics is much less evident.

The results of the Minnesota study are still incompletely reported and based on too small a sample to be conclusive. However, extensive testing continues, and further information from this project is being awaited eagerly as the sample expands. So far the major areas of concordance found for the twins are in their ability test performances, in indices of activity level and sociability, and in their patterns of brain waves.

Approach to Change: Biological Therapies

As we saw, the trait approach suggests that some psychological dispositions may have biological roots. If problematic behaviors, such as severe depression, reflect biological dispositions and biochemical problems, might they also respond to biological treatment? Researchers have actively pursued this question. If the cause is biochemical it also makes good sense to search for the cure through biochemical means.

Biological treatments attempt to change an individual's mood or behavior by direct intervention in bodily processes. These techniques include destruction of brain tissue by surgical operation, the electrical induction of convulsions by shock treatments, and the administration of drugs that cause chemical changes in bodily processes. Some biological methods have been valuable in the treatment or prevention of certain patterns of disturbed behaviors that result from physiological disorders. For example, general paresis (an organic psychosis caused by syphilis) may be controlled with antibiotics; mental problems associated with pellagra (a disorder produced by a vitamin deficiency) have been minimized through vitamin treatment; and barbiturates have helped people who have epilepsy. In all these cases biological therapy changes the bodily processes believed to be responsible for the troublesome behavior. In other efforts biological methods have been tried to treat behavior disturbances that seem not to have specific physiological causes.

Chemotherapy, or treatment with drugs, has so far proved to be the most promising biological therapy for psychological problems. The types of drugs used for specific purposes are summarized in Table 7-7.

Antidepressants. The *antidepressants,* or psychic energizers, are used to elevate the mood of depressed individuals. Some of these drugs (the tricyclics) appear to be effective with particular types of depressed individuals (e.g., Davis et al., 1967; Klein et al., 1980). Others (the monoamine oxidase inhibitors) do not appear to be as effective and may have more serious side effects, including a possibly fatal interaction with other drugs and foods.

Major Tranquilizers. The *phenothiazines* (most notably chlorpromazine) have proved to be so useful in managing schizophrenic patients that they are referred to as *antipsychotic drugs.* Their use in mental hospitals has been widespread since the 1950s and has changed the character of many hospitals, eliminating the need for locked wards and straitjackets. Discharged patients are often on maintenance dos-

Table 7-7
Some Drugs Used in Chemotherapy

Type of Drug	Application	Therapeutic Effectiveness
Antidepressants	Depression	Not fully substantiated but appear effective for elevating mood in some people
Major tranquilizers	Schizophrenia	Well substantiated: get patients out of hospitals, have practically eliminated need for restraints in hospitals
Minor tranquilizers	Anxiety, tension, milder forms of depression	Little controlled research; seem to slow down transmission of nerve impulses to the brain
Lithium	Manic behavior	Appears effective
Methadone (a synthetic narcotic)	Heroin addiction	Substantial: may eliminate craving for heroin; blocks "highs"

NOTE: These drugs are classified according to their effects on behavior not according to their chemical composition. Chemically dissimilar drugs can produce similar effects.

ages of these drugs and must occasionally return to the hospital for dose level adjustments.

The major tranquilizers have potentially serious side effects that may include motor disturbances, low blood pressure, and jaundice. There are also unpleasant subjective effects such as fatigue, blurred vision, and mouth dryness, which may explain why patients on their own may simply stop taking these drugs and often have to return to the hospital for an extended stay.

Minor Tranquilizers. The barbiturates were the first widely used minor tranquilizers—drugs which relieve anxiety that is not severe. But barbiturates are potentially addictive and were often used to commit suicide, so new drugs were developed. Perhaps the most widely used of these drugs is a synthetic chemical known by its trade name, *Valium*. Valium is the medicine most frequently prescribed in the United States today; Americans spend almost half a billion dollars a year on it.

Valium, like its predecessors the barbiturates, acts on the limbic system of the brain. In addition, Valium relaxes the muscles (which makes it effective in treating

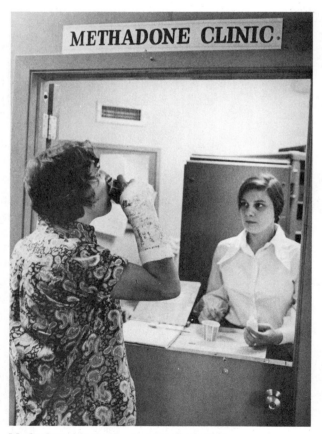

Methadone blocks the craving for heroin.

muscle spasm) and affects the electrical systems of the brain, thus making it useful in the treatment of some convulsive disorders. Although Valium is believed by some to be addictive, it seems less harmful than the barbiturates and other drugs of abuse. However, it readily crosses the placental barrier, and its potential effects on a developing fetus are not yet fully known. Since over two-thirds of Valium users are women, this is a significant and potentially dangerous side effect. Some people, especially the elderly, may become confused and agitated by Valium instead of being calmed by it. Valium is also widely used in nursing homes and by persons who are not institutionalized. Some of these individuals might feel better if they were given a simple placebo, and others might benefit from some other form of therapy or from a change in the conditions in their lives. Meanwhile, physicians continue to write Valium prescriptions, and the drug is used by millions of Americans in an attempt to reduce their anxieties.

Other widely used drugs include *lithium,* which is intended to reduce manic behavior and some forms of depression, and *methadone,* which appears promising for the treatment of heroin addiction (e.g., Dole et al., 1968). Methadone, which is itself addictive, blocks the craving for heroin and prevents "highs" if heroin is taken. A variety of psychostimulants, such as *Ritalin,* are also used extensively to treat impulse disorders and severe attention deficits.

As this brief survey suggests, some drugs appear to be positive contributors to a treatment program for some disorders. However, no drug by itself constitutes an adequate complete treatment for psychological problems. To the extent that the person's difficulties reflect problems of living, it would be naive to think that drugs can substitute completely for learning and practicing more effective ways to cope with the continuous challenges of life. And the fact that most drugs have negative side effects makes it all the more important to seek psychological treatment for psychological problems wherever possible.

SUMMARY EVALUATION OF THE TRAIT APPROACH

As Part III, the Trait Approach, concludes, it is time to summarize its main strengths and weaknesses. The major points are shown in Table 7-8. Examples and evidence for each point may be found by reviewing the last three chapters. As suggested at the end of Part II, it is a good review exercise to add to the Table any additional strengths or weaknesses you see and to illustrate them as fully as possible with specific examples.

Strengths and Weaknesses

On the positive side, we saw that the trait approach provided essential contributions to the quantification and objective measurement of personality dimensions. Tests like the MMPI and many others remain basic tools for the study of how individuals and groups differ. Trait measures help not only to describe important differences between people but also to assess the effects of any treatments or changes. Thus they help the researcher to see how people change—or remain stable—as a function of age and all sorts of life experiences.

Table 7-8
Summary Evaluation of the Trait Approach

Strengths	Weaknesses
Objective measurement, quantification, development of tests and research tools	Lack of explanatory theoretical concepts
Basic methodological contributions for evaluating test results and measuring treatment effects	Does not generate treatments
Useful for summarizing and predicting broad behavioral trends, especially for large samples and groups	Difficulty explaining or predicting specific behavior, especially for individual cases
Detects stable overall trends and differences	Underestimates role of situations
Calls attention to biological, genetic, and chemical bases of behavior	Underestimates role of social learning and experience

The trait approach allows a great deal of information to be condensed quantitatively in the form of summary scores. These summaries in turn let us see stable trends by averaging together many observations in statistical, quantitative terms. In this way one can detect the general "gist" of what individuals or groups "are like," and obtain a broad overview that compresses much information. For example, one can estimate "on the average" how one person or group differs from another on whatever measures or occasions one wants to sample. For many goals, the results allow predictions of stable future trends that can be extremely useful. The trait approach also is valuable in calling attention to the possible biological foundations of personality and social behavior.

On the critical side, the summaries of trends and tendencies provided by trait measures are just that and no more; they are summaries, not explanations. The trait approach provides relatively little in the way of psychological theory and does not say much about the "why" or "when" of personality and social behavior. Likewise, it is mute about psychological treatment and the conditions that lead to human change. The approach implies a high degree of stability in human qualities. Although some of these qualities may arise from experience, there also may be biochemical, genetic, and constitutional foundations for personality and individual differences. Valuable research into the biochemical and genetic bases of personality is now underway. Ultimately the yield from such research may help in the diagnosis and treatment of an array of human problems not yet imaginable in biochemical terms. If so, the approach may make a great contribution to treatment, but that possibility lies in the future.

We have seen that a major strength of the trait approach is that it condenses much information into averages and overall trends. For some critics that strength is also a serious liability. They see the trait approach as underestimating the role of the psychological situation and the human potential for variability and change. They also question the utility of the approach for dealing with individuals, either to predict their specific behavior in specific contexts or to design constructive psychological treatments for their unique circumstances.

Overview of the Approach

To complete our overview of the trait approach, it is helpful to summarize some of its main points. So much has been done within the framework of this approach that it becomes easy to lose its essential characteristics. Table 7-9 summarizes these characteristics. It reminds you that the main aim of the trait approach was to provide methods to infer and quantify people's social-personal traits. These traits were assumed to be stable and broadly consistent dispositions that underlie a wide range of behaviors across a number of related situations.

Traits are inferred from questionnaires, ratings, and other reports about the subject's dispositions. The subject's reports are taken as direct signs of the relevant dispositions. For example, the more often you rate yourself as aggressive, the more you are assumed to have an aggressive disposition. The focus of research is on measurement: to develop quantitative ways of describing important individual differences and their patternings. Traditionally, the trait approach has recognized that behavior varies with changes in the situation, but has focused on individual differences in response to the same situation. More recently, theorists and researchers have begun to try to take systematic account of the situation. They also have begun to see traits as "act trends," summaries of behavior, rather than as explanations. And they continue to explore the possible biochemical and genetic roots of personality and of psychological problems.

Table 7-9
Summary Overview of Trait Approach

Basic units	Inferred trait dispositions.
Causes of behavior	Generalized (consistent, stable) dispositions; biochemical (e.g., genetic) causes for some dispositions.
Favored data	Test responses (e.g., on questionnaires).
Observed responses used as	Direct signs (indicators) of dispositions.
Research focus	Measurement (test construction), description of individual differences and their patterning; heritability of personality
Approach to personality change	Not much concerned with change: Search for consistent, stable characteristics; biochemical treatments for disorders.
Role of situation	Acknowledged but of secondary interest until recently.

SUMMARY

1. Extensive individual differences in self-control have been found. Measures of "ego-control" and "ego-resiliency" are related to other relevant ratings and competencies throughout the course of development, establishing many meaningful patterns of coherence.

2. There are great individual differences in perceived control over outcomes and perceived responsibility for the things that happen. Differences among people in perceived control have been conceptualized on a dimension of "internal-external" control of reinforcement. An individual's status on this dimension is related to many other aspects of his personality and may affect his interpretation of different situations.

3. What people do depends on numerous moderating conditions. Evidence for the existence of broad traits has been questioned severely—and defended vigorously. On the other hand, although specific behavior changes across situations, there is evidence for the stability and coherence of lives even over long periods of time. While measures of traits are often not able to predict single acts, they may be able to predict a pooled combination of many behaviors relevant to one trait.

4. Complex interactions among dispositional and situational variables influence behavior. The relationship between any two variables—a child's dependency and his school achievements, for example—may be moderated by many other variables, such as his age, IQ, anxiety, the type of task, and the conditions of testing.

Recent studies of dispositions have tried to analyze the role of situations and of conditions as well as of individual differences.

5. One attempt to characterize the "personality" of situations is based on the description of the personality traits of individuals who function especially well in a particular situation. The psychological similarity of two situations can then be evaluated in terms of the similarity of the trait portraits of individuals who function best in them.

6. Biological treatments for psychological disorders now favor chemotherapy, which makes use of a variety of drugs. Several drugs appear to be helpful aids in treatment. They facilitate but cannot by themselves substitute for more effective coping patterns to deal with the problems of living.

7. The trait approach also continues to stimulate research into the possible genetic and biochemical bases of both normal and abnormal personality traits, and the results so far are encouraging and provocative.

8. The main strengths and weaknesses and basic features of the trait approach were summarized.

PART FOUR
PHENOMENOLOGICAL APPROACHES

Chapter 8

Phenomenological Approaches: Conceptions

The theorists discussed in this part insist that we must examine the nature of subjective experience; we must see how people perceive their world. For example, we cannot understand anxiety without understanding how the individual experiences it. We begin, therefore with a sample of such personal experience in the form of a self-description by a college student about to take a final examination:

> When I think about the exam, I really feel sick . . . so much depends on it. I know I'm not prepared, at least not as much as I should be, but I keep hoping that I can sort of

snow my way through it. He [the professor] said we would get to choose two of three essay questions. I've heard about his questions . . . they sort of cover the whole course, but they're still pretty general. Maybe I'll be able to mention a few of the right names and places. He can't expect us to put down everything in two hours . . . I keep trying to remember some of the things he said in class, but my mind keeps wandering. God, my folks—What will they think if I don't pass and can't graduate? Will they have a fit! Boy! I can see their faces. Worse yet, I can hear their voices: "And with all the money we spent on your education." Mom's going to be hurt. She'll let me know I let her down. She'll be a martyr: "Well, Roger, didn't you realize how this reflects on us? Didn't you know how much we worked and saved so you could get an education? . . . You were probably too busy with other things. I don't know what I'm going to tell your aunt and uncle. They were planning to come to the graduation you know." Hell! What about me? What'll I do if I don't graduate? How about the plans I made? I had a good job lined up with that company. They really sounded like they wanted me, like I was going to be somebody. . . . And what about the car? I had it all planned out. I was going to pay seventy a month and still have enough left for fun. I've got to pass. Oh hell! What about Anne [girlfriend]? She's counting on my graduating. We had plans. What will she think? She knows I'm no brain, but . . . hell, I won't be anybody. I've got to find some way to remember those names. If I can just get him to think that I really know that material, but don't have time to put it all down. If I can just . . . if . . . too goddam many ifs. Poor dad. He'll really be hurt. All the plans we made—all the . . . I was going to be somebody. What did he say? "People will respect you. People respect a college graduate. You'll be something more than a storekeeper." What am I going to do. God, I can't think. You know, I might just luck out. I've done it before. He could ask just the right questions. What could he ask? Boy! I feel like I want to vomit. Do you think others are as scared as I am? They probably know it all or don't give a damn. I'll bet you most of them have parents who can set them up whether they have college degrees or not. God, it means so much to me. I've got to pass. I've just got to. Dammit, what are those names? What could he ask? I can't think . . . I can't. . . . Maybe if I had a beer I'd be able to relax a little. Is there anybody around who wants to get a beer? God, I don't want to go alone. Who wants to go to the show? What the hell am I thinking about? I've got to study. . . . I can't. What's going to happen to me? . . . The whole damn world is coming apart (Fischer, 1970, pp. 121–122).

Feelings and thoughts like those reported by this student are the raw materials of theories that deal with the self and with the person's subjective, internal experiences and personal concepts. There are many complexities and variations in the orientation to personality presented in this chapter. In spite of these variations, however, a few fundamental themes emerge.

To simplify, we will call the orientation in this chapter "phenomenological," a term that refers to the individual's experience as he or she perceives it, because that is its most basic theme. Some of the positions here have been given other labels also, such as "self" theories, "construct" theories, "humanistic" theories, "cognitive" theories, and "existential" theories. Most phenomenological theories are distinctive both in the concepts they reject and in the ones they emphasize. They tend to reject most of the dynamic and motivational concepts of psychoanalytic theories and also most of the assumptions of trait theories. Instead, they emphasize people's immediate experiences and their current relationships, perceptions, and encounters. The person thus is viewed as an experiencing being, rather than as a "personality structure" or as a set of "psychodynamics" and long-term dispositions. The focus is on the individual's subjective experience, feelings, personal view of the world and self, and private concepts. Most of the approaches discussed in this chapter also stress people's positive strivings and their tendencies toward growth and self-actualization.

Most of the theories presented here are concerned broadly with cognition—with how we know and understand the world and ourselves. An interest in cognition implies attention to the internal or mental processes through which individuals "code" and categorize information. Influenced by the Swiss psychologist Jean Piaget, cognitive theories call attention to the active ways in which the mind generates meaning and experience. Ulric Neisser, for example, puts it this way (1967, p. 3): "Whether beautiful or ugly or just conveniently at hand, the world of experience is produced by the man who experiences it." That statement, of course, does not imply that there is no "real" world of objects—houses, mountains, people, tables, books—and it does not suggest that the "environment" is a fiction that does not affect our private experience. The cognitive position stresses, however, that "we have no direct immediate access to the world, nor to any of its properties. . . . Whatever we know about reality has been *mediated,* not only by the organs of sense but by complex systems which interpret and reinterpret sensory information" (Neisser, 1967, p. 3).

Some personality psychologists concerned with cognition have tried to understand how the individual perceives, thinks, interprets, and experiences the world; that is, they have tried to grasp the individual's point of view. Their focus is on persons and events of life as seen by the perceiver. In sum, they are most interested in the person's experience as he or she perceives and categorizes it—the person's *phenomenology.* Ideally, they would like to look at the world through the "subject's" eyes and to stand in that person's shoes, to experience a bit of what it is to *be* that person. This phenomenological view is the main concern of the present chapter.

SOURCES OF THE PHENOMENOLOGICAL APPROACH

The orientation presented in this chapter has numerous sources. Among the many early theorists who were fascinated with the self were William James, George H. Mead, and John Dewey. Another early theorist concerned with the self was Carl Jung. As early as the start of the century, Jung called attention to the organism's strivings for self-realization and integration. He believed in creative processes that go beyond the basic instincts of Freudian psychology. Also important were Gestalt psychology and existential philosophy. Given all these contributors, it becomes a bit arbitrary to select a few for detailed exposition. Therefore, you should consider the ideas that are presented next as merely representative.

Allport's Contribution: Functional Autonomy and the Proprium (Self)

Gordon Allport recognized that some common traits might be shared by all people in varying degrees. Some of his other ideas are most relevant to a phenomenological approach, however, and fit best in the present chapter. Allport emphasizes the *uniqueness* of the individual and of the integrated patterns that distinguish each person. He also notes the *lack of motivational continuity* during the individual's life and criticizes the Freudian emphasis on the enduring role of sexual and aggressive motives.

According to Allport, behavior is motivated originally by instincts, but later it may sustain itself indefinitely without biological reinforcement. Allport sees most normal adult motives as no longer having a functional relation to their historical roots. "Motives are contemporary. . . . Whatever drives must drive now. . . . The character of motives alters so radically from infancy to maturity that we may speak of adult motives as *supplanting* the motives of infancy" (1940, p. 545). This idea has been called "functional autonomy" to indicate that a habit, say practicing the violin at a certain hour each day, need not be tied to any basic motive of infancy. The extent to which an individual's motives are autonomous is a measure of maturity, according to Allport.

Allport thus stresses the contemporaneity of motives (1961). In his view, the past is not important unless it can be shown to be active in the present. He believes that historical facts about a person's past, while helping to reveal the total course of the individual's life, do not adequately explain the person's conduct today. In his words, "Past motives explain nothing unless they are also present motives" (1961, p. 220).

While fully recognizing the unity of growth in personality development, Allport emphasizes that later motives do not necessarily depend on earlier ones. Although the life of a plant is continuous with that of its seed, the seed no longer feeds and sustains the mature plant. In human terms, while a pianist may have been spurred to mastery of the piano through the need to overcome inferiority feelings, the later love of music is functionally autonomous from its origins.

Allport was also one of the strongest advocates of the self as a key feature of personality. To avoid a homunculus or manikin-in-the-mind conception of self, he has coined the term *proprium*. In his view, the proprium contains the root of the consistency that characterizes attitudes, goals, and values. This proprium is not innate (a newborn does not have a self); it develops in time. It provides a sense of self-identity, self-esteem, and self-image.

In addition to deemphasizing the person's early motivations and distant past, Allport focuses on the individual's currently perceived experiences, his or her phenomenological self and unique pattern of adaptation. He also favors a *wholistic* view of the individual as an integrated, biosocial organism, rather than as a bundle of traits and motives. Table 8-1 summarizes some of Allport's main ideas about individuality.

Lewin's Life Space

Still another important post-Freudian influence came from field theories (e.g., Lewin, 1936). These positions construed behavior as determined by the person's psychological life space—by the events that exist in the total psychological situation at the moment—rather than by past events or enduring, situation-free dispositions. The most elegant formulation of this position was Kurt Lewin's "field theory."

Table 8-1
Some Distinguishing Features of Individuality According to Allport (1961)

1. Motives become independent of their roots *(functional autonomy)*.

2. A *proprium* or self develops, characterized by:

    bodily sense
    self-identity
    self-image
    self-esteem
    self-extension
    rational thought

3. A *unique,* integrated pattern of adaptation marks the person as a whole.

The field concept of physics leading to Einstein's theory of relativity was the inspiration for Kurt Lewin's theory of personality. Einstein's concept of "fields of force" had an expression in the Gestalt movement of psychology, which asserted that each part of a whole is dependent upon every other part. The Gestaltists applied the notion of a field of interrelated components primarily to perception.

Kurt Lewin (1890–1947)

They proposed that the way in which an object is perceived depends upon the total context or configuration of its surroundings. What is perceived depends on the *relationships* among components of a perceptual field, rather than on the fixed characteristics of the individual components.

Lewin defined *life space* as the totality of facts that determine the behavior (*B*) of an individual at a certain moment. The life space includes the person (*P*) and the psychological environment (*E*), as depicted in Figure 8-1. Thus behavior is a function of the person and the environment, as expressed in the formula
$$B = f(P, E).$$

Lewin also discussed the question of the temporal relationship of an event and the conditions that produce it. Generally this question concerns whether past events only, or future events also, can cause change. Ordinary cause, based on the notion of causation in classical physics, assumes that something past is the cause of present events. Teleological theories assume that future events influence present events. Lewin's thesis is that neither past nor future, by definition, exists at the present moment and therefore neither can have an effect at the present. Past events have a position in the historical causal chains whose interweavings create the present situation, but only those events that are functioning in the present situation need to be taken into account. Such events are, by definition, current or momentary. In other words, only present facts can cause present behavior.

To represent the life space, Lewin therefore took into account only that which is contemporary. He termed this the principle of *contemporaneity* (Lewin, 1936). This does not mean the field theorists are not interested in historical problems or in the effects of previous experience. As Lewin (1951) pointed out, field theorists have enlarged the psychological experiment to include situations that contain a history that is systematically created throughout hours or weeks. For example, college students in an experiment might be given repeated failure experiences (on a series of achievement tasks) during several sessions. The effects of these experiences on the students' subsequent aspirations and expectations for success might then be measured.

The boundaries between the person and the psychological environment and between the life space and the physical world are *permeable,* that is, they can be

Figure 8-1
Lewin's Life Space

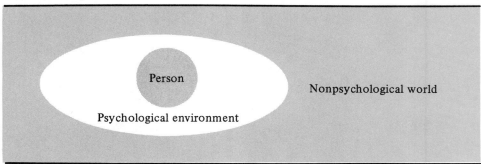

The life space contains the person in his or her psychological environment, which is delineated by a boundary (the ellipse) from the nonpsychological world.

crossed easily. That makes prediction difficult because one cannot be sure before-hand when and what facts will permeate a boundary and influence a fact from another region. Lewin asserts that the psychologist might therefore concentrate on describing and explaining the concrete psychological situation in terms of field theory rather than attempt prediction.

Lewin (1935) rejected the notion of constant, entity-like personality characteristics such as unchanging traits. As a result of dynamic forces, psychological reality is always changing. The environment of the individual does not serve merely to facilitate tendencies that are permanent in the person's nature (1936). Habits are not frozen associations, but rather the result of forces in the organism and its life space.

Lewin was similarly dissatisfied with the usual concept of needs. In descriptions of psychological reality, Lewin said, the needs that are producing effects in the momentary situation are the only ones that have to be represented. A need in Lewin's theory corresponds to a tension system of the inner-person region. Lewin was also interested in reward and punishment. Instead of the hedonistic pleasure-pain formulations of early learning theorists, Lewin construed rewards as devices for controlling behavior in momentary situations by causing changes in the psychological environment and in the tension systems of the person.

For Lewin, behavior and development are functions of the same structural and dynamic factors. Both are a function of the person and the psychological environment. In general, with increasing maturity there is greater differentiation of the person and the psychological environment.

Lewin's field theory had a major impact on experimental social psychology. His students extended his ideas and pursued them through ingenious experiments designed to alter the subject's life space—by altering perceptions about the self, about other people, about events. The effects of these alterations on attitudes, aspirations, task persistence, and other indices were then examined carefully. Until recently Lewin's influence on personality psychology has been less extensive. There is now, however, an increasing recognition of the importance of the psychological situation in studies of traits and motives (e.g., Magnusson, 1980; Mischel, 1984).

Phenomenology and Existentialism: The Here and Now

Carl Rogers and George A. Kelly developed positions in which private experiences, subjective perceptions, and the self all have an important part. Somewhat similar themes emphasizing the role of higher-order "positive" motives—growth, fulfillment, and the self and its actualization—have been developed by Abraham Maslow and others. According to Maslow, for example, humans are innately good. Growth motivation moves the individual through hierarchically ordered degrees of health to ultimate self-actualization. "Every person is, in part, his own project, and makes himself" (Maslow, 1965, p. 308). Behavior is seen as goal directed, striving, purposeful, and motivated by higher actualization needs rather than by primary biological drives alone.

The ideas of most of these theorists have much in common with the existential philosophical position developed by such European thinkers and writers as Kierkegaard, Sartre, and Camus and by the Swiss psychiatrists Binswanger and Boss. The key features of their orientation are expressed by Rollo May, an American proponent of existential psychology. Thinking about a patient of his in psychotherapy, May recognizes that he has available all sorts of information about her, such as hypotheses from her Rorschach and diagnoses from her neurologist. He then comments (1961, p. 26):

> But if, as I sit here, I am chiefly thinking of these *whys* and *hows* of the way the problem came about, I will have grasped everything *except the most important thing of all, the existing person.* Indeed, I will have grasped everything except the only real source of data I have, namely, this experiencing human being, this person now emerging, becoming, "building world," as the existential psychologists put it, immediately in this room with me.

May's remarks point to the existentialist's focus on phenomenological experience, on the "here and now" rather than on distant historical causes in the person's early childhood. Furthermore, the existential orientation sees the human being as capable of choice and responsibility in the moment rather than as the victim of unconscious forces or of habits from the past.

The Swiss existential psychiatrist Binswanger commented that Freudian theory pictured human beings not yet as people in the full sense, but only as creatures buffeted about by life. Binswanger believes that for a person to be fully himself— that is, to be truly realized or actualized as a human being—he must "look fate in the face." In his view, the fact that human life is determined by forces and conditions is only one side of the truth. The other side is that we ourselves "determine these forces as our fate" (cited in May, 1961, p. 252). Thus in the phenomenological and existential orientation, humans are seen as beings whose actualization requires much more than the fulfillment of biological needs and of sexual and aggressive instincts.

The existentialists propose that we are inevitably the builders of our own lives and, more specifically, that each person is:

1. a *choosing* agent, unable to avoid choices throughout the course of life
2. a *free* agent, who freely sets life goals
3. a *responsible* agent, accountable personally for his or her life choices

Our existence in life is given but our essence is what we make of life, how meaningfully and responsibly we construct it. This is an often painful, isolated, agonizing enterprise. To find satisfying values, to guide our lives accordingly, to give life meaning—these goals are all part of the existential quest, and they require the "courage to be"—the courage to break from blind conformity to the group and to strive instead for self-fulfillment by seeking greater self-definition and authenticity.

Finally, to grasp what it means to *be* also requires being in constant touch with the awareness of nonbeing, of alienation, of nothingness, and ultimately of the inevitability of death, everyone's unavoidable fate. The awareness of this inevitable fate and what that implies produces *existential anxiety*. The antidote for such anxiety is to face and live our lives responsibly, meaningfully, and with courage and awareness of our potential for continuous choice and growth.

To understand some of the main features of the existential and phenomenological orientation more closely, we shall consider the ideas of one of its most articulate proponents, Carl Rogers, in the next section.

CARL ROGERS' SELF THEORY

Unique Experience: The Subjective World

Rogers' theory of personality emphasizes the unique, subjective experience of the person. He believes that the way you see and interpret the events in your life determines how you respond to them—that is, how you behave. Each person dwells in a subjective world, and even the so-called objective world of the scientist is a product of subjective perceptions, purposes, and choices. Because no one else, no matter how hard he tries, can completely assume another person's "internal frame of reference," the person himself has the greatest potential for awareness of what reality is for him. In other words, each person potentially is the world's best expert on himself and has the best information about himself.

Carl Rogers (b. 1902)

Rogers emphasized the tendency of the organism to actualize itself.

In Rogers' view, "behavior is typically the goal-directed attempt of the organism to satisfy its needs as experienced, in the field as perceived" (1951, p. 491). The emphasis is on the person's perceptions as the determinants of his or her actions: How one sees and interprets events determines how one reacts to them.

Self-Actualization

Like most phenomenologists, Rogers wants to abandon specific motivational constructs and views the organism as functioning as an organized whole. He maintains that "there is one central source of energy in the human organism; that it is a function of the whole organism rather than some portion of it; and that it is perhaps best conceptualized as a tendency toward fulfillment, toward actualization, toward the maintenance and enhancement of the organism" (1963, p. 6). Thus the inherent tendency of the organism is to actualize itself. "Motivation" then becomes not a special construct but an overall characteristic of simply being alive.

In line with his essentially positive view of human nature, Rogers asserts that emotions are beneficial to adjustment. Instead of stressing the disruptive effects of anxiety, Rogers believes that "emotion accompanies and in general facilitates . . . goal-directed behavior, . . . the intensity of the emotion being related to the perceived significance of the behavior for the maintenance and enhancement of the organism" (1951, p. 493).

The organism in the course of actualizing itself engages in a valuing process. Experiences that are perceived as enhancing it are valued positively (and approached). Experiences that are perceived as negating enhancement or maintenance of the organism are valued negatively (and avoided). "The organism has one basic tendency and striving—to actualize, maintain, and enhance the experiencing organism" (Rogers, 1951, p. 487).

The Self

The self is a central concept for most phenomenological theories, and it also is basic for Rogers. Indeed, his theory is often referred to as a self theory of personality. The self or self-concept (the two terms mean the same thing for Rogers) is an "organized, consistent, conceptual gestalt composed of perceptions of the characteristics of the 'I' or 'me' and the perceptions of the relationships of the 'I' or 'me' to others and to various aspects of life, together with the values attached to these perceptions" (Rogers, 1959, p. 200). As a result of interaction with the environment, a portion of the perceptual field gradually becomes differentiated into the self. This perceived self (self-concept) influences perception and behavior. That is, the interpretation of the self—as strong or weak, for example—affects how one perceives the rest of one's world.

The experiences of the self become invested with values. These values are the result of direct experience with the environment, or they may be introjected or taken over from others. For example, a young child finds it organismically enjoyable to relieve himself whenever he experiences physiological tension in the bowel or bladder. However, he may sometimes also experience parental words and actions indicating that such behavior is bad, and that he is not lovable when he does this. A conflict then develops that may result in distortion and denial of experience. That is, the parental attitudes may be experienced as if they were based on the evidence of the child's own experience. In this example, the satisfaction of defecating may start to be experienced as bad even though a more accurate symbolization would be that it is often experienced as organismically satisfying. Rogers goes on to suggest that in bowel training, denial or distortion of experience may be avoided if the parent is able genuinely to accept the child's feelings and at the same time accepts his or her own feelings.

Consistency and Positive Regard

Rogers proposes two systems: the self (self-concept) and the organism. The two systems may be in opposition or in harmony. When these systems are in opposition or incongruence, the result is maladjustment, for then the self becomes rigidly organized, losing contact with actual organismic experience and filled with tensions. Perception is selective: we try to perceive experiences in ways consistent with the self-concept. The self-concept thus serves as a frame of reference for evaluating and monitoring the actual experiences of the organism. Experiences that are inconsistent with the self may be perceived as threats, and the more threat there is the more rigid and defensive the self structure becomes to maintain itself. At the same time, the self-concept becomes less congruent with organismic reality and loses contact with the actual experiences of the organism.

Rogers (1959) assumes a universal need for positive regard. This need develops as the awareness of the self emerges and leads the person to desire acceptance and love from the important people in his life. Sometimes they may accept him conditionally (i.e. depending on his specific behavior), or they may accept him in his own right and give him unconditional regard. The person needs positive regard not only from others but also from his self. The need for self-regard develops out of self-experiences associated with the satisfaction or frustration of the need for positive regard. If a person experiences only unconditional positive regard, his self-regard also would be unconditional. In that case the needs for positive regard and self-regard would never be at variance with "organismic evaluation." Such a state would represent genuine psychological adjustment and full functioning.

Most people do not achieve such ideal adjustment. Often a self-experience is avoided or sought only because it is less (or more) worthy of self-regard. For example, a child may experience anger toward her mother but avoids accepting that feeling because she wants to be a "good girl." When that happens, Rogers speaks of the individual's having acquired a "condition of worth." Experiences that are in accord with the individual's conditions of worth tend to be perceived accurately in awareness, but experiences that violate the conditions of worth may be denied to awareness and distorted grossly. When there is a significant amount of incongruence between the individual's self-concept and her evaluation of an experience, then defenses may become unable to work successfully. For example, if a young woman persistently experiences herself as painfully dissatisfied and "unhappy" in her efforts at schoolwork, but views herself as having to "succeed at college" in order to be an adequate person, she may experience great strain in her defensive efforts.

Rogers' theory, like Freud's, posits that accurate awareness of experiences may be threatening to the self and therefore may be prevented. Anxiety in Rogers' theory might be interpreted as the tension exhibited by the organized concept of the self when it senses (without full awareness, i.e., by "subceptions") that the recognition or symbolization of certain experiences would be destructive of its organization (1951). If a person's concept of the self has been built around his "masculinity," for example, experiences that might imply that he has some homosexual tendencies would threaten him severely. Anxiety thus involves a basic threat to the self, and defenses are erected to avoid it.

"Client-centered" (Rogerian) therapy seeks to bring about the harmonious interaction of the self and the organism. It tries to facilitate a greater congruence between the conceptual structure of the self and the phenomenal field of experience. The warm and unconditionally accepting attitude of the counselor hopefully enables the client to perceive and examine experiences that are inconsistent with the current self-structure. The client can then revise this self-structure to permit it to assimilate these inconsistent experiences. According to Rogers, the client gradually reorganizes the self-concept to bring it into line with the reality of organismic experience: "He will *be,* in more unified fashion, what he organismically *is,* and this seems to be the essence of therapy" (1955, p. 269). In recent years Rogers

(1980) has moved beyond individual client-centered therapy to form and lead many encounter groups intended to encourage psychological growth (see Chapter 9 and *In Focus 8.1*).

In sum, Rogers' theory highlights many of the chief points of the phenomenological and humanistic approach to personality. It emphasizes the person's perceived reality, subjective experiences, organismic striving for actualization, the potential for growth and freedom. It rejects or deemphasizes specific biological drives. It focuses on the experienced self rather than on historical causes or stable trait structures. A unique feature of Rogers' position is his emphasis on unconditional acceptance as a requisite for self-regard. Other theorists have emphasized different aspects of experience in their formulations. One of the most influential of these positions is George Kelly's theory, which is discussed in the next section.

GEORGE KELLY'S PSYCHOLOGY OF PERSONAL CONSTRUCTS

We all know that "The map is not the terrain." Yet the two are often confused. Psychologically it is equally true that our constructs and abstractions about behavior are not the same as the behaviors that are being categorized. In addition to acting as motivated organisms, people also are perceivers and construers of behav-

George A. Kelly (1905–1967)

Looking back at the almost 50 years of his contributions to psychology, Rogers (1974) tried to pinpoint the essence of his approach. In his view, his most fundamental idea was that:

> . . . the individual has within himself vast resources for self-understanding, for altering his self-concept, his attitudes, and his self-directed behavior—and that these resources can be tapped if only a definable climate of facilitative psychological attitudes can be provided (Rogers, 1974, p. 116).

Such a climate for growth requires an atmosphere in which feelings can be confronted, expressed, and accepted fully and freely. His continued emphasis on the person's potential freedom, the hallmark of a humanistic orientation, remains unchanged:

> My experience in therapy and in groups makes it impossible for me to deny the reality and significance of human choice. To me it is not an illusion that man is to some degree the architect of himself . . . for me the humanistic approach is the only possible one. It is for each person, however, to follow the pathway—behavioristic or humanistic—that he finds most congenial (Rogers, 1974, p. 119).

In the same humanistic vein he regrets modern technology and calls for autonomy and self-exploration:

> Our culture, increasingly based on the conquest of nature and the control of man, is in decline. Emerging through the ruins is the new person, highly aware, self-directing, an explorer of inner, perhaps more than outer, space, scornful of the conformity of institutions and the dogma of authority. He does not believe in being behaviorally shaped, or in shaping the behavior of others. He is most assuredly humanistic rather than technological. In my judgment he has a high probability of survival (Rogers, 1974, p. 119).

ior: They generate abstractions about themselves and others. These hypotheses and constructions have long intrigued psychologists interested in subjective states, in phenomenology, and in the experience of the self.

The Subject's Constructs

In the psychodynamic approach, the motive is the chief unit, unconscious conflicts are the processes of greatest interest, and the clinical judge is the favored instrument. Kelly's (1955) personal construct theory, in contrast, seeks to illuminate the person's own constructs rather than the hypotheses of the psychologist. Its main units are personal constructs—the ways we represent or view our own experiences. Rather than seeing people as victimized by their impulses and defenses, this position views the human being as an active, ever-changing creator of hypotheses.

According to Kelly, trait psychology tries to find the subject's place on the *theorist's* personality dimension. "Personal construct theory" instead tries to see how the subject sees and aligns events on *his or her own* dimensions. It is Kelly's hope to discover the nature of the subject's construct dimensions rather than to locate his position on the dimensions of the psychologist's theory. If next week's test is important to you, Kelly wants to explore how you see it, what it means to you, not what your score is on a scale of test-taking anxiety.

People as Scientists

The psychology of personal constructs explores the subjective maps that people generate in coping with the psychological terrain of their lives. Kelly emphasizes that, just like the scientist who studies them, human subjects also construe or abstract behavior, categorizing, interpreting, labeling, and judging themselves and their world. The individuals assessed by psychologists are themselves assessors who evaluate and construe their own behavior; they even assess the personality psychologists who try to assess them. Constructions and hypotheses about behavior are formulated by all persons regardless of their formal degrees and credentials as scientists. According to Kelly it is these constructions, and not merely simple physical responses, that must be studied in an adequate approach to personality. Categorizing behavior is equally evident when a psychotic patient describes his personal, private ideas in therapy and when a scientist discusses her favorite constructs and theories at a professional meeting. Both people represent the environment internally and express their representations and private experiences in their psychological constructions. Personal constructions, and not objective behavior descriptions on clear dimensions, confront the personality psychologist.

Kelly notes that most psychological scientists view themselves as motivated to achieve cognitive clarity and to understand phenomena, including their own lives. Yet the subjects of their theories, unlike the theorists themselves, are seen as unaware victims of psychic forces and traits that they can neither understand nor control. Kelly tries to remove this discrepancy between the theorist and the subject and to treat all people as if they were scientists.

Just like the scientist, subjects generate constructs and hypotheses with which they try to anticipate and control events in their lives. Therefore to understand the subject, one has to understand his or her constructs or private personality theory. To study an individual's constructs one has to find behavioral examples or "referents" for them. We cannot know what another person means when she says, "I have too much ego," or "I am not a friendly person," or "I may be falling in love," unless she gives us behavioral examples. Examples (referents) are required whether the construct is personal, for example the way a patient construes herself "as a woman," or theoretical, as when a psychologist talks about "introversion" or "ego defenses." Constructs can become known only through behavior.

Constructive Alternativism: Many Ways to See

The same events can be alternatively categorized. While people may not always be able to change events, they can always construe them differently. That is what Kelly meant by "constructive alternativism." To illustrate, consider this event: A boy drops his mother's favorite vase. What does it mean? The event is simply that the vase has been broken. Yet ask the child's psychoanalyst and he may point to the boy's unconscious hostility; ask the mother and she tells you how "mean" he is; his father says he is "spoiled;" the child's teacher may see the event as evidence of the child's "laziness" and chronic "clumsiness;" grandmother calls it just an "accident;" and the child himself may construe the event as reflecting his "stupidity." While the event cannot be undone—the vase is broken—its interpretation is open to alternative constructions, and these may lead to different courses of action.

Kelly's theory began with this fundamental postulate: "A person's processes are psychologically channelized by the ways in which he anticipates events" (Kelly, 1955, p. 46). Phrased differently, this postulate means that a person's activities are guided (stabilized, channelized) by the constructs (ways) he or she uses to predict (anticipate) events. This postulate shares with other phenomenological theories an emphasis on the person's subjective view, but it is more specific in its focus on how the individual predicts or anticipates events. The postulate is further elaborated by a set of formal corollaries. Although the details of the theory need not concern us here, several of the main ideas require comment.

Kelly is concerned with the *convenience* of constructs rather than with their absolute truth. Rather than try to assess whether a particular construct is true, Kelly attends to its convenience or utility for the construer. For example, rather than try to assess whether or not a client is "really a latent homosexual" or "really going crazy," he tries to discover the implications for the client's life of construing himself in that way. If the construction is not convenient, then the task is to find a better alternative—that is, one that predicts better and leads to better outcomes. Just as a psychologist may get stuck with an inadequate theory, so his subjects also may impale themselves on their constructions and construe themselves into a dilemma. Individuals may torture themselves into believing that "I am not worthy enough" or "I am not successful enough," as if these verdicts were matters of undisputable fact rather than constructions and hypotheses about behavior. The job of psychotherapy is to provide the conditions in which personal constructs can be elaborated, tested for their implications, and, if necessary, modified. Just like the scientist, the subject needs the chance to test personal constructs and to validate or invalidate them, progressively modifying them in the light of new experience.

Roles: Many Ways to Be

Kelly's emphasis on roles and role enactments also merit special attention. Rather than seeing humans as possessing fairly stable, broadly generalized traits, Kelly saw them as capable of enacting many different roles and of engaging in continuous change. A role, for Kelly, is an attempt to see another person through the other's glasses—that is, to look at a person through *his or her* constructs—and to structure one's actions in that light. To enact a role requires that behavior be guided by perception of the other person's viewpoint. Thus to "role play" your mother, for example, you would have to try to see things (including yourself) as she does, "through her eyes," and to act in light of those perceptions. You would try to behave as if you really were your mother. Kelly used the technique of role playing extensively as a therapeutic procedure designed to help persons gain new perspectives and to generate more convenient ways of living.

People Are What They Make of Themselves

Like other phenomenologists, Kelly rejects the idea of specific motives. His view of human nature focuses on how people construe themselves and on what they do in the light of those constructs. Kelly (like Rogers) believes that no special concepts are required to understand why people are motivated and active: Every person is motivated "for no other reason than that he is alive" (Kelly, 1958, p. 49). For Kelly, the concept of motivation "can appear only as a redundancy" (1958, p. 50).

He believes, like many existentialists, that the individual *is* what he *does* and comes to know his nature by seeing what he is doing. Starting from his clinical experiences with troubled college students in Fort Hays, Kansas, where he taught for many years, Kelly independently reached a position that overlaps remarkably with the views of such European existential philosophers as Sartre (1956). In Sartre's (1956) existentialist conception, "existence precedes essence": There is no human nature—man simply *is,* and he is nothing else but what he "makes of himself."

THE SEARCH FOR SELF-ACTUALIZATION

Kelly believes that his theory, though it focuses on the person's constructs, is not purely concerned with cognitive and intellectual functions. Constructs, he says, often are not verbal, and they may have highly emotional ingredients. Nevertheless some critics find that his view of the scientist neglects the person as an emotional being. Since Kelly's work, many phenomenologically oriented psychologistshave become increasingly committed to the affective, nonverbal components of experience. This search for feeling is seen in numerous recent psychological movements, both within psychology as a formal discipline and in the larger social scene.

The concern with feelings, the sense of being "out of touch" and isolated from emotional experiences, is illustrated poignantly in these excerpts from a troubled college student's letter:

> Long ago I lost touch with my body—my brain became separated from my body, and started commanding it. My body turned into just a machine for transporting my brain around from place to place to talk unfeelingly and analytically with other detached brains. I was glad it was a big and efficient machine—but I thought it was the inferior part of me, and that my brain should be in charge and call the tune for my feelings, letting the "positive" ones out and keeping the "negative" ones safely tucked in. . . .
>
> But now I feel lost in that head, out of phase with people—and somehow I want to reach them and my own guts—to know what I really feel, and stop all these precious intellectual games—to really live and not just to exist—So what do I do now?

The idea expressed by this distressed student is shared by many others who want "to make contact" emotionally, both with themselves and with other people.

Expanding Consciousness

Probably the most dramatic and controversial manifestation of this trend to achieve deeper feeling was the effort to expand consciousness and emotional experiences by means of psychedelic drugs. Initially drugs such as psilocybin and LSD were advocated most energetically by Timothy Leary and Richard Alpert when they were psychologists at Harvard in 1961 and 1962. In the 1960s the "mind-expanding" movement through drug-induced "trips" or psychic "voyages" gained many enthusiastic participants. Although drawing heavily on Freudian dynamic psychology for its interpretations, this movement had a different purpose from that espoused by most neo-analytic followers of Freud. The neo-analysts emphasized "ego psychology" and the impulse-free (or "conflict-free") spheres of the ego and of rational control processes. Many advocates of consciousness expansion, instead, seemed to seek a return of the "primacy of the id"—a focus on feeling and fantasy, on "primary processes" rather than on logic and rational thought. This effort to capture pure feeling, to experience more closely one's bodily states, to escape from "ego" and "superego" and societal constraints, and to live fully in the "here and now," was seen most vividly in the "hippie" movement and the "drug culture" of the 1960s.

Such drugs as LSD undoubtedly produce major alterations in subjective experience, including the intensification of feelings (e.g., Leary, Litwin & Metzner, 1963), but enthusiasm for them was soon tempered by the recognition that they entail serious risks. While the much less controversial drug, marijuana, has received increasing acceptance, there also has been a trend to search for greater awareness without the aid of any drugs.

Away from Alienation

Several routes to increasing awareness have relied on psychological experiences rather than on drugs. These efforts include meditation (Ornstein, 1972), encounter groups, and "marathons" of the type developed at the Esalen Institute in Big Sur, California (Schutz, 1967). While meditative techniques have been based mainly on Oriental religious sources (Ornstein & Naranjo, 1971), the encounter or "sensitivity training" movement has drawn on various role-play and psychodrama techniques, on existential philosophy, and on Freudian dynamic psychology. The resulting syntheses are seen in the ideas of the "Gestalt therapy" of Fritz Perls (1969), in the efforts to expand human awareness and to achieve "joy" and true communication (e.g., Schutz, 1967), and in the pursuit of "peak experiences" and "self-actualization" (e.g., Maslow, 1971). Because the implications of these positions are most relevant for psychotherapy and personality change they will be discussed in that context in Chapter 9; also see *In Focus 8.2.*

In Focus 8.2
Toward Fulfillment: Maslow's Self-Actualizing Person

One of the most influential spokespersons for the importance of becoming "in touch" with one's true feelings and fulfilling oneself totally was Abraham Maslow (1968, 1971). Maslow's theory overlaps considerably with that of Rogers. He also emphasized human beings' vast positive potential for growth and fulfillment. The striving toward actualization of this potential is a basic quality of being human:

Man demonstrates *in his own nature* a pressure toward fuller and fuller Being, more and more perfect actualization of his humanness in exactly the same naturalistic, scientific sense that an acorn may be said to be "pressing toward" being an oak tree, or that a tiger can be observed to "push toward" being tigerish, or a horse toward being equine. . . (Maslow, 1968, p. 160).

Maslow's commitment was to study "optimal man" and to discover the

In a "peak experience" the person may achieve a moment of fulfillment and joy.

Figure 8-2
Maslow's Hierarchy of Needs

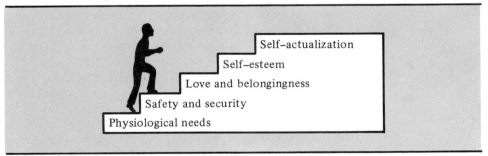

Maslow arranges motives in a hierarchy ascending from such basic physiological needs as hunger and thirst through safety and love needs to needs for esteem, (e.g., feeling competent), and ultimately, self-actualization—the full realization of one's human potential, as in creativity. The lower needs are more powerful and demand satisfaction first. The higher needs have less influence on behavior but are more distinctly human. Generally, higher needs do not become a focus until lower ones have been at least partly satisfied.

qualities of those people who seemed to be closest to realizing all their potentialities. In his view, one has higher "growth needs"—needs for self-actualization fulfillment—that emerge when more primitive needs (*physiological needs, safety needs, needs for belongingness and self-esteem*) are satisfied (see Figure 8-2). Maslow wanted to focus on the qualities of feeling and experience that seem to distinguish self-actualizing, fully functioning people. Therefore, he searched for the attributes that seemed to mark such people as Beethoven, Einstein, Jefferson, Lincoln, Walt Whitman, as well as some of the individuals he knew personally and admired most. These positive qualities are elaborated as part of the humanistic view of the "healthy personality" in Chapter 9.

Self-actualization may be seen not only as a human need and as a quality of certain people, but also as a subjective experience that many of us may have, even if only momentarily, at some points in life. Maslow called this special state a "peak experience"; a temporary experience of fulfillment and joy in which the person loses self-centeredness and (in varying degrees of intensity) feels a nonstriving happiness, a moment of perfection. Words that may be used to describe this state include "aliveness," "beauty," "ecstasy," "effortlessness," "uniqueness," and "wholeness." Such peak experiences have been reported in many contexts, including the esthetic appreciation of nature and beauty, worship, intimate relationships with others, and creative activities.

COMMON THEMES AND ISSUES

The approaches surveyed in this chapter are quite diverse and far more complex than a brief summary suggests. In spite of their diversity, these approaches share a focus on the self-as-experienced, on situations as perceived, on personal constructs, on feelings, and on the possibility of freedom. They search for data and methods that explore how people can disclose and reveal themselves more fully and honestly. They also see greater self-awareness, consistency, and self-acceptance as crucial aspects of personal growth and actualization.

The existential belief that "man is what he makes of himself" and what he conceives himself to be is extremely appealing to many people. It also raises some key issues. First, psychologists committed to a deterministic view of science have to ask what are the *causes* that govern what individuals make of themselves and conceive themselves to be—how do individuals come to make themselves and conceive themselves in particular ways? While philosophers may put the springs of action and cognition into the will (as Sartre does), the scientifically oriented psychologist seeks the variables that account for the phenomena of being and will itself. While able to accept in part the idea that individuals are what they make of themselves, the psychologist as a scientist has to go further and search for the conditions that make them, including those conditions that influence (or make) their self-conceptions.

The existential idea that the person is "in possession" of himself or herself, rather than possessed by a human nature, and that people are what they make of themselves, has profound implications for the study of personality. Instead of a search for where the individual stands with regard to the assessor's dimensions, the assessor's task becomes the elaboration of what the individual is making of herself. To the extent that assessors seek a full account, however, they also must search for the causes of that existence. This last step is where most psychologists concerned with observable causes part company with the existentialist. It is also the point at which many psychologists have chosen for themselves a humanistic existentialism rather than a deterministic psychology.

Are Cognitions the Causes of Behavior?

In spite of the obvious importance of personal constructs and other cognitions, one cannot assume that they are the main causes of the person's behavior. Verbal constructs and cognitions do not always cause or even influence nonverbal behavior and the things we do. The relations between personal concepts and other behaviors often are quite indirect and remote. Changes in personal constructs—or in opinions, beliefs, or values—do not always produce important behavior changes (Festinger, 1964). Often cognitive and value changes may *follow* as a function of particular behavioral performances, rather than serve as the causes for these performances (e.g., Bem, 1972; Festinger, 1957). That is, constructs and cognitions may be realigned to make them consistent with behavior and may be used to justify that behavior. The issues and evidence on this topic are discussed in later chapters.

Is the Self a ''Doer''?

Phenomenological accounts of the self in personality have been criticized most strongly for being descriptive rather than explanatory (see Brewster Smith's 1950 discussion). In his analysis, Smith distinguished between two different meanings of the self. One meaning of the self is as the *doer* of behavior. That meaning refers to the diverse processes that comprise the individual's personality. The self as doer is simply a summary term for these processes. The second meaning is the *self-as-object*. This definition refers to the person's concepts and attitudes about himself.

Smith argues that this distinction between the self-as-doer or process, and the phenomenal construct of the self—that is, the self-as-object perceived by the individual—has been confused by phenomenologists. He notes that Rogers, for example, talks about the self this way:

> When the self is free from any threat of attack or likelihood of attack, then it is possible for the self to consider these hitherto rejected perceptions, to make new differentiations, and to reintegrate the self in such a way as to include them (Rogers, 1947, p. 365).

Smith questions these feats of the self, commenting on the confusion between the self as a causal agent and the self as an experienced phenomenon:

> Can a phenomenal self consider perceptions and reintegrate itself . . . , or is this rather double-talk resulting from the attempt to make one good concept do the work of two? (Smith, 1950, p. 520)

Thus Smith faulted self theorists for endowing the self-as-object (which is a concept that the individual has about himself) with all sorts of causal powers, such as the ability to evaluate itself, guard itself, and change itself. Similar criticisms have been made repeatedly (e.g., Skinner, 1964).

The Self as a Basic Schema (Category)

There certainly have been many problems with the definition of "self" and its place in personality theory. But these difficulties should not obscure the enduring and central importance of the self as an integrative personality construct. The challenge will be to avoid endowing the self with mysterious powers without losing its subjective reality. Subjectively, there is little doubt of the "I," "me," or "self" as a basic reference point around which experiences and the sense of personal identity itself seem to be organized. There have also been some promising efforts to treat the self not as a "thing" but as a schema, cognitive category, or map that serves as a vital frame of reference for processing and evaluating experiences. This cognitive approach to the self promises to be researchable as well as theoretically appealing (e.g., Markus, 1977; Markus & Smith, 1981), as discussed in Chapter 10.

SUMMARY

1. The diverse theories discussed in this chapter all reject specific motivational and dynamic concepts. Instead they focus on the immediate perceived experience and concepts of individuals, and on their strivings toward growth and self-actualization.

2. Allport's theory of personality stresses the functional autonomy of motives and argues that motives that are functioning currently in the mature individual may be independent of their historical roots. He gives central importance to the phenomenological or perceived self.

3. Lewin's field theory introduces the notion of life space and the importance of the psychological environment. His theory stresses the immediate relationships between person and environment and elements in the environment, rather than dealing with these as absolute entities. Contemporaneity is an important feature of this viewpoint. Lewin was dissatisfied with the usual concepts of traits and needs and saw behavior and development as functions of dynamic changes in the psychological environment and in the tension systems of the person.

4. Many of the positions discussed in this chapter have in common an interest in subjective experience and a positive view of human nature.

The human being is seen as purposeful and striving toward self-fulfillment, not simply as driven by unconscious forces and motivated by the necessity to satisfy biological needs.

5. The existentialists focus on the "here and now." They emphasize that we build our own lives, and that each person is a choosing, free, responsible agent.

6. Carl Rogers' theory is illustrative of the central characteristics of the phenomenological approach to personality. The emphasis is on the person's unique experienced reality. In this theory the *self* (self-concept) is a conscious perception of self-as-object. This self-concept develops as the result of direct experience with the environment and may also incorporate the perceptions of others. The experienced self in turn influences perception and behavior. Maladjustment occurs when the sense of self and a person's perceptions and experiences are in opposition and disharmony.

7. George Kelly's theory stresses the necessity of understanding the individual's own dimensions, categories, and hypotheses rather than viewing him or her in terms of the psychologist's constructs. It also emphasizes the convenience of the person's hypotheses and constructs for deal-

ing with experience. Role play may help the person to select and practice more satisfactory, convenient modes of construing the world in alternative ways.

8. Meditation and encounter groups have been favored by movements that emphasize nonverbal, emotional components of experience and existence. Some of these approaches seek to explore and expand consciousness and awareness through a variety of techniques aimed at escape from the "reality-oriented ego" into more genuine feelings and enhanced sensitivity. Others search for fulfillment through self-actualization and "peak experiences," as Maslow emphasized.

9. The phenomenological emphasis has made many contributions. Nevertheless, it also has been criticized. A focus on people's subjective perceptions and cognitions does not necessarily uncover the causes of their behavior. Sometimes self theorists seem to confuse the self as an experienced phenomenon and as an agent determining behavior.

Chapter 9

The Internal View

The phenomenological ideas discussed in Chapter 8 deeply influence both personality assessment and change. As we saw, the main feature of the phenomenological orientation is its emphasis on the person's experience as he or she perceives it. In Kelly's phrase, if a man's private domain is ignored "it becomes necessary to explain him as an inert object wafted about in a public domain by external forces, or as a solitary datum sitting on its own continuum" (1955, p. 39). On the other hand, if different individuals are to be construed within the same general system of laws, then commonalities and generalizations also must be discovered. To study the individual's experiences within the framework of scientific rules, methods have to be found to reach those private experiences and to bring them into view. In this chapter we will consider some of the methods intended to let us glimpse the internal view.

PEOPLE AS THEIR OWN EXPERTS

Phenomenologists like Rogers and Kelly seek to go beyond introspection and to anchor their theories to objective and scientific methods. In Rogers' view, for example, the therapist enters the internal world of the client's perceptions not by introspection but by observation and inference (1947). A concern with objectivity is reflected in Rogers' extensive efforts to study persons empirically, and these efforts are what place his work in the domain of psychology rather than philosophy. The same concern with objective measurement of subjective experience has characterized Kelly's approach to assessment. This chapter considers some of the main efforts that have been made by phenomenologically oriented psychologists to study experience objectively and to provide strategies for personal growth and awareness.

Gary W.'s Self-Conceptualization

Phenomenological study begins with the person's own viewpoint. To approach that viewpoint one may begin with the individual's self-presentation, as expressed in the way he depicts and describes himself. Some of the raw data of phenomenology are illustrated in the following self-description recorded by Gary W. when he was asked to describe himself as a person.

Excerpts from Gary's Self-Description:

I'm twenty-five years old, and a college graduate. I'm in business school working toward an MBA.

I'm an introspective sort of person—not very outgoing. Not particularly good in social situations. Though I'm not a good leader and I wouldn't be a good politician, I'm shrewd enough that I'll be a good businessman. Right now I'm being considered for an important job that means a lot to me and I'm sweating it. I know the powers at the office have their doubts about me but I'm sure I could make it—I'm positive. I can think ahead and no one will take advantage of me. I know how to work toward a goal and stick with whatever I start to the end—bitter or not.

The only thing that really gets me is speaking in a large group. Talking in front of a lot of people. I don't know what it is, but sometimes I get so nervous and confused I literally can't talk! I feel my heart is going to thump itself to death. I guess I'm afraid that they're all criticizing me. Like they're almost *hoping* I'll get caught with my pants down. Maybe I shouldn't care so much what other people think of me—but it does get to me, and it hurts—and I wind up sweating buckets and with my foot in my mouth.

I'm pretty good with women, but I've never found one that I want to spend the rest of my life with. Meanwhile I'm enjoying the freewheelin' life. I hope someday to find a girl who is both attractive and level-headed. A girl who is warm and good but not dominating and who'll be faithful but still lead a life of her own. Not depend on me for every little thing.

My childhood was fairly typical middle-class, uptight. I have an older brother. We used to fight with each other a lot, you know, the way kids do. Now we're not so competitive. We've grown up and made peace with each other—maybe it's just an armistice, but I think it may be a real peace—if peace ever really exists. I guess it was his accident that was the turning point. He got pretty smashed up in a car crash and I guess I thought, "There but for the grace of God. . . . " I count a lot on being physically up to par.

Dad wasn't around much when we were growing up. He was having business troubles and worried a lot. He and mother seemed to get along in a low-key sort of way. But I guess there must have been some friction because they're splitting now—getting divorced. I guess it doesn't matter now—I mean my brother and I have been on our own for some time. Still, I feel sorry for my Dad—his life looks like a waste and he is a wreck. A walking tragedy.

My strengths are my persistence and my stamina and guts—you need them in this world. Shrewdness. My weaknesses are my feeling that when it comes to the crunch you can't really trust anybody or anything. You never know who's going to put you down or what accident of fate lies around the corner. You try and try—and in the end it's probably all in the cards.

Well, I guess that's about it. I mean, is there anything else you want to know?

Can People Assess Themselves Accurately?

How can we begin to interpret Gary's self-portrait? It is possible to proceed in terms of one's favorite theory, construing Gary's statements as reflections of his traits, or as signs of his dynamics, or as indicative of his social learning history, or as clues to the social forces that are molding him. But can one also make Gary's comments a bridge for understanding his private viewpoint, for glimpsing his own personality theory and for seeing his self-conceptions?

Because each of us is intimately familiar with his own conscious, perceived reality, it may seem deceptively simple to reach out and see another person's subjective world. In fact, we of course cannot "crawl into another person's skin and peer out at the world through his eyes," but we can "start by making inferences based primarily upon what we see him doing rather than upon what we have seen other people doing" (Kelly, 1955, p. 42). That is, we can try to attend to him rather than to our stereotypes and theoretical constructs.

A most direct way to inquire about another person's experience is to ask him, just as Gary was asked, to depict himself. Virtually all approaches to personality have asked people for self-reports. In most orientations these reports have served primarily as cues from which to infer the individual's underlying personality structure and dynamics. Perhaps because of the assumption that people engage in extensive unconscious distortion, the subject's own reports generally have been used as a basis for the clinician (or the test) to generate inferences and predictions about him, rather than as a means of conveying the subject's view of himself.

Can people be "experts" about themselves? Can they assess themselves? Can their reports serve as reliable and valid indices of their behavior? For example, in his self-appraisal Gary predicts that he can succeed in the job for which he is being considered. Is this self-assessment accurate, or is it a defensive hope, or an opportunistic ploy, or a belated effort at self-persuasion?

Some studies have tried to examine whether people can assess and predict their own behavior adequately. If they cannot, then the value of phenomenological inquiries would be limited severely; if they can, then it may be not only interesting but also useful to listen to their self-assessments most seriously. To establish the utility of a person's direct report about himself, you must compare it with the predictions about him that can be made from other data sources. For example, you must compare the individual's self-reports with the statements drawn from sophisticated psychometric tests or from well-trained clinical judges who use such techniques as the interview and the projective test to infer the subject's attributes.

It has been a surprise for many psychologists to learn that simple self-reports may be as valid as, and sometimes better predictors than more sophisticated, complex, and indirect tests designed to disclose underlying personality. Thus, Marks, Stauffacher, and Lyle (1963) tried to predict future adjustment for schizophrenic patients. They found that simple self-reports on attitude scales (like the California *F* Scale, discussed in Chapter 6) may yield better predictions than did psychometrically more sophisticated scales. Simple attitude statements (on the California *F* Scale) have also been one of the best predictors of success in the Peace Corps; they have been more accurate than far more costly personality inferences. Interviews and pooled global ratings from experts did not prove nearly as accurate as self-reports were (Mischel, 1965). Another study found that two extremely simple self-ratings (one on "adjustment" and one on "introversion-extraversion") may be as stable and useful as are inferences from factor scores based on sophisticated personality-rating schedules (Peterson, 1965). Three studies designed to test the same personality characteristics both by direct and indirect measures generally found the direct measures to be better (Scott & Johnson, 1972).

At first glance evidence for the value of direct self-reports might seem more relevant to the trait approaches discussed in Chapters 5 and 6 (since many trait measures rely on self-reports) than to phenomenology. In fact, the evidence in this section does not speak to the question of the nature of personality traits; it merely shows that people can report directly about their own behavior with as much or better accuracy than we can get from other more indirect inferences and information about them (Mischel, 1972, 1981). In sum, useful information about people may be obtained most directly by simply asking them. These conclusions seem to hold for such diverse areas as college achievement, job and professional success, treatment outcomes in psychotherapy, rehospitalization for psychiatric patients, and parole violations for delinquent children (e.g., Merluzzi et al., 1981; Mischel, 1981).

TECHNIQUES FOR STUDYING SUBJECTIVE EXPERIENCE

Thus it seems under some conditions people may be able to report and predict their own behavior at least as accurately as experts can make inferences about them. Consequently, it often is reasonable to ask the person directly how he or she will behave, and in many instances the self-statements obtained may be as accurate as, or better than, any other data sources. Of course people do not always predict their own behavior accurately. Sometimes individuals lack either the information or the motivation to foretell their own behavior. Even if a criminal plans to steal again we cannot expect him to say so to the examining prosecutor at his trial. Moreover, many future behaviors may be determined by variables not in the person's control (e.g., other people, accidents). The obtained findings do suggest that techniques designed to obtain direct self-estimates and self-predictions merit serious attention.

One especially useful rating technique for obtaining reports about the self, the Q-technique or Q-sort, was already discussed in Chapter 6 as a tool for studying individual differences. For many phenomenologically oriented psychologists, self-statements from Q-sorts may be of interest in themselves. The phenomenologist simply wants to see the person's self-characterization for its own sake. It is possible to use techniques like the Q-sort to assess how persons describe themselves both as they really view themselves ("real self") and as they would like to be ("ideal self"). Often the difference between these two measures is especially informative.

Interviews

Most modern phenomenologists have recognized that self-reports may not reveal everything important about behavior and may not give a complete picture of personality. Persons may be conscious of the reasons for their behavior but be unable or unwilling to report them. Or they may not be conscious of all their experiences, in which case they cannot communicate them no matter how hard they try. In spite of these limitations, such phenomenologists as Rogers prefer the client's frame of reference as the vantage point for understanding. The psychologist's task, in Rogers' view, is to provide conditions that are conducive to growth and that facilitate free exploration of feelings and self.

One cannot expect people to be honest about themselves when they fear that their statements may incriminate them or lead to negative decisions about their future. In order for a person to reveal private feelings, he or she needs a nonthreatening atmosphere that allays anxieties, reduces inhibitions, and fosters self-disclosure (Jourard, 1967). Phenomenologically oriented psychologists therefore pay much attention to creating conditions of acceptance, warmth, and empathy in which the individual may feel more at ease for open self-exploration. These conditions of acceptance are illustrated vividly in "client-centered" (Rogerian) therapy, discussed later in this chapter. Rogerians have not only tried to create conditions conducive to personal growth; they also have studied those conditions in the interview.

In their earliest efforts the approach was informal. They selected excerpts from recorded interviews in client-centered therapy mainly to document how the clients' verbalizations reflect their self-pictures, and how these pictures change in the course of therapy (e.g., Rogers, 1942; Rogers & Dymond, 1954). Since these early beginnings, the content analysis of interview protocols has become a systematic research method. Going far beyond the mere tape recording of interviews, researchers have devised theory-relevant categories for reliably scoring the client's expressions. For example, many investigators have scored changes in self-references on various dimensions during therapy. They have grouped these self-references into such categories as positive or approving self-references, negative or disapproving self-references, ambivalent self-references, and ambiguous self-references. The scores obtained could then be correlated with other aspects of the therapy, such as the point in the relationship at which they occurred, or the association among diverse types of changes as therapy progressed. For example, it has been possible to try to test propositions such as the idea that increasing acceptance of self leads to increasing acceptance of others. Research in this vein has been vigorous and extensive (e.g., Chodorkoff, 1954; Marsden, 1971; Truax & Mitchell, 1971).

Rogerians have not been the only ones to attempt content analysis of verbal behavior in interviews. The technique of scoring content has been favored in descriptive studies of all sorts of psychotherapy and not just in phenomenological approaches. A typical question in psychodynamically oriented therapy, for example, might trace changes in types of conflict expressed in various phases in psychotherapy. To illustrate, Figure 9-1 depicts the percentage of total statements judged to deal with general hostility conflict as opposed to sex conflict in the course of the first fifteen psychotherapy hours (Murray, Auld, & White, 1954). As the figure suggests, sexual conflicts began to be expressed increasingly in later sessions, whereas more general conflicts were readily verbalized in earlier phases of the relationship. These content analyses, of course, depend on the clinician's infer-

Figure 9-1
General Hostility Conflict and Sex Conflict Statements

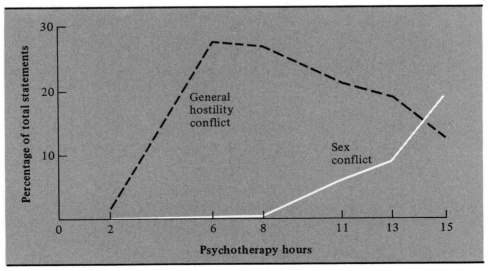

General hostility conflict statements about husband, and sex conflict statements about husband, in six random selected therapy hours with one client
From Murray, Auld, & White (1954).

ences about the underlying meaning of the client's statements; they do not reflect the subject's phenomenology directly.

As these studies indicate, phenomenological data from the interview have been objectified and investigated with diverse research strategies guided by many different theoretical viewpoints. While the interview is a favorite tool for the phenomenologist, the data from the interview can be analyzed in many different ways. In general, the interview continues to be, for most of the major theoretical orientations, a source of data for personality assessments. Its popularity probably reflects its great flexibility and the vast range of topics that it can cover rapidly.

Many phenomenologically oriented psychologists use the interview to observe how the individual interprets himself and describes his experiences. They employ the interview as a direct sample of the person's self-description (the ways he sees and presents himself) regardless of the validity of the data he provides as "signs" of his nontest behaviors or of his psychodynamics. They seek to create an atmosphere conducive to honest self-disclosure, an atmosphere in which self-revelation is actively encouraged (e.g., Jourard, 1974).

The Semantic Differential

Another route for phenomenologically oriented assessment has been developed to study meanings. This technique, the "semantic differential," yields ratings of the meaning of the persons, events, or concepts the investigator wants to study.

On the semantic differential test the meanings of diverse words, phrases, and concepts are rated on many scales (Osgood, Suci, & Tannenbaum, 1957). Raters (or subjects) are supplied with a stimulus word like "feather," or "me," or "my father," or with a phrase like "my ideal self," and are asked to rate each stimulus on a seven-point, bipolar scale. Polar adjectives like "rough–smooth" or "fair–unfair" are the extremes of each scale. Raters are instructed to mark the point that most nearly indicates the meaning of the stimulus concept for them. For example, you might be asked to rate "my ideal self" on scales like those shown in Table 9-1. To see what that is like, you should try it for yourself, both for the concepts suggested and for any others you find interesting for yourself. The technique is both objective and flexible. It permits investigation of how people describe themselves and others, as well as how special experiences (for example, psychotherapy) affect them.

A great deal of research has repeatedly indicated that three main factors tend to emerge when the results are analyzed. A primary *evaluative* (good–bad) factor seems to be the most important (Kim & Rosenberg, 1980). In other words, evaluations in such terms as "good–bad" enter most extensively into how people characterize themselves, their experiences, and other people. The two other factors are *potency,* represented by scale items like hard–soft, masculine–feminine, strong–weak, and *activity,* tapped by scales like active–passive, excitable–calm, and hot–cold (Mulaik, 1964; Vernon, 1964).

Exploring Personal Constructs

Suppose that you see a person quietly letting herself be abused by someone else. You might conclude that the person is "submissive." Yet the same behavior might

Table 9-1
Examples of Concepts and Rating Scales from the Semantic Differential

Concepts whose meanings are rated:
My Actual Self
My Ideal Self
Masculinity
Foreigner
Mother

Scales for rating the meaning of each concept:

strong	___:___:___:___:___:___	weak
pleasant	___:___:___:___:___:___	unpleasant
hard	___:___:___:___:___:___	soft
safe	___:___:___:___:___:___	dangerous
fair	___:___:___:___:___:___	unfair
active	___:___:___:___:___:___	passive

NOTE: As an exercise, provide these ratings yourself for each concept.
SOURCE: Based on Osgood, Suci, & Tannenbaum, 1957.

be construed by other observers as sensitive, cautious, intelligent, tactful, or polite. Recall that George Kelly (1955) emphasized that different people may construe the same event differently and that every event can be construed in alternative ways.

The personal construct is the central unit of George Kelly's theory. Kelly's operation for measuring a construct is best seen in his Role Construct Repertory Test or "Rep" Test. On the Rep Test subjects may list many people or things that are important to them (e.g., self, mother, brother). After they list these items (or the assessor lists them), they consider them in groups of three. In each triad they have to indicate how two items are similar to each other and different from the third. In this way the subjective dimensions of similarity among events, and the subjective opposites of those dimensions, may be evoked systematically (Table 9-2). It is also possible to study the characteristics of the peoples' construct systems—for example, the number of different constructs they have in their construct repertory.

Table 9-2
Elaboration of Personal Constructs: Examples from Gary W.

1. List the three most important people in your life:
    me   my brother   my father
   How are any two of these alike and different from the third?
    My brother and I both know how to be tough and succeed, no matter what—my father is soft, knocked out, defeated by life.

2. Think of yourself now, five years ago, and five years from now. How are any two of these alike and different from the third?
    Five years ago I was warmer, more open and responsive to others than I am now. Now I'm mostly a scheming brain. Five years from now I hope to have recaptured some of that feeling and to be more like I was five years ago.

Like the semantic differential, the Rep Test is a flexible instrument that can be adapted for many different purposes, and it provides a convenient and fairly simple way to begin the exploration of personal constructs. Some examples, taken from the study of Gary W., are shown in Table 9-2 (which illustrates the general type of procedure that may be used to elaborate personal constructs).

Research on the temporal stability of personal constructs from Kelly's Rep Test indicates a good deal of consistency over time (Bonarius, 1965). For example, a high retest correlation (.79) was found for constructs after a two-week interval (Landfield, Stern, & Fjeld, 1961), and factor analyses of the Rep test suggest that its main factor is stable (Pedersen, 1958), and thus that an individual's main constructs may be relatively permanent.

According to Kelly, the individuals' personal constructs gradually become elaborated through their answers on the Rep Test, and through their behaviors in the interview and on other tests. To illustrate some features of the assessment of personal constructs, here is an analysis of our case based on how Gary spontaneously elaborates and contrasts the constructs with which he views the world. What follows are excerpts from an attempt by an assessor to summarize some of Gary's main conceptions.

A Personal Construct Conceptualization of Gary W.

Rationality-Emotionality is a construct dimension that seems to be of considerable importance for Gary. This construct is elaborated most clearly when he is discussing his interpersonal relationships. A sexual relationship with a woman is described in such terms as "spiritual," "instinctive," "sublime," and "beyond rationality." It is characterized by intense feeling and the primacy of emotions, and it is based on physical attraction. Real friendships, in contrast, are based upon verbalizable grounds—rational bases such as interests and ways of thinking that are common to both parties.

The distinction between the rational and the emotional is echoed when Gary describes his worries in terms of those that are "rational" versus those that are "immediate and threatening." In discussing anger, he says that he has learned to cover up his feelings, but that his emotions sometimes "surface." He no longer gets violently angry, as he did when he was a child, but is "controlled," "stony," and "devious." He gives the most positive evaluation to reason, and contrasts what is reasonable with what is "worthless."

Transposed onto a time line, his distinction between reason and emotion forms part of the contrast between adults and children. After he was about 12 years old, Gary "psyched out" his father, so the latter was no longer his "enemy" but instead became his "friendly, rational adviser." He also describes shifts in his relations with his mother and with his brother that apparently involve handling his feelings toward them in a less explosive way.

Power and control versus dependence and weakness seems to be a major dimension on which adults and children differ. Adults are the enemies of children.

In his interview descriptions of his childhood experiences, what parental figures require of a child is typically the opposite of what the child wants. Gary describes life as a child as involving "denial, helplessness, nothing and nobody on my side." It was a time when he "couldn't control events," when he was being "manipulated" and "shamed." Gary contrasts foresight, and events that he can plan and control, with accidents, terror, and the unpredictable.

Defeat-Success is a closely related dimension around which a number of constructs are clustered. Defeat is defined in terms of lack of money, passivity, compliance, dependence, frustration, undermined masculinity, and physical pain. Success means money, activity, freedom, independence, control, and being a "real" man.

Security-Liberty is another major dimension for Gary. In describing jobs, acquaintances, and life styles, he talks in terms of "the ordinary 9 to 5 job complete with wife, kids, and mortgage," versus the "free and easy life." "Blind obedience" is contrasted to "judging the issues for oneself." Gary describes himself as being "uncertain," and contrasts being free-wheeling with plodding determination. He sees himself as being currently without "acceptance" and "success" and he feels "cut off." His own "procrastination" hinders his "drive," but he hopes his "ambition will win out" and gain him both security and liberty.

As far as *role conceptions* are concerned, Gary now sees his father as "emasculated" and "knocked out," although once he saw him as "a giant" and as his "enemy." The father seems to have moved along the conceptual continuum from "power and control" to a point where he is seen as inadequate and as being competition no longer. He dislikes his father for the middle-class values that he feels he represents and for his passivity. There is also the implication that he resents his father for not comparing favorably with his mother. The turning point in Gary's feelings for his brother, whom he disliked for sharing many of their father's qualities, came when his brother was smashed up in a car crash. He now sees him as less conventional, more humorous and self-examining.

Gary sees his mother, and ideal women in general, as "independent partners" rather than "devouring" sources of affection. Instead of making their families central in importance, they achieve success and recognition in work outside their home. They keep the male "alive" by providing stimulation through their competence, which extends even to athletics, rather than being dependent and "clinging." Gary sees himself as similar to his mother and says he loves her best, next to himself. On the more negative side, he sees his mother as frigid and incapable of expressing affection. However, in view of his own evaluation of emotionality, this criticism is a highly qualified one. He sees his mother as having in many ways been the cause of his father's defeat, but constantly adds that she did not intend this result and feels bad about it, that it was a by-product of other admirable qualities she possesses.

His relationship with his mother is characterized by control of expression of both anger and love. He sees her dominating tendencies as dangerous, as evidenced by his childhood conception of her as omniscient and omnipotent. This fear seems to have generalized to his grandmother and to other women, as evidenced by his TAT stories.

In his relationships with women there seems to be a general distinction between sex objects and companions. In describing a sexual relationship that he felt had no potentialities for friendship, Gary says, "If we hadn't been able to 'make it' we would have stopped seeing each other." He generally prefers women who are stimulating and challenging, though he fears all forms of domination, through either authority or emotional ties.

In his relationships with men outside his family, Gary prefers distance and respect and finds that closeness leads to friction, as with his present roommate. At school he found two older men whom he could look up to: a teacher to whom he was grateful for not being "wishy-washy" and another person whom he describes as being a "real man." (Ways to obtain more information about personal constructs are discussed in *In Focus 9.1.*)

Nonverbal Communication

Techniques like the semantic differential and the Rep Test sample what people *say*—that is, their verbal behavior. But significant communication among people is often nonverbal—it can involve facial expressions, movements, and gestures. Nonverbal expressions have intrigued psychologists of many theoretical orientations who are interested in the subject's perceptions and inner states. Researchers explore the possible meanings and effects of such nonverbal expressions as eye contact and the stare.

It has been found, for example, that when an interviewer evaluates subjects positively they increase eye contact with him; when he evaluates them negatively, they decrease eye contact with him (Exline & Winters, 1965). The effects of eye contact seem to interact with the verbal content conveyed in the relationship. One study varied whether an interviewer looked at the subject frequently or hardly at all, and whether the conversation was positive or threatening (Ellsworth & Carlsmith, 1968). When the verbal content was positive, more frequent eye contact produced more positive evaluations of the interviewer. In contrast, when the verbal content was negative more frequent eye contact produced more negative evaluation.

Although much is still unknown about nonverbal communication, many results have been encouraging. It has been shown, for instance, that "when people look at the faces of other people, they can obtain information about happiness, surprise, fear, anger, disgust/contempt, interest, and sadness. . . . Such information can be

Some of Gary's main constructs emerged from his self-descriptions and verbalizations. When people start to express their constructs, they usually begin with very diffuse, oversimplified, global terms. For example, Gary called himself "shrewd," "too shy," "too sharp." He also said he wanted to "feel more real," to "adjust better," and to "be happier."

What can the construct assessor do with these verbalizations? As we have seen in earlier chapters, psychodynamically oriented clinicians rely chiefly on their intuitive inferences about the symbolic and dynamic meanings of verbal behavior. Personal construct assessors recognize that talk about private experiences and feelings tends to be ambiguous. For example, statements of the kind commonly presented in clinical contexts, like "I feel so lost," generally are not clear. Instead of inquiring into *why* the person feels "lost," personal construct assessments try to discover referents for just *what* the statement means. An adequate personal construct assessment of what people say involves the analysis of what they mean. For this purpose the assessor's initial task is like the one faced when we want to understand a foreign language. Trait-oriented psychometric assessments either

investigate the accuracy of the persons' statements as indices of their nontest behavior, or treat their verbalizations as signs of their position on a personality dimension. A personal construct analysis of language, on the other hand, is completely different. The main aim of such an analysis is to decipher the content of what is being conveyed and to discover its behavioral referents and consequences; its aim is not to translate what is said into signs of underlying motives, of unconscious processes, or of personality dimensions.

Often it is hard to find the words for personal constructs. Just as the psychologist interested in such concepts as extraversion, indentity, or anxiety must find public referents to help specify what he or she means, so must the client find public referents for his or her private concepts, difficulties, and aspirations.

In sum, Kelly urges a specific and elaborate inquiry into personal constructs by obtaining numerous behavioral examples as referents for them. Kelly has described in detail many techniques to explore the conditions under which the individual's particular constructions about emotional reactions may emerge and change (1955).

interpreted, without any special training, by those who see the face . . . " (Ekman, Friesen, & Ellsworth, 1972, pp. 176–177).

ADAPTATION, DEVIANCE, AND CHANGE

The phenomenological orientation also has had profound influences on applied approaches to psychological "health," to problematic behavior, and to personality change.

The Healthy Personality

The phenomenological orientation implies a "humanistic" view of adaptation and deviance. There are many variations, but in general personal genuineness, honesty about one's own feelings, self-awareness, and self-acceptance are positively valued;

"self-realization," the ultimate in fulfillment, involves a continuous quest to know oneself and to actualize one's potentialities for full awareness and growth as a human being. Denouncing "adjustment" to society and to other people's values as the road to dehumanization, the quest is to know oneself deeply and to be true to one's own feelings without disguise, to be oneself in the "here and now." Conversely, human problems are seen as rooted in distortions of one's own perceptions and experiences in the service of furthering the expectations of society, including the dictates of one's own self-concept with its needs for "positive regard" (Chapter 8).

A description of the "healthy" personality from a humanistic viewpoint is provided by Maslow (1968), whose characterization of the qualities of "self-actualizing" people is summarized in Table 9-3. Slightly different, but overlapping, perspectives come from other humanistic spokesmen (e.g., Jourard, 1974).

In sum, in spite of its many different versions, the phenomenological-humanistic orientation tends to view "healthy people" as those who:

1. become aware of themselves, their feelings, and their limits; accept themselves, their lives, and what they make of their lives as their own responsibility; have "the courage to be."
2. experience the "here-and-now;" are not trapped to live in the past or to dwell in the future through anxious expectations and distorted defenses.
3. realize their potentialities; have autonomy and are not trapped by their own self-concepts or the expectations of others and society.

METHODS FOR GROWTH

To help achieve these ideals, several avenues for constructive personality change have been favored by advocates of the phenomenological approach, as discussed next.

Client-Centered Psychotherapy

One of the most influential applications of the phenomenological approach was the "client-centered" therapy developed by Carl Rogers (Chapter 8). Rogers rejected most of Freud's concepts regarding the nature of psychodynamics and psychosexual development. He also avoided all diagnostic terms, refusing to put his labels on the client. He maintained, however, the interview format for psychotherapy (using a face-to-face arrangement rather than the orthodox psychoanalyst's couch for the client). Rogers and his students focused on the client-clinician relationship. Usually they required many fewer sessions than did psychoanalytic therapy, and they dealt more with current than with historical concerns in the client's life.

For Rogers (1959) the therapist's main task is to provide an atmosphere in which the client can be more fully open to her own "organismic" experience. To achieve a growth-conducive atmosphere, the clinician must view the client as intrinsically good and capable of self-development. The clinician's function is to be nonevaluative and to convey a sense of unconditional acceptance and regard for the client. To reach the client effectively the clinician must be "genuine" and "con-

Table 9-3
Some Qualities of Maslow's "Self-Actualizing" People

1. Able to perceive reality accurately and efficiently.
2. Accepting of self, of others, and of the world.
3. Spontaneous and natural, particularly in thought and emotion.
4. Problem-centered: concerned with problems outside themselves and capable of retaining a broad perspective.
5. Need and desire solitude and privacy; can rely on their own potentialities and resources.
6. Autonomous: relatively independent of extrinsic satisfactions, for example, acceptance or popularity.
7. Capable of a continued freshness of appreciation of even the simplest, most commonplace experiences (for example, a sunset, a flower, or another person).
8. Experience "mystic" or "oceanic" feelings in which they feel out of time and place and at one with nature.
9. Have a sense of identification with humankind as a whole.
10. Form their deepest ties with relatively few others.
11. Truly democratic; unprejudiced and respectful of all others.
12. Ethical, able to discriminate between means and ends.
13. Thoughtful, philosophical, unhostile sense of humor; laugh at the human condition, not at a particular individual.
14. Creative and inventive, not necessarily possessing great talents, but a naive and unspoiled freshness of approach.
15. Capable of some detachment from the culture in which they live, recognizing the necessity for change and improvement.

SOURCE: Based on Maslow, 1968.

gruent"—an open, trustworthy, warm person without a facade. The congruent therapist, according to Rogers, feels free to "be himself" and to accept himself and the client fully and immediately in the therapeutic encounter, and he conveys this openness to the client by simply being himself. When a genuinely accepting, unconditional relationship is established, the client will become less afraid to face and accept her own feelings and experiences. Becoming open to the experience of herself as she is, she can reorganize her self-structure. Now, it is hoped, she will accept experiences that she had previously denied or distorted (because they did not fit her self-concept) and thus achieve greater internal congruity and self-actualization.

Rogers thus sought an empathetic, interview-based relationship therapy. He renounced the Freudian focus on psychodynamics and transference. Instead, he wanted to provide the client an unconditionally accepting relationship—an atmosphere conducive to "growth" (self-actualization). In this relationship the focus is on empathic understanding and acceptance of feelings rather than interpretation, although the latter is not excluded. The clinician is relatively "nondirective;" the objective is to let the client direct the interview while the clinician attempts to accurately reflect and clarify the feelings that emerge.

In client-centered therapy (now also called "person-centered"), permissiveness and unqualified acceptance on the part of the therapist provide an atmosphere favorable to personal honesty. Psychologists are urged to abandon their "objective" measurement orientation and their concern with tests. Instead, they should try to learn from the client how he or she thinks, understands, and feels. "The best vantage point for understanding behavior is from the internal frame of reference of the individual himself" (Rogers, 1951, p. 494). Although their focus is on empathy, the Rogerians have not neglected objective research into the relationship, as was noted earlier in this chapter in the context of interview research. As a result, Rogerians have helped to illuminate some of the processes that occur during client-centered therapy and also have provided considerable evidence concerning its effectiveness (e.g., Truax & Mitchell, 1971).

Client-centered psychotherapy has been shown to produce some significant alterations. An extensive review of outcome research indicated that some clients may improve significantly (on measures of self-concept change), while others deteriorate significantly during treatment (Bergin, 1966). Bergin's review concluded that some forms of Rogerian psychotherapy may cause clients to become either significantly better or worse than untreated controls. For example, Gendlin (1962) reported detrimental effects from client-centered relationship therapy for some people, especially those diagnosed schizophrenic. Consequently, therapy research needs to try to identify the characteristics of clients, clinicians, and client-clinician combinations that might predispose particular forms of therapy to success or failure (e.g., Bergin, 1971). If these attributes can be isolated it might be possible to offer particular forms of client-centered therapy only to those who can benefit from them.

It is evident that Rogers' client-centered psychotherapy differs in many ways from Freudian psychotherapy. Indeed, when Rogers first proposed his techniques they were considered revolutionary. Sometimes his approach to psychotherapy is even described as the polar opposite of Freud's. While there are major differences between Freudian and Rogerian approaches to psychotherapy, on closer inspection there also are some fundamental similarities. Both approaches retain a verbal, interview format for psychotherapy; both focus on the client-clinician relationship; both are primarily concerned with feelings; both emphasize the importance of unconscious processes (defense, repression); both consider increased awareness and acceptance of unconscious feelings to be major goals of psychotherapy.

To be sure, the two approaches differ in their focus. They differ in the specific content that they believe is repressed (e.g., id impulses versus organismic experiences), in the motives they consider most important (e.g., sex and aggression versus self-realization), and in the specific insights they hope will be achieved in psychotherapy (the unconscious becomes conscious and conflict is resolved versus organismic experience is accepted and the self becomes congruent with it). But these differences should not obscure the fact that both approaches are forms of relationship treatment that emphasize awareness of hypothesized unconscious feelings and the need for the client to accept those feelings.

Phenomenologically Oriented Groups

As part of the search for growth and expanded awareness, in the 1960s and 1970s a variety of group treatments became popular. These group experiences go beyond the verbal exchange of the traditional client-clinician interview and seek to achieve better communication and contact among a group of people as well as to increase each individual's insight and self-awareness. This trend toward group experiences is found in diverse forms, especially in encounter groups and marathons like those developed at the Esalen Institute in California (Schutz, 1967) and in the "Gestalt therapy" of Fritz Perls (1969).

Encounter groups have many different labels, such as human-relations training group (T-group), sensitivity training group, personal growth group, and include many varieties of experiences, but in this discussion the focus is on their common qualities.

Schutz (1967) in his book *Joy* noted that encounter group methods involve *doing* something, not just talking. The aim is to help people to experience, to feel, to make life more vital. In this quest he advocated a host of group methods that include body exercises, wordless meetings, group fantasy, and physical "games." These games range from gentle face and body explorations by mutual touching and holding to physically aggressive encounters involving shoving, pushing, and hitting. In many activities the group leaders and group members interpret the meaning of the members' behavior as their encounters occur.

Elliot Aronson (1972, p. 238) described what is learned in group experiences this way: " . . . in a psychology course I learn how people behave; in a T-group I

Proponents of encounter groups emphasize their value for enhancing contact and communication among many people, not just those with severe problems.

learn how I behave. But I learn much more than that: I also learn how others see me, how my behavior affects them, and how I am affected by other people." Referring to the process through which such learning occurs, Aronson (p. 239) emphasizes learning-by-doing; " . . . people learn by trying things out, by getting in touch with their feelings and by expressing those feelings to other people, either verbally or nonverbally." Such a process requires an atmosphere of trust so that members learn not how they are "supposed" to behave but rather what they really feel and how others view them.

At a theoretical level, the encounter group movement involves a complex synthesis of both Freudian and Rogerian concepts with a focus on nonverbal experiences and self-discovery. The psychodynamic motivational framework is largely retained and is used in many of the interpretations, but it is implemented by direct "acting-out" procedures for expressing feelings through action in the group, by body contact designed to increase awareness of body feelings, and by games to encourage the expression of affection and aggression. Thus many of Freud's and Rogers' ideas have been transferred from the consulting room to the group encounter, and from verbal expression to body awareness and physical expression. Indeed, Carl Rogers (1970) developed and extended many of his theoretical concepts to the encounter experience and has become one of its leading advocates. Rather than talking about impulses, feelings, and fantasies, the individual is encouraged to act them out in the group. For example, rather than talk about repressed feelings of anger toward his father the individual enacts his feelings, pummelling a pillow while screaming "I hate you Dad, I hate you."

Many of these therapies are phenomenologically oriented and seem to emphasize the achievement of greater consciousness and personal integration. The aim is to help individuals to gain awareness, self-acceptance, and spontaneity and ultimately to achieve fulfillment and joy. The objective seems to include a feeling of wholeness and of independence and autonomy. Such a concern with "doing your own thing" and achieving self-acceptance characterizes the "Gestalt therapy" advocated by Fritz Perls (1969). The philosophy of that position is summarized in the "prayer" of Gestalt therapy (Perls, 1969, p. 4):

> I do my thing, and you do your thing
> I am not in this world to live up
>   to your expectations
> And you are not in this world to
>   live up to mine.
> You are you and I am I
> And if by chance we find each
>   other, it's beautiful.
> If not, it can't be helped.

Effects of Encounter Groups

Many people have reported positive changes as a result of group experiences. To illustrate, consider this testimonial cited by Rogers (1970, p. 129):

> I still can't believe the experience that I had during the workshop. I have come to see myself in a completely new perspective. Before I was "the handsome" but cold person

insofar as personal relationships go. People wanted to approach me but I was afraid to let them come close as it might endanger me and I would have to give a little of myself. Since the institute I have not been afraid to be *human*. I express myself quite well and also am likeable and also can love. I go out now and use these emotions as part of me.

While such reports are encouraging they of course are not firm evidence, and they are offset in part by reports of negative experiences and "bad trips" (e.g., Lieberman et al., 1973). Some behavior changes do seem to emerge, but their interpretation is beset by many methodological difficulties (Campbell & Dunnette, 1968). When careful control groups are used some doubt is raised if the gains from encounter experience reflect more than the enthusiastic expectancies of the group members. For example, people in weekend encounter groups showed more rated improvement than did those who remained in an at-home control group: but improvement in the encounter groups did not differ from that found in an on-site control group whose participants believed they were in an encounter group although they only had recreational activities (McCardel & Murray, 1974).

Nevertheless, a number of experimental studies indicate specific changes that may occur in some types of groups. These changes include a decrease in ethnic prejudice (Rubin, 1967), an increase in empathy (Dunnette, 1969) and in susceptibility to being hypnotized (Tart, 1970), and an increased belief by subjects that their behavior is under their own control (Diamond & Shapiro, 1973). This evidence is accompanied by a greater awareness on the part of encounter group enthusiasts that not all groups are for all people, that bad as well as good experiences may occur, and that coerciveness in groups is a real hazard that needs to be avoided (Aronson, 1972).

Meditation

As Eastern cultures have long known, and as Western cultures have recently learned, meditation can have powerful effects on subjective experience. The term "meditation"

> refers to a set of techniques which are the product of another type of psychology, one that aims at personal rather than intellectual knowledge. As such, the exercises are designed to produce an alteration in consciousness—a shift away from the active, outward-oriented, linear mode and toward the receptive and quiescent mode, and usually a shift from an external focus of attention to an internal one (Ornstein, 1972, p. 107).

Transcendental Meditation. Students, businessmen, athletes, ministers, senators, and secretaries are among the more than 600,000 people in the United States alone who enthusiastically endorse one version of meditation called *transcendental meditation (TM)*. Introduced into the United States in 1959 by Maharishi Mahesh Yogi, a Hindu monk, TM in the public's mind has changed over the years from counterculture fad to mainstream respectability as it became one of the largest and fastest-growing movements of the 1970s. TM is defined as a state of restful alertness from which one is said to emerge with added energy and greater mind-body coordination. It is practiced during two daily periods of twenty minutes each. The meditator sits comfortably with eyes closed and mentally repeats a Sanskrit word called a "mantra."

Table 9-4
The Mechanics of Meditation

1. Sit in a comfortable position in a quiet environment, eyes closed.

2. Deeply relax all muscles.

3. Concentrate on breathing in and out through your nose. As you breathe out, repeat a single syllable, sound, or word such as "one" silently to yourself.

4. Disregard other thoughts, adopt a passive attitude, and do not try to "force" anything to happen.

5. Practice twice daily for twenty-minute periods at least two hours after any meal. (The digestive process seems to interfere with the elicitation of the expected changes.)

SOURCE: Adapted from Benson, 1975.

Maharishi and his movement maintain that the technique of TM can be learned only from specially trained TM teachers, who charge a substantial fee. One of the pioneer researchers into the effects of TM, Herbert Benson, a Harvard cardiologist, disagrees (1975). He believes that the same kind of meditation can be self-taught with a one-page instruction sheet, achieving the same measurable results (see Table 9-4).

The goal of TM is to bring about greater use of an individual's full potential. Those who practice TM report that they have more physical energy, are more mentally alert, less tense, and better able to cope with stress. There are also reports of improved physical health as a result of regular and sustained TM practice.

Effects of Meditation. Scientific research into the effects of TM indicates that there are direct physical responses to meditation. These changes include decreased rate of metabolism (decreased oxygen consumption) and an increase in alpha waves (slow brain-wave patterns). Although TM was initially introduced as a technique for expanding consciousness, the current emphasis is on reducing stress and achieving such special effects as lowering blood pressure and increasing energy and powers of concentration.

The research publicized by the TM movement is open to criticism. The fact that many of the researchers are dedicated meditators themselves makes it possible that their results and interpretations may be unintentionally biased. Perhaps most important, the characteristic brain-wave pattern that the TM movement claims to be a sign of the "alert reverie" produced by meditation does not appear to be unique to meditation (Pagano et al., 1976). It can occur, for example, in hypnosis when a state of deep relaxation is suggested. And Benson's (1975) relaxation technique (see Table 9-4) produces the same reductions in oxygen consumption and respiration rate that are produced during transcendental meditation without the expense and the complex rituals of meditation training. In reply, those committed to the movement argue that TM produces a wide range of more fundamental changes than relaxation, including a tremendous improvement in the quality of life. Perhaps because the subjective experience produced by meditation may appear unique to the meditators, they often continue to claim that meditation is a distinct state of consciousness in spite of the contradictory physiological evidence.

The Uses of Meditation. Meditation has been practiced throughout the ages, usually within a religious context. It seems to have few undesirable side effects, and many subjectively positive effects have been reported by its practitioners. However, most researchers agree that meditation should not be practiced in excess (more than the prescribed two brief periods a day), that it cannot be substituted entirely for sleep, and that it should be used only with medical care and supervision in the treatment of such disorders as high blood pressure. For many meditators, the most important use of meditation is to achieve the mystical experience (discussed in *In Focus 9.2*).

The Person's Experience and the Unconscious

For many years most psychologists slighted people's perceptions and constructs and did not consider them as phenomena of interest in their own right. They preferred, instead, to infer what dispositions and motives might underlie the person's phenomenology and behavior.

The historical neglect of the subject's viewpoint probably has many reasons. One was the belief that because of unconscious distortions and defenses, people's self-appraisals were biased and inaccurate. Some psychologists thus refrained from studying the perceptions, concepts, and reasons of the individual because they felt these data were not really scientific. But it is entirely legitimate philosophically and logically to take account of individuals' reported subjective perceptions—the rules

Group meditation.

Achievement of the special state of consciousness claimed by various methods of meditation appears to depend on stopping the flow of consciousness. It is as if the normal stream of consciousness is like an ongoing motion picture film, while in meditation one stops the motion, freezes a single frame, concentrates on it, and holds it focused in consciousness (e.g., Mandler, 1975; Ornstein, 1972).

In Zen one moves to this state of "stopping the flow" by exercises in which one starts by counting breaths and then concentrates on breathing itself. In Yoga (as in TM) one uses a *mantra* (words which repeat easily). As Ornstein (1972) notes, many prayers also consist of repetitive, monotonous chants. In his view the common theme underlying diverse methods of meditation is that in each there is an active restriction of awareness to a "single, unchanging process," and a withdrawal of attention from ordinary thought. The crucial step seems to be to

Table 9-5
Some Qualities Claimed for the Mystical Experience

Quality	Description
Unity	The hallmark of the mystic experience: experiencing oneself as one with the universe or with God.
Ineffability	The impossibility of describing the experience in words or by reference to experiences of ordinary life.
Intense realness and feelings of absolute truth	Sensations and ideas seem as real as objects do ordinarily. Insights are intuitively felt to be a more fundamental form of reality than the phenomena of ordinary consciousness.
Sacredness	Sense of awe, reverence, inspiration.
Unusual percepts	Perceptions such as of encompassing light and infinite energy which seem very distinct from perceptions of the phenomena of the natural world.

they use and the reasons they give to explain their own actions (T. Mischel, 1964). It is not legitimate, however, to assume that these rules and reasons are useful bases for predicting what individuals will do—their behavior—in other situations. The links between persons' reported feelings and beliefs and their other behaviors must be demonstrated empirically.

Another reason for neglecting the subject's viewpoint in personality study was the difficulty of finding objective methods of studying private experiences. But while such experiences are obviously difficult to study, they demand attention and are extremely important. Objecting to the neglect of the "subject's" private experience in psychology, the phenomenological orientation in the last few decades has sought to explore the individual's perceptions and personal constructs. This movement, under the leadership of such theorists as Rogers and Kelly, has had a major impact on the study of personality.

maintain a single object as the focus of awareness during a long period of time.

The various meditation methods also appear to share a common purpose: they all are devoted to creating or enhancing a subjective state that is an essentially mystical experience. As with other experiences, it is difficult to communicate just what is felt, and it is impossible to "prove it" in any objective sense. While there are many variations in reports about mystical experiences, certain qualities are mentioned frequently, as summarized in Table 9-5. It seems likely that rather than a single mystical experience there are many varieties of these experiences. The particular one that is felt will depend on the particular person's interpretations of the total situation at the moment. Our cognitions and expectations are crucial in deciding what is a "peak experience," "a mystical experience," or a "high."

Table 9-5 *(continued)*

Quality	Description
Transcendence of time and space	Loss of usual time sense and of three-dimensional perspective.
Paradoxicality	Experiences that violate the laws of logic but are felt to be true. For example, something has both a quality (personal, for example) and its opposite (impersonal).
Transiency	Mystical consciousness is temporary; the person returns to everyday consciousness.
Positive changes in attitudes and behavior	As a result of mystical experiences, individuals report renewed self-confidence, greater acceptance of self and openness with others, greater commitment to values, and expanded awareness and appreciation.

SOURCE: Deikman, 1972; Pahnke & Richards, 1972.

Although the phenomenological orientation focuses on the subject's viewpoint, in some of its variations it also seeks to infer his or her unconscious characteristics and conflicts. For example, Carl Rogers in some of his formulations (e.g., 1963), has emphasized integration, unity, and people's achieving congruence with their "inner organismic processes." Rogers thought that these organismic processes were often unconscious. As a result of unfortunate socialization procedures in our culture persons often become dissociated, "consciously behaving in terms of static constructs and abstractions and unconsciously behaving in terms of the actualizing tendency" (Rogers, 1963, p. 20).

Encounter groups (Schutz, 1967) also pay considerable attention to unconscious processes. In this sense they also depend, just as psychodynamic theorists do, on clinical inferences about the person's behaviors as signs whose meaning individuals themselves do not know consciously. The emphasis on interpretation of underlying meanings is evident in this excerpt from a typical introduction to an encounter session provided by the "trainer" (leader):

> . . . you, not me, decide what to do in here, such as the topic you want to talk about or the activities you try . . . but I can be counted on to ask, "What's going on?" The idea is to try to understand not only what we do or say—the content level—but also the feelings underneath, the processes going on (Lakin, 1972, p. 20).

Except for the fact that the setting is a group in which the members will be active and participate in the interpretation, this orientation may not be very different from the type supplied in more traditional psychotherapy. As such, the problems of reliability and validity found in connection with clinical judgment (Chapter 3) apply here just as strongly. It of course may be argued that group members are always entirely free to reject any interpretations they feel do not fit them. But such "resistance" may require more independence than can be expected realistically. To try to guard against poor group practices, many advocates of encounter experiences note the importance of the leader's competence and experience and urge that prospective members choose their groups with the greatest care, cautioning "Let the buyer beware!"

To the extent that psychologists accept the idea that unconscious processes are key determinants, and rely on clinical judgment to infer them, they face all the dilemmas previously discussed in the context of clinical judgment. But no methodological difficulties should deter psychologists from listening more closely to what their "subjects" can tell them.

SUMMARY

1. The assessment techniques discussed in this chapter represent attempts to study the person's subjective experience within the framework of scientific rules. Most phenomenologically oriented personality psychologists try to bring the individual's private experiences into the public domain by studying subjective experiences with objective techniques. This chapter has shown that the phenomenological orientation to personality has available a variety of methods for studying personal meanings and experiences objectively. The phenomenological approach hence is not merely a point of view about personality; it also offers distinctive techniques for studying persons.

2. Gary W.'s self-conceptualization serves as an example of the raw data of phenomenology. In the phenomenological view, the person may be his or her own best assessor. Research indicates that self-assessment has yielded predictions as accurate as those from more sophisticated personality tests, from combinations of tests, from clinical judgments, and from complex statistical analyses. Thus the person may be a good predictor of his or her own behavior for such diverse outcomes as success in college, in jobs, and in psychotherapy.

3. One especially useful technique for obtaining a person's self-appraisal is the Q-sort. These Q-sorts may be used for self-description, to describe the ideal self, or to describe a relationship.

4. The interview has been favored by phenomenologically oriented psychologists. Through empathy the interviewer tries to explore the persons's feelings and self-concepts and to see the world from his or her framework and viewpoint. Content analysis has been used by Carl Rogers and others in research on processes in the interview.

5. The "semantic differential" is a rating technique that permits the objective assessment of the meaning of the rater's words and concepts. Research with these scales reveals an evaluative, a potency, and an activity factor. These three factors are similar to those found often in trait ratings of persons.

6. The Role Construct Repertory (Rep) Test was devised by George Kelly to systematically study personal constructs. The test tries to explore the subjective dimensions of similarity among events (people or things) and the subjective opposites of those dimensions as the individual construes them. Interviews and other techniques (such as the TAT) also may be used to elaborate personal constructs more fully. A personal construct conceptualization of Gary W. illustrates some of the main features of the personal construct approach to phenomenology.

7. Recently attention has been given to the importance of nonverbal expressions, movements, and gestures.

8. The phenomenological orientation also has influenced views of what constitutes healthy personality and it has significant practical applications for personality change. Most influential have been Rogers' client-centered therapy and a variety of encounter group experiences. These methods offer potential gains for some people but may be hazardous under certain conditions.

9. In other directions, efforts have been made to explore the use of meditation to change consciousness and to increase personal awareness.

10. Usually phenomenological analyses focus on experience and perceptions. Sometimes, however, extensive inferences are made about unconscious problems and conflicts beyond the individual's awareness. Then the psychologist faces all the problems encountered in psychodynamic efforts to make clinical inferences. It is necessary to demonstrate the reliability and validity of the clinician's inferences, regardless of his or her particular theoretical orientation.

Chapter 10

Social Cognition, the Self, and Emotion

The phenomenological approach is currently pursued in two quite different directions. Its most direct influence has been on clinical practice and humanistically-oriented forms of enhancing personal growth and self-actualization. This line of influence was stimulated mostly by the ideas of Rogers and Maslow, and some of these applications were noted in Chapters 8 and 9. A second direction has been more indirect, although equally important in psychology. It consists of a renewed interest by researchers in such phenomenologically-favored topics as the self, emotion, and the intuitive expertise and limits of the lay person's naive theories and social perceptions. This work, often on the edge between personality and social psychology, owes much historically to George Kelly, a pioneer of cognitive psychology; to Kurt Lewin (p. 196), a founder of social psychology; and to Gordon Allport, a leader in the study of the "self." It might, however, seem very alien to Rogers and Maslow. A main theme in this stream of research is "social cognition."

"Social cognition" refers to how we perceive, know, and understand social stimuli, including ourselves and other people. A focus on social cognition and on people as "knowers" and "perceivers" of behavior, including their own emotions and behavior, is, of course, central to some of the phenomenological, cognitive, and self-theories discussed in Chapters 8 and 9.

Recall, for example, Kelly's (1955) belief that in everyday life all people, not just professional psychologists, function like scientists. They observe themselves and the world, develop expectations, try to make sense of their experience and form theories. The ways we see the social world—our social cognitions—are the bases for how we relate to each other and to ourselves. Our perceptions and judgments of people, of their social behavior and emotions, and of ourselves, are the topics of this chapter. The results of research on these topics help to extend the value of the phenomenological and cognitive approach in new directions. You will see that while the research in this chapter owes much to the phenomenological orientation, it has gone far beyond it. Both its methods and its findings would surprise some of the original theorists discussed earlier—but that can be a promising sign of progress.

FORMING IMPRESSIONS

To understand how enduring impressions about the self are formed, one may begin by seeing how we form impressions about other people. Indeed the processes of forming self-impressions and of forming impressions of others may be identical (Bem, 1972; Kelley, 1973).

When you think about other people you do not describe their actions objectively, nor do you analyze their specific responses in relation to particular stimuli. Instead, you form broad impressions about their characteristics as people, evaluate their intentions, and assess their worth.

Causal Attributions: Why Did He (She) Do It?

As a first step in judging others, we often ask ourselves why they acted as they did. Why did she not keep our appointment? Why did he seem so distant last night? Why did the professor seem to make a special effort to chat with me at the party? These questions all inquire into the causes of people's behavior: they deal with the *causal attribution* of behavior. They ask, what is responsible for particular actions, to what can a given pattern of behavior be attributed? In our interactions with each other each person is both a source of behavior and an "attributor," an analyzer of the reasons underlying behavior, including his or her own. The answers to our questions about attribution—about the causes of behavior—influence our subsequent understanding of the interaction, our feelings about the other person, and our choice of further action.

In everyday relationships, judgments of a person's actions depend on the perceived intentions of the actor (Heider, 1958; Weiner, 1974). Whether the actions seem deliberate or accidental is especially important. Did the waiter spill the soup accidentally, or was he deliberately rude? If you trip over my foot, your reaction will depend on whether you think I deliberately tripped you. Similarly, a dropped plate, an error in making change at the cash register, a passing friend who does not say hello—the meaning of each of these acts, and hence their impact, depends on the observer's inferences about the intentions motivating it (Jones & Davis, 1965; Kelley, 1973).

Attribution Biases: Internal Causes

Although people can and do distinguish between different types of causes, they show systematic bias toward certain kinds of attributions. One of these biases is toward internal (dispositional) rather than external (situational) causes to explain behavior.

We readily use behavioral cues to infer purposeful dispositions and motives in others and ourselves, even when the cues are trivial and momentary. The simplest behavior may be taken as a sign of underlying motives and traits as the perceiver quickly jumps from observed acts to hypothetical dispositions. Even moving geometric shapes may be credited with purposes and emotions ranging from anger through fear (Michotte, 1954).

When observers watch a disk, a large triangle, and a small triangle moving about, they tend to interpret the shapes as if they were people embroiled in interpersonal conflicts and competitions: the large triangle is viewed as aggressive, the small one as heroic, and the disk as timid and feminine (Heider & Simmel, 1944). Obviously people do not really believe that such moving shapes or cartoon pictures have psychological qualities, but they do readily endow almost any agent of behavior with motives, wishes, and traits, especially when conditions are ambiguous.

Indeed, historians tell us that ancient physicists often personified inanimate objects by giving them dispositions and attributing motives and wills to them. According to Butterfield (1965), Aristotle contended that a falling body accelerated because it became more jubilant as it approached the ground. While modern man is more sophisticated, the tendency to attribute motives as causes, especially in explaining the behavior of other people, persists.

When explaining other people's behavior, we easily invoke their consistent personality dispositions as causes. Harry is the type of person who is quiet at parties; Mary had a car accident because she is careless. However, when asked to explain our own behavior, we may be more alert to specific conditions: "I was quiet because the party was boring." Jones and Nisbett (1971) believe that "actors tend to attribute the causes of their behavior to stimuli inherent in the situation while observers tend to attribute behavior to stable dispositions of the actor" (p. 58).

One possible reason for this seeming paradox may be that when we try to understand ourselves, we have more information available concerning the diversity and complexity of the situations that we encounter in our lives. But because we observe others in only narrow contexts, we may tend to overgeneralize from their behavior in those few instances and treat every sample of their behavior as if it were typical.

In sum, we tend to overattribute consistent dispositions to others and to minimize the role of the situation in our explanations of their behavior (Nisbett & Ross, 1980). Once these attributions have been made, we tend to stick to them even in the face of strong disconfirming evidence, sometimes believing our incorrect intuitions more than the objective data (Ross, 1977).

The Illusion of Control and Meaningfulness

Although we may tend to explain our own behavior in situational terms while explaining others' behavior in trait terms, this does not imply that we see our actions as due to chance. On the contrary, there is a strong bias to see everyone's behavior as meaningful, orderly, and *not* the result of chance even when it is random.

This common attributional bias is known to anyone who has ever watched behavior in a casino. If you watched such behavior closely, you probably noticed how often gamblers act as if they can control chance by shaking the dice just right, or waiting to approach the roulette wheel at the perfect moment, or pulling the slot machine levers with a special little ritual. Gamblers are not unique in believing they can control chance events.

Even when something is clearly the result of chance (like the cards one draws in a poker game), people may see it as potentially controllable and not just luck. There is a deep human tendency to see the world as predictable, orderly, and controllable rather than random and chaotic. We expect a "just world" (Heider, 1958), a world in which the things that happen to people are deserved and caused by them—even things like whether or not they win a lottery, get cancer, or are raped and murdered. Much research (reviewed by Langer, 1977) suggests that people often do not discriminate between objectively controllable and uncontrollable events. Instead they seem to have the "illusion of control," acting as if they can even control events that actually are pure chance. Moreover, this bias is self-enhancing: we are more likely to see ourselves as causally responsible for our actions when they have positive rather than negative outcomes. When we do well or win, it is to our personal credit; when we do badly or lose, we could not help it (e.g., Fitch, 1970; Wortman et al., 1973). Even when outcomes are negative, as in a tragic accident, we may find it hard to cope with events unless we somehow can see them as "just," meaningful, and orderly.

Expectations and Implicit Personality Theories

In our culture, individuals who wear glasses tend to be seen as more intelligent, industrious, and reliable than those who do not (Manz & Lueck, 1968); attractive children are credited as being more intelligent, popular, and likely to go to college (Clifford & Walster, 1973); and if a woman's glance is directed straight ahead, making eye contact with the perceiver, she will be judged more favorably than if her eyes are downcast (Tankard, 1970). Thus, people who share a particular culture develop many similar expectations about stimulus meanings and learn similar interpretations of all sorts of cues.

The resulting stereotypes may be very useful for certain forms of communication because they allow us to categorize people and experiences easily. They may also be tragic, as when physical handicaps or deficits become the grounds for ridicule and rejection among children and ethnic cues become the basis for bitter prejudice. But for good or ill, the expectations of the perceiver influence the perceptions formed of people.

The perceiver's ideas about what traits go with or relate to other traits seem to form larger networks of relationships. These patterns of expected associations are called *implicit personality theories* (Schneider, 1973). Our implicit personality theories may lead us to overgeneralize from the behaviors we actually observe and infer that when a person seems to have one trait that other related traits will also be there, whether or not they really are (Berman & Kenny, 1976). On the basis of a few observations (watching a couple of friendly acts performed by an attractive woman with a warm smile, for example) we may begin to form an impression of a total consistent personality that goes far beyond the actual information we have.

The significance of the perceiver's theory was highlighted in a study in which boys and girls living together at a camp gave free verbal descriptions of each other. The investigators coded these descriptions into categories (Dornbusch et al., 1965). There were several conditions: either one child described two others, or two children described the same child, or two children described two different others. The most similar descriptions were found when the same perceiver (A) rated different children (B and C); these descriptions overlapped more than when the same child (B) was described by different perceivers (A and C). The total results thus showed that the children's categories and interpersonal perceptions depended more on the perceiver than on the child who was being perceived. Other research also indicates that while ratings by others generally do relate to the qualities of the rated person (Block, 1971), they are heavily colored by the ideas and expectations of the rater (e.g., Mischel, 1968, 1973) and by the rater's notions of what traits go with what other traits (Shweder, 1975)—that is, expectations about types of people.

Does this mean that our categories about other people are merely illusions in the head of the perceiver? Such pure illusions seem unlikely. Certain patterns of behavior probably tend to occur more often in reality; therefore, we also learn to expect them. For example, there may be a tendency for sociable behavior to co-occur with talkative and active behavior in certain types of persons (e.g., extraverts), just as sweet songs, feathers, and wings tend to co-occur in certain birds (e.g., canaries). The behavior of people is far from perfectly patterned, but it is also far from random. Ideas about peoples' traits arise from an interaction between the beliefs of observers and the characteristics of the observed (Cantor & Mischel, 1979).

The Uses and Abuses of Categorizing People

Our categories about the likely traits and behaviors of different types of people have several functions. First, and perhaps most importantly, such categories allow us to structure and give coherence to our knowledge about people in general, providing expectations about typical behaviors for different types of people. Such categories guide and make more efficient our understanding of people's behavior and attributes. Having typed a person as being more or less a particular sort (e.g., an extravert, a "P.R. type," a neurotic), one is guided by general expectations about what that type of person is or is not likely to do. This reduces the range of actions expected from the person in particular situations ("Jack is the sort of man who always would be fun to have at a party"). Finally, when necessary, these categories can provide information to fill out one's incomplete impressions. All of these functions simplify and make more efficient our knowledge of people. In this sense, they are "cognitively economical." For example, when someone fits well in a particular category like "extravert" (or has been labeled as a member of that category), not only does memory for details of the person's behavior improve in general (e.g., Cantor & Mischel, 1977, 1979), but also attributes commonly associated with that category are attributed more freely to that person (e.g., Snyder & Uranowitz, 1978; Tsujimoto, 1978).

The functions of categorizing are sometimes abbreviated as "cognitive economics." These cognitive economics are a mixed blessing. A reliance on preconceived categories to structure one's perceptions of people has its costs as well as its value. One cost is that one tends to attribute the characteristics associated with a category to each member, even when those characteristics may not fit the individual ("He's a Republican; therefore conservative." "She was a mental patient; therefore unstable"). Such attributions may constrain and bias our perceptions and actions toward the people we categorize. By searching for "good fits" to our general type cate-

Six candidates for a school board election. From their appearance, what impressions do you get of their probable attitudes and personal qualities?

Stereotypes are formed quickly—sometimes with unfortunate results.

gories, we may misjudge—and mistreat—individuals who do not really fit our preconceptions (see *In Focus 10.1*).

The expectancies or hypotheses we form about people may affect not only how we feel and act, but also how other people begin to act and reciprocate. Ideas in the head of the perceiver may gradually shape the responses of the person who is perceived and not just the one who is doing the perceiving (Snyder, 1979).

Evidence for these claims comes from a series of experiments by Snyder and Swann (1978) with college women. Some women volunteers served as interviewers, others were interviewed, and all conversations were recorded. Some interviewers were led initially to hypothesize that they were interviewing either an extravert or an introvert. In fact, they were assigned interviewees purely by chance.

In Focus 10.1
Social Inference: The Fallible Judge

"Base-rate data" are data or information about the average incidence (frequency) of an event in the population. For example, in one mental hospital the base rate for suicide attempts is less than one percent, meaning that among the patients in that hospital fewer than one percent actually attempt suicide. Suppose you learn that Tom W., a patient in the hospital, is described as "a very depressive type," often thinks about the uselessness of his life, was recently deserted by his wife, complains constantly about his unhappiness and misery, and prefers to stay indoors by himself all day. If asked to predict the probability that Tom would commit suicide, you might well be tempted to predict a considerably higher likelihood than the one percent base rate suggests. If so, you would be acting like most people, including well-trained clinicians, because most of us tend to ignore base-rate information in favor of

more vivid or salient data, such as personality descriptions, even if they are sketchy and of dubious reliability (e.g., Kahneman & Tversky, 1973; Nisbett & Borgida, 1975). When information comes in the form of dry background statistics, base rates, or abstract logical arguments, it may have little impact on our concrete social judgments, even when the data are solidly reliable and logically should be persuasive.

Thus, Nisbett and his associates (1976) found that when people are asked to predict who had helped a stranger in distress, they were swayed by their intuitive impressions of the potential helpers' personalities while totally ignoring the relevant base rates—base rates showing that surprisingly few people had helped at all. The base rates should have led them to *not* predict helping; the personality information won out, however, and led them to *over*predict helping on

Interviewers who thought that they were interviewing an extravert (or introvert in other conditions) asked questions designed to confirm their expectations. Most interestingly, in their search for evidence to confirm their hypotheses, they unwittingly induced the interviewed person to act in ways that would confirm their expectations. That is, the interviewer's hypotheses led the interviewers to behave in ways that forced confirmation from the other person regardless of the other person's actual personality. Specifically, when the interviewer hypothesized that she was interviewing an extravert, that person soon began to act more like an extravert (more confident, more poised, more energetic, as rated by independent judges). Conversely, when the interviewer hypothesized that she was interviewing an introvert, that person's behavior tended to shift toward greater introversion, thereby helping to confirm the interviewer's introversion hypothesis. As the researchers note, to the degree that people use strategies that coerce confirmation for their hypotheses about other people, they may be creating a world in which their beliefs about those people can never be proved wrong.

Our stereotypes and expectations about personality types can even produce "retrospective distortions," leading us to reorganize how we recall information learned earlier. This point was illustrated in a study that began by having subjects read a narrative case history about the life of a woman named Betty K (Snyder & Uranowitz, 1978). This account contained a mass of information about Betty's early home life, relations with parents, and social life in high school and college (for example, she went on dates in high school but did not have a steady boyfriend). After they read the narrative, some subjects were led to believe that during her

the part of people who seemed like helpful types.

The same researchers also compared the impact of reliable statistical information with less reliable but more concrete, vivid firsthand information on college students' choice of courses. Specifically, they let some subjects (in the base-rate condition) read ratings of courses on five-point scales (from excellent to poor), based on the evaluations culled from the 26 to 142 students who had taken the courses before. A second group heard a few brief remarks about the courses from two or three students firsthand. The subjects' course choices were much more influenced by the less extensive but more vivid data from the "face-to-face" remarks they heard than by the base rates from *all* the people who had taken the course. As the authors noted, we all often ignore the kinds of statistics and abstract information

that are supposed to be logically compelling in favor of less reliable but more vivid, concrete, emotionally involving data. That may be why, for example, so many people ignored ponderous AMA statistics about the importance of early detection for cancer but were personally moved to seek checkups when the mastectomies of celebrities were publicized.

Vivid, concrete facts are more influential than pallid abstractions. We can also see the importance of "concreteness" and of highly individualized or personalized experience when we look at the perception of responsibility. While we may be remarkably unmoved by reports about thousands of people killed in earthquakes, wars, or other disasters we may become personally distressed by a vivid concrete description of the plight of a single victim.

senior year of college Betty adopted a lesbian life style; others were told that during her senior year she fell in love with a man whom she married. Later all subjects were tested for their ability to recognize accurately the many things they had read about Betty. The results indicated that the "lesbian" or "married" stereotype significantly influenced their memory. Subjects selectively reconstructed and affirmed those events that confirmed and strengthened their new view of Betty. For example, those who thought Betty was now a lesbian remembered and affirmed those aspects of her past consistent with a lesbian stereotype.

Combining Information

Almost any cues—sex, clothing, facial expression, attractiveness, context—may be used in forming an impression. And the first available cues obtained about a person, even when they are minimal, tend to be given considerable weight, often biasing one to take later information less seriously. In other words, the sequence of the information is important. For example, if subjects learn that a stranger is intelligent, industrious, impulsive, critical, stubborn, and envious, their impression of him is more positive, and they more readily attribute other good traits to him than if they learn that he is envious, stubborn, critical, impulsive, industrious, and intelligent (Asch, 1946).

A great deal of research has explored the processes through which new information may be added, combined, and integrated into the total perception. In general, first impressions tend to be very important and are given extra weight in the total impression. This bias in favor of initial information is called the *primacy effect*. The first pieces of information may serve as a kind of conceptual anchor that influences the interpretation of subsequent information.

The most promising theory proposes a process in which every piece of information is averaged into the total impression, although later information may be given a lesser weight and discounted (e.g., Anderson, 1965, 1974). This *averaging model* suggests that the total dimension such as "liking," appears to involve an averaging of all the information given. Consider, for example, how much you would like a person who is described as sincere, ambitious, honest, warm, unpopular, and shy. Research indicates that the final liking one has for a stimulus person is a function of the averaging of the evaluation of each trait that the stimulus person appears to have (Anderson, 1974).

The same processes that influence our impressions of others also affect how we come to view ourselves. The next section considers this process, as we turn to research on the self and self-conceptions.

SELF-CONCEPTS: SEEING OURSELVES

For the phenomenological theorists, "the self" is a most important concept. William James (1890) almost a century ago suggested two different aspects of the self. First, one may think of the self as the *actor* or "subject"; this is the "I" who knows and does things. The "I" is an active observer; the "I" also acts in the world and tries to control it. The second aspect of the self is an *object;* it is the "Me," the observed. The "Me" is what one sees when attention is focused on the self.

In the course of growth the child develops and increasingly rich sense of himself or herself as an active agent, an "I" separate from other people and objects. A sense also develops of a "Me" that has defining features and qualities. The child learns to identify the characteristics that define his or her self, and comes even to recognize how the "Me" changes with age. In this process a self-theory develops. This theory is a construction, a set of concepts about the self. It is created by the child from experience, but it in turn affects future experience (Harter, 1983; Epstein, 1973, 1983; Wiley, 1979).

The individual's self-concepts are not a simple mirror-like reflection of some absolute reality. Rather, self-concepts, like impressions of other people and of the world, involve an integration and organization of a tremendous amount of information (Harter, 1983). Although self-concepts are not a mirror of reality, they are correlated with the outcomes that the person has obtained throughout the past and expects to obtain in the future (Wiley, 1979). The roots of our self-concepts are the impressions and evaluations that other people have of us in our interactions with them through the course of life.

Self-Schemata

Self-concepts, also called *"self-schemata"* (Markus, 1977), include generalizations about oneself like "I am an independent person" or "I tend to lean on people." Self-schemata are cognitions that arise from past experiences and, once formed, guide how we deal with new information related to the self. To illustrate, if you have strong self-schemata about being extremely dependent, passive, and conforming, you would process and remember information relevant to those schemata more quickly and effectively than do people for whom those schemata are not personally relevant (Markus, 1977). People have better recall for information about traits that they believe describe them than for traits that are not self-descriptive (Rogers, 1977; Rogers, Kuiper, & Kirker, 1977). Thus we give things relevant to the self special cognitive treatment, for example by being more oriented and attentive toward them.

Self-Esteem

One of the most critical aspects of the self-concept is "self-esteem" (Harter, 1983). Self-esteem refers to the individual's personal judgment of his or her own worth (e.g., Coopersmith, 1967). Epstein (1973) reasons that the major function of the individual's self-theory is to optimize positive experience (pleasure rather than pain), especially by maintaining sufficient self-esteem. Self-esteem is such an important aspect of the self-concept that the two terms are often used as if they were the same. Although "self-esteem" is sometimes discussed as if it were a single entity, persons evaluate their functioning in different areas of life discriminatively. These self-evaluations reflect in part the feedback that they continuously get from the environment as they learn about themselves (see *In Focus 10.2*).

To explore the nature of self-esteem in personality development, Coopersmith (1967, 1968) studied a sample of normal, middle-class urban boys from preadolescence to early adulthood. He examined their family backgrounds through interviews and exposed the children to diverse personality and ability tests. For example, he assessed how high the children set their goals in situations such as the "bean bag" study illustrated in Figure 10-1. He then analyzed the

Figure 10-1
Self-Esteem and Goal-Setting

The more distant the target that the child selects in the "beanbag game" the higher the score that he could win but the greater the risk of failing.
From Coopersmith (1968.)

Figure 10-2
Percentage of Children in Each Self-Esteem Group Rated Negatively by Their Mothers

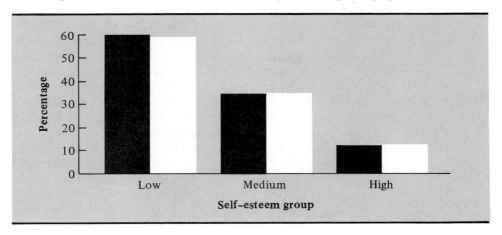

Children with lower self-esteem were appraised more often by their mothers as having marked, frequent problems (black bars) rather than limited, infrequent ones, and also as being relatively destructive (white bars) rather than nondestructive.
Based on data from Coopersmith (1967.)

patterns that emerged.

His results suggest that children with high self-esteem tend to be those who are more esteemed and more competent; they also tend to be those who are exposed to parental models who display high self-esteem (Coopersmith, 1967, 1968). Some of the specific characterizations associated with self-esteem in the boys are summarized in Figure 10-2.

Coopersmith found that if he categorized the boys into three levels or degrees of self-esteem (low, medium, and high), certain traits seemed to best fit each level. Although there were many exceptions, and the relationships generally were of only modest strength, some consistent trends emerged (see Figure 10-2).

Coopersmith noted some of the trait terms that seem to best fit boys of different degrees of self-esteem; examples of these relationships are summarized in Table 10-1. As these examples suggest, the high-self-esteem youngsters seemed to be the ones who felt and behaved more competently. Presumably these qualities helped them to achieve more recognition and self-satisfaction and, in turn, their self-esteem was strengthened by their achievements.

Table 10-1
Examples of Trait Terms Characterizing Boys of High and Low Self-Esteem

Self-Esteem	Descriptive Trait Terms
High	Active, expressive, successful; little childhood destructiveness and not much anxiety; self-confident, optimistic.
Low	Discouraged, felt depressed, unlovable, fearful of angering others, isolated from others; shrank away from being noticed.

SOURCE: Based on Coopersmith, 1968.

Expectancies for Success

In one approach, self-concepts about one's adequacy may be thought of as consisting of both highly situation-specific, self-relevant performance expectancies and more generalized expectancies. According to Rotter (1954), "specific expectancies" refer to the individual's expectancies that a particular set of behaviors on his or her part will lead to particular outcomes (reinforcements) in the specific situation. "Generalized expectancies" refer to somewhat broader expectations regarding the probable outcomes of the person's behavior based on past experiences and total history in similar situations. Both kinds of expectancies regarding future performance depend on information about past performance. The precise relationships between performance, performance feedback, and changes in the person's expectancies about herself have been studied extensively (e.g., Weiner, 1972).

While self-concept changes are related to the feedback that individuals get about themselves, the relationship may be influenced by many important variables (Wiley, 1979). For example, people who are highly oriented to achievement and who are anxious to avoid failure may react quite differently to failure experiences than do people who are low in achievement striving (e.g., Atkinson & Feather, 1966; Heckhausen, 1969; Weiner, 1965, 1974). Depending on such moderating variables, the person may adopt many different strategies to cope with performance feedback. Hence self-concept changes are not a direct reflection of performance feedback; they are influenced by many other factors (e.g., Harter, 1983).

Self-Efficacy

Self-efficacy is a more specific concept than self-esteem. Self-efficacy refers to the individual's belief that he or she can successfully execute the behaviors required by a particular situation. Such perceptions of one's own efficacy may importantly guide and direct one's behavior. The close connection between high self-efficacy expectations and effective performance is illustrated in studies of people who received various treatments to help reduce their fear of snakes. A consistently high association was found between the degree to which persons improved from treatment (becoming able to handle snakes fearlessly) and their perceived self-efficacy (Bandura, 1977). So if we assess perceived self-efficacy, (asking people to specifically predict their ability to do a given act successfully), we can predict the relevant behavior with impressive accuracy (Bandura & Adams, 1977). Results of this kind suggest strong and clear links between self-perceptions of one's competence and the ability to actually behave competently. Once again we see that when the right questions are asked people can be excellent predictors of their own behaviors. The concept of self-efficacy is important for understanding how people cope and deal with life's challenges. We will refer to it again in later chapters.

The Self-Perception of Helplessness versus Mastery

When people believe that there is nothing they can do to control negative or painful outcomes they may come to expect that they are *helpless* (Seligman, 1975). That is, they may learn to expect that aversive outcomes are uncontrollable, that there is nothing they can do. In that state, they also may become apathetic, despondent, and slow to learn that they actually *can* control the outcomes. Such states of helplessness may generalize, persist, and involve feelings of depression or sadness. The state of helplessness may have especially negative and persistent effects when the person believes that it reflects his or her own enduring, widespread internal qualities (e.g., "I'm incompetent") rather than that it is to more momentary, external, or situational considerations (Abramson, Seligman, & Teasdale, 1978). Thus the person's attributions have an important part in determining how a state of helplessness affects that person.

Following frustration in the form of failure on a task, some individuals "fall apart" and their performance deteriorates. But other people actually improve. What causes these two different types of responses to the frustration of failure? One important cause may be how the person interprets the reasons for the experience. Children who believe their failure is due to lack of ability (called "helpless children") were found to perform more poorly after they experienced failure than did those who see their failure as due to lack of effort (called "mastery-oriented" children). Indeed, the "mastery-oriented" children often actually performed better after failure. Most encouraging, training the helpless children (those who attribute their failure to lack of ability) to view outcomes as the result of their own effort, results in their improved performance after a failure experience (Dweck, 1975).

When faced with failure, helpless children seem to have self-defeating thoughts that virtually guarantee further failure. This became clear when groups of helpless and mastery-oriented fifth-graders were instructed "to think out loud" while solving problems. When children in the two groups began to experience failure, they soon said very different things to themselves. The helpless children made statements reflecting their loss or lack of ability, such as "I'm getting confused" and "I never did have a good memory" (Diener & Dweck, 1978, p. 458). None of the mastery-oriented children made lack-of-ability statements. Instead, these children seemed to search for a remedy rather than for a cause for their failure. They gave themselves instructions that could improve their performance, such as "I should slow down and try to figure this out" and "The harder it gets, the harder I need to try." The mastery-oriented children also made statements about their degree of effort and concentration. The helpless children made many statements that were irrelevant to the solution and that usually were ineffective strategies for problem solving (see Table 10-2). For example, one helpless male repeatedly chose the brown-colored shape, saying "chocolate cake" in spite of the experimenter's repeated feedback of "wrong." Finally, the attitudes of the two groups toward the task differed markedly. Even after several failures, mastery-oriented children remained positive and optimistic about the possibility of success, while helpless children expressed negative feelings and resignation, declaring, for example, "I give up."

Self-Consciousness

Much of what we do is "mindless" (Langer, 1978), guided by more-or-less automatic routines or "scripts" that are familiar and require little active attention (Abelson, 1976). In a fast-food restaurant, or at a football game, for example, we tend to act out more or less automatic routines.

Under such conditions, the self plays little role and we do not experience self-

Table 10-2
Coping Strategies of Helpless and Mastery-Oriented Children

Helpless Children	Mastery-Oriented Children
Attributions for failure "I'm getting confused"	*Self-instructions to improve performance* "The harder it gets, the harder I need to try"
Solution irrelevant statements "There is a talent show this weekend, and I am going to be Shirley Temple"	*Self-monitoring statements* About degree of effort or concentration (no examples given) *Positive prognosis statements* "I've almost got it now"
Statements of negative affect "This isn't fun anymore"	*Statements of positive affect* "I love a challenge"

SOURCE: Based on Diener & Dweck, 1978.

awareness; that is, we do not focus on ourselves. But one of the distinctive properties of the self is its capacity to be conscious of itself; its ability to take itself as the object of its own attention. This idea of taking oneself as the object of one's attention is central to the theory of self-awareness (e.g., Duval & Wicklund, 1972). The theory holds that attention can be directed inward toward the self; that is, it can be "self-focused." Or, alternatively, attention can be directed outward toward the environment. Self-focus has been created experimentally simply by confronting people with a mirror (or camera lens). The self-focused individual tends to be more likely to conform to personal standards for behavior and to societal values than will the less self-aware person. And self-aware people tend to be more honest, helpful, and work harder. They also may be more aware of their dominant feelings or attributes in the situation, and generally show greater consistency and self-attention (Wicklund & Frey, 1980).

Self-focus or "self-consciousness" also has been measured as a personal disposition by questions like those shown in Table 10-3. People who are high in self-consciousness on this test do indeed seem to be more aware of themselves as objects (Carver & Scheier, 1978; Scheier & Carver, 1980), and tend to show many of the characteristics that can be induced when self-focus is created experimentally. But self-consciousness may not be a single dimension of individual differences. For some people self-consciousness is mostly a matter of how others view them, a concern with public reactions. For other individuals, however, self-consciousness is a private matter, and refers to awareness of one's own thoughts, feelings, and

Table 10-3
High Self-Consciousness Items*

Private	Public
I'm generally attentive to my inner feelings.	I'm concerned about the way I present myself.
I'm always trying to figure myself out.	I'm concerned about what other people think of me.

*Examples from the private and public subscales of the Self-Consciousness Scale
SOURCE: Fenigstein, Scheier, & Buss, 1975.

motives. Notice that different types of items are used to try to measure these two kinds of self-consciousness—a public type and a private type.

Perceived Consistency: Stability of Self

Perhaps the most compelling quality of the private or "phenomenological" self is its perceived continuity and consistency. The experience of subjective continuity in ourselves—of basic oneness and durability in the self—seems to be a fundamental feature of personality. Indeed the loss of a feeling of consistency and identity may be a chief characteristic of personality disorganization, as is seen in schizophrenic patients who sometimes report vividly experiencing two distinct selves, one of them disembodied (Laing, 1965).

It seems remarkable how each of us normally manages to reconcile seemingly diverse behaviors into one self-consistent whole. A man may steal on one occasion, lie on another, donate generously to charity on a third, cheat on a fourth, and still readily construe himself as "basically honest and moral." People often seem to be able to transform their seemingly discrepant behaviors into a constructed continuity, making unified wholes out of almost anything (Mischel, 1969). How does this process work?

Probably many complex factors are involved (Mischel, 1973, 1979), but part of the answer to this question may be that people tend to reduce cognitive inconsistencies and, in general, to simplify information so that they can deal with it (Nisbett & Ross, 1980; Tversky & Kahneman, 1974). The overall evidence from many sources (clinical, experimental, developmental, correlational) suggests that the human mind may function like an extraordinarily effective reducing valve that creates and maintains the perception of continuity even in the face of perpetual, observed changes in actual behavior. The striving for self-consistency that the phenomenologists emphasize (e.g., Rogers, 1951), has received support in the work of other researchers working on related topics (e.g., Aronson & Mettee, 1968; Cooper & Fazio, 1984; Festinger, 1957).

In general, the self-concepts reported on many personality questionnaires seem to show a good deal of stability (Byrne, 1966; Gough, 1957; Mischel, 1968). As previously discussed, personal constructs as measured by Kelly's Role Construct Repertory Test (Rep Test) also show much consistency over time (Bonarius, 1965). Thus our cognitive constructions about ourselves and the world—our personal theories about ourselves and those around us—tend to be relatively stable and resistant to change (Nisbett & Ross, 1980), as are our attitudes and values (E. L. Kelly, 1955).

THE EXPERIENCE OF EMOTIONS

Another basic quality of the self is the subjective experience of emotions; we are aware of our own feelings and of our many different emotional states. This subjective impression—of fear, joy, anger, pride, shame—is a distinctive quality of self-perception.

In the popular view emotions are the elements of life that give it intensity and zest. Love and hate, anger and fear, euphoria and depression make life colorful. Emotions seem to range from the mildest promptings to the most profound passions and from the most positive to the most negative feelings. The English vocabulary gives us names for this vast experimental range, from subtle sensations such as pleasure or annoyance to intense emotions such as ecstasy, sorrow, joy, and hate.

Bodily Changes in Emotion

Visceral or physiological reactions in the body are an important part of emotional experience. Such phrases as "took my breath away," "makes my heart race," and "choked up with emotion" suggest that emotional states involve bodily changes. In fact, the activation of the sympathetic division of the autonomic nervous system produces many of the physiological changes that we experience in intense emotional states. These bodily changes include:

1. Channeling of the blood supply to the muscles and brain.
2. Slowing down of stomach and intestinal activity.
3. Increase in heart rate and blood pressure.
4. Widening of the pupils of the eyes.
5. Increase in rates of metabolism and respiration.
6. Increase in sugar content of the blood.
7. Decrease in electrical resistance of the skin.
8. Increase in speed of the blood's ability to clot.
9. "Goose pimples" resulting from the erection of hairs on the skin.

These changes are sometimes referred to as the "fight or flight" reaction because they are considered to be the body's emergency reaction system to threat and danger. They enable the organism to cope rapidly and effectively with environmental dangers, in part by providing the alertness and energy necessary for survival in the face of attack. In humans the arousal pattern can lead to a wide variety of behaviors and can be elicited in response to situations that do not objectively endanger survival, as when you face a French examination or walk into the boss's office to ask for a raise. Bodily changes play a role in emotion, but how this works is the subject of several theories.

Theories of Emotional Experience

Several theories have been proposed to help understand what happens in emotion. Let us consider some of the major positions.

The James-Lange Theory. Historically, a central question for students of emotion has been: What is the temporal relation between physiological arousal and the perception or experience of emotional feelings? On the basis of introspection, it often seems as if such feelings as anger, excitement, fear, and joy come first and then produce the physical components of the particular emotion. We become sad and then cry; we feel happy and then laugh. But an early theory of emotion proposed the opposite sequence. William James, an American psychologist, suggested in 1890 that felt experiences follow physiological reactions. For example, we cry first and then feel sad rather than cry because we feel sad. A Danish physiologist, Carl Lange, developed similar ideas at the same time as James. To credit him also, the notion that physiological responses precede and determine emotional experience is often referred to as the *James-Lange theory* of emotion.

Cannon's Criticisms. Important objections to the James-Lange theory were made by American physiologist Walter B. Cannon (1929). He noted the frequent absence of distinct visceral changes associated with different emotions and the fact that any visceral changes often are relatively slow while many emotional experiences are immediate. Cannon also noted the occurrence of emotional experiences in surgical patients whose viscera had been separated from the central nervous system, suggesting that emotional feelings are possible in the absence of feedback to the brain from the viscera. Moreover, individuals in whom visceral changes were artificially produced (e.g., by drugs) reported emotional experiences that seemed "unreal." This finding was constructed by Cannon as evidence that visceral changes were not sufficient to produce full-blown emotional experience.

The Cognitive-Physiological Theory. Currently, the most widely accepted theory is the *cognitive-physiological theory* developed by Stanley Schachter. His research suggests that in the epinephrine experiment described below, emotion may seem to involve two factors: a diffuse physiological arousal state and the way the person interprets it.

Distinguishing Between Emotions: How Do You Know What You Feel?

Are the internal visceral responses that accompany emotional experiences different for such feelings as joy, anger, happiness, anxiety, yearning, and disgust? Most of us surely feel that emotions like fear and anger seem to involve unmistakably distinct internal cues. In accord with the subjective conviction that clearly different emotions exist, psychologists and physiologists for many years tried to differentiate emotional states into specific types and to discover the particular patterns of bodily activity that might accompany each of these states. The general result of a good deal of investigation appears to be that, though there are sometimes subtle differences in the patterns of physiological responses associated with different emotions (e.g., Ax, 1953; Tourangeau & Ellsworth, 1978), what they have in common is far more striking. A diffuse state of general physiological arousal seems to characterize different emotional experiences.

Nevertheless, we all have the subjective impression of experiencing distinctly different feelings such as anger and euphoria. How can one account for these subjectively different experiences if the bodily arousal underlying them is the same? Discriminations among emotions are influenced by situational cues and do not necessarily require distinctive visceral changes. On the basis of situational cues, the individual may label his or her state cognitively, assigning a name to the arousal.

In Focus 10.3 Recognizing Emotions Universally

Are different emotional states associated with distinctive facial expressions? In 1872 Charles Darwin proposed that certain innate and universal facial expressions of emotional states exist in man. Later, psychologists challenged this notion, maintaining that the meaning of any facial expression depends on the culture of the expresser and the observer (e.g., LaBarre,

1947; Birdwhistell, 1970). But there now is evidence for widespread agreement about the emotional meaning of certain facial expressions (Ekman, Friesen, & Ellsworth, 1972; Ekman, 1982).

In studies of thirteen literate and two isolated preliterate cultures the same facial expressions were found to be associated with the same emotions. Individuals from

Table 10-4
Judgments of Emotion in Five Cultures

	Percentage Agreeing That the Photograph Showed the Indicated Emotion				
	United States (N = 99)	Brazil (N = 40)	Chile (N = 119)	Argentina (N = 168)	Japan (N = 29)
Happiness	97%	95%	95%	98%	100%
Disgust	92%	97%	92%	92%	90%
Surprise	95%	87%	93%	95%	100%

Thus emotions may involve at least two components: a state of general physiological arousal and a cognitive appraisal of the situation (Schachter, 1964).

Often the source of emotional arousal is easy to identify. When faced by an attacking animal or by an impending car crash, the source of excitement is self-evident. The label attached to the experience in these cases depends on the source—the stimulus producing the arousal. Thus the emotional response to an attacking animal is probably *fear,* identified by the fact that a dangerous animal is approaching. Identification of the emotion also depends on the person's goal-directed response when confronted by the stimulus. For example, attempted escape

these widely different cultures were shown photographs of faces such as those shown in Table 10-4 and were asked to categorize the emotion expressed in each. There was substantial agreement in the recognition and labeling of expressions indicating happiness, sadness, anger, fear, disgust, and surprise.

The universality of facial muscle movements in emotional expression is also supported by careful recordings of these movements in individuals from widely different cultures (Ekman, 1972). Americans and New Guineans asked to show how they would look in various situations (e.g., "Your child has died") made similar facial muscle movements. And Japanese and Americans watching a stress film spontaneously made similar muscle movements.

Table 10-4 *(Continued)*

	Percentage Agreeing That the Photograph Showed the Indicated Emotion				
	United States (N = 99)	Brazil (N = 40)	Chile (N = 119)	Argentina (N = 168)	Japan (N = 29)
Sadness	84%	59%	88%	78%	62%
Anger	67%	90%	94%	90%	90%
Fear	85%	67%	68%	54%	66%

SOURCE: Based on Ekman, 1973, p. 207

from the animal also leads to calling the emotion "fear". These examples illustrate that the label for the emotion depends in part on the *source* of arousal and in part on the *response* to it.

The emotional meaning attributed to arousing stimuli and response patterns depends on previous experience and expectations. This point becomes most evident from anthropological reports of differences among cultures in the ways in which feelings are expressed. Visitors to a strange culture would make many mistakes if they tried to assess the meaning of emotional expressions in terms of their own social learning history. A Masai warrior honors a young man who looks promising by spitting in his face, an Andaman Islander greets a visitor by sitting down on his lap and sobbing his salutation tearfully, a scolded Chinese schoolboy takes a reprimand with cheerful grinning as a sign of his respect, and to show anger Navajo and Apache Indians lower the voice instead of raising it (Opler, 1967).

Within each culture people reach good agreement about the meaning of emotional cues. But these observations of the importance of culture coexist with the possibility that certain facial expressions seem to have a universal meaning (as discussed *In Focus 10.3*). The emotions of anger, happiness, disgust, sadness, fear, and surprise, shown in photographs of faces, tended to be correctly identified in a variety of extremely different cultures (Ekman, 1982).

Sometimes persons cannot correctly identify the source of their own arousal and are uncertain about their response to it. Under these ambiguous conditions cognitive and social variables play an especially dominant part in determining the experience. Depending on the cognitive label assigned, the context, and social cues from other people, the individual might experience the same physiological arousal pattern in alternative ways, as discussed next.

Cognition and Emotion

How we know what we feel under ambigous conditions has been explored in several experiments by Stanley Schachter (1964). In one study, supposedly attempting to investigate the effects of vitamins on visual skills, college students received an injection of epinephrine, a drug that increases heart rate and raises blood sugar levels, thus producing physiological arousal (Schachter & Singer, 1962). Some subjects were told what to expect from the injections, others were told nothing, and a third group was misinformed—that is, they were told that their hands and feet would feel numb and that they would have an itch and a slight headache, none of which would actually be a result of the epinephrine injection. A control group received a saline injection that has no physiological effect.

Next each subject was left alone in a waiting room with a person who appeared to be another subject but who actually served as the experimenter's confederate. In one condition the confederate behaved in an angry, aggressive, and insulting fashion; in another condition he was wild and euphoric, laughing, throwing paper airplanes, and playing games. Those subjects who had been given the arousing drug and had been uninformed or misinformed concerning its effects were most suscep-

reported feeling angry if the confederate in their case displayed angry behavior and euphoric if the confederate was euphoric (see Table 10-5 and Figure 10-3).

The emotional experiences of aroused subjects who had been given an appropriate explanantion for their bodily arousal, on the other hand, were influenced very little by the confederate. This finding supported the hypothesis that an individual who has a plausible explanation for his state of arousal does not depend on momentary situational cues to evaluate and label his experiences. But a person who cannot plausibly explain his aroused state must label his emotions on the basis of whatever cues the environment provides.

In sum, Schachter's "cognitive-pysiological theory" suggests that emotions may depend on two factors:

1. A state of physiological arousal, and
2. An interpretation of the causes responsible for the arousal.

When we do not have an explanation for a state of arousal, we become dependent on situational cues to understand what we are feeling. But if the arousal is completely explained—if one knows it is caused by an injection, for example—one does not have to use the present situation to interpret it.

Schachter's work helps us to understand behavior in everyday situations when individuals are unsure about the sources of their own arousal, uncertain about what is making them emotional. In such cases the same pattern of physiological arousal (such as increased heart rate and blood pressure) may be experienced as anything from euphoria to anger, depending on the context in which it occurs and the way it is interpreted. Of course, in many life situations the source of the emotional arousal is easy to identify, and the emotion is readily labeled. An approaching grizzly bear or a car coming head-on would result in an emotional response labeled fear with little hesitation. In sum, the subjective experience of emotion often seems to be labeled from contextual cues, and we know what we feel partly by seeing where we are and what is happening. To understand another person's emotional experiences fully we have to consider the person in the context and the complex

Table 10-5
Emotion Reported in Various Conditions

Drug Treatment	Modeled Behavior	
	Euphoria	Anger
Control injection (not aroused)	Little euphoria	Little anger
Epinephrine, informed	Little euphoria	Little anger
Epinephrine, uninformed	More euphoria	More anger
Epinephrine, misinformed	Much euphoria	(Not tested)

SOURCE: Based on Schachter & Singer, 1962.

Figure 10-3
The Schachter Experiments

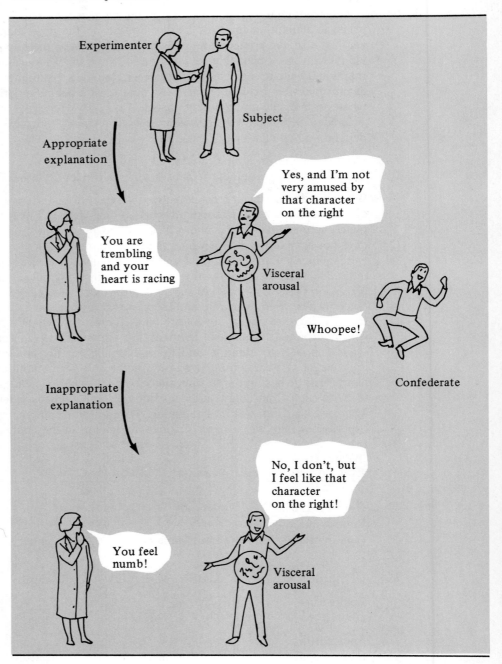

From Mandler (1962).

relations between the contextual variations and subjective experience; to understand our own feelings, we may have to do the same.

Schachter has also applied his theory to try to understand the effects of smoking marihuana. In his view, labels are attached to the physiological changes accompanying marihuana intoxication. The smoker must decide whether dizziness, misjudgments of time and distance, and the other effects of the drug are pleasant or not. Situational cues enter into these judgments. For example, if the setting is pleasant and includes warm, supportive models who enjoy smoking, one is likely to have a positive experience, but under different circumstances or expectations the same physical arousal pattern may be labeled very differently.

The Schachter and Singer (1962) experiment has been challenged by new research that questions their conclusions (Maslach, 1979; Marshall & Zimbardo, 1979). Schachter and Singer (1979), however, continue to maintain their interpretation, and rebuke their sharp critics with equal vigor. What shall we conclude? A good deal of evidence indicates that we often do use external information to judge our inner states. But there also may be important exceptions. Indeed, many different types of information may influence how we experience, judge, and label our inner states (Leventhal, 1984; Schneider, Hastorf, & Ellsworth, 1979). Human emotions remain as complex and intriguing to understand scientifically as they are to deal with in life.

The Flow of Emotions and Behavior

Feelings are not static: They ebb and flow, changing over time as new information becomes available. As one psychologist notes, "Anger suddenly melts and changes

The experienced emotion depends on how the aroused state is interpreted.

to guilt, depression, relief, or love; anxiety changes to relief or euphoria; guilt changes to anger" (Lazarus, 1974, p. 24).

Thus our emotions tend to be complex states based on continuously changing feedback from the situation and our own reactions to it. The intensity and quality of the emotional reaction change as the cognitive appraisal (interpretation) of the total context changes. For example, in coping with potential danger and stress, one's subjective experiences vary depending on one's shifting expectations about being able to master the danger or tolerate the stress. When we think we can cope, we may feel challenged; when we expect to be overcome, we may feel threatened or helpless.

Feelings not only color our inner states, they also influence our judgment, memory, and behavior (e.g. Bower, 1981). When people are "feeling good," for example, they may behave quite differently than when they experience negative emotions or are in a more or less neutral mood. Even seemingly minor experiences (such as finding a coin in a phone booth) can have enough emotional impact to influence action and make us, for instance, act kind or selfish, generous or stingy (Isen & Levin, 1972). For example, after people were made to feel good by succeeding on a task, they made more generous donations to a worthy cause (Isen, 1970). After people in a shopping mall received free gifts (note pad for women, nail clippers for the men), they also made more positive evaluations of the performance and service records of products they owned when asked to rate them in an independent survey (Isen et al., 1978).

Causal Attributions and Emotions

The close links between cognition and emotion are also seen if we examine how "causal attributions" influence our emotional responses. For example, we may see the same event—say getting an A on an exam—as due to internal causes (such as high ability or hard work) or as due to external causes (such as the ease of the task or good luck). How we feel about the grade depends on whether we see it as due to internal or external causes. Generally, "pride and shame are maximized when achievement outcomes are ascribed internally, and minimized when success and failure are attributed to external causes " (Weiner, 1974, p. 11). In other words, a success that is perceived to be the result of one's ability or effort (internal causes) produces more positive feelings about oneself than does the same success when it is viewed as merely reflecting luck or an easy task (external causes). Conversely, we feel worse (e.g., experience "shame") when we perceive our failure as reflecting low ability or insufficient effort than when it is seen as due to bad luck or the difficulty of the particular task. For example, being fired from a job for one's incompetence has a different emotional impact than does being fired because the firm went bankrupt.

Not surprisingly, our perceptions of these causes may be biased in self-enhancing ways (Epstein, 1973; Greenwald, 1980; Harter, 1983). For example, we are more likely to see ourselves as responsible for our actions when they have positive rather than negative outcomes. When we do well or succeed, it is to our personal credit; when we do badly or fail it is because we could not help it (e.g. Schneider, Hastorf, & Ellsworth, 1979; Wortman et al., 1973).

SUMMARY EVALUATION OF THE PHENOMENOLOGICAL APPROACH

As Part Four, The Phenomenological Approach, concludes, it is time to summarize its main strengths and weaknesses and its basic features. Chapters 8, 9, and 10 showed that this approach includes a wide range of theories and research. The approach also has been undergoing much change and an important evolution. There is a gradual shift from a concern with broad theories of the self, personal growth, and humanistic values to a more specific focus on careful research into particular aspects of the self, emotion, social perception, and social cognition.

Strengths and Weaknesses

Many of the general strengths of the approach (see Table 10-6) have remained stable. The approach continues to focus on important, previously neglected topics: the self, emotions, current subjective experience, and social perceptions are still its principal concerns. As such, the phenomenological approach in its modern versions remains an appealing alternative to excessively narrow, mechanistic views of personality.

The phenomenological focus on the present and on the future, on the "here and now" as experienced, as well as on the future as anticipated, is seen by many psychologists as a strength. Historically, this focus came as a welcome correction to an excessive emphasis in previous approaches on the individual's history and early roots. Of course, every advantage also has a possible disadvantage. For some personality psychologists, the phenomenologists neglect the past and fail to provide an adequate account of personality development, stability, and change.

The original phenomenological theorists, like Rogers and Kelly, writing more than thirty years ago, were lone voices calling for a new kind of personality psychology. They wanted to make central such topics as the person's subjective perceptions in the "here-and-now," personal feelings and emotions, and the importance of the self. At the time, little formal research was available on these topics.

Table 10-6
Summary Evaluation of the Phenomenological Approach

Strengths	Weaknesses
Focus on previously neglected topics: person's subjective current experiences, emotions, and perceptions; the self studied scientifically	Difficulty relating perceptions and personal experiences to objective conditions and external causes
Focus on present and future	Neglect of past history and development
View of persons as scientists and potential experts—but capable of systematic errors and distortions	Persons may be biased perceivers and reporters; difficult to objectify personal experiences
Focus on healthy personality, and positive strivings	Excessive reliance on personal growth; not applicable to severely disturbed, poorly functioning persons

Therefore many of the original theoretical statements were more an inspired call for a new focus than a building of a science with systematic observations. It is a great tribute to the early theorists in this approach that many of the topics they championed are being investigated decades later with fresh and intense new interest (e.g., Harter, 1983; Kihlstrom & Cantor, 1984; Gergen, 1984; Zajonc, 1980).

The new research directions show historical continuity with some pioneers within the approach, like Kurt Lewin who led the way toward the experimental study of how people experience the "life space" at any given moment. They also owe much to the ideas of George Kelly. On the other hand, some of the new work might seem alien to some of the humanistically-oriented thinkers, like Rogers and Maslow, who are associated historically with the phenomenological approach. They would not have anticipated that the "self," one of their favorite topics, would be receiving so much research attention in experimental studies like those reviewed in this chapter. And they might feel that such experiments are too narrow and do not really capture the essential qualities of the self that they had in mind. But then, sometimes scientific progress is most interesting when it moves in unpredictable directions!

Methodologically, the approach has shown increasing ingenuity and sophistication. That is seen in the clever ways that difficult topics are being opened to systematic research. There are plenty of examples throughout this chapter. The "self" is no longer just an abstraction: it is a topic of active investigation. The same is true for the topic of emotions. This increasing research sophistication suggests that some of the weaknesses listed in Table 10-6 actually are becoming less serious and even irrelevant. Ways are being found, for example, to link social cognitions more clearly to social conditions.

Likewise, the processes through which self-perceptions influence behavior are becoming increasingly accessible to study. We saw for example, that peoples' perceptions of control are being related to the social conditions that enhance or decrease those perceptions. It is hoped that these encouraging developments will make the weaknesses shown in Table 10-6 increasingly obsolete in future years. Likewise, research on these topics no longer relies just on self-reports but includes all sorts of behavior. It is also exciting that aspects of the phenomenological approach continue to be applied in new ways to the understanding and therapeutic modification of problematic behavior, as you will see in subsequent chapters.

Thirty years ago, the fact that people are sometimes biased in their perceptions and therefore may be inaccurate sources of information was seen as a liability of the approach. It was seen, for example, as limiting the accuracy and value of phenomenological assessments and insights. More recently, the possible biases and cognitive simplifications of the perceiver, rather than being dismissed as merely unreliable, have become major topics of scientific interest in their own right (e.g., Kahneman & Tversky, 1984). For example, the topic of how the self knows itself and others is beginning to get the attention it deserves (e.g., Berkowitz, 1984; Gergen, 1984).

The evolution of the phenomenological approach owes much to a growing link between the ideas of personality theorists like George Kelly and cognitive psychology more generally. In the last few decades cognitive psychology has become a central area of the field of psychology, especially important to both social and personality psychologists. This new interest in cognition reflects the realization that how people perceive themselves and their experiences crucially influences their behavior. You saw examples of this focus throughout this chapter.

The phenomenological orientation discussed in Part Four is not only cognitive; it also began with a humanistic focus. Theorists like Maslow called attention to higher-order human needs, such as self-actualization. For Carl Rogers the conditions under which organismic experiences and genuineness were possible were of great importance. The humanistic commitment to enhance personal growth and the human potential has in part been absorbed into some forms of psychotherapy. Encounter groups, family therapy, and various forms of counseling and community service all show the influence of the humanistic movement.

At the same time, the humanistic side of the phenomenological orientation continues in an active dialogue with the behavioral approach to personality, discussed in Part Five (e.g., Rychlak, 1981; Wandersman et al., 1976). Some of this dialogue raises questions about the usefulness of concepts like self-actualization for designing treatments to help severely disturbed people. Critics point out that Rogers and Kelly both built their theories with healthy college students as their clients in therapy. The ideas of these theorists may have had their greatest appeal and relevance

Table 10-7
Summary Overview of Phenomenological Approaches

Basic units	The experienced self; personal constructs and self-concepts; subjective feeling and perceptions; attributions.
Causes of behavior	Self-concepts and underlying feelings and conflicts; attributions and expectations.
	Free (not mechanistic or predetermined) choices; what one "makes of oneself."
Favored data	Self-disclosure and personal constructs (about self and others); self-reports.
Observed responses used as	Signs (of the person's inner states, perceptions, or emotions).
Research focus	Self-concepts; self-awareness and expression; human potential and self-actualization; emotion; attribution.
Approach to personality change	By increased awareness, personal honesty, internal consistency, and self-acceptance.
Role of situation	As the context for experience and choice; focus on the situation-as-perceived.

to young, well-functioning people in search of personal growth. The applications of these ideas may be less clear for the severely malfunctioning, and the severely disadvantaged socially, culturally, and economically.

Overview

In sum, many psychologists welcome the emphasis on the person's cognitions, feelings, and personal interpretations of experience stressed by the theories discussed in Part Four. This concern with how individuals construe events and see themselves and the world has been a most influential force, and it has generated a great deal of research. The resulting contributions are widely acknowledged. Some of the main features of phenomenological approaches are summarized in Table 10-7, which shows some of their shared characteristics.

SUMMARY

1. People actively organize and interpret the information provided by the social world. This process is called "social cognition." It includes how we form impressions, make inferences, and attribute motives for behavior.

2. There is a bias to explain behavior (particularly others' behavior) in terms of internal dispositions, rather than external or situational causes. We also tend to see events as controllable and meaningful, even when they are objectively the result of chance. We tend to see positive outcomes as more under our personal control than negative outcomes. Individuals who view tragic accidents as unavoidable or as meaningful in some way cope better than those who see the accident as a chance occurrence, as avoidable, or who blame others for its happening.

3. Perceptions of people are influenced by the perceiver's expectations. For example, we expect certain traits (such as warmth, generosity, and happiness) to "go together." Such expectations, or implicit personality theories, are probably based on the actual co-occurrence of these behaviors in some people. Simplifying and organizing information about others is often efficient but also may result in unfair or inaccurate stereotypes.

4. Trait impressions tend to remain relatively stable. Inconsistent behavior is often attributed to temporary, external causes or reinterpreted in terms of an underlying consistency. Our own behavior toward others is affected by the way we label them, and we may elicit from others the very behavior that we expect, thus confirming our expectations.

5. The sequence in which information is received also affects the impression. In forming a total impression of another we may average the evaluations of each perceived trait, although we may give extra weight to the earliest information. Vivid, concrete, emotionally involving data tend to be more influential than more abstract or statistical information.

6. Self-concepts (or "self-schemata") develop as a result of the outcomes a person has obtained in the past and expects to obtain in the future. Self-esteem is an important aspect of the self-concept. Concepts of adequacy or ability with regard to particular performance areas have been studied extensively. Specific self-concepts about performance level tend to depend on the feedback the person received from past performance. These expectancies may generalize to other situations to

the degree that the situations are perceived as similar.

7. Perceptions of self-efficacy and of helplessness are closely related to a person's behavior. For example, self-efficacy expectations predict improvement in treatment: People who expect to do well, really do well. Likewise, children who are helpless (believe failure is due to their lack of ability) do perform more poorly after a failure experience than do children who see their failure as due to a lack of effort.

8. Self-awareness can be created experimentally or studied as individual differences on such dimensions as self-consciousness.

9. We tend to perceive people and ourselves as basically consistent even in the face of seemingly contradictory evidence from behavior. People may strive to maintain a sense of consistency, especially about important concepts like the self.

10. The James-Lange theory originally proposed that the subjective experience of an emotion follows rather than precedes the physiological reaction that accompanies an emotional state. First we cry, then we feel sad. Cannon raised some important objections to this theory, noting that bodily changes and subjective experience in emotion may occur simultaneously. Schachter's cognitive-physiological theory of emotion emphasizes the way the individual interprets his or her diffuse state of physiological arousal.

11. In the perception of feelings, although we may subjectively experience distinct emotions, corresponding distinct patterns of physiological responses generally have not been found. Instead, a diffuse state of general physiological arousal may characterize the various emotional experiences. The discriminations that we make among emotions are affected by cognitions and situational cues. The source of the arousal and the person's response to it affect the cognitive appraisal of that arousal and the label that the individual attaches to it. The meaning of arousal stimuli and response patterns depends on many considerations.

12. When you cannot easily identify the source of your own arousal and are uncertain about your response to it, cognitive and social variables may strongly determine your experience. If you are in an aroused physiological state that you cannot explain plausibly, you may label this state in accord with the environmental cues and cognitions about them so as to explain the state reasonably.

13. Emotional reactions to an event also depend on its perceived causes. For example, a success that is seen as due to one's own ability or efforts (internal causes) produces more feelings of pride than does the same event when it is seen as due to luck or the easiness of the task (external causes).

14. Strengths and weaknesses of the phenomenological approach were summarized and its main features were discussed.

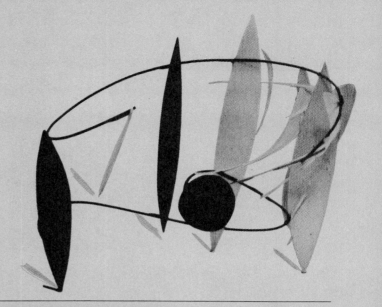

PART FIVE
THE BEHAVIORAL APPROACH

Chapter 11

Behavioral Conceptions: Beginnings

Within the broad boundaries set by inherited limitations, people become what they are mainly through learning. Through learning, things that attract one person may come to repel another, just as one individual's passions may become another's nightmares. There is a substantial amount of knowledge about human learning, and it can be harnessed to influence human behavior for good or for ill.

In this chapter and in Chapter 12, you will find some approaches to personality that utilize the principles of learning to analyze and change behavior and to understand personality. These approaches are called behavioral theories or learning theories and several varieties have been formulated. In this chapter we will consider some of the original concepts of this approach; in later chapters we will examine its more recent developments and applications.

ORIENTATION: FOCUS ON BEHAVIOR

We can know people only by examining their behavior—the things they say and do. Thus, all psychological approaches are based on the study of behavior, but they differ in how the behavior is used. Both the trait approach and the psychodynamic approach use behaviors as signs, inferring attributes or motives from the observable things the individual does. In the behavioral approach, by contrast, the observed behavior is of interest in itself.

Behaviorists sample the individual's behaviors but generally do not interpret them as signs (indicators) of the person's motives, traits, real or ideal selves, or other attributes. They try to sample the relevant behavior directly. For example, a behaviorist might try to sample Gary's behaviors to find out just what he does before speeches, without drawing any inferences from them about his underlying anxiety, insecurity, or other personal qualities. To the degree that theorists limit themselves to behavior, their definition of personality itself becomes equated with the whole of an individual's behaviors: the person *is* what the person *does*. But *why* do people do what they do?

Rejection of Inferred Motives: A Science of *Behavior*

To explain behavior, theorists in the past have hypothesized many human motives. Theories concerning motivation have helped to reveal the variety and complexity of human strivings, and also have contributed to the development of research about their causes. Investigators of motives originally were inspired by the model of experimental research on biological drives in animals. In animal studies of motivation, the hypothesized need of the animal (its hunger or sex drive, for example) has been linked clearly to observable conditions manipulated in the laboratory. For example, the strength of the hunger drive may be inferred in part from the amount of time that the animal has been deprived of food. When a dog has not been fed for two days, we may safely say that it has a high hunger drive. In such cases, references to drives and motives are straight forward. Likewise, some careful investigations of hypothesized higher-order motives in people have specified clearly the objective conditions that define the motive (e.g., McClelland et al., 1953).

Less rigorous applications of motivational theory to personality, however, may use motives loosely (for example as "wishes" and "desires"), and their value as explanations of behavior is open to serious question. The tendency to invoke motives as explanations of why people behave as they do is understandable, because that is how we "explain" behavior in common sense terms. To explain why a child spent an unusual amount of time cleaning and grooming himself neatly, we easily might say "because he had strong cleanliness needs" or "because he had a compulsive desire for order." Such hypotheses about motives may sound like explanations, but they tell us little unless the motive is defined objectively and unless the causes of the motive itself are established. What makes the child have

B.F. Skinner (b. 1904)

"cleanliness needs"? What determines his "compulsive desires"? Why does he "wish" to be clean?

B. F. Skinner, a pioneer in the behavioral approach, has criticized many concepts regarding human needs as being no more than motivational labels attached to human activities. Thus orderly behavior may be attributed to a motive for orderliness, submissive behavior to submissiveness needs, exploratory behavior to the need to explore, and so on. To avoid such circular reasoning and to untangle explaining from naming, behaviorally oriented psychologists like Skinner prefer to analyze behaviors in terms of the observable events and conditions that seem to vary with them. Hence they refuse to posit specific motivations for behavior. Rather, they try to discover the external events that strengthen its future likelihood and that maintain or change it. This approach leads to questions like: When does that child's cleaning activity increase, and when does it decrease in relation to observable changes in the environment (e.g., how the parents respond to the behavior)?

For Skinner, psychology is the science of behavior: inferences about unobservable states and motives are not adequate explanations, and they add nothing to a scientific account of the conditions controlling behavior. "Motivation" is simply the result of depriving or satiating an organism of some substance such as water or food for a given period of time. Thus a "drive" is just a convenient way of referring to the observable effects of such deprivation or satiation. Likewise, Skinner avoids any inferences about internal "conflicts," preferring an experimental analysis of the stimulus conditions that seem to control the particular behavior in the situation. In his words:

> Man, we once believed, was free to express himself in art, music, and literature, to inquire into nature, to seek salvation in his own way. He could initiate action and make spontaneous and capricious changes of course. . . . But science insists that action is initiated by forces impinging upon the individual, and that caprice is only another name for behavior for which we have not yet found a cause (Skinner, 1955, pp. 52–53).

The essence of Skinner's behavioristic view is the belief that our behavior is shaped by the external environment, not by motives, dispositions, or "selves" that are "in" the person.

Basic Strategy

Skinner's work is based on the premise that a genuine science of human behavior is not only possible but desirable. In his view, science should try to predict and determine experimentally the behavior of the individual organism (Skinner, 1974).

Skinner proposes a "functional analysis" of the organism as a behaving system. Such an analysis tries to link the organism's behavior to the precise conditions that control or determine it. Skinner's approach therefore concentrates on the observ-

Ivan Pavlov (1849–1936)

able covariations between "independent variables" (stimulus events) and "dependent variables" (response patterns). The variables in a functional analysis, according to Skinner, must be external, observable, and described in physical and quantitative terms. It will not do to say that a child becomes concerned with cleanliness when she "fears her father's disapproval;" one must specify the exact ways that changes in the father's specific behavior (e.g., his praise) are related to specific changes in what the child does (e.g., how much she washes her hands per hour).

Skinner contends that the laboratory offers the best chance of obtaining a scientific analysis of behavior; in it, variables can be brought under the control of experimental manipulation. Furthermore, the experimental study of behavior has much to gain from dealing with the behavior of animals below the complex human level. Science, Skinner points out, advances from the simple to the complex and is constantly concerned with whether the processes and laws discovered at one stage are adequate for the next.

CLASSICAL CONDITIONING

Like most other experimental psychologists, Skinner recognized the importance of the type of "classical" or "respondent" conditioning initially discovered at the turn of the century by Ivan Pavlov, the Russian physiologist. To understand Skinner's own contributions, we must consider first the nature of classical conditioning. Classical conditioning (conditioned-response learning) is a type of learning (emphasized by Pavlov) in which a neutral stimulus (e.g., a bell) becomes conditioned by being paired or associated with an unconditioned stimulus (one that is naturally powerful).

How Classical Conditioning Works

A dog automatically salivates when food is in its mouth. The response of salivation is a *reflex* or *unconditioned response* (UCR): it is natural and does not have to be learned. Like most other reflexes, in humans and in animals alike, salivation helps the organism adjust or adapt: the saliva aids in digesting the food. Stimuli that elicit unconditioned responses are called *unconditioned stimuli* (UCS). The unconditioned stimulus (food in this example) can elicit behavior without any prior learning.

Any dog owner knows that a hungry dog may salivate at the mere sight of food, before it gets any in its mouth. The dog may even begin to salivate at the sight of the empty dish in which the food is usually served. Salivating to the sight of the empty dish that has been associated with food is an example of a learned or *conditioned response* (CR). The stimulus that elicits a conditioned response is called a *conditioned* (learned) *stimulus* (CS): its impact on behavior is not automatic but depends on learning.

Pavlov discovered some of the ways in which such neutral stimuli as lights and metronome clicks could become conditioned stimuli capable of eliciting responses like salivating. His pioneering experiments with dogs began with his repeatedly making a certain sound whenever he gave his dogs their food. After a while he found that the dogs salivated to the sound even when it was no longer followed by

Table 11-1
The Language of Classical Conditioning

Term	Definition
Unconditioned stimulus (UCS)	A stimulus to which one automatically, naturally responds without learning to do so.
Unconditioned response (UR)	The unlearned response one naturally makes to an unconditioned stimulus. The response may be positive or negative (for example, salivating when food is placed in the mouth; jerking your hand away from a hot stove).
Conditioned stimulus (CS)	A previously neutral stimulus to which one learns to respond after it has been paired or associated with an unconditioned stimulus.
Conditioned response (CR)	The learned response to a conditioned stimulus. This response was previously made only to an unconditioned stimulus, but now it is made to a conditioned stimulus as a result of the pairing of the two stimuli.

food: *conditioning* had occurred. This type of learning is what we now call classical conditioning.

To sum up, in classical conditioning the subject is repeatedly exposed to a neutral stimulus (that is, one that elicits no special response) together with an unconditioned stimulus that elicits an unconditioned response. When this association becomes strong enough, the neutral stimulus by itself may begin to elicit a response similar to the one produced by the unconditioned stimulus. (See Tables 11-1 and 11-2 for basic definitions and examples.)

Most experiments in classical conditioning are performed in the laboratory, but the knowledge they have generated may help us to understand many things that

Table 11-2
Examples of Possible Effects of Classical Conditioning

Before Conditioning	After Conditioning
Dog knocks child over. (UCS) Child cries. (UCR)	Dog Approaches. (CS) Child cries. (CR)
Mother feeds and cuddles baby. (UCS) Baby relaxes. (UCR)	Baby smells mother's perfume. (CS) Baby relaxes. (CR)
Car accident injures woman. (UCS) Woman is afraid. (UCR)	Woman thinks about getting in car. (CS) Woman is afraid. (CR)
Man drives across a swaying bridge. (UCS) Man is afraid. (UCR)	Man approaches another bridge. (CS) He is afraid and avoids bridge. (CR)
Mother discovers her daughter masturbating, scolds her, slaps her hands. (UCS) Daughter is hurt and afraid. (UCR)	Daughter looks at her nude body. (CS) Daughter feels anxious and negative about her body, particularly her genitals. (CR)

happen outside the laboratory, such as the development of affections and attractions (e.g., Byrne, 1969; Lott & Lott, 1968). For example, a liking for particular people and things may depend on the degree to which they have been associated with positive or pleasant experiences (Griffitt & Guay, 1969). If so, one's affection for a friend may be directly related to the degree to which he or she has been associated with gratifications for oneself.

Now consider the development of fear. How do initially neutral (or even positive) stimuli acquire the power to evoke fear? Suppose for example, a person repeatedly sees a light and experiences an electric shock simultaneously. In time, the light by itself may come to evoke some of the emotional reaction produced by the shock. Neutral stimuli that are closely associated in time with any pain-producing stimulus then become conditioned stimuli that may elicit fear and avoidance reactions. Thus the seemingly irrational fears that some people have may reflect a conditioned association between previously neutral stimuli and painful events.

Classical conditioning may influence development throughout a person's life. If, for example, sexual curiosity and fear-producing experiences (such as severe punishment) are closely associated for a child, fear may be generated by various aspects of the individual's sexual behavior even after there is no longer any danger of punishment. And conditioning can spread as well as persist: the girl who is made to feel bad about touching her genitals may also become anxious about other forms

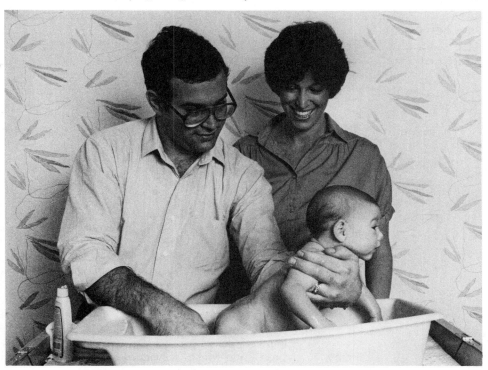

How much we like a person may depend on the degree to which he or she has been associated with gratification.

of sexual expression; she may even develop fears about her whole body and herself as a person.

Case Example: Little Albert

Watson and Reynor (1920) induced a severe fear of rats in a little boy named Albert, who had not been afraid of rats before. This was done by classical conditioning: just as Albert would reach for the rat, the experimenters would make a loud noise that frightened him. After he had experienced the rat and the aversive noise several times in close association, he developed a strong fear of the rat.

Albert's fear generalized so that later, when shown a variety of new furry stimuli such as cats, cotton, fur coats, human hair, and wool, he responded with obvious fear to them as well. His fear had spread to these new objects even though they had never been paired with the noise. This is a human example of the kind of learning found when rats who were shocked in a white compartment began to respond fearfully to the compartment itself even when the shock no longer occurred (Miller, 1948). The case of Little Albert has become one of the many bases for applications of classical conditioning to the analysis and treatment of human problems (Chapter 14; see also *In Focus 11.1*).

In Focus 11.1
The Behavioral Challenge to the Psychodynamic Theory of Neurosis

Differences between theoretical approaches are seen most clearly when applied to the same case. Behavior theorists have strongly challenged Freud's theory of neurosis by reanalyzing in learning terms a case that he presented. Recall that Freud's view of how neuroses develop begins with the child's aggressive or sexual impulses, which seek direct, immediate release. Because expression of these impulses may be punished severely, the child may become anxious about his own impulses and try to repress them. But the impulses continue to seek release and become increasingly pent up. Eventually they may be impossible to repress, and components of them may break through, creating further anxiety. To reduce this anxiety, the person may attempt a variety of defense mechanisms. In neurosis these defenses begin to break down: the unacceptable impulses start to express themselves indirectly and symbolically in various disguised forms, such as in phobias or obsessive-compulsive thoughts and actions. The roots of

neurosis, in Freud's view, are always in childhood:

> It seems that neuroses are acquired only in early childhood (up to the age of six), even though their symptoms may not make their appearance till much later. The childhood neurosis may become manifest for a short time or may even be overlooked. In every case the later neurotic illness links up with the prelude in childhood (Freud, 1933, pp. 41–42).

An example from Freud's theory is his published case of Little Hans. Hans was a five-year-old boy who developed a horse phobia. He was afraid of being bitten by a horse and, after seeing a horse hitched to a wagon slip and fall on a street near his home, began to dread going out. Freud interpreted the phobia as an expression of the child's psychodynamic conflicts. These conflicts included his desires to seduce his mother and replace his father. These desires, in turn, made him fear castration by the father; symbolically, the horse came to represent the dreaded father.

Higher-Order Conditioning

When a previously neutral stimulus, such as a light, a bell, or a face, has become a conditioned stimulus through its association with an unconditioned stimulus, such as food or pain, it can in turn modify one's reactions to another neutral stimulus by being associated with it. This process is called *higher-order conditioning*. It was demonstrated when Pavlov found that after a metronome sound had become a conditioned stimulus (by being paired with food), it could itself be paired with a neutral stimulus (such as a black triangle) and, as a result of that association, the neutral stimulus would also elicit the unconditioned response of salivation. In people, words and other complex symbols can be powerful conditioned stimuli capable of evoking emotional responses through higher-order conditioning.

A wide variety of stimuli, including activities, individuals, groups, and events, are valued according to their associations with positive or negative outcomes and even mere labels. For example, when neutral items are paired with words like "dirty" and "ugly," they take on negative valuations, but the same items become positively evaluated when they have been associated with words like "beautiful" and "happy" (Staats & Staats, 1957). Likewise, the names of countries and political parties and the sight of national flags can come to arouse intense positive or negative feelings depending on their earlier associations. The Russian patriot who

---

A behavioral analysis of this case, however, explains Hans's phobia without invoking any internal conflicts or symbolism (Wolpe & Rachman, 1960). Namely, the scene Hans witnessed of a horse falling down and bleeding on the street was sufficiently frightening to the young child to produce fear. In turn, the fear generalized to all horses and resulted in Hans's avoidance behavior. Thus a simple conditioning process might explain a phobia: since the horse was part of an intensely frightening experience, it became a conditioned stimulus for anxiety, and the anxiety generalized to other horses.

As this example illustrates, the behavioral view of neurosis is concerned with anxiety and avoidance no less than the psychodynamic view, but it tries to link them to external circumstances rather than to internal conflicts (Redd et al., 1978). Through direct or vicarious frightening experiences people often develop anxiety in response to particular objects, persons, or situations. Not only encountering these events in reality but even just thinking about them may be upsetting. These emotional reactions may generalize and take many forms. Common examples include muscle tensions and fatigue and intense fear reactions to seemingly neutral stimuli.

Psychodynamic and behavioral theorists do agree that the neurotic individual may make all sorts of efforts to escape and avoid painful feelings. Many of his avoidance attempts may be maintained persistently because they serve to terminate the pain. For example, such elaborate avoidance defenses as obsessive-compulsive rituals, in the form of handwashing for many hours, may be maintained because they reduce the person's anxiety (e.g., Wolpe, 1963). In addition, attention and sympathy from relatives and friends for being sick or relief from pressures and obligations can also serve to maintain the anxious person's avoidance patterns by providing reinforcement for them.

A fear may generalize to stimuli similar to the one that initially produced it.

feels deep emotion at the playing of "The Internationale" is unlikely to have similar feelings for the "The Star-Spangled Banner."

OPERANT CONDITIONING

Skinner incorporated into his position many concepts regarding classical conditioning, but he concentrated on another kind of learning that is different in some ways from classical conditioning. He contends (1953) that most human social behavior consists of freely emitted response patterns, or *operants*. Even a little baby shows much spontaneous behavior: it reaches up to a mobile, turns its head, looks at objects, cries and gurgles, and moves its arms and legs. Through such operants the organism operates on its environment, changing it and, in turn, being changed by it.

How Operant Conditioning Works

Operant behavior is modified by its consequences: the outcome of any operant response (or pattern of responses) determines how likely it is that the subject will perform similar responses in the future. If a response has favorable (reinforcing) consequences, the subject is more likely to perform it again in similar situations. Contrary to some widespread misconceptions, "reinforcers" or favorable outcomes are not restricted to such primitive rewards as food pellets or sexual satisfactions. Almost all events may serve as reinforcers, including such cognitive gratifications as information (Jones, 1966) or the achievement of competence. Such learning, based on the consequences produced by responses, is called *operant conditioning* (or, in earlier usage, trial-and-error or instrumental learning).

When the consequences of a response pattern change, the probability of it and of similar response patterns occurring again also changes. If a little boy whines and clings to his mother and she drops everything in an attempt to appease him, the chances increase that he will behave in this way in the future. If she systematically ignores the behavior, however, and consistently fails to react to it, the chances decrease that the child will continue to behave this way.

In Skinner's research on operant conditioning the typical experiment involves an animal or a person freely performing (emitting) operant responses. The experimenter has preselected a particular class of responses to reinforce (e.g., a young child successfully using a potty-training chair or an adult using personal pronouns in an interview). When the selected operant response is made (the child urinates in the potty or the adult says, "I," "you," "she," and so on), the reinforcement occurs: the child gets a small toy; the interviewer nods or murmurs "good." Figure 11-1 illustrates what happens in operant conditioning.

The outcomes a person obtains for a particular behavior influence his or her future behavior. A child's refusal to eat may gain attention from a father usually too busy to pay the child much attention. Since the child's behavior is reinforced by the attention, she may refuse to eat again. If she is offered special treat foods in an effort to tempt her, she may quickly turn into a finicky eater with limited food preferences. By changing the outcomes of responses, reinforcing previously unreinforced behaviors or discontinuing reinforcement for other behaviors, even behavior patterns that seem deeply ingrained may be changed.

Influenced by Skinner, many psychologists have tried to modify maladaptive behavior by altering the consequences to which it leads. Working with people who have severe behavioral problems, they attempt to remove reinforcement for dis-

Figure 11-1
Operant Conditioning

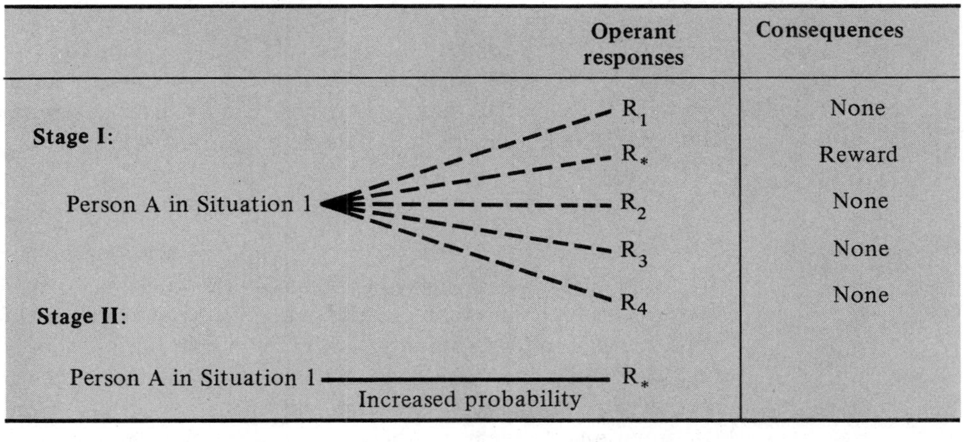

	Operant responses	Consequences
Stage I:	R_1	None
	R_*	Reward
Person A in Situation 1	R_2	None
	R_3	None
	R_4	None
Stage II:		
Person A in Situation 1	R_*	
	Increased probability	

A person performs (emits) many operant responses in any given situation. If one operant is followed by a favorable outcome (reward) in that situation, the person will be more likely to perform that operant again in a similar situation.

advantageous behavior and to make attention, praise, or other reinforcement contingent on the occurrence of more adaptive advantageous behavior. Learning programs of this type follow a set of definite steps. First, the problem behaviors are carefully defined and their frequency in a naturalistic context is measured. Next, one observes and records the reinforcing consequences that seem to maintain the behaviors. Guided by this analysis, the relearning program is designed and put into effect. Finally, the resulting changes are assessed over a period of time.

For example, in one case parents sought help because their three-year-old daughter developed regressive behaviors and reverted to crawling rather than walking. This regression produced serious problems for the child and the family. An analysis of the girl's behavior suggested that her regressive, babyish actions were being encouraged and maintained unwittingly by the attention they brought her. Therefore, an effort was made to rearrange the response-reinforcement patterns so that crawling and infantile acts were not rewarded by the attention of worried adults. Instead, attention and other rewards were made contingent on more adaptive and age-appropriate behaviors, such as jumping, running, and walking, thereby increasing these desirable behaviors while the infantile ones decreased (Harris et al., 1964).

Conditioned Generalized Reinforcers

As noted before, neutral stimuli may acquire value and become conditioned reinforcers when they become associated with other stimuli that already have reinforcing powers and emotion-arousing properties. Conditioned reinforcers become *generalized* when they are paired with more than one primary reinforcer. A good example of a conditioned generalized reinforcer is money, because it can provide so many different primary gratifications (food, shelter, comfort, medical help, and alleviation of pain). Gradually generalized reinforcers may become quite potent even when the primary reinforcers upon which they were initially based do not accompany them any more. Some people, for example, seem to learn to love money for its own sake and work to amass "paper profits" that they never trade in for primary rewards.

Some generalized reinforcers are obvious—like money—but others are subtle and involve complex social relationships. Attention and social approval from people who are likely to supply reinforcement—such as parents, a loved one, or a teacher—often are especially strong generalized reinforcers.

Discrimination and Generalization in Everyday Life

Discriminative stimuli indicate when an operant response will or will not have favorable consequences. Without such signals we would not know in advance the outcomes to which different behaviors are likely to lead and life would be chaotic. With the help of discriminative stimuli we learn to stop the car when coming to a railroad crossing; to eat certain foods with forks and spoons and to continue to eat others with our fingers; to shout and cheer at football games, but not at course examinations; to wear warmer clothes when the temperature starts to drop and to shed them when it becomes hot; to stop at red traffic lights and to go when they turn green.

When a particular response or pattern of responses is reinforced in the presence of one stimulus but not in the presence of others, discrimination occurs. It may be all right to belch in your own room when alone or with close friends but less acceptable to do so when talking to a faculty advisor in her office. Discrimination results from the reinforcement or condoning of behavior in some situations but not in others. The individual is more likely to display the behavior in those situations in which it will probably be reinforced than in those in which it is unlikely to be reinforced.

If a response pattern is uniformly rewarded in many conditions or situations, *generalization* occurs. For example, a child is likely to develop generalized aggressive patterns if he is encouraged or allowed to behave aggressively with his parents and teachers as well as with his siblings and classmates and when visiting other families as well as when at school and at home. Generalization depends on the similarity among stimulus situations. Stimuli that are physically similar or that have similar meanings result in the greatest generalization.

The socialization of children is based on discrimination training. For example, children must learn to control their bowel and bladder functions so that defecation and urination occur only in some situations and not in others. Active exploration of the toy box or the sandbox is permitted and encouraged, while forays into the medicine chest or mother's jewel box have quite different outcomes. As a result of

"Generalized reinforcers" often are subtle and involve complex human relationships.

such "discrimination" training, the child's behavior begins to depend on the specific conditions in which it unfolds.

When behavior yields similar consequences in a broad variety of settings, it can be expected to generalize from one situation to another. For example, if a little girl easily gets help in solving problems at home, at school, with parents, teachers, and siblings, she may develop widespread dependency. In contrast, when certain behaviors, such as curiosity, are punished in some situations but not in others, consistencies across the different situations should not be expected. A child becomes increasingly discriminating as the various roles of sibling, student, lover, and many more are learned. Each of these roles implies its own distinct set of appropriate behaviors in particular situations.

Shaping Behavior by Successive Approximations

Before a response can be reinforced, it must occur. Extremely complex responses, such as saying new words in a foreign language, are unlikely ever to be performed spontaneously by the learner. If you do not know how to say "How do you do?" in Greek, you are unlikely ever to come out with the right phrase spontaneously, no matter how many sounds you utter. To try to overcome this problem, and to help an organism form new responses, Skinnerians often use a procedure called "shaping."

Shaping is a technique for producing successively closer approximations to a particular desired behavior. It consists of carefully observing and immediately rewarding any small variations of the behavior in the desired direction as they are spontaneously performed by the organism. At first, a large class of responses is reinforced; then gradually the class is narrowed, and reinforcement is given only for closer approximations to the final form of the desired behavior. For example, when teaching a pigeon to stand only in the center of a large bull's-eye target painted on the floor, one might reward the bird for standing increasingly close to the center.

The Patterning of Outcomes: Schedules of Reinforcement

The patterning or sequencing ("scheduling") of reinforcement affects the future occurrence and strength of the reinforced behavior (e.g., Ferster & Skinner, 1957). Sometimes the scheduling of reinforcement may be even more important than the nature of the reinforcer (Morse & Kelleher, 1966). Continuous reinforcement usually increases the speed with which responses are learned. Intermittent reinforcement tends to produce more stable behavior that is more persistently maintained when reinforcement stops. For example, rewarding temper tantrums intermittently (by occasionally attending to them in an irregular pattern) may make them very durable. Since many potentially maladaptive behaviors, such as physical aggression and immature dependency, are rewarded intermittently, they can become very hard to eliminate.

Different schedules have different influences on operant responses. Operant strength is measured by the *rate of responses:* the more frequently a response is made in a given period of time, the greater its rate (and inferred strength).

Continuous reinforcement (CRF) is a schedule on which a behavior is reinforced every time it occurs. Responses are usually learned most quickly with continuous reinforcement. A child would become toilet trained more quickly if he were praised and rewarded for each successful attempt. While continuous reinforcement is easy to create in a laboratory, in life it is a rare experience; a *partial reinforcement* or intermittent schedule, in which a response is reinforced only some of the time, is much more common. We see partial reinforcement when a child's bids for attention succeed only occasionally in getting the parent to attend, or when the same sales pitch produces a sale once in a while, or when the gambler hits the jackpot but only in-between many losing bets.

Behavior that has received partial reinforcement often becomes hard to eliminate even when reinforcement is withdrawn altogether. A mother who intermittently and irregularly gives in to her child's nighttime bids for attention (crying, calling for a drink of water, or for just one more story) may find the child's behavior very durable and unresponsive to her attempts to stop it by ignoring it. Many potentially maladaptive behaviors (facial tics, physical aggression, immature dependency) are hard to eliminate because they are rewarded intermittently.

The child with a speck of grit in her eye who successfully follows her father's instruction to blink to get it out may keep on blinking periodically long after the eye is clear of irritation. If her blinks are further reinforced by her parents' occasional attention (whether troubled concern or agitated pleas to "stop doing that!"), she may develop an unattractive facial tic that is extremely resistant to extinction. Likewise, as has often been noted, the gambler who once hit a jackpot may persist for a long time even when the payoff becomes zero. The persistence of behavior after partial reinforcement suggests that when one has experienced only occasional, irregular, and unpredictable reinforcement for a response, one continues to expect possible rewards for a long time after the rewards have totally stopped.

Superstitions: Getting Reinforced into Irrationality

The relationship between the occurrence of an operant response and the reinforcement that follows it is often causal. For example, turn the door knob and the door opens, the outcome reinforcing the action. Consequently in the future we are likely to turn door knobs to enter and leave rooms, and our behavior at the door seems rational. Often, however, the response-reinforcement relationship may be quite accidental, and then bizarre and seemingly superstitious behavior may be produced. For example, a primitive tribe may persist in offering human sacrifices to the gods to end severe droughts because occasionally a sacrifice has been followed by rain.

The genesis of superstition, according to Skinner, may be demonstrated by giving a pigeon a bit of food at regular intervals—say every fifteen seconds—regardless of what he is doing. Skinner (1953, p. 85) describes the strange rituals that may be conditioned in this way:

> When food is first given, the pigeon will be behaving in some way—if only standing still—and conditioning will take place. It is then more probably that the same behavior will be in progress when food is given again. If this proves to be the case, the "operant"

will be further strengthened. If not, some other behavior will be strengthened. Eventually a given bit of behavior reaches a frequency at which it is often reinforced. It then becomes a permanent part of the repertoire of the bird, even though the food has been given by a clock which is unrelated to the bird's behavior. Conspicuous responses which have been established in this way include turning sharply to one side, hopping from one foot to the other and back, bowing and scraping, turning around, strutting, and raising the head. The topography of the behavior may continue to drift with further reinforcements, since slight modifications in the form of response may coincide with the receipt of food.

It may seem amusing to watch pigeons generate elaborate superstitious rituals and bizarre behaviors as a result of accidental reinforcement contingencies. It is tragic, however, if people inadvertently become bizarre and develop neurotic symptom syndromes in fundamentally similar ways. According to many Skinnerians, there is much overlap between the ways in which pigeons become victimized by the scheduling of reinforcement and the manner in which people may become twisted by the response-reinforcement arrangements in their lives. These ideas have been widely applied in both analyses and modifications of human problems (Chapters 13 and 14). They also have been severely criticized (see *In Focus 11.2*).

In Focus 11.2
Humanistic Criticisms of Behaviorism

We have seen that radical behaviorists refuse to invoke qualities of the person as causes of his behavior and attribute causal control instead to the environment. "Whatever we do," Skinner asserts (1971, p. 188), "and hence however we perceive it, the fact remains that it is the environment which acts upon the perceiving person, not the perceiving person who acts upon the environment." Such assertions have led to charges that behaviorally oriented psychologists overemphasize the environment and the situation while "losing the person" (Bowers, 1973; Carlson, 1971). Closely related to these criticisms is the protest against the behavioral approach in general developed by humanistic psychologists like Carl Rogers (Chapter 8). From the humanistic perspective behaviorism is said to dehumanize the person, to neglect his potential for freedom, and to overlook his consciousness while focusing on observable behavior and environmental conditions. Some humanistic psychologists believe behaviorists may have literally "lost man's mind."

We are all familiar with the image of the white-coated behaviorist scheming to manipulate society into creating robotlike creatures whose buttons are controlled by laboratory assistants trained to condition people into puppets. Fears of behaviorism are not limited to the popular mass media. Sidney Jourard, a humanistic psychologist, says:

I have always been uneasy about the behavioristic approach to man, because it appeals to the power motive in the behavior scientist. Moreover, research in behaviorism is frequently funded by agencies interested in controlling the behavior and experience of others, not necessarily with their knowledge or consent nor always with the best interest of the controllees at heart (1974, pp. 20–21).

This comment is representative of the humanistic distrust of behaviorism. The heart of the humanistic protest is the belief that behaviorally oriented psychologists treat and manipulate people as if they were externally controlled rather than free, self-determining beings responsible for their own growth and actions.

Skinner himself has tried to answer

Punishment

Skinner focused on the role of rewards, but punishment or "aversive stimulation" is also important. In laboratory studies of anxiety the unconditioned stimulus is usually a painful electric shock and the stimulus to be conditioned is a discrete event such as a distinctive neutral tone or a buzzer. Generally human life is not that simple and neat. Often "aversive stimuli" involve punishments that are administered in less obvious and less controlled ways. These punishments may be conveyed subtly, by facial expressions and words rather than by brute force, and in extremely complicated patterns, by the same individuals who also nurture the child, giving love and other positive reinforcement. Moreover, the events that are punished often involve more than specific responses; they sometimes entail long sequences of overt and covert behavior.

The behaviors that are considered inappropriate and punishable depend on such variables as the child's age and sex as well as the situation. Obviously the helplessness and passivity that are acceptable in a young child may be maladaptive in an older one, and the traits valued in a girl may not be valued in a boy. While the mother may deliberately encourage her son's dependency and discourage his

---

these criticisms. Among the accusations against behaviorism he lists the following:

1. It ignores consciousness, feelings, and states of minds.
2. It neglects innate endowment and argues that all behavior is acquired during the lifetime of the individual.
3. It formulates behavior simply as a set of responses to stimuli, thus representing a person as an automaton, robot, puppet, or machine.
4. It does not attempt to account for cognitive processes.
5. It has no place for intention or purpose.
6. It cannot explain creative achievements–in art, for example, or in music, literature, science, or mathematics.
7. It assigns no role to a self or sense of self.
8. It is necessarily superficial and cannot deal with the depths of the mind or personality.
9. It limits itself to the prediction and control of behavior and misses the essential nature or being of man.
10. It works with animals, particularly with white rats, but not with people, and its picture of human behavior is therefore confined to those features which human beings share with animals. (Skinner, 1974, pp. ix–x).

In addition, Skinner lists ten more objections, including the belief that it neglects the uniqueness of the individual in its concern with general principles, fosters an antidemocratic atmosphere in the relations between subject and experimenter, manipulates people, and dehumanizes man. Skinner provides a detailed, point-by-point rebuttal and concludes that all these accusations are wrong, but most humanists, not surprisingly, remain unconvinced, and the controversy continues. Within the behavioral approach itself, there has been increasing responsiveness to the objections against radical behaviorism, as the next chapters show.

aggressiveness, his school peers may do the reverse, ridiculing dependency at school and modeling and rewarding aggression and self-assertion. Given this, the influence of punishment on personality development is, not surprisingly, both important and complex (e.g., Aronfreed, 1968; Walters & Grusec, 1977).

A careful review of research on the effects of punishment upon children's behavior concluded, in part, that:

> aversive stimulation, if well timed, consistent, and sufficiently intense, may create conditions that accelerate the socialization process, provided that the socialization agents also provide information concerning alternative prosocial behavior and positively reinforce any such behavior that occurs (Walters & Parke, 1967, p. 218).

The important point to remember here is that when punishment is speedy and specific it may suppress undesirable behavior, but it cannot teach the child desirable alternatives. Therefore, parents should use positive techniques to show and reinforce appropriate behavior that the child can employ in place of the unacceptable response that has to be suppressed (e.g., Walters & Parke, 1967). In that way the learner will develop a new response that *can* be made without getting punished. Without such a positive alternative, the child faces a dilemma in which total avoidance may seem the only possible route. Punishment may have very unfortunate effects when the child believes there is no way in which he or she can prevent further punishment and cope. If you become convinced that no potentially successful actions are open to you, that you can do nothing right, depression and hopelessness may follow (Seligman, 1975).

SUMMARY

1. B. F. Skinner's approach refuses to infer drives or other internal motivational forces or traits. Analysis of the stimulus conditions controlling behavior replaces inferences about internal conflicts and underlying motives. Skinner's conceptualization leads to the analysis of behavior in terms of conditioning processes.

2. In classical conditioning, a potent and a neutral stimulus event have been paired together so that eventually the previously neutral event alone evokes portions of the same response that the potent one did initially. Classical conditioning principles have been extended to explain some complex social phenomena and neurotic or abnormal behaviors such as irrational fears.

3. In *operant conditioning* behavior patterns may be modified by changing the consequences (reinforcements) to which they lead. Information

and attention, as well as food and sexual gratification, are among the many outcomes that can serve as reinforcers and increase the probability of a particular behavior in operant conditioning.

4. Discrimination learning is fundamental in the socialization process. In almost every culture, growing up requires learning numerous behaviors that are acceptable and expected under some circumstances but prohibited or punished under others, producing many discriminations. When behavior yields similar consequences under many conditions, generalization occurs and the individual may display similar behavior patterns across diverse settings. Similarity in meaning as well as in physical characteristics results in increased generalization.

5. The patterning or sequencing of the outcomes produced by a particular behavior can be even more important than the type of outcome itself. While continuous reward or reinforcement for behavior may result in faster learning, irregular or intermittent reinforcement often produces more stable behavior that persists even when reinforcement is withdrawn. In life situations many potentially maladaptive behaviors are rewarded irregularly and may therefore become very resistant to change.

6. The influence of punishment is complex and depends on many conditions, such as its timing. Unlike conditions in laboratory studies of punishment, in the child's life punishment is often subtle and indirect. Punishment in socialization depends on many contingencies, such as the child's age and sex as well as the type of behavior and the setting.

Chapter 12

Social Learning and Cognition

SOCIAL LEARNING: BEHAVIOR THEORY BECOMES COGNITIVE

In recent years, many of the original learning concepts have been liberalized and integrated with ideas and findings from other areas. Probably most important is the increasing attention to the person's cognitions—to what the person knows, thinks, believes, and expects. This trend may be called the growing "cognitivization" of behavior theory. It takes many forms, as the following sections discuss, and even includes a name change: the newer approaches tend to be called "social learning" or "cognitive social learning" theories.

Expectancies and Values

J. B. Rotter (1954, 1972) introduced this more cognitive element to personality-oriented learning theories. He emphasizes the individual's subjective expectations about future outcomes and the subjective value of reinforcements in the person's psychological situation. In Rotter's theory, the probability that a particular pattern of behavior will occur depends on the individual's expectancies concerning the outcomes to which his or her behavior will lead and the perceived values of those outcomes. For example, whether a girl behaves dependently or self-assertively with her teacher depends on her expectations regarding the probable consequences (e.g., attention, disapproval, affection) of either behavior and the value to her of those consequences.

To predict behavior we must estimate the individual's relevant expectancies and values in the particular situation. Subjective expectancies about probable outcomes reflect past learning experiences in similar situations. That is, expectations are a function of the person's past reinforcement. Likewise, the subjective values of outcomes are a function of prior learning. Specific expectancies, in Rotter's formulation, are easily modifiable by even seemingly minor alterations in the individual's situation. "Generalized expectancies" are assumed to be more consistent and stable across situations. Thus generalized expectancies are more like traits, although they are construed as learned expectations.

Expectancies and values also have remained central concepts in more recent social learning formulations. For example, they are seen as important qualities of the person that help guide choices among available action alternatives in the situation (Bandura, 1977, Mischel, 1973).

The Role of Awareness in Learning

When you are aware of the contingencies and rules governing the consequences to which your responses will lead, you learn better (Bandura, 1969). Under many conditions private expectations and hypotheses about what is happening may affect actions much more than does the objective reality of the rules and reinforcements that actually govern the outcomes of behaviors. Thus awareness of the relevant rules and contingencies greatly facilitates learning.

Consider, for example, an experimenter who gave social reinforcement (saying "Mmm-hmm") to college students when they said human nouns (e.g., "girl") in a word-naming task. Not surprisingly, subjects who became aware of the contingency for reinforcement (i.e., guessed correctly that social reinforcement from the experimenter depended on their saying human nouns) greatly increased their output of human nouns (DeNike, 1964). Those who remained unaware of the contingency did as poorly as subjects in a control group, who were reinforced randomly for 10

Albert Bandura (b. 1925)

percent of their responses (see Figure 12-1, Part *A*). Most interesting, the students showed no appreciable improvement in their performance until they correctly discerned the contingency for reinforcement; as soon as they became aware of the contingency they gave dramatically more human noun responses (Figure 12-1, *B*).

Rules and Symbolic Processes

Instructions and rules also can improve learning greatly. Rules help us to link discrete bits of information and powerfully affect our ability to learn and remember those materials (e.g., Anderson & Bower, 1973). In child-rearing it helps not only to reward appropriate behavior but also to specify the relevant rule. In addition to praising kind behaviors, for example, the parent might describe what exactly is being rewarded, as, "That's good: I like it when you are nice and gentle with your baby sister." If parents state the rules governing reinforcement, children can more readily learn the standards that they are supposed to adopt (e.g., Aronfreed, 1966). When children are informed that particular performance patterns are good and that others are unsatisfactory, they adopt the appropriate standards more easily than when there are no clear verbal rules (Liebert & Allen, 1967).

Rules also may affect classical conditioning. Suppose, for example, that a person has been conditioned in an experiment to fear a light because it is repeatedly paired with electric shock. Now if the experimenter tells her that the light (the conditioned stimulus) will not be connected again with the electric shock, her emotional reactions to the conditioned stimulus can quickly extinguish (Bandura, 1969). On later trials she can see the light without becoming aroused.

Figure 12-1
Awareness and Verbal Conditioning

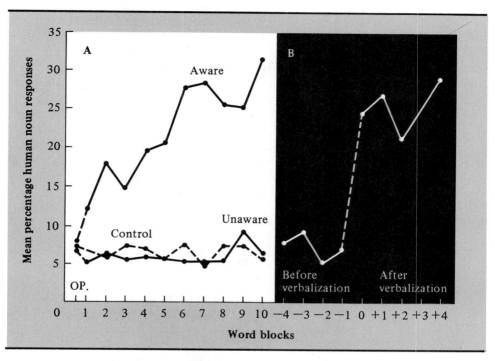

A, Mean percentage of human noun responses given by the aware, unaware, and control groups on each word block during the conditioning task. *B,* Mean percentage of human noun responses given by subjects in the aware group before and after they verbalized the reinforcement contingency correctly.

Adapted by Spielberger & DeNike (1966), from DeNike (1964).

OBSERVATIONAL (COGNITIVE) LEARNING

Reinforcement has powerful influences on behavior in a great variety of situations. But people also learn a great deal by observing others, not merely by experiencing rewards for what they do themselves. Much social learning occurs through observation without any direct rewards or reinforcement administered to the learner. Classical and operant conditioning, as discussed in Chapter 11, are important types of learning, but so is learning through observation.

Learning Through Observation

Learning without direct reinforcement is sometimes called *modeling,* sometimes *cognitive* or *observational learning.* All these terms refer to the acquisition of knowledge and potential behavior without the learner's receiving direct external reinforcement for that behavior. In fact, observational learning can occur without the person's ever performing the learned response at all. You can learn a lot about travel to the moon, for example, without ever going there yourself.

Observational learning occurs when people watch others or when they attend to their surroundings, to physical events, or to symbols such as words or pictures. Albert Bandura (1969, 1986) for the last three decades has led the way in the analysis of observational learning and its relevance for personality. Much human learning, from table manners and interpersonal relations to school and work, depends on observation of this kind rather than on direct reinforcement for a particular action. Nor is the observation itself always direct. We learn much from what others observe and then tell us about. The mass media, which are highly effective means of communicating experiences and observations, contribute heavily to the enormous amount we learn about the environment and the behavior of others.

The influence of observational learning through the mass media is seen in the contagion of aggression that has spread through the United States as a result of so many people's watching television violence. Although the television networks deny it, watching violence on television can have definite negative effects on viewers (Liebert, 1972; Murray, 1973). For example, after observing segments of aggressive films (from "The Untouchables"), children were more willing to hurt others than after viewing a neutral program that featured a track race (Liebert & Baron, 1972). Similarly, after watching violent cartoons for some time, children became more assaultive toward their peers than other youngsters who had viewed nonviolent cartoons for the same period of time (Steuer, Applefield, & Smith, 1971).

Completely new response patterns can be learned simply by observation of others performing them. Observation is of especially great importance for learning a language. Bandura (1977) emphasizes the advantages of observation for language learning compared to direct reinforcement for uttering the right sounds. He notes that exposure to models who speak the language leads to relatively rapid acquisition, while shaping would take much longer.

Children learn partly through observation and imitation.

Acquisition versus Performance: Knowing versus Doing

What a person is able to do in any given situation is often very different from what he actually does. No one does everything he has learned and is capable of doing. Many twelve-year-old children know how to suck their thumbs as well as three-year-olds, but few do. Even among three-year-olds there are striking individual differences in the amount of time they spend sucking their thumbs, though they are all equally able to do it. Likewise, men and women in our culture are equally capable of using eggbeaters and driving racing cars, but the sexes have differed markedly in how often they engage in these activities. In each of these instances we are distinguishing between the learning or *acquisition* of behaviors and their *performance* or enactment.

Human learning (acquisition) of new behavior is not dependent on reinforcement, though this may help (e.g., Bandura & Walters, 1963). Learning (acquisition) is mainly regulated by what we observe, perceive, and know rather than by conditioning and direct reinforcement. What a person can do, thus, depends on acquired knowledge and skills rather than on incentives or reinforcement.However, when it comes to performance, to what the person actually does, then incentives, values, and expected outcomes become crucial. A person's choice of what to do in a particular situation depends on such considerations as the outcomes expected for the different choices available in the particular context and their subjective values.

It is often difficult to discover a person's potential (previously learned) response patterns. We can only observe the person's performance. If one does not, for example, swear, play aggressively, cook, or fondle kittens, it may be because that individual never learned these behaviors. On the other hand, these responses may be potentially available, but the incentives provided in the situation may not elicit them. The introduction of a more potent incentive may readily produce the behavior, revealing that it has been learned but was not performed because the rewards offered were not powerful enough.

Observing Other People's Outcomes: What Happens to Them Might Happen to You

Valuable information about the possible consequences of various behaviors is gained from observing what happens to others when they engage in similar behaviors. Your expectations about the outcomes of a particular course of action depend not only on what has happened to you in the past when you behaved similarly in a similar situation, but also on what you have observed happening to others.

We are more likely to do something if we have observed another person (model) obtain positive consequences for a similar response. Seeing other children praised for cooperative play, for example, makes a child more likely to behave cooperatively in similar situations. If, on the other hand, models are punished for a particular pattern of behavior such as cooperation, observers are less likely to display similar behavior.

In one study, young children in a preschool watched a film of an adult hitting and kicking a Bobo doll and displaying other novel aggressive responses (Bandura, 1965). (See Figure 12-2.) The consequences to the adult of behaving aggressively varied for different groups of children. One group saw a film strip in which the

Figure 12-2
After Watching Films of an Aggressive Model Who Punched, Pummeled, and Hurled a Bobo Doll, These Children Spontaneously Imitated the Model's Aggressiveness When Put in a Similar Situation

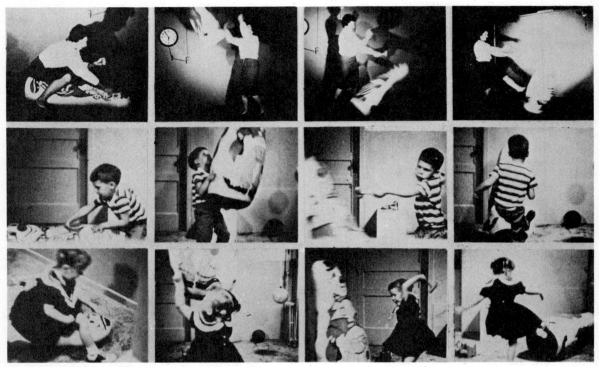

From Bandura (1965).

adult's aggressive behavior was punished, a second saw it rewarded, and a third group saw no consequences of any kind for the model. A fourth group saw no film at all. The children were then presented with the Bobo doll and their behavior was observed and recorded. Those who had observed aggressive behaviors modeled and rewarded imitated tham most; those who saw no aggressive model showed the least aggression.

When the children who had seen the film were told they would receive a small prize if they could reproduce all the modeled behaviors, the differences between the group that had watched different films (with different consequences to the model) were wiped out. All the children seem to have learned the model's behavior equally well, regardless of the reinforcing consequences. The observation of different consequences for the model's aggressive behavior increased or decreased the children's spontaneous performance of such behavior but not their knowledge of what the model had done.

Although laboratory studies offer clear demonstrations of the importance of expected consequences, examples from life are more dramatic. Consider, for instance, the role of modeling in airline hijackings (Bandura, 1973). Air piracy was unknown in the United States until 1961. At that time some successful hijackings of Cuban airliners to Miami were followed by a wave of hijackings, reaching a crest of eighty-seven airplance piracies in 1969. Fresh impetus came from news of a hijacker who successfully parachuted from an airliner with a huge sum of extorted money. Finally, hijackings were seemingly extinguished in the United States when new security procedures greatly decreased the chances of success and stern sanctions punished the offenders.

An equally dramatic modeling effect on a worldwide scale was the rash of kidnappings following the well-publicized abduction of Patricia Hearst in 1974. Within less than a month an unprecedented outbreak of kidnappings followed in the United States and in Europe and Latin America as well. Ransom demands ranged from $1 million to more than $20 million. In addition to the many actual kidnappings, kidnap threats escalated. The kidnappers seemed to have little in common, and their motives ranged from political revolution to cash.

In sum, you do not have to perform particular actions yourself in order to learn about them and their consequences; the observed as well as the directly experienced consequences of performances influence subsequent behavior. You do not have to rob a bank to learn that it is punishable; you do not have to be arrested for hijacking to learn about its consequences; and you do not have to rescue a burning child from a fire or return found money to discover that such acts are considered good. Information that alters the person's anticipations of the probable outcomes to which a behavior will lead changes the probability that he will perform that behavior. Models inform us of the probable consequences of particular behaviors and thus affect the likelihood that we will perform them. Observation also influences the emotions we experience (see *In Focus 12.1*).

What Occurs in Observational Learning?

The existence and importance of observational (cognitive) learning has been demonstrated often. But just what is learned through observation? Modeling has been shown to teach effectively rules of language, abstract principles and concepts, creative and novel ways of solving problems, and many other rule-regulated strategies for coping inventively with difficult tasks (Zimmerman & Rosenthal, 1974). Rather than learn specific stimulus–response associations through observation, we seem to acquire rules in this way. These rules can be applied to many new instances, permitting us to generate adaptive new behaviors that go far beyond simple mimicry or rote repetition of what was previously observed. The products of observational learning thus appear to include rules and competencies for constructing (generating) novel behavior in related new situations. In addition to fostering such competencies, observation also informs us about the probable outcomes to be expected for particular behaviors, often much more efficiently than do other forms of learning.

Now consider briefly the basic processes that occur in observational learning. These processes have four components: attention, retention, reproduction, and motivation (Bandura, 1977).

To learn from observation it is obviously essential to *attend* to the distinctive features of the modeled behavior. Models would have little longterm impact if we did not *remember* (retain) their behavior after watching it. Consequently, organiz-

In Focus 12.1
Vicarious
Conditioning:
He Gets
Shocked, You
Get Frightened

A person does not need to have a direct experience with a stimulus to learn an emotional response to it. By observing the emotional reactions of others to a stimulus, it is possible vicariously to learn an intense emotional response to that stimulus. You may become "vicariously conditioned" when you observe repeated contiguity (association) between a stimulus and an emotional response exhibited by another person without receiving any direct positive or aversive stimulation yourself.

In one study adults observed another person making fear responses in reaction to the sound of a buzzer supposedly associated with the onset of an electric shock. (Actually the person was a confederate of the experimenter and only feigned fear without getting any shocks.) Gradually, after repeatedly watching the pairing of the buzzer and the fear responses made by the confederate, the observers themselves developed a measurable physiological fear response to the sound of the buzzer alone (Berger, 1962).

Vicarious conditioning can help explain the development of emotional behavior—for example, fear of dogs or snakes—in people who have had no direct experiences with the emotion-provoking stimuli. A person may come to fear the animal just from observing the emotional reaction of another person to the same animal or even from reading about it. Likewise, a girl whose mother repeatedly reveals inhibited attitudes toward men and sex might adopt some of her mother's attitudes without ever having a traumatic sexual experience herself. Thus previously neutral stimuli may come to elicit strong emotional responses by merely being observed under appropriate conditions (e.g., Venn & Short, 1973).

Observational learning can help remove fears and other strong emotional reactions as well as teach them. A group of preschool children who were intensely afraid of dogs watched from a safe distance while a fearless model (another preschool child) played with a dog (Bandura, Grusec, & Menlove, 1967). The model began by briefly petting the dog through the bars of a playpen in which the animal was confined and became progressively bolder over a series of eight short sessions. In the final session the child model joined the dog inside the playpen, fed it weiners and milk from a baby bottle, and hugged it joyfully. Fearful children who observed the model later showed less fear and approached dogs more than did equally fearful children who had not had the opportunity to observe the model.

ing and rehearsing what was observed are important ingredients of learning from models. Especially when the behavior involves complex motor activities (as in swimming, driving, or tennis), the observer also must be able to put together physically the components of the action. Such *motor reproduction* requires accurate self-observation and feedback during rehearsal. For example, it is essential to observe the consequences of particular movements on the steering wheel, and on the gas and brake pedals of the car, when learning to park. Finally, to go from knowledge to performance the observer must have the *motivation* (reinforcement) to enact the behaviors that he or she has learned.

The Role of Self-Efficacy

Although many different techniques may all produce changes in behavior, might they all work through the same basic mechanism? Bandura (1978, 1982) has proposed that there is such a common mechanism: people's expectations of self-efficacy. As previously discussed, self-efficacy is the belief that one can personally master a particular behavior. Behavior therapy works, according to Bandura, by increasing efficacy expectations and thus leading people to believe that they can cope with the difficult situations that previously threatened them. In this view, individuals will try to overcome a particular fear to the extent that they expect they can do so successfully. Any methods that strengthen expectancies of personal efficacy (mastery) will therefore help the person. The best methods will be the ones that give the person the most direct, compelling success experiences, thereby increasing efficacy expectancies most. For example, actually climbing a fire escape successfully is a better way to overcome a fear of heights than just thinking about it because it provides a more complete success experience and a stronger expectation for future mastery.

Summary of Three Types of Learning

Table 12-1 summarizes the three types of learning discussed so far: classical conditioning, operant conditioning (both discussed in Chapter 11), and observational learning. There is much overlap between these types of learning, but each has some

Table 12-1
Summary of Three Types of Learning

Type	Arrangement	Effect	Example	Interpretation
Classical conditioning	A neutral stimulus (e.g., a bell) repeatedly and closely precedes a powerful unconditioned stimulus (e.g., food).	The originally neutral stimulus becomes a conditioned stimulus—that is, acquires some of the impact of the powerful unconditioned stimulus.	Bell begins to elicit a salivary response, even when not paired with food.	Organism learns that the conditioned stimulus (bell) signals (predicts) the occurrence of the unconditioned stimulus (food).
Operant conditioning	A freely emitted response (operant) is repeatedly followed by a favorable outcome (reinforcement).	The operant increases in frequency.	If crying is followed by attention, its frequency is increased.	Organism learns that this response will produce that particular outcome.
Observational learning	Observer attends to a modeled sequence of novel behavior.	Observer becomes capable of enacting the sequence. The frequency of performing it and related behaviors may change.	Watching unusual forms of violence on TV.	Through observation the ability to reconstruct the behavior is acquired; its enactment depends on expected outcomes.

relatively distinct features, as indicated in the table, and each has a place within current social learning theory.

SOME IMPLICATIONS OF SOCIAL LEARNING FOR STUDYING PERSONS

Social learning theory influences ideas about the nature of personality traits and has many implications for how to think about people and how to study them.

Consistency and Discriminativeness in Personality

Recall that trait theories hypothesize broad dispositions and cross-situational consistencies as the basic units of personality (Chapter 5). In contrast, social learning theory suggests that a person will behave consistently across situations only to the extent that similar behavior leads, or is expected to lead, to similar consequences across those conditions (Mischel, 1968). Most social behaviors are not uniformly rewarded across different settings or situations. For example, while physical aggression is encouraged among boys sparring in the gym, it is not supported when the boys aggress toward their fathers or their younger siblings. Consequently sharp discriminations develop, the individual becoming aggressive in one context and not in the other (Bandura, 1973).

Guided by the idea that behavior depends on its probable outcomes, social learning theorists anticipate "behavioral specificity" rather than trait consistency across conditions in which there are different discriminative stimuli. On the other hand, if responses are uniformly rewarded across diverse conditions, "generalization" occurs, and the person will show similar behaviors across many situations. For example, a boy whose father reinforces him for physical aggressiveness everywhere might become broadly aggressive and fight with his siblings as well as with his friends in many settings at home and at school. Thus, depending on conditions, the same person might show a trait like aggressiveness across several contexts or might be highly discriminative and behave one way in some settings but quite differently in others.

Consider a woman who seems hostile and fiercely independent some of the time but passive and dependent on other occasions. What is she really like? Which one of these two patterns reflects the woman that she really is? Is one pattern in the service of the other, or might both be in the service of a third motive? Must she be a really aggressive person with a facade of passivity—or is she a warm, passive-dependent woman with a surface defense of aggressiveness? Social learning theory suggests that it is possible for her to be *all* of these—a hostile, fiercely independent, passive, dependent, aggressive, warm person all in one (Mischel, 1969). Of course which of these she is at any particular moment would not be random and capricious; it would depend on who she is with, when, how, and much, much more. But each of these aspects of her self may be a quite genuine and real aspect of her total being.

Focus on Current Social Behavior

Social learning assessments do not describe people in generalized trait terms, sort them into type categories, or infer their conflicts and motives (Mischel, 1968,

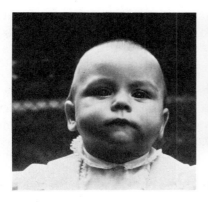

Even the young child processes information actively and is not an empty organism.

1981). Instead they sample what the individual does now in relation to the conditions in which he or she does it. In this sense, assessment involves an exploration of the unique aspects of the single person by analyzing how he or she changes in response to changes in stimulus conditions.

Social learning approaches to personality thus pay less attention to motivational and dispositional constructs and instead look more at behavior, and at the functional relations between what the person does and the psychological conditions of his or her life. What people do, of course, includes much more than motor acts. Far more than rats and other lower organisms that have been favorite subjects in experiments, humans do exceedingly complex and varied things, and they do them in their heads and guts as well as with their hands and feet. But to understand these complex activities, social learning theorists suggest that it might be wiser to spend more time looking at what people are doing rather than try to infer their global motives and traits.

Recall that trait theories emphasize differences *between* people in their response to the same stimulus. In contrast, social learning theories emphasize differences in the behavior of the *same* person as a result of even slight changes in conditions. This emphasis on the role of the stimulus in the regulation of the individual's behavior is indicated in Figure 12-3. Social learning analyses try to discover the impact or meaning of particular stimulus conditions in the person's life by observing how

Figure 12-3
The Social Behavior Approach Emphasizes That the Same Person Behaves Differently in Response to Various Psychological Situations (Stimuli)

Stimulus 1 (criticism from teacher) —— Response A (excuses and denial)

Stimulus 2 (criticism from mother) —— Response B (anger)

Stimulus 3 (rejection from girlfriend) —— Response C (remorse) —— Person 1

Stimulus 4 (hostility from peer) —— Response D (aggression)

Stimulus 5 (scolding from father) —— Response E (apology)

changes in those conditions alter what he or she expects, thinks, and does. In turn, the influence of changing expectations on subsequent behavior also are systematically examined (e.g., Merluzzi et al., 1981).

The Active Organism

An emphasis on the role of stimulus conditions is easily misinterpreted as implying a passive view of people—an image of organisms that are empty except for some psychological glue that cements or bonds a bundle of responses automatically to impinging external stimuli. Behavioral analyses attend to the exact covariations between changing conditions and the individual's changing behavior. But while alterations in conditions may come to regulate the individual's behavior, it is the person—not the stimulus or the situation—that is alive and that does the acting. Responses reside only in organisms, not in inanimate stimuli or conditions. Moreover, many of the "stimuli" that influence people are social in nature and in fact include other people; humans actively "shape" their world as much as they are shaped by it.

Social learning approaches recognize that the individual is not a passive bundle of responses. We have long learning histories and long memories, and much of what has happened to us gets internalized and affects all our current responses and future expectations. We interpret ourselves and our behavior—we evaluate, judge, and regulate our own performance. In addition to being rewarded and punished by the external environment, people learn to monitor and evaluate their own behavior and to reward and punish themselves, thus modifying their own behavior and influencing their environment (Bandura, 1971, 1986; Mischel, 1973, 1984). The principles that govern whether we reward or condemn our own behavior have been given much attention in social learning theory. The conditions that control the choice of self-administered rewards and punishments, and their relevance for the maintenance and modification of behavior, will be discussed in later chapters.

The Complexity of Social Learning

Most contemporary social behavior theories recognize that people may generate patterns of behavior in complex ways; they do not simply emit conditioned responses to stimuli. The complexity of the "rule systems" that may regulate how persons generate behavior may be seen best in language learning. Children's acquisition of the grammatical system of their language is an extraordinary accomplishment whose mechanisms still are not understood fully (e.g., Chomsky, 1965). It is also widely agreed that how people interpret and perceive internal and external stimuli influence how they ultimately react to them. While early "stimulus-response" theories often left a void between the stimulus and the response, more current learning approaches recognize that the organism is an alive, active processor and storehouse of information rather than a thoughtless, unfeeling automaton. Research and theorizing, however, investigate what people are *doing* (including what they are doing in their heads) rather than try to infer the global motives, dispositions, or traits that they *have*.

Although current behavior theories acknowledge the existence of internal states and processes, they emphasize that these internal events can only be studied through their behavioral referents and manifestations—such as self-reports or physiological measures of emotionality. Social learning approaches, like all other objective approaches, therefore have to rely on behavior as the basis of their observations.

"Preparedness:" Biological Constraints

While social learning theories emphasize learning, they recognize that the structure and capacities of the organism limit what it can learn and do. Granted that learning is crucially important, within every species and every individual there are structurally imposed limits on potential behavior, as for example, in the limits of human memory (e.g., Miller, 1956). Behavioral learning theories have to recognize that response capacities are restricted by the capacities and characteristics of the organism.

These "built-in" restrictions may even affect the ease with which different types of associations can be learned. For example, people often develop severe fears of snakes and dogs, but rarely for electric outlets, in spite of their potential hazards. Why? Might some types of stimuli be more likely to become "conditioned" stimuli for different species? (See *In Focus 12.2.*)

Summary

In sum, according to social learning theories, direct and vicarious (observed) learning experiences determine the potential behaviors available to the individual. The person's choice among those behavioral alternatives depends on the probable consequences expected in that particular situation.

Even subtle changes in the situation may alter expectancies about the probable consequences of behavior. Therefore behavior is often specific for a situation, and individuals show great discrimination in what they do.

Social learning theories seek to analyze the conditions that covary with changes in what people do. The focus therefore is on current behavior change in response to simulus changes, rather than on inferences about global dispositions. But while the focus is on what the person is doing now, the behaviors studied include self-regulatory and self-control patterns, and the things the individual expects and does privately and covertly. Similarly, while the emphasis is on the "stimulus" or situation, the stimulus often is exceedingly complex—including, for example, instructions, information and other people's behavior.

COGNITIVE SOCIAL LEARNING PERSON VARIABLES

People are confronted with a potential flood of stimuli; how are these stimuli selected, perceived, processed, interpreted, and used by the individual?

Theorists in the social learning approach have begun to seek more adequate conceptualizations of individual differences or "person variables." In recent years a great deal of personality research has focused on the processes through which social behaviors are acquired, evoked, maintained, and modified. Throughout Part Five

For many years, most psychologists who studied learning searched for general laws of learning that would hold for all species and for all types of responses and stimuli. Generally, they paid little attention to differences in learning among species and assumed that any such species-specific differences were relatively unimportant; the "laws" of conditioning should be universal, they thought, and would apply broadly. This assumption is now seriously challenged.

Instinctive Drift

Many amusement centers feature exhibits that show what odd things animals can be taught to do. Hungry chickens, for example, can be trained through standard techniques of operant conditioning to do things that are very unusual for chickens: for instance, they can be trained to deliver plastic capsules to outstretched human hands. Similarly, hungry pigs can be trained to put coins in "piggy" banks (Breland & Breland, 1966). But animal trainers also report that after a while the chickens begin to throw the capsules on the ground and peck at them and the pigs pause to "root" the coins (manipulate them with their snouts). Note that the animals do this in spite of the fact that through these behaviors the rewards given for the learned responses are postponed or even forfeited. In fact, the tendencies to peck and root grow stronger and stronger with more time. This gradual shift away from a conditioned response toward one that is made naturally by the animal in its usual environment (even though it means giving up rewards) is called *instinctive drift*. In the view of some psychologists, findings like these suggest that innate predispositions limit what organisms can learn.

Biological "Preparedness"

It is true that all associations between stimuli are not formed with equal ease. For example, rats fed a distinctively flavored new food and then made sick to their stomachs will avoid that food even if their illness does not occur until twelve hours later. If the same food is followed by electric shock, however, the rat does not learn to avoid eating it, even when the shock is delivered immediately (Garcia, McGowan, & Green, 1972). These variations in the ease of associating different types of events are believed by some scientists to be evidence of selective *biological preparedness*. They believe that organisms are biologically prepared to learn some associations or pairings more readily than others. It also has been speculated that the differences found between species in the types of associations learned readily may reflect differences in what it is necessary to learn in the evolutionary struggle for survival (Seligman, 1971; Seligman & Hager, 1972).

you see examples of these processes (such as observational learning.) Much less attention has been given to the psychological *products* within the individual of cognitive development and social learning experiences. A comprehensive psychology of personality also must attend to person variables that are the products of each individual's total history and that, in turn, regulate how new experiences affect him or her.

The person variables to be discussed in this section were proposed to provide a synthesis of seemingly promising constructs about persons developed in the areas of cognition and social learning (Mischel, 1973, 1984); hence they are called "*cognitive social learning* person variables." These variables were not expected to provide ways to accurately predict broadly cross-situational behavioral differences

On the other hand, evidence that learning in animals, especially lower animals, is constrained by their biological capacities does not necessarily mean that humans are innately programmed in favor of specific associations (Bandura, 1977). Indeed, such preprogramming in humans might be very disadvantageous in evolution because of our need to adapt to more complex and rapidly changing circumstances—circumstances that we ourselves often create. The human ability to symbolize experience allows enormous potential for learning. The extraordinary variety of human behaviors is well documented both by formal evidence and by casual observation. While chickens and pigs may have serious biological learning constraints, people are generally not so prewired, according to the counterargument. For example, in humans, taste aversions may be acquired in a number of different ways. The pairing of electric shocks, or even of nauseating thoughts, with the sight, smell, and taste of alcoholic drinks is as effective as drug-induced nausea in producing a temporary avoidance of alcohol by alcoholics.

Even in animals, differences between species in what can be learned easily are not necessarily the result of biologically built-in preparedness. For example, differences in the ease with which rats learn to associate taste and stomach upset may be due to their ability to discriminate between particular stimuli and to associate paired events over time rather than be due to an inborn preparedness to associate only certain types of stimuli (Krane & Wagner, 1975). Thus some stimulus relationships may be more readily learned by both humans and by lower organisms because the events covary in ways that make it easier to recognize their covariation in the environment. A rat can be taught in one trial to avoid shock from a grid floor if it can escape to a compartment with a smooth black floor. It takes close to ten trials to learn to avoid the shock when the escape compartment has a grid floor continuous with that of a shock compartment (Testa, 1974). Little Albert was conditioned by Watson and Raynor to fear rabbits by pairing the appearance of the rabbit with a loud noise. But a student of Watson's was unable to produce fears when either a block of wood or a dark curtain was paired with the noise. The argument that people are disposed biologically to fear things that have threatened human survival throughout evolution is intriguing (Seligman, 1971). But as Bandura warns; "It remains to be demonstrated whether the events people fear are better predicted from their threat to survival or from the degree to which they are correlated with direct, vicarious, and symbolic aversive experiences" (1977, p. 75).

between persons. But these variables suggest useful ways of conceptualizing and studying specifically how the qualities of the person influence the impact of stimuli ("environments," "situations," "treatments") and how each person generates distinctive complex behavior patterns in interaction with the conditions of his or her life.

First, one must deal with the individual's *competencies* to construct (generate) diverse behaviors under appropriate conditions. Next, one must consider the individual's *encoding* and categorization of situations. A comprehensive analysis of the behaviors a person performs in particular situations also requires attention to his or her *expectancies* about outcomes, the *subjective values* of such outcomes, and his or her *self-regulatory systems and plans*. The following five sections discuss each of

Walter Mischel (b. 1930)

these person variables. While these variables obviously overlap and interact, each may provide distinctive information about the individual and each may be measured objectively and studied systematically.

Competencies: What *Can* You Do?

Through direct and observational learning each individual acquires information about the world and his or her relationship to it. As a result of learning and cognitive development each of us develops competencies to construct (create, generate) many cognitions and behaviors. Our competencies include such knowledge as the rules that guide conduct, the concepts generated about self and others (Chapter 10), and a host of interpersonal and physical skills.

The concept of "competencies" refers to the individual's abilities to transform and use information actively and to create thoughts and actions (as in problem-solving), rather than to a store of static cognitions and responses that one "has" in some mechanical storehouse. Each individual acquires the capacity to actively construct a multitude of potential behaviors with the knowledge and skills available to him or her. Great differences between persons exist in the range and quality of the cognitive and behavioral patterns that they can generate. That becomes obvious from even casual comparison of the different competencies, for example, of a professional weight lifter, a chemist, a retardate, an opera star, or a convicted forger.

Different individuals may encode even the same situation in different ways.

Encoding Strategies: How Do You See It?

People differ greatly in how they encode (represent, symbolize) and group information from stimulus inputs. The same "hot weather" that upsets one person may be a joy for another who views it as a chance to go to the beach. A stimulus perceived as "dangerous" or "threatening" by one person may be seen as "challenging" or "thrilling" by the one next to her. The "environment," the "situation," the "stimulus" are perceived, coded, and categorized by each person, and these cognitive operations influence the impact that they have.

People can readily perform *cognitive transformations* on stimuli, focusing on selected aspects of the objective stimulus (e.g., the taste versus the shape of a food object); such selective attention, interpretation, and categorization change the impact the stimulus exerts on behavior (Geer, Davison & Gatchel, 1970; Holmes & Houston, 1974). How we encode and selectively attend to observed behavioral sequences also greatly influences what we learn and subsequently can do. Clearly, different persons may group and encode the same events and behaviors in different ways (e.g., Argyle & Little, 1972) and selectively attend to different kinds of information (Bower, 1981).

People abstract and infer traits and other dispositions to describe and explain their experience and themselves, just as professional psychologists do. It would be strange if personality psychologists ignored the concepts, perceptions, and experiences of those whom they are studying. We noted before that people categorize their own personal qualities in relatively stable trait terms (e.g., on self-ratings and self-report questionnaires). These self-categorizations, while often only complexly related to nonverbal behavior, may be relatively durable and generalized (Chapter 10).

Expectancies: What Will Happen?

So far the person variables considered deal with what the individual *can* do and how one categorizes (codes) events. But we also must move from what we know and how we perceive (categorize) events to what we *do,* from potential behaviors to actual performance in specific situations. This move requires attention to the determinants of *performance*. For this purpose, the person variables of greatest interest are the individual's expectancies. If you cheat on the final exam and are caught, what do you expect will be the consequences? If you tell your friend what you really think of him, what will happen to your relationship? If you switch to another career plan, what will be the probable effects?

To predict specific behavior in a particular situation it is essential to consider the individual's specific expectancies about the consequences of different behavioral possibilities in that situation. These expectancies guide the person's selection (choice) of behaviors from among the many which he or she is capable of constructing within any situation. We generate behavior in light of our expectancies even when they are not in line with the objective conditions in the situation. If you expect to be attacked you become vigilant even if your fears later turn out to have been unjustified.

One type of expectancy concerns *behavior-outcome relations.* These *behavior-outcome expectancies* (hypotheses, contingency rules) represent the "if _____, then _____," relations between behavioral alternatives and expected probable outcomes in particular situations. In any given situation, we generate the response pattern that we expect is most likely to lead to the most subjectively valuable outcomes (consequences) in that situation (e.g., Mischel, 1973; Rotter, 1954). In the absence of new information about the behavior-outcome expectancies in any situation, one's performance will depend on one's previous behavior-outcome expectancies in similar situations. That is, if you do not know exactly what to expect in a new situation (a first job interview, for example) you are guided by your previous expectancies based on experiences in similar past situations. This point is illustrated in a study that showed that the expectancies people brought to a situation influenced their behavior in the situation when no other relevant information was available (Mischel & Staub, 1965). But the same study also showed that new information about probable outcomes in the particular situation may quickly overcome the original expectancies. The new information produces highly specific situational expectancies that influence performance most significantly.

Adaptive performance requires the recognition and appreciation of new contingencies. To cope with the environment effectively, we must identify new contingencies as quickly as possible and reorganize behavior in the light of the new expectancies. Strongly established behavior-outcome expectancies may handicap our ability to adapt to changes in contingencies. Indeed, "defensive reactions" may be seen in part as a failure to adapt to new contingencies because one is still behaving in response to old contingencies that are no longer valid. For example, if on the basis of past experiences a man overgeneralizes and becomes convinced that people will take advantage of him unless he is hostile toward everyone, his own suspicious, aggressive behavior may prevent him from ever being able to disconfirm his belief, even when people are trying to be considerate. The "maladaptive" individual is behaving in accord with expectancies that do not adequately represent the actual behavior-outcome rules in his or her current life situation.

A closely related second type of expectancy concerns *stimulus-outcome relations.* The outcomes we expect depend on a multitude of stimulus conditions. These stimuli ("signs") essentially "predict" for us other events that are likely to occur. More precisely, each of us learns that certain events (cues, stimuli) predict certain other events. Outside the artificial restrictions of the laboratory, in the human interactions of life, the "stimuli" that predict outcomes often are the social behaviors of others in particular contexts. The meanings attributed to those stimuli hinge on learned associations between behavioral signs and outcomes.

For example, through learning, "shifty eyes," "tight lips," "lean and hungry looks," obese body build, age, sex, eye contact, posture, gestures, and many even subtler behavioral cues (e.g., regarding the status and power of others) come to predict for us other behaviors correlated with them. If your friend nods "understandingly" when you start to talk frankly about a personal problem you will proceed differently than if she taps her foot "impatiently," gets up abruptly, or yawns. Each of these "signs" implies a very different outcome in the particular situation. Some expected stimulus-outcome associations presumably reflect the perceiver's idiosyncratic (unique) learning history, and his or her own evolving personal rules about stimulus meanings. Many of these associations, however, are likely to be widely shared by members of the same culture who have a common language for verbal and nonverbal communication.

Finally, a third type of expectancy consists of *self-efficacy expectations:* the person's confidence that he or she *can* perform a particular behavior, like handling a snake or taking an exam. Measures of these expectations predict with considerable accuracy the person's actual ability to perform the relevant acts. And therapeutic improvement of efficacy expectancies in turn allows the person to function more effectively (Bandura, 1978).

Subjective Values: What Is It Worth?

Two individuals who have similar expectancies nevertheless may act differently if the outcomes they expect have different *values* for them (e.g., Rotter, 1954, 1972). For example, if everyone in a group expects that approval from a teacher depends on saying certain things, there may be differences in how often they are said due to differences in the perceived value of obtaining the teacher's approval. Praise from the teacher may be important for a youngster striving for grades, but not for a rebellious adolescent who rejects school. Such differences reflect the degree to which different individuals value the same expected outcome. What delights one person may repel his or her neighbor. Therefore it is necessary to consider still another variable: the subjective (perceived) value for individuals of particular classes of events, that is, their stimulus preferences and aversions, their likes and dislikes, their positive and negative values.

Self-Regulatory Systems and Plans: How Can You Achieve It?

While behavior depends to a considerable extent on externally administered consequences for actions, people regulate their own behavior by self-imposed goals (standards) and self-produced consequences. Even in the absence of external constraints and social monitors, we set performance goals for ourselves. We react with self-criticism or self-satisfaction to our behavior depending on how well it matches our expectations and standards. The expert sprinter who falls below his past record may condemn himself bitterly; the same performance by a less experienced runner who has lower standards may produce self-congratulation and joy.

Another feature of self-regulatory systems is the person's adoption of *contingency rules* and *plans* that guide his or her behavior in the absence of, and sometimes in spite of, immediate external situational pressures. Such rules specify the kinds of behavior appropriate (expected) under particular conditions, the performance levels (standards, goals) which the behavior must achieve, and the consequences (positive and negative) of attaining or failing to reach those standards. Plans also specify the sequence and organization of behavior patterns (e.g., Miller, Galanter, & Pribram, 1960; Schank & Abelson, 1977). Individuals differ with respect to each of the components of self-regulation depending on their unique earlier histories.

Self-regulation provides a route through which we can influence our environment substantially, overcoming "stimulus control" (the power of the situation). We can actively *select* the situations to which we expose ourselves, in a sense creating our own environment, entering some settings but not others, making decisions about what to do and what not to do. Such active choice, rather than automatic responding, may be facilitated by thinking and planning and by rearranging the environment itself to make it more favorable for one's objectives. If one cannot study well in the midst of noise one may try to find a quiet place for work or attempt to soundproof one's room as much as possible. Even when the environment cannot be changed physically (by rearranging it or by leaving it altogether and entering another setting), it may be possible to *transform* it psychologically by self-instructions and ideation as in mental self-distractions or, conversely, concentrated attention (e.g., Mischel, 1984).

Summary of Person Variables

To summarize, individual differences in behavior may be due to differences in each of the discussed person variables (summarized in Table 12–2) and in their interactions. First, individuals differ in their *competencies,* i.e., in their ability to gen-

Table 12-2
Summary of Cognitive Social Learning Person Variables

1. COMPETENCIES: ability to construct (generate) particular cognitions and behaviors. Related to measures of IQ, social and cognitive (mental) maturity and competence, ego development, social-intellectual achievements and skills. Refers to what the person knows and *can* do.
2. ENCODING STRATEGIES AND PERSONAL CONSTRUCTS: units for categorizing events, people, and the self.
3. EXPECTANCIES: behavior-outcome and stimulus-outcome relations in particular situations; self-efficacy or confidence that one can perform the necessary behavior.
4. SUBJECTIVE VALUES: motivating and arousing stimuli, incentives, and aversions.
5. SELF-REGULATORY SYSTEMS AND PLANS: rules and self-reactions for performance and for the organization of complex behavior sequences.

SOURCE: Adapted from Mischel, 1973.

erate cognitions and actions. For example, because of differences in skill and earlier learning, individual differences may arise in cognitive-intellective achievements. Differences in behavior also may reflect differences in how individuals *categorize* (encode) a particular situation. That is, people differ in how they encode, group, and label events and in how they construe themselves and others. Performance differences in any situation depend on differences in *expectancies* and specifically on differences in the expected outcomes associated with particular response patterns and stimuli. Differences in performance also may be due to differences in the subjective *values* of the expected outcomes in the situation. Finally, individual differences may reflect differences in the *self-regulatory systems and plans* that each individual brings to the situation. Obviously these person variables should be seen as just one way to view individual differences from a perspective that emphasizes cognition and social learning. Surely it is not the only way to view major differences among people, as is evident from the many alternative personality approaches discussed throughout this volume.

SUMMARY

1. Contemporary social learning theories (also called "social behavior" or "social learning" theories) recognize that the human being is a complex and active interpreter of the world. Nevertheless, they still tend to focus on what people are *doing* rather than on their underlying dispositions. They seek to understand the stimulus conditions influencing action and cognition.

2. J. B. Rotter introduced the notion of *expectancy* to personality-oriented learning theories. Expectancies about the consequences of behavior and the value to the person of those consequences determine choices. These expectancies and values are learned from past reinforcement.

3. Recent social learning theories emphasize observational learning. Complex and important potential behavior can be acquired without external reinforcement to the learner. Observational learning without direct reinforcement may account for the learning of many novel responses. Outcomes, incentives, and reinforcements are important, however, as determinants of what the person does in a particular situation, that is, which response one selects from the repertoire of alternatives available.

4. Social learning theory does not posit the existence of broad traits or dispositions. Instead, it views both consistency and discriminativeness in behavior as dependent on the conditions of learning and the cues in the situation.

5. Social behavior analyses study the covarying changes of conditions and behavior. Both the conditions and the behaviors may be exceedingly complex; they may involve much more than simple physical stimulus attributes. An especially important aspect of personality involves the person's self-reactions and self-regulation of outcomes that do not depend simply on the external environment.

6. Social behavior theory searches for causes in the current conditions that demonstrably control the person's present behaviors. This emphasis contrasts with traditional dynamic theories, which infer the person's motives, conflicts, and dispositions from behavioral "signs" and which construe behaviors as being in the service of underlying motives and their dynamic transformations.

7. Although behavior theories focus on learning, they recognize that an organisms's inborn capacities limit what can be learned. There is some controversy about the degree to which people are innately "prepared" to learn certain associations (for example, specific fears) more easily than other associations.

8. The focus of social behavior theory is on what people are doing in the "here and now" rather than on reconstructions of their psychic history. There is a refusal to hypothesize drives, forces, motives, and other broad dispositions as explanations, and an emphasis on the individual's potential for change.

9. Person variables are the products within the individual of cognitive development and social learning history. They in turn regulate the meaning of new experiences for the individual. They are an attempted synthesis based on cognitive and social learning psychology.

10. Person variables include the individual's competencies, encoding strategies and personal constructs, expectancies about probable outcomes, subjective values, and self-regulatory systems and plans.

Chapter 13
Analyzing Behavior

Each of the different behavioral approaches to personality has led to somewhat different applications. Psychologists influenced by B. F. Skinner's formulations often began by studying pigeons and other animals in the laboratory. More recently they have applied their ideas to clinical settings and devised assessments and behavior change programs for a wide range of human problems. The assessment and modification of complex behavior in diverse clinical and experimental settings also has been guided by various other social learning theories. This chapter considers the applications of the behavioral approach to assessment; Chapter 14 examines the applications to behavior change.

CHARACTERISTICS OF BEHAVIORAL ASSESSMENTS

Behavioral assessments emphasize stimulus conditions as regulators of behavior. Rather than seeking behavioral signs of the individual's general traits and motives, behavioral approaches have focused on the specific conditions and processes—both "inside" and "outside" the person—that might govern his or her behavior. For this purpose behaviorally oriented psychologists often followed an experimental strategy in which stimulus conditions are varied so that one can observe systematically any changes in the behavior of interest in relation to the changing conditions.

In one sense, all psychological approaches are based on behavioral observation: check marks on MMPI answer sheets and stories in response to inkblots obviously are behaviors just as much as crying or running or fighting. Moreover, we saw that the dynamic approach also samples such lifelike behaviors as bridge-building under stress. The difference between approaches depends on how these behaviors are used. As we saw, in the dynamic orientation the observed behaviors serve as highly indirect *signs* (symptoms) of the dispositions and motives that might underlie them. In contrast, in behavior assessments the observed behavior is treated as a *sample,* and interest is focused on how the specific sampled behavior is affected by alterations in conditions. Behavioral approaches thus seek to directly assess stimulus-response covariations.

Case Example: Conditions Controlling Gary's Anxiety

The general strategy of behavior assessment can be illustrated by once again considering the case of Gary W. An assessment of Gary in the framework of a behavioral orientation obviously would focus on his behavior in relation to stimulus conditions. But what behaviors, and in relation to which conditions? Rather than seeking a portrait of Gary's personality and behavior "in general," or an estimate of his "average" or dominant attributes, a behavioral perspective dictates a much more specific focus. The particular behavior patterns selected for study depend on the particular problem that requires investigation. In clinical situations, priorities are indicated by the client; in research contexts, they are selected by the investigator.

During his first term of graduate school Gary found himself troubled enough to seek help at the school's counseling center. As part of the behavioral assessment that followed, Gary was asked to list and rank in order of importance the three problems that he found most distressing in himself and that he wanted to change if possible. He listed "feeling anxious and losing my grip" as his greatest problem. To assess the behavioral referents for his felt "anxiety," Gary was asked to specify in more detail just what changes in himself indicated to him that he was or was not anxious and "losing his grip."

He indicated that when he became anxious he felt changes in his heart rate, became tense, perspired, and found it most difficult to speak coherently. Next, to explore the covariation between increases and decreases in this state and changes in stimulus conditions, Gary was asked to keep an hour-by-hour diary sampling most of the waking hours during the daytime for a period of two weeks and indicating the type of activity that occurred during each hour. Discussion with him of this record suggested that anxiety tended to occur primarily in connection with public speaking occasions—specifically, in classroom situations in which he was required to speak before a group. As indicated by the summary shown in Table

Table 13-1
Occurrence of Gary's Self-Reported Anxiety Attacks in Relation to Public Speaking

Occurrence of Anxiety	Hours with Anxiety (10)	Hours without Anxiety (80)
Within 1 hour of public speaking	9 (90%)	0 (0%)
No public speaking within 1 hour	1 (10%)	80 (100%)

13–1, only on one occasion that was not close in time to public speaking did Gary find himself highly anxious. That occasion turned out to be one in which he was brooding in his room, thinking about his public speaking failures in the classroom.

Having established a covariation between the occurrence of anxiety and public speaking in the social-evaluative conditions of the classroom, his assessors identified the specific components of the public speaking situation that led to relatively more and less anxiety. The purpose here was to establish a hierarchy of anxiety-evoking stimuli ranging from the mild to the exceedingly severe. This hierarchy then was used in a treatment designed to gradually desensitize Gary to these fear stimuli by "systematic desensitization" (described in Chapter 14).

Note that this behavioral assessment of Gary is quite specific: It is not an effort to characterize his whole personality, to describe "what he is like," or to infer his motives and dynamics. Instead, the assessment restricts itself to some clearly described problems and tries to analyze them in objective terms without going beyond the observed relations. Moreover, the analysis focuses on the *conditions* in which Gary's behavior occurs and on the covariation between those conditions and his problem. Behavior assessment tends to be focused assessment, usually concentrating on those aspects of behavior that can be changed and that require change. Indeed, as you will see often in this chapter, behavior assessment and behavior change (treatment) are closely connected.

The foregoing assessment of Gary illustrates one rather crude way to study stimulus-response covariations. Of course there are many different ways in which these covariations can be sampled (see *In Focus 13.1*). This chapter illustrates some of the main tactics developed for the direct measurement of human behavior within the framework of the social behavior orientation.

DIRECT BEHAVIOR MEASUREMENT

For many purposes in personality study it is important to sample and observe behavior in carefully structured, lifelike situations. In clinical applications, direct observation may give both client and assessor an opportunity to assess life problems and to select treatment objectives. Direct observation of behavior samples also may be used to assess the relative efficacy of various treatment procedures. Finally, behavior sampling has an important part in experimental research on personality.

The types of data collected in the behavioral approach include situational samples of both nonverbal and verbal behavior, as well as physiological measurements

Different approaches to personality can lead to quite different interpretations of the same case. This point is illustrated in the case of "Pearson Brack" (Grinker & Spiegel, 1945, pp. 197–207; Mischel, 1968).

Pearson Brack was a bombardier in the Tunisian theater of operations during World War II. During Brack's ninth mission his airplane was severely damaged by flak. It suddenly jolted and rolled, and then began to dive. The pilot regained control of the plane just in time to avoid crashing. During the plane's fall, however, Brack was hurled violently against the bombsight and was seriously injured. After his return from this mission he was hospitalized for a month and then, seemingly recovered, was returned to flight duty. On his next two missions, the tenth and eleventh, he fainted, and gradually his problem was brought to the attention of a psychodynamically oriented psychiatrist. Direct observations revealed that Brack's tendency to faint seemed specifically linked to being at an altitude of about 10,000 feet.

After intensive interviews, the psychiatrist concluded that Brack's fainting was connected to deep, underlying anxieties rooted in his childhood experiences. Brack was viewed as a basically immature person with long-standing insecurity who had inadequately identified with his father. The near-fatal plane incident was seen as essentially trivial, except in so far as it precipitated anxiety in an already insecure and immature individual.

In contrast, a behavioral analysis of the same case (Mischel, 1968) emphasized the severe emotional trauma that might have been conditioned to altitude cues during the mishap. That is, if Brack's injury occurred at about 10,000 feet, then any altitude cues present at that time might have become conditioned stimuli capable of eliciting a traumatic reaction (such as fainting). In that case, every time Brack later reexperienced cues connected with the accident (such as being in a plane at a comparable altitude), he would again become emotionally debilitated. In fact, when Brack was taken up in an airplane for further assessments, it was found that his emotional upset and fear occurred only around that altitude.

From the viewpoint of behavior theory, the relevant causes of Brack's problem were the conditions that seemed to control its occurrence, in this instance altitude cues that may have been associated with the trauma. But from the perspective of psychodynamic theory, the causes were Brack's inferred underlying anxiety and its antecedents in childhood. The key point is that different approaches to personality and assessment can lead to quite different interpretations of the same case.

of emotional reactions. In addition, a comprehensive assessment often includes an analysis of effective rewards or reinforcing stimuli in the person's life. Examples of all of these measures are given in the following sections.

Situational Behavior Sampling

Lovaas and his associates (1965b) wanted a comprehensive description that would contain not only the behaviors the subject performed but also the duration and the specific time of onset of each type of behavior. Such detailed information is needed if one wants to determine the covariations among an individual's specific behaviors, or their alterations in relation to various changes in the environment and in the behavior of other people.

Lovaas and his collaborators devised an apparatus that consists of a panel of buttons that are depressed by the observer. Each button represents a category of behavior (for example, "talking," "running," "sitting alone") and is attached to an automatic pen-recorder. Whenever a button is depressed, the corresponding pen on the recorder is activated. A continuous record is thus provided.

The observer presses the button when the subject starts the specific behavior designated by that button and does not release the button until that behavior stops. The observer after a little practice can devote his whole attention to watching what the subject is doing and yet record up to twelve different categories of behavior without looking at the button panel. The apparatus permits a record that is precise enough to include duration and the specific time of onset of each behavior. The method can then be applied to discover covariations among the individual's different behaviors and between his behavior and that of other people in the situation.

Even without the aid of such sophisticated apparatus, there have been many attempts to measure important interpersonal and emotional behaviors precisely. Some impressive examples come from assessments of the intensity or magnitude of such emotional behaviors as seemingly irrational fears (phobias).

The strength of diverse avoidance behaviors has been assessed reliably in clinical situations by exposing fearful individuals to series of real or symbolic fear-inducing stimuli. For example, fear of heights was assessed by measuring the distance that the phobic person could climb on a metal fire escape (Lazarus, 1961). The same people were assessed again after receiving therapy to reduce their fears. In this phase, the subjects were invited to ascend eight stories by elevator to a roof garden and to count the passing cars below for two minutes. Claustrophobic behavior— fear of closed spaces—was measured by asking each person to sit in a cubicle containing large French windows opening onto a balcony. The assessor shut the windows and slowly moved a large screen nearer and nearer to the subject, thus gradually constricting her space. Of course each subject was free to open the windows, and thereby to terminate the procedure, whenever she wished, although she was instructed to persevere as long as possible. The measure of claustrophobia was the least distance at which the person could tolerate the screen. As another example, Table 13-2 shows a checklist for performance anxieties before making a public speech.

Another study assessed nursery-school children's fear of dogs (Bandura, Grusec, & Menlove, 1966). Each child was led into a room containing, in the far corner, a playpen in which a dog was enclosed. The chidren's approach behavior was scaled objectively according to how near they ventured toward the animal. To get the highest scores the child had to climb into the playpen and sit in it while playing with the dog.

Direct behavior sampling has also been tried extensively in the analysis of psychotic behavior. One study, for instance, employed a time-sampling technique. At regular thirty-minute intervals, psychiatric nurses sought out and observed each hospitalized patient for periods of one to three minutes, without directly interacting with him (Ayllon & Haughton, 1964). The behavior observed in each sample was classified for the occurrence of three previously defined behaviors (for example, psychotic talk), and the time-check recordings were used to compute the relative frequency of the various behaviors. This time-sampling technique was supple-

Table 13-2
Timed Behavioral Checklist for Performance Anxiety

Behavior Observed	Time Period							
	1	2	3	4	5	6	7	8
1. Paces								
2. Sways								
3. Shuffles feet								
4. Knees tremble								
5. Extraneous arm and hand movement (swings, scratches, toys, etc.)								
6. Arms rigid								
7. Hands restrained (in pockets, behind back, clasped)								
8. Hand tremors								
9. No eye contact								
10. Face muscles tense (drawn, tics, grimaces)								
11. Face "deadpan"								
12. Face pale								
13. Face flushed (blushes)								
14. Moistens lips								
15. Swallows								
16. Clears throat								
17. Breathes heavily								
18. Perspires (face, hands, armpits)								
19. Voice quivers								
20. Speech blocks or stammers								

SOURCE: Paul, 1966.

mented by recordings of all the interactions between patient and nurses (such as each time the patient entered the nursing office). The resulting data served as a basis for designing and evaluating a treatment program. Equally clever ways of sampling and recording family interactions that occur naturally in the home were developed by Patterson and his associates (1976). They studied highly aggressive children in the contexts of everyday family life, for example at dinner. The attempt was to analyze the exact conditions under which aggression would occur more or less.

Verbal Behavior

What people say—their "verbal behavior"—may be just as important as what they do nonverbally. Most personality assessors, guided by trait and psychodynamic theories, have focused on verbalizations as signs of personality, rather than as descriptions of reactions to stimulus conditions. In social behavior assessment, on the other hand, what the person says is intended to help define the relevant stimuli and the response patterns that they have come to evoke and to specify the covariations between them. For example, a number of self-report techniques have been used to sample specific self-reported fears (Geer, 1965; Lang & Lazovik, 1963; Wolpe & Lang, 1964). These schedules list many items that were found to elicit frequent anxiety in patients. The respondent indicates on scales the degree of disturbance provoked by such items as strangers, bats, ugly people, mice, making mistakes, and looking foolish.

As was illustrated in the assessment of Gary's public speaking anxieties, a daily record may provide another valuable first step in the identification of problem-producing stimuli. Many behaviorally oriented clinicians routinely ask their clients to keep specific records listing the exact conditions under which their anxieties and problems seem to increase or decrease (Wolpe & Lazarus, 1966). The person may be asked to prepare by himself lists of all the stimulus conditions or events that create discomfort, distress, or other painful emotional reactions.

Measuring Expectancies

As part of their increasing use of cognitive constructs, social learning theorists have paid more attention to the measurement of people's cognitive (mental) activities, especially their expectancies (Bandura, 1978, 1982; Merluzzi et al., 1981). This new focus reflects the belief that the impact of the environment depends on what the individual knows, expects, and values (Mischel, 1973, 1983). Self-efficacy expectations, defined as the person's conviction that he or she can execute the behavior required by a particular situation, have been shown to be especially important predictors of behavior (Bandura, 1986). Therefore there have been many attempts to measure such expectations.

Self-efficacy is assessed by asking the person to indicate the degree of confidence that he or she can do a particular task. For example, Bandura et al. (1985) wanted to assess the recovery of patients who had suffered heart attacks. A large number of tasks were described to the patients. These included such potentially stressful things as driving a few blocks in the neighborhood, driving on a freeway, driving on a narrow mountain road. They also included situations that would induce other kinds of emotional strain, as illustrated in Table 13-3. For each item the respondent indicates the confidence level for being able to do the task.

Self-efficacy measures seem to predict the relevant behaviors at high levels of accuracy. For example, a consistently strong association was found between rated self-efficacy and the degree to which people showed increased approach behavior toward previously feared objects after they had received treatment for their fears (Bandura, Adams, & Beyer, 1977).

Table 13-3
Measuring Self-Efficacy Expectancies

Listed below are situations that can arouse anxiety, annoyance, and anger. Imagine the feelings you might have in each situation, such as your heart beats faster and your muscles tense. Indicate whether you could tolerate now the emotional strain caused by each of the situations.

Under the column marked *Can Do,* check (√) the tasks or activities you expect you could do *now.*

For the tasks you check under *Can Do,* indicate in the column marked *Confidence* how confident you are that you could do the task. Rate your degree of confidence using a number from 10 to 100 on the scale below.

10	20	30	40	50	60	70	80	90	100
Quite Uncertain				Moderately Certain					Certain

	Can Do	Confidence
Attend a social gathering at which there is no one you know.	_____	_____
At a social gathering, approach a group of strangers, introduce yourself and join in the conversation.	_____	_____
At a social gathering, discuss a controversial topic (politics, religion, philosphy of life, etc.) with people whose views differ greatly from yours.	_____	_____
Be served by a salesperson, receptionist, or waiter whose behavior you find irritating.	_____	_____
Complain about poor service to an unsympathetic sales or repair person	_____	_____
When complaining about bad service, insist on seeing the manager if you are not satisfied	_____	_____
In a public place, ask a stranger to stop doing something that annoys you, such as cutting in line, talking in a movie, or smoking in a no-smoking area.	_____	_____
Ask neighbors to correct a problem for which they are responsible, such as making noise at night, not controlling children or pets.	_____	_____
At work, reprimand an uncooperative subordinate.	_____	_____

SOURCE: Examples selected from Bandura et al., 1985.

Measurement of Bodily Changes

Measures of bodily changes in response to stimulation also provide important information, especially when the stimuli are stressful or arousing. Various indirect measures of bodily reactions during emotional activity have been developed. One of

Figure 13-1
Heart Rhythm in an Elderly Subject

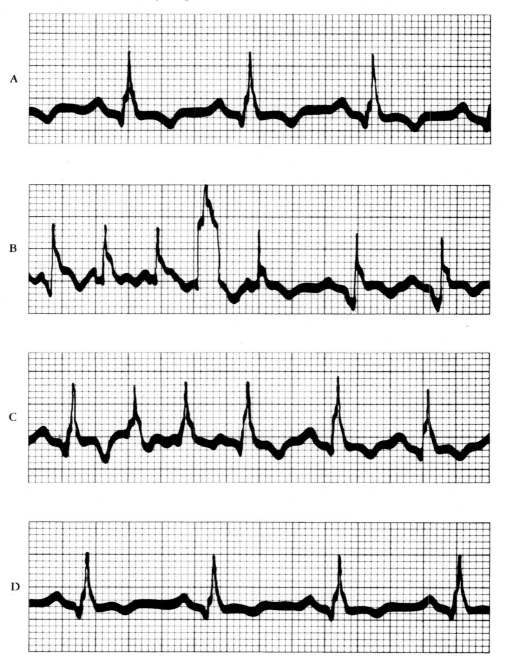

A, Normal heart rhythm (control level, rate 80). *B* and *C,* Initial beats show an abnormally irregular heartbeat during extreme emotional arousal. Last two beats show the heart rate has increased to 115. *D,* Following the end of arousal, heart rate returns to control level; abnormal beating is no longer present.
Courtesy of George Prozan, M.D.

323

the most convenient methods is the polygraph recording of some of the critical effects produced by the bodily activity involved in the reactions of the autonomic nervous system. The polygraph apparatus contains a series of devices that translate indices of body changes into a visual record by deflecting a pen across a moving paper chart.

One popular component of polygraphic measurement is the *electrocardiogram* (EKG). As the heart beats its muscular contractions produce patterns of electrical activity that may be detected by electrodes placed near the heart on the body surface. Figure 13-1 shows a record of heartbeats monitored by the polygraph, the area from one peak to another on the record representing one beat of the heart. An especially useful index of heart activity is based on the *rate* at which the person's heart is beating: It is measured in terms of the time between each beat on the electrocardiogram.

In a basically similar manner, changes in blood volume may be recorded by means of a *plethysmograph.* Other examples of valuable indices include changes in the electrical activity of the skin due to sweating (recorded by a galvanometer and called the *galvanic skin response* or GSR), changes in blood pressure, and changes in muscular activity.

Intense emotional arousal is generally accompanied by high levels of "activation" (e.g., Malmo, 1959). That is shown by increases in the activity of the cerebral cortex, increases in muscle tension and, at the behavioral level, increasingly vigorous activity and excitement. The degree of activation in the cerebral cortex may be inferred from "brain waves" recorded by the electroencephalograph (EEG), as illustrated in the records shown in Figure 13-2. As the EEG patterns in this figure indicate, the frequency, amplitude, and other characteristics of brain waves vary according to the subject's degree of behavioral arousal and excitement.

Finding Effective Rewards

So far we have considered the direct measurement of various responses. Behavior assessments, however, analyze not just what people do (and say and feel), but also the conditions that regulate or determine what they do. For that reason, behavior assessments have to find the rewards or reinforcers that may be influencing a person's behavior. If discovered, these reinforcers also can serve as incentives in therapy programs to help modify behavior in more positive or advantageous directions as discussed in Chapter 14. Psychologists who emphasize the role of reinforcement in human behavior have devoted much attention to discovering and measuring effective reinforcers. People's actual choices in lifelike situations, as well as their verbal preferences or ratings, reveal some of the potent reinforcers that influence them. The reinforcement value of particular stimuli also may be assessed directly by observing their effects on the individual's performance (e.g., Weir, 1965).

Primary reinforcers like food, and generalized conditioned reinforcers such as praise, social approval, and money, are effective for most people. Sometimes, however, it is difficult to find potent reinforcers that would be feasible to manipulate. In some learning situations with children or with chronic behavior problems it has been especially difficult to find realistic and effective reinforcers. For example, in one programmed instruction project, the investigators tried to use social approval

Figure 13-2
Various Human EEG Patterns under Several Arousal States

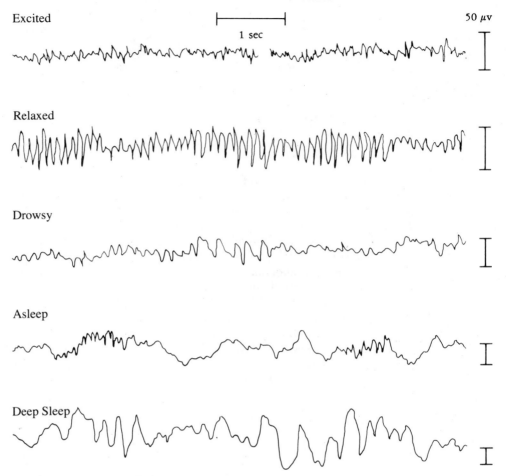

Excited

1 sec

50 μv

Relaxed

Drowsy

Asleep

Deep Sleep

SOURCE: From H. Jasper, in Penfield and Erickson, *Epilepsy and Cerebral Localization,* 1941. Courtesy of Charles C. Thomas, Publisher, Springfield, Ill.

and information feedback about test results as reinforcers for their pupils (Birnbrauer, Bijou, Wolf, & Kidder, 1965). The investigators soon discovered that right and wrong answers seemed to be one and the same to the children. Indeed, often the children did not even look at the answers the teaching programs supplied. Learning academic subjects was of little value to these children, and the researchers had to find better reinforcers. In other situations it has been discovered that such social rewards as praise may have little value with disturbed or delinquent patients (e.g., Atkinson, 1957; Cairns, 1959). Sometimes smiles and praise from the clinician may even lead to anxiety and hostility rather than to the intended beneficial effects.

With disturbed groups (such as hospitalized schizophrenic patients), many of the usual reinforcers prove to be ineffective, especially with people who have spent

Table 13-4
Mean Tokens Exchanged for Various Available Reinforcers
(By 8 Patients During 42 Days)

Reinforcers	Mean Tokens Paid	Number of Patients Paying Any Tokens
Privacy	1352.25	8
Commissary items	969.62	8
Leave from ward	616.37	8
Social interaction with staff	3.75	3
Recreational opportunities	2.37	5
Devotional opportunities	.62	3

SOURCE: Based on Ayllon and Azrin, 1965.

many years living in the back wards of a mental hospital. Ayllon and Azrin (1965) have shown how effective reinforcers can be discovered for seemingly unmotivated psychotic patients. These reinforcers then can serve to motivate the patients to engage in more adaptive behavior.

As a first step the patients were observed directly in the ward to discover their most frequent behaviors in situations that permitted them freedom to do what they wished. Throughout the day observers carefully recorded the things the patients did, or tried to do, without pressures from the staff. The frequency of these activities provided an index of their potential values as reinforcers.

Six categories of reinforcers were established on the basis of extensive observation. These categories were: privacy, leave from the ward, social interactions with the staff, devotional opportunities, recreational opportunities, and items from the hospital canteen. "Privacy," for example, included such freedoms as choice of bedroom or of eating group, and getting a personal cabinet, a room-divider screen, or other means of preserving autonomy. "Recreational opportunities" included exclusive use of a radio or television set, attending movies and dances, and similar entertainments.

The patients could obtain each of the reinforcers with a specific number of tokens, and they earned these tokens by participating in such rehabilitative functions as self-care and job training. A sensitive index of the subjective reinforcement value of the available activities is obtained by considering the outcomes for which the patients later chose to exchange most of their tokens. Over forty-two days the mean tokens exchanged by eight patients for the available reinforcers are shown in Table 13-4. Note that chances to interact socially with the staff and opportunity for recreation and spiritual devotion are most unpopular. These results suggest that, with chronic hospitalized patients such as these, therapy programs that rely primarily on social motivations would not fare well. Instead, such reinforcers as privacy, autonomy, and freedom might be the most effective incentives.

ASSESSING THE CONDITIONS CONTROLLING BEHAVIOR

To assess behavior fully, behavior theorists believe that we have to identify the conditions that control it. But how do we know whether or not a response pattern is really controlled or caused by a particular set of conditions? Behaviorally oriented psychologists test the conditions by introducing a change and observing whether or not it produces the expected modification in behavior. They ask: Does a systematic change in stimulus conditions (a "treatment") in fact change the particular response pattern that it supposedly controls? If we hypothesize that a child's reading problem is caused by poor vision, we would expect appropriate treatment (such as corrective eye glasses or corrective surgery) to be followed by a change in the behavior (that is, an improvement in reading). The same should be true for psychological causes. For example, if we believe that the child's reading difficulty is caused by an emotional problem in her relation to her mother, we should try to show that the appropriate change in that relationship will yield the expected improvement in reading. That is, to understand behavior fully we need to know the conditions that cause it. We can be most confident that we understand those conditions when we can show that a change in them yields the predicted change in the response pattern.

A rigid distinction between behavior assessment and treatment (i.e., behavior change) thus is neither meaningful nor possible. Indeed, some of the most important innovations in behavior assessment have grown out of therapeutic efforts to modify problematic behavior (discussed in Chapter 14). A main characteristic of these assessment methods is that they are linked closely to behavior change and cannot really be separated from it.

Functional Analyses

The close connection between behavior assessment and behavior change is most evident in "functional analyses"—that is, analyses of the precise covariations between changes in stimulus conditions and changes in a selected behavior pattern. Such functional analyses are the foundations of behavior assessments, and they are illustrated most clearly in studies that try to change behavior systematically. The basic steps may be seen in a study that was designed to help a girl in nursery school as discussed in *In Focus 13.2*.

A similar type of functional analysis was conducted by Bijou (1965). In this case, a mother had many problems with her six-year-old son, whom she described as extremely overdemanding. The mother first was oriented to the procedures and data collection techniques of the researchers, and the general assessment strategy was formulated and discussed. The mother and son next were asked to play in a playroom as they normally would at home. After receiving the family's consent, observers monitored and recorded these interactions from an adjacent observation room.

The mother's verbal and nonverbal immediate reactions to each of her child's behaviors were recorded with great care. For example, "excessive demandingness" was defined, in part, as verbal demands by the child to the mother, like "You go there and I'll stay here!" or "No, that's wrong! Do it this way." These behaviors were observed directly in the interaction between mother and child in the play room. After each instance of demanding behavior from the child, the mother's immediate reactions were scored. These data provided information about the maternal behaviors that might be reinforcing and maintaining the child's demandingness with her.

Ann was a bright four-year-old from an upper-middle-class background who increasingly isolated herself from children in her nursery school (Allen et al., 1964). At the same time she developed various ingenious techniques to gain prolonged attention from the adults around her. She successfully coerced attention from her teachers, who found her many mental and physical skills highly attractive. Gradually, however, her efforts to maintain adult attention led her to become extremely isolated from other children.

Soon Ann was isolating herself most of the time from other youngsters. This seemed to be happening because most of the attention that adults were giving her was contingent, quite unintentionally, upon behaviors that were incompatible with Ann's relating to other children. Precisely those activities that led Ann away from play with her own peers were being unwittingly reinforced by the attention that her teachers showered on her. The more distressing and problematic Ann's behavior became, the more it elicited interest and close attention from her deeply concerned teachers.

Ann was slipping into a vicious cycle that had to be interrupted. A therapeutic plan was formed where Ann no longer received adult attention for her isolate behavior and her attempts at solitary interactions with adults. At the same time the adults gave her attention only when she played with other children. That is, attention from adults became contingent on her playing with her peers.

As part of the assessment, two observers continuously sampled and recorded Ann's proximity to and interactions with adults and children in school at regular ten-second intervals. The therapeutic plan was instituted after five days of base-line data had been recorded. Now whenever Ann started to interact with children an adult quickly attended to her, rewarding her participation in the group's play activities. Even approximations to social play, such as standing or playing near another child, were followed promptly by attention from a teacher. This attention was designed to further encourage Ann's interactions with other children. For example: ''You three girls have a cozy house. Here are some more cups, Ann, for your tea party.'' Whenever Ann began to leave the group or attempted to make solitary contacts with adults, the teachers stopped attending to her.

Figure 13-3 summarizes the effects of the change in the consequences to Ann for isolate behavior with her peers. Notice that in the base-line period before the new response-reinforcement contingencies were instituted Ann was spending only about 10 percent of her school time interacting with other children and 40 percent with adults. For about half the time she was altogether solitary. As soon as the contingencies were changed and adults attended to Ann only when she was near children, her behavior changed quickly in accord with the new contingencies. When adult-child interactions were no longer followed by attention, they quickly diminished to less than 20 percent. On the first day of this new arrangement (day six), Ann spent almost 60 percent of her time with peers.

To assess the effects of reinforcement more precisely, the procedures were reversed on days twelve to sixteen. Adults again rewarded Ann with their attention

The assessors then tested experimentally whether or not the mother's observed responses to the child's demands were really maintaining his behavior. In this period the mother was counseled to try different reactions to the child's inappropriate behaviors, such as ignoring them totally. She was simultaneously helped to explore experimentally some new reactions to the child's more adaptive, prosocial behaviors (like cooperative play) that would help to strengthen these new behav-

Figure 13-3
Percentages of Time Spent by Ann in Social Interaction During Approximately Two
Hours of Each Morning Session

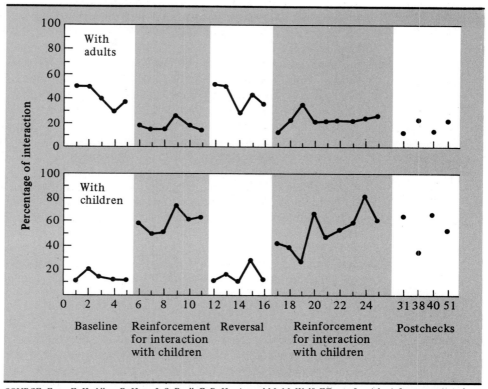

SOURCE: From E. K. Allen, B. Hart, J. S. Buell, F. R. Harris, and M. M. Wolf. Effects of social reinforcement on isolate
behavior of a nursery school child. *Child Development,* copyright 1964 by the Society for Research in Child Development,
Inc., *35,* No. 2, 310

for interacting with them and disregarded her interactions with children. Under these conditions (the "reversal" days in Figure 13-3), Ann's previous behavior reappeared immediately. In a final shift (beginning on day seventeen), in which attention from adults again became contingent upon Ann's interacting with children, her contact with peers increased to about 60 percent. After the end of the special reinforcement procedures (day twenty-five), periodic postchecks indicated that Ann's increased play behavior with peers tended to remain fairly stable.

iors. The subsequent interactions were again observed, assessed, and progressively modified as necessary to increasingly achieve the selected therapeutic goals. Thus personality assessment and behavior change become inextricably fused: the assessments guide the therapeutic program, and the efficacy of the treatment program is in turn continuously assessed.

The same basic designs and concepts have been extended to assess and modify important interpersonal behaviors within the home. In these studies, at the parent's request, the problematic parent-child relationship is observed directly in the home. When distressing interpersonal dilemmas are found, the parent is helped to change his behavior toward the child. These changes are designed, practiced, and assessed in everyday home situations in ways that ultimately lead to a more satisfying relationship (e.g., Hawkins et al., 1966; Patterson, 1976; Rekers & Lovaas, 1974; Wahler et al., 1965).

A final example of functional analysis comes from a series of studies (Lovaas, Freitag, Gold, & Kassorla, 1965a) assessing the conditions controlling self-destructive behavior in a psychotic nine-year-old girl. This child was extensively and severely self-destructive, tormenting herself violently. Her tragic repertoire included banging her head and arms and pinching and slapping herself repeatedly. Her intensely maladaptive behaviors dated back at least to her third year of life, and currently she engaged in almost no appropriate social activities. Her self-destructive tortures included sticking her head in an electric wall heater, thus setting her hair on fire. She spent much time in repetitive and stereotyped physical self-stimulation, and her interactions with others were minimal.

To explore the possible conditions controlling the child's self-destructiveness, the investigators studied how changes in selected variables affected the child's objectively measured self-destructive behavior. These assessments were made over a period of many sessions. One of the most important parts of the study investigated systematically any changes in the girl's self-destructive behavior following withdrawal of reinforcement (in the form of attention) for previously rewarded behavior.

The child's self-destructiveness seemed to increase most when attention was withdrawn from response patterns for which she previously had been reinforced. Thus the withdrawal of attention (reinforcement) from a previously reinforced response appeared to be the critical stimulus for her self-destructive behavior. The assessors interpreted their results to suggest that whenever her previously reinforced responses began to be unattended by others (extinguished), the girl could consistently reinstate the reinforcement (attention) by hurting herself.

Hurting oneself is painful, but sometimes it may be the only way to obtain such valued outcomes as parental attention. Experimenting with matches and stoves may be dangerous and potentially painful, but it also attracts mother's interest quickly. Thus the same stimulus that supplies pain can also lead to positive consequences and hence may serve to support seemingly bizarre behaviors—such as self-destructive acts. A complete analysis must deal with all the acquired meanings of a stimulus for the individual—not just the normative ones.

A complete analysis also must consider the total relations among stimulus conditions rather than focus on single aspects of reinforcement in isolation. These assessments showed, for example, that this child was highly discriminating in the very particular times and circumstances during which she became self-destructive. For example, massive withdrawal of attention—as when the experimenter withheld attention from an entire session—did not affect her self-destructive behavior. In contrast, the removal of smiles and attention only for previously reinforced responses led to radical changes in her behavior.

ADAPTATION AND DEVIANCE

Behavioral theories influence radically how one thinks about adaptation and deviance, as this section shows.

Evaluating the Consequences of Behavior, Not the Person

The behavioral approach avoids evaluating the health, adequacy, or abnormality of the person or personality as a whole. Instead, when judgments must be made, they focus on evalutation of the individual's specific behaviors. Behaviors are evaluated on the basis of the kinds of consequences that they produce for the person who generates them and for other people who are affected by them. "Advantageous" (adaptive, constructive) behaviors are those whose consequences are judged to be favorable; conversely, "disadvantageous" (problematic, maladaptive, destructive) behaviors are those that yield negative effects.

Evaluations about the positive or negative consequences of behavior are social and ethical judgments that depend on the values and standards of the community that makes them. Advantageous behaviors are those judged to have positive personal and interpersonal consequences (e.g., helping people "feel good," or increasing constructive, creative outcomes) without any aversive impact on others. Behaviors that have negative, life-threatening, destructive consequences, or those that endanger the full potentialities of the person or other people (e.g., debilitating fears, homicidal attempts), would be considered maladaptive.

The behavioral approach also implies a high value for the development of the

Judgments about behavior depend on the values and standards of the community.

individual's total competencies and skills so that he or she can maximize opportunities and options. Similarly, the person must be able to discern the important contingencies and rules of reinforcement in his or her life in order to maximize satisfactions and minimize aversize, disadvantageous outcomes. To be able to overcome unfavorable environments and life conditions, a high premium is also put on the development of effective strategies for self-control and for modifying the impact of the environment itself to make it more favorable.

Beyond these generalizations, the behavioral approach to deviance has sharply attacked the traditional "disease" models that view problematic (deviant, disadvantageous) behaviors as symptoms of an underlying mental illness, as discussed next.

Disease Models

Historically, with the growth of modern biology and medicine, disease explanations of abnormal behavior became especially favored. At the turn of this century the discovery and cure of a psychotic disorder stemming from syphilis ("general paresis") greatly reinforced the belief that deviant behavior might be a sign of organic disease. Similarly, more recent findings concerning biochemical and genetic antecedents in certain forms of mental deficiency (discussed in Chapter 7) bolstered the biological approach to psychological problems.

In the biological view, deviant behaviors are construed as symptoms of underlying organic pathology. Different types or patterns of deviant behavior (e.g., delusions, depression) presumably might be linked to different types of pathology (e.g., brain infections, tumors), just as different symptoms of physical disease may be attributed to particular underlying organic causes. As noted previously (Chapter 7), research continues in the search for organic causes of psychological problems, but at present most difficulties in social behavior appear to be "functional" (nonorganic). Nevertheless, the disease view is still widely used as an *analogy* for conceptualizing psychological problems even when no physical disease has been implicated. In this quasi-disease approach the person is seen as a "patient" whose deviant behaviors are considered "symptoms" of underlying *mental* or emotional pathology comparable to a physical disease like influenza or cancer. The patient's disturbed behavior is not the focus of interest because it is seen as merely symptomatic of underlying pathology, as was illustrated in the psychodynamic approach to problematic behaviors.

Criticisms of Disease Models

Behaviorally oriented critics argue that while the disease model may be appropriate for the analysis and treatment of physical illness in medicine, it is not useful for conceptualizing psychological problems (e.g., Bandura, 1969; Krasner & Ullmann, 1973). When there are no identified discrete organic causes (like germs) that can be tied clearly to social behavior, speculations about hypothesized pathology cannot help the troubled person. On the contrary, conceptualizing behavior in terms of diseases whose properties and physiological bases are not established can divert the assessor from the psychological and life conditions that influence the maladaptive behavior. The disease model may also lead to an unfortunate emphasis on psychiatric hospitalization, rather than on new learning experiences in life settings and on social education.

Szasz (1960) has been a foremost critic of the "disease approach" to psychological problems. He believes that to speak of "mental illness" as if it were a disease-like sickness is to subscribe to a myth. He contends that the so-called sick person has problems of living and is not a victim of "demons, witches, fate, or mental illness" (Szasz, 1960, p. 118). The term "mental illness" may have had some value initially in that it permitted troubled and unusual individuals to be considered "sick" rather than morally tainted. But while shielding individuals from social criticism, the concept of mental illness also divests them of the privileges and human rights that are part of responsibility. Szasz maintains that hospitalized, legally committed mental patients in fact lose their basic freedoms and are victimized by society rather than by a disease.

Moreover, the widespread practice of construing the whole person as either "sick" or "healthy" is often unjust, because a person may function perfectly well in many aspects of life and be incompetent or deficient only in some domains. In fact, most "mentally ill" individuals are capable of much adequate and responsible behavior and show impairments that are relatively specific rather than generalized (Fairweather, Sanders, Cressler, & Maynard, 1969). Therefore many therapists bemoan the "common tendency to classify people as either sick or well, even though a person's social status *should* primarily be determined by her ability to assume particular rights and duties" (Fairweather et al., 1969, p. 18).

Some of the essentials of the criticisms of the disease model were put this way: "A child who strangles kittens or spits at his mother does not have a disease although he does have something that somebody judges to be a problem" (Peterson, 1968, p. 5). But no matter how deserved some of the criticisms of the disease model may seem to be, it is essential to keep an open mind. It is quite possible that future research may reveal distinctive pathology, genetic patterns, or brain or hormonal problems correlated with at least some patterns of deviant behavior that now are considered to be of psychological origin (for further discussion, see *In Focus 13.3*).

Deviance as Problematic Behavior

Even severe critics of the disease model generally recognize that at least some patterns of behavior may exist in many cultures or even everywhere. But they still insist that the vast bulk of human problems reflect unfortunate social histories and environments. They therefore focus their attention on the disadvantageous behaviors themselves. Rather than viewing maladaptive patterns as merely symptoms or signs of underlying diseases or dynamics, this view rejects the symptom-disease distinction and concentrates on the individual's problematic behaviors. For example, rather than seeing an individual's fear of snakes as possibly symbolic of unconscious sexual conflicts, the behavior therapist deals with the snake phobia itself and attempts to treat it in its own right. Thus in the behavioral approach the focus shifts from hypothesized but unobservable physical or mental disorders in the person to problematic behaviors. The focus on behavior was illustrated in the assessment of

The medical model or disease approach to psychological problems has become highly controversial. Some consider it misguided because they believe psychological problems, unlike physical illness, are not caused by underlying agents such as germs that can be closely tied to a pattern of symptoms (e.g., Szasz, 1970; Ullmann & Krasner, 1969). The "symptoms" of deviance are problematic social behaviors; it may not be much help to search for an underlying disease as the cause. Moreover, while it may appear to be more humane to consider troubled people ill than to consider them evil or possessed, the people who have been labeled mentally ill may lose many of their human rights and responsibilities and may be stigmatized and victimized by society in many ways, such as job and social discrimination.

In one study normal individuals (doctors, psychologists, and graduate students) participated in a research project in which they admitted themselves to psychiatric hospitals and then, during their confinement, proceeded to behave rationally. What happened to them dramatically illustrates some of the hazards of the diagnostic system and the medical model or disease approach (Rosenhan, 1973). These individuals were consistently treated by the hospital staff (who did not know their true identity) as if they were insane as soon as they were admitted to the hospital and labeled psychotic. Even when their behavior was completely rational and normal, they were still treated as insane by the staff, although some of the other patients suspected that they did not really belong there.

Thomas S. Szasz, himself a psychiatrist

Hospitalization may increase people's sense of isolation by removing them even further from the life that they must learn to face.

has become the most controversial and outspoken challenger of the tendency to view deviant behavior as a sign of mental illness. He says:

> My aim is to suggest that the phenomena now called mental illness be looked at afresh . . . that they be removed from the category of illnesses . . . and regarded as the expressions of man's struggle with the problem of *how* he should live (Szasz, 1960, p. 113).

An emphasis on treating psychiatric problems as problems of living can have many beneficial effects. For example, it can help reduce the tendency to stigmatize people as ill or crazy whenever their behavior upsets us or is socially deviant. As many anthropologists have pointed out often, what seems normal in one culture may seem bizarre or abnormal in another. However, a closer look at diverse cultures yields some surprising results. A careful analysis of the Eskimos on an Alaskan island and a Yoruba group in Nigeria, for example, indicated that they both have a word translatable as "insanity" (Murphy, 1976). The word is used to label conduct consistent with the Western definition of schizophrenia, such as hearing voices, talking to oneself, and having outbreaks of violence. In both cultures, people who consistently show such conduct are considered ill and seek the help of native healers. In the words of the anthropologist who studied them, in both the Eskimo and Yoruba cultures, the labels for insanity

> refer to beliefs, feelings, and actions that are thought to emanate from the mind or inner state of an individual and to be essentially beyond his control; the afflicted persons seek the aid of healers; the afflictions bear strong resemblance to what we call schizophrenia. Of signal importance is the fact that the labels of insanity refer not to single specific attributes but to a pattern of several interlinked phenomena. Almost everywhere a pattern composed of hallucinations, delusions, disorientations, and behavioral aberrations appears to identify the idea of "losing one's mind," even though the content of these manifestations is colored by cultural beliefs (Murphy 1976, p. 1027).

In sum, at least certain human problems—subsumed in our culture under the broad label "schizophrenia"—involve more than specific violations of the social norms of the particular society: they appear widely enough to indicate a type of affliction that may be shared "by virtually all mankind" (Murphy, 1976, p. 1027). Such findings strengthen the view that at least some "problems of living" may turn out to have a genetic and "diseaselike" character (Kety, et al., 1975). The degree to which that is true is likely to be hotly disputed for many years.

The Rights of Mental Patients

Although many experts see Szasz's strong attacks on psychiatry (1960, 1970) as too extreme, he has made important points and championed some worthy causes. His basic concern is with individual freedom, including the person's right to be grossly deviant from the prevailing conventions of society. But rather than urge that people be held less responsible for their actions, he insists that legal responsibility should apply to everyone, even those who defy conventions. And with legal responsibility come legal rights, requiring the protection of the civil liberties of people judged mentally ill. Szasz's goals include the abolition of involuntary hospitalization, the retention of civil rights as a citizen even when one is hospitalized, and the abolition of the insanity plea in criminal cases except when even lay people would agree that the criminal was wildly insane, a "raving maniac."

While Szasz's position seemed radical when first proposed, it has gained increasing acceptance in social policy. There has been a growing awareness that the rights of hospitalized mental patients may be jeopardized. In a landmark decision, the United States Supreme Court ruled in 1975 that "mental illness alone is not a sufficient basis for denying an individual his fundamental right to liberty." Specifically, an involuntarily hospitalized patient who is not dangerous to himself or others has a right to be released (see Figure 13–4).

Figure 13-4
Notice on the Legal Rights of Patients Following the 1975 Supreme Court Decision

NOTICE TO PATIENTS

The United States Supreme Court recently ruled that a mental patient who has been involuntarily hospitalized, who is not dangerous to himself or to others, who is receiving only custodial care, and who is capable of living safely in the community has a constitutional right to liberty--that is, has a right to be released from the hospital. The Supreme Court's opinion is available for patients to read.

If you think that the Supreme Court ruling may have a bearing on your present status, please feel free to discuss the matter with the hospital staff. In addition, if you wish to talk with an attorney about the meaning of the Supreme Court decision and how it may apply to you, the Superintendent has a list of legal organizations that may be of assistance. The staff will be glad to aid anyone who wishes to contact a lawyer.

From NIMH (1975).

Gary in this chapter. Rather than infer Gary's traits and motives, or try to reconstruct his history, the troublesome behaviors (e.g., anxiety related to public speaking) were identified so that they could be modified directly.

The social behavior orientation to deviance usually assumes a fundamental *continuity between normal and abnormal behavior* (e.g., Bandura 1977; Kanfer & Phillips, 1970; Ullmann & Krasner, 1969). Rather than attributing deviance to distinct pathology or basically different conditions, one sees it as governed by the same laws that might (under other specific circumstances) lead to adequate or even creative behavior. That is, normal and abnormal behavior are not viewed as distinctly separate entities; instead, all behavior—regardless of its social value—is analyzed in the same terms. For example, observational learning processes are basically the same regardless of whether a child's parental models are criminals or pillars of social virtue: The behaviors the child learns will be different in these two cases but the learning principles will be the same. Similarly, reinforcement principles presumably are the same regardless of whether incompetent behaviors or creative ones are reinforced. Thus disadvantageous interpersonal behaviors and deviance may result from inadequate or inappropriate social learning in regard to any (or all) aspects of personal adaptation (Part Six of this book). Examples of disadvantageous behaviors include antisocial reactions to frustration, excessive avoidance patterns in the face of stress and threat, unduly severe self-evaluations, and negative self-concepts. Belief in the continuity of normal and abnormal behavior also implies that the same basic strategies may be used to understand and study disadvantageous behaviors and more normative behaviors.

The emphasis on the specificity of behavior implies that an individual may engage in deviant or disadvantageous behaviors only under some conditions and not under others. A boy may be hyperaggressive at school but not at home, failing in schoolwork but excelling in sports, popular with boys but terrified of girls. Gary may be anxious about public speaking but quite calm when facing sports competitions and even when climbing hazardous mountain peaks. In the behavioral orientation, therefore, one does not characterize the person as normal or deviant, and concentrates instead on identifying specific problematic behaviors and the situations in which they occur.

Finally, attention is devoted to the *current,* immediate causes of behaviors rather than to their historical development in early childhood. This focus on current causes implies a belief that behavior change techniques can be used to modify problems regardless of their historical beginnings in the individual's past. Regardless of *why* Gary developed public speaking anxiety, behavior therapists want to modify the fears that trouble him now.

SUMMARY

1. Although there are various behavioral approaches to personality, their methods have in common the careful measurement of behavior in relation to specific stimulus conditions. Behavioral observation is common to all psychological approaches: It is the use that is made of the data obtained that distinguishes between approaches. In the psychodynamic orientation behaviors serve as indirect *signs* of hypothesized underlying dispositions and motives. Behavioral approaches

treat observed behavior as a *sample,* and the focus is on how the specific sample is affected by variations in the stimulus conditions.

2. Analyses of the case of Gary W. illustrates the behavioral assessment of anxiety: Rather than attempting to make statements concerning underlying motives and conflicts, the search is for how changes in stimulus conditions produce changes in the response patterns of interest.

3. Ways in which behavior may be measured directly include situational behavior sampling, both verbal and nonverbal, and the physiological measurement of emotional reactions. In behavior sampling, the emphasis is on detailed information concerning the onset, magnitude, and duration of the behaviors of interest and the circumstances of their occurrence. The subject may supply this information through various self-report techniques such as daily records, lists of problematic situations, or responses on preset survey scales (schedules). Polygraphic measurement of bodily changes includes indices of heart rate, changes in blood volume and blood pressure, changes in muscular activitiy and in sweat gland activity. Brain waves also provide clues about changes in activity level.

4. The assessment of the reinforcing value of stimuli may be made from an individual's choices in lifelike situations, verbal preferences and ratings, or the observed effects of various stimuli on actual behavior. In clinical work it may be especially important to discover rewards that are effective for the individual concerned. Sometimes the usual reinforcers are not effective and new ones must be sought to facilitate therapeutic progress.

5. Functional analyses, the foundations of behavior assessments, are illustrated by studies of single cases. Careful observation of the behavior in question as it naturally occurs suggests what specific conditions maintain this behavior. Then systematic changes are made in those conditions until the problem behavior no longer occurs and more satisfying behaviors are substituted.

6. Behaviorally oriented approaches to adaptation and deviance propose an alternative to both psychiatric diseases and inferred psychodynamics. They suggest, instead, a focus directly on the behaviors themselves and on what the person does rather than his or her hypothesized underlying mental diseases or dynamics.

Chapter 14

Behavior Change and Personality

The most important applications of behavioral approaches have been their innovations for producing change. Traditional approaches to personality change emphasized insight, awareness, and the acceptance of feelings. In recent years social behavior theories have been leading to new methods of behavior change based on specific learning experiences. These learning forms of therapy have three main common features:

1. They attempt to modify the problematic behavior itself; therefore they are called "behavior therapies."
2. Like the social behavior theories and assessments that guide them, behavior therapies emphasize the individual's current behaviors rather than the historical origins of his or her problems.
3. Most behavior therapists assume that disadvantageous or "deviant" behavior can be understood and changed by the same learning principles that govern normal behavior.

Traditionally, "normal" personality psychology was sharply distinguished from the study of abnormal personality. Recently this distinction is becoming blurred. Behavior therapists are trying to show that they can use the same psychological principles to modify all sorts of human problems, regardless of the specific type of problem or its severity. Indeed they prefer to treat severely disturbed human behaviors—such as longstanding, bizarre difficulties that have been highly resistant to other forms of treatment—to demonstrate the power of their methods.

The methods and findings of behavior therapy challenge traditional concepts about normal and abnormal personality and the conditions necessary for personality change in highly disturbed, as well as in more adaptive, people. Finally, behavior therapies are having an increasingly important impact not only on techniques for treating people but also on theories about the basic nature of personality. In this chapter, you will learn about the strategies of behavior therapy and the implications for the conception of personality.

BEHAVIOR THERAPY: BASIC STRATEGIES

In this section we will consider some of the main techniques and findings of behavior therapy based on the concepts of learning theories. Later we shall examine some of the implications for theorizing about personality.

Desensitization: Overcoming Anxiety

Learning principles for therapeutic behavior change have been available for more than fifty years, but until recently they were only rarely applied because most therapists were afraid that "symptom substitution" would occur. They believed that the removal of problematic behaviors would be followed by other symptoms that might be even worse than the original ones. Joseph Wolpe, a psychiatrist who became skeptical about psychoanalytic theory, took the risk of attempting direct behavior modification with many of his patients. In 1958 he published a book describing a method of "systematic desensitization" based on the principle of classical conditioning.

Wolpe was impressed by the work of such early learning theorists as Pavlov and believed that neurosis involves maladaptive learned habits, especially anxiety (fear) responses. In neurotic behavior, he hypothesized, anxiety has become the conditioned response to stimuli that are not anxiety-provoking for other people. He reasoned that therapy might help the neurotic individual to inhibit anxiety by *counterconditioning* him to make a competing (antagonistic) response to anxiety eliciting stimuli. In his words, "If a response antagonistic to anxiety can be made to occur in the presence of anxiety-evoking stimuli so that it is accompanied by a complete or partial suppression of the anxiety responses, the bond between these stimuli and the anxiety response will be weakened" (Wolpe, 1958, p. 71). His attempt to desensitize the individual to anxiety-evoking stimuli includes three steps (summarized in Table 14-1).

1. *Establishing the anxiety stimulus hierarchy.* First the situations that evoke distressing emotional arousal and avoidance are identified. That is done with a detailed assessment usually conducted through interviews. Sometimes a person has many areas of anxiety, such as fear of failure, self-doubts, dating, guilt about sex, and so on. Regardless of how many areas or "themes" there are, each is treated separately. For each theme the person grades or ranks the component stimuli on a hierarchy of severity ranging from the most to the least intensely anxiety-provoking events (see Table 14-2). For example, a person who is terrified of public speaking might consider "reading about speeches while alone in my room," a mildly anxiety-provoking stimulus, while "walking up before the audience to present the speech" might create severe anxiety in him (e.g., Paul, 1966). In Gary's case, "the minute before starting a formal speech" was the most anxiety provoking, while "watching a friend practice a speech" and "taking notes in the library for a speech" were only moderately disturbing. As another example, a woman who sought treatment for sexual dysfunction indicated that "being kissed on cheeks and forehead" evoked merely mild anxiety but thinking about items like "having

Table 14-1
Three Basic Steps in the Desensitization of Anxiety

Step	Example
1. Establishing the anxiety stimulus hierarchy: anxiety-evoking situations ranked from least to most severe	Low anxiety: reading about speeches alone in your room Intermediate anxiety: getting dressed in the morning on which you are to give a speech High anxiety: presenting a speech before an audience
2. Learning an incompatible response	Learning deep muscle relaxation by tensing and relaxing various muscle groups (head, shoulders, arms), deep breathing techniques, and similar methods
3. Counterconditioning: learning to make the incompatible response to items in the hierarchy	Practicing relaxation responses to the lowest item on the hierarchy and moving gradually to higher items.

Table 14-2
Items of Different Severity From Four Anxiety Hierarchies*

| Severity (Degree of Anxiety) | Anxiety Hierarchies (Themes) | | | |
	1 Interpersonal Rejection	2 Guilt About Work	3 Test-Taking	4 Expressing Anger
Low	Thinking about calling Mary (a new girlfriend) tonight	Thinking "I still haven't answered all my mail"	Getting the reading list for the course	Watching strangers quarrel in street
Intermediate	Asking for a date on the telephone	Taking off an hour for lunch	Studying at my desk the night before the final	My brother shouts at his best friend
High	Trying a first kiss	Going to a movie instead of working	Sitting in the examination room waiting for the test to be handed out	Saying "No! I don't want to!" to mother

*These items are examples from much longer hierarchies.

intercourse in the nude while sitting on husband's lap" produced the most intense anxiety in her (Lazarus, 1963).

2. *Training the incompatible response (relaxation).* After identifying and grading the stimuli that evoke anxiety, the person needs to learn responses that can be used later to inhibit anxiety. Wolpe prefers to use relaxation responses because they can be taught easily and are always inherently incompatible with anxiety: no one can be relaxed and anxious simultaneously. The therapist helps the client to learn to relax by elaborate instructions that teach first to tense and then to relax parts of the body (arms, shoulders, neck, head) until gradually an almost hypnotic state of total calm and deep muscle relaxation is achieved (see *In Focus 14.1*). Most people can learn how to relax within a few sessions. The critical problem is to learn to relax to anxiety-evoking stimuli, and that task is attempted in the next phase.

3. *Associating anxiety stimuli and incompatible responses.* In the critical phase, counterconditioning, the client is helped to relax deeply while presented with the least anxiety-arousing stimulus from the previously established hierarchy. The stimulus event usually is described verbally or presented symbolically (in a picture) while the client is deeply relaxed and calm. As the therapist says the words for the item the client tries to generate the most vivid image of it that his or her imagination can form. As soon as the client can concentrate on this item while remaining calm, the next, more severe item from the hierarchy is introduced until, step by step, the entire hierarchy is mastered.

If at any point in the procedure the client begins to become anxious while presented with an anxiety stimulus, he or she signals the therapist. The client is

The technique of desensitization is used most often to reduce anxiety as, for example, in phobias, compulsions, and various patterns of general apprehension and avoidance. As a first step, the fearful person is taught to relax deeply. While reclining comfortably he gets instructions like these:

> Your whole body is becoming heavier. . . all your muscles are relaxing more and more. Your arms are becoming very relaxed. *(Pause)* Your shoulders. *(Pause)* Your neck. *(Pause)* Now the muscles of your jaws . . . your tongue . . . *(Pause)* and your eyes . . . very relaxed. Your forehead . . . very relaxed . . . noticing that as you become more relaxed you're feeling more and more calm. *(Pause)* Very relaxed . . . relaxing any part of your face which feel the least bit tense. *(Pause)* Now, back down to your neck . . . your shoulders . . . your chest . . . your buttocks . . . your thighs . . . your legs . . . your feet . . . very, very relaxed. *(Pause)* Feeling very at ease and very comfortable (Morris, 1975, p. 244).

An exciting program at a special research and treatment center for children with asthma combined training in relaxation with biofeedback techniques. This combination was used to teach the children how they can control their respiratory disorder themselves rather than relying solely on medication or on the help of doctors and nurses (Creer, 1974).

The children are first taught a sequence of steps toward deep relaxation. As they are practicing these relaxation techniques, they are given feedback through earphones that deliver a clicking sound in proportion to the child's muscular tension: the less tension, the fewer the clicks. The relaxation is combined in a standard desensitization procedure with stimuli that the child has identified as anxiety arousing (e.g., waking in the night and having to come to the hospital for treatment). Immediate improvement was observed in these children after they used the relaxation and biofeedback techniques. The children seemed to be increasing their capacities and learning new skills (such as more efficient expiratory flow) for relieving their distress whenever and wherever an asthma attack may occur. Note that this therapy program combined the procedure of substituting relaxation for anxious responses with the technique of providing feedback to reinforce the child for relaxing.

promptly instructed to discontinue the image of the stimulus until calm again. Then a somewhat less severe item from the hierarchy is presented so that he or she can concentrate on it without anxiety. After that, the client is ready to advance to the next item in the anxiety hierarchy and the step-by-step progress up the list can be resumed.

In sum, the desensitization (counterconditioning) procedure attempts to make responses strongly antagonistic to anxiety (such as relaxation) occur in the presence of mildly anxiety-evoking stimuli. The incompatible response then will at least partially prevent the anxiety response. In that way, the association between the aversive stimulus and anxiety becomes reduced, while the association of the stimulus with the relaxation reaction becomes strengthened (e.g., Guthrie, 1935, Wolpe, 1958).

Desensitization has been used to modify diverse avoidance patterns and "neurotic" behaviors as well as specific fears. Wolpe (1963), for example, treated an adolescent boy who had a severe hand-washing compulsion. This boy often spent up to three-quarters of an hour in an elaborate ritual of cleaning his genitals after urination and then devoted up to two hours to washing his hands. Wolpe noted that the youngster's washing rituals were always precipitated by urination. Consequently, the boy was desensitized to stimulus hierarchies that dealt with urine and urination. Wolpe reported excellent and rapid progress. When urination no longer provoked anxiety, the boy abandoned his cleanliness ritual.

Clinical reports of successful desensitization may be encouraging, but they do not prove that the clinical procedure, rather than other things in the client's life, was responsible for the observed improvement. More conclusive evidence has come from controlled experiments. The findings from these studies generally indicate that desensitization is a valuable method for modifying phobias and reducing anxiety (Kazdin & Wilson, 1978; Wilson & O'Leary, 1980).

One careful experiment, for example, studied the efficacy of desensitization for treating intense public-speaking anxieties (Paul, 1966). Students who had severe anxieties about speaking in public were assigned to one of four conditions. In one group they received Wolpe's desensitization treatment, learning to relax to progressively more threatening imagined situations connected with public speaking. Students in a second condition received brief traditional, insight-oriented psychotherapy from an expert clinician. In a third condition the students served as control subjects, obtaining only placebo "tranquilizers" and bogus training allegedly designed to help them "handle stress." Thus these subjects were given attention but received no specific treatment. In each of the above conditions the students had five contact hours over a six-week period for their treatments, so that all were given the same amount of time. A fourth group was used as a no-treatment control, taking a pre- and post-treatment assessment battery of tests but receiving no special treatment.

Before and after treatment all students were assessed by tests, ratings, and observations of their behavior. Public-speaking anxiety was measured through self-report, physiologically and behaviorally (by observations of actual public-speaking behavior under stress). As Figure 14-1 indicates, systematic desensitization was consistently the best treatment. Brief insight-oriented psychotherapy did not differ from attention-placebo, although people in both these conditions obtained greater anxiety reduction (on some measures) than did the untreated controls. On the physiological measures, only the desensitization group showed a significant reduction in anxiety when compared to the no-treatment controls. A follow-up on the test battery six weeks later, and another one two years later, found that improvement was maintained (Paul, 1966, 1967). There were no indications of "symptom substitution." On the contrary, students who had received the counterconditioning treatment in addition to becoming desensitized to public-speaking anxiety, also improved in overall college grades when compared to students in the other conditions (Paul & Shannon, 1966).

Observational Learning (Modeling)

In treatment by observational learning, or modeling, the individual observes another (the model) who displays more appropriate or adaptive behavior sequences. The model may be observed live or, in some cases, on film. Modeling techniques have been used to modify fears and other strong emotional reactions with dramatic success. For example, an important experiment compared the effects

Figure 14-1
Mean Reduction in Anxiety (from Pretest to Posttest) in Each of Three Measures

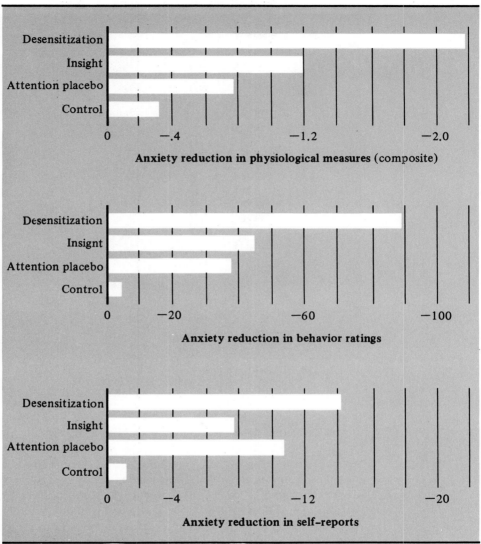

Anxiety reduction in physiological measures (composite)

Anxiety reduction in behavior ratings

Anxiety reduction in self-reports

Adapted from Paul (1966).

of modeling and desensitization treatments in removing phobic behavior (Bandura, Blanchard, & Ritter, 1969). Teen-age and adult volunteers with intense fear of snakes were assigned to three treatment groups and a nontreated control group.

One group of subjects was trained to relax while visualizing progressively stronger fear-arousing scenes involving snakes (systematic desensitization treatment). A second group of fearful people saw films in which fearless children and adults interacted in a progressively bold fashion with a snake (symbolic modeling treatment). In early scenes the models handled only plastic snakes. Later scenes

Figure 14-2
Photographs of Children and Adults Modeling Progressively Bolder Interactions with a King Snake

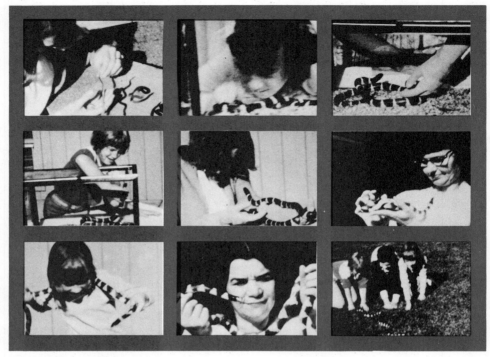

From Bandura, Blanchard, and Ritter (1969).

showed models touching, holding, and allowing a large snake to crawl freely over them (see Figure 14-2). Subjects were instructed in relaxation techniques to use during the showing of the film and were able to regulate the film presentation, stopping the film and reversing it back to an earlier, less threatening scene if they became too anxious. When they were able to stay relaxed during the previously threatening scene, they moved on to the next scene.

The third group received a treatment that combined live modeling with guided participation. The fearful subjects watched live models boldly handing the snake. At first subjects watched through an observation window; later the model handled the snake directly in front of them. The model then gradually led the subject into handling the snake at first with gloves and then with bare hands. The model's physical guidance was gradually reduced until the subjects themselves were able to perform all the prescribed activities with the snake. It was found that modeling with guided participation was the most powerful of the three methods, almost completely removing the fearful behavior in everyone who received this treatment. In this group the participants tended to be amazed at how quickly and thoroughly they had been able to overcome their deep fear.

The volunteers in all groups were tested for the strength of their fear and avoidance of snakes before and after completion of their respective treatments. They

Figure 14-3
Effects of Modeling and Desensitizations on the Development of Approach Responses to Previously Feared Stimuli

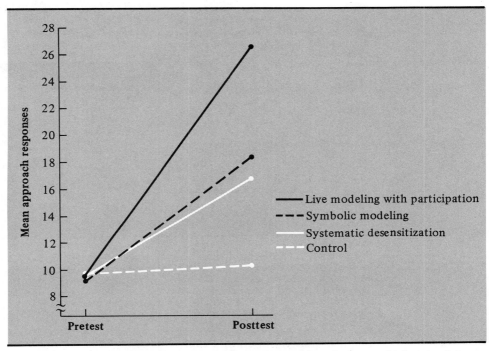

Mean number of approach responses performed by subjects before and after receiving their respective treatments.
From Bandura, Blanchard, & Ritter (1969).

also completed an extensive fear inventory. Some of the main results are shown in Figures 14-3 and 14-4. Of the three methods, modeling with guided participation was most powerful; it produced virtually complete removal of phobic behavior in every subject.

Snake fears have received much attention because of the symbolic sexual significance attributed to them by psychoanalytic theory (Brill, 1949). If such phobias are symbolic of an underlying psychodynamic problem (as is postulated by psychoanalytic theory), then a genuine cure of the phobia cannot be achieved without first modifying the unconscious conflicts supposedly symbolized by the phobic symptom. Many behavior therapists have eliminated these phobias directly without any exploration of their possible unconscious meanings and historical etiology to obtain enduring improvement (e.g., Lang & Lazovick, 1963). The success of such direct methods (Bandura, 1977) contradicts predictions of psychoanalytic theorists and is of considerable theoretical and practical significance.

Modeling also has been used to help people overcome shyness and assert themselves more effectively when they feel they should. Assertive skills may be sought by anyone who wishes to be more effective with other people, whether roommates,

Figure 14-4
Reduction in Fear Levels after Modeling and Desensitization Treatments

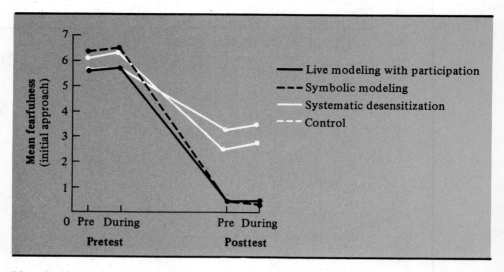

Mean level of fear arousal associated with approach responses that subjects performed before treatment and the fear levels reported in the post treatment period for the same subset of approach responses. (*Pre* refers to the intensity of fear subjects experienced when each snake approach response was described to them, and *Dur* signifies the fear level they reported while actually performing the corresponding behavior).
From Bandura, Blanchard, & Ritter (1969).

a boss, spouse, or parent. People who are unable to be assertive, who cannot stand up for their rights, may not only be exploited and deprived by others but may feel ineffective and incompetent and lack self-esteem. Thus *assertiveness training* may have many positive effects on one's life. The procedure may include observation of models who assert themselves effectively. This step may be followed by role playing with the therapist and by rehearsing more assertive responses, first in safe situations and ultimately in real life when the assertive responses are needed.

Improvement in assertive behavior may be achieved by *covert modeling* as well as by observation of live models who display assertiveness. In covert modeling, unassertive individuals imagine scenes in which a model performs assertively when it is appropriate. Here is a typical scene:

The person (model) is dining with friends in a restaurant. He (she) orders a steak instructing the waiter that it be rare. The steak arrives and as the person cuts into it, it is apparent that something is wrong. He (she) signals the waiter, who comes to the table. The person says, "This steak is medium; I ordered it rare. Please take this back and bring me a rare one" (Adapted from Kazdin, 1974, p. 242).

To measure assertive behavior, people may be presented with interpersonal situations that require assertive responses, and their assertiveness or lack of it is observed and recorded. Examples of such situations are:

1. Your boss asks you to work late when you already have plans.
2. Friends interrupt your studying.

3. The laundry has lost your cleaning.
4. In a long ticket line outside a theater, two people cut in directly in front of you.

In a typical study, subjects were asked to imagine that they were actually in these situations and to respond accordingly. The responses were recorded and judges rated them for assertiveness (McFall & Marston, 1970), thus providing a measure against which subsequent changes could be compared.

Conditioned Aversion: Making Stimuli Unattractive

While some people suffer because they have learned to react negatively to certain situations, others are plagued because they become pleasurably aroused by stimuli that most people in the culture find neutral or even aversive. One example of this problem is fetishistic behavior, in which the person may become sexually excited by such objects as undergarments. In these cases, things that are neutral or even disgusting for most people have acquired the power to produce pleasurable emotional arousal. While such reactions may provide the person with some immediate pleasure, they often are severely disadvantageous in their long-term consequences for the individual. They may, for example, provoke severe guilt and negative self-reactions, as well as scorn and punishment from others, and therefore treatment is needed if the person desires change.

A positively valued stimulus may be neutralized by counterconditioning if it is presented with stimuli that evoke extremely unpleasant reactions. Gradually, as a result of repeated pairings, the previously positive stimulus acquires some of the aversive emotional properties evoked by the noxious events with which it has been associated.

One young man developed an intense attraction to girdles and became anxious unless he wore one throughout the day (Clark, 1963). His unusual fetish had many debilitating effects on other aspects of his life. For example, his relations with his wife suffered severely because he compulsively wore her undergarments; he also was unable to work without his fetishes. A careful assessment revealed that some of the main fetishistic objects that aroused him included stockings and girdles as well as photos of girdle wearers. To obtain help, the client voluntarily hospitalized himself. During a period of one week, drug-induced nausea was repeatedly paired with presentations of the fetishistic objects. He was encouraged to wear the undergarments and to contemplate fetishistic pictures while he became increasingly sick from the medication. As his nausea developed, he also listened to a recording that he had made earlier on which he had described his fetishistic pleasures in elaborate detail. These treatments occurred about twice daily. Follow-up tests administered three weeks later, and again three months after therapy, indicated that the client was back at work "enjoying a normal sex life and symptom free" (Clark, 1963, p. 405).

Might such counterconditioning produce too much generalization? For example, might counterconditioning a man who has a fetishistic attraction to women's undergarments cause him to lose not only his interest in the fetish but also in women? In one study (Gelder & Marks, 1969; Marks & Gelder, 1967), many fetishists and transvestites received electric shock while they engaged in their deviant acts either overtly or in imagination. For example, one transvestite was aversively counterconditioned to a series of items including panties, pajamas, and a slip—one item at a time. His excitement (measured by erectile responses) diminished only to the specifically counterconditioned items and did not generalize to untreated ones. Thus, after completion of the aversion therapy the client remained responsive to appropriate heterosexual stimuli (such as female nude photos), but his sexual arousal to the specific deviant fetish was eliminated. Human learning often is highly discriminative: The effects of conditioning depend on the specific stimuli conditioned and do not necessarily entail massively generalized changes. Systematic counterconditioning has also been attempted with other unfortunate addictions such as alcoholism (Bandura, 1969B).

Psychologists are reluctant to use treatments that inflict pain on a troubled person. However, it must be remembered that aversion therapies usually are attempted after other forms of help (such as interview therapies) have been tried unsuccessfully. In some cases aversion treatments have come as a last resort in lieu of more drastic treatments, such as long imprisonment or irreversible brain surgery (Rachman & Hodgeson, 1980; Raymond, 1956).

Aversion therapies usually are not imposed on the client: they are voluntary and the person submits to it with full knowledge and consent, except when legal authorities have charge of the case. Indeed it is this very dependence on the client's cooperation that limits the efficacy of the treatment. That is, after the initial counterconditioning trials the client often may revert to his or her fetish without submitting voluntarily to further treatment. Since it becomes impractical to hospitalize him continuously or remove him from exposure to the problematic stimuli, he must learn to administer aversive stimulation to himself whenever necessary. For example, he may be taught to administer electric shock to himself from a small portable, battery-operated apparatus concealed in his clothing, or to induce aversive thoughts or imagery whenever he experiences the problematic urges. Thus, counterconditioning procedures ultimately provide the individual with a form of *self*-control. Whether or not he continues to practice and seek this self-control is up to him. And whether or not he practices self-control determines how effectively his new behavior will be maintained.

Changing the Consequences of Behavior

Many psychologists have tried to modify maladaptive behaviors by changing the consequences to which those behaviors lead. Guided to a large extent by B. F. Skinner's ideas about learning, they try to withdraw reinforcement for undesired behavior and to make attention, approval, or other reinforcement contingent on the occurrence of more appropriate, advantageous behavior. Their basic procedure (discussed in Chapter 13 as it bears on assessment) is well illustrated in the work of Hawkins and his colleagues (1966).

Hawkins' case was Peter, a young child of low intelligence. Peter was brought to a clinic by his mother because he was "hyperactive" and "unmanageable." Because the problems seemed to involve the relations between Peter and his mother, he was assessed and treated directly in his home. His mother served as a therapist under the guidance of the professional workers.

A first task was to specify the problematic behaviors. Direct observations of Peter in the home revealed the following problems to be among the most common and disturbing ones:

1. biting his shirt or arm
2. sticking his tongue out
3. hitting and kicking himself, other people, or objects
4. using derogatory names
5. removing his clothing and threatening to remove it.

The frequency of these and similar behaviors was carefully recorded at ten-second intervals during one-hour observation sessions in the home. After the first assessments were completed, the mother was helped to recognize the occurrence of Peter's nine most objectionable behaviors. Whenever these occurred during subsequent one-hour sessions at home she was taught to respond to them with definite steps. These steps involved signaling to Peter when his behavior became disruptive and, if a verbal warning failed, isolating him briefly in a separated, locked "time out" room without toys and other attractions. Release from the room (and reinstatement of play, attention, and nurturance) was contingent on Peter's terminating the tantrum and showing more reasonable, less destructive behavior. This arrangement was opposite to the one the mother may have inadvertently used in the past, when she became increasingly concerned and attentive (even if distressed) as Peter became increasingly wild. Subsequent assessment revealed that the new regimen was effective in minimizing Peter's outbursts. While apparently helpful to Peter's development, however, the modification of his trantrums may have been just one step toward the more extensive help he needed.

Using a combination of modeling and reinforcement procedures, Lovaas and his coworkers (1966) modified the deficient speech and social behaviors of severely disturbed ("autistic") children who were unable to talk. First the therapist modeled the sounds himself. He rewarded the child only for vocalizing the modeled sounds within a specified time interval. As the child's proficiency increased the therapist proceeded to utter more complicated verbal units. Gradually training progressed from sounds to words and phrases. As the training continued, rewards from the therapist became contingent on the child's reproducing increasingly more elaborate verbalizations more skillfully (i.e., more quickly and accurately). The combination of modeling and reinforcement procedures gradually helped the child to learn more complex meanings and complicated speech. Research like this shows the value of wisely used reinforcement, but rewards also may be hazardous, as discussed in *In Focus 14.2*.

People often are judged maladjusted mainly because they have not learned how to perform the behavior patterns necessary to effectively meet the social or vocational demands they encounter. They cannot behave appropriately because they lack the skills required for successful functioning. For example, the socially deprived, economically underprivileged person may suffer because he or she never has acquired the response patterns and competencies needed to obtain success and

Food treats and physical comfort and affection have been used as rewards to help severely disturbed children to improve their verbal and social skills.
Photos courtesy of Dr. Ivor Lovaas, UCLA.

avoid failure in school and in vocational and interpersonal situations. Similarly, the high school dropout in our culture does indeed carry an enduring handicap. Behavioral inadequacies, if widespread, may lead to many other problems, including severe emotional distress and avoidance patterns to escape the unhappy consequences of failure and incompetence. Many special learning programs have been designed to teach people a variety of problem-solving strategies and cognitive skills (e.g., Bijou, 1965), to improve classroom learning (Birnbrauer et al., 1965), to help rehabilitate psychotic children (Ferster & DeMyer, 1961), to assist families to cope with serious conduct disorders displayed by their children (Patterson, 1974), and to help achieve many other changes in behavior (Karoly, 1980).

Rewards are important for effective behavior, but they can be used unwisely. A major purpose of effective therapy (and socialization), is to wean the individual away from external controls and rewards so that his behavior becomes increasingly guided and supported by intrinsic gratifications—that is, satisfactions closely connected with the activity itself. Therefore it is essential to use rewards or incentives only to the extent necessary to initiate and sustain prosocial (adaptive, desirable) behavior.

External incentives may be important in order to encourage a person to try activities that have not yet become attractive for him or her. When rewards are used to call attention to a good job, or to an individual's competence at an activity, they may actually bolster interest. They provide positive performance feedback and supply tangible evidence of excellence (Harackiewicz, Manderlink, & Sansone, 1984). Approval and praise from parents for trying to play a violin, for example, may be helpful first steps in encouraging the child's earliest musical interest. But when the youngster begins to experience activity-generated satisfactions (e.g., from playing the music itself), it becomes important to avoid excessive external rewards. Too much reward would be unnecessary and possibly harmful, leading the child to play for the wrong reasons and making him or her prone to lose interest easily when the external rewards are reduced or stopped altogether (Lepper, Greene, & Nisbett, 1973). The same consideration would apply to the encouragement of such prosocial activities as concern for fairness, empathy, helpfulness, responsiveness to the needs of other people, and attention to the long-term consequences of one's behavior and not just to its immediate payoffs. While such sensitivities would initially be encouraged by external rewards, ultimately they should be sustained by gratification from the activities themselves.

In sum, "overjustification" of an activity by excessive external reward may interfere with the satisfactions (intrinsic interests) that would otherwise be generated by the activity itself. Excessive external rewards may even have boomerang effects and lead the recipient to devalue and resist the rewarded activity. Such resistance is especially likely in a culture that values autonomy and freedom, for any seemingly undue or exaggerated external rewards may be seen as pressures and may lead to intense, though possibly covert, resistance (e.g., Brehm, 1966).

Stimulus Control

An effective way to improve performance is to bring it under *stimulus control;* that is, allow the behavior only under certain restricted conditions. The stimulus control strategy is illustrated in a treatment to help people who suffer from insomnia (Bootzin, 1973).

The basic reasoning was simple. Many people find it hard to sleep because the bed and bedtime have become associated for them with all sorts of activities that are incompatible with falling asleep. For example, they use bedtime to rehash the day's happenings and worry about the next day and its problems. Therefore treatment should separate cues for such extraneous activities from cues for going to sleep. To achieve that aim, the patients were advised to follow these instructions (Bootzin, 1973):

1. Lie down intending to go to sleep only when you are sleepy.
2. Do not use your bed for anything except sleep; that is, do not read, watch television,

or eat in bed. Sexual activity is the only exception to this rule. On such occasions, the instructions are to be followed afterward when you intend to go to sleep.

3. If you find yourself unable to fall asleep, get up and go into another room. Stay up as long as you wish and then return to the bedroom to sleep. Although we do not want you to watch the clock, we want you to get out of bed if you do not fall asleep immediately. Remember the goal is to associate your bed with falling asleep quickly! If you are in bed more than about ten minutes without falling asleep and have not gotten up, you are not following this instruction.

4. If you still cannot fall asleep, repeat step 3. Do this as often as is necessary throughout the night.

5. Set your alarm and get up at the same time every morning no matter how much sleep you got during the night. This will help your body acquire a consistent sleep rhythm.

6. Do not nap during the day.

These stimulus control instructions proved to be highly effective. Patients in this treatment learned to fall asleep sooner and sleep longer; they also reported feeling better on awakening (compared to a no-treatment group). Similar procedures have been applied successfully to bring many other problem behaviors under stimulus control.

Therapeutic Communities

There also have been efforts to modify the behavior problems of groups of people by altering the reinforcement they get in their environment. Much of this work has been conducted with hospitalized adult patients diagnosed as chronic schizophrenics (e.g., Atthowe & Krasner, 1968; Ayllon & Azrin, 1965; Fairweather, 1964, 1967). Many of the patients treated in these studies were hospitalized in the first place because of severe behavioral inadequacies. Moreover, their initial inadequacy and dependency problems usually became much worse as a result of the mental hospital regime in which they lived. The hospital routine tends to "institutionalize" the patient, discouraging individuality and fostering dependency by removal of privacy, fixed daily routines for eating, medication, and cleaning, and reinforcement (by privileges and praise) for passive, docile conformity. After being institutionalized for many years under such a regime, patients tend to become progressively more deficient in interpersonal and vocational skills, and increasingly dependent upon the hospital. With passing years they lose whatever contacts with family and relatives they may have had in the "outside world," and their prospects of ever achieving a life beyond the institutional shelter approach zero. Here is one comment on the typical plight of the long-term mental hospital patient:

The great majority of patients still remain untreated. Recent statistics indicate that the median age of state mental hospital patients is approximately 65 years. This means that half of all patients in state mental hospitals are at such an advanced age that vocational opportunities are almost totally lacking and family ties have usually been broken. Even if there were nothing wrong with them, it would be difficult to discharge them into the outside world, since the outside world has no place for them. The longer these patients remain in the mental hospital, the more severe their behavioral problems seem to grow. One currently hears the phrases "hospitalism" and "institutionalization," which describe a state of apathy and lack of motivation that is acquired by a stay at a mental hospital. The hospital community is usually geared to providing the biological necessities of life, and perhaps some minimal level of recreational opportunities, but the overall relationship is a parasitic dependency in which the patient need not function in order to obtain most, if not all, of the activities or privileges that might still be of interest to him (Ayllon & Azrin, 1968, p. 3).

To help overcome this grim situation, programs with these patients have attempted to increase their independence and to help them achieve more adequate self-care and autonomy by creating a more appropriately motivating environment. Reinforcement is made contingent on their becoming more independent, first in the simplest functions, such as grooming and self-feeding and then, gradually, in more complex and interpersonal areas such as work and social relations (e.g., Ayllon & Azrin, 1965).

Some behavior change programs minimize the role of the professional therapeutic agent as a controller of the client's behaviors. They try to transfer responsibility to the client and his or her peer group as rapidly as feasible. An outstanding example is the therapeutic community designed by Fairweather to rehabilitate chronic psychotics who had been hospitalized for years. This program tried to move long-term schizophrenics out of the hospital and into a specially designed patient lodge located in the larger community as rapidly as possible. Fairweather recognized that many psychotic patients who have undergone more than two years of hospitalization become "marginal men" who continue to remain in the hospital and, if discharged, are returned to the hospital within a few months (Fairweather, 1964). Therefore he tried to develop small social systems that could function in the community itself and provide these individuals with more autonomy. He tried to organize this social system so that the members would regulate and discipline each other and share all responsibility for the step-by-step progress of their community.

To start, a group of patients were organized in the hospital and lived and worked together in a special ward. The patients were given the greatest autonomy possible over their own behavior throughout the program. They had to make increasingly complex and difficult decisions about their collective behavior, beginning with the simplest functions (e.g., self-care, dressing). The entire group was held responsible for the behavior of all its members at each stage of the program and advanced through a carefully graded series of steps; each new step required new responsibilities but also provided more privileges (e.g., weekend passes). Reinforcement (progress to the next step) was always contingent upon success at the earlier, prerequisite step.

Soon the group moved from the hospital to the lodge, and after a month there they began to function as a basically independent, self-sufficient organization. For example, they organized and maintained a commercial and residential janitorial and yard service employing their own members, took care of their own records, arranged their transportation, and assumed responsibility for their own living, working, and health arrangements. Consultants to the lodge were gradually replaced by nonprofessional volunteers and then slowly were withdrawn completely. In time the patients themselves fully assumed such responsible roles as nurse and work manager. Within three years all external help was withdrawn, and the expatients then remained together freely as an autonomous, self-sufficient group in the community (Fairweather 1967; Fairweather et al., 1969).

It would be naive to think that the lodge program quickly transformed these schizophrenics who had been hospitalized for years into totally new individuals. It did, however, provide a degree of competent and self-sufficient functioning to a group that previously had been considered virtually hopeless and had been utterly dependent on caretakers in a hospital. Especially noteworthy is that it did so at a cost in professional time and money that was vastly cheaper than confining the patients to the custodial care of the hospital. Expatients living in the lodge remained in the community much longer, and were employed much more steadily, than matched patients in control groups, who were simply released from the hospital (Fairweather et al., 1969).

Contingency Contracting

A move to enroll the person actively in his or her own behavior change program whenever possible is reflected in the use of "contingency contracting" (e.g., Rimm & Masters, 1974; Thoresen & Mahoney, 1974). An example was the treatment of "Miss X" for drug abuse as described by Boudin (1972). Miss X, a heavy user of amphetamines, made a contingency contract with her therapist. She gave him $500 (all of her money) in ten signed checks of $50 each and committed him to send a check to the Ku Klux Klan (her least favorite organization) whenever she violated any step in a series of mutually agreed upon specific actions for curbing her drug use. After applying the contract for three months, a follow-up for a two-year period indicated that Miss X did not return to amphetamine use. The principle of contingency contracting can be extended to a wide variety of commitments in which the client explicitly authorizes the therapist to use rewards and punishments to encourage more advantageous behaviors in ways formally agreed upon in advance.

Contracts for self-reward in which one gives oneself money for the purchase of special items and entertainment when certain goals are reached also may be used to lose weight (Mahoney, 1974; Mahoney, Moura, & Wade, 1973). A typical behavioral contract is shown in Figure 14-5. Behavior contracts can also be drawn up between the individual and persons other than the therapist. Such contracts have been used effectively to help delinquents and their families improve their relationships (Stuart, 1971). The responsibilities that the adolescent must fulfill and the privileges that will be gained on fulfillment are clearly stated in the contracts (see Table 14-3). Penalties for failing to comply are determined in advance and bonuses are provided for extended periods of fulfilling all responsibilities. These penalties and bonuses help to assure the adolescent's sustained participation and the family's faithfulness in keeping their promises.

BEHAVIOR THERAPY: EXTENSIONS

So far we have discussed examples of some of the main behavior change strategies. In clinical practice, their applications often become more complicated.

From the Global to the Specific

Behavior therapists usually have treated specific, clearly definable behaviors, such as concrete fears, fetishes, speech problems, sexual handicaps, and motivational

Figure 14-5
An Example of a Behavioral Contract

Name _____   Date _____

Agreement: During the next _____ days, if I

successfully (specify desired behavior)

_____

_____

then I will reward myself with (specify reward) _____

_____.

I will be consistent in rewarding myself if I perform the

above specified behaviors and I will not reward myself

if I don't perform them. If earned, my self-reward will

be received before (date) _____.

Signature _____

Witness _____

Witness: Please contact the above person on or before

the self-reward date to determine whether (a)

the desired behavior was successfully

performed, and (b) the self-reward was

appropriately administered. Your

encouragement of consistency and persistence

will be appreciated.

From Mahoney & Mahoney (1976).

deficits. Many people, however, suffer from much more diffuse problems. A person may complain, for example, of an "identity crisis," "feeling miserable," "wasting my life," or may even say "I hate my personality" or "I am lost—I just don't know what's wrong." People tend to conceptualize themselves in broad trait terms rather than in behavioral descriptions. When a person begins to describe herself she may

Table 14-3
Typical Responsibilities and Privileges Used in Behavioral Contracts with Juvenile Delinquents and Their Families

Responsibilities
School attendance
Grades
Curfew hours
Household chores
Informing parents of whereabouts

Privileges
Free time
Spending money
Choice of hair and dress styles
Use of the family car

say "I am too timid" or "I am an introvert"; she probably will not say "My heart rate seems to increase sharply and I feel dizzy and start to stutter when I have to address a group of strangers in a new situation, especially in a social setting." Thus while in some cases the treatment objectives are self-evident (as when a person is terrified of birds), in most cases it is not so easy to specify just what requires treatment and the particular behaviors that should be the goals of treatment

In these cases the client describes her problems and objectives in vague terms with broad, global labels. The clinician's task then must be to help her elaborate and examine what she means in behavioral terms (e.g., Mischel, 1968). This may be done by written reports such as diary records, by direct discussion, or by asking the person to perform in specially structured situations in which the stimulus conditions are deliberately and systematically varied, as in an experiment.

If a person describes himself as, for example, "depressed," the clinician can explore with him just when he feels depression and when he does not. To specify examples or behavioral referents for depression, the clinician inquires into just what happens when the client feels more depressed and less depressed and the changes that occur in him and in his behavior when he experiences the depression. For example, the clinician might ask, "How do you know when you are depressed?" The purpose of these probes is to obtain behavioral examples for subjective experiences, not to validate or invalidate the truth or falsity of the client's phenomenology. The goal here is the discovery of the behaviors that are problematic for him and the conditions governing them.

Similarly, role-play situations may be used in which the meaning of the complaint is explored thoroughly. Suppose a client complains of not being sufficiently "aggressive and assertive." To understand what she means by that construct the assessor could ask her to indicate when she feels insufficiently "aggressive and assertive." Suppose she mentions "when I first meet a new person." The assessor then might suggest a role play and take the part of a person who is just being introduced to the client. In this role situation the client then has to respond as she would in real life. Afterward the roles may be reversed and explored further. These procedures should help to clarify the construct "aggressive-assertive" and to see its relations to the client's behavior. The role plays can be quite specific—for example, first meeting with a potential employer, asking an attractive man for a date, or having to criticize a "subordinate" at work. Note that these procedures are quite consistent with the ideas initially proposed by George Kelly (1955), discussed in the context of the phenomenological approach.

An adequate assessment should make it possible to convert global problems into behavioral terms. On closer analysis, one young man's "existential neurosis," for example, translated in part to such tangibles as his current academic failures at school, his inadequate acceptance by peers in social relations, his frustrations due to the recent breakup of his engagement, and his indecision about vocational objectives. Each of these problems was treatable, and their improvement increased his sense of well-being.

Combining Principles

In contemporary applications, behavior therapists generally combine diverse social influence and learning methods, rather than favoring only one. For example, to

Table 14-4
Summary of Some Techniques Used in Behavioral Treatment

Technique	Method	Application
Counterconditioning: desensitization and aversive conditioning	Stimuli that evoke problem responses are paired with incompatible responses.	Treatment of phobias by pairing feared stimuli (snakes, heights) with relaxation. Treatment of addictions. For example, pairing alcohol with nausea or cigarettes with thoughts of cancer.
Modeling (observation)	The client observes an individual (model) engage in the desirable behavior successfully. In participant modeling the client attempts the behavior under the guidance of the model.	For acquiring complex, novel responses in a relatively short time (as in assertiveness training) and for overcoming fear. Symbolic presentations of the model (on film) also may be useful.
Contingency management	New consequences for behavior are introduced. Reinforcement for maladaptive behavior is withdrawn and approval and other rewards are made contingent on more advantageous behavior.	Used with children and hard-to-reach hospitalized patients. Often combined with modeling in the teaching of new skills.
Self-management	Evaluative and reinforcing functions are transferred from change agents (therapists, parent, teacher) to the individual.	Enables the individual to control his own behavior with minimum external constraints and artificial inducements.

In Focus 14.3
Improving Sexual Performance

One of the most important areas of performance concern for many people is sex. Today both men and women tend to feel that total sexual responsiveness is part of maturity. Sometimes sexual performance is hindered by physiological impairments such as low hormone levels. Far more often fear or disgust interfere with natural responsiveness.

William H. Masters and Virginia Johnson (1970) have done groundbreaking and controversial research and therapy (called conjoint marital unit therapy) in human sexual behavior. They believe that sexual inadequacies, no matter how they originated, are often maintained by fears that cripple sexual performance. Usually fear about performance leads a person to develop an anxious "spectator role" that interferes with his or her natural responsiveness. The therapy program they have developed for married couples therefore tries to reduce performance fears.

In their therapy with married couples Masters and Johnson find that every sexually dysfunctional marital unit is handicapped by insecurity in sexual matters. Partners also often feel incomplete as individuals and believe that their efficiency even in nonsexual situations is impaired. Many of the couples that enter the intensive two-week Masters and Johnson program have had problems for many years and have tried other forms of counseling and therapy, including advice from their clergymen and extensive psychoanalysis. In some couples the lines of communication have so broken down that they have not been able to discuss their sexual (or other) problems openly with each other.

In the treatment program, each couple meets with a male-female therapy team to facilitate frank communication. Both partners undergo complete physical examinations so that any physical problems contributing to their distress can be discovered and dealt with. A complete case history is also recorded, plus an assessment of each partner's ideas about what is necessary and what is permissible in a sexual relationship. The couple is expressly forbidden to engage in sexual activity for the first few days of therapy. At the end of the third day the partners are instructed to embark on a program of *sensate focus*. Sensate focus (focusing on sensual pleasure) is one of the most important steps in overcoming performance fears and becoming a participant in sexual enjoyment rather than a spectator concerned with how he or she is doing. With suggestions from the therapists and the other marital partner, the "giving" partner sensually pleasures the "getting" partner in order both to give and to discover sensate pleasures in a series of increasingly erotic explorations. The marital partners exchange roles of giving (pleasuring) and getting (being pleasured). The partners are explicitly required not to engage in sexual intercourse during this phase of therapy. In this way the performance anxiety is removed from the situation. Each partner in turn can concentrate on sexual thoughts and feelings and allow his or her natural responses and feelings of pleasure to occur. Gradually the two people in the relationship tend to develop increasingly intimate and pleasurable contact in slow steps. Most couples subsequently begin to have more mutually satisfying sexual relations.

---

train highly passive persons to become more assertive there have been ingenious combinations of behavioral rehearsal, modeling, and coaching (e.g., McFall & Twentyman, 1973). Innovative treatment strategies also have been developed for social action programs and educational problems in the classroom (e.g., O'Leary & Kent, 1973), and combinations of modeling and direct reinforcement tactics

Table 14-5
Three Mechanisms Linking Behavior to Physical Disease

Mechanism	Examples
Direct physiological effects	Changes in body functioning due to psychological stimuli such as stress
Health-impairing habits and behavior	Smoking, excessive alcohol use, poor diet, lack of exercise, and poor hygienic habits
Reactions to illness and the sick role	Delay in seeking medical care, failure to comply with treatment or rehabilitation regimen

SOURCE: Based on Krantz, Grunberg, & Baum, 1985.

have been devised for the treatment of severely disturbed (autistic) children (Lovaas et al., 1967) and for reducing cross-sex behavior (Rekers & Lovaas, 1974). In a similar vein, a number of learning-based methods have been synthesized in a step-by-step program of arousing experiences designed to increase sexual responsivity in nonorgasmic women (LoPicolo & Lobitz, 1972). The use of learning principles is also evident in the well-publicized program of Masters and Johnson (1970) for the treatment of sexual inadequacy in both sexes (see *In Focus 14.3*). The hallmark of all these programs is that they search for the most effective combinations of treatments possible and do not confine themselves to a single method, while still adhering to the general orientation of the behavioral approach. Table 14-4 summarizes some of the major methods that may be used in various combinations to fit the particular problem.

Community Health: Behavioral Medicine

An especially exciting new direction for the combination of influence procedures is in the application of behavioral approaches to health. Behavior and physical health are closely connected. Table 14-5 summarizes three ways in which behavior and physical disease may be linked. The specific mechanisms through which stress and illness may be linked are a special topic in its own right (discussed in Chapter 15). Examples of how health-impairing behaviors and poor reactions to illness can be improved through behavioral intervention are considered next. These efforts combine various social influence procedures to change behaviors that affect health (e.g., Krantz, Grunberg, & Baum, 1985). The new field that devotes itself to such efforts is called "behavioral medicine."

The acid test of social influence procedures is their ability to change important attitudes and behavior in real-life situations, not just in momentary laboratory demonstrations. The combination of diverse change principles is seen clearly in the new field of "behavioral medicine," aimed at improving health self-care. One large-scale effort is trying to apply the principles of social influence for community betterment. Specifically, in 1972 a long-term field experiment intended to reduce the risk of cardiovascular disease was launched in three northern California communities (Farquhar et al., 1977). In two of these communities there were extensive mass-media campaigns using standard social influence procedures (such as giving information to change attitudes, exposure to models). In one community, face-to-face counseling was also provided for a small sample of individuals judged to be at high risk of coronary disease. Both mass-media and face-to-face instruction were aimed at modifying four of the important risk factors for cardiovascular disease: cigarette smoking, obesity, high blood pressure, and high levels of cholesterol in the blood. A third community served as a control, receiving no educational campaign.

Among the unusual aspects of the study were:

1. Participants were randomly selected from open communities, providing a better basis for generalizations about future public health education efforts.
2. The mass-media materials attempted to teach specific necessary behaviors and skills (for example, food selection and preparation) in addition to providing information aimed at changing attitudes and motives relevant to reducing the four risk factors. The mass-media campaign included about fifty television spots, over one hundred radio spots, hours of television and radio programming, regular newspaper columns, advertisements, and stories, community posters, billboards, and printed matter mailed to the participants.
3. Diverse methods of social influence, attitude and behavior change, and self-control training were used in both the face-to-face instruction and the mass-media approaches.
4. Before the campaign began, participants were interviewed to determine their knowledge about the probable causes of coronary disease and the specific measures that may reduce risk (e.g., reduction of saturated fat in the diet, exercise, avoidance of cigarette smoking). The campaign was then designed to provide the specific knowledge and skills necessary to accomplish and maintain the necessary behavior changes (e.g., caloric reduction in the daily diet, reduced alcohol intake and smoking, increased physical activity).

At the end of the two years the risk of cardiovascular disease increased in the community which had not received the educational campaign. In the two treatment communities there was a substantial and sustained decrease in risk as measured by risk-factor knowledge, saturated fat intake, cigarette use, blood pressure, and blood cholesterol levels. In the community where there was some face-to-face counseling with high-risk individuals, there was a greater increase in knowledge about coronary disease and a reduction of smoking and weight after one year. By the end of the second year, however, the decrease was similar in both treatment communities. The authors concluded, "These results strongly suggest that mass media educational campaigns directed at entire communities may be very effective in reducing the risk of cardiovascular disease" (Farquhar et al., 1977, p. 1192). The results also show that social influence procedures may be effectively employed for the good of the community in life-enhancing and even lifesaving ways.

Cognitive Behavior Modification and Restructuring

Behavior therapists increasingly draw on cognitive methods. These cognitive methods include helping clients to talk to themselves differently (e.g., Beck et al., 1979; Meichenbaum, 1977) to manage stress better (discussed in Chapter 15), and other forms of mental problem solving (Goldfried & Goldfried, 1980; Mahoney, 1974).

An important example is *cognitive restructuring:* ways to view problems differently by thinking about them more constructively and less irrationally. One of the most influential forms of cognitive restructuring is Albert Ellis's (1962, 1977) Rational Emotive Therapy. This approach is based on the idea that irrational beliefs produce irrational behaviors. It follows that if people are taught to think more rationally their behavior will become less irrational and their emotional problems will be reduced.

Some very common irrational beliefs, according to Ellis, are the ones summarized in Table 14-6. These beliefs are irrational in the sense that they do not accurately represent the individual's real world. Reacting to situations on the basis of such irrational beliefs will produce ineffective behavior and such maladaptive emotions as anxiety and depression. Irrational beliefs may be revised by rational restructuring, as when a person who believes she must be loved by everybody rethinks this potentially debilitating attitude and realizes its impossibility.

Some evidence supports the value of rational emotive therapy. For instance, self-verbalizations (how one talks to oneself) can affect emotional arousal (e.g., Russell & Brandsma, 1974). Irrational self-statements do seem to be associated with maladaptive emotional reactions (e.g., Goldfried & Sobocinski, 1975) and many problem behaviors may be reduced by teaching clients to restructure (revise) their irrational self-statements. Some of Ellis's techniques and concepts are therefore now

Table 14-6
Widespread Irrational Beliefs

1. An adult human must be loved or approved by almost everyone.
2. In order to feel worthwhile, a person must be competent in all possible respects.
3. People who are bad, wicked, or villainous should be blamed and punished severely.
4. When things are not the way you want them to be it is a catastrophe.
5. People have little or no control over the external causes of the bad things that happen to them.
6. The best way to handle a dangerous or fear-producing event is to worry about it and dwell on it.
7. It is easier to avoid certain life difficulties and responsibilities than it is to face them.
8. One needs to depend on others and to rely on someone stronger than oneself.
9. One's present behavior is determined primarily by one's past history.
10. One should be upset by the problems of others.
11. There is always a perfect solution to a human problem, and it is essential to find it.

SOURCE: Based on Ellis, 1962.

being used by many behavior therapists. While the approach seems promising, the relations between attitudes and actions are more complex than Ellis's theory suggests, and his position tends to oversimplify the complex and multiple determinants of behavior. Rational restructuring may help some people with some problems, but it is only one cognitive technique among many potentially fruitful alternatives. Its value still has to be tested further, and although the evidence to favor it so far is encouraging it is not yet conclusive (Rachman & Wilson, 1980; Wilson & O'Leary, 1980). Closely related to it are attempts to change the self-negating and self-defeating cognitions that may underlie depression, discussed next.

Cognitive Therapy: Beck's Approach

Aaron T. Beck has developed a somewhat similar form of cognitive therapy that he has applied systematically to the treatment of depression. He defines cognitive therapy this way:

> Cognitive therapy is an active, directive, time-limited, structured approach used to treat a variety of psychiatric disorders (for example, depression, anxiety, phobias, pain problems, etc.). It is based on an underlying theoretical rationale that an individual's affect and behavior are largely determined by the way in which he structures the world . . . His cognitions (verbal or pictorial "events" in his stream of consciousness) are based on attitudes or assumptions (schemas), developed from previous experiences. For example, if a person interprets all his experiences in terms of whether he is competent and adequate, his thinking may be dominated by the schema, "Unless I do everything perfectly, I'm a failure." Consequently, he reacts to situations in terms of adequacy even when they are unrelated to whether or not he is personally competent (Beck, Rush, Shaw, & Emery, 1979, p. 3).

There are five basic steps in Beck's version of cognitive therapy:

1. Patients first learn to recognize and monitor their negative, automatic thoughts. These thoughts are "dysfunctional," that is, ineffective and lead to serious dilemmas.
2. They are taught to recognize the connections between these negative thoughts (cognitions), the emotions they create, and their own actions. (See Figure 14-6 for examples of connections between thoughts and emotions.)
3. They learn to examine the evidence for and against their distorted automatic thoughts.
4. They substitute for these distorted negative thoughts more realistic interpretations.
5. They are taught to identify and change the inappropriate assumptions that predisposed them to distort their experiences. Examples of such assumptions are shown in Figure 14-7.

A variety of ingenious techniques have been developed to encourage people to undertake these five basic steps and to use them effectively to alter their actions, thoughts, and feelings. The following excerpt from Beck's therapy illustrates how patients can be helped to change dysfunctional beliefs. The intent is to help the patient see how the unfortunate assumption or belief becomes a self-fulfilling

Figure 14-6
Examples of Connections between Negative Automatic Thoughts and Emotion

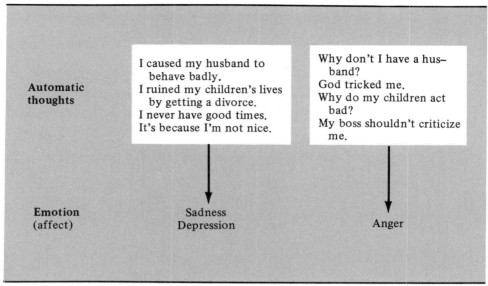

Adapted from Beck et al. (1979, p. 250.)

prophecy: it traps the believer into the very same dilemma that the belief was designed to avoid in the first place. The therapist in this excerpt tries to illuminate these self-fulfilling assumptions.

PATIENT: Not being loved leads automatically to unhappiness.
THERAPIST: Not being loved is a "nonevent." How can a nonevent lead automatically to something?
P: I just don't believe anyone could be happy without being loved.

Figure 14-7
Examples of Assumptions that Encourage Depression

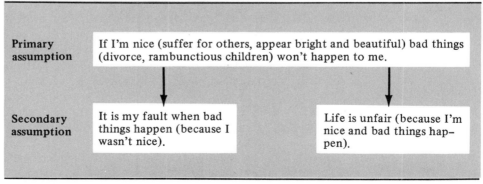

Adapted from Beck et al. (1979, p. 250.)

T: This is your belief. If you believe something, this belief will dictate your emotional reactions.

P: I don't understand that.

T: If you believe something, you're going to act and feel as if it were true, whether it is or not.

P: You mean if I believe I'll be unhappy without love, it's only my belief causing my unhappiness?

T: And when you feel unhappy, you probably say to yourself, "See, I was right. If I don't have love, I am bound to be unhappy."

P: How can I get out of this trap?

T: You could experiment with your belief about having to be loved. Force yourself to suspend this belief and see what happens. Pay attention to the natural consequences of not being loved, not the consequences created by your belief. For example, can you picture yourself on a tropical island with all the delicious fruits and other food available?

P: Yes, it looks pretty good.

T: Now, imagine that there are primitive people on the island. They are friendly and helpful, but they do not love you. None of them loves you.

P: I can picture that.

T: How do you feel in your fantasy?

P: Relaxed and comfortable.

T: So you can see that it does not necessarily follow that if you aren't loved, you will be unhappy (Beck et al., 1979, p. 260).

These assumptions in turn may lead to negative automatic thoughts and emotions shown in Figure 14-7.

Cognitive therapy of this sort appears to be a promising part of treatment for depression and related emotional and behavioral problems. Its value has been explored in a large number of studies with subjects ranging from those with mild problems to hospitalized severely depressive patients. The results seem to be consistently encouraging, indicating improvement from treatment greater than that found for individuals who remain in no-treatment control or other comparison conditions (Beck, et al., 1979).

A Caution

Behavior therapies have been criticized on many grounds. It has been noted, for example, that some therapies that are at best loosely connected with learning theory claim to be derived from it, that the actual practice of behavior therapy may include many uncontrolled and unreported factors, and that learning theory itself often may be inadequate to deal with complex life phenomena (Breger & McGaugh, 1965). Moreover, the efficacy—and limitations—of particular forms of behavior modification for particular types of problems still needs much more research. Too many claims for the value of behavior change strategies rest on case studies rather than on large scale comparisons among different methods. In addition to asking "does it work?" about each type of change strategy, one must ask "does it work better than other available alternatives?"

Critics of behavior therapies rightly note that the history of therapeutic efforts to achieve personality change is full of promising false starts and of movements whose claims and enthusiasms greatly exceeded their ultimate results. Even supporters of behavior therapy recognize that its adoption is not without danger:

> There are hazards in the rapid growth of behavior therapies: that a premature orthodoxy may develop, that claims to scientific roots will not be translated into scientific appraisal and renovation, that a new generation of practitioners may be created whose lack of awareness of unresolved basic theoretical and empirical questions would create undeserved longevity for still another generation of ineffective techniques, that safeguards by society in the use of clinical behavior-control methods will not be sufficient to protect individual rights or to avoid premature social experimentation with unforeseen negative effects. However, the potential benefits, given sufficient critical evaluation and constructive research, are at least equally great (Phillips & Kanfer, 1969, p. 122).

Behavior Therapy and Ethics

In the popular media, and even within the profession of psychology, behavior therapists are sometimes presented as power-hungry manipulators interested in controlling the conduct and experience of other people, often without their consent and even against their best interests. Undoubtedly, some serious abuses exist, especially when the subjects are captives, as in prison populations. Obviously, there are great differences among behavior therapists in their sensitivity to ethical issues. In fact, it is misleading to speak of behavior therapy or behavior modification as if these terms referred to a single approach applied by a single group. There are many behavior therapies and many ways to modify behavior.

Unfortunately, due to misrepresentation in the media, for many people the term "behavior modification" has come to stand for the sinister brainwashing portrayed in fiction and movies. Behavior modification should mean no more and no less than the application of psychological principles to produce a desired change in behavior. Such applications are found in routine educational efforts of the sort common in school systems and in every attempt, explicit or implicit, to exert an influence on behavior, including in our daily relations. When you smile at some of your friend's comments, ignore or frown at others, you are modifying her behavior. Obviously, psychological principles can be used ethically or unethically, effectively or absurdly, wisely or foolishly.

In addition to becoming increasingly sensitive to ethical issues, perhaps the best way for behavior therapists to avoid abuses is to emphasize *self*-control by the client rather than external control by the therapist. A focus on "power to the person" (Mahoney, 1974) means that the client chooses the therapeutic objectives and voluntarily implements the methods for achieving them. (For example, clients select their dieting goals, record their weight, and reward themselves for pounds lost.) A vital goal of behavior change methods should be to increase the individual's competence and independence as quickly as possible so that any external control by the therapist can be eliminated rapidly. Individuals who have learned to regulate and direct their own behavior will also be better equipped to resist the pressures of the environment and to pursue their desired goals even when circumstancesare difficult.

In sum, probably the best way to assure that behavior therapies will not be abusive is to enroll the client actively in every step of the procedures, from the selection of goals to the implementation of each therapeutic step. The client's voluntary participation in behavior therapies may not only be ethically desirable; it may also be important for effective behavior change to be achieved at all. People who do not want their behavior changed generally can and do subvert the efforts of others who are trying to change them involuntarily.

BEHAVIOR CHANGE AND PERSONALITY CHANGE

Critics recognize that behavior therapy may produce alterations in the individual's specific behavior, but they question the genuineness and "depth" of such behavior modification. Their doubts seem to center on several points.

Is There Transfer? Moving Into Life

Will beneficial effects achieved in behavior therapy *transfer* or generalize to the life situations in which the person must actually function on his own? Will a timid person who has practiced more assertive behaviors in the safety of the therapist's office really become more masterful on the job? Will he become more confident with the headwaiter who snubs him? Will a person who has learned to think calmly about taking tests during desensitization in the therapist's office also become calm when she must actually take examinations?

Generalization is helped to the degree that the stimulus conditions sampled in treatment are similar to those in the life situation in which the new behaviors will be used. Therefore behavior therapists try to introduce into treatment situations that closely approximate the life situations in which behavior change is desired. For example, if a person can think calmly about public speaking but becomes upset when he tries it, treatment might teach him to speak calmly in public rather than to think about it in private. Similarly, if a person is able to take examinations effectively but devalues and derogates her own achievements, an appropriate treatment might help her to reevaluate her performance rather than to change her test-taking skills. In other words, treatment should be directed as closely and specifically as possible to the intended terminal behaviors or objectives.

Just like the social behavior theories that guide them, behavior therapies emphasize that a person's behavior tends to be specific to particular stimulus conditions. Therefore they try to fit what is practiced in therapy with the behavioral objectives desired in the person's life. Consider, for example, a client who wants to improve his relations with his wife. The behavior therapist probably would focus on movement toward specific objectives in the marriage, such as improvements in sexual techniques and better forms of communication. One might also try specific changes in the assignment of roles and responsibilities with regard to financial decisions, recreational choices, household chores. Much lower priority would be given to more global aspects of the client's attitudes toward women in general (e.g., his feelings toward his mother). In treatment those behaviors would be encouraged and practiced that would be most similar to the ones the client wants to achieve in his daily life.

Toward Community Psychology

To facilitate generalization many therapists also believe it is best if the treatment occurs in the relevant life setting rather than in an artificial one like a laboratory or a clinic. Therefore they are bringing their treatment services into the community rather than waiting for people to be brought to mental hospitals or other institutions. (This trend has even become part of a new field within psychology called "community psychology.") For example, just as academic learning programs for children are conducted in schools so may social learning programs for youngsters with interpersonal problems be located in the school system itself. Similarly, if parent-child relations are problematic, it may be better to have consultants observe and help to modify the problems where they occur—in the home—rather than transport the family to a clinic. Moreover, in these settings, teachers, the parents, friends, and other professionals may be enrolled to help in the treatment process (e.g., Patterson, 1976). To help a married couple, it may be more appropriate to work with their relationship directly, treating the couple together rather than each mate in isolation. There is a trend now to engage in the treatment process the people with whom the client has important daily relations, rather than rely on repeated contacts with clinics, hospitals, special agencies, and professional personnel. Similarly, group situations often are better than treating the individual alone, especially if improving relations with other people is one of the treatment objectives. For example, Paul and Shannon (1966) found that the group provided a setting in which anxious students could spontaneously and naturally extinguish many of their social fears through their own mutually supportive interactions. Community centers, settlement houses and clubs, civic organizations, school systems, all provide opportunities for bringing behavior change programs to the community.

A concern with community-oriented action programs and with "preventive health" of course has not been limited to advocates of behavior modification. In recent years an increasing number of psychologists, guided by many different theoretical orientations, have noted that effective programs to deal with the enormous problems of people in our society will have to go beyond the "patching and healing" of psychologically wrecked individuals. Like the individual's biological health, psychological adaptation hinges on the condition of one's personal environment. There is a psychological as well as a biological ecology, an intimate, continuous interplay of people and environment. A destructive psychological environment that submits people to excessive stress, insufficient gratification, confusing and conflicting demands, frustrating routines, can create havoc in human lives more quickly than any therapy can repair them. A satisfying life requires a satisfying environment. An adequate approach to psychological welfare will have to be concerned with prevention of problems before they become too difficult to handle, and with the construction of a psychological environment in which people can live without debilitatingly twisting themselves and each other.

Toward Self-Management: From External to Internal

Ideally, behavior change programs are designed to increase individuals' independence and competence as rapidly as possible so that external control of their behavior by the therapeutic regime can be reduced and ended quickly. Many techniques can help to achieve that objective (e.g., Bandura, 1969; Kanfer, 1980; Kazdin & Wilson, 1978; Rachman & Wilson, 1980). Carefully dispensed external reinforcement (like tokens or praise) may be necessary at first to help a disturbed child learn to speak, read, and write. But the satisfactions deriving from these new activities, once they begin to be mastered, will help maintain and develop them further in their own right, even when the therapist's help is gradually withdrawn.

The young child who is learning to play the piano may at first be highly dependent on praise, attention, treats, and parental guidance to induce him or her to practice. However, to the extent that the learning program is structured effectively, piano practice will be increasingly supported by the pleasure of the activity (e.g., the sounds produced and the satisfactions and "sense of competence" from playing). If the learning experience is successful, in time the child "wants to play" and "loves the piano." There is a shift from performing to please others to performing to please oneself, a transition from behavior for the sake of the "extrinsic" rewards it yields to behavior for "its own sake"—that is, for "intrinsic rewards." The behavior that offers the intrinsic rewards for which people strive may range from painting miniatures to racing sports cars, from playing the flute to wrestling, from climbing rocks to yoga exercises, from lifting weights to gourmet cooking.

Whether or not an activity becomes intrinsically rewarding may have less to do

Gradually there may be a shift from performing for external rewards to performing for its own sake.

with the activity than with how it was learned and the conditions influencing its performance. Often in the course of socialization the conditions of learning inadvertently are poorly arranged. We see that when activities like piano practice or schoolwork become occasions for tension and family quarrels rather than for satisfaction and personal achievement. But often even under difficult conditions a variety of "self management" strategies allow people to master all sorts of achievements and skills that characterize human accomplishments. The processes involved in this "mastery" have become a major topic in their own right, as will be discussed later (Chapter 16).

Symptom Substitution?

Do behavior therapies neglect the causes of the person's problematic behavior and thus leave the "roots" unchanged while modifying only the "superficial" or "symptomatic" behaviors? It is often charged that behavior therapists ignore the basic or underlying causes of problems. Advocates of behavior therapy insist that they do seek causes but that they search for *observable* causes controlling the current problem, not its historically distant antecedents nor its hypothesized but unobservable psychodynamic mechanisms. This search for observable variables and conditions controlling the behavior of interest was demonstrated most clearly in the functional analyses discussed in Chapter 13. Traditional, insight-oriented approaches have looked, instead, for historical roots in the person's past and for theoretical mechanisms in the form of psychodynamics. The difference between these two approaches thus is not that one looks for causes whereas the other does not: Both approaches search for causes but they disagree about what those causes really are.

> All analyses of behavior seek causes; the difference between social behavior and [psychodynamic] analyses is in whether current controlling causes or historically distant antecedents are invoked. Behavioral analyses seek the current variables and conditions controlling the behavior of interest. Traditional [psychodynamic] theories have looked, instead, for historical roots and developmental etiology (Mischel, 1968, p. 264).

Traditional approaches ask about their patient, "Why did she become this kind of person?" Behavioral approaches ask, "What is now causing her to behave as she does and what would have to be modified to change her behavior?"

Does a neglect in treatment of the psychodynamics hypothesized by traditional therapies produce symptom substitution? In spite of many initial fears about possible symptom substitution, behavior change programs of the kind discussed in the preceding sections tend to be the most effective methods presently available; the changed behaviors are not automatically replaced by other problematic ones (e.g., Davison, 1968; Kazdin & Wilson, 1978; Lang & Lazovik, 1963; Paul, 1966; Rachman, 1967; Rachman & Wilson, 1980). On the contrary, when people are liberated from debilitating emotional reactions and defensive avoidance patterns, they generally tend to become able to function more effectively in other areas as well. As was noted years ago:

> Unfortunately, psychotherapists seem to have stressed the hypothetical dangers of only curing the symptoms, while ignoring the very real dangers of the harm that is done by not curing them (Grossberg, 1964, p. 83).

Fear of symptom substitution is no longer the deterrent to direct behavior modification it once appeared to be, but many thorny theoretical and practical issues still remain. For example, the exact meaning of "symptom" often is not defined in theoretical discussions of symptom substitution, so that one is unsure about what might constitute a substituted symptom. How many weeks, months, or years might have to elapse before the substituted symptom can be expected to emerge? If the symptom is disguised in another form just how would we distinguish it from a problem that is wholly new? If a person whose snake phobia was removed develops problems at work or with his wife three years later, is he showing symptom substitution or new problems? In its extreme form the idea of symptom substitution may be untestable, because one cannot know what is a substituted symptom and what is a new problem.

On the other hand, some enthusiastic proponents of behavior modification overlook the complexity of the client's problems. They may oversimplify the difficulties into one or two discrete phobias when in fact the client may have many other difficulties. In that case, it would not be surprising to find that even after removal of the initial problem the individual still is beset with such other psychological troubles as self-doubts, feelings of worthlessness, and so on. Such a condition of course would imply that the person had an incomplete treatment rather than that symptom substitution had occurred. It would be extremely naive to think that reducing Gary's public speaking anxiety, for example, would make his life free of all other problems. Whatever other difficulties he might have would still require attention in their own right.

In sum, to avoid the emergence of disadvantageous behaviors, a comprehensive program must provide the person with more adaptive ways of dealing with life; such a program may have to go beyond merely reducing the most obvious problems. Behavior modification does not automatically produce generalized positive effects that remove all the person's troubles.

Behavior Change and Self-Concept Change

Often when competence improves so do self-reactions. Self-concepts tend to reflect the individual's actual competencies: self-perceptions include the information that we get about the adequacy of our own behaviors. The individual who learns to perform more competently achieves more gratification and is also likely to develop more positive attitudes toward himself or herself. As a result of being able to overcome fears and anxieties one should also become more confident. Reducing Gary's fears of public speaking would not be a cure-all, but it might certainly help him to feel more positively about himself and would open alternatives (e.g., in his career opportunities) otherwise closed to him. But while this is often true, it does not always happen. Indeed critics of behavior therapy note that people may suffer not because their behavior is inadequate but because they evaluate it improperly. That is, some people have problems with distorted self-concepts more than with performance.

Behavior theorists consider such self-concept problems to be just as much behavior problems as any other difficulties; in these cases, the behaviors are self-evaluation and self-labeling. Often a person labels himself and reacts to his own behaviors very differently than do the people around him and the rest of society. A successful Mafia leader, for example, may experience few immediate aversive personal consequences although his activities lead to severe distress for others. On the other hand, an esteemed financier may receive the rewards and praise of society while he is privately unhappy enough to contemplate suicide. Or a popular college student who is the prom queen of her school might have secret doubts about her sexual adequacy and femininity and might be torturing herself with these fears.

Thus many human problems involve inappropriate self-evaluations and self-reactions. In these cases the difficulty often may be the person's appraisal of his or her performances and attributes rather than their actual quality and competence level. For example, a student may react self-punitively to his scholastic achievements even when their objective quality is high. The student who is badly upset with himself for an occasional "low A" may need help with self-assessment rather than with school work. From the viewpoint of behavior theory such problems should be treatable by the same learning principles used to change any other type of behavior. The mechanisms involved in both the growth and treatment of self-evaluative problems are starting to receive the attention they deserve (Bandura, 1986).

Am I What I Do? Genuine Change

What happens when the conditions of reinforcement change stably in a person's life? What happens, for example, to the mother-dependent little boy when he finds that his school peers begin to have less tolerance for his "babyish" attention-getting bids and instead esteem assertiveness and self-confident independence? Usually the child's behavior will change in accord with the new contingencies. If the contingencies remain stable, so does the child's new pattern; if the contingencies shift, so does the behavior. Then what has happened to the child's dependency trait?

Many theorists would argue that the basic personality structure remains and that merely its overt manifestation has altered. But is this just a "symptom" change that does not really affect the personality structure that generated it and the psychological life space in which it occurs? Advocates of behavior theory contend that to treat persons as truly active and dynamic, we must recognize that they change as their behaviors do. A behavioral view sees behavior change in an individual not as a merely superficial overlay. Behavior theory insists that to find out what a person *is* we need to know what he or she *does;* and if actions change then so does the person. Behavior theorists emphasize that discontinuities—real ones and not merely superficial or trivial surface changes—are part of the genuine phenomena of personality (Mischel, 1973). They believe that an adequate conceptualization of personality has to recognize that people can change as the conditions of their lives change.

SUMMARY EVALUATION OF THE BEHAVIORAL APPROACH

It is time to pause and evaluate the main ideas that have been discussed in the chapters devoted to the behavioral approach. (See Table 14-7).

Table 14-7
Summary Evaluation of the Behavioral Approach

Strengths	Weaknesses
Concepts based on principles of general psychology; benefits from basic research on learning, cognition, etc.	Concepts not integrated into a distinctive, comprehensive, systematic theory of personality
Methods based on experimental psychology and behavior analysis; allow rigorous testing of concepts and the efficacy of treatments	Neglect of problems that do not lend themselves to study by available methods
Systematic development of principles for behavior change; useful for behavior change	Insufficient attention to stable characteristics that resist change
Focus on observable behavior and the psychological environment	Insufficient attention to genetic and biochemical causes

Strengths and Weaknesses

Early efforts to apply concepts from learning theories to personality relied on "stimulus-response" formulations that came from laboratory research on simple learning with lower animals. These efforts drew mostly on the principles of classical and operant conditioning, discussed in Chapter 11. Many psychologists recognized that these principles might be useful for treatment of at least some human behavior problems such as specific fears. Most psychologists, however, were concerned that the early behavioral work was based largely on studies with lower animals constrained in artificial laboratory situations. Elegant experiments were done on the behavior of rats running in mazes and of pigeons pecking on levers as food pellets dropped down. But how could one extend the results from these studies meaningfully to the complex lives of people under the often unpredictable social conditions of real life?

Critics severely and powerfully attacked early behaviorism as far too simplistic to permit a reasonable account of such everyday human behavior as language (e.g., Chomsky, 1965). If the early behavioral conceptions could not deal adequately with how people talked and thought—and they could not—then how could they possibly address the complex phenomena of personality?

At the same time (before the 1960s), most clinicians saw behavioral concepts as too superficial and even dangerous to be applied usefully to troubled people. Partially in response to these challenges, behaviorally-oriented workers attempted some applications of their ideas and methods with human subjects. They began in the last two decades to treat some of the most difficult behavioral problems that had resisted other forms of therapy. For example, they were allowed to try to treat hospitalized people who were so severely disturbed that there was little to lose by attempting experimental innovations with them after other available methods had proved to be unsuccessful. You saw many examples of these applications in the treatment and assessment of disturbed mental patients in Chapters 13 and 14.

Some impressive studies of effective human behavior change emerged and gained some credibility as possible treatment methods (e.g., Ullmann & Krasner, 1969; Krasner & Ullmann, 1973). The systematic rigor of the work was widely appreciated, but severe doubts remained about the relevance of the approach for understanding personality and complex social behavior.

Sharing these same concerns, a number of theorists attempted to make learning and behavior theories more cognitive and "social." They preferred to study complex social learning rather than simple animal response (e.g., Bandura, 1969; Bandura & Walters, 1963; Mischel, 1968; Rotter, 1954). They drew on a wide range of phenomena and principles. Although they remained committed to the understanding and analysis of behavior from the perspective of learning theory, they tried to develop a more comprehensive, yet rigorous, approach to personality.

Most of these developments still emphasized what a person *does* rather than trying to infer the attributes he or she *has* (Mischel, 1968). But most current social learning theories do not limit themselves to simple reinforcement principles. Contemporary social learning formulations rather than neglect cognitive processes, rely heavily on them in their account of the development of all complex social behaviors. They increasingly use such cognitive concepts as expectancies, values, and even "self" in their theorizing, their research, and their applications.

The early forms of the behavioral approach were criticized as too narrow; the later forms tended to seek greater breadth and to integrate a variety of concepts from many areas of psychology into a larger framework. This trend toward a broad integration of concepts within social learning theory may be seen as both positive and negative.

On the positive side, a cumulative science develops by gathering and integrating the best available concepts supported by the best available research. A theory of personality is broadened by including useful concepts from all areas of the field, including cognition, rather than limiting itself to a few favorite ideas. On the negative side, increasing breadth and integration may be seen as decreasing a theory's distinctiveness and incisiveness. It allows many alternative explanations and interpretations: the cost of breadth may be an increase in looseness and a loss of uniqueness. Severe critics doubt that social learning theory provides a distinctive account of personality in any special way.

Some critics appreciate the contributions of behavioral approaches for applied purposes but still fault them for overemphasizing the "stimulus" or "situation" (e.g., Adinolfi, 1971; Alker, 1972; Bowers, 1973). They view this overemphasis as part of a "situationism in psychology" that erroneously minimizes the importance of dispositional or intrapsychic determinants such as traits (Bowers, 1973; Carlson, 1971). In reply, later versions of social learning theory have explicitly rejected the idea that situations are the only (or even the main) determinants of behavior. Indeed, they emphasize the reciprocal (mutual) interaction between the person and the situation, noting that people change situations actively and are not merely passively "shaped" by them (Bandura, 1977, 1986; Mischel, 1973, 1984). They also insist that a full account of behavior must pay attention to the person's "self-system"; the standards and rules used in self-control, and the expectations and plans about what one can and cannot do successfully in the future.

One of the persistent concerns about behavioral approaches is whether they really contribute to an understanding of the phenomena of interest to personality psychologists. Do they merely translate those phenomena into the language of learning, cognition, and general psychology, or do they help clarify and explain them? Do they even deal with them? An early worry about the behavioral approach was that it did not even try to study complex and distinctively human qualities. Indeed some critics charged that behavioral psychologists only study what is easy to study with available methods rather than turn to study what is worth studying.

While this criticism may once have hit the mark, in more recent years, social learning theorists have included an increasingly wide range of topics in their research and theorizing. Among the areas of intense activity has been personality development (e.g., Bandura & Walters, 1963), personal control (e.g., Rotter, Chance, & Phares, 1972), self-regulation (e.g., Kanfer, 1980), morality and sex

---

In Focus 14.4
Behavior Theory and Existentialism: Unexpected Similarities

Psychological theories sometimes have unexpected similarities. The behavioral approach involves a focus on what the person is doing in the here and now, rather than on reconstructions of personal history, and a reluctance to hypothesize drives, forces, motives, and other psychic dispositions as explanations. All these features, surprisingly, are not unique to a behavioral position. They just as fully seem to describe the platform of some existentially oriented and phenomenological psychologists (Chapter 8). Thus, the behavioral focus on what the person is doing, rather than on attributes or motives, also fits the existential doctrine. As Sartre put it, "existence precedes essence." He meant by that phase that

> man first of all exists, encounters himself, surges up in the world—and defines himself afterwards. If man as the existentialist sees him is not definable, it is because to begin with he is nothing. He will not be anything until later, and then he will be what he makes of himself. Thus, there is no human nature. . . . Man simply is (Sartre, 1965, p. 28).

A rejection of preconceptions about motives, traits, and the content of human nature is hardly unique to behavior theorists. George Kelly in his "personal construct theory" (Chapter 8) meant something similar when he said, "I am what I do," and urged that to know what one is one must look at what one does.

Behavior theories also share with phenomenological theories the belief that it is impossible to conceptualize people apart from the context or environment (the "field") in which they exist.

The possible compatibility between modern behavior theory and the existential-phenomenological orientation seems to hinge on several common qualities. Both share a focus on the here and now and a reluctance to posit specific motivational and trait constructs. Both emphasize what the person is doing—"where he is at"—rather than the constructs of the psychologist who studies him. Both share a disinterest in distant historical reconstruction and a concern with new action possibilities for the individual. These commonalities are impressive.

The overlap between the behavioral and existential-phenomenological orientation seems intriguing, especially because historically the latter developed in part as a protest against early behavioral approaches.

---

differences (e.g., Mischel & Mischel, 1976), and aggression (e.g., Bandura, 1973, 1986). As you will see in the final part of this book, few topics in personality psychology have been uninfluenced by the behavioral approach. Only time will allow a deep evaluation of the quality of the impact, but there is little doubt that its magnitude is great—and sometimes surprising (see *In Focus 14.4*).

Overview of the Approach

Table 14-8 summarizes the main characteristics of social behavior approaches. The table condenses points from both the more traditional behavioral and the newer, more cognitive social learning versions of these approaches.

However, the two positions may have one critical incompatibility. The existentialist takes the philosophical position that the individual is responsible, and attributes to him or her the ultimate causes of behavior. In Sartre's phrase, a person "is what he wills to be" (1956, p. 291). Though a behavior theorist may share Sartre's desire to put "every man in possession of himself," rather than allow him to be possessed by psychic forces, a behavioral analysis of causation cannot begin with the person's will as the fundamental cause of what he does, nor can it end with his constructs as a final explanation of his behavior.

George Kelly (personal communication, 1965) once emphasized his belief that personal constructs are the basic units and that it is personal constructs, rather than stimuli, that determine behavior. He recalled vividly from his Navy experience during World War II how very differently he related to the same officer on different occasions depending on how, at the time, he construed that officer. He remembered that the captain seemed diffferent to him in an informal role, chatting with his jacket off, from the way he seemed when he wore his officer's coat. You see, Kelly said, it is not the stimulus—the captain—but how I construed him that channelized my reactions to him.

But a social behavior theorist would find this story an excellent example, not of "construct control," but of "stimulus control": with his four stripes on, you see the captain one way; without his four stripes, you see him differently. To understand the construct change, in the behavioral view, you have to include in your understanding how those four stripes came to control it.

The phenomenological and behavioral positions differ in their focus of attention: the former seeks to know and understand the subject's experience; the behaviorally oriented psychologist also wants to clarify the conditions that control the subject's ultimate behavior, including the events that control constructs, cognitions, and feelings.

Is a reasonable synthesis of phenomenological psychology and social learning theory possible? Perhaps. Such a synthesis would require the ability to view people both as active construers who perceive, interpret, and influence the environment and themselves, and as creatures in nature, continuously responsive to the conditions of their lives.

Table 14-8
Summary Overview of Social Behavior Approaches

Basic units	Behavior-in-situation.
Causes of behavior	Prior learning and expectations and cues in situation (including the behavior of others).
Favored data	Direct observations of behavior in the target situation.
Observed responses used as	Behavior samples.
Research focus	Behavior change; analysis of conditions controlling behavior; self-control.
Approach to personality change	By changing conditions; by experiences that modify expectations and values; by altering self-reactions and self-efficacy.
Role of situation	Provides important information; interacts reciprocally with person.

SUMMARY

1. Behavior therapies attempt to modify disadvantageous behavior directly by planned relearning experiences and by rearranging stimulus conditions.

2. Systematic desensitization is used to help people overcome fears or anxieties. In this procedure, the individual is exposed cognitively (i.e., in imagination) to increasingly severe samples of aversive or fear-arousing stimuli; simultaneously she is helped to make responses incompatible with anxiety, such as muscle relaxation. Gradually the anxiety evoked by the aversive stimulus is reduced and the stimulus is neutralized.

3. Just as strong emotional reactions may be acquired by observing the reactions of models, so may they be modified by observing models who display more appropriate reactions. In addition to modeling fearless behavior, the model also may guide the phobic person directly to behave more bravely when faced with the anxiety-producing stimulus.

4. It is possible to neutralize a positive arousing stimulus (e.g., a fetishistic object) by repeatedly pairing it with one that is very aversive (e.g., shock). Periodic follow-up treatments help to sustain the new emotional reactions.

5. Maladaptive behaviors also may be modified by changing the consequences to which they lead. The basic procedure is to withdraw attention, approval, or other positive consequences from the maladaptive behavior and to make rewards contingent instead on the occurrence of more advantageous behavior. First the naturally occuring response-reinforcement contingencies are identified; then new and more advantageous response-reinforcement relations are instituted.

6. In some of the newest behavior change programs, responsibility is transferred as quickly as possible from the therapist to the client and his peer group. In one therapeutic community, chronic psychotics who had been hospitalized for many years were organized on a special ward.

Their autonomy was gradually increased, and their rewards were made contingent on their increasingly responsible self-management as a group.

7. People often describe their problems and their objectives in broad terms so that it is difficult to specify the particular behaviors that need to be changed. In these cases a first step may be to help the client to elaborate his or her difficulties as precisely as possible in behavioral terms.

8. In everyday life, as well as in psychotherapy, several different forms of behavior therapy may occur simultaneously. Current behavior therapies often combine several learning strategies, such as modeling, desensitization, direct reward, rather than confining themselves to one.

9. There is much controversy with regard to the depth and endurance of behavior change. Some of the most important questions concern transfer of gains to life situations, the capacity of the individual for self-control independent of the therapeutic regime, the possibility of symptom substitution, and the adequacy of behavior change techniques to deal with a person's self-concepts. Basically, these questions ask, does behavior change entail genuine, durable change—that is, basic personality change—or is it restricted to relatively minor, specific behaviors that have limited applicability to major life problems?

10. To facilitate transfer from treatment to life, one introduces into treatment stimulus conditions that are as similar as possible to the life situations in which the new behaviors will be used. Treatment samples the relevant situations and occurs in the same life setting in which improvement is desired.

11. By achieving greater competence and gratifications from his or her new, more adequate behaviors, the individual should become able to function increasingly without external reinforcement and support. New behavior change methods encourage self-management so that individuals may gain relative independence and control of their own behavior as rapidly as possible.

12. Many learning programs to eliminate maladaptive behaviors have shown promising results. The modified behaviors are not automatically replaced by other problematic ones; there is more evidence for positive generalization than for symptom substitution, although the theoretical issues are complex.

13. Often people suffer because they evaluate their behavior improperly. Behavior theorists believe they can modify problems stemming from inappropriate self-assessments by the same learning principles used to change other types of maladaptive behavior.

14. Social behavior theories contend that people are what they do. Therefore behavior change is the prerequisite for any alteration in personality. In that view, there is no personality change apart from behavior change, although the behaviors involved often may be covert and subtle, as in thoughts and self-evaluations.

15. Surprisingly, current behavior theories share common features with phenomenological approaches. In the phenomenological approach of George Kelly, for example, we know a woman by what we see her doing. Curiously, a similar statement could come from contemporary behavior theorists. Another similarity between the social behavior approach and the phenomenological orientation is that both favor concentrating on the "here-and-now" rather than on inferences about the person's past. But the approaches also differ importantly.

16. The main features of the behavioral approach were summarized and evaluated.

PART SIX
ADAPTATION AND
THE COPING PROCESS

The previous parts provided broad overviews of major approaches to personality and of the main ideas and applications associated with each. In this part the focus will shift from conceptualizing individuals to the basic processes involved in personal adaptation and coping. Investigators of personality have been guided by each of the major theoretical orientations and, most often, by a mixture that draws on some ideas from many conceptualizations. Hence in practice it becomes difficult to separate the contributions of various theories. Nevertheless, wherever possible, we shall point out major differences between orientations. Our main interest will be how the individual adapts and copes with the stresses and challenges of life. Topics include how people deal with frustration, aggression, conflict, and anxiety. We also will consider how people develop sexual identities, and what determines such important behaviors as aggression and altruism. Finally, we will return to one of the most enduring and central issues in psychology: how can we conceptualize the interaction of the person and the conditions of his or her life?

Chapter 15

Coping with Frustration, Anxiety, and Stress

In this chapter we turn to personal and interpersonal adaptation and examine how people cope with the psychological challenges that face them throughout the life cycle.

In earlier chapters you saw that theories such as Freud's and Erikson's (Chapter 2) highlight some common problems and milestones often found in development.

Just as there are many different approaches to personality, there are several different ways to conceptualize such human qualities as adjustment, normality, and mental health. There is no universal agreement even about the best definitions of such concepts. Indeed, it may be easier to find agreement about what a normal adaptive, healthy person is not than about what he or she is. Throughout this text you have seen that different theories suggest different conceptions of adaptive, positive behavior.

What Is Adjustment?

Clearly, a normal or adjusted person is not one who is always happy and free of problems and conflicts. To be totally without troubles and worries might indicate ignorance about oneself and the world more than it indicates normality.

Can one find any consensus about the qualities of positive psychological adjustment? There do seem to be some shared themes. For example, such terms as "personal responsibility," "self-control," and "social responsibility" often occur in descriptions of the ideal. In addition, humanistically oriented psychologists emphasize a humanistic ethic that values such qualities as mutuality and genuineness in human relations, a here-and-now perspective, and a search for growth rather than a mere conformity to social pressures and demands (see Table 15-2). In this regard,

recall also Maslow's view of the self-actualizing person.

In general, the humanistic orientation describes healthy people as those who:

Are aware of themselves and their experiences.

Are able to accept themselves as they are.

Take responsibility for their own lives.

Do not distort their genuine feelings.

Realize their potentialities as fully as possible.

Are not trapped by false expectations.

Finally, there are voices pleading that concepts like normality and adjustment be eliminated altogether in psychology. As one critic puts it, we need a shift in perspective away from "one which looks upon man as normal or abnormal or

Table 15-2
Examples of Positive Values in a Humanistic Ethic

Genuineness in relationships

"Play" as well as "work"

Here-and-now perspective

Acceptance of such emotions as pain, grief, anger

Search for growth experiences

Involvement and willingness to risk

SOURCE: Based on Bugental, 1971.

They paint a general picture of human adaptation in broad strokes. While such global portraits may be fascinating and often compelling, they reflect the intuitions of the theorist and his personal clinical experience. As a result, they tend to miss much of the great variety, and many of the specific features, of the actual process of coping with life's stresses and challenges as experienced by different people throughout their development. Examples of the range of potential life problems and crises are summarized in Table 15-1. Some of the issues and findings emerging

somewhere in between to one which views him as having varying potentialities and limitations under varying conditions" (Friedes, 1960, p. 132). Thus, rather than debate about some abstract ideal or norm that would apply to everyone, one would seek to encourage the realization of each person's competencies to the greatest degree possible in the specific circumstance of that individual's life.

What Makes People Happy?

In spite of much abstract debate among professionals about the nature of adjustment, until recently little was known about people's own views of what they want from life and what makes them happy or miserable. Extensive surveys exploring factors associated with what people call happiness suggest that some of our traditional beliefs about both the causes and the nature of happiness may be incorrect (Freedman, 1978). Some of the main findings include the following:

1. Childhood. An unhappy childhood, including parents' divorce or death and physical and psychological problems, does not necessarily result in an unhappy adult. A warm relationship between parents may produce a happy child, but not necessarily a happy adult. Guilt seems more closely related to adult happiness; those who often feel guilty as children describe themselves as less optimistic and less happy as adults. Guilty children are more likely to feel lonely and worthless and to have fears, anxieties, and insomnia as adults.

2. Having Everything—Isn't It. Some people are happy although they appear to have little reason to be, while others who seem to have every reason for happiness are chronically unhappy. People seem to get used to whatever they have in life, after which only deviations from this level can make them happy or unhappy.

3. Expectations. People who get more in life than they thought they would tend to be happier than those who achieve what they or others expected them to achieve. If expectations are unrealistically high (and cannot be achieved), disappointment and unhappiness are inevitable.

4. Rose-Colored Glasses and Self-Confidence. Happy and unhappy people behave differently. Happy people seek out experiences that make them happy, make the most of what they have, and enjoy life more; unhappy people do the opposite. Happy people seem to have self-confidence in their guiding values, a belief that life has meaning and direction, and a belief that it is possible to control the good and bad things that happen. Self-confidence and self-esteem seem to be associated with a high potential for happiness.

5. Social Factors. On the whole, married people say they are happier than singles; divorced individuals are the least happy. For unmarried individuals good friends and a satisfying social life are closely related to general happiness. Both men and women report love is the most important single element in happiness. Job satisfaction is also rated as important.

from studies of this coping process will be discussed in the rest of this chapter and throughout this part of the text.

As people try to meet the diverse challenges of life they face many threats to their adjustment. In this chapter we begin by considering the adjustment concept itself (see *In Focus 15.1*). Then we turn to two aspects of the coping process that are of great interest to personality theorists of all orientations: frustration and anxiety.

Table 15-1
Examples of the Range of Potential Life Crises and Sources of Stress

Developmental life transitions	Entering kindergarten
	Moving and changing schools
	Parental divorce
	Death of a parent or sibling
	Entering college
	Sexual intimacy
	Marriage and parenthood
	Retirement
	Death of a spouse or child
Unusual stresses	Imprisonment
	Exile and repatriation
	Atomic and natural disasters
	Rape
	Serious illness

SOURCE: Based on Moos, 1976.

FRUSTRATION

Throughout the lifespan, a basic fact of human adaptation is that to survive one must cope with frustration. Frustration is potentially everywhere and spares no one: a pacifier falls from the mouth of an infant too young to retrieve it; your flight is delayed and you miss Thanksgiving dinner with the family; a stroke victim struggles to find the words to make a simple request.

Frustration Defined

Frustration occurs when a sequence of goal-directed behavior is interrupted so that its completion, and the attainment of the desired goals, is blocked or delayed (see Fig. 15-1). Thus in frustration there is a thwarting of expected goal attainment. The closer one gets to completion of the goal-directed activity, and the more one expects to complete it, the more intense is the frustration of being interrupted or blocked (Haner & Brown, 1955). In other words, frustration is worst when one has built up expectations and then is stopped from fulfilling them.

Figure 15-1
Frustration Occurs when Goal-Directed Behavior is Blocked or Interrupted Before its Completion. It is Greatest when the Blocked Behavior Pattern Has Often Led to the Expected Outcome in the Past

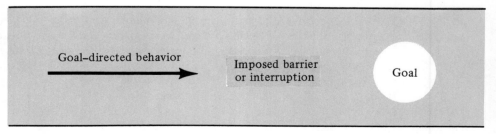

Frustrations may be especially painful when they are caused by the person's own condition and when they persist. For example, the child with a new but enduring physical handicap—such as blindness after an accident—faces a world filled with frustration. Less obvious but often more painful are the effects of the individual's own failures or incompetence—the flunked examination, the bungled job interview, the inept social encounter that leads to rejection.

Perhaps the worst frustrations are those in which control over one's own life is interrupted and one is placed in captivity (e.g., Biderman, 1967). The slave or the political prisoner, and even the involuntary military conscript, provide vivid examples of adaptation to total interruption of a life resulting in a massive disorganization of habitual behavior patterns.

In common-sense terms, frustration is most bitter when the person has built up high hopes and then is prevented from realizing them. The disgruntlement of disadvantaged minority groups, for example, seems to become most painful after they have started to build expectations for a better life. Frustration seems to be most keen when an important built-up hope or expectancy is disappointed. As was noted many years ago by de Tocqueville: "Patiently endured so long as it seemed beyond redress, a grievance comes to appear intolerable once the possibility of removing it crosses men's minds" (cited in Rubin, 1968). Indeed, as history shows, political dictators sometimes have shared de Tocqueville's insight and have proceeded to "treat" the disappointments of their people by systematically eliminating their hopes.

Thus the experience of frustration involves a thwarting of expected goal attainment. These expectations of gratification are the result of the individual's learning experiences. That is, the actions that we expect to execute smoothly and without interruption are those that have been "overlearned" or repeatedly practiced successfully on past occasions (Mandler, 1964). The more overlearned the sequence, the more arousing its disruption tends to be and the more aversive is the delay of expected gratification or goal attainment.

Emotional Arousal

Intense frustration leads to a state of emotional arousal. Numerous bodily changes occur during high states of arousal and involve a variety of "autonomic" events. These are physiological changes mediated by the autonomic nervous system. Such bodily changes may include an increase in heart rate and blood pressure, sweating, and vasoconstriction in the fingers (Elliott, 1974). We saw how some of these bodily changes may be measured in Chapter 13.

The emotional arousal produced by frustration is often seen in an increase in the vigor of behavior (Amsel & Roussel, 1952). Increased vigor produced by frustration has been found, for example, in the form of more energetic plunger-pulling or lever-pushing by children after frustration in experimental game situations (e.g., Haner & Brown, 1955; Holton, 1961). Similarly, frustrated rats have been shown to display dramatic increases in energetic behavior. It is not clear whether increased vigor of responses after thwarting is an intrinsic effect of frustration or a well-learned common reaction to it.

Persistence

Usually a first reaction to the interruption of behavior is to attempt to persist with the blocked sequence (Mandler, 1964). The cliché, "If at first you don't succeed, try again," fits the repetitive behavior typically found in first reactions to an imposed delay—as when one vainly repeats jiggling the stuck key in the lock, usually more and more vigorously, or when the toddler whose mother disappears behind the kitchen door starts pushing against it more and more forcefully, with increasing distress.

Frustration and Aggression

How one copes with frustration is a crucial aspect of adaptation to the stresses of life. In early work it was often believed that frustration has certain inevitable effects on behavior. For example, the classic *frustration-aggression hypothesis* (Dollard et

Frustration is worse when built-up hopes cannot be filled.

al., 1939) asserted that all frustrations increase the probability of an aggressive reaction and that all aggression presupposes the existence of prior frustration.

The frustration-aggression hypothesis conceptualized aggression as an unlearned drive or instinct. This hypothesis assumed that the aggressive instinct evolved biologically as a mechanism for coping with frustrations, especially those that threaten the organism's survival. It was hypothesized that this instinct to inflict harm or injury on others made it possible for the individual to survive in competition with other members of the species.

In light of much research, the frustration-aggression hypothesis proved too simple and required serious changes (e.g., Bandura, 1973; Berkowitz, 1969). Specifically, the following has become plain:

1. Aggressive reactions can and do happen without any prior frustration. For example, unfrustrated preschool children watched an adult model physically attack a Bobo doll. Later, after the model had left the room, these children readily imitated the model's aggressiveness and violently attacked the doll (Bandura & Walters, 1963).
2. Although aggression often may occur after frustration, it is certainly not the only possible reaction to frustration. There are great differences among people in their response to frustration, and even the same person may react to particular frustrations differently, depending on the specific situation.

Frustration Has Diverse Effects

One often reacts aggressively when frustrated because aggressive reactions seem likely to work effectively to remove the frustration. The child that keeps banging against the shut door is likely to get in, just as the more violent spouse in a family quarrel is likely to have his or her own way, at least temporarily.

In our society, forceful, assertive, dominating behavior is attended to and often rewarded. The aggressive executive, the child who "acts out," the prisoners who "riot," the employees who go on strike, all demand—and get—attention. Their aggressiveness may also remove barriers effectively and produce personal gain and social power. Such frequent rewards for aggressive behavior in our society help to explain why violence is a frequent response to frustration.

Aggression, however, does not have to follow frustration. The choice of behaviors after frustration is governed by the same principles as other socially learned response patterns: peoples' experiences in related situations and their expectancies concerning the probable outcomes of the alternative actions available now determine what they will do (see Chapter 12). If aggression is expected to work and pay off best, it will occur; if nonaggressive ways of coping are expected to be the best ones in the situation, then they will occur. (The topic of aggression is discussed further in Chapter 18.)

Alternative Ways of Coping

Behavior in the face of frustration is often unconstructive and negative. This point was made in a classic experiment (Barker, Dembo, & Lewin, 1941) in which indi-

Figure 15-2
The Frustration Situation

From Barker et al., (1941).

vidual nursery school children engaged in a free-play situation with a set of standard play materials. Their play was rated for its constructiveness: elaborate games and stories were scored high and simply handling the materials was scored low.

Next the children were frustrated. Some much more attractive toys were mixed in with the standard play materials, and when the child was deeply engrossed in play, the experimenter removed the attractive toys to a part of the room in full view of the child but made inaccessible by a locked wire-screen wall (see Figure 15-2).

The frustrated, unhappy children now played much less creatively with the standard toys than they had during the initial free-play period. Their play became more infantile (e.g., simple scribbling with crayons) and aggressive (breaking the toys). Some kicked the barrier or tried to go around it. Some pleaded with the experimenter. Almost all the children whimpered or complained.

Under other conditions, however, frustration may have different effects. In an experiment with small groups of children (Davitz, 1952), some of the groups received praise and approval for cooperative and constructive behavior in competitive games during training sessions. Other groups were rewarded for making aggressive responses during these sessions. Then the children were frustrated by interruption of a film they were watching just as it approached its climax and by being required to return the candy that had been given to them earlier. Analyses of the children's responses to these frustrations indicated that those previously rewarded for constructiveness responded more constructively; those rewarded for aggression reacted more aggressively.

How people respond to frustration also depends on how they interpret the situation. For example, if one interprets a frustration so that instead of seeming arbitrarily imposed it appears somehow reasonable, one becomes less angry (Pastore, 1952). In one study, children lost a cash prize because of another child's clumsiness. Children who heard the explanation that the clumsy child was sleepy and upset expressed less aggression than did those youngsters who had not gotten this interpretation of the cause of frustration (Mallick & McCandless, 1966). The child's ability to cope with frustration also may be related to his or her competence and self-esteem.

Competence and Self-Esteem

The ability to cope successfully with frustration increases enormously in the course of cognitive and language development. As children become better able to reason and solve problems, to use language, to anticipate consequences, and to plan for the future, their ability to cope with frustration also grows impressively (Harter, 1983).

Some researchers have been exploring the origins of competence by observing young children who come from families that have already produced other extremely competent older children (White et al., 1976). Careful observation of young children in their homes suggests that the foundations for competence may be established by the age of three years.

Several types of early experience seem especially important for the development of the child's basic linguistic, intellectual, and social skills. White emphasizes the amount of "live" language the child gets: the more, the better. Live language comes from adults talking directly to the child, not from overheard speech or exposure to language on television and radio. When characterizing parents who seem to rear exceptionally competent children, White notes that they appear to be excellent designers and organizers of their child's environment and firm disciplinarians who also display great affection for their child. These parents tend to let the child initiate social interactions with them and are responsive to the child and ready to serve as "personal consultants" in brief episodes when the child needs them.

The child's increasing competence is also reflected in the development of self-esteem: as children acquire greater mastery, they develop positive concepts about themselves and their personal worth. (Coopersmith, 1967). For example, boys with high self-esteem tend to be described as more effective and more competent. Children who have high self-esteem tend to be those who are more esteemed, more competent, and who have parents who have high self-esteem, as was noted earlier (Chapter 10).

Apathy and Helplessness

We already saw that under some conditions individuals may develop a sense of apathy and helplessness in the face of frustration. Such reactions as withdrawal, listlessness, and seeming emotional indifference are sometimes found among war prisoners and inmates of concentration camps. The victims seem to have given up totally, presumably overwhelmed by their inability to do anything that will change their desperate lot.

Experiments with animals also are relevant for understanding responses to extreme frustration. Consider, for example, a dog who first is placed in a situation where he can do nothing to end or escape an electric shock delivered to his feet through an electrified grid on the floor. Later he may sit passively and endure the shocks even though he can escape them now by jumping to a nearby compartment. Such a state of *learned helplessness* may persist and be very hard to remedy (Seligman, 1975, 1978). It also has been found that children who believe they cannot control their environment may become its passive victims, withdrawing from problems rather than coping with them actively (e.g., Diener & Dweck, 1978).

Dramatic examples of learned helplessness may be found among the children of America's migrant families whose plight was described by Coles (1970). He notes that unlike typical children in the middle class, migrant children soon discover that their shouts and screams will not necessarily bring any relief from their pains and frustrations. Consider this description by a migrant mother of her own helpless feelings in the face of her children's suffering:

> My children, they suffer, I know. They hurts, and I can't stop it. I just have to pray that they'll stay alive, somehow. They gets the colic, and I don't know what to do. One of them, he can't breathe right and his chest, it's in trouble. I can hear the noise inside when he takes his breaths. The worst thing, if you ask me, is the bites they get. It makes them unhappy, real unhappy. They itches and scratches and bleeds, and oh, it's the worst. They must want to tear all their skin off, but you can't do that. There'd still be mosquitoes and ants and rats and like that around and they'd be after your insides then, if the skin was all gone. That's what would happen then. But I say to myself it's life, the way living

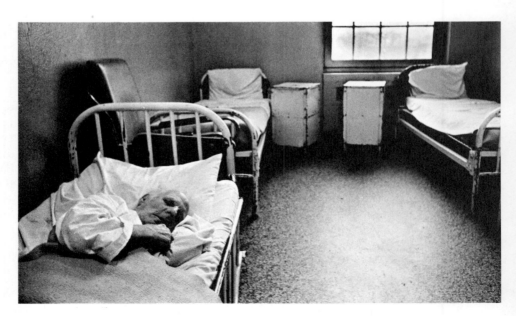

Learned helplessness may lead to depression and hopelessness

is, and there's not much to do but accept what happens. Do you have a choice but to accept? That's what I'd like to ask you, yes sir. Once, when I was little, I seem to recall asking my uncle if there wasn't something you could do, but he said no, there wasn't, and to hush up. So I did. Now I have to tell my kids the same, that you don't go around complaining—you just don't (Coles, 1970, pp. 9–10).

Indeed, a good deal of research with humans now suggests that when people believe they cannot control events and outcomes they gradually do develop a sense of helplessness (e.g., Wortman & Brehm, 1975) and even severe depression (see *In Focus 15.2*). Conversely, when people are led to believe that they can make an impact on their environment, that they can influence and control events, they become more alert, happier—and may even live longer. For example, one group of institutionalized elderly adults was given opportunities for making decisions actively and for being personally responsible for something outside of themselves (a plant). Soon these people began to feel and act more competent (relative to comparison groups who were kept in the usual passive institutional routine and who had all the decisions made for them by the staff). A follow-up eighteen months later showed that in the active responsibility groups only half as many people had died as in the comparison group (Rodin & Langer, 1977).

Perceived Control: It Helps to Think You Have It

An excellent protection against helplessness, depression, and apathy is a belief that one can control and change the events in one's life through one's own actions. As previously noted (Chapter 7), such a belief is called an *internal* (rather than external) *locus of control* (e.g., Phares, 1976; Rotter, 1966). It arises from experiences leading to expectations that one can influence one's own conditions and fate. In contrast, some people may believe they can exercise no control over what happens to them; they believe in an *external locus of control.* An individual with such beliefs may feel that personal achievements, successes, and failures all come from fate or luck and therefore cannot be influenced by himself or herself.

To illustrate, one person with an extreme belief in external locus of control was described as showing

> a curious mixture of calmness and anxiety. On some occasions he seemed uneasy, as if he realized how ill-prepared he was to cope with a potentially overpowering world. On other occasions he was relaxed, as if to say "I know things are beyond my control and that my efforts are not really very important, so why should I get upset? Whatever will be, will be" (Phares, 1976, p. 4).

While such extremes are sometimes found, most people tend to have a mixture of beliefs. They expect that some outcomes (under some conditions) are within their internal control while other outcomes are not (Lao, 1970; Mischel, 1973; Phares, 1976).

A belief in internal locus of control is important for many aspects of coping. But also remember the old saying that wisdom requires knowing the difference between what one can change and what one cannot: while it may be best to cope actively with what one can change, it is also important to learn to accept what one cannot control (Miller, 1980). Above all, it may be crucial to discriminate accurately between the things one can change and those that one cannot.

In Focus 15.2
Depression As Insufficient Reinforcement

When people feel they cannot tolerate the frustrations in their lives, they may become depressed, sometimes to a severe degree. In the extreme, they may lose interest in all activities and virtually stop behaving, often spending a great deal of time in bed. They tend to become very sad and are filled with feelings of worthlessness and physical complaints.

There is general agreement that the behaviors listed in Table 15-3 characterize depressed people as a group. Each depressed individual displays his or her own combination of any of these behaviors, often including deep unhappiness, emotional numbness and loss of interest, withdrawal from normal activities, and profoundly negative feelings about oneself and life.

But why? Perceived helplessness may play a part in depression, but there also may be other causes. According to one promising theory, depression may be understood as a result of a persistent lack of gratification or positive outcomes (reinforcement) for the person's own behavior (Lewinsohn, 1975). That is, depressed persons feel bad and withdraw from life because their environments are consistently unresponsive to them and fail to provide enough positive consequences for what they are doing. The situation is analogous to an extinction schedule in which reinforcement for a behavior is

Table 15-3
Some Indicators of Depression

Mood
　　Feel sad and blue most of the time
　　No longer enjoy things they used to
　　General loss of feeling
　　Fatigue, apathy, boredom
　　Loss of interest in eating, sex, and other activities

Physical symptoms
　　Headaches
　　Difficulty sleeping
　　Gastrointestinal symptoms (indigestion, constipation)
　　Weight loss—loss of appetite
　　Vague physical complaints

Behaviors
　　Unsociable—often alone
　　Unable to work, less sexual activity
　　Complaining, worrying, weeping
　　Neglect appearance
　　Speak little (speech is slow, monotonous, soft)

Ideation
　　Low self-esteem ("I'm no good")
　　Pessimism ("Things will always be bad for me")
　　Guilt, failure, self-blame, self-criticism
　　Feel isolated, powerless, helpless
　　Suicidal wishes ("I wish I were dead." "I want to kill myself.")

SOURCE: Based on Lewinsohn, 1975.

withdrawn until gradually the behavior itself stops. In the case of the depressed person, the only reinforcement that does continue tends to be in the form of attention and sympathy from relatives and friends for the very behaviors that are maladaptive: weeping, complaining, talking about suicide. These depressive behaviors are so unpleasant that they soon alienate most people in the depressed person's environment, thus producing further isolation, lack of reinforcement, and unhappiness in a vicious cycle of increasing misery and increasing withdrawal.

Depressed people, according to this theory, may suffer from three basic problems. First, they tend to find relatively few events and activities gratifying. Second, they tend to live in environments in which reinforcement is not readily available for their adaptive behaviors. For example, they may live highly isolated lives, as often happens with older people alone in impersonal rooming houses, or

with younger people in large universities that make them feel lost. Third, they lack the skills and are deficient in the behaviors that are needed to elicit positive reactions from other people. For example, they may be shy and socially awkward, making gratifying relationships with others very difficult. It follows that they in turn develop feelings such as "I'm not likable," or even "I'm no good." The essentials of the theory are shown schematically in Figure 15-3.

Although the theory has not been tested conclusively, a good deal of evidence is consistent with it. For example, depressed people do seem to elicit fewer behaviors from other people and thus presumably get less social reinforcement from them. Depressed people also tend to engage in fewer pleasant activities and enjoy such events less than do nondepressed individuals (Lewinsohn, 1975).

This concept of depression immediately suggests a treatment strategy: increase the rate of positive reinforcement for the

Figure 15-3
Schematic Representation of Lewinsohn's Theory of Depression

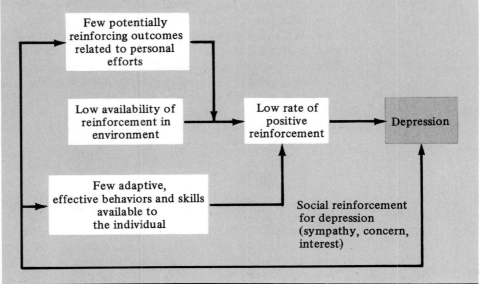

Based on Lewinsohn (1975).

depressed person's adaptive efforts. Note that such a plan would require increasing the rate of positive outcomes received by depressed people contingent on their own behavior; it does not mean simply giving more rewards regardless of what the individual does. The crucial point is to increase depressed peoples' expectations that their own efforts and actions will yield positive consequences for them, thereby enhancing their involvement in life and reducing their sense of helplessness (Seligman, et al., 1979) as well as their feelings of hopelessness.

ANXIETY AND STRESS

Dealing with frustration is only one part of the process of adaptation. Equally important is how the person manages the emotion that has been an enduring focus for most personality theorists: anxiety.

Theoretical Views of Anxiety

Each of the major theoretical orientations conceptualizes anxiety somewhat differently, in accord with its own views of what is threatening for people. For example, Freudian formulations emphasize the breakthrough into consciousness of unacceptable impulses. Learning theories focus on association with painful or aversive stimulation, and phenomenological-existential theories stress the perception of a basic threat to the self or to the individual's very existence as a personality (e.g., May, 1950). Other formulations view anxiety mainly as a state of distress and helplessness in which the organism has no alternatives (Mandler & Watson, 1966) or as a "disease of overarousal" (Malmo, 1957). Taken together these definitions provide a glimpse of the great variety of events that may be subjectively dangerous for any particular individual and that may create anxiety.

There is no reason to restrict the meaning of anxiety to any single conception. Indeed, each individual has a somewhat different, personal set of threats that create greatest anxiety. Because each person can conceptualize arousal states in somewhat different ways, the experiences under the label "anxiety" may be almost endless, and they range from birth traumas to death fears. Therefore rather than seek a universally acceptable definition of anxiety, it may be more fruitful to examine how anxiety can be measured and to consider its causes, consequences, and correlates.

The Meaning of Anxiety

Anxiety is most simply defined as an acquired (learned) fear; for the moment we will employ the terms *anxiety* and *fear* interchangeably, although they are often used in somewhat differernt ways. Examples of anxiety are all around us: the student who is anxious about taking examinations, the businessperson with anxiety about the financial future, the teen-age boy who is anxious about his appearance and sex appeal, and the child who wakes up anxious from a nightmare.

Although different individuals experience anxiety in different ways, the following three elements often are found (Maher, 1966):

1. A conscious feeling of fear and danger, without the ability to identify immediate objective threats that could account for these feelings.
2. A pattern of physiological arousal and bodily distress that may include miscellaneous physical changes and complaints. Common examples include *cardiovascular* symptoms (heart palpitations, faintness, increased blood pressure, pulse changes); *respiratory* complaints (breathlessness, feeling of suffocation); and *gastrointestinal* symptoms (diarrhea, nausea, vomiting). If the anxiety persists, the prolonged physical reactions to it may have chronic effects on each of these bodily systems. In addition the person's agitation may be reflected in sleeplessness, frequent urination, perspiration, muscular tensions, fatigue, and other signs of upset and distress.
3. A disruption or disorganization of effective problem-solving and cognitive control, including difficulty in thinking clearly and coping effectively with environmental demands.

From Trauma to Anxiety

Probably the clearest examples of anxiety reactions occur after the individual has experienced a life-threatening danger or trauma. A near-fatal automobile accident, an almost catastrophic combat experience, an airplane crash—such intense episodes of stress are often followed by anxiety. After the actual dangers have passed, stimuli that remind the individual of those dangers, or signs that lead him or her to expect new dangers, may reactivate anxiety that may persist or recur after the trauma is over.

After severe trauma, the victim is more likely to respond anxiously to other stress stimuli that occur later in life (Archibald & Tuddenham, 1965). Surviving victims of Nazi concentration camps, for example, sometimes continued for years to be hypersensitive to threat stimuli and to react to stress readily with anxiety and sleep disturbances (Chodoff, 1963). These observations support the idea that anxiety involves a learned fear reaction that is highly resistant to extinction and that may be evoked by diverse stimuli similar to those that originally were traumatic. That is, the fear evoked by the traumatic stimuli may be reactivated and also may *generalize* to stimuli associated with the traumatic episode. For example, after a child has been attacked and bitten by a dog, her fear reaction may generalize to other dogs, animals, fur, places similar to the one in which the attack occurred, and so on (Figure 15-4). Moreover, if the generalization stimuli are very remote from the original traumatic stimulus, the person may be unable to see the connection between the two and the anxiety may appear (even to her) particularly irrational. Suppose, for example, that the child becomes afraid of the room in which the dog bit her and of similar rooms. If the connection between her new fear of rooms and the dog's attack is not recognized, the fear of rooms now may seem especially bizarre.

From a learning point of view, anxieties after traumas, like other learned fears,

Figure 15-4
From Trauma to Anxiety

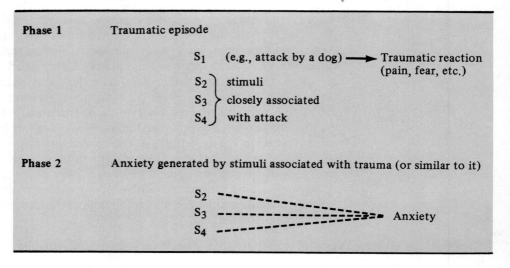

Phase 1　　Traumatic episode

S_1　(e.g., attack by a dog) ⟶ Traumatic reaction
(pain, fear, etc.)

S_2 ⎫ stimuli
S_3 ⎬ closely associated
S_4 ⎭ with attack

Phase 2　　Anxiety generated by stimuli associated with trauma (or similar to it)

S_2
S_3 ----- Anxiety
S_4

may be interpreted in accord with conditioning principles. If neutral stimuli have been associated with aversive events or outcomes, then they also may come to elicit anxiety in their own right. Such aversively conditioned emotional reactions may also generalize extensively to new stimuli (Figure 15-4). Clinical examples of aversive arousal and avoidance include many phobic and anxious reactions to objects, people, and social and interpersonal situations. Not only external events, but also their symbolic representations in the form of words or of thoughts and fantasies, may create painful emotions. In our example of the child traumatized by the dog, even thinking about the incident, or the room in which it occurred, or similar rooms may terrify the youngster.

Stimuli closer or more relevant to those associated with emotional arousal tend to elicit stronger reactions. In one study, novice sports parachutists and control subjects were administered a specially constructed word association test (Epstein & Fenz, 1962; Fenz, 1964). The words contained four levels of relevance to parachuting. Throughout the word association tests, subjects' physiological reactions (GSR) were recorded to measure their emotional arousal in response to the various stimulus words. One testing occurred two weeks before the scheduled jump, another testing was done the day before the jump, and a final test was on the day of the parachute jump.

The results showed more arousal in parachutists for parachute-relevant words. The effect was greatest for the words most relevant to parachuting, and the gradient of arousal was highest and steepest when the testing time was closer to the emotion-arousing parachute jump itself.

Traumas often may lead to anxiety, but many other effects are also possible. One study examined differences between children in Israeli settlements subjected to frequent artillery shellings during Arab-Israeli conflicts and those from comparable settlements that were not shelled (Ziv, Kruglanski, & Shulman, 1974). The children in the shelled settlements appeared to cope actively with the stress and did so in ways that were supported by the social norms in their community. Specifically, they developed greater patriotism for the settlement in which they resided, showed more externally oriented aggressiveness, and became more appreciative of courage as a personality trait.

Anxiety and Avoidance

Because anxiety is aversive we usually try to reduce or avoid it. When the dangerous event is external—like an attacker—anxiety may be reduced by physical escape from the threatening situation or by other forms of problem-solving (such as calling for help). The reduction of the anxiety state in turn reinforces the behaviors that led to the relief. Consequently the person's successful escape or avoidance behaviors become strengthened.

The strengthening of successful escape behaviors may be adaptive to the extent that one can then more readily avoid similar future dangers. On the other hand, because the escape pattern was reinforced, the person may continue to avoid similar situations in the future when in fact they are no longer dangerous. That is, previously reinforced quick escape and avoidance maneuvers may prevent the person from learning that the danger feared is no longer there or that its aversive effects can be mastered. The child who was bitten by a dog and then runs away from all dogs has no chance to learn that most dogs are friendly. In that case the fearful person continues to defensively avoid similar or related situations instead of unlearning his or her fear of them. Hence avoidance reactions may be highly persistent (Seligman, 1975).

Reinforced escape and avoidance patterns, if widely generalized, may have debilitating consequences. As an example, consider the case of a little girl who has been sexually molested by an intruder at home. As a result of this traumatic experience the child may acquire a phobic reaction, not just to the painful encounter and the man who terrified her, but also to other men and to many aspects of sexual experience and intimacy. Her subsequent refusal of dates and her generalized avoidance of closeness with men would make it increasingly difficult for her to overcome her anxieties and to develop satisfying heterosexual relationships.

Anxiety and Conflict

Avoidance reactions may become most problematic when the threat stimuli persist and cannot be escaped by moving away from them physically. Often individuals cannot escape from the sources of possible anxiety around them by simply avoiding them. This is true when they depend upon and love the very people who threaten them.

In the course of socialization the same significant persons who nurture and care for the child and to whom the child becomes most deeply attached, are also the ones who discipline and punish him or her. For example, the same mother who reinforces the child with her attention and social approval may cause pain and anxiety. Thus the same social stimulus—the mother, in this example—that has been associated with positive rewards and gratification is also connected with pain because of the punishments she dispenses and the rewards that she withholds from the child. The phenomena of "ambivalence" and "conflict" may result whenever the same persons or objects who evoke positive feelings and approach tendencies are also the sources for negative emotions and avoidance reactions. This duality is common in life and it does not end with childhood. In an adult's life, for example, the same spouse who gives love may also be the source of many bitter frustrations. Hence, mixed feelings develop.

Just how the individual will feel and react in relation to these ambivalence-producing stimuli depends on many considerations. For example, a child may be harshly punished by his father when he is physically aggressive to his baby sister, but may be warmly praised by his father when he is physically self-assertive with

---

In Focus 15.3
Types of Conflict

Individuals may experience conflict when they want to pursue two or more goals that are mutually exclusive. For example, a person may want to spend the evening with a friend but thinks he should prepare for an examination facing him the next morning; or she may want to express her anger at her parents but also does not want to hurt them. When an individual must choose among incompatible alternatives, he or she may undergo conflict.

Neal Miller's (1959) conceptualization of conflict hypothesizes *approach* and *avoidance* tendencies. For example, in an "approach-approach" conflict the person is torn, at least momentarily, between two desirable goals. Conversely, people often face "avoidance-avoidance" conflicts between two undesirable alternatives: to study tediously for a dull subject or flunk the examination, for example. The individual may wish to avoid both of these aversive events, but each time he starts to move away from his desk he reminds himself how awful it would be to fail the test.

Some of the most difficult conflicts involve goals or incentives that are both positive and negative in value. These are the goals toward which we have "mixed feelings" or ambivalent attitudes. For example, we may want the pleasure of a gourmet treat but not the calories, or we may desire the fun of a vacation spree but not the expense, or we may love

certain aspects of a parent but hate others.

You also will recall that approach-avoidance conflicts had a predominant place in Freud's hypotheses regarding intrapsychic clashes—for example, between id impulses and inhibitory anxieties.

Miller's original theory of conflict was based on a number of animal experiments (e.g., Brown, 1942, 1948; Miller, 1959). In one study, for example, hungry rats learned how to run down an alley to get food at a distinctive point in the maze. To generate "ambivalence" (approach-avoidance tendencies), the rats were given a quick electric shock while they were eating. To test the resulting conflict, the rats were later placed again at the start of the alley. The hungry rat now started toward the food but halted and hesitated before reaching it. The distance from the food at which he stopped could be changed by manipulating either the amount of his hunger or the strength of the electric shock.

Miller applied the concept of *goal gradients* to analyze conflict. Goal gradients are changes in response strength as a function of distance from the goal object. To assess the strength of approach and avoidance tendencies at different points from the goal, a harness apparatus was devised to measure a rat's pull toward a positive reinforcement (food) or away from a negative reinforcement (shock).

---

peers. If that happens consistently he soon may learn to expect positive gratification from his father in one context but punishment and aversive consequences in the other context. Thus in one situation he will expect praise and love from the same father who is the source of his anxiety in the second situation. These situations will be discriminated clearly, and anxiety associated with uncertainty and conflict therefore will probably be minimal. (For a discussion of types of conflict, see *In Focus 15.3*)

Anxiety may be much higher, however, when the child is uncertain about the behaviors that will lead to punishment and those that will not, and when she does not feel that she can control the important aversive outcomes in her life. It may be especially difficult for a child to cope adequately if punishment from the parent

---

The light harness enabled the experimenter to restrain the rat for a moment along the route to the goal and measure (in grams) the strength of the animal's pull on the harness at each test point (Brown, 1948). The rats pulled harder when they were restrained nearer the goal than when they were restrained farther away from it. This finding is evidenced by the slope of the approach gradient (shown in Figure 15-5) connecting the near test point and the far test point.

Similar procedures were used with rats who received an electric shock at the end of the alley. When these animals were later placed at the same point in the alley where they had been shocked before (but now with no shock), they ran away from the spot. Moreover, the nearer the rats were to that spot when tested in the restraining harness, the harder they generally pulled to get away (Figure 15-5). The steeper slope of the avoidance gradient (when compared to the approach gradient) is especially noteworthy. It indicates that the strength of the avoidance tendency increases more quickly with nearness than does the tendency to approach.

Figure 15-5
Approach and Avoidance Gradients

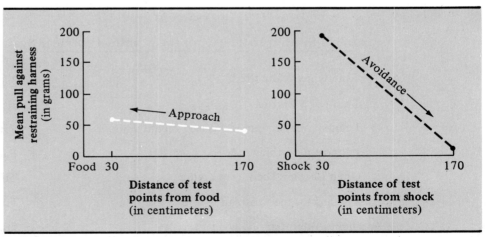

Adapted from Brown (1948).

(and other important people) is unpredictable and inconsistent so that she is unsure of what to expect. In that case the child may experience a more generalized dread, because threat and punishment are possible at almost any time and place.

Trait Anxiety

A distinction has been made between *state* and *trait* anxiety (Spielberger, 1966). State anxiety refers to a person's momentary or situational anxiety and it varies in intensity over time and across settings. Trait anxiety, in contrast, refers to one's more stable, characteristic overall level of anxiety. Usually trait anxiety is measured by the person's self-report on questionnaires.

Anxiety inventories ask people to report the extent to which various anxiety responses generally characterize them. The MMPI is the forerunner and model for most anxiety questionnaires. For example, the most popular anxiety test, the Manifest Anxiety Scale or MAS (Taylor, 1953) borrowed from the pool of MMPI items. Construction of the scale started with selection of 200 items from the MMPI. These items were given to five clinical psychologists with instructions to identify those that seemed to tap anxiety. To facilitate judgment, the clinicians were given a lengthy description of anxiety reaction. Gradually the best items were selected and the meaning of the resulting scale was elaborated through extensive research. The items on anxiety scales like the MAS deal with various forms of anxiety such as feeling uneasy, worrying, perspiring, and experiencing unhappiness and discomfort (see Table 15-4).

Relations Among Measures

Are people who feel anxious in some situations likely to feel anxious in many other situations? For instance, are people who are anxious about taking tests also likely to worry more about their health or their family? The basic question is: Does "anxiety" constitute a broadly generalized trait? To study this question, investigators

Table 15-4
Items Similar to Those on the Manifest Anxiety Scale

Item	High Anxiety Response
I rarely get really tired.	False
I am not a worrier.	False
I cannot keep my mind focused on anything.	True
I almost never blush.	False
Often I cannot keep from crying.	True
It's hard for me to attend to a job.	True
Often I think I am no good.	True

[The subject must respond "true" or "false."]

assess the correlations among people's anxiety responses on diverse measures (Sarason, 1978).

Substantial correlations are often found among different self-report anxiety questionnaires that deal with topics like "test anxiety" (anxiety about taking tests) or more "general anxiety" reactions (e.g., Sarason et al., 1960; Ruebush, 1963). For example, the correlation between scores on the Test Anxiety Scale for Children and the General Anxiety Scale for Children tends to be highly significant. The associations become smaller, however, when anxiety is measured by diverse methods, involving response modes and formats other than questionnaires—for example, measures of physiological (autonomic) arousal and actual avoidance behavior. The correlations are highest for people who are most extreme in their self-reported anxiety (very high or very low).

Anxiety and Performance: Effects of Arousal

Sometimes a public speaker has his speech well learned and strong motivation to give it—and yet his performance falls apart because of stage fright. In situations that range from preparing for examinations to making love, people often suffer

Figure 15-6
Hypothetical U-Shape Relation between the Effective Level of Functioning and the Level of Arousal. Note the Characteristic Inverted U Shape

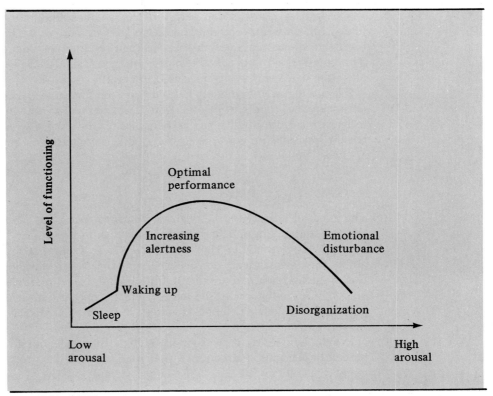

From Hebb (1972).

Table 15-5
Items Like Those Used to Measure Self-Reported Anxiety

Work upsets me easily. (true)

When I am embarrassed, I blush beet-red, which is very annoying. (true)

I never lose sleep worrying. (false)

I lack self-confidence. (true)

I always feel I can overcome any difficulties I have. (false)

I am a good sleeper.(false)

Answers in parentheses are scored as high anxiety.

from anxiety that gravely impairs their performance. How does anxiety undermine performance? In part, the problem for the anxious person is too much emotional arousal. The relationship between level of emotional arousal and the effectiveness of performance may be pictured as an inverted U (see Figure 15-6). When emotional arousal is very low or absent, performance tends to be poor because the person is practically asleep; when arousal is extremely high, there is too much stimulation and performance deteriorates because the person becomes swamped. Hence, performance tends to be most efficient when arousal is at a moderate level and the person is alert without being overwhelmed.

The impact of anxiety on performance has been studied more closely than that of any other form of emotional arousal. One strategy of studying this relationship has been to examine the links between self-reported test anxiety (fears associated with being tested) and actual test performance. Table 15-5 gives some more examples of how test anxiety is measured in current research.

In general, whether anxiety helps or hurts performance depends both on the level of anxiety and on the difficulty of the task. Individuals who are very anxious tend to learn a simple conditioned response faster than those who are low in anxiety, but this relationship is reversed when the learning task is complex (e.g., Spence & Spence, 1964).

Anxiety and Ability

The effect of anxiety on the quality of performance also depends on one's ability. College students in one study were grouped into five ability levels based on tests of scholastic aptitude as shown in Figure 15-7. Note that in the middle range of ability, anxious students achieved poorer grades than did those with low anxiety. But at the extreme ends of the ability range the level of anxiety did not influence grades. For students with the lowest ability, college grades reflected mainly their poor ability. Likewise, the best students did well regardless of anxiety level (Spielberger, 1962).

In sum, anxiety about tests is related to performance, but the relationship is complex. It depends on instruction, task difficulty, and ability, to name but a few of the many relevant variables.

Figure 15-7
Mean Grade-Point Averages for High- and Low-Anxiety College Students at Five Levels of Scholastic Ability

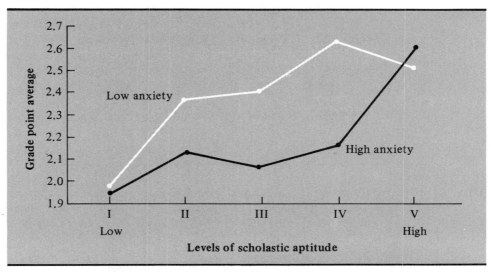

Adapted from Spielberger (1962); drawn from data in Sarason (1961).

Interfering Self-Preoccupying Thoughts

Anxiety interferes most with effective performance when it arouses anxious, self-preoccupying thoughts (e.g., "I'm no good at this—I'll never be able to do it") in the stressed person. These thoughts compete and interfere with task-relevant

The possible impact of anxiety on performance depends both on the person and the situation.

thoughts (e.g., "Now I have to recheck my answers"). The result is that performance (as well as the subject) suffers (Sarason, 1979). The interference from self-preoccupying thoughts tends to be greatest when the task-to-be-done is complex and requires many competing responses. One just cannot be full of negative thoughts about oneself and simultaneously concentrate effectively on difficult work. Likewise, as the motivation to do well increases (as when success on the task is especially important), the highly anxious person may become particularly handicapped. That happens because under such highly motivating conditions test-anxious people tend to catastrophize and become even more negatively self-preoccupied, dwelling on how poorly they are doing. In contrast, the less anxious pay attention to the task and concentrate on how to master it effectively.

In Focus 15.4
How to Talk to Yourself Better: Changing Internal Monologues

To perform more competently in the face of stress, it may help to "inoculate" oneself to it. One successful training program aims to modify both one's appraisal of the fearful situation and one's expectancies about being able to cope with it. To accomplish these aims, anxious people may be taught better ways to talk to themselves while anticipating and handling stressful situations. The idea is simply that if you improve your internal monologue, if you talk to yourself better, you will be able to cope more effectively. Examples of potentially useful self-

Table 15-6
Examples of Coping Self-Statements

Preparing for a Stressor
  What is it I have to do?
  I can develop a plan to deal with it.
  Just think about what I can do about it. That's better than getting anxious.
  No negative self-statements, just think rationally.
  Don't worry. Worry won't help anything.
  Maybe what I think is anxiety is eagerness to confront it.

Confronting and Handling a Stressor
  I can meet this challenge.
  One step at a time; I can handle the situation.
  Don't think about fear—just about what I have to do. Stay relevant.
  This anxiety is what the doctor said I would feel. It's a reminder to use my coping exercises.
  This tenseness can be an ally, a cue to cope.
  Relax; I'm in control. Take a slow, deep breath. Ah, good.

Coping with the Feeling of Being Overwhelmed
  When fear comes, just pause.
  Keep focus on the present; what is it I have to do?

The Role of Expectancies: Think Success

In part, anxiety sabotages performance by creating negative expectancies:the person who expects failure is likely to fulfill his prophecy. If people who expect to fail are led to think they can do better, will their performance actually improve? One study of academically borderline college freshmen examined just this question (Meichenbaum & Smart, 1971) and, as was discussed in Chapter 1, concluded that students who were led to expect success in fact became more successful in their school work.

The power of positive thinking is shown even more dramatically through "mental practice." In one experiment, subjects were instructed to imagine throwing darts

---

statements are shown in Table 15-6. Since failure often occurs because people become upset by their own thoughts and fears of failure, it follows that a more positive monologue increases the chances for more competent performance. Whether or not you can perform effectively and fearlessly (and calmly drape a six-foot King snake around your neck, for example) may depend most importantly on whether or not you expect that you can do it (Bandura, 1978). And such expectations of competence, in turn, depend on just what you say to yourself.

Table 15-6 (*continued*)

Let me label my fear from 0 to 10 and watch it change.
I was supposed to expect my fear to rise.
Don't try to eliminate fear totally; just keep it manageable.
I can convince myself to do it. I can reason my fear away.
It will be over shortly.
It's not the worst thing that can happen.
Just think about something else.
Do something that will prevent me from thinking about fear.
Just describe what is around me. That way I won't think about worrying.

Reinforcing Self-Statements
It worked; I was able to do it.
Wait until I tell my therapist about this.
It wasn't as bad as I expected.
I made more out of the fear than it was worth.
My damn ideas—that's the problem. When I control them, I control my fear.
It's getting better each time I use the procedures.
I'm really pleased with the progress I'm making.
I did it!

SOURCE: From Meichenbaum and Cameron, 1974.

at a target (Powell, 1973). Half the subjects were asked to imagine that their darts were hitting near the target's center; the other half imagined that their darts were striking outside the target area. Dart throwing improved significantly for people who had imagined successful performances during mental practice but not for those who had imagined poor performances. The moral is plain: think success!

Stress: It Depends on How You See It

Anxiety is a concept closely related to "stress." "Stress" has been the label used to classify a host of potentially unpleasant or dangerous events that include unavoidable pain, excessive noise and fatigue under strenuous work conditions, and traumatic dangers, as well as more routine life changes.

Just what is a "stressful" event? To answer this question, thousands of people were asked to rate the severity of many life changes (from vacations through divorce and the terminal illness of a loved one), yielding scales of Social Readjustment (e.g., Holmes & Masuda, 1974; Holmes & Rahe, 1967). The events listed in Table 15-7 are ranked in terms of the amount of readjustment that each life change seems to require.

People respond on this scale by indicating which life events they have experienced within the last year. Their score reflects their degree of recent life change (in life-change units). This score serves as the measure of current degree of stress: the more change, the more stress.

Generally, a significant but modest association has been found between degree of stress and physical illness. More stressful life events take a somewhat greater physical and emotional toll on most—but not all—people (e.g., Rabkin & Struening, 1976). Some people may be more psychologically hardy than others; they resist illness even when faced with highly stressful life events. For example, business executives who express attitudes of vigorousness about life, of being more oriented to challenge, also may experience less illness than do those who express opposite attitudes while encountering similarly high levels of stress (Kobasa, 1979). The people who face stress but remain healthy thus seem to perceive change not as a threat but as a challenge and an opportunity (Kobasa, Maddi, & Kahn, 1982). For example, rather than seeing a job loss as a terrible setback, they view it as a chance for a more challenging new career.

These results underline that the cognitive appraisal of a stress—how it is viewed by the person—may be more important than the amount of stress (change) that actually occurs in the environment. Whether or not one believes that one can cope with the stress, for example, influences how one reacts to it. This point has been made most clearly by R. S. Lazarus and colleagues. They have demonstrated repeatedly that just how stress is cognitively appraised critically influences how one experiences it and copes with it (e.g., Lazarus, 1976; Lazarus & Alfert, 1964). Just as one's thoughts during a test affect performance on it, so does the appraisal of any stressful event influence its impact on the perceiver (Lazarus, 1981).

Reducing the Impact of Stress

The negative effects of stress often are reduced if individuals know when to expect the stressful event and believe they can do something to control it. For example,

Table 15-7
Measuring Stress as Degree of Life Change: The Social Readjustment Rating Scale

Life Change	Life-Change Units
Death of spouse	100
Divorce	73
Marital separation	65
Jail term	63
Death of close family member	63
Personal injury or illness	53
Marriage	50
Fired at work	47
Marital reconciliation	45
Retirement	45
Change in health of family member	44
Pregnancy	40
Sex difficulties	39
Gain of new family member	39
Business readjustment	39
Change in financial state	38
Death of close friend	37
Change to different line of work	36
Change in number of arguments with spouse	35
Mortgage or loan for major purchase (e.g., home)	31
Foreclosure of mortgage or loan	30
Change in responsibilities at work	29
Son or daughter leaving home	29
Trouble with in-laws	29
Outstanding personal achievement	28
Wife begins or stops work	26
Begin or end school	26
Change in living conditions	25
Revision of personal habits	24
Trouble with boss	23
Change in work hours or conditions	20
Change in residence	20
Change in schools	20
Change in recreation	19
Change in church activities	19
Change in social activities	18
Mortgage or loan for lesser purchase (e.g., car, TV)	17
Change in sleeping habits	16
Change in number of family get-togethers	15
Change in eating habits	15
Vacation	13
Minor violations of the law	11

Note: The larger the life-change unit the greater the amount of readjustment required by the life change.
SOURCE: Adapted from Holmes and Rahe, 1967.

409

college women were exposed to a stressful noise that occurred either at a predictable time or unpredictably and then had to work on a task (Glass et al., 1969). Their tolerance for frustration and the quality of their performance were impaired only when the noise was unpredictable. Equally interesting, the negative effects could be reduced considerably if during the stress period the subjects believed they could do something to control the end of the stress. Other work also supports the conclusion that generally most people tend to become less upset when they think they can predict and control stressful or painful events (Staub et al., 1971).

Similar conclusions come from animal studies in which it is permissible to create much stronger stresses. In one study, for example, two groups of rats were exposed to equal amounts of electric shock. One group was allowed to learn and make a simple coping response (such as rotating a small wheel) to escape the shock; the other group received identical shocks but had no coping response available (Weiss, 1971a). The rats that could make the simple coping response developed far fewer stomach lesions (ulcers). But this conclusion held only if the coping response provided a simple, straightforward way of effectively avoiding the shock (Weiss, 1971b). When stress cannot be avoided, other strategies are required.

To master stressful situations that we cannot avoid or change, a strategy of detachment to reduce personal involvement is often effective. Examples come from interviews with medical students who had to witness a medical autopsy for the first time (Lief & Fox, 1963). The students may be helped to cope with their distress by the many aspects of the autopsy procedure that appear to have been designed as an institutionalized ritual to make detachment easier.

The autopsy room itself is arranged to provide a sterile, clinical, impersonal atmosphere. The face and genitalia of the corpse are kept covered, and after the vital organs have been removed, the body is taken out of the room. A detached, scientific, professional stance further helps to keep the whole procedure distant and impersonal.

Not surprisingly, experimental research also confirms that an attitude of detachment helps people react more calmly when exposed to gory scenes portraying bloody accidents and death (Koriat et al., 1972) or when expecting electric shock (Holmes & Houston, 1974). These results are consistent with reports showing that soldiers may immunize themselves against emotion by distancing themselves psychologically from their victims, for example, by calling them "gooks" and labeling them as subhumans. While highly effective for reducing feeling, a detachment strategy to reduce emotionality can easily be misused, producing callous, insensitive attitudes and cold-bloodedness toward others.

The type of cognitive strategy that helps one to deal best with stress depends on the individual. Recall, for example, the individual differences in the tendency to use distraction and to "blunt" rather than to sensitize or "monitor," discussed in the chapter on repression as a mechanism of defense (Chapter 4). The point to remember is that such preferences in the type of information sought for dealing with stress affect how the person copes best with stress; while one strategy helps some people, the opposite strategy may help others.

Reactions to stress depend also on the individual's psychological environment. For example, people generally deal better with stress (and are less likely to respond to it with illness) when they have social ties and supports, such as spouses, rela-

Table 15-8
Summary of Some Major Influences Determining Coping Responses

Cognitive appraisal

Perception of control and competence

Predictability of stress

Availability of social supports and sharing

tives, close friends, and groups to which they belong (e.g., Antonovsky, 1979). Coping is also better when people can share their stressful experience with others (Nilson and associates, 1981). When people work together in response to a common stress, such as an earthquake disaster or the bombing raids of war, they seem to focus less on their personal problems and more on the common goal of survival. When people are members of a group to which they "belong," they can receive emotional support, help with problems, and even a boost to self-esteem (e.g., Cobb, 1976; Cohen & McKay, 1984).

Overview

In this chapter we have considered the nature and sources of frustration and anxiety. We also considered the closely related concept of stress. We noted some of the many influences that determine jointly how people cope with the problems and challenges of life and its stream of changes. Because so many variables may be involved, it helps to summarize some of the main ones that have been identified, as listed in Table 15-8.

SUMMARY

1. Coping with frustration is a basic challenge throughout development. Frustration occurs when attainment of an expected goal is blocked. The stronger the expectation, the greater the frustration. The frustration-aggression hypothesis assumes that aggression is an instinctive and inevitable response to frustration. Research has shown, however, that aggressive reactions may occur without prior frustration and that aggression, although a frequent reaction to frustration, is not the only possible one.

2. The responses people make to frustration depend on their experiences in similar situations, the alternative actions available to them, and their expectations about the probable outcomes of these alternatives. Reactions to frustration are likely to be aggressive if aggression has worked in the past to end frustration. Frustration may have other negative effects, such as unconstructive behavior, when better alternatives are neither available nor encouraged. But if nonaggressive, constructive reactions to frustration are encouraged and rewarded, they become more likely.

3. Children who have positive concepts about themselves (high self-esteem) tend to be esteemed by others, to behave competently, and to have parents who model high self-esteem. Experiments with animals, and observations of people, suggest that situations in which there is no way of escaping frustration or punishment may result in states of withdrawal and helplessness.

4. A promising theory of depression suggests that the misery of depressed people reflects insufficient gratification from the environment for their own behavior. Depressed people are caught in a vicious cycle of lack of reinforcement for their own efforts, leading to greater withdrawal from other people and, in turn, increased depression.

5. Anxiety may be defined as an acquired (learned) fear. The experience of anxiety involves an intense feeling of fear or dread of impending danger accompanied by a state of autonomic physiological arousal. Often anxiety leads to difficulty in thinking clearly and coping effectively with environmental demands.

6. Each major personality theory has conceptualized anxiety in somewhat different ways. Thus Freudian formulations, for example, emphasize the breakthrough into consciousness of unacceptable impulses; learning theories focus on association with painful or aversive stimulation; and phenomenological-existential theories stress the perception of a basic threat to the self.

7. Life-threatening dangers or "traumas" result in the clearest examples of intense anxiety reactions. Moreover, a person's traumatic fear may generalize so that events and cognitions closely associated with the original traumatic experiences may later evoke anxiety even after the objective danger is gone. If the anxiety spreads to stimuli remote from the traumatic stimulus, the connection may not be apparent and the anxiety may seem particularly irrational. Under some conditions, however, traumas may lead to active coping rather than to generalized anxiety.

8. Avoidance or escape behaviors performed in a state of anxiety become strengthened when they are successful in reducing the anxiety state. Ambivalence and conflict may result when the same persons (or events) are associated with both positive and aversive experience, as happens commonly in life. The very people the child loves and depends upon also may threaten and punish him or her. Different types of conflict were described.

9. Individual differences in trait anxiety usually are measured by a self-report inventory on which subjects indicate the extent to which various fears characterize them. Anxiety is not a situation-free personality trait. Anxiety reactions depend on the exact stimulus conditions and response mode measured, as well as on the individual.

10. Anxiety affects the quality of performance. The exact effect of arousal level on performance depends on many variables, both in the person and in the specific situation. For example, anxiety hurts performance especially when it arouses negative, self-preoccupying thoughts.

11. Raising people's expectations about the likelihood of success can actually improve their performance in both physical skills and college courses. Directly modifying a person's private self-statements in a stressful situation may improve his or her competence in coping with stress.

12. The concept of "stress" was discussed; the cognitive appraisal of stress influences its impact.

Chapter 16
Self-Regulation and Mastery

Successful coping with the challenges of life requires the ability to resist situational pressures and to effectively exert control when it is appropriate to do so. In this chapter we will discuss some of the many ways in which individuals solve problems, evaluate and regulate their own behavior, and achieve mastery as they cope with the world and try to reach their personal goals. You saw in the last chapter that expectancies that one can succeed and control outcomes greatly help in the coping process. You will learn in this chapter about a number of important strategies that allow mastery and the successful pursuit of difficult goals.

FRUSTRATION TOLERANCE AND VOLUNTARY DELAY

The human ability to control events has intrigued not only philosophers and psychologists but most laymen as well. This concern is reflected in such diverse concepts as "willpower," "mastery," and "competence," and in their psychological opposites, such as "helplessness" and "hopelessness." All of these concepts involve the idea of volition ("will") and deal with the ability of individuals to affect their own outcomes and to influence their personal environments. Sometimes this influence is judged to be for the social good, and therefore prosocial or "moral;" often it is not. Always it involves the individual's efforts to modify conditions and to self-regulate and increase mastery in the light of particular goals.

One especially striking characteristic of human "will" is that people frequently impose barriers on themselves, interrupting their own behavior and delaying available gratification. When a delay of gratification is imposed on an individual by external conditions or forces we talk about "frustration" (Chapter 15); when the delay is self-imposed we call it "self-control."

Delay of Gratification

The ability to voluntarily refuse immediate gratification, to tolerate self-imposed delays of reward, is at the core of most concepts of "will power" and "ego strength." It is hard to imagine civilization without such self-imposed delays. Learning to wait for desired outcomes and to behave in the light of expected future consequences is essential for the successful achievement of long-term, distant goals. Every person must learn to defer impulses and to express them only under special conditions of time and place, as seen in toilet training. Similarly, enormously complex chains of deferred gratification are required for people to achieve the delayed rewards provided by our culture's social system and institutions.

Consider, for example, the self-imposed deferrals of pleasure required to achieve occupational objectives such as careers in medicine or science. The route to such a goal involves a continuous series of delays of gratification, as seen in the progression from one grade to the next, and from one barrier to another in the long course from occupational choice to occupational success. In social relationships the culture also requires delays, as seen in the expectation that people should postpone sexual relations, marriage, and children until they are "ready for them." Although judgments of what constitutes such readiness differ greatly across cultures and among different people, some norms concerning appropriate timing are found in every society.

The importance of self-control patterns that require delay of gratification has been widely recognized by theorists from Freud to the present. The concept of voluntary postponement of gratifications for the sake of more distant, long-term gains is fundamental for many conceptualizations of complex human behavior and personality development (e.g., Harter, 1983; Kanfer & Karoly, 1972; Kopp, 1982).

Should Gratification Be Delayed?

The cultural norm of impulse delay is expressed most clearly in the so-called Protestant Ethic, with its puritanical demands for self-restraint and its negative attitude toward pleasure. Understandably there are many strong reactions against such extremes of self-denial. Some thoughtful people question the wisdom of building a society on endless chains of deferred gratification. Others have experimented with more utopian societies, seeking simpler forms for the creation of a more satisfying community. The goals that people struggle toward in our society and the barriers that both they and the society impose need to be questioned. But although the particular goals and frustrations may change, it is difficult to conceive of organized life without some delays and barriers. Even the simplest agricultural or folk community needs both delay and planning. The issue therefore is not delay of gratification in itself, but when, how, and for what one should delay.

Learning to Choose Delayed Gratification

The extreme self-imposed delay is symbolized by the ethics of puritanism. This extreme contrasts sharply with the inadequate voluntary delay and the deficiencies in self-control that seem to characterize many people in our society. Inadequate delay patterns often are partial causes of antisocial and criminal behavior (including violence and physical aggression). People who cannot delay gratification also may fail to achieve reasonable work and interpersonal satisfactions (Mowrer & Ullmann, 1945). Thus while some personal and social problems stem from excessive frustration, others result from the failure of individuals to learn and practice appropriate patterns of delay and restraint. Indeed, deficiencies in voluntary delay may cause frustration and may victimize the individual by guaranteeing an endless chain of failure experiences in our culture. Consider, for example, the "high school dropout" who leaves school because he cannot tolerate postponing pleasures and working for more distant goals. His school failure in turn may sentence him to future vocational hardships and prevent him from achieving durable satisfactions. Given the serious social problems associated with the inability to delay rewards, it becomes important to understand the causes of voluntary delay behavior.

One research program has studied delay of reward and self-control with direct behavioral measures (Mischel, 1966, 1974). In this research subjects usually have to choose among actual alternatives that vary in delay time and value. For example, they choose between immediate smaller versus delayed larger rewards in realistic situations. Preschool children, for instance, are given a choice between getting a less valuable but immediate reward or a more attractive reward for which they must wait. This type of choice situation is depicted in Figure 16-1.

The figure shows the "clown box" with two windows displaying the two items in the choice (Mischel, 1970). The window in front of the smaller reward can be opened at once, whereas the window displaying the larger reward remains sealed for a predetermined time period. By depositing a token in the appropriate slot (in the clown's hands) the child may choose whether he or she wants to open the window in front of the smaller reward now or wait for the other window to spring open after a specified delay time. Basically similar choices involving age-appropriate out-

Figure 16-1
A Set of Paired Rewards in Place in the Magic Clown Surprise Box

From Mischel (1970).

comes have been presented to older children and adults by means of questionnaires that describe the choices verbally.

To a considerable degree a person's willingness to defer gratification depends on the outcomes that she expects from her choice (Mischel, 1966, 1968). Of particular importance are the individual's expectations that future (delayed) rewards for which one would have to work and wait would actually materialize, and their relative value. Such expectations or feelings of trust depend, in turn, on the person's history of prior promise-keeping and on past reinforcement for waiting behavior and for other forms of planful, goal-directed self-control. When the attainment of delayed gratification requires the person to reach particular achievement levels, then the willingness to work and wait for these future outcomes also hinges on expectations that one can adequately fulfill the necessary contingencies (Mischel & Staub, 1965). These expectations depend not only on direct personal experiences, but also on the observation of the behavior of social models, such as peers, parents, and teachers.

Effects of Models

Laboratory experiments have investigated most precisely the determinants of preferences for immediate, less valuable as opposed to more desirable but delayed outcomes. To illustrate this type of experiment, here is one example in some detail.

Bandura and Mischel (1965) hypothesized that self-imposed delay of reward would be determined in part by the delay patterns displayed by social models. In the initial phase of this experiment many children were administered a series of paired rewards. In each of these pairs they were asked to select either a small reward that could be obtained immediately, or a more valued item contingent on a delay period ranging from one to four weeks. For example, children chose between a smaller, immediately available candy bar and a larger one that required waiting. From the total pool of subjects those falling in the extreme upper and lower 25 percent of scores were selected for the succeeding phases of the experiment.

Children from each of these extreme groups (who exhibited predominantly either delayed-reward or immediate-reward patterns of behavior) were then assigned to treatment conditions. In one treatment children observed a live adult model who exhibited delay-of-reward responses counter to their own self-gratification pattern. For example, if the child was initially high in delay preferences, the adult model consistently chose immediate rewards. (He selected, for instance, a cheaper set of plastic chess figures immediately instead of a more attractive set available a week later.) The model also explained his choices. For example, he said: "Chess figures are chess figures. I can get much use out of the plastic ones right away." Or he commented: "You probably have noticed that I am a person who likes things now. One can spend so much time in life waiting that one never gets around to really living. . . ." Conversely, children who initially displayed strong immediate reward preferences were exposed to models who chose delayed, costlier rewards. In other treatment groups children were similarly exposed to a model displaying delay-of-reward behavior opposite to their own, with the exception that the model's responses were presented only in written form rather than "live." In a final condition children had no exposure to any models.

Right after the experimental procedure the children's delay-of-reward responses were measured. To test the generality and stability of changes in delay behavior, they were reassessed by a different experimenter in a different social setting approximately one month later. The overall results revealed strong effects. Figure

Figure 16-2
Effects of Modeling on Delay of Gratification

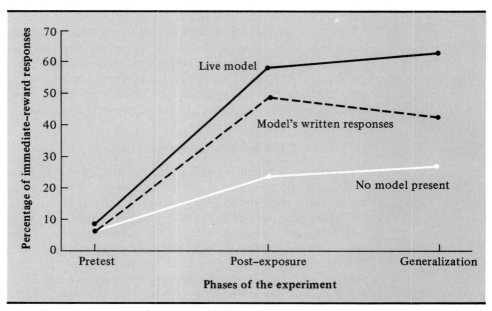

Mean percentage of immediate-reward responses by high-delay children on each of three test periods for each of three experimental conditions.
Adapted from Bandura & Mischel (1965).

417

16-2, for example, shows the mean percentage of immediate-reward responses produced by the high-delay children in each of the test periods as a function of treatment conditions. Children who had shown a predominantly delayed-reward pattern displayed an increased preference for immediate and less valuable rewards after observing models favoring immediate gratification; conversely, those who had exhibited a marked preference for immediate rewards increased and maintained their willingness to wait for more valuable but delayed reinforcers following exposure to models displaying high-delay behavior. The effects of seeing the model's written responses were similar to those of watching live models, although less pronounced and less generalized.

Similar effects occurred when similar procedures were extended to a population of young prison inmates. Specifically, exposure to high-delay peer models substantially increased delay of gratification in 18- to 20-year-old inmates who initially had displayed an extreme preference for immediate rewards (Stumphauzer, 1972). The effects showed some generalization and were maintained in a follow-up one month later.

COPING WITH SELF-IMPOSED DELAY

Given that one has chosen to wait for a larger deferred gratification, how can the delay period be managed?

Theoretical Predictions

Freud (1911) provided one of the few theoretical discussions of how delay of gratification may be bridged. According to the psychoanalytic formulation, ideation arises initially when there is a block or delay in the process of direct gratification (Rapaport, 1967). During such externally imposed delay, according to Freud, the child constructs a "hallucinatory image" of the physically absent, need-satisfying object. This mental image provides fantasy satisfactions (e.g., Freud, 1911; Singer, 1955). But in spite of much psychoanalytic theorizing and speculation about the role of the mental representation of blocked gratifications in the development of delaying capacity, the exact process remains far from clear (e.g., Kopp, 1982).

A Method for Observing Waiting

To study this problem a method was constructed in which very young (preschool) children would be willing to remain in an experimental room, waiting entirely alone for at least a short time without becoming upset (Mischel & Ebbesen, 1970). After the usual play periods for building rapport, each child was taught a "game" in which she could immediately call the experimenter by a simple signal. This step was practiced repeatedly, until the child clearly understood that she could immediately end her waiting period in the room simply by signaling for the experimenter, who regularly returned from outside as soon as the child signaled. Next, the child was introduced to the relevant contingency.

She was shown two objects (e.g., food treats), one of which she clearly preferred (as determined by pretesting). To attain the preferred object she had to wait for it until the experimenter returned "by himself." The child was, however, entirely free throughout the waiting period to signal at any time for the experimenter to return; if she signaled she could have the less preferred object at once but had to forego the more desirable one.

The Value of Not Thinking

To manipulate the extent to which children could attend to the reward objects while they were waiting, the rewards were removed from the experimental room in all combinations, creating four conditions with respect to the objects available for attention. Examples are shown in Figure 16-3. In one condition, the children waited with both the immediate (less preferred) and the delayed (more preferred) reward facing them in the experimental room so that they could attend to both outcomes. In another group neither reward was available for the subject's attention, both having been removed from sight. In the remaining two groups either the delayed reward only or the immediate reward only was available for attention while the child waited. The measure was the length of time before each child voluntarily stopped waiting.

The initial theorizing about delay behavior led to predictions of results that were the direct opposite of the obtained findings (shown in Figure 16-4). It was predicted that attention to the outcomes available in the choice situation while waiting would enhance delay behavior; instead it sharply reduced delay of gratification. The children waited longest when no rewards were available for attention.

One of the most striking delay strategies used by some youngsters was as simple as it was effective. These children seemed to manage to wait for the preferred reward for long periods apparently by converting the aversive waiting situation into a more pleasant, nonwaiting one. They seemed to do this by elaborate self-distraction techniques through which they spent their time psychologically doing something (almost anything) other than waiting. Rather than focusing prolonged attention on the objects for which they were waiting, they avoided looking at them. Some of these children covered their eyes with their hands, rested their heads on their arms, or found other similar techniques for averting their eyes from the

Figure 16-3
Waiting for Delayed Gratification

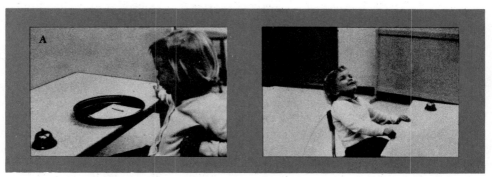

Based on Mischel, Ebbesen, and Zeiss (1972).

Figure 16-4
Effects of Attention on Delay of Gratification

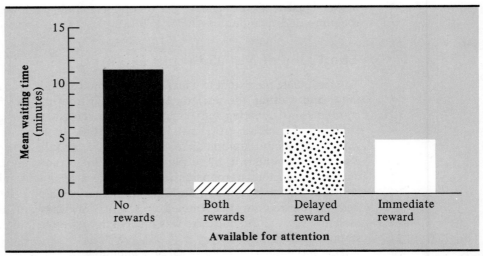

Based on data from Mischel and Ebbesen (1970).

reward objects. Others seemed to try to reduce the frustration of delay of reward by generating their own diversions: they talked to themselves, sang, invented games with their hands and feet, and when all other distractions seemed exhausted, even tried to fall asleep during the waiting situation—as one child successfully did.

These observations suggest that diverting yourself from attention to the delayed reward stimulus (while maintaining behavior directed toward its ultimate attainment) may be a key step in bridging temporal delay of reward. That is, learning *not* to think about what you are awaiting may enhance effective delay of gratification much more than does ideating about the outcomes.

These observations seem consistent with theoretical considerations that focus on the aversiveness of frustration and delayed rewards. If wanting something but not being able to have it is actively aversive, it seems likely that cues that enhance the salience of the desired but still unavailable (delayed) reward should increase the aversiveness of the delay period. In that case, the greater and more vivid the anticipation of reward, the greater the frustration generated by its delay. When hungry, for example, it is easier to wait for supper if one is not confronted with the sight and smell of food.

This line of reasoning would suggest that conditions that decrease people's attention to the blocked reward—and that distract them by internal or overt activity from the frustrative delay of reward—would make it less aversive for them to continue their goal-directed waiting and hence permit them to wait longer for gratifications. In other words, just as cognitive avoidance and "blunting" through self-distraction may facilitate coping with anxiety (as noted in Chapter 15) so may it help individuals to cope with other aversive stimuli, such as the frustration of waiting and wanting something that they cannot have yet.

Self-Distraction to Cope with Frustration

If these ideas are correct then delay of gratification and frustration tolerance should be enhanced when the person can readily transform the aversive waiting period into a more pleasant, nonwaiting situation. He might do that by converting his attention and thoughts away from the frustrative components of delay of gratification and thinking instead about other things. Such distractions can be achieved if he can engage in activities, overtly or mentally, during the delay period that help him to suppress or decrease cognitively the aversiveness of waiting for the delayed but preferred outcome.

If that is true then voluntary delay of reward should be aided by any overt or covert activities that serve as distractors from the rewards and thus from the aversiveness of wanting them but not having them. Through such distraction the individual should be able to convert the frustrative delay-of-reward situation into a psychologically less aversive condition. Therefore motoric activities and internal cognitions and fantasy that can distract the individual from the rewards potentially available in the situation should increase the length of time that he will delay gratification for the sake of the more valuable reward.

Follow-up studies support this reasoning (Mischel, Ebbesen, & Zeiss, 1972). Children waited much longer for a preferred reward when they were distracted cognitively from the goal objects than when they directly attended to them. Another experiment demonstrated that only certain cognitive events (thinking "fun things") served as effective ideational distractors. Thinking "sad thoughts" produced short delay times similar to thinking about the rewards themselves. In a final experiment the delayed rewards were physically not available for direct attention during the delayed period. The children's attention to the absent rewards was manipulated cognitively by prior instructions.

It was found that cognitions directed toward the rewards while the children waited greatly reduced, rather than enhanced, the length of time that the children were able to delay gratification. Thus attentional and cognitive mechanisms that enhance the salience of the rewards substantially shortened the length of voluntary delay of gratification. In contrast, distractions from the rewards, overtly or cognitively, facilitated waiting for preferred but delayed reinforcement.

These results seem to contradict the notion that "will power" requires one to bear up and force oneself to maintain directed attention to things that are aversive, difficult, or boring. Rather than trying to maintain aversive activities such as delay of reward through "acts of will" and focused attention, effective self-control may hinge on *transforming* the difficult into the easy, the aversive into the pleasant, the boring into the interesting, while still maintaining the task-required activity on which the ultimate reward depends.

You can create such transformations either by engaging in the appropriate overt distracting activity or changing your own mental content and ideation. A good way to master the difficult or aversive thus may be to think or do something pleasant while performing the necessary, task-relevant response (e.g., waiting, working). Rather than "willing" oneself to heroic bravery one needs to perform the necessary "difficult" response while engaging in another one cognitively (Mischel, 1984).

Cognitive Transformations and Delay

If the young child is left during the waiting period with the actual reward objects (e.g., pretzels or marshmallows) in front of him, through instructions he can cognitively transform them in many ways that enable him to wait for long time periods (e.g., Mischel & Baker, 1975). If he cognitively transforms the reward stimulus, for example, by thinking about the pretzel sticks in front of him as little brown logs, or by thinking about the marshmallows as round white clouds or as cotton balls, he may wait long and patiently. Conversely, if the child has been instructed to focus cognitively on the arousing (consummatory) qualities of the reward objects, such as the pretzel's crunchy, salty taste or the chewy, sweet, soft taste of the marshmallows, he tends to be able to wait only a short time. Similarly, through instruction the children can easily transform the real objects (present in front of them) into a "color picture in your head," or they can transform the picture of the objects (presented on a slide projected on a screen in front of them) into the "real" objects by pretending in imagination that they are actually there on a plate in front of them (Moore, Mischel, & Zeiss, 1976).

Thus what is in the children's heads—not what is physically in front of them—determines their ability to delay. Regardless of the stimulus in their visual field, if they imagine the real objects as present they cannot wait long for them. But if they imagine pictures (abstract representations) of the objects they can wait for long time periods (and even longer than when they are simply distracting themselves with abstract representations of objects that are comparable but not relevant to the rewards for which they are waiting). Through instructions about what to imagine during the delay period, it is possible to completely alter (even to reverse) the effects of the physically present reward stimuli in the situation, and to cognitively control delay behavior (Mischel & Moore, 1980). But while in experiments the experimenter provides instructions (which the subject often obligingly follows) about how to construe the stimulus situation, in life the "subjects" supply their own instructions and may transform the situation in many alternative ways.

Summary

Taken collectively, research on delay-of-gratification and tolerance for self-imposed frustration suggests a two-part process. First, consider the determinants of the *choice* to undergo frustrative delay for the sake of preferred delayed outcomes. This choice is influenced mainly by expectations concerning the probable consequences of the choice. These consequences include the relative subjective values of the immediate and delayed outcomes themselves as well as other probable reinforcing outcomes associated with each alternative. Expectancies about these outcomes depend on direct and vicarious past experiences and trust relationships, modeling cues, the specific contingencies in the choice, and so on (e.g., Mischel, 1966). So if you really expect to get the delayed reward, and want it, you are more likely to wait for it.

Second, once the choice to self-impose delay of gratification has been made, effective delay depends on cognitive and overt self-distractions to reduce the aversiveness of the self-imposed frustration. For this purpose, the person needs to avoid the goal objects, generating his or her own distractions while maintaining the necessary behavior on which goal-attainment is contingent. An effective way of coping with the frustrations imposed by delay in many life situations is to transform the aversive delay period cognitively into a more positive or interesting experience. This can be achieved by doing something else, overtly or internally, while continuing to wait for the desired goal, or by cognitively transforming the desired goal objects to reduce their excessively arousing qualities. So if you can make the waiting easier for yourself, you are more likely to wait successfully.

Early, Delay Predicts Later Personality

We saw before that a child's momentary mental representation of the outcomes in the delay situation influences his or her waiting time. Indeed it is possible to predict how long children will tend to wait from knowledge of the psychological conditions in which they are waiting. But individual differences in waiting time in the delay situation, regardless of condition, are not trivial matters. They are, instead, robust features of an important and enduring personal competence. There is significant continuity between the preschooler's delay time while waiting for a couple of pretzels or marshmallows and independent ratings of his or her perceived cognitive and social competence made by the parents a dozen years later (Mischel, 1984).

To illustrate, we know that the preschool child who delays effectively in some contexts may not do so in other, even slightly different situations, showing much cross-context discriminativeness (Mischel & Peake, 1982). However, there also are

---

In Focus 16.1
The Growth of Self-Control Knowledge

We now know a good deal about what makes it harder or easier for young children to delay gratification. When and how do the children themselves acquire knowledge of the "delay rules" that make waiting less frustrating? For example, does the preschool child know that thinking about the arousing, desirable qualities of the rewards (the pretzel's crunchy taste, for instance) will make self-imposed delay more difficult? Questions of this sort have begun to be explored (e.g., Yates & Mischel, 1979) and the results suggest that children's understanding and knowledge of effective delay rules show a clear progression in the course of development (Mischel & Mischel, 1983).

Most children below the age of about four years do not seem to generate clear or effective strategies for delay; indeed they sometimes even make waiting more difficult for themselves by focusing on

what they want but cannot have (Mischel, 1981). By the age of five to six years they know that covering the rewards will help them wait for them while looking at the rewards or thinking about them will make it difficult. By third grade children spontaneously generate and reasonably justify a number of potentially viable strategies and clearly understand the basic principles of resistance to temptation. For example, avoid looking at the rewards because: "If I'm looking at them all the time, it will make me hungry . . . and I'd want to ring the bell." Often they also indicate the value of distraction from the rewards, or of negative ideation designed to make them less tempting ("Think about gum stuck all over them"). And by the time they reach sixth grade, children show considerable sophistication, utilizing ideal strategies that allow them to delay gratification with relative ease.

---

significant continuities linking the preschooler's delay time in these experiments to indices of his or her cognitive and social competence, coping skills, and school performance years later (Mischel, 1984). For example, the number of seconds preschoolers delayed the first time they had a chance to do so regardless of the specific delay situation they encountered, significantly predicts their social competence as high school juniors and seniors as rated by their parents (Mischel, 1983). A clear picture seems to be emerging of adolescent correlates significantly associated with preschool delay in the experimental situation a decade earlier. Table 16-1 shows significant relations between the child's preschool delay time and mother's and father's composited ratings (on Q-sorts) years later. (These children's mean age at first delay was about four years; it was about 17 years at the time of the parental ratings).

The correlations give a general picture of the child who delayed in preschool developing into an adolescent who is seen as attentive and able to concentrate, able to express ideas well, responsive to reason, competent, skillful, planful, able to think ahead, and able to cope and deal with stress maturely. The strength of these

Table 16-1
Examples of Parental Ratings of Adolescents Correlated Significantly with Their Delay Time as Preschoolers (N = 77)

Positive Correlates (the preschooler who delayed more tends to become an adolescent who):
  Is attentive and able to concentrate
  Is verbally fluent, can express ideas well
  Uses and responds to reason
  Is competent, skillful
  Is planful, thinks ahead
  Is self-reliant, confident, trusts own judgment
  Is curious and exploring, eager to learn, open
  Is resourceful in initiating activities
  Appears to have high intellectual capacity
  Has high standards of performance for self

Negative Correlates (the preschooler who delayed less tends to become an adolescent who):
  Tends to go to pieces under stress, becomes rattled
  Reverts to more immature behavior under stress
  Appears to feel unworthy, thinks of himself as bad
  Is restless and fidgety
  Is shy and reserved, makes social contacts slowly
  Tends to withdraw and disengage himself under stress
  Shows specific mannerisms or behavioral rituals
  Is stubborn
  Turns anxious when his environment is unpredictable
  Is unable to delay gratification

Note: Based on mother-father composite ratings on 100 items.
SOURCE: Based on data from Mischel, 1983, 1984.

relations is modest, but the correlations seem impressive given that they span a lengthy period of development and are based on the child's preschool behavior objectively assessed in seconds of delay time. Perhaps most encouraging, the attributes suggested by the adolescent ratings are consistent with the cognitive competences essential for delay revealed by the experimental research. The total results indicate the essential ingredient for effective delay in the waiting paradigm may be the ability to divert and control attention. To wait successfully, the child must focus attention away from the frustrativeness of the waiting situation and the "hot" arousing stimulus pull of the rewards (e.g., how good they taste) while maintaining a more abstract "cool" representation of the rewards for which he or she is waiting (Mischel, 1981).

These qualities also are likely to be major ingredients of the "cognitive social competence" proposed as a basic person variable in the cognitive social learning approach (Chapter 12). Further, they seem to relate to the "ego resiliency" construct suggested in other investigations of child development and personality coherence (e.g., Block & Block, 1980, discussed in Chapter 7).

Cognitive Transformations to Reduce Stress

The discussion in this section has focused on voluntary delay of gratification, but the findings fit those from many other areas of self-regulation (e.g., Harter, 1983; Kopp, 1982). For example, not surprisingly it helps to distract oneself when trying to endure various kinds of pain and stress (e.g., Kanfer & Seidner, 1973). A good deal of related research also leads to the conclusion that self-distraction, when possible, can be an excellent way to reduce unavoidable stresses like unpleasant medical examinations (Miller, 1980; Miller & Green 1985).

People also feel better if they use cognitive transformations to redefine stressful situations in more positive ways (Holmes & Houston, 1974). When stress and pain are inevitable (as in patients awaiting major surgery), the adage to look for the silver lining and to "accentuate the positive" may be wise. In one study, surgical patients were helped to reconstrue their threatening ordeal (Langer, Janis, & Wolfer, 1975). For example, they were encouraged to focus on the hospital experience as an escape from pressure and a "vacation" with a chance to relax, and were given other similar techniques for emphasizing the positive side. These patients tended to cope better with their traumas, seeming to experience less stress and requesting fewer pain relievers and sedatives.

SELF-REACTIONS: ACHIEVING MASTERY

People judge and evaluate their own behavior and reward and punish themselves. In the typical animal laboratory the organisms perform, and the experimenter or her apparatus reinforces them at predetermined points. Unlike the animals in the researcher's laboratory, people exert considerable control over the rewarding and punishing resources available to them. They congratulate themselves for their own characteristics and actions; they praise or abuse their own achievements; and they self-administer social and material rewards and punishments from the enormous array freely available to them.

A critical aspect of self-regulation thus stems from the fact that people assess and monitor themselves. Self-praise and censure, self-imposed treats and punishments, self-indulgence and self-laceration are signs of this pervasive human tendency to congratulate and condemn oneself. People learn to set their own performance standards and to make their own self-reward contingent upon their achieving these self-prescribed criteria. To adequately understand human social behavior, we must know how people self-administer and regulate rewards and punishments that are in their own control (e.g., Masters & Mokros, 1974), and how this self-regulation develops and grows (Harter, 1983), allowing them to achieve increasing mastery in the pursuit of their goals.

Studying Self-Reinforcement

To investigate self-reward and self-punishment, a method has been developed in which subjects (usually grade-school children) work on a performance task that seemingly requires skill (e.g., Bandura & Kupers, 1964). They have free access to a large supply of rewards (e.g., assorted candies, tokens exchangeable for prizes, small toys, and desirable trinkets). The experiments are designed so that the child's information about his level or quality of performance can be manipulated readily. For example, many of these studies use a realistic looking electronic bowling game on which the child bowls and receives feedback in the form of scores automatically illuminated on a display panel. The scores may be programmed by the experimenter so that the child gets fixed, predetermined feedback although he thinks the scores reflect his real performance.

Effects of Models

One study, for example, tested the hypothesis that patterns of self-reinforcement are acquired imitatively (Bandura & Kupers, 1964). Children in one group observed either peer or adult models who adopted a high criterion for self-reinforcement during a bowling game like the one described. In this condition the model praised and rewarded his performance (by helping himself to freely available treats) only when his bowling scores were high. When the model's scores were low he refrained from self-reward. In a second group children were exposed to models who exhibited a similar pattern of self-reward and self-disapproval except that these models adopted a relatively low criterion. Children in a control group observed no models. Tests of self-reward after exposure to the models revealed that the children's reinforcement patterns closely matched those of the model they had observed.

Figure 16-5 shows the children's self-reward when they achieved low, moderate, and high performance levels for bowling in each condition. Note that the children who initially were exposed to high-standard adults are the ones who later made their own self-reinforcement almost always contingent on high levels of performance. In contrast, children who had observed low-standard models, or no models, were relatively more casual and lenient in their self-reinforcement; they treated themselves generously even after moderate or mediocre achievements.

Figure 16-5
Self-Reinforcement at Each Performance Level by Control Children and Those Exposed to Adults Modeling High and Low Standards for Self-Reward

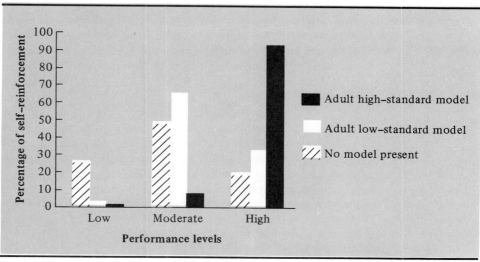

Adapted from Bandura and Kupers (1964).

Do As I Say or Do As I Do?

How does the relationship between the standards that the socialization agent practices and those that he "preaches" to the child affect his impact on the child's subsequent self-control? Take, for example, the common case of the parent who tries to instill self-control in his child while he himself models self-indulgence. Consider the father who regularly urges his son to study hard while he himself lounges in front of the television set. When researchers refer to "consistency" in child-rearing practices they usually mean consistency in direct training techniques across different situations; almost no attention has been given to the effects of consistency or discrepancy between direct training and modeling procedures. When an adult model acts one way himself but imposes opposite demands on the child, how will the child act afterwards when he is on his own: Will he do what the model did himself or what the model asked him to do? To investigate this question, Mischel and Liebert (1966) studied the effects of discrepancies in the stringency of the self-reward standards used by an adult and the criteria she imposed on a child.

In this study children participated with a female adult model in a task (the bowling game) that seemingly required skill but on which scores were experimentally controlled. Both the model and the subject had free access to a large supply of tokens that could be exchanged later for attractive rewards and prizes. In one condition, the model rewarded herself only for high performances but guided the subject to reward himself for lower achievements; in a second condition the model rewarded herself for low performances but led the subject to reward himself only for high achievements; in the third group the model rewarded herself only for high performances and guided the child to reward himself only for equally high achievements. After exposure to these experimental procedures the children's self-reward patterns displayed in the model's absence were observed and scored through a one-way mirror.

When the observed and imposed criteria were consistent they later were adopted and maintained readily by all children. The experiment illustrated that self-reactions are affected jointly by the criteria displayed by social models and the standards directly imposed on the child. The children's self-reward patterns were determined by a predictable interaction of both observational and direct training processes. As Figure 16-6 indicates, when the modeled and imposed standards were consistently high, the children adopted them uniformly. When they were inconsistent, the children who had been allowed to be lenient (although the model was stringent) all remained lenient. Those who had been trained to be stringent by a model who herself was lenient seemed conflicted, and about half of them remained stringent and half became lenient.

Finally, in a posttest the children demonstrated the game to a younger child, still in the absence of external constraints and of the experimenter herself. It was found that the children consistently both demonstrated and imposed on their peers the same standards that they had adopted for themselves, hence transmitting their own learned self-reward criteria to others.

Control of Internal States

The work discussed so far in this chapter merely provided some selected examples from a huge area of research (e.g. Kopp, 1982). To illustrate another direction, there are some fascinating but unexpected parallels between two seemingly extremely different methods to gain control. These are the efforts to achieve control

Figure 16-6
Self-Reward and Reward of Other Child, As a Function of the Initial Criteria Exhibited by the Model and Imposed on the Subject

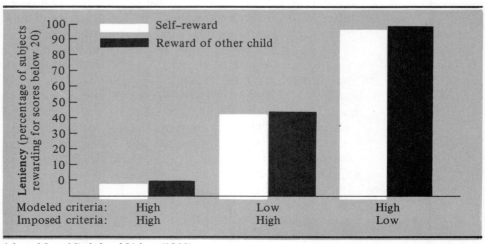

Adapted from Mischel and Liebert (1966).

of internal bodily responses through biofeedback (and "operant conditioning") on the one hand (see *In Focus 16.2*) and, on the other hand, the attempts of mystics (including those influenced by Zen, Yoga, and other "esoteric" traditions) to get into closer contact with their bodily states and internal "signals." Both strategies involve observing (monitoring) one's own inner states and changing them through some internal, and perhaps indescribable, effort. Ornstein (1972, pp. 195–196) compares the two strategies this way:

> There are, now, two major procedures available for contacting the weak signals within. In the esoteric traditions, one tries to turn off the competing activity, to turn day into night, so that the subtle signals are perceptible. In the newly developed feedback system, the "stars" are brought to consciousness by another method. The faint signals *themselves* are amplified, to make them perceptible even in the brilliance of the daylight. In the esoteric traditions, the "noise" is lessened; in biofeedback research, the "signal" is strengthened. In both cases, when these normally unconscious processes enter consciousness, we can receive this subtle information, and can learn to control what was previously an "unconscious" or "autonomic" process.

The Challenge of Obesity

The problem of obesity is one of the major challenges to students of self-regualtion. Only humans and the animals we have domesticated often become obese. Obesity is prevalent in our society and constitutes a major health hazard. Wild animals regulate their food intake in accordance with their physiological needs, but for us and the animals we feed, the natural balance between food intake and energy output is often upset. Why?

External versus Internal Cues for Eating. Some research suggests that people who overeat use cues for eating that others do not. Compared to obese or overweight individuals, people of normal weight seem to rely more on internal cues such as contractions of the stomach, which occur increasingly with time elapsed since last eating. Fat people eat more when they think it is dinner time, even though the clock may have been rigged, than when they think it is earlier than their usual dinner time (Schachter & Gross, 1968). They eat just as much or more when they are emotionally upset as when they are calm; they also eat as much when their stomachs are full as when they are empty (Schachter et al., 1968). And fat people may be more influenced by the taste of a particular food. For example, they ate more of a delicious ice cream and less of a somewhat bitter one than did normal subjects (Nisbett, 1968). Just listening to mouth-watering descriptions of food leads overweight people to consume much more than do individuals of normal weight under the same conditions (Rodin, 1981).

In individuals of normal weight there is a more direct correspondence between stomach activity and reports of experienced hunger (Stunkard & Koch, 1964). It is harder for people of normal weight than for the obese to go without food when fasting for religious reasons or when adjusting to time-zone changes (Goldman et al., 1968). The differences between normals and the obese are especially striking if food-related cues are absent. When obese individuals fed themselves a bland liquid formula in a situation lacking the social or aesthetic aspects of more typical meals, they consumed less than one-fourth of their calculated calorie needs. But

Inside our bodies a multitude of internal or *visceral responses* occur without our thinking about them, including changes in the secretions of the glands, the pumping action of the heart, and the electrical waves of the brain during emotional arousal. While Western scientists were labeling the system responsible for the control of this internal environment "automatic" or "autonomic" because of its seemingly involuntary character, Eastern mystics and yogis were demonstrating a remarkable degree of control over it in their own bodies. At the start of the twentieth century, British colonists reported that yogis could reduce their own metabolism while being buried alive for days and could even reduce their pulse to such an extent that their hearts seemed to have stopped. Today, instead of dismissing such reports as exaggerations or chicanery, researchers are investigating how voluntary control of visceral responses can be achieved.

One important clue came from the use of *biofeedback* techniques for the control of such voluntary activity as the practice of motor skills. In daily life, learning often is speeded and improved by feedback. After rolling a bowling ball down the alley we observe the consequences of the movements we made a moment ago. The

Figure 16-7
Biofeedback to Train a Patient to Control His Heart Rate

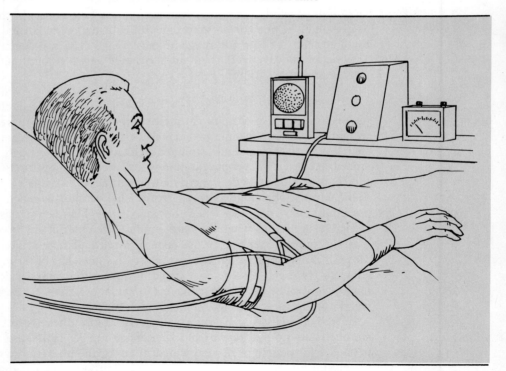

The patient watches a "traffic sign" on which red, yellow, and green lights signal how he is doing continuously as he tries to control his heart rate. On the left side of the table an intercom allows communication with the doctor. A meter (at right) shows the percentage of time the patient is mastering the task.

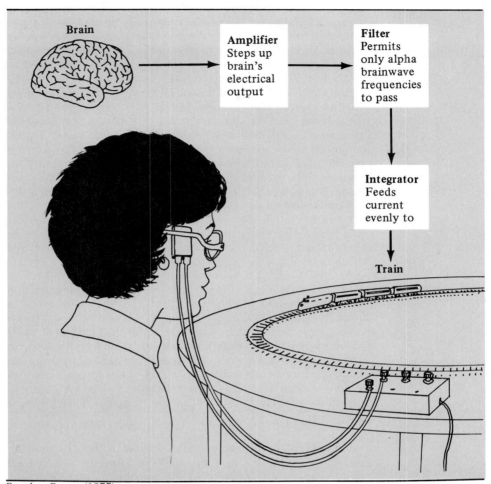

Based on Brown (1975).

consequences, whether a strike or a gutter ball, provide information regarding the effectiveness of our movements, and we adjust our behavior in an attempt to make a strike more likely next time. Similarly, the cook who tastes the soup and then adds some salt and the guitarist who refingers a chord to achieve the desired sound are using feedback to achieve the consequences that they desire.

What is distinctive about biofeedback is that it provides feedback from such internal sources as one's own glands, heart, blood vessels, and bioelectric brain rhythms, which we are ordinarily not aware of. We can then use this information to modify activity in the body parts themselves. The use of biofeedback in muscle relaxation provides an illustration. The activity of muscles controlled by the somatic, or voluntary, nervous system is detected, amplified, and presented through a loudspeaker. This feedback permits the individual to be aware of even the most minute tension in those muscles. When he gets such feedback information, the person can use various techniques to reduce the muscular tension. Such relaxation has proved to be useful clinically for the treatment of headaches and insomnia (Budzynski, Stoyva, & Adler, 1970). But this example involves muscles that are controlled by the voluntary nervous system. Can the same strategy also influence activities controlled by the autonomic nervous system which has traditionally been assumed to be involuntary and automatic? Pioneering studies by Neal Miller (1974) and others suggest an affirmative answer.

In one study baboons were rewarded with food for increasing their blood pressure and were punished with electric shock when they failed to do so. Under these conditions the baboons were able to maintain significant elevation in their blood pressure for periods of up to twelve hours (Harris et al., 1973). Similarly, in a striking experiment with humans, six patients suffering from high blood pressure were able to reduce it when decreases in blood pressure were rewarded by money or presentations of slides of scenes from around the world (Schwartz, 1973). The

general procedure is shown in Figure 16-7. To demonstrate that brain waves can also be controlled, a person's amplified brain-wave output was hooked up to a small electric train (Brown, 1975). (See Figure 16-8.) The system was designed so that alpha waves (the rhythms associated with restful, pleasant feelings) would make the train run, and beta waves (a higher-frequency, lower-amplitude pattern associated with problem solving) would bring the train to a stop. When the person is made so vividly aware of which type of brain wave he is producing, he learns to produce more alpha to keep the train running.

Visceral training has been used successfully to treat patients with abnormal heart rhythms of a type associated with sudden death (Engel & Bleecker, 1974; Weiss & Engel, 1971). In the training situation, the patient sits in front of three colored lights: green, red, and yellow. When the green light flashes, it is a signal for the patient to try to speed up the rate of his heartbeat. Red means to slow down heart rate and yellow means heart rate is in the desirable range.

First the patient learns to speed up and slow down his heart rate by a few beats

normal individuals took enough formula in this situation to maintain their body weight (Hashim & Van Itallie, 1965). However, when food cues are prominent (e.g., when tempting food snacks can be seen) obese subjects will work much harder to obtain the food than when food cues are minimal. Normal subjects are relatively unaffected in food-directed efforts by prominent food cues (Johnson, 1974).

In sum, overweight individuals are easily influenced by external cues for eating. They are more susceptible to such cues for eating as time of day, sight and smell of food, the attractiveness of the food and the setting in which it is served, and the sight of other people eating. They seem to be less influenced by signals from their own bodies.

Obesity and Biology. While obese and normal-weight individuals seem to engage in different eating behaviors, the causal links between these eating patterns and obesity have not been firmly established and we do not know the relative contributions of biological and psychosocial factors. But there are some suggestive rela-

per minute. This convinces him that he can actually control his heart. Next he learns to hold his heart rate within a narrow range. Heart rates that are too fast cause the red light to flash; too slow heart rates (which typically follow a too rapid rate) activate the green light. The patient learns to identify these abnormal heart rhythm sequences and to suppress them. When his control is well established, the feedback from the lights is gradually phased out by omitting it on an increasing number of trials. This procedure helps the patient to determine by himself whether or not his heart rate is correct and enables him to transfer his control from the laboratory to everyday life. Follow-up studies, which measured the patients' heart rates while they performed their normal activities, suggested that most of the nine patients who were studied retained good control of their heart rhythms even after many months.

Such results are encouraging, but whether or not the learned modifications in visceral activity can be made large enough to be valuable for the practical treatment of many serious medical disorders remains debatable. Most of the effects reported so far have been limited in magnitude and duration. The means by which the obtained modifications are achieved also remain uncertain. Some investigators believe that a learned modification of the voluntary (somatic) nervous system is at the basis of all so-called autonomic learning effects. In their view, the obtained findings may be achieved in the same way that you can increase your heart rate by running up a flight of stairs or by imagining that you are about to take an important examination. Other researchers hold that such deliberate intervention is not required and that autonomic learning can occur directly. At present, various experiments can be cited to support either view. Of greatest significance is the finding that visceral responses can be changed by operant conditioning and the hope that such learning can be harnessed effectively in the future for the treatment of a variety of disorders. As Neal Miller (1974), a leader in this area of investigation has urged, at this point researchers should be bold in what they attempt but cautious in what they claim.

tions between biology and obesity. For example, the eating behavior of obese people resembles that of rats who have lesions in their feeding centers (the ventromedial nucleus of the hypothalamus). Both the rats and obese people eat less often than normals, but when they do eat, they eat faster and they eat more (Schachter & Rodin, 1974).

Using such evidence but going beyond it, one investigator, Nisbett, suggested that the association between weight and eating behavior is biologically rooted (1972). In Nisbett's view, some individuals are biologically programmed to be fat. To support his notion, he points to striking parallels between the behavior of obese and hungry individuals, noting that overweight people often behave as if they were always hungry. A physiological index, the presence of free fatty acids in the blood stream of overweight individuals seems to support this hypothesis. Some other research also supports this view. For example, infants with overweight parents were more responsive to food cues and preferred sugar solutions more than did infants whose parents were of normal weight (Milstein, 1980).

But while biology may well play a role in obesity, psychological considerations are also likely to be important. What you weigh depends on what you eat and on the energy you expend, and people are capable of controlling both their food intake and their energy output. In a society in which parents often use food treats like candy and desserts as rewards, in which food products are sold in vending machines and advertised on television, and in which fast-food chains dot every highway, it is not surprising that eating becomes more than a response to physiological needs for many individuals.

The Control of Weight

The possible biological roots of human obesity may make it especially difficult for the overweight to achieve better control of their weight. While weight loss is often obtained in response to crash diets and other dietary regimes, a common problem appears to be that the weight loss is difficult to maintain: often the dieter seems to lose much weight quickly, but six months later is back to the prediet weight. Regardless of the possible roots of obesity, ways are needed to help people control their own weight enduringly.

Many investigators have been searching for better techniques for sustained weight control. At present, prospects seem best for programs that make it possible for the dieter to eat nutritious and palatable foods while gradually losing weight and maintaining the losses. Listed below are the main steps of these programs. You will note that they illustrate the general principles for self-control summarized in Table 16-2.

1. The dieter practices *self-observation,* keeping careful records and monitoring his or her own weight regularly. Daily records of the type and amount of food eaten and the events surrounding eating are important for establishing a base line and sometimes promote weight loss just by themselves (Mahoney, 1974).

Table 16-2
Some Methods to Increase Self-Control

Method	Definition	Example
Self-observation	Systematic observation of one's own behavior	A dieter records everything she eats.
Stimulus control	The performance of certain behaviors only in the presence of certain cues	A person studies only in a special place at special times.
Self-reinforcement	Providing positive consequences to oneself, contingent on desired behavior	A student rewards herself (e.g., with new clothes) for achieving specified grades.
Self-instruction	Talking to oneself to control one's behavior	An impulsive child is taught to think: "go slow," "work carefully."

SOURCE: Based on Kazdin, 1975, p. 194ff.

2. The dieter establishes reasonable *specific goals* for weight loss. Usually a weekly goal of between one and two pounds is realistic. The total number of pounds to be lost should also be specific. Crash diets are to be avoided because they may be harmful to health, are often unpleasant, and do not insure that the weight will not be regained quickly.
3. The dieter practices *stimulus control,* eating in only one place and doing nothing else while eating. For example, The dieter does not watch television or read when eating (Stuart, 1967).
4. *Self-reinforcement:* The dieter rewards himself for improving eating behavior and losing weight. Friends and relatives may help by providing social reinforcement for improvement (Mahoney, 1974).
5. *Incompatible responses:* One does things that prevent inappropriate eating. When tempted to eat, for example, the dieter may go for a walk, drink water, eat only in the presence of someone who will make it embarrassing to overeat, look at the diet plan or weight charts, or think about wanting to be more attractive and not wanting to stay overweight (Rimm & Masters, 1974).
6. The dieter can reduce the attractiveness of especially troublesome foods by *self-instructions* or by imagining a scene combining the problem food with aversive images that induce nausea (Stuart, 1967).

Weight control programs of this sort have yielded some positive results, not just for immediate weight loss but for a loss (averaging about twenty pounds) sustained after a one-year follow-up (Craighead, Stunkard, & O'Brien, 1981). These investigators compared the five groups shown in Table 16-3. Subjects in all three treatment groups also received nutritional counseling (including low-calorie diets), and information about exercise.

Interestingly, the best long-term results were obtained for the group that received behavior modification only, unassisted by any appetite-suppressant drug (fenfluramine). In contrast, the group that combined the appetite-suppressant drug with behavior modification lost more weight initially (almost thirty-four pounds), but had regained more weight after one year (see Table 16-3).

Why did subjects who received behavior modification without drugs maintain their weight loss best? It is plausible that these individuals attributed their weight

Table 16-3
Effects of Treatment on Weight Loss

Group	Weight Loss	
	After Treatment	After One Year
Treatments		
Behavior modification only	24.0	19.8
Drug therapy only	31.9	13.8
Combined	33.7	10.1
Controls		
Waiting list	2.9 gain	————
Physician office visits for weight control	13.2	————

SOURCE: Adapted from Craighead, Stunkard, & O'Brien, 1981.

loss more to their own efforts (compared to those who were also aided with the drug). As a result they may have developed a greater sense of self-efficacy that helped them to more enduringly withstand temptations and avoid a return to old eating habits. The drug-assisted group, on the other hand, may have seen their initial weight loss as due to the medication, and when it was withdrawn they gave in more to their renewed hunger.

Planning and Future Orientation

As people develop, they become increasingly able to think of the future, using rules and plans to guide their behavior and to cope with situational pressures and frustrations (Kopp, 1982). Such rules and plans help a person organize complex behavior patterns into orderly, effective sequences over long time periods (e.g., Miller, Gallanter, & Pribram, 1960) and thus achieve life goals more effectively.

Through plans and other forms of self-regulation we can influence the environment's effect on us and exert control over it (e.g., Patterson & Mischel, 1976). We can actively choose the situations to which we expose ourselves, in a sense creating our own environment, entering some settings but not others, anticipating different possibilities, and deciding what to do and what not to do. We can plan for the winter, for example, long before the storm hits by preparing snow tires and chains to avoid getting stuck. Although we cannot change the weather itself, we can plan vacations that will remove us from a harsh environment, at least for a while, or we can even move permanently.

Increasing Self-Control and Mastery: Making the Difficult Easier

This section summarizes some of the many promising methods to improve self-control. Among other things, such methods have made it easier for people to diet, give up smoking, or overcome fears (Mahoney, 1974; Yates, 1985). Four types of methods successfully used for this purpose were shown in Table 16-2.

You already saw that the first type of method, *self-observation,* involves carefully monitoring one's own behavior, as when a dieter records the time and place of everything he or she eats. In the second type, *stimulus control,* one learns to do certain things (studying, for example) only in certain places (at a certain desk, perhaps) and at certain times. You already saw the applications of this method to treat insomnia. *Self-reinforcement* consists of making desired outcomes contingent on first reaching specific goals, as when one postpones a coffee break until half the reading assignment has been completed. *Self-instruction* involves explicit self-directions that help the individual to resist the pressures of the situation and to pursue, instead, more difficult but desired objectives. Self-instructions can be used to help sustain continued work and effort even under difficult conditions (e.g., Kanfer & Zich, 1974; Meichenbaum & Goodman, 1971). To illustrate, young children can resist transgression better if they are first given a verbalization ("I must not turn around and look at the toy") to repeat to themselves later when they are alone and tempted (Hartig & Kanfer, 1973). Similarly, fearful people may be able to cope

Table 16-4
Examples of Self-Statements Used to Increase Creativity

Be creative, be unique.
Break away from the obvious, the commonplace.
Think of something no one else will think of.
Just be free-wheeling.
If you push yourself you can be creative.
Quantity helps breed quality.

Size up the problem; what is it you have to do?
You have to put elements together differently.
Use different analogies.
You're in a rut—okay try something new.
Take a rest now; who knows when the ideas will visit again.

Release controls; let your mind wander.
Free-associate; let ideas flow.
Relax—just let it happen.
Let your ideas play.
Ideas will be a surprise.
Refer to your experience; just view it differently.

SOURCE: From Meichenbaum, 1974, p. 15.

better if they learn and practice calming, problem-solving self-instructions which they can say to themselves when they must actually face the stressful situations (Meichenbaum, 1974).

Self-instructions also have been applied to help increase creativity. For this purpose one researcher has urged college students to modify what they say to themselves. Statements like those in Table 16-4 were modeled by the psychologist and then practiced by the students. The groups given self-instructional training showed increased creativity (compared to control groups) on some measures and reported that their training generalized to help them take a more creative approach to their academic and personal problems (Meichenbaum, 1974). The approach appears to have promise in helping people overcome the rigidity that often blocks creative solutions.

SUMMARY

1. People learn to evaluate and control their own behavior and act in the light of future-oriented considerations. There have been many approaches to understand these processes. Some studies on self-control have explored the individual's willingness to delay immediate, smaller gratification for the sake of delayed but larger rewards and goals.

2. The person's subjective expectations concerning the outcome of his choice influence his willingness to select delayed rather than immediate gratification. Will the delayed rewards for which one postpones immediate satisfaction actually materialize? Will they be worthwhile? Will one be able to earn them? A person's answers to these questions depend partly on his

or her past history and on relevant social models. For example, after children were exposed to the patterns of delayed or immediate gratification displayed by social models, their own choices changed in accord with the preferences they had observed.

3. How can people delay gratification for the sake of preferred but delayed outcomes? When young children attended to the available outcomes while waiting they were less able to wait for them. Thus under some conditions *not* thinking about the desired outcomes seems to enhance effective delay behavior. Delay of gratification may be helped by cognitive and overt self-distractions to reduce the aversiveness of waiting.

4. In the course of development, children acquire knowledge of effective rules for delay of gratification so that they can increasingly engage in the self-distractions and cognitive activities that make waiting less frustrating. Early delay behavior may be related to aspects of personality years later.

5. People learn to set their own performance standards and to make their self-reward contingent upon achievement of the self-prescribed criteria. Children's patterns of self-reward are influenced by the models whom they have observed, as well as by standards imposed on them through direct training.

6. Apart from self-reward, people show other diverse forms of self-regulation such as self-punishment, conscience, and guilt after transgression. Even in the area of visceral and glandular responses, which are generally thought of as "involuntary," some mastery and self-control may be achieved, since these responses can be sensitively influenced by appropriate rewards or feedback. Some parallels were noted between "biofeedback" research and esoteric techniques to achieve greater contact with one's own bodily states.

7. The problem of obesity is especially challenging. The obese appear to be strongly influenced by external cues for eating. Self-control may be helped by planning in advance to perform such behaviors as eating only in certain places at certain times (stimulus control), by systematically observing one's own behavior, and by self-rewarding specified achievements.

8. Rules and plans contribute to self-regulation and help us to cope with frustrations. Increasing autonomy from situational pressures is achieved by selecting the environments to which we expose ourselves and anticipating future possibilities before they occur. Among the many promising methods for the improvement of self-control are self-instructions (to resist temptation, solve problems, or calm oneself) and self-reinforcement for desired behaviors.

Chapter 17
Sex Roles and Identity

This chapter examines how boys and girls gradually become psychological males or females. These processes illustrate many of the most important features of personality development.

This chapter thus is concerned with psychological sex differences in social behavior and with how these personality differences develop. The focus will be on the development of sex differences in social behavior rather than on the physiology and biology of sexual behavior itself. The development of psychological sex differences serves as an illustration of the development of personality differences in general, but it is also fascinating in its own right.

Sexual preferences and orientations (one's preferred sexual partners and activities) emerge as a result of many critical steps in development. Some important phases include the following (Cairns, 1979, p. 296):

1. Genes and hormones interact to form sexual structures before birth.
2. The child's gender at birth is recognized and permanently categorized by parents and society. The child acquires a gender self-concept, a recognition of his or her permanent sex in the preschool years. Society's expectations about appropriate sexual behavior, and the pressures and examples of peers, are influences throughout childhood.
3. In adolescence and throughout adulthood social influences persist. The individual continues to interact with others and with the standards of society, and these interactions further influence his or her sexual preferences, values, and styles.

Almost universally an individual's gender is one of the most powerful determinants of how other people treat him or her. Gender also influences the views the individual develops about himself or herself. Established invariantly at birth, biological sex soon begins to direct much of one's psychological and social development, identity, and roles and values. Moreover, it continues to have a dominant influence throughout life. Probably no other categorization is more important psychologically than the one that sorts people into male and female and their characteristics into masculine and feminine. And in recent years probably no other categorization has become more controversial. The controversy is based on many challenges to conventional, rigid sex roles and stereotypes about what it means to be a man or a woman.

Some of the issues raised by these challenges to traditional notions about sexual identity will be discussed later in this chapter. But first we will consider some of the personality differences found between the sexes. Then we will examine their causes and consequences.

PSYCHOLOGICAL SEX DIFFERENCES

In some respects the differences between the sexes, not only biologically but psychologically, may seem self-evident. On closer examination, however, the nature of the psychological differences between the sexes is not nearly as simple as it may seem.

Perceived Sex Differences: Examples

Before examining formal studies on sex typing, it is informative to consider sex differences as seen by a young woman—call her "Amy Wilson"—when asked, during the course of her development. Here are excerpts from Amy's comments at four ages.

At Age 3½ Amy's Concepts about Sex Differences Were Still Vague and Primarily Limited to Trying to Distinguish the Roles of Mother and Father:

Q. How are boys and girls different?

A. They're good (both boys and girls)—and they fight a little bit. They laugh sometimes.

Q. What do boys do that girls don't do? And what do girls do that boys don't?

A. They play outside with their daddies. They play outside with their selves and they swing around on the glider—they play outside with their mother.

Q. And when they grow up?

A. Boys be daddies. Girls be mommies, and have babies in their tummies. Mommies feed children and babies and daddies.

Q. And what do daddies do?

A. They wash the dishes.

When interviewed 18 months later at age 5, Amy made a more differentiated analysis. She recognized biological and role differences and focused mainly on sex differences in aggressive behavior:

Q. How are boys and girls different?

A. Boys have penises and girls have vaginas.

Q. How else?

A. Boys make money to buy food. Girls want their children not to make too much noise. Boys work—sometimes help the mother, sometimes play with their children. Mothers—they try not to scream. Boys can grow up to be a gardener and girls want their children to be very, very quiet and good.

Q. What are the girl-things you do?

A. I play on swings and slides; I paint and make good art pictures. Boys play on slides and do the things girls do too; when they grow up they work and don't do the things girls do any more.

Q. Do you want to be a girl or boy?

A. A girl! I don't want to be a boy because they fight, hit girls, say I wanna kill you, fight their teachers, and get spanked—that's why I don't want to be a boy.

Q. Why do you do the girl-things you do?

A. Because I'm a girl—that's why I don't fight.

Q. Why don't you fight?

A. Because I don't want to—because it isn't nice—because then I would get punishment.

Q. Do boys get punished for fighting?

A. Yes, but they don't think they will—they're not so scared.

The analysis of role differentiation becomes increasingly sophisticated with age, as Amy's comments at age 7½ reveal:

Q. How are boys and girls different?
A. Men are much stronger than women. Boys grow up to be daddies, girls grow up to be mommies, and mothers have babies.
Q. How else?
A. Girls have more feelings. Boys have more strength.
Q. What are some of the girl-things you do?
A. Play handball—that's what girls and boys do, play two square, go on the slide. Sing, dance, spell. You mean what are the girl-things I do with no boys included? I don't play baseball, I don't play stick ball, I don't play hot box.
Q. Do you want to be a girl or boy?
A. A girl. Well, sometimes I wish I were a boy and sometimes I wish I weren't.
Q. Why?
A. Being a boy I could do scary things. For girls I would wear fancy dresses and be rich—live in a fancy mansion.
Q. Why do you do the girl-things you do?
A. Because I want to—I just do—I like the sport of it.
Q. What would happen if you did boy-things?
A. Oh I do boy-things sometimes, but there's nothing wrong with it.
Q. How come you don't like fighting?
A. Because girls don't fight—I guess they're too dainty. If you fight you can get in trouble. I guess boys are rougher, have more strength, don't tell on each other so much and so don't get into trouble so much.

Interviewed again at age 30, Amy Wilson gave this mature and subtle picture of sex roles and personality:

Q. How are men and women different psychologically?
A. I don't think there are many innate psychological differences between men and women. The differences within each sex are much greater than between the sexes. . . . I do feel that although it has become much more acceptable, even encouraged, for women to be strong and assertive, men still aren't as free to express their nurturing, sensitive qualities.
Q. What do men do that women don't do?
A. In this country, at least, there aren't many things that men do that women don't do. Well . . . but while many women are entering traditionally male fields, there are still not nearly as many women as men in positions of power.
Q. Would you rather be a man or a women?
A. I'm very happy to be a woman. In the last few decades, women's roles have expanded; women are freer to be independent and to strive for

achievement in business and professional fields. But the burden of balancing a full-time career and raising a family presents a real challenge!

Q. What are some of the things you like most?

A. I like to feel I'm really stretching myself . . . at work, by taking on difficult projects and not letting the fear of failing keep me from trying my hardest. . . . I also love being with my family on vacation when the pressures of work and school aren't there so we can really have fun together.

To discover personality differences between the sexes systematically, many researchers have tried to measure differences in the frequency or in the amount of particular behavior patterns typically displayed by males and females. In our culture the two behavior patterns with regard to which sex differences have received most research attention are behaviors aimed at inflicting injury on others *(aggression)* and at eliciting attention and help from others *(dependency)*. Some of the main sex differences found for aggression and dependency respectively are reviewed briefly in the following sections and are summarized in Table 17-1.

Aggression

Aggression is one of the key variables defining masculine and feminine behavior (Frieze et al., 1978; Sears, 1963, 1965). Sex differences in aggression have been found as early as the age of three years. Boys are physically more aggressive and

Table 17-1
Some Representative Psychological Sex Differences

Behavior	Greater in
Physical and antisocial aggression (e.g., physical quarrels, fights, hyperaggressiveness, playful rough-housing)	Boys
Rated aggressiveness	Boys
Self-rated aggressiveness	Boys
Dependency, passivity	Girls (sometimes but not always: generally inconclusive)
Verbal ability	Girls (beginning at age 11 years)

SOURCES: Maccoby & Jacklin, 1974a, b; Maccoby, 1980.

show more "negativistic" behavior; negative attention getting, antisocial aggression, and physical aggression are more characteristic of boys than of girls. Boys also participate in more physical quarrels in nursery school, have more aggressive contact with their peers, initiate more fights and conflicts, and tend to resist attack more often. These results (Table 17-1) appear to have considerable generality across cultures (Whiting & Whiting, 1969). Rating studies provide similar findings, judges rating boys as more negativistic and as generally more aggressive than girls.

The sexes also differ in their self-concepts with regard to aggression. Self-ratings indicate that boys see themselves as more directly and overtly aggressive, especially after their hostility has been aroused experimentally. Greater self-reported overt aggressiveness by males holds for a wide age range, having been found for people aged from fifteen to sixty-four (Bennett & Cohen, 1959). Projective tests also indicate more direct aggression and hostility expressed by males (e.g., Gordon & Smith, 1965). But sometimes women can be more aggresive than men (see *In Focus 17.1*).

Dependency

Sex differences in dependency or help-seeking have also been studied thoroughly. In nursery school children, not many major differences have been found between the sexes on most dependency measures. At later ages (teens and college), however, girls sometimes seem to be more dependent, passive, and conforming than males (see Table 17-1), although the differences are often weak and inconclusive. Most of the findings are based on self-reports and trait ratings of dependency. Therefore it is difficult to separate the degree to which they reflect widely shared stereotypes that women are supposed to be more dependent from differences in the degrees of actual dependency displayed by women versus men. Some evidence suggests that females may conform more than males, but certain factors may

---

**In Focus 17.1
When Are
Women More
Aggressive
than Men?**

In an experiment by Taylor and Epstein (1967) male and female college students believed they were in a competitive situation with male and female opponents. The fictitious opponents administered increasing amounts of electric shock to the students. The shock was not actually delivered, but its amplitude was made known. The students were instructed to set the amount of shock they wanted their opponent to receive in turn. The aggressiveness of the students was measured by the amount of shock they selected to administer.

There were no differences between sexes when the opponent was believed to be a female. Both sexes administered less shock to the female than to the male opponent even when the female opponent administered increasingly higher levels of shock. This finding was expected in view of our culture's sanctions against physical aggression toward women. But most interesting, the female subjects became more aggressive than the males to aggressive opponents they believed to be male and gave them extremely strong shocks.

In sum, the subjects' use of physical punishment depended on their own sex as well as that of the other person: both males and females were highly discriminative in their use of physical punishment, and women under some conditions were capable of being more physically aggressive than men.

reverse this difference (e.g., Sampson & Hancock, 1967). For example, Iscoe and his colleagues (1964) report a significant race-by-sex interaction in conformity behavior. In this study, white females conformed more than white males, while black males were more conforming than black females. On the whole, girls are not more "suggestible" or susceptible to social pressure than boys (Maccoby & Jacklin, 1974b). Contrary to the stereotypes, females do not turn out to be more dependent in their behavior than are males (Frieze et al., 1978).

Although most research on sex differences has concentrated on aggression and dependency, other areas have not been ignored. For example, possible differences in such behavior as cooperation, mothering, helping, and empathy have been studied. Generally, the existence and extent of strong sex differences in these areas remain inconclusive (Frieze et al., 1978). In addition to studying differences on numerous personality variables, researchers have also explored sex differences in cognitive and intellectual functioning and in other domains (e.g., Maccoby & Jacklin, 1974b).

Intellectual-Cognitive Functions

Studies of American youngsters indicate, in general, that girls tend to do better than boys on tests of verbal ability. Girls, for example, tend to speak sooner and to be better in verbal articulation, word fluency, vocabulary, grammar, and spelling (e.g., Gesell et al., 1940; Irwin & Chen, 1946). Once one moves out of the American white middle-class group, however, the general superiority of girls to boys in verbal intellectual skills becomes more complex. Anastasi and D'Angelo (1952), for example, compared black and white preschool children in language development and found a significant sex-by-race interaction. That is, white girls were superior to white boys, while black boys were superior to black girls in length and maturity of verbal responses in a standard test situation. Still another study of children in Bristol, England, suggested that the verbal superiority often found in females may be culture bound (Dunsdon & Fraser-Roberts, 1957). A random sample of all the schoolchildren showed boys to be superior on four oral vocabulary tests. But in spite of exceptions, females generally tend to be superior on tests of verbal ability, beginning at about age eleven years and extending at least through the high school years and perhaps beyond them (Maccoby & Jacklin, 1974a).

Sex differences are less clear on verbal reasoning tests, such as analogies. Sometimes boys do better on these tests (Klausmeier & Wiersma, 1964, 1965; McNemar, 1942), sometimes girls (Lee, 1965); and sometimes there is no difference (Bennett et al., 1959). Girls do learn to read sooner than boys (Balow, 1963; Anderson et al., 1957). Other studies show, however, that boys catch up by about the age of ten.

In general, the finding of some cultural variations indicated above limits conclusions. And although girls may be superior to boys at an early age, boys may catch up or even excel later. Moreover, even though some sex differences in intellectual abilities have been found reliably, many of these differences tend to be small. This means that a child's sex may be a relatively minor factor in determining his or her mental ability in a particular area. In any classroom some boys probably will be superior to girls in vocabulary, and some girls will excel in spatial ability.

Sex differences have also been reported in a cognitive style described as "analytic" or field-independent as opposed to global or field-dependent (Witkin et al., 1962). The two measures most frequently employed in research on these styles are the Embedded Figures Test and the Rod and Frame Test. In the first, subjects have to find a simple hidden figure embedded in a more complex stimulus array. In the Rod and Frame Test a rod within a frame is projected on the wall of a darkened room, and the subject has to adjust the rod to the vertical as the frame is tilted. Boys and men tend to perform better and faster on these tasks than girls and women do, although sex differences are not found before the early school years (Maccoby, 1966). Witkin and his co-workers reported consistent sex differences only at age seventeen and after, and once again the variations within each sex were greater than the consistent differences between the sexes.

In spite of some reported sex differences in cognitive styles, a close analysis of the total research on this topic indicates that the conclusions must be highly qualified. After an exhaustive review, Maccoby and Jacklin (1974a, p. 110) conclude that the belief that boys are more "analytic" than girls is one of many myths about sex differences. In fact, on cognitive style tests: "Boys are superior only on problems that require visual discrimination or manipulation of objects set in a larger context; this superiority seems to be accounted for by spatial ability . . . and does not imply a general analytic superiority (p. 110)." Thus, boys tend to excel in visual-spatial ability but not in more general analytic skills. This difference seems to begin in early adolescence.

In sum, a variety of sex differences have been found, especially on indices of physical aggression and on certain aspects of cognitive functioning. These average differences are important. However, within each of these domains there is considerable variability in the behavior of the same individual across situations. An individual's sex-typed behaviors may be relatively specific rather than highly generalized. A young boy may, for example, be good at baseball and still love painting, and he may like to tinker with tools and play with soldiers. The same child may also be extremely dependent on his mother's attention, may even like to dress his sister's dolls, may cry easily if he is hurt, but also may fight aggressively when peers provoke him.

Sex-Role Stereotypes and Identity

We all share global stereotypes about masculine and feminine traits based on average differences between the sexes. A "real" boy in the United States is supposed to do such things as climb trees, dirty his knees, and disdain girls, while a "real" girl plays with dolls, jumps rope, and loves hopscotch (Brown, 1965). These stereotypes serve as bases for judging others. Sex-role stereotypes may also function as standards by which people evaluate themselves.

Sex-role stereotypes are widely shared within a particular culture and to some extent across cultures (e.g., D'Andrade, 1966). Even within a relatively homogeneous subculture, however, individuals may vary in the degree to which they adopt sanctioned sex-role standards. For example, children, especially girls, from homes and schools that stressed individualized development departed more from conventional sex-role standards than did children from more traditional backgrounds (Minuchin, 1965).

Sex-role identity refers to the "degree to which an individual regards himself as masculine or feminine" (Kagan, 1964, p. 144). Kagan's formulation of sex-role identity stresses the person's global concept of his or her own overall masculinity or femininity. As he puts it (1964, p. 144):

> The degree of match or mismatch between the sex-role standards of the culture and the individual's assessment of his own overt and covert attributes provides him with a partial answer to the question, "How masculine (or feminine) am I?"

In the years since this simple conception of sex-role identity was proposed, it has become plain that the matter is more complex (J. H. Block, 1973). An increasing number of people are unwilling to either ask or answer the traditional question "How masculine (or feminine) am I?" in the conventional ways. Some of the many controversies that surround the topic of sex-role identity are discussed later in this chapter.

THE DEVELOPMENT OF SEX-TYPING

In order to understand psychological sex differences properly one has to consider their development. Often the extensive investigations on the development of sex roles are grouped under the heading of "sex typing." *Sex typing* is the process whereby the individual comes to acquire, to value, and to practice (perform) sex-typed behavior patterns—that is, patterns that are considered appropriate for one sex but not for the opposite sex. What are the causes of sex-typed behavior?

Biological Determinants

The biological differences between the sexes are important in the development of psychological characteristics. For example, the fact that women bear children whereas men do not dictates many other differences in life roles. Beyond differences in the physical characteristics of the sexes, however, the biological or physiological approach has emphasized the possible effects of sex hormones on the development of psychological differences in nonsexual human behavior.

This biological emphasis is seen in the work of such researchers as Broverman and his associates (1968). These investigators suggest that sex differences in cognitive abilities reflect complex sex differences in biochemistry. They suggest that the relationships involved can be understood best by studying changes in people's cognitive processes induced by such organismic changes as variations in hormone levels and the administration of drugs. They speculate that "the sex differences in performances of simple perceptual-motor and inhibitory restructuring tasks are related, in part at least, to the differential effects of the 'sex' steroid hormones on activation and inhibition neural processes" (p. 42). The work of Broverman and his associates seems provocative, but for obvious ethical and practical reasons there has been little systematic experimentation with people on the possible role of sex hormones in the development of psychological sex differences (but see *In Focus 17.2*).

Some researchers have concentrated on sex differences in newborns in order to study possible innate sex differences before socialization practices exert their effects massively. Human neonatal behavior indicates some sex differences in activity level and in reactivity to a variety of stimuli. For example, sex differences occur in infants' responses to facial stimuli during the first year of life (Lewis, 1969). Girls vocalized and smiled more and showed greater differential expression to the facial stimuli, although boys looked longer. At age two to three months, girls are more sensitive to skin exposure than boys (Wolff, 1965). Newborn females seem to react more to the removal of a covering blanket, and show lower thresholds to air-jet stimulation of the abdomen (Bell & Costello, 1964). Newborn boys raise

---

In Focus 17.2
Two Sexes in One Body

"It's a girl" or "it's a boy" is typically the first identification given a newborn in the delivery room. In most cases this assignment is unambiguous because the newborn's internal biological sexuality corresponds to its external sex organs. But sometimes a *hermaphrodite* is born—an individual who has both male and female sex organs. The designation of a hermaphrodite as either male or female is ambiguous and may be incorrect in terms of the individual's genetic sex. Children have been born with male genitals and reared as boys until tests found that they were genetic (chromosomal) females and further examination revealed that they had internal female sex organs.

One study followed nineteen hermaphrodites who were designated and reared as the sex opposite their chromosomal sex. Without exception, the sex role and orientation adopted by these individuals was in accordance with their designated sex and rearing (Hampson, 1965). In another report, a group of hermaphroditic individuals who had been reared as females in accordance with their external genitalia behaved and dressed as females throughout their lives and chose male marriage partners even though they had a male hormone pattern, possessed internal male genitalia, and were genetically male (Money, 1965, a,b). These studies demonstrate the impact of

the psychological sex role to which a child is assigned. Early assignment and the psychological variables that establish and maintain a sex role may, as in these cases, override hormonal influences.

But these findings do not mean that sex roles are entirely learned. The greater aggressiveness of males observed in virtually all human societies, and in animal species closely related to man as well, supports the existence of some biologically based psychological sex differences (Diamond, 1976; Maccoby & Jacklin, 1974b). While the issue of possible interrelations between hormones, brain functions, and behavior is far from settled, there is no doubt that social learning plays a large part in the development of sex roles. In Maccoby's words,

> the sex-typed attributes of personality and temperament . . . are the product of the interweaving of differential social demands with certain biological determinants that help to produce or augment differential cultural demands upon the two sexes. The biological underpinnings . . . set . . . limits to the range of variation of these demands from one cultural setting to another. Still, within these limits considerable variation does occur, between families, between cultures, and in the nature of the behavior that a social group stereotypes as "feminine" or "masculine" (1966, p. 50).

---

their heads higher than newborn girls do (Bell & Darling, 1965), and there are also sex differences in infant play behavior (Goldberg & Lewis, 1969).

The interpretation sometimes drawn from these early sex differences in response to stimulation is that they are innate. But as in other domains of personality, nature and nurture—heredity and environment—tend to be deeply and often inextricably entwined, as discussed in *In Focus 17.2*.

While biological limits and constraints have been recognized and acknowledged, most psychologists. have emphasized socialization and cognitive processes as the causes of psychological sex-role characteristics.

Cognition and Consistency Strivings

In the course of development young children soon recognize their sexual identity or gender. They rapidly develop a conception of their permanent sexual identity through the same observational and cognitive processes that permit them to understand the invariable identity of physical objects in the environment (Kohlberg, 1966). These concepts seem to occur early in development, generally before the age of five years. By the time children reach school age they clearly have learned the concepts "male" and "female" (Hartup & Zook, 1960; Kagan, Hosken, & Watson, 1961). Early during the course of socialization they also rapidly learn the stereotypes about masculinity and femininity prevalent in their subculture.

Sex-role concepts and stereotypes probably arise in part from children's observations of sex differences in bodily structure and capacities. When they reach the age of four or five years, children become distinctly aware of adult sex differences in size and strength. These perceived differences in turn may be associated with concepts about sex differences in power.

Some theorists emphasize the importance of cognitive strivings for consistency, and view consistency motivation as the crux of sex-role development. According to Lawrence Kohlberg, cognitive self-categorizations as "boy" or "girl" are made as reality judgments early in the child's development. Once formed, these judgments tend to be fairly irreversible, being maintained by the physical reality of one's sex: a person is male or female forever. Kohlberg's cognitive-developmental formulation gives this direct self-categorization of gender central importance as the fundamental organizer of sex-role attitudes and values:

> Basic self-categorizations determine basic valuings. Once the boy has stably categorized himself as male he then values positively those objects and acts consistent with his gender identity (1966, p. 89).

Kohlberg's theorizing assumes that strong tendencies or strivings toward cognitive consistency lead the person to acquire values consistent with his cognitive judgments about himself (as discussed in Chapter 10). Granting the existence of such powerful strivings for cognitive consistency, just what are the processes through which the individual adopts his specific values and behaviors from among the many possibilities that could be consistent with his gender?

Kohlberg hypothesizes that after the child has categorized himself as male or female he then values positively whatever is consistent with his gender identity. That hypothesis is provocative. However, one has to explain how the boy learns and selects the particular sets of sex-typed behaviors that he adopts from the vast array that could be "consistent with his gender." There are many different appropriate ways of being a boy or a girl, and even more diverse ways of being a man or a woman, in any given culture. Boys and girls are exposed to a great variety of potentially appropriate sex-typed behaviors by same-sex models. From this diverse array of gender-consistent possibilities, they select and choose discriminatively. To understand sex typing fully we must account for individual differences in sex-typed behavior *within* each sex and not just for modal differences between the sexes. It is therefore necessary to go beyond cognitive self-categorization and consistency strivings to consider social learning.

Social Learning

Social learning theorists find it helpful to distinguish between the mechanisms through which individuals learn sex-typed behaviors and those that regulate their selection of particular sex-typed behaviors from the repertoire that is already available. As we have stressed before, people obviously do not perform all the behaviors

The performance of sex-typed behavior depends on the expected consequences.

that they have learned and could enact. Members of each sex know a great deal about the role behaviors of both sexes. In our culture both men and women know, for example, how to fight aggressively, and how to use cosmetics, although they differ in the frequency with which they perform these activities.

The acquisitional (learning) phases of sex typing involve cognitive and observational processes through which concepts and potential behaviors are learned. On the other hand, the individual's choice of selection of sex-typed behaviors from the available array that she already has mastered and knows how to execute depends on motivational and situational considerations. This distinction between acquisition and response selection is not limited to sex typing; it has also been made for all other aspects of social behavior by most current social learning theories. We are referring here to the previously discussed view that the acquisition of novel responses is regulated by sensory, attentional, and cognitive processes, but that direct and vicarious reinforcement is the important regulator of response selection in performance.

Boys and girls discover quickly that the consequences for many of the things that they try are affected by their sex. Indeed, that is exactly the meaning of "sex-typed" behaviors: their appropriateness depends on the sex of the person who displays them. Sex-typed behaviors are those that are typically more expected and approved for one sex than for the other and that lead to different outcomes or consequences when performed by males as opposed to females in the particular community. Because they yield differential consequences for males and females, these sex-typed behaviors come to be performed with different frequency by the sexes and to have different value for them. Thus a person's sex influences the consequences she gets for many of the things she does and affects how people relate to her as well as how she reacts to herself.

Child-Rearing Practices

Parents, teachers, and other significant social agents tend to reward sex-appropriate behaviors and to punish or ignore sex-inappropriate responses. Even young children soon learn that their parents expect boys and girls to behave differently. For example, a group of five-year-olds were shown a series of paired pictures illustrating masculine and feminine activities (Fauls & Smith, 1956). The children were asked which activity Mother and Father would prefer for boys and girls (e.g., "Which does Mother want the boy to do?"). Children of both sexes indicated that parents wanted the child to perform sex-appropriate activities more often than sex-inappropriate activities. But with the current trend toward more fluid conceptions of masculinity and femininity, notions of appropriate behavior for each sex may be becoming more flexible.

Parents tend to rear boys and girls most differently in the area of *aggression* (Sears, Maccoby, & Levin, 1957). Boys were given greater freedom in the expression of aggression toward the parents and toward other children. Girls were more often praised for "good" behavior and more often subjected to withdrawal of love for "bad" behavior. These reported differences are not strong, but they are consistent with the cultural sanction of physical aggression in males. "Prosocial" aggressions (verbalizations about the goodness or badness of behavior and verbal threats) are more acceptable for girls but are considered "sissyish" for boys. These results are consistent with the sex differences discussed earlier showing that boys are more frequently physically aggressive, while girls display more prosocial and verbal aggression.

Although parents tend to sanction physical aggression for boys more than for girls, they are not indiscriminate. They obviously do not condone aggression for boys regardless of circumstances and setting. This fact is illustrated in the finding that boys who were aggressive at school had parents who encouraged aggression toward peers; many of these boys, however, were nonaggressive at home, and their parents indeed punished aggression at home (Bandura, 1960).

Laboratory studies have demonstrated that permissiveness for dependency, and reward for dependency, increased children's dependency behavior. Heathers (1953), for example, found that children who accepted help from the experimenter in a difficult situation tended to have parents who encouraged them to depend on others rather than to be independent. Similarly, a field study by Bandura (1960) indicated, among other results, that parents who reward dependency have children who tend to display a high degree of dependency behavior.

In spite of the belief that boys and girls may be socialized differently by their parents, the degree to which parents really treat the sexes differently is not clear. For example, overall evidence for different treatments is not strong, according to the review by Maccoby and Jacklin (1974b). In their view, although parents may react sharply when their children violate narrowly defined sex typing (as when boys want to play with dolls and dresses), evidence for clear differences in how parents react to sons and daughters in such areas as aggression and dependency is less clear. But other reviews point out that society shapes males and females in quite different ways with clear and often painful costs for both sexes (Block, 1973). Even when parents do not consistently respond differently to boys and girls, there are many other social forces that encourage sex differences in social behavior. These influences include the behaviors modeled by the child's peers, and the rules learned about what it means to be a boy or girl—rules that are learned cognitively and by observation without any direct "shaping" or reinforcement of the child.

Social Structure

To understand socialization and especially the development of psychological sex differences fully, we must recognize the role of the social system in which the individual lives. The emphasis on the person in psychology must not obscure the intimate dependence of personality on environment—and the vital role of social forces, institutions, and groups in molding that environment throughout the person's development.

Even within any one broad culture there are important differences among the component subcultures. For example, the extent to which children develop traditional sex-role concepts and sex typing depends on the degree to which they participate in a subculture that shares, models, and encourages those traditional attitudes and values (Minuchin, 1965).

On the other hand, some sex differences in socialization are found cross-culturally (Barry, Bacon, & Child, 1957). Two competent judges rated the socialization data from 110 cultures, a majority of which were nonliterate. They judged sex differences in socialization on five variables: nurturance, obedience, responsibility, achievement, and self-reliance. The differences they found in childhood socialization pressures on these five variables are summarized in Table 17-2.

As Table 17-2 indicates, not only in our society but also in many other cultures, girls are socialized to become nurturant, obedient, and responsible, whereas boys are socialized toward greater self-reliance and achievement striving. However, there were exceptions. Since there were some reversals, and since many cultures showed no detectable sex differences on these dimensions, the evidence favors the role of socially learned rather than biologically established determinants. Nevertheless, many of the sex differences in social behavior obtained cross-culturally may partly reflect the widespread adaptation of cultures to universal biological variables such as child-bearing. The authors commented on the differences they obtained as follows:

> The observed differences in the socialization of boys and girls are consistent with certain universal tendencies in the differentiation of adult sex role. In the economic sphere, men are more frequently allotted tasks that involve leaving home and engaging in activities where a high level of skill yields important returns; hunting is a prime example. Emphasis on training in self-reliance and achievement for boys would function as preparation for such an economic role. Women, on the other hand, are more frequently allotted tasks at or near home that minister most immediately to the needs of others (such as cooking and water carrying); these activities have a nurturant character, and in their pursuit a responsible carrying out of established routines is likely to be more important than the development of an especially high order of skill. Thus training in nurturance, responsibility, and, less clearly, obedience, may contribute to preparation for this economic role. These consistencies with adult role go beyond the economic sphere, of course. Participation in warfare, as a male prerogative, calls for self-reliance and a high order of skill where survival or death is the immediate issue. The childbearing which is biologically assigned to women, and the child care which is socially assigned primarily to them, lead to nurturant behavior and often call for a more continuous responsibility than do the tasks carried out by men. Most of these distinctions in adult role are not inevitable, but the biological differences between the sexes strongly predispose the distinction of role, if made, to be in a uniform direction (Barry, Bacon, & Child, 1957, pp. 328–329).

Table 17-2
Ratings of Cultures for Sex Differences in Childhood Socialization
Pressure on Five Variables

Variable	Number of Cultures	Both Judges Rate Socialization Pressure Higher for	
		Girls	Boys
Nurturance	33	17	0
Obedience	69	6	0
Responsibility	84	25	2
Achievement	31	0	17
Self-reliance	82	0	64

SOURCE: Adapted from Barry, Bacon, & Child, 1957.

Moderator Variables

Although the consequences produced by any behavior depend in part on the person's sex, they also hinge on numerous other considerations. These considerations include: the type of behavior, the situation in which it occurs, the individual's age, status, and other characteristics. Studies of child-rearing practices show the many variables that moderate the exact effects of the child's sex.

These practices depend not only on the sex of the child but also on the sex of the parent. For example, Rothbart and Maccoby (1966) found complex interactions between sex of parent and sex of child. Parents of preschool children listened to tape-recorded statements of a child's voice and indicated what they would say or do to their own sons or daughters in response to each statement. Mothers' reactions showed almost no overall average difference from fathers' reactions, but sex of parent did interact with sex of child. Mothers tended to be more permissive toward sons than toward daughters. But fathers tended to be more attentive and permissive toward their daughters than their sons. This interaction was most pronounced when the child expressed pain (complaining that the baby had stepped on its hand).

The researchers concluded that inconsistency between parents with regard to sex-typed behavior seems to be the rule and also that a parent's reactions could vary from one behavior area to another. The exact form of a behavior, the child's sex, and the sex of the parent reacting to it are all important variables in determining the consequences of the behavior. If parental reactions hinge on numerous situational variables, then global concepts like parental "permissiveness" may be of only limited value in understanding how children develop.

The behaviors that are sex typed, the consequences for appropriate and inappropriate sex typing, the sex-role models that are valued and those that are disapproved, all change significantly and repeatedly in the course of the individual's development. Most psychological studies of the development of personality in general and of sex typing in particular have been conducted with young children (usually under age seven) as the subjects. Yet some of the most important aspects of personality, and of distinctively male and female behavior, emerge at later ages—at and after puberty. It is at these later times that the individual practices adult sex-role behavior, not during the child's dress-up play in his parent's shoes, but in actuality and in his or her own right.

In early adulthood, rather than in childhood, sex-typed expectations become relevant for a host of new interpersonal and sexual behaviors. During adolescence, for example, we can see most clearly sex differences in character, in the cultivation of skills, and in the expression of sexual feelings (Douvan & Kaye, 1957; Harris, 1959). Some of the dramatic differences in sex-typed behaviors that commence in adolescence do not end there and continue to influence the individual for many years. Throughout their lives the role expectations and the role behaviors of the sexes differ in numerous critical respects. These patterns continue to change. They come under new influences as appropriate role demands and role models vary, and as the consequences for particular forms of sex-typed behavior shift, in accord with changes throughout the individual's life and in the larger culture. A male who shows tenderness may be mocked as an adolescent boy on the ballfield, but cherished for the same quality by a spouse in later years.

In sum, sex-typed response patterns often are affected by the situation in which they are made and by such variables as the individual's age and the sex of the other persons in the situation. In research many interactions occur between the experimenter's sex and the sex of the subject. The reinforcing consequences produced by behavior depend not only on the performer's sex and on the content of the behavior, but also on his or her age and the particular circumstances. Individuals learn to discriminate sharply in their behaviors, moderating their actions in the light of the probable consequences they may produce. Again we see that many conditions may combine to determine what the individual does. In addition, it is possible that these conditions may to some degree include innate differences between the sexes in their readiness to learn certain behaviors. In some readings of the state of research, this seems true in the case of aggression (Hernstein & Wilson, 1985; Maccoby & Jacklin, 1974b), but that interpretation remains controversial.

Correlates of Sex-Typing

There are enormous individual differences in masculinity-femininity. As with most other dimensions of personality, research has revealed extensive correlations between masculinity-femininity indices and other personality measures. One set of investigations has studied the relations between indices of personality adjustment and sex typing. It was found that adolescent boys who had highly masculine interests (on the Strong Vocational Interest Test) when compared to those with highly feminine interests, had more positive self-concepts and more self-confidence on the TAT (Mussen, 1961). The children with more masculine interests were also rated by peers as more masculine.

The adolescents in Mussen's studies were reexamined to assess their adjustment when they reached their late thirties. Using many personality measures, Mussen compared the men who as adolescents had expressed more traditionally masculine interests with those who had reported more feminine interests.

> Comparison of the ratings assigned to the two groups showed that in adulthood, as during adolescence, those who had relatively feminine interest patterns manifested more of the "emotional-expressive" role characteristics—e.g., they were rated as more dependent but more social in orientation. In contrast, those with highly masculine adolescent interest patterns possessed, in their late teens and in their late thirties, more active, "instrumental" characteristics: greater self-sufficiency, less social orientation and, in adulthood, less introspectiveness. There was little congruence between the adolescent and adult statuses of the two groups with respect to several other characteristics, however. During adolescence, highly masculine subjects possessed more self-confidence and greater feelings of adequacy than the other group, but as adults, they were relatively lacking in qualities of leadership, dominance, self-confidence, and self-acceptance (Mussen, 1962, p. 440).

Thus sex-appropriate identification in adolescence is not a fixed sign of an overall enduring adjustment pattern. Adolescents who have stereotyped masculine interests may adjust more happily during adolescence and are rated more positively at that time. Middle-class adolescents who profess stereotypically masculine interests, attitudes, and values probably would fare better, especially with their peers, than would boys who express strongly feminine interests. These adolescent sex-typed preferences, however, do not guarantee a generalized pattern of adjustment for life. Indeed, Mussen (1962, p. 440) pointed out that:

> In general there seems to have been a shift in the self-concepts of the two groups in adulthood, the originally highly masculine boys apparently feeling less positive about themselves after adolescence, and, correlatively, the less masculine groups changing in a favorable direction.

Stability of Sex-Typed Behaviors

There are sex differences in the durability of various sex-typed behavior patterns. Kagan and Moss (1962) found some significant consistency between childhood and early adulthood ratings of achievement behavior, sex-typed activity and spontaneity for both sexes. Certain other variables, like dependency and aggression, were stable for one sex but not for the other. In particular, childhood dependency and passivity were related to adult dependency and passivity for women, but not for men. Conversely, "the developmental consistency for aggression was noticeably greater for males" (p. 95). They suggested that these sex-linked differences in the continuity of behaviors may reflect differences in their "congruence with traditional standards for sex-role characteristics" (p. 268).

CHANGING STEREOTYPES AND SEX-ROLE BIAS

In recent years there have been some dramatic challenges to conventional sex roles in our culture. Such challenges may be seen in the women's movement and in changing concepts of sex differences and sex roles.

Sex-Role Bias in Society

There has been a growing recognition in psychology, as well as in the women's movement, that psychologists, teachers, and parents should not unquestioningly perpetuate stereotyped sex roles (Bardwick, 1972; J. H. Block, 1973; Dweck, 1975). To automatically encourage boys and girls to accept the stereotyped roles society expects them to play may prevent each person from realizing his or her full potential. The sex-role ideology, explicit or implicit, prevalent in the United States has been accused of producing an unfortunate "homogenization" of American women (Bem & Bem, 1972). It has been pointed out that there is widespread acceptance in America of an "unconscious ideology" about women. This ideology is reflected in the fact that the majority of American women end up in virtually the *same* role, that of homemaker, often combined with a dead-end job (e.g., sales clerk, secretary, factory worker). A woman often is consigned to her role on the basis of sex, without regard to her unique abilities and capacities. The American ideology regarding the female sex tends to close options to women and constrict " . . . the emerging self-image of the female child and the nature of her aspirations from the very beginning . . ." (Bem & Bem, 1972, p. 7). In contrast, a male may

Sex-role stereotypes should not prevent each person from realizing his or her full potential.

be more likely to become whatever his talents and interests permit him to be, with greater diversity in his occupational potential.

The same authors contend further that the American male also may be disadvantaged by the prevailing ideology; for example, he may be discouraged from developing such desirable traits as tenderness and sensitivity on the grounds that those qualities are "unmanly." Further, the relationship between males and females may suffer from the inequities in current sex-role stereotypes. Once we become conscious of this destructive ideology, changes may be necessary: (1) to prevent discrimination (at the legal and economic levels); (2) to avoid constrictive, personally debilitating sex-role socialization; and (3) to encourage institutions and ideologies that will nullify the presumed incompatibility of family and career for women in our society.

Many statements have been made about the constricted and inequitable nature of the traditional female sex roles and some of these assertions have been seen as unfounded propaganda by critics (e.g., Dechter, 1972). Although arguments have been abundant on all sides of this heated social issue, there has been some work on bias due to sex roles (e.g., Frieze et al. 1978). For example, it has been asserted widely that clear sex-role stereotypes which prevent the full expression of individuality in interests and abilities are imparted early to children. A study of elementary school reading textbooks examined the treatment of males and females in the stories to which school children are routinely exposed (C. Jacklin and H. Mischel, 1973). The results were quite clear. Female characters in the children's reading texts were consistently underrepresented and were rarely main figures in the stories. Males were the heroes, carried the action, and experienced more positive consequences as a result of their own efforts and initiative. In contrast, females were passive, and whatever positive consequences they received came from the situation (e.g., from what others did for them, from luck) rather than from their own actions and initiative. These inequitable portraits of males and females became even stronger as the series of books progressed from kindergarten through third grade.

Sex-Role Stereotyping in Psychology

Sex-role stereotyping has been laid squarely at the door of psychology itself in a study by Broverman, et al. (1970). Clinically trained psychologists, psychiatrists, and social workers were asked to describe a healthy, mature, socially competent (*a*) man; (*b*) woman; (*c*) adult, sex unspecified. Judgments of what characterized mentally healthy males and females differed in a way congruent with stereotypic sex-role differences (see Table 17-3 for examples). The qualities used to define mental health for an ideal adult (of unspecified sex) closely resembled those attri-

---

In Focus 17.3
Do Women Fear Success?

In an influential study of achievement fantasies in women, Horner (1972) asked female college students to tell a story based on the following cue: "After first-term finals Ann finds herself at the top of her medical school class." Over 65 percent of the stories told by the women about Ann contained negative responses (e.g., anxiety, guilt, loss of femininity, social rejection) and indicated an avoidance of success. The women's denial of Ann's achievements often went to extremes, as when their stories put down Ann's success to a failure of the computer in grading or to a fluke, or described it as something that Ann will not be able to keep up. College men were asked to tell a story about the same situation, except that the actor was John instead of Ann. The men's responses to John were negative in only 10 percent of their stories, indicating little or no avoidance of success.

To account for this difference between the sexes, Horner hypothesized the motive of *fear of success* in women. In her view, this motive occurs often in women but very rarely in men and arises from women's expectancy that achievement-related success will be followed by negative consequences in our culture. For example, a woman expects (fears) that success in a career such as medicine will conflict with (undermine) her femininity and her attractiveness as a person. Horner believes that "in order to feel or appear more feminine women disguise their abilities and withdraw from the mainstream of thought, nontraditional aspiration, and achievement in our society" (1972, p. 67).

Horner's hypothesis that women have a fear of success motive has been challenged by the results of several subsequent studies. One of them used the same story about Ann but gave it to males as well as females (Monahan, Kuhn, and Shaver, 1974). Both males and females were also asked to tell stories about John (see Table 17-4). Once again, females expressed negative themes to the cue involving Ann's success. For example:

Soon Ann became one of the leading doctors in the world. When she was in France, she met an American man. They both fell in love. Soon they were married. But after they had their first child, Ann turned all her attention to her work. So they got divorced. Ann was always involved in her work. The only people she talked to were fellow doctors and nurses. Soon she got very ill and

Table 17-3
Examples of Traits Attributed by Clinicians to "Healthy" Women
Compared to "Healthy" Men

"Healthy" Women Are Less	"Healthy" Women Are More
independent	submissive
adventurous	easily influenced
aggressive	excitable in minor crises
competitive	conceited about their appearance

SOURCE: Based on data from Broverman et al., 1970.

butes judged healthy for men but differed significantly from those considered to be healthy for women. For example, the healthy adult of unspecified sex was described as dominant, independent, adventurous, aggressive, and competitive. These adjectives were also used to describe the healthy adult male. In contrast, the healthy adult female was described as more submissive, less independent, less adventurous, less aggressive, less competitive, more easily influenced, more excit-

died. No one even went to her funeral because she was very mean (Monahan et al., 1974, pp. 62–63).

Interestingly, the results also showed that males responded negatively to female success—even more often, in fact, than did the females. But few subjects, whether male or female, gave negative responses to the story of male success. Thus the sex of the actor presented in the cue, rather than the sex of the subject telling the story, appears to be the critical determinant. Rather than reflecting a special fear of success motive that is unique to women, the stories told by both sexes may simply reflect their negative stereotypes and expectancies about a woman who succeeds in a traditionally masculine field such as medicine. As Table 17-4 summarizes, negative stories were told frequently about a successful female medical student and infrequently about a successful male medical student, regardless of the sex of the storyteller.

Table 17-4
Summary of Some Studies on Fear of Success

Study	Sex of Subjects	Story Cue: "After first-term finals———finds herself (himself) at the top of her (his) medical school class."	Percent of Subjects Telling Negative Stories[a]
Horner	F	Ann	High
1969	M	John	Low
Monahan	F	Ann	High
et al.,	M	Ann	High
1974	F	John	Low
	M	John	Low

[a]High indicates over 50 percent and low indicates under 50 percent.

able in minor crises, and more conceited about her appearance. As the authors noted (p. 5), "this constellation seems a most unusual way of describing any mature, healthy individual." Moreover, this negative assessment of women was shared equally by the women professionals and by the men.

The implication is that a woman who is assertive and independent, or who is aggressive and adventurous, is likely to be judged maladjusted, while the same qualities in a male (or in a person of unspecified sex) are considered assets. In addition, stereotypic masculine traits (such as "very aggressive," "very worldly," "very logical") were seen twice as often as more desirable than were stereotypic feminine traits. Among the few feminine traits seen as desirable were "very talkative," "very tactful," and "very gentle." In sum, the overall results suggest that not only is "healthy male" synonymous with "healthy adult" and antithetical to "healthy female," but masculine traits are the ones that tend to be seen as desirable. In contrast, most feminine traits are seen as undesirable, even in the eyes of well-trained psychologists, psychiatrists, and social workers.

Consequences of Sex-Role Stereotypes

Sexual stereotypes have many painful effects. One of these negative consequences was pointed out by Matina Horner (1969, 1972) who suggested that in our culture women develop a "motive to avoid success." According to Horner, for men success is perceived as compatible with their sense of masculinity. But for women success often is a conflict-producing, mixed blessing, because professional success may imply failure in the personal sphere, and the qualities demanded for success at work may conflict with those required for success as a women (see *In Focus 17.3*). Other researchers have disputed whether or not women really have a distinct motive to avoid success. But there tends to be agreement that in many instances in our culture success and failure have very different implications and consequences for men and women. For example, when a woman does succeed on a task considered "masculine," her performance is as likely to be attributed to her luck as to her skill (Deaux & Emswiller, 1974; see Figure 17-1).

Especially discouraging is the finding that when more women enter a high-status profession, its perceived prestige declines. Male and female college students were led to believe that certain high-status professions (e.g., college professor and physician) would have an influx of women. They rated the fields as less prestigeful and desirable than a control group informed that the proportions of women in these fields would remain stable and low. This devaluation was expressed equally by women and by men (Touhey, 1974).

Also unjust and frustrating is the fact that some professional work may be judged less favorably when it is done by women than by men, even when the work is identical (Goldberg, 1967). In this line of research, subjects were asked to judge a series of professional articles. The identical articles were shown as authored by either males or females simply by varying the name on them (e.g., John Simpson or Joan Simpson). Goldberg's results suggested that when U.S. college women were the judges they devalued the achievements of other women and they did so even in fields that are traditionally associated with women, such as dietetics and primary education.

Figure 17-1
What Is Skill for the Male May Be Luck for the Female

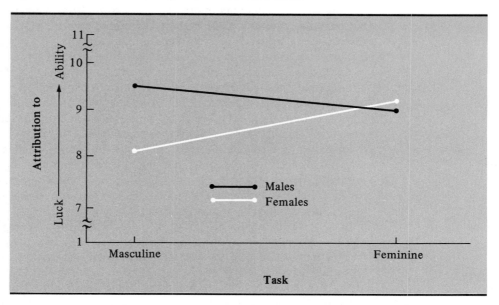

Graph showing that when females were able to find hidden pictures of such items as tire jacks and wrenches (masculine tasks) in a larger picture, their success was attributed partly to their luck, whereas the performance of males on this task was credited more to their skill. When the task was to discover hidden pictures of mops and double boilers (feminine tasks) the performance of both sexes was judged to be due to their ability to the same degree.

Adapted from Deaux & Emswiller (1974, p. 82).

A group of later studies, conducted in both the United States and Israel with both males and females, questions the existence of a generalized preference for male expertise (H. Mischel, 1974). Using the same method as Goldberg, this study found that professional sex bias in the United States depended on the particular field in which work was judged. Judges of both sexes preferred authors whose sex was the same as that normative for (or stereotypically associated with) the professional field in which the article was written. For example, bias was in favor of a female author in primary education but in favor of a male author in law. Israeli subjects subscribed to the same stereotypes as the U.S. subjects regarding the sex association of the diverse fields, but did not show the evaluative biases found in the United States. These results highlight the complexity and specificity of existing sex biases, and show that they are double-edged, with discrimination against men (when they are in stereotypically female fields) as well as against women (when they venture into male-dominated fields).

Toward Androgyny?

Alert to the negative effects of rigid traditional sex-role stereotypes, Sandra Bem (1975) questioned the very notion of "masculinity" and "femininity" as two opposite ends of a single dimension. She reasoned that this bipolar dimension has obscured the possibility that individuals might be "androgynous," i.e., *both* masculine *and* feminine, as those terms are usually defined. Moreover, traditionally narrow sex-role concepts might inhibit persons from behaving flexibly across situations that threaten their stereotypes about sex-appropriate behavior. In this research, androgynous persons were defined as those who are not rigidly sex typed but instead endorse masculine and feminine attributes equally. Specifically, an individual who endorses both types of attributes equally is defined as having an androgynous sex role (see Table 17-5). According to Bem, these individuals, whether male or female, may be more flexible (e.g., resisting social pressure to conform) than those who are more traditionally sex typed. Although much more research is needed before firm conclusions can be reached, Bem (p. 643) speculates that the sex-role flexibility of androgynous people "enables them to engage in situationally effective behavior without regard for its stereotype as masculine or feminine. Accordingly, it may well be—as the women's liberation movement has urged—that the androgynous individual will someday come to define a new and more human standard of psychological health."

In spite of its appealing qualities, the concept of psychological androgyny has not escaped criticism, both of its measurement (Pedhazur & Tetenbaum, 1979) and of its rationale (Locksley & Colten, 1979). For example, consider the notion that androgynous people are better adjusted because they have greater flexibility in their behavior as a consequence of not being confined by sex stereotypes. A series of studies examined this idea by giving subjects Bem's questionnaire for sex-role preferences. Subjects were scored for degree of androgyny versus traditional masculinity or femininity. The same subjects also were given many other measures, including those of self-esteem, helplessness, sexual maturity, and personal adjustment (Jones, Chernovertz, & Hansson, 1978). The hypothesis of better adjustment for the androgynous was not confirmed. On the contrary, for both sexes high mas-

Table 17-5

Examples of Items on the Masculinity and Femininity Scales of Bem's Androgyny Test

Masculine Items	Feminine Items
Acts as a leader	Affectionate
Analytical	Compassionate
Competitive	Feminine
Forceful	Gullible
Individualistic	Sensitive to the needs of others
Self-reliant	Sympathetic
Willing to take a stand	Warm

1	2	3	4	5	6	7
Never or Almost Never True	Usually Not True	Sometimes but Infrequently True	Occasionally True	Often True	Usually True	Always or Almost Always True

NOTE: On the test the items are mixed together. For each item the subject is asked to describe himself or herself by marking the appropriate number.
SOURCE: Based on Bem, 1974 (by permission).

culinity scores (rather than androgyny) tended to predict better flexibility and overall adjustment. Other studies, nevertheless, suggest that people who have an androgynous sex role orientation do tend to view themselves as better adjusted (Flaherty and Dusek, 1980). Clear conclusions are thus hard to reach at this point.

Androgyny does not provide a simple path in a society that continues to reinforce traditional sex roles. In American society currently, the potentially creative woman experiences considerable conflict. On the one hand she seeks to pursue creative, achievement-oriented activities that traditionally are viewed as "masculine." On the other hand, she continues to experience pressure towards "sex-appropriate, feminine" characteristics (Harrington & Andersen, 1981). Reconciling these opposing pressures is hardly an easy task.

Results of the type reviewed in this section should sensitize psychologists against perpetuating traditional stereotypic conceptions of masculinity and femininity. Most psychologists would probably agree that concepts like "sex-appropriate behavior" (used throughout this chapter) merely describe the existing norms and practices of the culture. They would insist that they do not necessarily endorse those norms. Yet we have seen that psychologists—just like most other people— may inadvertently perpetuate sex-role stereotypes. Fortunately, there appears to be a growing recognition that the conventional practices of society—which often may constrict human potentialities for both sexes—must not be confused with the ideals toward which its members should strive.

SUMMARY

1. Psychological sex differences and the sex-typing processes through which they develop are crucial aspects of personality. Sex typing is illustrated by self-reports about perceived sex differences at different ages, from childhood to maturity, in the life of one person.

2. Aggressive behavior is one of the main dimensions on which sex differences have been consistently found. Boys show more physical aggression and antisocial aggression than girls as early as age three years. These differences appear cross-culturally in rating studies, self-ratings, and projective tests.

3. Some sex differences have been found in intellectual functioning. Beginning early in adolescence boys tend to excel in visual-spatial ability; girls tend to have greater verbal ability.

4. Sex-role stereotypes are widely shared ideas about what is masculine and what is feminine, on the basis of average differences between the sexes within the culture. These stereotypes may serve as standards for judging and evaluating one's own behavior as well as for judging others. There are great individual differences in the degree to which people adopt particular sex-role standards.

5. Sex typing is the development of patterns of behavior considered appropriate for one sex but not the other. The development of sex roles and sex typing involves biological determinants as well as learning and cognitive processes.

6. The biological or physiological approach emphasizes the possible effect of sex hormones on the development of differences even in nonsexual human behavior. Research with lower animals suggests interrelations between hormonal conditions, brain functions, and behavior. Studies with hermaphrodites dramatize the importance of the psychological gender role assigned to the child.

Research with newborns suggests some sex differences in activity and sensitivity to a variety of stimuli.

7. Cognitive-developmental theory emphasizes the striving for cognitive consistency as a determinant of sex roles. According to this theory, once the cognitive self-categorization of "boy" or "girl" is made, then positive valuation of objects and behaviors consistent with this gender identity follows.

8. Social learning theories stress that children within every culture learn quite early about sex differences in behavior. Through observational learning children of both sexes know about, and are capable of performing, many role behaviors from both sexes. The sexes differ, however, in the frequency with which they perform these activities and in how they value them.

9. In the social learning view, because sex-typed behaviors yield different consequences when displayed by males and by females they rapidly become valued and practiced differentially by boys and by girls. Sex is an important determinant of how other people react to you and of how you react to yourself.

10. Parents and other significant social agents may encourage the child's sex-appropriate behavior and ignore or punish sex-inappropriate behaviors in the course of development. Aggression is the area in which boys and girls probably are reared most differently. Parents probably permit more physical aggression in boys than in girls. This sanction is not indiscriminate, however. Parents teach their children to discriminate in the expression of aggression with regard to circumstances and setting. The degree to which parents treat the sexes differently is not firmly established.

11. Social forces, institutions, and groups have a vital role in the development of psychological sex differences throughout the life cycle. Cultures differ in their sex-role standards, and even within a given culture there may be important subcultural differences. However, some cross-cultural differences in sex-role socialization have been found repeatedly. Many of the cross-culturally obtained sex differences in social behavior may partly reflect the widespread adaptation of cultures to universal sex differences in biological variables such as child-bearing.

12. Not only the child's sex, but also the sex of the people who react to her, can be important "moderators" determining some of the consequences she receives for her sex-typed behavior. There are many interactions, for example, between the sex of the parent and the sex of the child with respect to particular behaviors and situations. Thus in addition to the child's own sex, such other variables as age, the sex of other people in the situation, and the type of behavior also interact to influence the consequences for engaging in such sex-typed behaviors as aggression and dependency.

13. Within any society the role expectations and role behaviors of the sexes change significantly and repeatedly in the course of the individual's development. Some of the most important aspects of personality and of distinctively male and female behavior may emerge at and after puberty. Dramatic differences in sex-typed behaviors begin in adolescence and continue to influence the individual throughout life. Sex-typed behavior changes as important role models change and new role demands are experienced. Changes in the larger culture also can influence sex-typed behavior.

14. Many correlations exist between masculinity-femininity indices and other personality measures. For example, relations have been found between sex typing and such indices of personality adjustment as positive self-concepts and self-confidence.

15. Traditional sex-role stereotypes and sex-typing practices are being questioned and challenged increasingly. Sex-role biases are prevalent in society, including education and the mental health fields, and narrow sex-role stereotypes undoubtedly have negative, constrictive consequences that limit the human potentiality of both sexes. As part of the growing recognition of sex bias and the constriction produced by stereotypic sex-roles, there has been a move to measure—and perhaps encourage—increasing "androgyny" so that both sexes may achieve greater sex-role flexibility.

Chapter 18

Social Interaction: Attraction, Aggression, Altruism

We live in a world in which people constantly influence each other: advertisers pound us with endless messages to buy their products; educators try to "teach" children (to learn, to like their schools, to study); children and parents try to improve each other (to "grow up," to "understand," to "be reasonable"); politicians seek to win support for their policies (and their reelection); governments struggle for power (to expand or preserve their influence). Whether verbally or physically, by praise and flattery or by threats and brute force, intentionally or unwittingly, subtly or obviously, all of us are involved in almost continuous influence efforts, whether we like it or not. In this chapter we will survey some of the main forms of social interactions and social influence most relevant for understanding personality and complex social behavior. We will begin with interactions that involve attraction and liking. Then we will turn to aggression or hurting, and its psychological opposite, altruism or helping.

ATTRACTION AND LIKING

Our interactions with people depend greatly on how much we like them. What determines liking and attraction? Why do we like some people and dislike others? What conditions or qualities lead us to seek more contact with some people and to avoid others, to be responsive to some and indifferent to others?

Physical Attraction

The first thing that we notice about people is their physical appearance. Research verifies two facts that we may not want to admit: we like people who are physically attractive better than those who are not, and we attribute desirable qualities to attractive people (Berscheid & Walster, 1974).

In one study (Walster et al., 1966), freshmen males and females were randomly paired into couples as computer dates for a dance and then rated by judges for physical attractiveness. Halfway through the dance the participants answered questionnaires about how much they liked their date and whether they wanted to see him or her again. Intelligence, school grades, attitude similarity, and a variety of personality characteristics (e.g. dependence-independence, dominance-submission) were examined. The characteristic most closely linked with liking was physical attractiveness.

The power of physical attractiveness is not limited to feelings about members of the opposite sex. Using photographs, male and female college subjects were asked to rate peers on a variety of personality traits and to predict their future happiness. Predictions of happiness and attributions of the most desirable traits were significantly greater for the physically attractive people. This was true whether women were rating men or other women and whether men were rating women or other men (Dion et al., 1972).

Physical attractiveness influences our evaluations quite early in life and affects our judgments in a variety of areas. Nursery school children tend to like their physically attractive age mates better than their unattractive ones (Dion & Berscheid, 1971). Adults also are influenced by a child's physical attractiveness. For example, suppose a child performs an aggressive act such as throwing an ice-packed snowball at another child, hitting him and causing a deep cut. Adult judges tend to see such misdeeds as less likely to be the result of a stable antisocial disposition when they are performed by a physically attractive child than by an unattractive one. In addition, even severely aggressive acts are judged to be less serious when committed by an attractive child than by an unattractive one (Dion, 1972). In an experiment in which students played the role of jurors in a student court at college, they judged physically attractive defendants with less certainty of guilt and recommended less severe punishments for them than for unattractive defendants (Efran, 1974).

Just believing that an unseen person is physically attractive affects not only the believers' behavior, but the behavior of the other person as well (Snyder, Tanke, & Berscheid, 1977). In one study, college men talked for ten minutes by intercom telephone to unseen college women who they were told were either physically attractive or unattractive. Later, new subjects (who knew nothing about the study and did not know which women had been labeled "attractive" or "unattractive") rated tape recordings of these getting-acquainted conversations. Some raters heard only the woman's side of the conversation; other raters heard only the man's side of the conversation. The women were rated on such traits as "sociable," "poised," "sexually warm," and "outgoing." The analysis revealed that "what had initially been reality in the minds of the men had now become reality in the behavior of the women with whom they had interacted—a behavioral reality discernible even by naive observer judges, who had access *only* to tape recordings of the women's contributions to the conversations" (Snyder, Tanke, & Berscheid, 1977, p. 661).

Ratings of the men, from their conversations with women whom they believed to be either physically attractive or unattractive, revealed that the men's behavior may have elicited the differences found in the women's behavior. The judges rated men interacting with "attractive" women as more sociable, sexually warm, interesting, independent, and socially adept than men interacting with "unattractive" women. The total pattern of results suggests that the physical attractiveness stereotype can influence the behavior of the person who gets stereotyped as well as the behavior of the person who is applying the stereotype. If someone thinks you are attractive (or unattractive), he or she will relate differently to you; your behavior, in turn, also may change in line with his or her belief.

Competence

Although common sense suggests that we should like people who are competent, there is some conflicting evidence on this point. Elliot Aronson and his colleagues asked college students to rate the attractiveness of four persons: a person of superior ability who blundered (by spilling coffee on his new suit), a person of mediocre ability who performed the same blunder, and persons of superior and mediocre ability who did not blunder. The two highly competent persons were rated as most attractive, the two mediocre persons as least attractive (Figure 18-1). Interestingly, the superior person who spilled coffee was rated as more attractive than the one who did not blunder, while the mediocre person who committed the same blunder was rated as least attractive of all.

It would be misleading to conclude that generally people prefer someone who blunders to someone who is competent. On the contrary, we tend to behave rationally and to prefer a competent individual to a mediocre one. The research on the effects of committing a blunder or taking a "pratfall" merely suggests that under

Figure 18-1
Superior People Can Afford to be Human

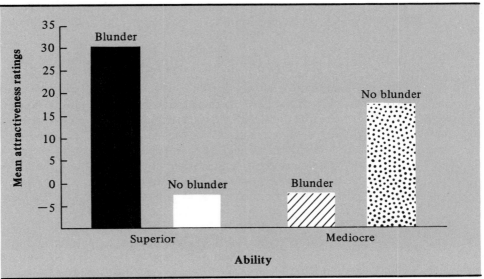

Aronson et al. (1966).

some special circumstances a competent person who is revealed to be capable of a blunder may seem more human and fallible and therefore may be seen as even more attractive. Aronson (1976) suggests that this increase in the attractiveness of a competent person who commits a blunder may occur especially when the perceiver feels an implicit threat of competition.

Similarity

People are likely to be drawn to those who seem similar to themselves. For example, at a party one tends to become interested in strangers who share one's ideas, values, and beliefs. The tendency of people to like others who are similar to themselves, and to like them better the more similar they are, is well documented in social psychology. We are attracted to people who seem similar to ourselves on dimensions that range from race and physical characteristics to intelligence and ability. It is similarity of attitude, however, that has been studied most extensively (Byrne, 1971).

Suppose that people are asked to rate the attractiveness of a stranger they have never met, a person represented only by his opinions on specific topics. The more similar these opinions are to the rater's, the greater the attraction. For example, in one study undergraduate couples participated in a computer-arranged dating program. The students gave more positive evaluations to potential dates whose responses to a personality attitude questionnaire were similar to their own (Byrne et al., 1970).

We also may tend to see the attitudes of those we already like as more similar to our own (e.g., Levinger & Breedlove, 1966). Under some circumstances, however, similarity breeds contempt. Female college students judging a peer who behaved pleasantly preferred her when they were led to believe that she was similar to them. But they disliked the similar person more when she behaved obnoxiously (e.g., by bragging) than did subjects who observed the same behavior from a person they believed to be dissimilar to them (Taylor & Mettee, 1971).

Reciprocity: We Like People Who Like Us

Generally, liking breeds liking. We like people who praise us, do nice things for us, and otherwise show their friendship and approval. However, it is important to believe that the signs of liking are honest and genuinely motivated rather than mere flattery or manipulation. Unrealistic and extreme compliments or expressions of liking clearly motivated by manipulative intent tend to arouse suspicion. Flattery will get you somewhere if it occurs in an area about which a person is uncertain or lacks confidence (Walster, 1965). For example, if you compliment an accomplished athlete on his social skills rather than on his obvious athletic prowess, he may be more inclined to like you (Jones, 1964).

The sequence through which we discover how another person feels about us can also be important. Consider, for example, a pattern in which you find that your roommate's liking for you remains at an even level, say six on a liking scale ranging from a low of one to a high of ten. Compare this with a sequence in which your roommate liked you only at a level of five when you first met but gradually came to rate you at a level of seven as your relationship developed, thus averaging out at six, just as in the first case. If you are like most people, you will prefer the roommate who esteems you more as time goes on, even though the average amount of gratification is the same (Aronson, 1976). The gain in liking may serve as a boost to one's self-esteem. But the gain must be gradual rather than abrupt to avoid the suspicion of insincerity. A good way to insure that someone will feel rejected and therefore dislike you is to react positively to them at first and then express increasingly negative feelings.

AGGRESSION

A glance at the front page of any newspaper documents that individuals, as well as groups and nations, all too often engage in aggression and violence that takes many forms, often with a tragic human price. Conversely, people are capable of helping each other in positive ways through altruistic behaviors. Aggression—and its psychological opposite, altruism (helping)—illustrate vividly both the influences that shape important social behaviors and the influence that those behaviors, in turn, exert on other people in the course of social life. Our look, first at aggression and then at altruism, will reveal that these seemingly opposite patterns actually depend on basically similar social-influence processes.

Defining Aggression

A businessman systematically forces his competitor out of business; a rejected lover strangles his girlfriend; an angry adolescent insults her mother; a soldier massacres innocent civilians; a little girl pinches her younger brother; a young woman shoplifts. Behaviors like these, in spite of their diversity, might all be considered instances of aggression. What is the underlying theme, the essence of aggression? Although aggressive behaviors may take many forms (physical assault, verbal abuse, a wordless snub), they share a common outcome—they all harm or injure another person. Often (but not always) aggressive behavior seems to be intentionally aimed at harming another. Unfortunately, such intentions may be hard to judge reliably, even in a court of law. For example, while the victim of the businessman may be sure that he was driven into bankruptcy by his competitor's mean, evil intentions, the one who won the struggle may see his actions as motivated by a commitment to his own family's financial needs and free enterprise. Nevertheless, there is usually little doubt in recognizing gross aggression. When people are robbed or beaten or raped or napalmed, the aggressive meaning of the action is obvious from its consequences.

In our society many types of aggression are not only allowed but actively encouraged. Aggressiveness in business, in sports, and even in some social relations is positively valued by many of us and even rewarded. But the same people who approve such socially acceptable forms of aggression share a fear and horror of being victimized by criminals. Physical assault is especially terrifying because it seems so unpredictable, uncontrollable and leaves one with a sense of helplessness, the potential victim of vandals, muggers, or terrorists. Consequently, even though the chances of being harmed or killed by a criminal are far less than those from driving an automobile, there is much greater concern with "crime in the streets" than with traffic safety. Because of its harmful, destructive impact on individuals and society, hurtful aggression is an especially important topic in psychology and has received much attention. First we will consider the Freudian view of aggression, then we will examine some alternative conceptions and research especially relevant for personality.

Inhibition and Anxiety

The Freudian conception of aggression was developed by Dollard and Miller (1950). Like Freud, they believed many socialization practices really teach children to fear their own angry feelings. They say (1950, p. 148): "We assume . . . that anger responses are produced by the innumerable and unavoidable frustration situations of child life. . . . Society takes a special stand toward such anger responses, generally inhibiting them and allowing them reign only in a few circumstances (self-defense, war, etc.)."

Again like Freud, Dollard and Miller believed that problems in development to a large extent are caused by punishment for aggression, which leads the person to become anxious about angry feelings. They comment (1950, p. 148): "Parents intuitively resent and fear the anger and rage of a child, and they have the support of the culture in suppressing its anger." Guided by the psychodynamic belief that unacceptable angry feelings are repressed but may return in disguised form as symptoms, they wrote (1950, p. 148): "Lift the veil of repression covering the childhood mental life of a neurotic person and you come at once upon the smoking responses of anger."

Conflict and Indirect Aggression

What happens to aggression when its expression is prevented? The answer partly depends on how aggression is conceptualized. Is aggression a drive-like natural impulse provoked by frustration? Or is it a learned but not inevitable response? First, consider aggression as a basic impulse or drive, as conceptualized both by psychodynamic theory and by Dollard and Miller (1950). This conceptualization was introduced in Chapter 15 but is examined here more fully.

Dollard and Miller hypothesized that frustration triggers the aggressive drive. They believed that aggression is the natural impulsive response to frustration. Often, however, it cannot be expressed directly against the perceived source of frustration. Blocking or inhibition may be caused by objective danger (such as realistic fear of retaliation). Or blocking may be due to anxiety about the expression of aggression. As a result, the individual becomes conflicted and experiences an approach-avoidance conflict between wanting to vent aggression and anxiety about the consequences of aggressiveness. To reduce this conflict, he or she may try to inhibit aggressive impulses.

Although the expression of aggressiveness may be inhibited, the impulse to aggress remains and presses for discharge in one form or another. According to psychodynamic theory, unexpressed impulses become "pent up" and must be released. Freud thought that impulses that are not discharged may gradually "build up" to the point where they lead to an explosive outburst. When direct expression and discharge are blocked, the drive may manifest itself indirectly in many forms.

Figure 18-2 shows some of these theoretical possibilities schematically. This scheme is suggested both by Freud's ideas on the nature of impulses and their

Figure 18-2
The Frustration-Aggression Hypothesis and Its Elaborations

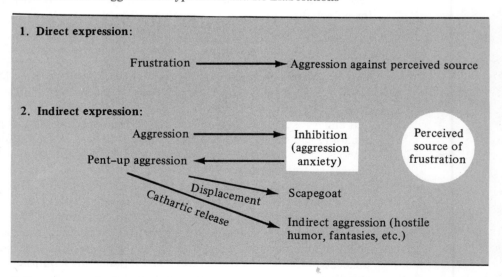

Frustration produces aggression: the aggressive impulse then is expressed directly or indirectly (e.g., through displacement). The form of expression depends on learned inhibitions and defenses.

transformation, and by Dollard and Miller's concepts concerning frustration-aggression. As the figure shows, aggressive impulses are triggered by frustration. When their direct discharge is blocked, they may be released indirectly through *displacement* to less threatening objects or by *catharsis.*

Displacement

Consider this example of displacement from Dollard and Miller (1950, pp. 432–433). George, a fourteen-year-old boy, had an arrangement with another boy for a Saturday outing to the country and planned the holiday carefully. On the morning of the trip the friend's mother called to say her son had a cold and could not go. Deeply disappointed, George pretended to his friend's mother that he accepted the circumstances and "he suppressed his anger since he had learned it was no use fighting the inevitable (p. 433)."

Later George started to play in his backyard where he happened to meet his twelve-year-old sister. As usual, she teased him a little, but this time George flared up, struck her, and the two wound up in an intense quarrel that their mother had to terminate. Dollard and Miller interpret this case as an example of how anger and aggression are called forth as prepotent responses to frustration but are quickly suppressed because of prior inhibition learning. But, in their view, the aggressive drive is not eliminated but merely suppressed and rechanneled, and it emerges in displaced form in the boy's attack on his younger sister.

According to Dollard and Miller, displacement of aggression depends on several factors, including similarity between the cause of frustration and the available targets for aggression. Their drive theory of aggression suggests that aggression may be displaced from the real target to safer, less threatening "scapegoats" (such as subordinates at work).

Catharsis: Effects of Expressing Aggression

To help release pent-up aggressive impulses in nondestructive ways, some theorists have encouraged therapeutic expression or "catharsis" of angry feelings by direct or vicarious participation in mildly aggressive enactments (e.g., violent plays). In its most extreme form, this position may suggest that frustrated people must cathart or vent their aggressive impulses gradually. Otherwise civilization faces the prospect of extreme violent outbursts of war and killing when the pent-up impulses burst forth uncontrollably. Critics attack this theory as a "drainage" or "pus" view of aggression. They suggest that catharsis, rather than draining off aggressiveness, much as pus is drained out of a festering wound, actually may lead to more aggressive behavior (Bandura, 1973).

The issue of whether permissible expression of aggression actually has any cathartic effect is still not fully settled by research. For example, if an individual is highly aroused, aggressive fantasy may reduce violence by providing a distraction that enables the person to cool off before acting (Berkowitz, 1969). Under some circumstances the expression of angry or negative feelings, combined with a reinterpretation of the situation, may help reduce aggression (Geen & Murray, 1975). But several studies indicate that engaging in aggressive fantasy may result in increased open aggression. In one study children showed more inappropriate aggression after playing with aggressive toys than after playing with neutral toys (Feshbach, 1956). And recent studies on the effect of exposure to televised violence on children's aggressive behavior strongly indicate that children become more aggressive as a result of such exposure. In general, the observation of violence leads to more aggression (Geen, 1978).

If direct or vicarious participation in aggressive behavior does not reduce emotional arousal, what can help angered people to overcome their feelings? Physiological studies have helped to clarify the ways in which a person can regain tranquility without acting out his or her angry feelings. Physiological measures of arousal have been used to determine whether a particular response is effective for reducing arousal (e.g., Stone & Hokanson, 1969). These studies have demonstrated that a variety of responses to pain and frustration, including friendliness toward the aggressor, can help reduce emotional arousal if the person believes that they will help end the pain or discomfort.

In sum, if aggressive behavior serves to reduce or end pain or threat, it may also reduce arousal. But if individuals can successfully cope with the source of harm or frustration by some other means, then they do not have to behave aggressively in order to reduce their arousal.

Alternative Views of Aggression

The conceptualization of aggression as the natural, drive-like reaction to frustration recognizes the importance of learning in the expression of aggression. But this view of aggression sees it as a basic drive that builds up and hence requires release either directly or indirectly. In the same vein, the ethologist Konrad Lorenz (1966) proposed that aggression in humans and other animals is a fighting instinct that is naturally directed at members of the same species. In his view, humans lack the innate inhibitions against hurting members of their own species that other animals have and are therefore in an especially dangerous, potentially tragic condition. Like Freud, Lorenz believes that aggression is inevitable and should be encouraged in modified forms toward socially acceptable substitute targets to drain off the instinctual impulses. He favors international sports competitons as one such outlet for the socially acceptable expression of aggression.

In contrast, several current learning theorists generally conceptualize aggression as learned response patterns and do not assume either instinctual or drive-like properties for them (Bandura, 1973; Berkowitz, 1970). They view frustration as potentially leading to many alternative responses, depending on the individual and the specific situation.

Aggression as Learned

The view that aggression is a basic human instinct that builds up and must be expressed in one form or another is directly opposed by social learning theory. Indeed, according to Bandura (1973, 1977), there is little evidence to support the belief in an inborn agressive drive, and such a belief may be popular mostly because it relieves people of taking responsibility for behaving in inhuman ways toward each other. Instead of an instinct or drive that must be expressed, Bandura (1973) offers an explanation of aggression as socially learned behavior. According to social learning theory, aggression is acquired and regulated by the same processes that govern other forms of social behavior. In that view, the belief that frustration inevitably triggers aggression has proved unjustified. Often aggression does follow frustration but not always, and not necessarily: constructive reactions such as cooperation and problem solving can and do occur when people learn that they are appropriate responses to frustration.

Like other emotions, aggression is seen as involving a general state of arousal whose meaning and consequences depend on the person's cognitive appraisal (interpretation) and expectations in the particular situation. Depending on these considerations, the same arousal state could lead to attack, to cooperation, or to some other response. Moreover, different people react differently when distressed by emotional arousal.

> Some people seek help and support; others increase achievement strivings; others show withdrawal and resignation; some aggress. . . . Others anesthetize themselves against a miserable existence with drugs or alcohol. (Bandura, 1973, pp. 53–54)

In the social learning approach to aggression, one must again recall the distinction between the acquisition (learning) of responses and their performance. Throughout social development people are exposed to all kinds of information enabling them to acquire aggressive skills. For example, by watching aggressive models on television, on film, and in real life at home, at school, and in the community, children in our culture quickly learn a great deal about how to behave aggressively. They learn how to hurt and insult verbally as well as how to use knives, guns, and many other methods of injuring others. Whether or not they actually behave aggressively in particular situations, however, depends on the expected consequences for aggression compared to the consequences for other possible actions in that specific context.

Any condition that increases the individual's expectation that aggression will be an appropriate response—that it will achieve desired results and pay off—increases the likelihood that the individual will perform an aggressive act. For example, cues indicating that aggressiveness will be rewarded (rather than punished or unrewarded) tend to encourage observers to behave aggressively. It also follows that any conditions that make aggression more difficult for the aggressor—for example, by leading him or her to feel sympathy for the victim—will reduce the likelihood of aggression. Some of the conditions that influence the occurrence of aggression are summarized in Table 18-1.

Table 18-1
Examples of Conditions That Enhance Aggression

Aggression Is Increased by	Research Source
Being attacked (insulted) by a nonpowerful aggressor (rather than by a powerful one)	Thibaut & Riecken (1955)
Watching aggressive models rewarded	Bandura, Ross, & Ross (1963)
Anonymity	Zimbardo (1969)
Distance from victim	Milgram (1965, 1974)

A

B

Milgram's experimental situation: *A.* The shock- generating machine. *B.* A "victim" being strapped down. *C.* The experimenter urges subject to continue shocking the victim. *D.* A subject refuses to obey further.

In Focus 18.1 Testing the Limits of Human Aggression: The Milgram Experiments

Imagine that you are participating in a learning experiment supposedly designed to test the effects of punishment on memory. The learner is in an adjoining room strapped into a chair with electrodes fastened to his wrists. He pushes a button to give his answers and you, the teacher, are instructed to give him a shock for every wrong answer. You are given a sample shock and are told that although the shocks may become extremely painful, they can cause no tissue damage. The shock generator has thirty voltage levels ranging from 15 to 450 volts and divided into eight descriptive categories, such as slight shock and very strong shock. The last two categories are labeled "danger: severe shock" and simply "XXX."

The experimenter has you begin with 15 volts and instructs you to increase the shock intensity by one level for each successive wrong response. As the experiment continues, you will be asked to administer shocks to the learner up to and including the XXX level. When the level reaches 300 volts, the learner pounds on the wall between you and the chair in which he is strapped. Now he no longer pushes the button to give his answers. At the 315-volt level he again pounds on the wall and then remains

silent. If you refuse to continue shocking him, the experimenter says:

1. "Please continue" or "Please go on."
2. "The experiment requires that you continue."
3. "It is absolutely essential that you continue."
4. "You have no other choice; you *must* go on."

What would you do? After describing the study in detail, Stanley Milgram asked a group of subjects this question. Each and every one of them said that at some point they would disobey the commands of the experimenter to deliver increasing amounts of shock. Often they gave moral reasons for their predicted disobedience, as did the person who said, "I do not think any experiment is worth inflicting strong shock on another human being. . . . I could not be the one to inflict . . . pain" (Milgram, 1974, p. 28).

In actual tests, however, when subjects were confronted with the demands in the situation described above, not a single one stopped before administering 300 volts and well over half went on until they reached the most potent shock available, two steps above the category labeled

C

D

"danger: severe shock." Although 35 percent of the subjects defied the experimenter at some point, the remaining 65 percent obeyed the orders to the end. In a pretest in which the victim made no objections (not banging on the wall or crying out in pain) all subjects, once commanded, went to the maximum shock level without hesitation. Protests from the victims were necessary to produce even a single instance of disobedience, and many subjects administered the maximum punishment ordered, even in the face of strong protests from the victims. Of course, the subjects believed that the shocks were actually being administered, although the victim was really a confederate who worked with the experimenter and received no shocks.

Thus far we have described the objective findings and methods. But the Milgram experiments also have had a tremendous emotional impact, not just on psychology but on society itself. (Indeed, the experiments became the basis of a nationally televised drama.) Reactions in the media and in the social sciences have ranged from disbelief that normal people would really follow orders to the point where they thought they were seriously injuring and even killing someone, to

outrage at the researchers for tricking subjects into engaging in such Nazi-like behavior to such an extreme degree.

How must the subjects have felt when they realized the implications of what they had done? How did they live with themselves knowing that they went to the brink of electrocuting an innocent victim just because an authority figure told them to? While some critics have been mostly angry at the researchers and the ethics of submitting subjects to such severe conflicts in a psychological experiment, the results are undeniable and raise deeply disturbing questions about human nature and the potential for mindless obedience on demand. Most of us feel that what happened in Nazi Germany, or in the massacres of innocent people throughout history, was perpetrated by cruel and peculiar twisted characters with whom we cannot identify personally— surely we are incapable of such atrocities. The Milgram studies can be criticized, but they cannot be dismissed: they testify that ordinary, normal human beings can become torturers and killers under conditions created with remarkable ease.

While many of the consequences that we expect come from outside circumstances, we also regulate our own actions through self-evaluation and self-administered consequences. Even in the absence of a policeman or any chance of detection, people may refuse to steal or vandalize because it would violate their own standards and lead them to condemn themselves.

To try to explain why aggression is so frequent in human conduct and to explore its possible reduction, Buss (1971, p. 17) theorized:

> There is a huge payoff for aggression in terms of money, prestige, and status. The scope of the problem is tremendous, but it is a small task to list the solutions. We need to realign our economy and law enforcement procedures so that criminal aggression does not pay, alter our national myths from war loving to peace loving attitudes, and revise our masculine role to exclude aggressiveness.

Much research has shown that aggression, like other social behaviors, is responsive to social influence and may increase or decrease predictably as social conditions change (see *In Focus 18.1*). In this section we will consider the most important social influences that produce aggression.

Resisting the Pressures to Aggress

The grim realities of the Milgram results *(In Focus 18.1)* may be counteracted in part when people realize that they—and not some external authority who gives the orders—have ultimate moral and personal responsibility for their own actions. The less responsible one is, the easier it may be to victimize that individual callously. Some support for these expectations may be found in Milgram's own studies. For example, when choice of shock level was left to the subject, the majority delivered the very lowest shock.

Table 18-2 lists some conditions that reduced obedience in the Milgram situation. The closer the victim, the less obedience. While only 35 percent defied the experimenter when the victim pounded on the wall and 37.5 percent did so when

Table 18-2
Some Conditions Reducing Obedience to Commands That Demand Aggression

Choice of aggression level (shock level) left to subject

Feedback, protestations from the victim (banging on the wall, cries of pain)

Proximity of the victim

Status of the victim. Compliance decreases if the victim's status is higher than that of the authority

Disagreement among authorities of equal status

Presence of defiant supporters: two peers of the subject who (by previous instruction) disobey

SOURCE: Based on data from Milgram, 1974.

the victim's verbal complaints could be heard clearly through the wall, the percentage of defiers jumped to 60 percent when the victim was in the same room with them and was visible as well as audible. And 70 percent defied when they had to place the victim's hand forcibly on the shock plate to deliver punishments at or beyond the 150-volt level. When they were only accessories to the act of shocking, and a confederate was the one who administered the shock, only three out of forty subjects defied at some point. The rest went all the way.

The Modeling of Aggression

In 1973, two days after the airing of *Fuzz,* a television movie, six young men in Boston beat a twenty-five-year-old woman until she agreed to douse herself with gasoline. She was left in flames and died within hours. In Miami a few weeks later, teenagers drenched three derelicts with lighter fluid and set them on fire. In both cases the attackers admitted that they had enacted a scene from the movie they had watched on television.

In 1974 three California girls, ranging in age from ten to fifteen years, brutally attacked a nine-year-old girl on the beach and assaulted her sexually with a soda bottle. Filing suit against the television network that had aired *Born Innocent,* the victim's attorney noted that two of the three atackers had seen the show four days earlier. It depicted a similar incident and, according to the girls, had influenced them.

On November 24, 1971, a commercial airliner with thirty-six passengers was hijacked by a young man. Claiming that his briefcase contained a bomb, he demanded and received $200,000 in cash and then parachuted from the plane to escape with his loot. Soon afterward there were fifteen attempted skyjackings in which the skyjackers demanded parachutes as well as cash.

Often modeling effects are not completely imitative, and the observers create variations on a theme. For example, in a 1976 television episode of *The Blue Knight* police serial, a gang of bandits used a bazooka mounted on the back of a white van to try to hijack an armored car loaded with cash. Shortly thereafter in Montreal, real-life criminals modified the script, successfully hijacking a Brink's armored car but with the aid of an antiaircraft gun, also mounted on the back of a white van.

Documented cases of the contagion of televised violence, although fairly rare, occur with alarming regularity over time (Bandura, 1973). In recent years there have been numerous commissions, a Surgeon General's Report (as reported in Murray et al., 1972), and half a dozen Senate and House hearings all indicating that exposure to televised violence increases aggressive behavior. Violence between cartoon characters may have similarly negative effects on children and typically occurs at the rate of one violent incident per minute in standard children's fare.

A great deal of experimental research confirms the informal observation of a close link between viewing televised aggression and behaving more aggressively (Geen, 1978). For example, children who regularly watched violent cartoons for a specified time each day became more assaultive toward their peers than did children who watched a comparable number of nonviolent cartoons (Steuer, Applefield, & Smith, 1971). The same general finding of negative effects from exposure

Figure 18-3
Average Intensity of Shocks Administered by Subjects as a Function of Diffusion of Their Responsibility and Dehumanization of the Victims

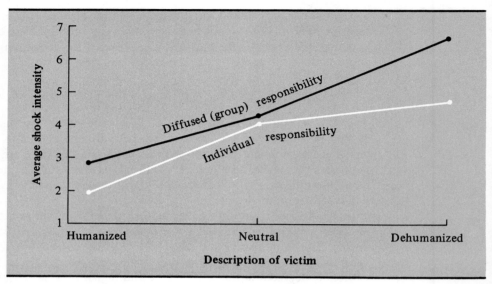

From Bandura et al. (1975).

to televised violence of various types has been obtained repeatedly (e.g., Bandura, 1973; Liebert, 1972; Murray, 1973), but this has had little impact on the policies of television networks.

Diffusion of Responsibility and Dehumanization

Aggression is likely to become especially intense when there is diffusion of responsibility and dehumanization of the victim. In one study, groups of three male college students were asked to supervise a team of decision makers supposedly working in a nearby room. As supervisors, the subjects were instructed to deliver electric shocks to the decision makers whenever they proposed an inadequate solution to a bargaining problem (Bandura, Underwood, & Fromson, 1975). The adequacy of the solution was indicated by a light, and the subjects were free to administer the shock in any of ten intensity levels from mild to painful. In fact, there were no decision makers and no shocks were actually delivered, just as in the previously discussed Milgram experiments.

Subjects were divided into two groups, individual responsibility and diffused responsibility. In the individual responsibility condition each subject was assigned to one person on the decision-making team and personally determined the shock level delivered. In the diffused responsibility condition, subjects were told that the levels of shock they selected were automatically averaged and that the average level was the one delivered to all the members of the decision-making team.

In addition, subjects in each responsibility condition overheard the decision makers characterized in one of three ways. In the humanized condition the victims were called "perceptive and understanding people"; in the dehumanized condition they were described as an "animalistic, rotten bunch"; and in the neutral condition nonevaluative references were made.

The results showed that dehumanization of the victims was the strongest determinant of aggression. Dehumanized victims—those who had been labeled as rotten animals—were punished more than twice as severely as humanized victims and considerably more severely than the neutral, unevaluated group. This pattern was found in both the diffused and individual responsibility conditions. Also as expected, more intense shock was given when responsibility was diffuse than when it was individual (see Figure 18-3).

After the experimental procedures, subjects answered questions about their reactions. When the victims had been divested of humanity, subjects often made self-absolving justifications and rarely condemned the punishment they had administered. They emphasized the benefits of punishment, saying, "It gets more efficiency out of the group," and absolved themselves of personal guilt: "As an acting supervisor it was my job to punish poor performance. . . . If doing my job as a supervisor means I must be a son of a bitch, so be it" (p. 261). In contrast, when the victim was humanized and the subject had personal (individual) responsibility, he would tend to say such things as, "Morally and ethically, I couldn't give a painful punishment."

In closely related research, Zimbardo (1969) investigated a special feature of diffused responsibility and dehumanization. He studied women in four-person groups. In some groups the women wore name tags and referred to each other by name. In other groups the subjects were "deindividuated"—they wore concealing gowns and hoods and remained nameless throughout the procedure (see photo).

Deindividuation increases aggression. When individuals wore gowns and hoods and were never called by name they delivered longer electric shocks than they did when their personal identities were known to the other members of the group.

When induced to give shocks to ostensible victims (actually confederates of the experimenter) visible through a one-way mirror, the deindividuated groups administered longer electric shocks than did groups whose members knew each other's real identities.

Self-Justification

People generally try to make their actions appear reasonable and appropriate, both to themselves and to others. Consider, for example, a college student who, serving as a subject in Milgram's aggression experiment, was ordered to administer electric shock to others. It is safe to assume that like everyone else the student wanted to do the right thing, to be a good, decent, sensible human being who could respect himself. If asked before participating in the experiment to predict what he would do in a similar situation, he would surely have said that it was wrong to hurt and endanger another human being and that he would not punish someone cruelly just because he was requested to. Yet, like most others, the student would probably administer severe electric shocks—during the experiment. How could he reconcile this discrepancy?

It is a familiar fact that people trying to justify themselves will rationalize even the most atrocious actions. As Hitler's henchmen often said about their participation in the systematic extermination of people in concentration camps, "I had to do my duty." Common variations on the same theme of self-justification include the use of moralistic labels and reasons (patriotism, honor, destiny, higher principles of justice) to excuse atrocious deeds by relabeling them and attributing them to the highest motives (Bandura, 1973). People also find ingenious ways to diffuse personal responsibility and to put the blame elsewhere so that they may continue to appear good and reasonable regardless of what they did.

Summary: Increasing Aggression

In sum, aggression—like other social behaviors—tends to increase when observers watch aggressive models, either directly in their own lives or through such media as television. When aggression is rewarded in society, either directly or vicariously, as when aggressive models become heroes, it becomes even more likely. Diffusing the responsibility for aggression also makes it much easier to aggress ("I'm just a cog in the machine"). And those who practice even extreme, cruel forms of aggression are likely to relabel their deeds ("I did what I had to") and to rationalize and moralize their acts to justify them.

ALTRUISM AND RESPONSIBILITY

Suppose that subjects are participating in an experiment, seated in separate booths, carrying on a conversation through an intercom system. One of the subjects is really a confederate of the experimenter and is the first to speak. He mentions that he is prone to seizures, begins to stammer, indicates one of his seizures is starting, and asks for help. The last sounds to be heard from him on the intercom are "I'm gonna die . . . er . . . er . . . er I'm . . . gonna die . . . er . . . er . . . [seizure] . . . er . . . [choke, then quiet]." When this experiment was actually conducted (Darley &

Latané, 1968), not one of the fifteen subjects responded to the confederates first request for help, only four came out of their booths when the choking occurred, and six never left their booths. Such seemingly inhuman apathy is not confined to the laboratory. Some years ago an event in New York gained national attention: thirty-eight neighbors heard Kitty Genovese's screams in the night and remained at their windows for half an hour as the young woman was slowly stabbed to death. Not one person helped, not even by telephoning the police. This incident was widely discussed, not because it was exceptional but because it seemed to symbolize much of the indifference to people that seems to characterize urban life. Moved by such incidents, social psychologists have begun to explore the reasons for them. They have been especially eager to discover the social conditions that might influence people to behave more altruistically. In contrast to aggressive behavior—that which is hurtful in intent and outcome—altruisticbehavior is helpful. It appears to be motivated by the desire to help even at some cost to the helper. Altruism, like other social behaviors, is influenced by many considerations and depends on the particular situation as well as on the person.

Increasing Altruism

Consider the following experiment. Subjects volunteer for a psychologicalstudy in which the experimenter, an attractive young woman, gives them a questionnaire to complete and then goes to an adjoining room. They hear the noise of a fall and her screams: "Oh, my God, my foot . . . I . . . I can't move . . . it. Oh . . . my ankle; I

Whether a bystander shows apathy or helpfulness partly depends on the number of bystanders.

. . . can't get this . . . thing . . . off me.'' After about a minute her pleas gradually fade out. Will they help? The answer depends in part on whether or not the subject is alone. When others are present, there is a diffusion of responsibility, and helping becomes less likely than when there is only one bystander and personal responsibility cannot be avoided. In the case of the moaning experimenter (who, of course, was simply following a script) 70 percent of those who were alone offered help, but only 40 percent of those who had a stranger as a partner acted to help (Latané & Rodin, 1969). In the same study, when subjects waited with a confederate of the experimenter who responded passively to the fall (shrugging his shoulders, for example, and continuing to work on the questionnaire), only 7 percent intervened to help. Other studies also support the view that bystander intervention in emergencies is less likely or slower when responsibility is diffused by an increase in the number of other people in the situation (e.g., Latané & Darley, 1968).

Note that the finding of decreased helping when there is a diffusion of responsibility is entirely consistent with the previously discussed conclusion that aggression increases when responsibility is diffused. That is, people are more likely to behave in cruel, unfeeling ways—aggressing more and helping less—in situations that free them of personal responsibility and dehumanize them or the people around them. Conversely, conditions that create face-to-face, humanizing contacts, reduce distance, and increase empathy and concern for the victim's welfare encourage one to be helpful (Staub, 1978).

Taken as a whole, the research on aggression and altruism provides a consistent picture: aggression and callousness blossom when individual responsibility is reduced and people are dehumanized or distanced from each other in ways that reduce empathy and concern for the welfare of the other person. The opposite conditions, responsibility and empathy, are likely to encourage altruism and enhance humane, moral conduct.

Morality and Personal Responsibility

In pursuing our goals and objectives we often face moral dilemmas and choices, as when our desires conflict with the welfare of others. The coping process involves not only increasing our control, but also facing and solving moral problems, coping with questions of right and wrong, fairness and justice.

Morality is one of the most enduring of human concerns. Gloomy warnings about the spread of moral decay seem to be confirmed by a glance at world affairs. Even if one does not think the holocaust is at hand, modern life is obviously full of violence; wars, intrigues, and corruption flourish throughout the world. Blatantly immoral behavior of all sorts, including murder, mass or individual, and every other conceivable kind of inhumane action are so commonplace that every child inevitably encounters them, at least on television. Given the importance of moral conduct for human affairs and society, the topic is an urgent one for the attention of psychologists concerned with the quality of personal development.

Moral Stages

One important approach to moral development is rooted in Piaget's theory of stages. Piaget described moral judgment and reasoning as developing through a succession of stages and changes in how the child organizes thoughts and perceptions of the social and moral order in which he or she lives.

According to Piaget (1932) the first of two clear-cut stages of moral judgment is defined as the stage of *objective responsibility*. In this stage children judge the gravity of a bad act in terms of the material damages it causes—that is, its consequences—regardless of what the guilty person intended. In the second stage, conduct is judged in terms of the person's intent rather than the material consequences of the conduct. This higher stage is defined as the *subjective responsibility* stage.

Influenced by Piaget but going far beyond him, Lawrence Kohlberg has proposed a more elaborate theory of moral development. According to Kohlberg (1969), six moral stages follow one another in an invariant and universal sequence. Each stage reflects increasing maturity in moral reasoning and depends on the one that precedes it (see Table 18-3). To assess a person's stage, Kohlberg has devel-

Table 18-3
Kohlberg's Six Moral Stages

Level I: Premoral	Stage 1: Orientation toward punishment and obedience. Deference to superior power. Goodness or badness is determined by the physical consequences of action.
	Stage 2: Right actions are those that satisfy needs (mainly one's own). People share but in a pragmatic way, not out of a sense of justice or loyalty.
Level II: Conventional	Stage 3: Good boy-nice girl orientation. Emphasis on conformity and on being "nice" to gain approval. Behavior that pleases or helps others and is approved by them is good behavior.
	Stage 4: Law-and-order orientation. Focus on authority, fixed rules, and the social order. Right behavior consists of maintaining the given social order for its own sake. Respect is earned by performing dutifully.
Level III: Postconventional	Stage 5: Social-contract legalistic orientation. Standards that have been agreed upon by the whole society define right action. Emphasis upon procedural (legal) rules for reaching consensus.
	Stage 6: Emphasis on decisions of conscience and self-chosen, abstract ethical principles that are logical, comprehensive, universal, and consistent. These abstract ethical principles are universal principles of justice, of equality of human rights, and of respect for the dignity of human beings as individuals.

SOURCE: Based on Kohlberg, 1969.

oped a system of scoring responses to hypothetical moral dilemmas such as this one:

> In Europe, a woman was near death from a very bad disease, a special kind of cancer. There was one drug that the doctors thought might save her. It was a form of radium that a druggist in the same town had recently discovered. The drug was expensive to make, but the druggist was charging ten times what the drug cost him to make. He paid $200 for the radium and charged $2,000 for a small dose of the drug. The sick woman's husband, Heinz, went to everyone he knew to borrow the money, but he could only get together about $1,000, which is half of what it cost. He told the druggist that his wife was dying, and asked him to sell it cheaper or let him pay later. But the druggist said, "No, I discovered the drug and I'm going to make money from it." So Heinz got desperate and broke into the man's store to steal the drug for his wife.
>
> Should the husband have done this? Why?

Here are some possible responses to this story that illustrate the six stages of moral development:

> Stage 1: He shouldn't steal because he might get caught and be put in jail.
>
> Stage 2: He needs his wife. He could get a new wife, but he'd still miss his old wife.
>
> Stage 3: Maybe they have children and the children need their mother. It would be wrong to let her die.
>
> Stage 4: God says: "Thou shalt not kill," and the druggist is killing the woman if he won't give the man the medicine for $1,000. He's still making a profit.
>
> Stage 5: It's wrong to steal, but the woman has the right to live. Heinz should complain to the authorities so they can settle the case.
>
> Stage 6: A person's life is more important than any other legal value. Heinz has the right to take the drug to save his wife's life—or any other person's life.

Critique of Moral Stages

Theories of moral stages have stimulated much interest and considerable supportive research but they have not gone unchallenged. One challenge has come from evidence that shows a person's stage of moral reasoning is modifiable when the person is exposed to relevant social learning experience (see *In Focus 18.2*).

Questioning the assumption of Piaget's theory of moral stages, Bandura and McDonald (1963) attempted to show that the moral judgments of children ranging in age from five to eleven years may be modified by exposure to models. Story situations based on Piaget (1932) were used to assess the children's level of moral judgment. The stories were presented in pairs, each of which described a well-intentioned act that resulted in considerable material damage and a selfishly or maliciously motivated act that produced minor consequences. The children were asked to judge who (which actor in each pair of stories) did the naughtier thing. They were then asked to explain their choices, and their answers were scored as to whether they were based on intent or on consequences.

On the basis of their initial pretest performance on a set of these stories, children who usually responded with moral judgments based on the magnitude of negative consequences (objective moral orientation) were placed in one group and children who usually responded with judgments based on intent (subjective moral orientation) in another. The experimental treatments consisted of combinations of modeling and reinforcement (of model, child, or both) of moral judgments at the level other than the one the child had shown in the pretest. For example, children who had responded primarily on the basis of an objective moral orientation were exposed to models reinforced for expressing a subjective moral orientation, and vice versa.

On a later test conducted in a new situation (in which the adult models were absent), the children displayed significant shifts from their initial dominant moral level. As a result of the modeling treatments (with or without reinforcement to the child), children belonging to the objective moral orientation group moved significantly to answers based on a subjective moral orientation, and those initially responding on the basis of a subjective moral orientation changed in the other direction. A more recent study using juvenile delinquents as the subjects has provided additional evidence of this modifiability, even when older children are the subjects (Prentice, 1972).

Acknowledging that learning experiences may have some effect, advocates of moral stage theory still believe that the nature and degree of such modifications are limited by the individual's particular stage position. For example, they believe that a person is more likely to move up only one step above his present level than to jump up several stages. So far, the existence of an inevitable sequence of moral stages remains an important but controversial proposition.

A second challenge to a moral stage theory comes from the fact that a person typically displays moral reasoning at several levels, not just at one stage. As Kohlberg himself reports (1969, p. 387), on the average somewhat less than 50 percent of a subject's moral judgments fit a single stage; the remainder show reasoning at stages both above and below the one to which the subject has been assigned. Among college students, "not one of the subjects studied employed moral reasoning that was exclusively rated at any single level of development" (Fishkin, Keniston, & MacKinnon, 1973, p. 114).

Finally, the applicability of Kohlberg's moral-stage views to women has been questioned intensely. In her book *In A Different Voice,* Carol Gilligan (1982) notes that men define and value themselves mostly in terms of success and autonomy. Women, however, define their identity through close relationships with people. They value themselves in terms of their ability to care and their role is that of nurturer, caretaker, and helpmate to men. Gilligan argues that while the men have been cared for by women, in the economic arrangements that they control they either assume or devalue that care. She also makes a case that in their psychological theories, including Kohlberg's (1969) moral theory, men reduce (to a lower stage) the value of the care and nurturance that women provide.

While the theory of moral stages is provocative, much more research will be needed before a final verdict can be reached about its value for the prediction and modification of moral conduct. The problem is likely to remain hotly debated— and intensively studied—for many years.

The main current alternative to the stage approach to moral development is the social learning view. Advocates of the social learning view argue that rather than acquiring a general conscience that governs all aspects of their self-control, people tend to develop subtler and subtler discriminations. If this view is correct, moral action depends on many variables, including the specific situation. The same individual who espouses high moral principles also may engage in harmful, aggressive actions against others who violate his conceptions of justice.

Social Learning View of Moral Development

A social learning view of morality begins with the concept of moral competence, which is the capacity to generate moral behavior (Mischel & Mischel, 1976). Moral competence includes the ability to reason about moral dilemmas (e.g., in the ways measured by Kohlberg). It also includes empathy skills and the ability to take account of the long-term consequences of different courses of action as they affect other people. While individuals certainly differ in their degree of moral competence, each one may also display much variation in both moral reasoning and moral conduct. In the social learning view such variety within the individual, as well as the differences between individuals, reflects the unique social learning history that each person has experienced and the situational considerations that are relevant at the moment to determine performance.

From Moral Competence to Moral Conduct

People who know how to behave competently in prosocial, constructive ways are capable of such behaviors, but whether or not they enact them at any given time (or choose, instead, less virtuous courses of action) depends on specific motivational and performance considerations in the particular psychological situation. The same person who is capable of the most virtuous moral conduct also may be capable of morally despicable action.

To predict specifically what people will do in a particular situation, a social

Moral Action and Self-Control: Becoming Responsible

Tests of moral maturity—that is, of moral reasoning—have usually consisted of asking how the individual would solve hypothetical moral dilemmas in stories. In real life, however, the successful realization of moral choices often depends on meeting long-term commitments that demand effective self-control and attention to the remote consequences of one's actions. Moral conduct requires one to honor one's commitments and obligations behaviorally, even (or especially) under difficult conditions, and not merely to endorse them in principle. Such prolonged self-control sequences may be helped by mature reasoning and judgment about justice. But they also depend on the ability to regulate one's own behavior even in the face of strong temptations and situational pressures for long periods and without the aid of any obvious or immediate external rewards and supports. Thus self-control is an important part of morality, for without it we cannot realize our moral ideals. Indeed, some philosophers suggest that all virtues are forms of self-control (Von Wright, 1963): to go from moral thought to moral conduct we must have self-control.

learning analysis of moral conduct considers their specific expectancies about the consequences of different behavioral possibilities in that situation and how they value those consequences. It is assumed that even the noblest altruism supported by the highest level of moral reasoning still depends on expected consequences, although the consequences may be far in the future and difficult even to identify clearly.

The behavior of young children may depend mainly on the immediate, concrete consequences they expect, but with greater maturity the evaluation and reinforcement of behaviors become increasingly free of immediate external rewards and punishments and start to include self-reactions and temporally distant and abstract considerations. This is not to say that the behavior no longer depends on expected consequences, but only that those consequences increasingly hinge on self-evaluations, on self-administered outcomes contingent upon achieving or violating one's own standards, and on more abstract, temporally distant consequences. An individual who says, for example, that a particular action is wrong because it violates universal standards of justice, or because it goes against his or her conscience, is still considering the consequences of the act but is evaluating them in more abstract terms that go beyond the immediate, externally administered outcomes for that individual and that take account of a long temporal span (e.g., Rachlin, 1973).

Critique of Social Learning View

The social learning view of moral development also has been criticized often and sharply. In its earlier versions it was charged with being too specific, mechanistic, and indifferent to cognitive activity. In more recent versions it has become more cognitively oriented and has even been called a cognitive-social learning approach (Mischel & Mischel, 1976). Nevertheless, it is still criticized by stage theorists for not taking enough account of stages in cognitive development and for overemphasizing situational, momentary factors that influence specific conduct rather than consistencies in moral thought.

Understandably, parents and educators are eager to know how to strengthen concern for others and altruistic behavior in the young. Responsible, helpful behavior can be encouraged by a wide variety of experiences, such as empathetic role playing, exchanging roles with others, and reasoning (e.g., Staub, 1978). For example, parents might say to their child, "When you forget to feed your pet, he will get hungry during the night" or "If you throw snow on their driveway, they will have to clean it up again." Experiences of this type help sensitize us to the consequences of our behavior for other people and not merely for ourselves. Not surprisingly, children learn concern for others most when they are given more than moral advice. Cross-cultural research suggests children's altruistic and helpful (rather than egoistic and selfish) tendencies may depend largely on the degree to which they are actually responsible for the maintenance of the family's welfare.

Children tend to be more altruistic when the culture requires them to assume more responsibilites, such as caring for younger siblings, animals, and other interpersonal obligations (Whiting & Whiting, 1969). Increasing responsibility for the welfare of others tends to generate increased altruism and helpfulness. Just as aggression feeds on aggression (e.g., Berkowitz, 1973), the development of responsible behavior and concern for others depends on positive experiences with mutual helpfulness and on exposure to models who value and communicate consideration and responsibility (e.g., Hoffman, 1975).

SUMMARY

1. We tend to like people who are physically attractive, competent, and similar to us and who sincerely reciprocate our liking. People who are competent tend to be perceived as more attractive, but under some circumstances some individuals may find a competent person who commits a blunder even more attractive. Generally, people tend to like others who are similar to them, but perceived similarity may make negatively evaluated behavior (such as bragging) seem even worse. Physical attractiveness strongly influences how a person is judged. Whether or not someone perceives you as attractive can even affect your behavior toward the perceiver.

2. Aggression is an innate instinct according to Freud, who believed that it can be redirected and modified so as to be expressed in acceptable ways but never blocked completely. Later theorists (Dollard and Miller) saw aggression as a natural drive response to frustration. In their view, when fear or anxiety about the punishing consequences of aggression prevents direct expression, release may be obtained through displacement toward a less threatening target or through catharsis, as in fantasy expressions and sports competitions. The ethologist Konrad Lorenz shares the instinct view of aggression and suggests that humans, unlike other animals, lack innate inhibitions against hurting members of their own species. The instinct position is rejected by social learning theorists.

3. In social learning theory, frustration produces a general state of arousal whose meaning and effect depend on the person's interpretation and expectations in the particular situation. If aggressive behavior is modeled and rewarded, the individual will respond to frustration and other situations aggressively. If aggression is expected to have negative consequences, it becomes less likely. Unlike psychodynamic instinct theory, social learning theory predicts that attempts to reduce aggression by direct or vicarious expression (catharsis) will fail. In fact, catharsis seems to have unreliable effects and sometimes even increases aggression. The emotional arousal that often accompanies aggressive behavior may be reduced by any responses that terminate or decrease threat or pain, including friendliness toward the aggressor.

4. The Milgram experiments demonstrated that, surprisingly, a majority of subjects would inflict what they believed to be severe shock on human victims in obedience to authority. Obedience to the commands of the experimenter was reduced when the victim protested, was visible, had physical contact with the punisher, or had greater status than the authority. In the Milgram experiments, as in other studies of conformity, observing even a single disobedient or noncomplying individual enabled subjects to resist the pressure to conform.

5. Aggressive and violent behaviors may also be used to exert influence. Aggressive behavior may take many forms, but the outcome—harming others—is the same. Aggression increases when its victims are dehumanized. For example, when victims were described as perceptive and understanding, they were given less shock than when they were described as "animalistic" and "rotten." When the responsibility for aggressive acts was diffused, more intense shocks were given than when subjects believed that they personally determined the shock level delivered to a particular victim. When people are anonymous (by wearing concealing clothes and remaining nameless, for example), they are more likely to be aggressive than when they cannot hide their real identity. Exposure to aggressive models in real life and on television also increases aggression.

6. Altruistic behavior is action that benefits another and appears motivated by a desire to be helpful, often at some cost to the helper. Helping decreases when there is a diffusion of responsibility, for example, when many possible helpers are available. Face-to-face contact with the needy person and expressions such as pain or urgency that promote empathy encourage altruism. The effects of these factors may be specific to the situation, however.

7. The findings on the determinants of aggression and altruism present a consistent picture. Lack of individual responsibility, distance, and dehumanization foster aggression and inhumanity, while their opposites encourage altruism and moral behavior.

8. Piaget described moral judgment and reasoning as developing through a series of successive stages in which there are fundamental changes in the way the child organizes his ideas and perceptions of the social and moral order of the world. Kohlberg's influential theory of moral development proposes six moral stages that follow one another in an unmodifiable sequence.

9. Moral judgments may be modified as a result of exposure to models. Critics question the invariant sequence of moral judgment stages. They note that the same individual typically makes different moral judgments at different levels, not all at a single level, and that the relationships between moral thought and moral action tend to be extremely complex.

10. The social learning view of moral development holds that moral action depends on many variables, including the individual's moral competence—the capacity to generate moral behavior—as well as the specific situation. Whether moral competence is translated into moral conduct depends on specific motivational and performance considerations, notably the individual's expectations about the consequences of different behavioral alternatives and the subjective value of those consequences. With increasing maturity, self-evaluation, internal standards, and abstract and temporally remote rewards and punishments become more important.

11. The development of responsible behavior and concern for others is fostered by experiences that sensitize individuals to the consequences of their behavior for others.

Chapter 19

The Interaction of Person and Situation

Personality psychologists want to clarify how psychological situations and personal dispositions interact. In this chapter we will consider the roles both of the environment and of individual differences in psychological characteristics. We will be especially concerned with how these two sources of influence interact and mutually determine behavior.

Social interactions depend not only on the people in them, but also on the environments in which they occur. The study of human behavior in relation to the environment from a psychological perspective is a rapidly growing field called "environmental psychology" (Stokols, 1978). Environmental psychology includes explorations of the specific effects of noise, temperature, and space on behavior. It also includes broader analyses of the interrelations between individuals and their social and physical environment (e.g., Proshansky, 1976). Environmental psychologists fuse the "basic" and "applied" perspectives, using scientific strategies to solve community problems, such as urban stress, the perceived quality of the environment, and the conservation of natural resources. Environmental psychologists study "the impact that physical and social environments have on human beings" (Moos & Insel, 1974, p. ix) and are concerned with "human problems in relation to an environment in which man is both victim and conquerer" (Proshansky et al., 1970, p. 4). Attention to the environment is a valuable new direction, helping to correct a tendency to study people while ignoring the close links between human experiences and the world in which those experiences occur. Hopefully, the findings of environmental psychology research will help us to optimize our environment and to design environments that fulfill the needs and goals of those who live in them.

Classifying Environments

Environments can be classified in many ways. One attempt to describe some of the many dimensions of environments was developed by Moos (1973, 1974) and is summarized in Table 19-1. The classification in Table 19-1 makes it clear that environments are complex and that they can be characterized in many ways from the weather to the buildings and settings, to the perceived social climates and the outcomes (reinforcements) that behaviors in that situation yield. Other schemes have tried to classify situations on the basis of their perceived similarity, emerging with such dimensions as "positive," "negative," "passive," "social," and "active" (e.g., Magnusson & Ekehammar, 1973). Of course, many different classifications are possible, depending on one's purpose, and there probably is no single "basic" taxonomy of situations: we can categorize situations in many different ways, focusing on many different features, from physical characteristics (e.g., heat, density) to perceived psychological qualities (e.g., degree to which a psychiatric hospital ward has a "democratic atmosphere" in the eyes of its patients or staff).

The Impact of Environments

Studies of environments lead to some general conclusions. First, within very broad limits people can and do tolerate a wide range of conditions and adapt to all sorts of environments. Within these broad limits one can learn to cope with such stresses as noise, crowding, and heat (e.g., Stokols, 1978). Obviously, the possible negative effects of these potential stresses depend both on the type of task on which performance is measured and on the characteristics of the individual. Perhaps most

Table 19-1
Some Dimensions of Human Environments

Dimensions	Examples
1. Ecological	Climate and geographical qualities; architectural and physical use of space and constraints (e.g., the walls of a prison)
2. Behavior settings	School, drugstore, football game, church
3. Organizational	Size and type of staff in a hospital; student/teacher ratio in a school; population density
4. Characteristics of inhabitants	Age, sex, abilities, status of members
5. Perceived social climate (psychosocial characteristics)	Nature and intensity of personal relations
6. Functional properties	Reinforcement consequences for particular behaviors in that situation

SOURCE: Based on Moos, 1973.

important, the impact of environments—like the impact of all stimuli—depends to a large degree on the total context and on how people view them. For example, when people believe they can predict or control a source of stress (such as noise), its negative impact may be minimized (Glass & Singer, 1972). Likewise, consider the impact of hot weather. To the trapped inhabitants of a city ghetto a heat wave may become the context of riots (Carlsmith & Anderson, 1979), but in the wealthy suburbs the same heat may become the cue for taking time off to relax at the community pool.

Scripts for Social Behavior

Environments and physical settings also affect interactions because they cue or trigger many of the routine "scripts" that guide much of our everyday social life (Abelson, 1976; Langer, 1978). For example, there are fairly standardized scripts for everyday familiar event sequences, guiding what we expect to do in the doctor's office, or in a fancy restaurant, or in a supermarket, or in a classroom, or at a cocktail party, or at a large family Thanksgiving dinner. Once we enter a setting, the relevant script is activated. Each of these scripts is like a "knowledge package" that summarizes our general notions about the appropriate flow of behavior in a particular setting. For example, in a fancy continental restaurant we expect to be seated, to order from menus, to wait for the food, to pay at the end, etc. Appropriate situational cues tend to activate or make available the relevant script, as when a reasonable, justified request for help encourages participation in the "request-for-a-favor" script (Langer, 1978). In the same vein, sociologists as well as philosophers and psychologists (e.g., Harré & Secord, 1973) have long called attention to the "dramatic-role" or "playlike" quality of many human scenarios. The physical environment provides the cues and supplies the stage on which we enact these daily dramas. The study of scripts and their effects on human interactions is sure to be one of the exciting research areas of the future.

The Meaning of Interaction

The increasing interest in environments expressed by personality psychologists reflects in part increased dissatisfaction with traditional personality theories that tried to understand people without adequately considering the specific conditions of the individual's life from moment to moment. It also reflects a recognition that many important human behaviors not only fluctuate as the situation changes but also depend crucially on the mutual (reciprocal) influence of the person and the situation; that is, their "interaction" or "transaction." We noted repeatedly throughout this book that the effects of conditions depend on the individuals in them, and that the *interaction* of individual differences and specific conditions is usually crucial. For example, the impact of different types of classroom arrangements depends on the particular students in them; small group discussion that might be helpful for some students might be a bore or even a handicap for others.

Some researchers hoped that studies of persons, environments, and their interaction would answer the question "are persons or situations more important for predicting behavior?" But the question serves mostly to stimulate futile debates. The answer must always depend on the particular situations and the particular persons sampled. The question of whether individual differences or situations are more important is an empty one that has no general answer. While some situations may be powerful determinants of behavior, others are trivial. The relative importance of individual differences and situations will depend on the situation selected, the type of behavior assessed, the particular individual differences sampled, and the purpose of the assessment (Magnusson & Endler, 1977; Mischel, 1973, 1984).

The Specific Effects of Situations

Situations tend to produce specific rather than generalized effects. Moreover, the effects are often weak (e.g., Sarason, Smith, & Diener, 1975). As one psychologist put it, "Although it is undoubtedly true that behavior is more situation specific than trait theory acknowledged . . . situations are more person specific than is commonly recognized" (Bowers, 1973, p. 307). That is, the impact of particular situations (or "treatments" in experimental and clinical contexts) depends on the particular people in them. A particular "enrichment" course, or creativity-training session, or therapy program might work well for some individuals but be ineffective (or even harmful) for others.

There is a growing belief throughout psychology and the social sciences that "treatments" may not have broad, highly generalized, stable effects. Specificity may occur because of the large range of different ways that different people may react to the "same" treatments and reinterpret them (e.g., Cronbach, 1975; Neisser, 1974). Thus, even a relatively simple "stimulus" or "situation" may produce a variety of often unpredictable specific (and weak) effects depending on a large number of variables. (Recall, for example, the many variables that may determine whether or not one chooses to delay gratification, discussed in Chapter 16.)

In sum, behavior is always determined by many variables. Thus, a focus on any one of them will lead to limited predictions and generalizations. This conclusion is not confined to the area of personality psychology. It has been reached for "treatments" as diverse as interview styles in psychotherapy, teaching practices and classroom arrangements in education, and instructions to aid recall in memory experiments. For example, a survey of research on memory concludes that: " . . . What is remembered in a given situation depends on the physical and psychological context in which the event was experienced, the knowledge and skills that the subject brings to the context, the situation in which we ask for evidence for remembering, and the relation of what the subject remembers to what the experimenter demands" (Jenkins, 1974, p. 793). The same conclusions probably apply as well to the subject matter studied in any other area of psychology.

As a consequence, it may become difficult to achieve broad, sweeping generalizations about human behavior; many qualifiers (moderators) must be appended to our "laws" about cause-and-effect relations—almost without exception and perhaps with no exceptions at all (Cronbach, 1975). On the other hand, while the need to qualify generalizations about human behavior complicates life for the social scientist, it does not prevent one from studying human affairs scientifically; it only dictates a respect for the complexity of the enterprise and alerts one to the dangers of oversimplifying the nature and causes of human behavior.

CONCEPTUALIZING INTERACTION

Throughout this book you have seen examples of person-situation interactions. Granted that both environments and individual differences are important and interact, how can the impact of situations be conceptualized?

The cognitive social learning variables described in Chapter 12 provide one step. Recall that these "person variables" are ways of thinking about individual differences from a perspective that blends contributions from personality and cognitive psychology. These variables refer to the products within the person of his or her cognitive development, social learning history, and genetic endowment. These variables include the person's *competencies* to construct or enact behaviors under appropriate conditions. One also has to consider the person's *encoding* and categorization; how individuals construe themselves, other people, and situations. To analyze performance in given situations also requires us to consider the person's *expectancies* about outcomes, the *subjective values* of such outcomes, and *self-regulatory systems* and *plans*. These variables are not meant to exclude others, but only to give examples of the kinds of person qualities that seem clearly related to basic psychological processes and that have a place in a comprehensive view of the individual. With these person variables as background, let us now consider more concretely how the interaction of persons and situations may work.

When Do Individual Differences Make a Difference?

The conditions or "situational variables" of the psychological environment provide the individual with information; this information influences person variables, thereby affecting how the individual thinks and acts under those conditions. "Situations" (environments) thus influence our behavior by affecting such person variables as how we encode the situation, the outcomes we expect, their subjective value for us, and our competencies.

Recognizing that the question "are persons or situations more important?" is misleading and unanswerable, one can now turn to the more interesting issue: *When* are situations most likely to exert powerful effects and, conversely, *when* are person variables likely to be most influential?

Psychological "situations" ("stimuli," "treatments") are powerful to the degree that they lead everyone to construe the particular events the same way, induce *uniform* expectancies regarding the most appropriate response pattern, provide adequate incentives for the performance of that response pattern, and require skills that everyone has to the same extent. A good example of a powerful stimulus is a red traffic light; it exerts powerful effects on the behavior of most motorists because they all know what it means, are motivated to obey it, and are capable of stopping when they see it. Therefore it would be easier to predict drivers' behavior at stop lights from knowing the color of the light than from making inferences about the "conformity," "cautiousness," or other traits of the drivers.

Conversely, situations are weak to the degree that they are not uniformly encoded, do not generate uniform expectancies concerning the desired behavior, do not offer sufficient incentives for its performance, or fail to provide the learning conditions required for successful genesis of the behavior. An extreme example of such a weak stimulus is the blank card on the TAT projective test (Chapter 3) with the instructions to create a story about what might be happening; clearly the answers will depend more on the story-tellers than on the card.

In sum, individual differences can determine behavior in a given situation strongly when the situation is ambiguously structured (as in projective testing). In that case, each person is uncertain about how to categorize the situation, has to structure it in his or her own terms, and has no clear expectations about the behaviors most likely to be appropriate (normative, reinforced) in that situation. To the degree that the situation is "unstructured" and the person expects that virtually all responses from him or her are equally likely to be appropriate (i.e., will lead to similar consequences), the significance of individual differences will be great. Conversely, when everyone expects that only *one* response will be appropriate (e.g., only one "right" answer on an achievement test, only one correct response for the driver when the traffic light turns red) and that no other responses are equally good, and all people are motivated and capable of making the appropriate response, then individual differences become minimal and situational effects dominate. Individual differences also may be seen when people know what is the appropriate behavior required by the situation but are unable to generate that behavior. That is, when we know what a situation demands, but cannot meet those demands, we may resort to more "typical" or characteristic forms of coping (see *In Focus 19.1*).

In Focus 19.1
Studying
Interactions:
When Are
Aggressive
Children
Aggressive?

Consistent individual differences may be revealed in situations that call for responses that individuals cannot make because they require competencies which they do not have. That is, when individuals are not able to cope appropriately with the challenges and requirements of the specific situation, their typical forms of dealing with stress may occur (e.g., Mischel, 1968, 1973; Moos, 1973; Olweus, 1977). Thus when the behaviors required in the situation for appropriate, competent functioning cannot be made, more generalized, characteristic types of maladaptive responses to the resulting stress may be seen.

Will increased consistency (of problematic behavior) really occur when the individual cannot cope with the immediate situation effectively? This question was examined in research with children characterized as generally either aggressive or withdrawn. These emotionally disturbed children were observed extensively in a summer camp residential facility over the course of several summers (Mischel, 1984; Wright, 1983).

It was anticipated that a child's "typical" levels of inappropriate (problematic, disadvantageous) behavior will occur in situations in which the child does not have the necessary competence to cope effectively. Thus, when the competencies required by the situation are moderate or low, cross-situational consistency of the child's problematic behavior will be modest; consistency will be greater when competency requirements exceed the child's competencies. It was expected that in such stressful situations, children characterized as generally aggressive will indeed show relatively consistent levels of aggression; those characterized as tending to withdraw will be relatively consistent in their levels of withdrawal. In sum, consistencies in problematic behavior should be more evident in those situations in which more adaptive, task-appropriate

behavior required by the context is beyond the person's available competencies.

To test this hypothesis, the researchers rated the cognitive and self-regulatory competency requirements of each of the situations sampled in two consecutive summers at the childrens' camp. Parallel assessments also were obtained of the childrens' competencies to meet those requirements. Examples of the items for rating the competency requirements of situations include: "This situation emphasizes delay of gratification, patience." "This situation emphasizes the ability to focus, concentrate, maintain good attention span." The items for the children were matched closely to those for the situations (e.g., "Is unable to delay gratification, to be patient.")

Using these ratings, the situations were divided into those requiring the highest versus the lowest cognitive and self-regulatory competence in relation to the competence levels of the children in them. The situations were regularly scheduled camp activities (e.g., music, athletics, cabin group meeting) in the daily schedule. In each, the childrens' behavior was observed and rated. For both aggression and withdrawal, the hypothesis was supported: significantly higher levels of cross-situational consistency were obtained for those situations whose competency requirements were higher (rather than lower) relative to the children's available competence.

The results just presented illustrate that there are regularities in typical forms of coping that become observable under predictable conditions. They show interactions in the form of consistencies for some types of behavior by some types of persons under some types of situations. In future research it will be challenging to explore the degree to which such "if ——
—— then ———— " regularities in behavior also can be identified for other behaviors and for people who are not characterized as maladaptive.

Behavioral Appropriateness and Situational Constraints

Social settings vary in the degree to which they prescribe and limit the range of expected and acceptable behavior for persons and hence permit the expression of individual differences (e.g., Barker, 1968; Price, 1974). In some settings the rules greatly limit the range of possible behavior (e.g., in church, at school, in a theater, at a conference). In other settings the range of possible behaviors is broad and often the individual can select, structure, and reorganize situations with few external constraints. Because in particular settings certain response patterns are rewarded (effective) while others are not, different settings may become the occasion for particular behaviors in different degrees.

Situations can be classified according to the range and type of behaviors considered appropriate within them. In one study, college students were asked to rate the appropriateness of fifteen behaviors in fifteen situations (Price & Bouffard, 1974). Examples of the behaviors are *run, belch, kiss, write, eat;* examples of the situations are *in class, on a date, on a bus, at a family dinner, in a restroom.* The average appropriateness ratings were calculated for each of the many combinations of behaviors and situations. These ratings could range from 0 ("the behavior is extremely inappropriate in this situation") to 9 ("the behavior is extremely appropriate in this situation"). To illustrate, Table 19-2 summarizes the average appropriateness ratings found for five behaviors in relation to five situations.

Analyses of this kind applied to a wide range of behaviors and situations can provide useful information. High values for a behavior indicate that it is considered appropriate in many situations, low values suggest that it is generally inappropriate. Likewise, the degree of *situational constraint* for a particular situation can be indexed simply by averaging the appropriateness ratings of the behaviors in that situation (e.g., the rows of Table 19-2). Situations that have high constraint tend to be seen as potentially embarrassing, as requiring more careful self-monitoring of one's behavior, and as demanding certain behaviors rather than others.

It would be especially interesting to examine the degree of *variation* among individuals (not just the average level) found for particular behaviors in particular situations. The most "powerful" situations would be those that usually allow little variation; the "weakest" situations would be those in which variation among people is typically high. Individual differences would be expected to exert the greatest

Table 19-2
Average Appropriateness Ratings for 5 Behaviors in 5 Situations

Situations	Behaviors				
	Run	Write	Mumble	Belch	Cry
Class	2.52	8.17	3.62	1.77	2.21
Family Dinner	2.56	2.58	2.54	2.50	3.21
Job Interview	1.94	4.85	1.31	1.21	1.37
Bar	1.96	5.38	6.21	5.04	3.44
Own Room	6.15	8.29	7.67	6.81	8.00

Note: The higher the number the higher the rated appropriateness of the behavior in the situation.
SOURCE: Based on data from Price & Bouffard, 1974.

influence in the weak (high variation) situations and to have the smallest effect in the powerful (low variation) ones. Parallel analyses would be made of the "difficulty level" of each situation in terms of its competence requirements, as discussed in *In Focus 19.1*.

Predicting from Situations and/or Persons

Although the psychology of personality cannot ignore the person, it is also true that behavior sometimes may be predicted and influenced simply from knowledge about relevant conditions. Consider, for example, studies that tried to predict the posthospital adjustment of mental patients. Accurate predictions of posthospital adjustment required knowledge of the environment in which the expatient would be living in the community—such as the availability of jobs and family support—rather than any measures of person variables or in-hospital behavior (e.g., Fairweather, 1967; Fairweather et al., 1969).

Likewise, to predict intellectual achievement it helps to take account of the degree to which the child's environment supports (models and reinforces) intellectual development (Wolf, 1966). And to predict whether or not people respond to stress with illness it helps to know the degree to which they have social supports (e.g., spouse, family) in their environments (Nilson et al., 1981). Finally, when powerful treatments are developed—such as modeling and desensitization therapies for phobias—predictions about outcomes may be useful when based on knowing the treatment to which the individual is assigned (e.g., Bandura, Blanchard, & Ritter, 1969; Bandura, 1986).

Social Interaction as a Reciprocal Influence Process

Some of the most striking differences between persons may be found not by studying how they react to the same situation but by analyzing their *selection* and construction of stimulus conditions. In the conditions of life outside the laboratory the psychological "stimuli" that people encounter involve other people and reciprocal relationships (e.g., with spouse, with boss, with children). We continuously influence the "situations" of our lives as well as being affected by them in a mutual, organic interaction (e.g., Raush et al., 1974). Such interactions reflect not only our reactions to conditions but also our active selection and modification of conditions through our own choices, cognitions, and actions (Wachtel, 1973). Different people select different settings for themselves; conversely, the settings that people select to be in may provide clues about their personal qualities (Eddy & Sinnett, 1973).

The analysis of complex social interactions (e.g., Patterson & Cobb, 1971; Patterson, 1976) vividly illustrates how each of us continuously selects, changes, and generates conditions just as much as we are affected by them. If you change your behavior toward another person he or she generally shows reciprocal changes in behavior toward you. In Raush's (1965, p. 492) studies of naturalistic interactions, for example, "the major determinant of an act was the immediately preceding act. Thus if you want to know what child B will do, the best single predictor is what child A did to B the moment before." Construed from the viewpoint of child A,

Person variables also influence the "situations" one
selects—including the people to whom one attends.

this means that A's own behavior determines B's reactions to him; if A provokes B, B will reciprocate aggressively. In that sense, the person is generating his or her own conditions.

The other side of the interaction is the fact that B's behavior is always constrained by what A did the moment before. Studies of the interactions among husbands and wives illustrate this point (Raush et al., 1974). In these studies, husband-wife interactions were observed as the couples coped with such conflicts as how to celebrate their first wedding anniversary when each had made different plans. For example, Bob has arranged and paid in advance for dinner at a restaurant, but Sue has spent half the day preparing for a special dinner at home. As the couple realize their conflict and try to resolve it, their interactions continuously reveal that each antecedent act (what Sue has just said to Bob) constrains each consequent act (how Bob responds).

The meaning and impact of each act also depends on such additional considerations as the total context in which it occurs as well as on the relationship and "style" that each couple develops. " . . . Situations thus 'inform' persons, selecting segments of personal experience; persons also inform situations, selecting segments to respond to" (Raush et al., 1974, p. 212).

Life-Span Development and Adaptation

Social interaction is a lifelong process. One's specific transactions with the environment continue to change throughout the life span (Baltes, 1979).

At different points in development the individual tends to experience different problems and challenges as the main sources of influence shift from parents to peers and spouses and offspring. The types of concerns dominant at any one time, and the sources of influence that seem most crucial, depend on the individual, on the phase of development that he or she has reached, and on the society he or she lives in. As the practices of society change, so do the typical problems and challenges found at different phases of life.

For example, a century or more ago adolescence was not the phenomenon it is now. Beginning fairly early in childhood most people worked long days and were quickly thrust into adult roles with little transition. In modern times, the prolonged period of schooling required for training highly skilled people in Western industrial societies has postponed the time at which most young people have to bear adult responsibilities. This period of enforced delay provides a fertile ground for many conflicts by placing the adolescent in an interim status—not really autonomous adult, not really dependent child.

Life in this phase may seem especially turbulent because this is the time most people have their first sexual encounters, become physically mature, and face difficult educational and career choices that will have lifelong consequences. Little wonder that modern adolescence has been characterized as a time of identity crises (Erikson, 1963). In our society, adolescence tends to be the period when the individual comes under strong peer pressure (Bronfenbrenner, 1970), attempts to accelerate the process of emancipation from the family, and tries to assess what his or her own values, beliefs, interests, and abilities really are.

When the person leaves the parental home, his or her new roles require new relationships that demand different resources and result in new outcomes. In time the adolescent becomes the parent; the cycle continues as the next generation tries to transmit its values and beliefs to its children. The responsibilities and crises of middle life then give way to those of advanced age, bringing new challenges and experiences that change one further as the interaction between person and conditions continues throughout life.

PERSONALITY IN PERSPECTIVE

As the student of personality reviews and concludes this book and forms an image of the field of personality psychology, it is easy to become lost in details, to "miss the forest for the trees." Now that this survey of personality ends, it is important to find a perspective from which to view and integrate what you have read throughout this text.

Overview of Approaches

As a first step, Table 19-3 summarizes again, in very brief form, the main approaches to personality that were considered earlier in the text. (Note that the behavioral approaches are divided into two separate columns to distinguish their earlier, more behavioristic versions from their newer, more cognitive and social learning developments, the applications for which were illustrated throughout the last five chapters.) Each approach points to different "truths," each suggests different routes, each yields different insights. Can all these coexist?

A Constructivist View

In one view, science is a search for *the* truth, *the* "reality:" The scientist tries to find what truly "is." An alternative view, called "constructivist," is emerging with some force in psychology, and it is linked more closely to a philosophy like George

Table 19-3
An Overview of Major Approaches to Personality: Alternative Perspectives

Characteristic	Approach				
	Psychodynamic	Trait	Phenomenological (Humanistic)	Behavioral	Cognitive-Social Learning
Belief as to basic causes of behavior	Underlying, stable motives and their unconscious transformations	Generalized (consistent, stable) dispositions	Self-concepts and underlying feelings	Prior learning and specific present situation	Specific person-situation interactions
Preferred data sources	Interpretations by expert judges	Global ratings	Self-disclosure and ratings	Direct observation of behavior in situation	Objective measures
Research focus	Personality dynamics and psychopathology	Measurement (test construction), description of individual differences and their patterning	Self-concepts, feelings, self-expression, human potential	Behavior change; analysis of conditions controlling behavior	Self-regulation, increasing personal control
Approach to personality change	By insight into motives underlying behavior	Unspecified (possibly genetic)	By increasing awareness, personal honesty, internal consistency, self-acceptance, perceived esteem and control	By changing conditions and responses directly	By changing expectancies, values, and other person variables

Kelly's constructive alternativism (Chapter 7). The constructivist view holds that there is no single correct reality, no one truth that exists "out there," waiting to be discovered. Rather, we invent or construct theories and concepts, very much like lenses, through which we view a complex and ever-changing world. What we see and find, then, depends on the particular lenses we have created and on where and how we look through them.

The analogy between theoretical conceptions and lenses is useful because it makes obvious the belief that one should not expect to use the same lenses for observing all things. No single set of lenses could possibly serve for viewing the stars, the molecules, and events in everyday life. Different purposes require different conceptions, and viewpoints that are helpful for some goals may not be useful or even relevant for other goals or other problems or at other times. Considering the advantages and disadvantages of such a constructivist view of science and social intervention, Sandra Scarr, an eminent developmental psychologist, comments:

> The disadvantage of this [constructivist] view over the current realism is that we may feel less certain of what we are doing. How can we know what is right, if there is no right? The feeling can resemble the loss of faith in a familiar and comforting religion. Theories make conflicting claims that cause us to think and choose—uncomfortable processes for many people. We are thrown onto our own resources to invent a plausible story in the face of certain ambiguity.
>
> The advantage of this view is that we can make more modest claims about the ultimate Truth, which leaves us less embarrassed when other theories replace our favorite view. A second and more important advantage is that we can modify our ineffective attempts to change others' behaviors more easily, because we recognize that we may have constructed the problem inappropriately for the time and space. It makes easier the invention of other questions and other approaches to a perceived problem (Scarr, 1985, pp. 511–512).

Inconsistencies or Coexisting Alternatives?

Throughout this text, the study of personality emerged with many themes that may seem to be mutually contradictory and confusing. Let us briefly consider some of the main themes from the study of personality that may appear especially paradoxical because, as the following list of examples shows, for each theme a seemingly contrary one also emerges:

Personality is stable. Personality is capable of change.

Dispositions are important. Situations are important.

Behavior depends on the social enviornment. Genetic and biological factors are foundations of social behavior.

People are consistent. People are inconsistent.

Humans are cognitive beings. Human are emotional beings.

Behavior is rational. Behavior is irrational.

Viewed from a constructivist framework, many of these apparent inconsistencies become less troubling. Each theme reflects not a preemptive reality that excludes the alternative, but a focus and an insight that are useful and valid for some purposes and for understanding some aspects of the different phenomena of personality. In that view, personality is both stable and capable of change, for example, and the two statements don't necesarily conflict. The questions rather, are when and how do we find stability, and when and how do we find change, and how can we best understand each phenomenon?

Multiple Dimensions with Multiple Determinants

Everyone recognizes and acknowledges the complexity of human beings. Obviously, people are not one-dimensional creatures, composed of any single characteristics. Rather, humans are a mix of features, a blend of dimensions, containing an often bewildering and seemingly contradictory set of aspects. We are rational and irrational, cognitive and emotional, stable and changeable, capable of creativity and altruism as much as of destructiveness and aggression. Although poets have long recognized and celebrated the diverse and seemingly contradictory qualities of human nature, in the study of personality it often is tempting to oversimplify them and to gloss over the multidimensional nature of personality.

A constructivist view seems well suited to the general characteristics of psychological variables. As has been emphasized repeatedly, most psychological variables operate not in isolation as single, separate causes or determinants, but rather they tend to be interrelated and interactive, as was illustrated earlier in this chapter. The variables involved throughout the coping process are related and interactive; they are dynamic elements rather than independent units. For each phenomenon of interest, the tasks are to study when and how the phenomenon occurs and to clarify the implications and consequences of viewing it from any given perspective for the particular goal one is trying to reach.

SUMMARY

1. The rapidly growing field of environmental psychology studies the relationship of human behavior to the environment in which it occurs. Environments can be classified in terms of many dimensions, from their physical properties to the way they are perceived by those who inhabit them.

2. One of the ways in which physical and social settings affect our behavior is by activating scripts. These "knowledge packages" summarize general and shared notions about the appropriate flow of behavior in the particular setting and may guide many social interactions more or less automatically.

3. Just as there is considerable "behavioral specificity," so also is there much specificity in the effects of most situations and treatments. While some conditions are powerful, others exert weak, specific, and ungeneralizable effects that require many qualifiers in efforts to find general laws about cause and effect relations.

4. Person variables help us to analyze the interaction of the individual and situations. Situations provide information that may affect each person variable—for example, the ability to generate behavior patterns, expectancies, the values placed on certain outcomes in the situation, the way the situation is construed. Powerful situations

are those which everyone construes the same way, in which everyone agrees about the most appropriate behavior and has adequate competence and incentives to enact it. When situations are less powerful and more ambiguous, individual differences tend to become more important.

5. When people cannot cope with the demands of the situation one may see their more characteristic ways of dealing with stress.

6. Behaviors and situations can be analyzed according to their range of appropriateness. Behaviors vary with regard to the range of situations in which they are appropriate; situations differ in the number and kinds of behavior they allow. (Compare, for example, football games, church services, and family mealtimes.)

7. The mutual, reciprocal influence between person and psychological conditions is a lifelong process of adaptation. It changes throughout the course of life-span development as different challenges and problems become dominant for the individual.

8. To place the study of personality in perspective, it helps to adapt a constructivist view of science. That view recognizes the legitimacy of alternative constructions for different purposes and different aspects of a phenomenon. It also takes into account the belief that complex human behavior is multiply determined by many interrelated and interacting variables from both outside and inside the person.

Glossary

Ability traits: Cattell's term for traits concerned with effectiveness in achieving a goal.

Adrenalin (epinephrine): Hormone secreted by the adrenal medulla that, along with noradrenalin, during emotional arousal raises blood pressure, influences heart rate, helps generate energy, and increases tension of skeletal muscles.

Aggression: Behavior motivated by the intent to hurt (which may or may not inflict harm).

Anaclitic identification: Hypothesized by Freud as the earliest form of identification based on the infant's intense dependency on the mother.

Anal stage: The second of Freud's psychosexual stages, it occurs during the child's second year. Pleasure is focused on the anus and on the retention and expulsion of feces.

Analytical psychology: Carl Jung's theory of personality. Humans are viewed as purposive and striving toward self-actualization. The unconscious includes a collective as well as a personal unconscious and is a healthy force.

Androgynous: Having the capability to perform both "masculine" and "feminine" behaviors.

Anima: In Jung's theory, the feminine, passive element in the unconscious of every male.

Animus: In Jung's theory, the masculine, assertive element in the unconscious of every female.

Anorexia nervosa: A disorder in which the individual (usually an adolescent female) refuses to eat, without any apparent cause, sometimes starving to death.

Antidepressants: Drugs used to elevate the mood of depressed individuals (see *chemotherapy*).

Antipsychotic drugs: (see *phenothiazine*).

Anxiety: A state of emotional arousal which may be experienced as a diffuse fear. In Freud's theory, the result of the struggle between an impulse and an inhibition.

Anxiety hierarchy: Ranking of events from the most to the least anxiety-arousing, used in desensitization treatment.

Anxiety neurosis: A neurotic condition in which the individual suffers from pervasive apprehension or fear without obvious specific cause (see *neurosis*).

Approach-approach conflict: A conflict that occurs when a person must choose one of several desirable alternatives (see *approach-avoidance conflict*).

Approach-avoidance conflict: A conflict that occurs when a person confronts an object or situation that has both positive and negative elements (see *approach-approach conflict*).

Archetypes: Jung's term for the contents of the *collective unconscious*—images or symbols expressing the inherited patterns for the organization of experience (e.g., mother archetype).

Assertiveness training: Training usually involving modeling and practice in developing and using effective assertive skills; a type of behavior therapy.

Attitudes: Positive or negative evaluative opinions or beliefs about an object, entity, or person.

Autism: A childhood form of severe psychological disorder in which there is an extreme lack of interest in reality and in other people; also a symptom of schizophrenia.

Availability heuristic: A rule that the more easily we can think of something, the more likely we believe it to be in reality.

Averaging model: Model of person perception suggesting that the total impression of a person is the result of the averaging of all the available information.

Aversion therapy: Procedures that pair attractive arousing, but problem-producing, stimuli with another stimulus that evokes extremely negative reactions. The positive stimulus comes to evoke some of the negative or aversive reactions or is at least neutralized. For example, alcohol may be paired with nausea-producing drugs.

Awareness: Most common synonym for consciousness in psychological usage.

Behavior: Includes emotions and covert mental activities, such as thoughts or "cognitions," as well as overt actions.

Behavior modification: Techniques used in behavior therapy which are derived from learning principles.

Behavior therapies: Therapies that try to change problem behaviors directly with techniques based on the concepts of learning theories.

Behavioral assessment: The analysis of how an individual's behavior changes in response to changing stimulus conditions.

Behavioral specificity: The dependence of a person's specific behavior on the particular situation in which it occurs.

Behaviorism: Approach to psychology emphasizing observable, objectively measurable behavior and the relationships between these behaviors and specific events or stimuli in the environment (see *stimulus-response psychology*).

Biofeedback: Use of equipment to provide immediate feedback about the activities of the autonomic and somatic systems; for example, giving information about heart rate or brainwaves to the person in whom they occur, at the time they occur.

Cardinal traits: Allport's term for a highly generalized disposition or characteristic that influences most aspects of an individual's behavior throughout life.

Castration anxiety: A male's fear of losing his penis. Freud believed this anxiety was central in the resolution of the Oedipus complex and in the boy's identification with his father.

Catharsis: The belief that the verbal or fantasy expression of an impulse leads to its reduction; a key concept in psychoanalytic theory.

Cathexis: Psychoanalytic term denoting the investment of instinctual impulses in objects.

Causal attribution: Perception (judgment) of the causes of behavior, either to internal or to external causes (see *locus of control*).

Central traits: Allport's term for a trait that is less important and pervasive than a cardinal trait, but which still influences much of a person's behavior.

Cerebrotonic: In Sheldon's typology, the temperament of the ectomorph, who has a well-developed brain. Characterized by artistic inclinations, introversion, and restraint (see *viscerotonic, somatotonic*).

Chemotherapy: With reference to psychology, the treatment of problems with such drugs as antidepressants and tranquilizers.

Choleric: One of the four temperaments of Hippocrates' typology. Choleric persons were supposedly irritable due to an excess of yellow bile.

Classical conditioning (conditioned-response learning): A type of learning, emphasized by Pavlov, in which the response to an unconditioned stimulus (e.g., food) becomes conditioned to a neutral stimulus (e.g., a bell) by being paired or associated with it.

Client-centered (Rogerian) therapy: Approach to therapy developed by Carl Rogers. Emphasizes a nonevaluative, accepting atmosphere conducive to honesty and concentrates on present relationships and feelings.

Clinical and counseling psychologists: Psychologists who conduct research and apply psychological principles to the evaluation and treatment of a variety of human problems such as mental deficiency, drug addiction, and psychoses.

Cognition: Refers to how we know the world through mental processes such as thinking, perceiving, and remembering.

Cognitive avoidance: Efforts to avoid painful thoughts, percepts, associations, or other cognitive events.

Cognitive consistency: Consonance among beliefs and perceptions. Research shows that in general people seek consistency, and tend to reduce inconsistency.

Cognitive dissonance: According to Festinger, an unpleasant state that occurs when a person knows that two things do not fit together. The theory of cognitive dissonance proposes that people try to reduce such discomfort by changing their cognitions or beliefs.

Cognitive learning: (see *observational learning*).

Cognitive-physiological theory of emotion: Theory of emotion developed by Schachter, stating that our experience of an emotion depends on the cognitive interpretation of physiological arousal. The same state of physiological arousal may be labeled differently under different circumstances. Also known as the two-factor theory of emotions.

Cognitive psychologists: Psychologists who study mental activity, focusing on the ways people process information in perception, memory, and thinking.

Cognitive restructuring: Therapeutic technique aimed at thinking about one's problems more constructively and less irrationally. Albert Ellis' Rational Emotive Therapy is a form of cognitive restructuring.

Cognitive social learning person variables: Person variables such as competencies, encoding strategies, personal constructs, expectancies, values, and plans that are the result of cognitive development and social learning history.

Cognitive styles: An individual's consistent ways of approaching and processing information, especially through perception, memory, and thought.

Collective unconscious: Inherited portion of the unconscious, as postulated by Jung. Consists of ancestral memories and archetypes.

Common traits: According to Allport, a trait that is shared in different degrees by many people.

Competence or "effectance" motivation: Desire to acquire mastery of a task for its own sake.

Competency: The individual's ability to transform and use information actively and to create thoughts and actions (as in problem solving).

Compliance: Public behavior changes in the form of conformity to rules or requests without accompanying internal changes (see *persuasion*).

Compulsions: A ritualistic behavior that the individual feels compelled to perform.

Concept formation: A type of thinking; requires the learning of categories and the rules for assigning instances to each category.

Concordance rate (in schizophrenia): Percent of pairs of twins in which the second twin is diagnosed as schizophrenic if the first twin has been diagnosed as schizophrenic. Higher for monozygotic twins.

Conditioned aversion: Conditioning in which a positive stimulus is repeatedly paired with a negative stimulus, resulting in the negative reaction being made to the formerly positive stimulus.

Conditioned reinforcers (secondary reinforcers): A stimulus that has become reinforcing as a result of its association with an unconditioned stimulus or a primary reinforcer.

Conditioned response: A learned response to a conditioned stimulus. A response previously made to an unconditioned stimulus is now made to a conditioned stimulus as the result of the pairing of the two stimuli.

Conditioned stimulus: A previously neutral stimulus to which one begins to respond distinctively after it has been paired with an unconditioned stimulus.

Conditioning: A basic form of learning (see also *classical conditioning; operant conditioning*).

Conflict: A state in which two or more opposing or mutually exclusive impulses, desires, or tendencies are present at the same time. In psychodynamic theory, continuous conflict within the personality arises from the struggle between the id, ego, and superego—between instinctual demands and the inhibitions that block them.

Consciousness: Total awareness; normal waking state.

Construct: In George Kelly's theory, a construct is a category that contains at least two individuals or events and excludes at least one other; it describes the way in which two things are seen as alike and as different from a third.

Construct validity: The process of establishing that the theory about what accounts for behaviors on a particular test is valid; involves validation of both the test and the theory that underlies it.

Construction competencies: A person variable that refers to the ability to construct (generate) particular cognitions and behaviors; what the individual knows and can do (see *person variables*).

Constructive alternativism: Recategorization of individuals or events to facilitate problem solving; a concept in George Kelly's theory.

Content validity: Establishes that the content of a test represents a larger category, that is, that the test items are relevant for what the tester intends to measure.

Contingencies: Conditions under which reinforcement will occur.

Contingency contracting (contracts): Contracts—made between an individual in treatment and his or her therapist—to achieve particular goals specifying the "contingencies" (conditions) under which positive or negative reinforcement may be given or withheld. For example, the person contracts to pay a disliked charity 50 dollars every time he or she smokes a cigarette, a

dieter contracts to buy new clothes after losing a certain amount of weight.

Contingent management: Technique of behavior change in which new consequences for a particular behavior are introduced. Rewards are made contingent on more advantageous behavior, and any reinforcement for maladaptive behavior is withdrawn.

Continuous reinforcement: Schedule of reinforcement in which a response is reinforced every time it occurs.

Control group: A group that does not receive the experimental treatment but is otherwise comparable to the experimental group. Responses by this group can be compared with those by the experimental group to measure any differences.

Correlation: The relationship between two variables or sets of measures. May be either positive or negative, and expressed quantitatively in a coefficient of correlation.

Correlation coefficient: Quantitative expression of correlation. Ranges from 0 to $+1$ or -1.

Counterconditioning: Replacement of a response to a stimulus by a new response in behavior therapy.

Covert modeling: A type of behavior therapy in which the individual imagines a model performing the desirable behavior in an appropriate situation (see *modeling*).

Criterion validity: A type of test validity. One form, *concurrent,* demonstrates relations between test scores and other current information from the same subjects. A second form, *predictive,* demonstrates a relation between test scores and later performance on a criterion, for example, college success.

Critical period: A point or age in development during which an organism is most ready to acquire particular patterns of behavior (see *imprinting*).

Cue: Stimulus that directs behavior, determining when, where, and how the response (behavior) will occur.

Defense mechanisms: According to Freud, ways in which the ego unconsciously tries to cope with unacceptable id impulses, as in repression, projection, reaction formation, sublimation, rationalization.

Defensive identificaton: (see *identification with the aggressor*).

Denial: In Freudian theory, a primitive defense mechanism in which a person denies a threatening impulse or event even though reality confirms it; the basis for development of repression.

Dependency: Behaviors aimed at eliciting attention and help from others.

Dependent variable: Aspect of the subject's behavior that is measured after the independent variable has been manipulated.

Depression: Extreme sadness, usually without personal loss, often accompanied by feelings of worthlessness and reduced activity level.

Depressive neurosis: A neurotic condition in which there is excessive sadness in reaction to a frustration, failure, or loss (see *neurosis*).

Desensitization: Method of eliminating anxiety or fear responses to a stimulus in which the individual learns to make an incompatible response, such as relaxation, to a series of increasingly anxiety-evoking stimuli.

Discrimination: Differential response to two stimuli, for example, returning a found wallet, but not a loose five-dollar bill; crying in your room but not in class.

Discriminative facility: Responsivity to changing conditions.

Discriminative stimulus: Stimulus that indicates when a response will or will not have favorable consequences.

Displacement: Redirecting an impulse toward a less threatening target; a key concept in psychoanalytic theory.

Dispositions: Attitudes, traits, motives, which cause a person to respond in typical ways.

Dissociative reaction: (see *hysterical neurosis*).

Dizygotic twins: Fraternal twins; two organisms that develop in the uterus at the same time but from two egg and two sperm cells; not genetically identical.

Double-blind method: Experimental procedure in which neither subjects nor experimenters know whether subjects are in experimental or control conditions.

Down's syndrome ("mongolism"): Genetic abnormality consisting of a third chromosome in the twenty-first chromosome pair. Causes severe mental retardation and a distinctive appearance.

Drive: Any strong stimuli (internal or external) which impel action.

Drive-conflict theory: Posits the simultaneous existence of drive-like forces (approach tendencies) and of inhibitory forces (avoidance tendencies).

DSM III: The current diagnostic and statistical manual of the American Psychiatric Association.

Dynamic psychology: Theories, such as psychoanalysis, which emphasize concepts that imply movement (process, motives, and development) in contrast to more static approaches such as trait theory.

Dynamic traits: Cattell's term for traits that are relevant to the individual's being "set into action" with respect to some goal.

Efficacy expectations: A person's specific expectancies about his or her ability to perform particular behaviors.

Ego: In Freudian theory, the conscious part of the personality which mediates between the demands of the id and of the world. Operates on the reality principle.

Ego-analysts: Followers of Freud (e.g., Anna Freud, Erik Erikson) who rejected Freud's emphasis on instinctual drives and stressed ego functions.

Ego-control: Degree of impulse control; important in delay of gratification, planfulness, and aggression inhibition (see also *ego-resiliency*).

Ego controls: Mechanisms through which people solve problems and control their own behavior.

Ego identity: According to Erikson, the individual's view of himself and of what others expect him to be; basic to the organization and development of personality.

Ego psychology: The variety of psychoanalytic theory that stresses ego functions and de-emphasizes instinctual drives.

Ego-resiliency: Refers to the individual's ability to adapt to environmental demands by appropriately modifying his or her habitual level of ego-control, thus functioning with some flexibility.

Electroencephalogram (EEG): Trace pattern recording the amplitude and frequency of brainwaves.

Electroencephalograph: Instrument that measures electrical activity within neural circuits of the brain.

Electroshock (convulsive) therapy: A treatment for psychological problems in which a strong electric current is passed through the brain, producing convulsions, unconsciousness, and loss of memory for events prior to the treatment. Used today primarily as a treatment for severe depression that has not responded to other types of treatment.

Emotional inoculation: A process in which forewarnings or some form of rehearsal are used to help a person to prepare himself or herself psychologically for a trauma and to cope with it better when it occurs.

Emotional insight: A process in which a person "works through" his or her problems and comes to understand and accept his or her impulses fully, not merely in an abstract, detached, rational way.

Emotional stability: The opposite of neuroticism, according to Eysenck, who views emotional stability-neuroticism as an important trait dimension.

Encoding strategies: A person variable that includes the individual's personal constructs and units for categorizing events and experience (see *person variables*).

Encounter group: A type of group therapy in which the emphasis on openness, honesty, trust, and acceptance in order to achieve increased self-awareness and sensitivity (see *human relations training group*).

Endomorph: One of Sheldon's somatotypes, characterized by a soft, round body with overdeveloped digestive viscera, and a sociable, relaxed, and food-loving (viscerotonic) temperament (see *ectomorph, mesomorph*).

Epinephrine: A hormone produced by the adrenal medulla during emotional arousal: it increases heart rate and raises blood-sugar levels (see *adrenalin*).

Existentialism: A theory that emphasizes freedom of choice and advocates taking full responsiblity for one's own existence and the realization of one's full potential.

Expectancies: A person variable that includes behavior-outcome and stimulus-outcome expectancies and guides an individual's choices.

Experiment: Attempt to manipulate a variable of interest while controlling all other conditions so that their influence can be discounted and the effects of the variable measured.

Extinction: The decrease in frequency of a response which follows the repetition of the response or, in classical conditioning, the repetition of the conditioned stimulus in the absence of the unconditioned stimulus.

Extravert: (1) In Jung's typology, the extravert is conventional, sociable, and outgoing and reacts to stress by trying to lose himself among people; (2) For Eysenck, extraversion-introversion is a dimension of personality along which all individuals can be placed at some point.

Extrinsic rewards: Rewards which are external to the behavior they are used to increase. For example, helping a disturbed child learn to speak by rewarding his or her efforts with food or hugs (see also *intrinsic rewards*).

Factor analysis: A mathematical procedure for sorting trait terms or test responses into clusters or factors; used in the development of tests designed to discover basic personality traits. It identifies items that are homogeneous or internally consistent and independent of others.

Fear of success: Motive to avoid success hypothesized in women to account for the finding that women may react negatively and with conflict to stories about successful women.

Feeling (in Jung's theory): One of Jung's four basic ways of experiencing or contacting the world, focusing on the emotional aspects of experience (see *intuition, sensing, thinking*).

Fetishistic behavior: Behavior resulting from the production of emotional arousal by things or events that are neutral or even aversive for most individuals, e.g., becoming sexually aroused by baby-carriages or nasal mucus.

Field theories: Positions that construe behavior as determined by the person's psychological life space—by the events in his or her total psychological situation at the moment—rather than by past events or by enduring , situation-free dispositions.

Fixation: A psychodynamic term referring to a process by which a person remains attached to a person or symbol appropriate to an earlier stage of development, and fails to progress satisfactorily through the stages of development.

Free association: A technique used in psychoanalytic therapy in which the patient is instructed to report whatever comes to mind, no matter how irrational it may seem.

Freudian "slips": Mistakes in speech, writing, or other behavior that Freud attributed to psychodynamic conflicts and believed revealed the underlying unconscious intention (see *defense mechanisms*).

Frustration: A state of arousal that may occur when a sequence of goal-directed behavior is interrupted and the desired goals are delayed or blocked.

Frustration-aggression hypothesis: Hypothesis that frustration is the primary cause of aggression, and that frustration always increases the probability of aggressive behavior.

Functional analysis: Behavioral analysis of the covariation between a particular behavior and the environmental conditions controlling it or covarying with it.

Functional autonomy (of motives): Gordon Allport's theory that most adult motives are independent of their instinctual roots. For example, a millionaire may continue to work for enjoyment and companionship though all his or her basic needs are met.

Functional psychoses: Extreme inability to meet the ordinary demands of life due to psychological rather than physical problems. Characterized by extreme behavior deficits and/or highly inappropriate thought, mood, and action, without known organic causes. May be divided into several subtypes including schizophrenia, the paranoid psychoses, and the affective psychoses.

Galvanic skin response or GSR: Changes in the electrical activity of the skin due to sweating, as recorded by a galvanometer, and used as an index of emotional state; for example, in a lie detector test.

Gender self-concept: A recognition of one's sex as a permanent characteristic.

Generalization: Responding in the same way to similar stimuli. For example, when a child who has been bitten by a dog becomes afraid of all dogs (see also *discrimination*).

Generalized expectancies: J. B. Rotter's term for expectancies about outcomes that determine behavior and are assumed to be consistent across situations.

Generalized mental ability: The generalized ability that some psychologists believe underlies success in many different mental tasks and measures of intelligence.

Genital stage: Last of Freud's psychosexual stages, in which the individual becomes capable of love and of adult sexual satisfaction.

Gestalt psychotherapy: An approach developed by F. Perls that aims at expanding the awareness of self and putting the person in touch with his or her own feelings and creative potential. Often practiced in groups, use is made of body exercises and the venting of emotions.

Goal gradients: Gradients of changes in response strength as a function of distance from a positive or negative reinforcement or goal.

Guided participation: Technique for treating phobias in which a model demonstrates appropriate interaction with a feared object and also guides the client through an increasingly difficult series of interactions or performances (see *modeling, observational learning*).

Hermaphrodite: A person who is born with both male and female sex organs and whose sex is therefore ambiguous.

Heroin: A physically addictive drug that depresses the central nervous system; can relieve pain, reduce hunger and sex drives, and provide a sense of euphoria.

Heuristics: Any strategy that increases the chances of finding a solution to a problem. Four main types are: means-end, working backwards, analogous plans, and simplification (see *availability heuristic*).

Hierarchical organization: The organization of information into increasingly broad categories.

Higher-order conditioning: Process that occurs when a conditioned stimulus modifies the response to a neutral stimulus with which it has become associated.

Higher-order motives: Certain hypothesized motives that, unlike thirst or hunger, do not involve specific physiological changes.

Human relations training group: A form of group therapy that emphasizes sensitivity training, self-awareness, personal growth, and both verbal and physical communication among group members. Also known as T-group.

Humanistic psychology: Approach to psychology emphasizing positive growth motives, feelings, self-awareness, and self-realization. The person is seen as an active agent whose behavior is purposeful, and who, in addition to being motivated by more primitive biological needs, is guided by higher growth motives that make self-actualization possible.

Hypochondriasis: Exaggerated attention to and anxiety about one's health.

Hysterical neurosis: A neurotic condition consisting of two subcategories: conversion reaction (physical symptoms such as paralysis or loss of sensation without organic cause) and dissociative reaction (disruption of a consistent unitary sense of self that may include amnesia, fugue, and/or multiple personality).

Id: In Freudian theory, the foundation of the personality, consisting of unconscious instincts and inherited biological drives; it operates on the pleasure principle.

Identification: (1) Similarity in behavior (including feelings and attitudes) between a child and the model with whom he or she identifies; (2) The child's motive or desire to be like the model; (3) The process through which the child takes on the attributes of the model.

Identification with the aggressor: According to Freud, the boy's castration anxiety and incestuous desires for his mother are resolved by identifying with his father (the "aggressor" or potential castrator) in the phallic stage of psychosexual development.

Identity crisis: According to Erikson, a point in psychosocial development when the adolescent or young adult defines his or her identity.

Implicit personality theories: Patterns of expected associations among personality traits.

Impulses: In psychoanalytic theory, instinctual impulses pass from the id to the ego where they are discharged, inhibited, diverted by the operation of a defense mechanism, or sublimated.

Incompatible response: Response whose performance precludes or prevents performance of another response, for example, relaxing to prevent anxiety; a step in some types of behavior therapy (see *counter-conditioning, desensitization*).

Independent variable: Stimulus or condition that the investigator systematically varies in an experiment.

Innate or primary biological needs: Inborn needs, such as the need for food, water, air, and warmth, which are essential for survival.

Insight: The intellectual and emotional understanding of one's motives and psychodynamics and the symbolic meaning of behavior.

Instinctive drift: A gradual shift away from a conditioned response toward one that is made more naturally by the animal in its usual environment. For example, a pig trained to deposit coins in a toy bank begins to put the coins on the ground and "root" them with its snout instead.

Instincts: Patterns of unlearned, innate, goal-directed and species-specific behavior.

Intellectualization: The tendency to deal with emotional conflicts in a detached, intellectual, and controlled manner.

Interscorer agreement: Degree of consistency among different judges scoring the same information. If scoring decisions are subjective, then it becomes especially necessary to demonstrate interscorer agreement.

Intrinsic motives: Motives (e.g., curiosity, achievement, affiliation, identity, stimulation, and social approval) that do not depend on the reduction of primary drives (such as hunger and sex), and do not have specific physiological correlates.

Intrinsic rewards: Rewards based on the properties of a behavior as distinguished from extrinsic or external rewards. For example, playing the piano for the sounds produced rather than for praise from another person.

Introversion-extraversion: Trait dimension based on Jung's typology, researched by Eysenck. The introvert is quiet and introspective, while the extravert is active and sociable (see *introvert, extravert*).

Introvert: According to Jung's typology, the introvert is shy, withdrawn, and prefers to be alone (see also *extravert*).

Intuition (in Jung's theory): One of Jung's four basic ways of experiencing or contacting the world, by quick guessing about what underlies sensory inputs (see *feeling, sensing, thinking*).

IQ (Intelligence Quotient): Concept formulated by Binet to summarize an individual's mental level based on test scores. IQ means "mental age" divided by chronological age $\times$ 100. The average IQ at any given chronological age is set to be 100.

James-Lange theory: Theory of emotion proposing that the emotional experience follows rather than precedes physiological reactions.

Latency period: In Freud's theory of psychosexual stages, the period between the phallic stage and the mature, genital stage, during which the child represses memories of infantile sexuality.

Learned helplessness: A condition in animals and humans which results from exposure to inescapable painful experiences in which passive endurance persists even when escape becomes possible.

Learned motivation: Dollard and Miller's concept for deriving human social behavior from its biological roots.

Libido: In Freudian theory, psychic energy that may be attached to different objects (e.g., to the mouth in the oral stage of psychosexual development).

Life space: Lewin's term for the determinants of an individual's behavior at a certain moment; it includes the person and his or her psychological environment.

Lithium: A drug sometimes used in efforts to reduce manic behavior; effects are still uncertain.

Locus of control: The source or cause to which one attributes control over the consequences of one's behavior, either "internal" (caused by the actor) or "external" (caused by the situation or by chance).

LSD (lysergic acid diathylamide): Best-known and most-used of the hallucinogens or "mind-altering" drugs, especially popular during the counterculture of the late 1960s.

Mandala: One of Jung's archetypes, a circle symbolizing the self and containing designs often divided into four parts.

Manic-depressive psychosis: An affective psychosis characterized by extreme happiness, sadness, or alternation between the two.

Mantra: A word or sound that is repeated in order to achieve the meditative state in yoga and in transcendental meditation.

Maturation: Development and growth with increasing age, primarily determined by genetic factors, and automatic when given the appropriate environment.

Melancholic: Describes one of the four temperaments of Hippocrates' typology. Melancholic persons were supposedly depressed due to an excess of black bile.

Mesomorph: One of Sheldon's somatotypes, characterized by a muscular, rectangular body and an assertive, energetic, and courageous (somatotonic) temperament (see *ectomorph, endomorph*).

Methadone: A drug that appears promising in the treatment of heroin addiction. Blocks the craving for heroin and prevents "high" if heroin is taken.

MMPI (Minnesota Multiphasic Personality Inventory): Most popular and influential personality questionnaire, consisting of over 500 statements to which the subject responds "true," "false," or "cannot say." Items cover a wide range of topics and have been grouped into nine clinical and three control scales. Scores are summarized in a profile.

Modeling: A technique used in behavior therapy in which the client observes the successful performance of the desirable behaviors by a live or symbolic model. Effective in teaching complex, novel responses in short time periods and in overcoming fears (see *observational learning, guided participation, covert modeling*).

Monozygotic twins: Identical twins; two organisms that develop from a single fertilized egg cell and share identical genes.

Moral anxiety: In Freud's theory, guilt about one's unacceptable feelings, thoughts, or deeds (see also *neurotic anxiety; reality anxiety*).

Moral competence: In the social learning view, the capacity to generate moral behavior.

Motivational determinism: Freud's belief that everything a person does may be determined by his or her pervasive, but unconscious, motives.

Multiple act criterion: A combination of many acts or behaviors that are expected to relate to a trait.

Need for positive regard: In Carl Rogers's theory, a universal need that may lead one to distort experiences that are inconsistent with positive self-regard (self-esteem).

Need to achieve: Motive to achieve and compete against standards of excellence.

Negative reinforcer: Any stimulus that increases the likelihood that a response associated with its termination or removal will occur again.

Neo-analysts: Psychoanalysts, such as Adler, Erikson, Sullivan, Fromm, and Horney, who elaborated and modified Freud's views, placing more emphasis on ego processes and sociocultural forces that Freud did. Also called Neo-Freudians.

Neobehaviorists: Term applied to B. F. Skinner and others who experimentally analyze the observable conditions controlling behavior.

Neurosis: A category of relatively mild maladjustment or deviance, in which the individual suffers from anxiety or fear without realistic justification; may include physical symptoms without organic cause (see *anxiety neurosis, hysterical neurosis, conversion reaction, dissociative reaction*).

Neurotic anxiety: In Freud's theory, fear that one's own impulses will go out of control and lead to punishment (see also *moral anxiety; reality anxiety*).

Neuroticism: The opposite of emotional stability, according to Eysenck, who views neuroticism-emotional stability as an important trait dimension.

Nonverbal communication: Communication without words, for example by gestures, facial expression, and eye contact.

Objective measures: Procedures used in the gathering, scoring, and interpretation of data that are standardized, reproducible, and usually involve structured responses.

Observational learning: The process of learning through observation of a live or symbolic model. Requires no direct reinforcement.

Obsession: A thought that repeatedly occupies attention although the person prefers to be rid of it.

Obsessive-compulsive neurosis: A neurotic condition in which there are disruptive, persistent thoughts and/or irresistible urges to repeat certain behaviors (e.g., washing one's hands hundreds of times daily) (see *neurosis*).

Oedipus complex: According to Freud, the love for the opposite-sex parent during the phallic stage of psychosexual development.

Operant: Freely emitted response pattern that operates on the environment; its future strength depends on its consequences.

Operant conditioning: The increase in frequency of an operant response after it has been followed by a favorable outcome (reinforced).

Oral stage: First of Freud's psychosexual stages, when pleasure is focused on the mouth and on the satisfactions of sucking and eating, as during the first year of life.

Organismic values: In Carl Rogers's theory, the actual values and true experiences of the organism.

Overjustification: Excessive external rewards for an activity; may interfere with the intrinsic or inherent gratification of the activity.

Paranoia: Psychosis characterized by delusions of grandeur and persecution, often organized into a coherent, internally consistent system.

Partial (intermittent) reinforcement schedule: Schedule of reinforcement in which a response is sometimes reinforced, sometimes not reinforced. The four types of partial reinforcement schedules are: fixed interval, fixed ratio, variable interval, variable ratio.

Peak experience: H. Maslow's term for a temporary experience of fulfillment and joy in which the person loses self-centeredness and (in varying degrees of intensity) feels a nonstriving happiness: a moment of perfection.

Penis envy: Envy of the male sex organ. Believed by Freud to be universal in women, to be responsible for women's castration complex, and to be central to the psychology of women.

Perceptual defense: Unconscious repressive mechanisms which screen and block threatening visual and auditory inputs.

Person perception: The process through which people form impressions of each other and of themselves.

Person variables: A set of cognitive and behavioral attributes, proposed in a cognitive-social learning approach to individual differences. Person variables include: construction competencies, encoding strategies, expectancies, values, and self-regulatory systems.

Personal construct theory: G. Kelly's theory that behavior is determined by the way an individual categorizes his or her experiences; personal constructs. This position views humans as active, ever-changing creators of hypotheses and players of multiple roles.

Personal constructs: Personal categories and labels; a concept in G. Kelly's theory.

Personality: Usually refers to the distinctive patterns of behavior (including thoughts and emotions) that characterize each individual's adaptation to the situations of his or her life.

Personality assessment: Efforts to measure and analyze an individual's behavior.

Personality coefficient: Phrase that describes the modest correlation (usually between .20 and .30) typically found in personality research linking responses on questionnaires to other behavior.

Personality structure: Allport's term for the individual's pattern of dispositions which he believed determined behavior.

Personality, study of: Seeks to generate theories about human nature and individuality and to understand the causes and meaning of important psychological differences among individuals.

Personologists: Those who study personality.

Persuasion: Changes in behavior in compliance to rules or requests, accompanied by alterations in beliefs and values (see *compliance*).

Persuasion inoculation: A technique intended to help a person resist influence: a weak attack is made upon the person's attitudes in order to stimulate the development of counterarguments in defense of these attitudes.

Phallic stage: Third of Freud's psychosexual stages (at about age five) when pleasure is focused on the genitals and both males and females experience the "Oedipus complex."

Phenomenological approach: Theory that emphasizes the person's experience as he or she perceives it.

Phenothiazines: "Major" tranquilizers useful in managing schizophrenic patients (also called "antipsychotic drugs").

Phlegmatic: Describes one of the four temperaments of Hippocrates' typology. Phlegmatic persons were supposedly calm and listless due to an excess of phlegm.

Phobic neurosis: A neurotic condition in which there is intense and excessive fear of objects or situations to an extent that interferes with the person's life (see *neurosis*).

PKU (phenylketonuria): A genetic abnormality in which the gene that produces a critical enzyme is missing. It results in mental retardation if not treated soon after birth.

Placebo: An inert substance administered to someone who believes it is an active drug.

Pleasure principle: In Freud's theory, the basis for id functioning. Irrational, seeks immediate satisfaction of instinctual impulses.

Plethysmograph: An instrument that records changes in blood volume.

Polygraph: An instrument used to measure several physiological responses at the same time (e.g., heart rate, respiration rate, and muscle tension), recording them by deflecting a pen across a moving paper chart.

Positive reinforcer: Any stimulus whose occurrence increases the likelihood that a response with which it has been associated will occur again.

Preparedness (biological preparedness): The capacity to acquire certain associations more easily than others (for example fear of snakes versus electrical outlets). Possibly innate.

Primacy effect: The tendency in perception or impression formation to give the initial information more weight than the subsequent information.

Primary drives: Inborn motives for behavior such as hunger, pain, sex.

Primary mental abilities: Irreducible mental abilities hypothesized by Thurstone and other factor analysts. They include memory, reasoning, and verbal and spatial abilities, and are said to underlie performance on intelligence tests.

Primary process thinking: Freud's term for the id's direct, reality-ignoring attempts to satisfy needs irrationally.

Primary reinforcer: An unconditioned or natural reinforcer that satisfies basic biological needs such as hunger or thirst.

Projection: A defense mechanism by which one attributes one's own unacceptable aspects or impulses to someone else.

Projective tests: Tests (such as the Rorschach or TAT) that present the individual with materials open to a wide variety of interpretations based on the belief that responses reveal important aspects of the respondent's personality central in psychodynamic assessment.

Proprium: G. Allport's term for the region of personality that contains the root of the consistency that characterizes attitudes, goals, and values. Not innate, it develops in time.

Prosocial aggressions: Verbal threats and statements about the goodness or badness of behavior.

Prototype: The best or most typical example of a category; for example a robin is a prototypical bird, an ostrich is not.

Psychedelic or consciousness-altering drugs: Drugs that affect mental processes, such as LSD.

Psychoanalytic therapy: Psychotherapy based on the ideas of Freud and his followers.

Psychodynamic approach: Theories that infer unconscious motives and conflicts and emphasize past experience, e.g., Freud's theory.

Psychodynamic behavior theory: Developed by John Dollard and Neal Miller in the late 1940s to integrate some of the fundamental ideas of psychoanalytic theory with the concepts and methods of experimental research on behavior and learning.

Psychogenic needs: Needs which are not physiologic such as achievement, affiliation, and competence.

Psychometric tests: Questionnaires, inventories, or rating scales that are objective and standardized.

Psychometric trait approach: Approach that emphasizes quantitative measurement of psychological qualities, comparing the responses of large groups of people under standard conditions, often by means of paper-and-pencil tests.

Psychosexual stages: According to Freudian theory, development occurs in a series of psychosexual stages. In each stage (oral, anal, phallic, and genital) pleasure is focused on a different part of the body.

Psychosis: Patterns of behavior diagnosed as signs of severe mental illness in which action, thinking, or mood problems cripple the individual's ability to function. Subtypes include schizophrenia, paranoid psychoses, and affective psychoses.

Psychosocial stages: Erikson's eight stages of development; extending throughout life, each stage centers around a "crisis" or set of problems and the individual's attempts to solve it.

Psychotherapy: Professional attempts to effect change in thought, mood, and/or behavior through verbal and symbolic techniques. Psychotherapy may be conducted by a variety of trained persons in a variety of settings.

Psychotic depression: Extreme sadness, often accompanied by feelings of worthlessness, fears, and loss of interest in eating, sex, and other activities. In psychotic depression there is usually no objective loss or failure experience in the person's life that can adequately explain the depression. In neurotic depression the depressed behavior may be an intense reaction to the death of a loved one or other loss or stress.

Q-sort technique, the: A method of obtaining trait ratings; consists of many cards, on each of which is printed a trait description. The rater groups the cards in a series of piles ranging from those which are least characteristic to those which are most characteristic of the rated person.

Radical behaviorism: The view that the science of human behavior should focus on the prediction and control of the behavior of individual organisms by studying stimulus-response relationships without attention to any intervening psychological steps.

Randomization: The assignment of research subjects to different conditions on the basis of chance. If many subjects are used, differences should average out, except for the effects produced by the experiment itself.

Rational emotive therapy: Albert Ellis' approach based on the idea that if people learn to think more rationally their behavior will become more rational and their emotional problems will be reduced.

Rational restructuring: Changing an individual's inaccurate (irrational) assumptions and beliefs so that they correspond more accurately to reality and produce less discomfort. A central focus in Ellis' rational-emotive therapy.

Rationalization: A defense mechanism that occurs when one makes something more acceptable by attributing it to more acceptable causes (see *defense mechanisms*).

Reaction formation: A defense mechanism that occurs when an anxiety-producing impulse is replaced in consciousness by its opposite.

Reality anxiety: In Freud's theory, the fear of real dangers in the external world (see also *moral anxiety; neurotic anxiety*).

Reality principle: In Freud's theory, the basis for ego functioning. Rational; dictates delay in the discharge of tension until environmental conditions are appropriate.

Reality testing: In psychodynamic theory, the process by which the ego forms a plan for the satisfaction of a need and then tests this plan in order to see whether or not it will work.

Regression: In psychodynamic theory, reversion to an earlier stage; the return of the libido to its former halting places in development.

Reinforcement: Any consequence that increases the likelihood that a response will be repeated.

Reinforcement learning theory: Theory

that reinforcement is necessary for learning to occur.

Reliability: Consistency or stability of a psychological test measured by a coefficient of correlation between scores on two halves of a test *(internal reliability),* alternate forms of the test, or retests with the same group of people being given the same test on two occasions *(temporal reliability). Interscorer agreement* is the degree to which different scorers arrive at the same judgments about the same test data.

Repression: According to psychoanalytic theory, an unconscious defense mechanism through which unacceptable (ego-threatening) material is kept from awareness. The repressed motives, ideas, conflicts, memories, etc., continue to influence behavior.

Repression-sensitization continuum: A dimension of differences in defensive patterns of perception ranging from avoiding the anxiety-arousing stimuli to approaching them more readily and being extravigilant or supersensitized to them.

Resistance: Difficulties in achieving progress in psychotherapy due to unconscious defenses as anxiety-producing material emerges during the treatment.

Response: Any observable, identifiable activity of an organism.

Response sets: Systematic ways of answering test or interview questions that are related to characteristics of the alternatives other than what the question is attempting to measure. Examples of response sets are *social desirability* (tendencies to endorse only socially desirable statements) and *yea-saying or acquiescence* (tendency to agree with items regardless of their content). Response sets hamper the interpretation of the test responses.

Role Play: A technique used in therapy by G. Kelly and others in which an individual behaves as if he or she were another person (a parent, for example) in order to gain new perspectives.

Rorschach: Projective test consisting of ten symmetrical inkblots to which the subject describes his or her reactions, stating what each blot looks like or might be.

Sanguine: Describes one of the four temperaments of Hippocrates' typology. Sanguine persons were supposedly optimistic due to an excess of blood.

Scapegoating: Directing aggression against a less powerful person or group than the one which is the source of the frustration or other antecedent of the aggression. Regarded by psychodynamic theory as a displacement of aggression, by social learning theory as the result of discrimination learning in which aggression against certain groups is modeled and highly rewarded.

Schedule of reinforcement: Pattern or sequence of reinforcement (e.g., number of responses or time interval before reinforcement is given).

Schema: Cognitive category that serves as a frame of reference for processing and evaluating experiences, for example *self-schema.*

Schemata: Cognitive structures or rules for processing information; believed by cognitive stage theorists to undergo fundamental transformations during development.

Schizophrenia: Most common form of psychosis. Prominent symptoms may include thought disorder, delusions, highly inappropriate or bizarre emotions, and hallucinations, all without known organic cause.

Secondary or learned drives: In psychodynamic behavior theory (Miller and Dollard), drives such as fear, which are acquired on the basis of primary (unlearned, innate) drives and whose reduction is reinforcing.

Secondary process thinking: In Freud's theory, the type of thinking characteristic of conscious mental activity. It obeys the laws of grammar and formal logic, uses bound energy, and is governed by the reality principle, i.e., reduces instinctual tension by adaptive behavior.

Secondary reinforcer: A stimulus that has become reinforcing as a result of its association with an unconditioned stimulus or primary reinforcer.

Secondary traits: Allport's term for dispositions that are narrower, more specific, and influence fewer behaviors than do central traits.

Selective perception: The interpretation of unclear events in accord with the individual's expectations and momentary states.

Self: In the theory of Carl Rogers, the conscious perception of oneself and the values attached to these perceptions.

Self-actualization: According to the humanistic view, the highest motive of human behavior, the motive to realize oneself fully as a person. Self-actualizing people are said to be characterized by self-acceptance, spontaneity, creativity, autonomy, concern for others, and mystical experiences.

Self-concept: In Carl Rogers's theory, the perception of oneself; may clash with one's "organismic values," producing conflict.

Self-efficacy: Bandura's term for the individual's beliefs about his or her own effectiveness; the expectation that one can successfully conduct the action required.

Self-efficacy expectations: The person's confidence that he or she *can* perform a particular behavior, like handling a snake or making a public speech.

Self-esteem: Refers to the individual's personal judgment of his or her own worth.

Self-focus: Process in which attention is directed inward toward the self. Also a personality trait similar to self-consciousness.

Self-instruction: Talking to oneself to control one's behavior; an aspect of some types of self-control training.

Self-management: A technique used in behavior therapy in which an individual evaluates and reinforces his or her own behavior in a systematic fashion.

Self-monitoring: Systematic self-observation and recording of progress in a behavior change program.

Self-observation: Systematic observation of one's own behavior; an important step in some types of behavior therapy.

Self-perception theory: Alternative to cognitive dissonance theory, proposing that when internal cues are weak or absent, a person judges his or her feelings and motives using the same information and reasoning that an outside observer would employ.

Self-realization: According to Jung, a basic goal of every individual, requiring reconciliation of complementary opposites in the personality (for example, conscious-unconscious, animus-anima).

Self-regulatory systems (plans): A person variable that includes the individual's rules, plans, and self-reactions for performance and for the organization of complex behavior sequences (see *person variables*).

Self-reinforcement: The process of providing positive consequences to oneself contingent upon enacting certain desired behaviors or achieving specific performance criteria (e.g., an A on an exam).

Self-report: Refers to any statements a person makes about himself or herself: "structured" self-reports are statements in which the form of reactions to items is restricted.

Self-schemata (or self-schema): Cognitions about the self that arise from past experience and guide the processing of new information.

Self-system: Includes the standards and rules used in self-control and the expectations about what one can do successfully.

Semantic differential: Technique for studying the meanings of concepts or words; the subject rates each concept or word in a list that has opposite words at each extreme (e.g., warm-cold) and five points in between.

Sensate focus: A method for overcoming sexual-performance fears in which the couple concentrates on sensual pleasures without engaging in sexual intercourse.

Sensing (in Jung's theory): One of Jung's four basic ways of experiencing or contacting the world, focusing on knowing through sensory systems (see *feeling, intuition, thinking*).

Sensory anaesthesia: Loss of sensory ability (e.g., blindness, deafness) or loss of feeling in a body part.

Sex-role identity: The degree to which an individual regards himself or herself as masculine or feminine.

Sex-typed behaviors: Behaviors that are considered appropriate for one sex but not for the opposite sex.

Sex-typing: The process whereby the individual comes to acquire, to value, and to practice (perform) sex-typed behaviors.

Shaping: Technique for producing successively better approximations of a behavior by reinforcing small variations in behavior in the desired direction and by reinforcing only increasingly close approximations to the desired behavior.

Single-blind method: An experimental procedure in which subjects do not know whether they are in experimental or control conditions.

Situationism: The study or explanation of behavior in terms of external stimuli, ignoring or deemphasizing organismic factors.

Social and personality psychologists: Psychologists who study individuals and groups in interaction with each other or in specially devised social and test situations.

Social cognition: Refers to the ways in which we perceive, know, and understand social stimuli, including ourselves and other people. The focus is on people as "knowers" and "perceivers" of behavior.

Social learning theory: Approach to psychology that emphasizes social learning and cognitive processes and the active interaction between the individual and his or her environment; has been applied especially to the analysis and treatment of complex social and abnormal behavior in the fields of clinical and personality psychology.

Somatotonic: In Sheldon's typology, the temperament of the mesomorph, who has a muscular body and is characterized by assertiveness, energy, and courage (see *cerebrotonic, viscerotonic*).

Somatotype: Body type; the basis of Sheldon's typology, linking character and body build.

Source traits: In R. B. Cattell's theory, the traits that constitute personality structure and determine surface traits and behavior.

Specific mental abilities: In contrast to generalized mental ability, specific mental abilities, different for different types of tests, are believed by some theorists to underlie performance on mental tasks (see *primary mental abilities*).

Spontaneous recovery: After a time, an apparently extinguished response may spontaneously reappear.

Stage theories: Theories that hypothesize fundamental transformations in development that follow a fixed and invariant sequence.

Standardized tests: Tests which apply the same procedures, materials, scoring, and interpretation to all subjects.

State anxiety: State anxiety is conceptualized as a person's momentary or situational anxiety and it varies in intensity over time and across settings.

Statisically significant: A research finding (e.g., a difference between two groups) is considered statistically significant when statistical tests indicate that it could not have occurred by chance except at an unlikely level of probability, for example, once in a hundred times.

Stereotype: Overly simple generalization about a group that leads one to believe that every member of the group possesses certain characteristics (e.g., the belief that all women are dependent).

Stimulus: (1) Any observable, identifiable event or situation inside or outside the organism; (2) The occasion for a response; (3) A specific type of energy coming to the sense organ (e.g., a sound wave).

Stimulus-resonse (S-R) psychology: Approach to psychology that emphasizes stimuli, responses, and their relationships, while avoiding all inferences about possible mental steps that take place between a given stimulus (S) and the response (R).

Stress: A psychological and physiological state that results from a broad range of potentially unpleasant or dangerous events, which include unavoidable pain, excessive noise and fatigue, and traumatic dangers.

Subception: Unconscious perception, or perception without full awareness.

Sublimation: A process through which socially unacceptable impulses are expressed in socially acceptable ways.

Superego: In Freud's theory, the conscience, made up of the internalized values of the parents; strives for self-control and perfection, is both unconscious and conscious.

Suppression: Occurs when one voluntarily

and consciously withholds a response or turns attention away from something (see also *repression*).

Surface traits: R. B. Cattell's term for clusters of observable trait elements (responses) that seem to go together; the manifestations of source traits.

Symptom substitution: The controversial psychoanalytic belief that new symptoms will automatically replace problematic behaviors that are removed directly (e.g., by behavior therapy) unless their underlying unconscious emotional causes also have been removed.

Systematic desensitization: A behavior therapy procedure designed to reduce incapacitating anxiety; an incompatible response (usually relaxation) is paired with progressively more anxiety-arousing situations until the individual is able to imagine or be in these situations without becoming anxious.

Temperament traits: R. B. Cattell's term for traits that determine emotional reactivity.

Testable: Term usually applied to a theory or hypothesis that means it is capable of being evaluated (confirmed or disproved) by empirical methods.

Test-retest reliability: A measure of the consistency or reliability over time obtained by comparing people's scores on a test on one occasion with their scores on the same test on a later occasion.

Thematic Apperception Test (TAT): Projective test consisting of a set of ambiguous pictures about which the subject is asked to make up an interesting story.

Thinking (in Jung's theory): One of Jung's four basic ways of experiencing or contacting the world, focusing on reasoning (see *feeling, intuition, sensing*).

Trait: A persistent (enduring) characteristic or dimension of individual differences. Defined by Allport as a generalized "neuropsychic system," distinctive to each person, that serves to unify many different stimuli .by leading the person to generate consistent responses to them.

Trait anxiety: A person's stable, characteristic overall level of anxiety (see also *state anxiety*).

Transcendental meditation (TM): A popular form of meditation in which the meditator sits comfortably with eyes closed and repeats a special Sanskrit word called a "mantra."

Transference: In psychoanalysis, the patient's response to the therapist as though the therapist were a parent or some other important figure from childhood. Considered an essential aspect of psychoanalytic therapy.

Trauma (psychological): Events that have a lasting negative effect on mental life.

Type A: A type of person characterized by a behavior pattern of competitive achievement striving, time urgency, aggressiveness, and hostility. Individuals of this type are believed to be coronary-prone.

Typology: Ways of categorizing individuals into discrete categories or types (e.g., male, female, depressed, optimistic).

Unconditioned response: The unlearned response one naturally makes to an unconditioned stimulus (e.g., withdraw the hand from a hot object).

Unconditioned stimulus: A stimulus to which one automatically, naturally responds without learning to do so (e.g., food, electric shock).

Unconscious: In psychoanalytic theory the part of the personality of which the ego is unaware.

Unconscious motives: Wishes or needs of which the individual is unaware but which influence both normal and abnormal behavior.

Unique traits: In Allport's theory, a trait that exists in only one individual and cannot be found in another in exactly the same form.

Validity: The degree to which a test measures what it is supposed to. Subcategories include (a) *content or face validity,* the extent to which the items on a test adequately represent a defined broader class of behavior; (b) *criterion validity,* the relationship between the obtained sample and other criterion data, either concurrently or predictively; (c) *construct validity,* the elaboration of the inferred traits determining test behavior.

Valium: A "minor" tranquilizer that acts on the limbic system of the brain and is the most frequently prescribed drug in the United States today.

Variable: An attribute, quality, or characteristic that may be given two or more values and measured or systematically varied.

Vicarious conditioning: Conditioning of response to a stimulus through observation.

Viscerotonic: In Sheldon's typology, the temperament of the endomorph, who has overdeveloped digestive viscera, and is characterized by sociability, relaxation, and love of eating (see *somatotonic, cerebrotonic*).

Working through: Process that occurs in psychoanalytic therapy when the patient, in the context of the transference relationship, re-examines his or her basic problems until their emotional roots are understood and learns to handle them more appropriately.

References

ABELSON, R. P. (1976). A script theory of understanding, attitude, and behavior. In J. Carroll & T. Payne (Eds.), *Cognition and social behavior*. Hillsdale, N.J.: Erlbaum.

ABRAMSON, L. Y., SELIGMAN, M. E. P., & TEASDALE, J. D. (1978). Learned helplessness in humans: Critique and reformation. *Journal of Abnormal Psychology, 87,* 49–74.

ADINOLFI, A. A. (1971). Relevance of person perception research to clinical psychology. *Journal of Consulting and Clinical Psychology, 37,* 167–176.

ADORNO, I. W., FRENKEL-BRUNSWIK, E., LEVINSON, D. J., & SANFORD, R. N. (1950). *The authoritarian personality.* New York: Harper & Row.

AJZEN, I., & FISHBEIN, M. (1977). Attitude-behavior relations: A theoretical analysis and review of empirical research. *Psychological Bulletin, 84,* 888–918.

ALKER, H. A. (1972). Is personality situationally specific or intrapsychically consistent? *Journal of Personality, 40,* 1–16.

ALLEN, E. K., HART, B. M., BUELL, J. S., HARRIS, F. R., & WOLF, M. M. (1964). Effects of social reinforcement on isolate behavior of a nursery school child. *Child Development, 35,* 511–518.

ALLPORT, G. W. (1937). *Personality: A psychological interpretation.* New York: Holt, Rinehart and Winston.

ALLPORT, G. W. (1940). Motivation in personality: Reply to Mr. Bertocci. *Psychological Review. 47,* 533–554.

ALLPORT, G. W. (1961). *Pattern and growth in personality.* New York: Holt, Rinehart and Winston.

ALLPORT, G. W. & ODBERT, H. S. (1936). Trait-names: A psycho-lexical study. *Psychological Monographs: General and Applied, 47* (1, Whole No. 211).

AMERICAN PSYCHOLOGICAL ASSOCIATION (1966). *Standards for educational and psychological tests and manuals.* Washington, D.C.: APA.

AMES, L. B., & WALKER, R. N. (1964). Prediction of later reading ability from kindergarten Rorschach and IQ scores. *Journal of Educational Psychology, 55,* 309–313.

AMSEL, A., & ROUSSEL, J. S. (1952). Motivational properties of frustration: I. Effect on a running response of the addition of frustration to the motivational complex. *Journal of Experimental Psychology. 43,* 363–368.

ANASTASI, A., & D'ANGELO, R. (1952). A comparison of Negro and white preschool children in language development and Goodenough Draw-a-Man I.Q. *Journal of Genetic Psychology, 81,* 147–165.

ANDERSON, I. H., HUGHES, B. O., & DIXON, W. R. (1957). The rate of reading development and its relation to age of learning to read, sex, and intelligence. *Journal of Educational Research. 50,* 481–494.

ANDERSON, J. R., & BOWER, G. H. (1973). *Human associative memory.* New York: Wiley.

ANDERSON, N. H. (1965). Primacy effects in personality impression formation using a generalized order effect paradigm. *Journal of Personality and Social Psychology, 2,* 1–9.

ANDERSON, N. H. (1974). Information integration theory: A brief survey. In D. H. Krautz, R. C. Atkinson, R. D. Luce, & P. Suppes (Eds.), *Contemporary developments in mathematical psychology.* San Francisco: Freeman.

ANTONOVSKY, A. (1979). *Health, stress and coping.* San Francisco: Jossey-Bass.

ARCHIBALD, H. C., & TUDDENHAM, R. D. (1965). Persistent stress reaction after combat. *Archives of General Psychiatry, 12,* 475–481.

AREND, R., GOVE, F. L., & SROUFE, L. A. (1979). Continuity of individual adaptation from infancy to kindergarten: A predictive study of ego-resiliency and curiosity in preschoolers. *Child Development, 50,* 950–959.

ARGYLE, M., & LITTLE, B. R. (1972). Do personality traits apply to social behavior? *Journal of Theory of Social Behavior* (Great Britain) *2,* 1–35.

ARKIN, A. M., ANTROBUS, J. S., & ELLMAN, J. (Eds.) (1978). *The mind in sleep: Psychology and psychophysiology.* Hillsdale, N.J.: Erlbaum.

ARONFREED, J. (1966). The internalization of social control through punishment: Experimental studies of the role of conditioning and the second signal system in the development of conscience. *Proceedings of the XVIIIth International Congress of Psychology.* Moscow, USSR, August, *35,* 219–230.

ARONFREED, J. (1968). *Conduct and conscience: The socialization of internalized control over behavior.* New York: Academic Press.

ARONSON, E. (1972). *The social animal.* San Francisco: Freeman.

ARONSON, E. (1976). *The social animal (2nd ed.).* San Francisco: Freeman.

ARONSON, E., & METTEE, D. (1968). Dishonest behavior as a function of differential levels of induced self-esteem. *Journal of Personality and Social Psychology, 9,* 121–127.

ARONSON, E., WILLERMAN, B., & FLOYD, J. (1966). The effect of a pratfall on increasing interpersonal attractiveness. *Psychonomic Science, 4,* 227–228.

ASCH, S. E. (1946). Forming impressions of personality. *Journal of Abnormal and Social Psychology, 41,* 258–290.

ASERINSKY, E., & KLEITMAN, N. (1953). Regularly occurring periods of eye motility, and concomitant phenomena, during sleep. *Science, 118,* 273–274.

ASERINSKY, E., & KLEITMAN, N. (1955). Two types of ocular motility occurring in sleep. *Journal of Applied Psychology, 8,* 1–10.

ATKINSON, J. W. (1957). Motivational determinants of risk-taking behavior. *Psychological Review, 64,* 359–372.

ATKINSON, J. W. (Ed.). (1958). *Motives in fantasy, action and society.* Princeton: Van Nostrand.

ATKINSON, J. W., & FEATHER, N. T. (1966). *A theory of achievement motivation.* New York: Wiley.

ATTHOWE, J. M., JR., & KRASNER, L. (1968). A preliminary report on the application of contingent reinforcement procedures (token economy) on a "chronic" psychiatric ward. *Journal of Abnormal Psychology, 73,* 37–43.

AX, A. F. (1953). The physiological differentiation between fear and anger in humans. *Psychosomatic Medicine, 15,* 433–442.

AYLLON, T., & AZRIN, N. H. (1965). The measurement and reinforcement of behavior of psychotics. *Journal of the Experimental Analysis of Behavior, 8,* 357–383.

AYLLON, T., & AZRIN, N. H. (1968). *The token economy.* New York: Appleton.

AYLLON, T., & HAUGHTON, E. (1964). Modification of symptomatic verbal behaviour of mental patients. *Behaviour Research and Therapy, 2,* 87–97.

BALOW, I. H. (1963). Sex differences in first grade reading. *Elementary English, 40,* 303–306.

BALTES, P. B. (1979). Life-span developmental psychology: Observations on history and theory. In P. B. Baltes & O. C. Brim, Jr. (Eds.), *Life-span development and behavior, Vol. 2.* New York: Academic Press.

BANDURA, A. (1960). Relationship of family patterns to child behavior disorders. Progress Report, U.S.P.H. Research Grant M-1734, Stanford University, Calif.

BANDURA, A. (1965). Vicarious processes: A case of no-trial learning. In L. Berkowitz (Ed.), *Advances in experimental social psychology, Vol.* II. New York: Academic Press, 1–55.

BANDURA, A. (1969). *Principles of behavior modification.* New York: Holt, Rinehart and Winston.

BANDURA, A. (1971). *Social learning theory.* Morristown, N.J.: General Learning Press.

BANDURA, A. (1973). *Aggression: A social learning analysis.* Englewood Cliffs, N.J.: Prentice-Hall.

BANDURA, A. (1977). *Social learning theory.* Englewood Cliffs, N.J.: Prentice-Hall.

BANDURA, A. (1978). Reflections on self-efficacy. In S. Rachman (Ed.), *Advances in behaviour research and therapy, Vol. 1.* Elmsford, N.Y.: Pergamon Press.

BANDURA, A. (1982). Self-efficacy mechanisms in human agency. *American Psychologist, 37,* 122–147.

BANDURA, A. (1986, In press). *Social foundations of thought and action: a social-cognitive theory.* Englewood Cliffs, N.J.: Prentice-Hall.

BANDURA, A., & ADAMS, N. E. (1977). Analysis of self-efficacy theory of behavioral change. *Cognitive Therapy and Research, 1,* 287–310.

BANDURA, A., ADAMS, N. E., & BEYER, J. (1977). Cognitive processes mediating behavioral change. *Journal of Personality and Social Psychology, 35,* 125–139.

BANDURA, A., BLANCHARD, E. B., & RITTER, B. (1969). Relative efficacy of desensitization and modeling approaches for inducing behavioral, affective, and attitudinal changes. *Journal of Personality and Social Psychology, 13,* 173–199.

BANDURA, A., GRUSEC, J. E., & MENLOVE, F. L. (1966). Observational learning as a function of symbolization and incentive set. *Child Development, 37,* 499–506.

BANDURA, A., GRUSEC, J. E., & MENLOVE, F. L. (1967). Vicarious extinction of avoidance behavior. *Journal of Personality and Social Psychology, 5,* 16–23.

BANDURA, A., & JEFFERY, R. W. (1973). Role of symbolic coding and rehearsal processes in observational learning. *Journal of Personality and Social Psychology, 26,* 122–130.

BANDURA, A., & KUPERS, C. J. (1964). Transmission of patterns of self-reinforcement through modeling. *Journal of Abnormal and Social Psychology, 69,* 1–9.

BANDURA, A., & MCDONALD, F. J. (1963). Influence of social reinforcement and the behavior of models in shaping children's moral judgments. *Journal of Abnormal Social Psychology, 67,* 274–281.

BANDURA, A., & MISCHEL, W. (1965). Modification of self-imposed delay of reward through exposure to live and symbolic models. *Journal of Personality and Social Psychology, 2,* 698–705.

BANDURA, A., ROSS, D., & ROSS, S. A. (1963). Imitation of film-mediated aggressive models. *Journal of Abnormal and Social Psychology, 66,* 3–11.

BANDURA, A., TAYLOR, C. B., EWART, C. K., MILLER, N. M., & DEBUSK, R. F. (1985). Exercise testing to enhance wives' confidence in their husbands' cardiac capability soon after clinically uncomplicated acute myocardial infarction. *American Journal of Cardiology, 55,* 635–638.

BANDURA, A., UNDERWOOD, B., & FROMSON, M. E. (1975). Disinhibition of aggression through diffusion of responsibility and dehumanization of victims. *Journal of Research in Personality, 9,* 253–269.

BANDURA, A., & WALTERS, R. H. (1963). *Social learning and personality development.* New York: Holt, Rinehart and Winston.

BARBER, T. X. (1970). *LSD, marihuana, yoga, and hypnosis.* Chicago: Aldine.

BARBER, T. X. (1972). Suggested "hypnotic" behavior: The trance paradigm versus an alternative paradigm. In E. Fromm & R. E. Shor (Eds.), *Hypnosis: Research developments and perspectives* (pp. 115–182). Chicago: Aldine-Atherton.

BARDWICK, J. (1972). *Psychology of women: A study of biocultural conflicts.* New York: Harper & Row.

BARKER, R. G. (1968). *Ecological psychology.* Stanford, Calif.: Stanford University Press.

BARKER, R. G., DEMBO, T., & LEWIN, K. (1941). Frustration and regression: An experiment with young children. *University of Iowa Studies in Child Welfare, 18* (Whole No. 386).

BARRY, H. B., III., BACON, M. K., & CHILD, I. L. (1957). A cross-cultural survey of some sex differences in socialization. *Journal of Abnormal and Social Psychology, 55,* 327–332.

BAVELAS, J. B. (1978). *Personality: Current theory and research.* Monterey, Calif.: Brooks-Cole.

BECK, A. T., RUSH, A. J., SHAW, B. F., & EMERY, G. (1979). *Cognitive therapy of depression.* New York: Guilford Press.

BELL, J. E. (1948). *Projective techniques.* New York: Longmans, Green.

BELL, R. Q., & COSTELLO, N. (1964). Three tests for sex differences in tactile sensitivity in the newborn. *Biologia Neonatorum, 7,* 335–347.

BELL, R. Q., & DARLING, J. (1965). The prone head reaction in the human newborn: Relationship with sex and tactile sensitivity. *Child Development, 36,* 943–949.

BELL, R. Q., WELLER, G., & WALDROP, M. (1971). Newborn and preschooler: Organization of behavior and relations between periods. *Monographs of the Society for Research in Child Development, 36* (Nos. 1, 2).

BEM, D. J., & ALLEN, A. (1974). On predicting some of the people some of the time: The search for cross-situational consistencies in behavior. *Psychological Review, 81,* 506–520.

BEM, D. J., & FUNDER, D. C. (1978). Predicting more of the people more of the time: Assessing the personality of situations. *Psychological Review, 85,* 485–501.

BEM, S. L. (1974). The measurement of psychological androgyny. *Journal of Consulting and Clinical Psychology, 42,* 155–162.

BEM, S. L. (1975). Sex-role adaptability: One consequence of psychological androgyny. *Journal of Personality and Social Psychology, 31,* 634–643.

BEM, S. L., & BEM, D. J. (1972). Homogenizing the American woman: The power of an unconscious ideology. Unpublished manuscript, Stanford University.

BENNETT, E. M., & COHEN, L. R. (1959). Personality patterns and contrasts. *Genetic Psychology Monographs, 59,* 101–155.

BENNETT, G. K., SEASHORE, H. G., & WESMAN, A. G. (1959). *Differential aptitudes test manual (3rd ed.).* New York: Psychological Corp.

BENSON, H. (1975). *The relaxation response.* New York: Morrow.

BERGER, S. M. (1962). Conditioning through vicarious instigation. *Psychological Review, 69,* 450–466.

BERGIN, A. E. (1966). Some implications of psychotherapy research for therapeutic practice. *Journal of Abnormal Psychology, 71,* 235–246.

BERGIN, A. E. (1971). The evaluation of therapeutic outcomes. In A. E. Bergin and S. I. Garfield (Eds.), *Handbook of psychotherapy and behavior change* (pp. 217–270). New York: Wiley.

BERKOWITZ, L. (1969). Control of aggression. *Review of Child Development Research, 3,* 95–140.

BERKOWITZ, L. (1970). The contagion of violence: An S-R mediational analysis of some effects of observed aggression. In M. Page (Ed.), *Nebraska symposium on motivation.* Lincoln: University of Nebraska Press.

References

BERKOWITZ, L. (1973). Words and symbols as stimuli to aggressive responses. In J. Knutoon (Ed.), *The control of aggression.* Chicago: Aldine.

BERKOWITZ, L. (Ed.). (1984). *Advances in experimental social psychology, Vol. 17. Theorizing in social psychology: Special topics.* New York: Academic Press.

BERMAN, J. S., & KENNY, D. A. (1976). Correlational bias in observer ratings. *Journal of Personality and Social Psychology, 34,* 263–273.

BERSCHEID, E., & WALSTER, E. (1974). Physical attractiveness. In L. Berkowitz (Ed.), *Advances in experimental social psychology, Vol. 7.* New York: Academic Press.

BIDERMAN, A. D. (1967). Life and death in extreme captivity situations. In M. H. Appley & R. Trumbull (Eds.), *Psychological stress* (pp. 242–277). New York: Appleton.

BIJOU, S. W. (1965). Experimental studies of child behavior, normal and deviant. In L. Krasner & L. P. Ullmann (Eds.), *Research in behavior modification* (pp. 56–81). New York: Holt, Rinehart and Winston.

BIRDWHISTELL, R. L. (1970). *Kinesics and context.* Philadelphia: University of Pennsylvania Press.

BIRNBRAUER, J. S., BIJOU, S. W., WOLF, M. M., & KIDDER, J. D. (1965). Programmed instruction in the classroom. In L. Ullmann & L. Krasner (Eds.), *Case studies in behavior modification.* New York: Holt, Rinehart and Winston.

BLOCK, J. (1961). *The Q-sort method in personality assessment and psychiatric research.* Springfield, Ill.: Charles C Thomas.

BLOCK, J. (1971). *Lives through time.* Berkeley : Bancroft.

BLOCK, J. (1977). Advancing the psychology of personality: Paradigmatic shift or improving the quality of research. In D. Magnusson & N. S. Endler (Eds.), *Personality at the crossroads: Current issues in interactional psychology.* Hillsdale, N.J.: Erlbaum.

BLOCK, J., & BLOCK, J. H. (1980). The role of ego-control and ego resiliency in the organization of behavior. In W. A. Collins (Ed.), *The Minnesota symposium on child psychology, Vol. 13.* Hillsdale, N.J.: Erlbaum (Wiley).

BLOCK, J., WEISS, D. S., & THORNE, A. (1979). How relevant is a semantic similarity interpretation of personality ratings? *Journal of Personality and Social Psychology, 37,* 1055–1074.

BLOCK, J. H. (1973). Conceptions of sex role: Some cross-cultural and longitudinal perspectives. *American Psychologist, 28,* 512–526.

BLOCK, J. H. & MARTIN, B. (1955). Predicting the behavior of children under frustration. *Journal of Abnormal and Social Psychology, 51,* 281–285.

BLUM, G. S. (1953). *Psychoanalytic theories of personality.* New York: McGraw-Hill.

BLUM, G. S. (1955). Perceptual defense revisited. *Journal of Abnormal and Social Psychology, 51,* 24–29.

BONARIUS, J. C. J. (1965). Research in the personal construct theory of George A. Kelly: Role construct repertory test and basic theory. In B. A. Maher (Ed.), *Progress in experimental personality research* (pp. 1–46). New York: Academic Press.

BOOTZIN, R. (1973). Stimulus control of insomnia (summary). Remarks in The Treatment of Sleep Disorders. Symposium presented at the meeting of the American Psychological Association, Montreal.

BOUCHARD, T. J., HESTON, L., ECKERT, E., KEYES, M., & RESNICK, S. (1981). The Minnesota study of twins reared apart: Project description and sample results in the developmental domain. *Twin research 3: Intelligence, personality and development.* New York: Alan R. Liss.

BOUDIN, H. M. (1972). Contingency contracting as a therapeutic tool in the deceleration of amphetamine use. *Behavior Therapy, 3,* 604–608.

BOWER, G. H. (1981). Mood and Memory. *American Psychologist, 36,* 129–148.

BOWERS, K. (1973). Situationism in psychology: An analysis and a critique. *Psychological Review, 80,* 307–336.

References

BRADY, J. P., & LEVITT, E. E. (1969). Hypnotically induced visual hallucinating. *Psychosomatic Medicine, 28,* 351–363.

BREGER, L., & McGAUGH, J. L. (1965). Critique and reformulation of "learning theory" approaches to psychotherapy and neurosis. *Psychological Bulletin, 63,* 338–358.

BREHM, J. W. (1968). *A theory of psychological reactance.* New York: Academic Press.

BRELAND, H. M. (1974). Birth order, family configuration, and verbal achievement. *Child Development, 45,* 1011–1019.

BRELAND, K., & BRELAND, M. (1966). *Animal behavior.* New York: Macmillan.

BRILL, A. A. (1949). *Basic principles of psychoanalysis.* Garden City, N.Y.: Doubleday.

BROADBENT, D. E. (1977). The hidden preattentive processes. *American Psychologist, 32,* 109–118.

BRONFENBRENNER, U. (1970). *Two worlds of childhood.* New York: Russell Sage.

BROVERMAN, D. M., KLAIBER, E. L., KOBAYASHI, Y., & VOGEL, W. (1968). Roles of activation and inhibition in sex differences in cognitive abilities. *Psychological Review, 75,* 23–50.

BROVERMAN, I. K., BROVERMAN, D. M., CLARKSON, F. E., ROSENKRANTZ, P. S., & VOGEL, S. R. (1970). Sex-role stereotypes and clinical judgments of mental health. *Journal of Consulting and Clinical Psychology, 34,* 1–7.

BROWN, B. (1975). *New mind, new body.* New York: Harper.

BROWN, J. S. (1942). The generalization of approach responses as a function of stimulus intensity and strength of motivation. *Journal of Comparative Psychology, 33,* 209–226.

BROWN, J. S. (1948). Gradients of approach and avoidance responses and their relation to level of motivation. *Journal of Comparative and Physiological Psychology, 41,* 450–465.

BROWN, R. (1965). *Social psychology.* New York: Free Press.

BRUNER, J. S., & GOODMAN, C. C. (1947). Value and need as organizing factors in perception. *Journal of Abnormal and Social Psychology, 42,* 33–44.

BRUNER, J. S., & POSTMAN, L. (1947). Emotional selectivity in perception and reaction. *Journal of Personality, 16,* 69–77.

BUDZYNSKI, T., STOYVA, J., & ADLER, C. (1970). Feedback-induced muscle relaxation. In T. Barber, L. DiCara, J. Kamiya, W. Miller, D. Shapiro, & J. Stoyva (Eds.), *Biofeedback and self-control.* Chicago: Aldine-Atherton.

BUGENTAL, J. F. T. (1971). The humanistic ethic—The individual in psychotherapy as a societal change agent. *Journal of Humanistic Psychology, 11,* 11–25.

BURTON, R. V. (1963). Generality of honesty reconsidered. *Psychological Review, 70,* 481–499.

BUSS, A. H. (1971). Aggression pays. In J. L. Singer (Ed.), *The control of aggression and violence.* New York: Academic Press.

BUSS, A. H., PLOMIN, R. & WILLERMAN, L. (1973). The inheritance of temperaments. *Journal of Personality, 41,* 513–524.

BUSS, D. M., & CRAIK, K. H. (1983). The act frequency approach to personality. *Psychological Review, 90,* 105–126.

BUTLER, J. M., & HAIGH, G. V. (1954). Changes in the relation between self-concepts and ideal concepts consequent upon client-centered counseling. In C. R. Rogers & R. F. Dymond (Eds.), *Psychotherapy and personality change: Co-ordinated studies in the client-centered approach* (pp. 55–76). Chicago: University of Chicago Press.

BUTTERFIELD, H. (1965). *The origins of modern science* New York: Free Press.

BYRNE, D. (1964). Repression-sensitization as a dimension of personality. In B. A. Maher (Ed.), *Progress in experimental personality research, Vol. 1.* New York: Academic Press.

BYRNE, D. (1966). *An introduction to personality.* Englewood Cliffs, N.J.: Prentice-Hall.

BYRNE, D. (1971). *The attraction paradigm.* New York: Academic Press.

BYRNE, D., ERVIN, C. R., & LAMBERTH, J. (1970). Continuity between the experimental study of attraction and real-life computer dating. *Journal of Personality and Social Psychology, 16,* 157–165.

CAIRNS, R. B. (1959). The influence of dependency-anxiety on the effectiveness of social reinforcers. Unpublished doctoral dissertation, Stanford University, Calif.

CAIRNS, R. B. (1979). *Social development.* San Francisco: Freeman.

CAMPBELL, D. T. (1960). Recommendations for APA Test Standards regarding construct, trait, or discriminant validity. *American Psychologist, 15,* 546–553.

CAMPBELL, D. T., & FISKE, D. W. (1959). Convergent and discriminant validation. *Psychological Bulletin, 56,* 81–105.

CAMPBELL, J., & DUNNETTE, M. (1968). Effectiveness of T-group experiences in managerial training and development. *Psychological Bulletin, 70,* 73–104.

CANNON, W. B. (1929). *Bodily changes in pain, hunger, fear and rage (2nd ed.).* New York: Appleton.

CANTOR, N., & MISCHEL, W. (1977). Traits as prototypes: Effects on recognition memory. *Journal of Personality and Social Psychology, 35,* 38–48.

CANTOR, N., & MISCHEL, W. (1979). Prototypes in person perception. In L. Berkowitz (Ed.), *Advances in experimental social psychology, Vol. 12.* New York: Academic Press.

CAREY, G., GOLDSMITH, H. H., TELLEGEN, A., & GOTTESMAN, I. I. (1978). Genetics and personality inventories: The limits of replication with twin data. *Behavior Genetics, 8,* 299–313.

CARLSMITH, J. M., & ANDERSON, C. A. (1979). Ambient temperature and the occurrence of collective violence: A new analysis. *Journal of Personality and Social Psychology, 37,* 337–344.

CARLSON, R. (1971). Where is the person in personality research? *Psychological Bulletin, 75,* 203–219.

CARTWRIGHT, D. S. (1978). *Introduction to personality.* Chicago: Rand McNally.

CARVER, C. S., COLEMAN, A. E., & GLASS, D. C. (1976). The coronary-prone behavior pattern and the suppression of fatigue on a treadmill test. *Journal of Personality and Social Psychology, 33,* 460–466.

CARVER, C. S., & SCHEIER, M. F. (1978). Self-focusing effects of dispositional self-consciousness, mirror presence, and audience presence. *Journal of Personality and Social Psychology, 36,* 324–322.

CATTELL, R. B. (1947). Confirmation and clarification of primary personality factors. *Psychometrika, 12,* 197–220.

CATTELL, R. B. (1950). *A systematic theoretical and factual study.* New York: McGraw-Hill.

CATTELL, R. B. (1957). *Personality and motivation structure and measurement.* Yonkers-on-Hudson: World Book.

CATTELL, R. B. (1965). *The scientific analysis of personality.* Baltimore: Penguin Books.

CHAPMAN, L. J., & CHAPMAN, J. P. (1969). Illusory correlations as an obstacle to the use of valid psychodiagnostic signs. *Journal of Abnormal Psychology, 74,* 271–280.

CHODOFF, P. (1963). Late effects of concentration camp syndrome. *Archives of General Psychiatry, 8,* 323–333.

CHODORKOFF, B. (1954). Self-perception, perceptual defense, and adjustment. *Journal of Abnormal and Social Psychology, 49,* 508–512.

CHOMSKY, N. (1965). *Aspects of the theroy of syntax.* Cambridge, Mass.: M.I.T. Press.

CLARK, D. F. (1963). Fetishism treated by negative conditioning. *British Journal of Psychiatry, 109,* 404–407.

CLIFFORD, M., & WALSTER, E. (1973). The effect of physical attractiveness on teacher expectations. *Sociology of Education, 46,* 248.

CLINE, V. B. Interpersonal perception. (1964). In B. A. Maher (Ed.), *Progress in experimental personality research, Vol. 1* (pp. 221–284). New York: Academic Press.

COBB, S. (1976). Social support as moderator of life stress. *Psychosomatic Medicine, 38,* 300–314.

COHEN, S., & McKAY, G. (1984). Social support, stress, and the buffering hypothesis: A theoretical analysis. In A. Baum, J. E. Singer, S. E. Taylor (Eds.), *Handbook of Psychology and Health: Vol. 4: Social Psychological Aspects of Health,* Hillsdale, N.J.: Erlbaum.

COLBY, K. M. (1951). *A primer for psychotherapists.* New York: Ronald.

COLES, R. (1970). *Uprooted children.* New York: Harper & Row.

COOPER, J., & FAZIO, R. H. (1984). A new look at dissonance theory. In L. Berkowitz (Ed.), *Advances in experimental social psychology, Vol. 17. Theorizing in social psychology: Special topics* (pp. 229–262). New York: Academic Press.

COOPERSMITH, S. (1967). *The antecedents of self-esteem.* San Francisco: Freeman.

COOPERSMITH, S. (1968). Studies in self-esteem. *Scientific American, 218* (2), 96–106.

COWEN, E. L., GARDNER, E. A., & ZAX, M. (1967). *Emergent approaches to mental health problems.* New York: Appleton.

CRAIGHEAD, L. W., STUNKARD, A. J., & O'BRIEN, R. M. (1981). Behavior therapy and pharmacotherapy for obesity. *Archives of General Psychiatry, 38,* 763–768.

CREER, T. (1974). Biofeedback and asthma. *Advances in Asthma and Allergy, 1,* 6–12.

CRONBACH, L. J. (1970). *Essentials of psychological testing.* New York: Harper.

CRONBACH, L. J. (1975). Beyond the two disciplines of scientific psychology. *American Psychologist, 30,* 116–127.

CROW, W. J. (1957). The effect of training upon accuracy and variability in interpersonal perception. *Journal of Abnormal and Social Psychology, 55,* 355–359.

CROW, W. J., & HAMMOND, K. R. (1957). The generality of accuracy and response sets in interpersonal perception. *Journal of Abnormal and Social Psychology, 54,* 384–390.

D'ANDRADE, R. G. (1966). Sex differences and cultural institutions. In E. E. Maccoby (ed.), *The development of sex differences* (pp. 174–204). Stanford, Calif.: Stanford University Press.

D'ANDRADE, R. G. (1974). Memory and the assessment of behavior. In H. Blalock (Ed.), *Measurement in the social sciences.* Chicago: Aldine.

DANET, B. N. (1965). Prediction of mental illness in college students on the basis of "nonpsychiatric" MMPI profiles. *Journal of Consulting Psychology, 29,* 577–580.

DARLEY, J. M., & LATANÉ, B. (1968). Bystander intervention in emergencies: Diffusion of responsibility. *Journal of Personality and Social Psychology, 8,* 377–383.

DAVIS, J. M., KLERMAN, G., & SCHILDKRAUT, J. (1967). Drugs used in the treatment of depression. In L. Efron, J. O. Cole, D. Levine, & J. R. Wittenborn, *Psychopharmocology: A review of progress.* Washington, D.C.: U.S. Clearing-House of Mental Health Information.

DAVISON, G. C. (1968). Systematic desensitization as a counterconditioning process. *Journal of Abnormal Psychology, 73,* 91–99.

DAVITZ, J. R. (1952). The effects of previous training on postfrustration behavior. *Journal of Abnormal and Social Psychology, 47,* 309–315.

DEAUX, K., & EMSWILLER, T. (1974). Explanation of successful performance on sex linked tasks: What is skill for the male is luck for the female. *Journal of Personality and Social Psychology, 29,* 80–85.

DECHTER, M. (1972). *The new chastity and other arguments against women's liberation.* New York: Coward McCann.

DEIKMAN, A. J. (1972). Deautomatization and the mystic experience. In C. Tart (Ed.), *Altered states of consciousness.* New York: Anchor.

DEMENT, W. C. (1967). Discussion. In S. S. Kety, E. V. Evarts, & H. L. Williams (Eds.), *Sleep and altered states of consciousness.* Baltimore, Md.: Williams and Wilkins.

DEMENT, W., & WOLPERT, E. A. (1958). The relation of eye movements, body motility and external stimuli to dream content. *Journal of Experimental Psychology, 55,* 543–553.

DENIKE, L. D. (1964). The temporal relationship between awareness and performance in verbal conditioning. *Journal of Experimental Psychology, 68,* 521–529.

DIAMOND, M. (1976). Human sexual development: Biological foundations. In F. A. Beach (Ed.),

Human sexuality in four perspectives (pp. 22–61). Baltimore: Johns Hopkins University Press.

DIAMOND, M. J. (1972). The use of observationally presented information to modify hypnotic susceptibility. *Journal of Abnormal Psychology, 79,* 174–180.

DIAMOND, M. J., & SHAPIRO, J. L. (1973). Changes in locus of control as a function of encounter group experiences: A study and replication. *Journal of Abnormal Psychology, 82,* 514–518.

DIENER, C. I., & DWECK, C. S. (1978). An analysis of learned helplessness: Continuous changes in performance, strategy, and achievement cognitions following failure. *Journal of Personality and Social Psychology, 36,* 451–462.

DION, K. K. (1972). Physical attractiveness and evaluations of children's transgressions. *Journal of Personality and Social Psychology, 24,* 207–213.

DION, K. K., & BERSCHEID, E. (1971). Physical attractiveness and sociometric choice in young children. Mimeographed research report, University of Minnesota.

DION, K. K., BERSCHEID, E., & WALSTER, E. (1972). What is beautiful is good. *Journal of Personality and Social Psychology, 24,* 285–290.

DIXON, N. F. (1971). *Subliminal perception: The nature of a controversy.* London: McGraw-Hill.

DIXON, N. F. (1981). *Preconscious processing.* New York: John Wiley & Sons.

DOLE, V. P., NYSWANDER, M. E., & WARNER, A. (1968). Successful treatment of 750 criminal addicts. *Journal of the American Medical Association, 206,* 2708–2711.

DOLLARD, J., DOOB, L. W., MILLER, N. E., MOWRER, O. H., & SEARS, R. R. (1939). *Frustration and aggression.* New Haven: Yale University Press.

DOLLARD, J., & MILLER, N. E. (1950). *Personality and psychotherapy: An analysis in terms of learning, thinking, and culture.* New York: McGraw-Hill.

DORNBUSCH, S. M., HASTORF, A. H., RICHARDSON, S. A., MUZZY, R. E., & VREELAND, R. S. (1965). The perceiver and the perceived: Their relative influence on the categories of interpersonal cognition. *Journal of Personality and Social Psychology, 1,* 434–440.

DOUVAN, E., & KAYE, C. (1957). *Adolescent girls.* Ann Arbor: Survey Research Center, University of Michigan.

DULANY, D. E., Jr. (1962). The place of hypotheses and intentions: An analysis of verbal control in verbal conditioning. In C. W. Eriksen (Ed.), *Behavior and awareness* (pp. 102–129). Durham, N.C.: Duke University Press.

DUNNETTE, M. D. (1969). People feeling: Joy, more joy, and the "slough of despond." *Journal of Applied Behavioral Science, 5,* 25–44.

DUNSDON, M. I., & FRASER-ROBERTS, J. A. (1957). A study of the performance of 2,000 children on four vocabulary tests. *British Journal of Statistical Psychology, 10,* 1–16.

DUVAL, S., & WICKLUND, R. A. (1972). *A theory of objective self-awareness.* New York: Academic Press.

DWECK, C. S. (1975). The role of expectations and attributions in the alleviation of learned helplessness. *Journal of Personality and Social Psychology, 31,* 674–685.

DWORKIN, R. H., BURKE, B. W., MAHER, B. A., & GOTTESMAN, I. I. (1977). Genetic influences on the organization and development of personality. *Developmental Psychology, 13,* 164–165.

D'ZURILLA, T. (1965). Recall efficiency and mediating cognitive events in "experimental repression." *Journal of Personality and Social Psychology, 1,* 253–257.

EDDY, G. L., & SINNETT, R. E. (1973). Behavior setting utilization by emotionally disturbed college students. *Journal of Consulting and Clinical Psychology, 40,* 210–216.

EFRAN, M. G. (1974). The effect of physical appearance on the judgment of guilt, interpersonal attraction, and severity of recommended punishment in a simulated jury task. *Journal of Research in Personality, 8,* 45–54.

EKMAN, P. (1973). Cross-cultural studies of facial expression. In P. Ekman (Ed.), *Darwin and facial expression.* New York: Academic Press.

EKMAN, P. (Ed.). (1982). *Emotion in the human face (2nd ed.)*. New York: Cambridge University Press.

EKMAN, P., FRIESEN, W. V. & ELLSWORTH, P. (1972). *Emotion in the human face*. Elmsford, N.Y.: Pergamon Press.

ELLIOTT, R. (1974). The motivational significance of heart rate. In P. A. Obrist, A. H. Black, J. Brener, & L. V. D. Cara (Eds.), *Cardiovascular psychophysiology: Current issues in response mechanisms, biofeedback, and methodology*. Chicago: Aldine.

ELLIS, A. (1962). *Reason and emotion is psychotherapy*. New York: Lyle Stuart.

ELLIS, A. (1977). Rational-emotive therapy: Research data that support the clinical and personality hypothesis of RET and other modes of cognitive behavior therapy. *The Counseling Psychologist, 7,* 2–42.

ELLSWORTH, P. C., & CARLSMITH, J. M. (1968). Effects of eye contact and verbal content on affective response to a dyadic interaction. *Journal of Personality and Social Psychology, 10,* 15–20.

ENDLER, N. S. (1973). The person versus the situation—A pseudo issue? *Journal of Personality, 41,* 287–303.

ENDLER, N. S., & HUNT, J. McV. (1969). Generalizability of contributions from sources of variance in the S-R inventories of anxiousness. *Journal of Personality, 37,* 1–24.

ENDLER, N. S., HUNT, J. M., & ROSENSTEIN, A. J. (1962). An S-R inventory of anxiousness. *Psychological Monographs, 76,* No. 536.

ENDLER, N. S., & OKADA, M. (1975). A multidimensional measure of trait anxiety: The S-R inventory of general trait anxiousness. *Journal of Consulting and Clinical Psychology, 43,* 319–329.

ENGEL, B. T., & BLEECKER, E. R. (1974). Application of operant conditioning techniques to the control of the cardiac arrhythmias. In P. A. Obrist, et al. (Eds.), *Cardiovascular psychophysiology*. Chicago: Aldine.

EPSTEIN, S. (1973). The self-concept revisited or a theory of a theory. *American Psychologist, 28,* 405–416.

EPSTEIN, S. (1977). Traits are alive and well. In D. Magnusson and N. Endler (Eds.), *Personality at the crossroads: Current issues in interactional psychology* (pp. 83–98). Hillsdale, N.J.: Erlbaum.

EPSTEIN, S. (1979). The stability of behavior: I. On predicting most of the people much of the time. *Journal of Personality and Social Psychology, 37,* 1097–1126.

EPSTEIN, S. (1983). Aggregation and beyond: Some basic issues on the prediction of behavior. *Journal of Personality, 51,* 360–392.

EPSTEIN, S., & FENZ, W. D. (1962). Theory and experiment on the measurement of approach-avoidance conflict. *Journal of Abnormal and Social Psychology, 64,* 97–112.

ERDELYI, M. H. (1974). A new look at the new look: Perceptual defense and vigilance. *Psychological Review, 81,* 1–25.

ERDELYI, M. H. (1985). *Psychoanalysis: Freud's cognitive psychology*. New York: W. H. Freeman & Company.

ERDELYI, M. H., & GOLDBERG, B. (1979). Let's now sweep repression under the rug: Towards a cognitive psychology of repression. In J. F. Kihlstrom & F. J. Evans (Eds.), *Functional disorders of memory*. Hillsdale, N.J.: Erlbaum.

ERIKSEN, C. W. (1952a). Defense against ego-threat in memory and perception. *Journal of Abnormal and Social Psychology, 47,* 230–235.

ERIKSEN, C. W. (1952b). Individual differences in defensive forgetting. *Journal of Experimental Psychology, 44,* 442–446.

ERIKSEN, C. W. (1958). Unconscious process. In M. R. Jones (Ed.), *Nebraska symposium on motivation* (pp. 169–227). Lincoln: University of Nebraska Press.

ERIKSEN, C. W. (1960). Discrimination and learning without awareness: A methodological survey and evaluation. *Psychological Review, 67,* 279–300.

ERIKSEN, C. W. (1966). Cognitive responses to internally cued anxiety. In C. D. Spielberger (Ed.), *Anxiety and behavior* (pp. 327–360). New York: Academic Press.

ERIKSEN, C. W., & KUETHE, J. L. (1956). Avoidance conditioning of verbal behavior without awareness: A paradigm of repression. *Journal of Abnormal and Social Psychology, 53,* 203–209.

ERIKSON, E. (1963). *Childhood and society.* New York: Norton.

ERIKSON, E. (1968). *Identity: Youth and crisis.* New York: Norton.

ERLENMEYER-KIMLING, L., & JARVIK, L. F. (1963). Genetics and intelligence: A review. *Science, 142,* 1477–1479.

EXLINE, R., & WINTERS, L. C. (1965). Affective relations and mutual glances in dyads. In S. Tomkins & C. Izard (Eds.), *Affect, cognition, and personality.* New York: Springer.

EYSENCK, H. J. (1952). The effects of psychotherapy: An evaluation. *Journal of Consulting Psychology, 16,* 319–324.

EYSENCK, H. J. (1961). The effects of psychotherapy. In H.J. Eysenck (Ed.), *Handbook of abnormal psychology: An experimental approach* (pp. 697–725). New York: Basic Books.

EYSENCK, H. J. (1973). Personality and the law of effect. In D. E. Berlyne & K. B. Madsen (Eds.), *Pleasure, reward, preference.* New York: Academic Press.

EYSENCK, H. J., & RACHMAN, S. (1965). *The causes and cures of neurosis: An introduction to modern behavior therapy based on learning theory and the principles of conditioning.* San Diego: Knapp.

FAIRWEATHER, G. W. (1964). *Social psychology in treating mental illness: An experimental approach.* New York: Wiley, 1964.

FAIRWEATHER, G. W. (1967). *Methods in experimental social innovation.* New York: Wiley.

FAIRWEATHER, G. W., SANDERS, D. H., CRESSLER, D. L., & MAYNARD, H. (1969). *Community life for the mentally ill: An alternative to institutional care.* Chicago: Aldine.

FARINA, A. (1972). *Schizophrenia.* Morristown, N.J.: General Learning Press.

FARQUHAR, J. W., WOOD, P. D., BREITROSE, H., HASKELL, W. L., MEYER, A. J., MACCOBY, N., ALEXANDER, J. K., BROWN, B. W., JR., McALISTER, A. L., NASH, J. D., & STERN, M. P. (1977). Community education for cardiovascular health. *The Lancet,* June 4.

FAULS, L. B., & SMITH, W. D. (1956). Sex-role learning of five-year-olds. *Journal of Genetic Psychology, 89,* 105–117.

FELDSTEIN, S. (1972). *Waking mentation and information processing following stage 1 REM deprivation in the sleep cycle.* Unpublished doctoral dissertation, City University of New York.

FENIGSTEIN, A., SCHEIER, M. F., & BUSS, A. H. (1975). Public and private self-consciousness: Assessment and theory. *Journal of Consulting and Clinical Psychology, 43,* 522–527.

FENZ, W. D. (1964). Conflict and stress as related to physiological activation and sensory, perceptual and cognitive functioning. *Psychological Monographs, 78,* No. 8, (Whole No. 585).

FERSTER, C. B., & DeMYER, M. K. (1961). The development of performances in autistic children in an automatically controlled environment. *Journal of Chronic Diseases, 13,* 312–345.

FERSTER, C. B., & SKINNER, B. F. (1957). *Schedules of reinforcement.* New York: Appleton.

FESHBACH, S. (1956). The catharsis hypothesis and some consequences of interaction with aggressive and neutral play objects. *Journal of Personality, 24,* 449–462.

FESTINGER, L. (1957). *A theory of cognitive dissonance.* Stanford: Stanford University Press.

FESTINGER, L. (1964). Behavioral support for opinion change. *Public Opinion Quarterly, 28,* 404–417.

FISCHER, W. F. (1970). *Theories of anxiety.* New York: Harper.

FISHKIN, J., KENISTON, K., & MACKINNON, C. (1973). Moral reasoning and political ideology. *Journal of Personality and Social Psychology, 27,* 109–119.

FITCH, G. (1970). Effects of self-esteem, perceived performance, and choice on causal attribution. *Journal of Personality and Social Psychology, 16,* 311–315.

FLAHERTY, J. F., & DUSEK, J. B. (1980). An investigation of the relationship between psychological androgyny and components of self-concept. *Journal of Personality and Social Psychology, 38,* 984–999.

FRANK, L. K. (1939). Projective methods for the study of personality. *Journal of Psychology, 8,* 389–413.

FREEDMAN, J. (1978). *Happy people.* New York: Harcourt.

FREIDES, D. (1960). Toward the elimination of the concept of normality. *Journal of Consulting Psychology, 24,* 128–133.

FREUD, S. (1901). Psychopathology of everyday life. *Standard edition, Vol. 6.* London: Hogarth, 1960.

FREUD, S. (1909). Leonardo da Vinci: A study in psychosexuality. *Standard edition, Vol. II.* London: Hogarth, 1957.

FREUD, S. (1911). Formulations regarding the two principles of mental functioning. *Collected papers, Vol. IV.* New York: Basic Books, 1959.

FREUD, S. (1915). Instincts and their vicissitudes. *Standard edition, Vol. 14.* London: Hogarth, 1957.

FREUD, S. (1917). On transformations of instinct as exemplified in anal eroticism. *Standard edition, Vol. 18.* London: Hogarth, 1955.

FREUD, S. (1920). *A general introduction to psychoanalysis.* New York: Boni and Liveright, 1924.

FREUD, S. (1933). *New introductory lectures on psychoanalysis,* W. J. H. Sproutt (trans.). New York: Norton.

FREUD, S. (1940). An outline of psychoanalysis. *International Journal of Psychoanalysis, 21,* 27–84.

FREUD, S. (1959). *Collected papers, Vols. I–V.* New York: Basic Books.

FRIEDMAN, M., & ROSENMAN, R. H. (1974). *Type A behavior and your heart.* New York: Knopf.

FRIEZE, I. H., PARSONS, J. E., JOHNSON, P. B., RUBLE, D. N., & ZELLMAN G. L. (1978). *Women and sex roles: A social psychological perspective.* New York: Norton.

FROMM, E. (1941). *Escape from freedom.* New York: Holt, Rinehart and Winston.

FROMM, E. (1947). *Man for himself.* New York: Holt, Rinehart and Winston.

GARCIA, J., McGOWAN, B. K., & GREEN, K. F. (1972). Biological constraints on conditioning. In A. H. Black & W. F. Prokasy (Eds.), *Classical conditioning II: Current research and theory.* New York: Appleton-Century-Crofts.

GARFIELD, S. L., & BERGIN, A. E. (1978). *Handbook of psychotherapy and behavior change.* New York: Wiley.

GEEN, R. G. (1978). Some effects of observing violence upon the behavior of the observer. In B. A. Maher (Ed.), *Progress in experimental personality research, Vol. 8.* New York: Academic Press.

GEER, J. H. (1965). The development of a scale to measure fear. *Behavior Research and Therapy, 3,* 45–53.

GEER, J. H., DAVISON, G. C., & GATCHEL, R. I. (1970). Reduction of stress in humans through nonveridical perceived control of aversive stimulation. *Journal of Personality and Social Psychology, 16,* 731–738.

GELDER, M. G., & MARKS, I. M. (1969). Aversion treatment in transvestism and transsexualism. In R. Green (Ed.), *Transexualism and sex reassignment.* Baltimore: Johns Hopkins Press.

GENDLIN, E. T. (1962). Client-centered developments and work with schizophrenics. *Journal of Counseling Psychology, 9,* 205–211.

GERGEN, K. J. (1971). *The concept of self.* New York: Holt, Rinehart and Winston.

GERGEN, K. J. (1984). Theory of the self: Impasse and evolution. In L. Berkowitz (Ed.),

Advances in experimental social psychology, Vol. 17. Theorizing in social psychology: Special topics (pp. 251–277). New York: Academic Press.

GESELL, A. (1940). *The first five years of life.* New York: Harper & Brothers.

GETZELS, J. W., & JACKSON, P. W. (1962). *Creativity and intelligence.* New York: Wiley.

GIESE, H., & SCHMIDT, S. (1968). *Studenten sexualität.* Hamburg: Rowohlt.

GILBERSTADT, H., & DUKER, J. (1965). *A handbook for clinical and actuarial MMPI interpretation.* Philadelphia: Saunders.

GILLIGAN, C. (1982). *In a different voice.* Cambridge, Mass.: Harvard University Press.

GLASS, D. C. (1968). Theories of consistency and the study of personality. In E. F. Borgatta & W. W. Lambert (Eds.), *Handbook of personality theory and research* (pp. 788–854). Chicago: Rand McNally.

GLASS, D. C. (1977). *Behavior patterns, stress, and coronary disease.* Hillsdale, N.J.: Erlbaum.

GLASS, D. C., & SINGER, J. E. (1972). *Urban stress.* New York: Academic Press.

GLASS, D. C., SINGER, J. E., & FRIEDMAN, L. N. (1969). Psychic costs of adaptation to an environmental stressor. *Journal of Personality and Social Psychology, 12,* 200–210.

GOLDBERG, L. R. (1959). The effectiveness of clinicians' judgments: The diagnosis of organic brain damage from the Bender-Gestalt test. *Journal of Consulting Psychology, 23,* 25–33.

GOLDBERG, L. R. (1973). The exploitation of the English Language for the development of a descriptive personality taxonomy. Paper delivered at the 81st Annual Convention of the American Psychological Association, Montreal, Canada.

GOLDBERG, L. R., & WERTS, C. E. (1966). The reliability of clinician's judgments: A multitrait-multimethod approach. *Journal of Consulting Psychology, 30,* 199–206.

GOLDBERG, P. A. (1967). Misogyny and the college girl. Paper presented at Eastern Psychological Association, Boston, Mass.

GOLDBERG, S., & LEWIS, M. (1969). Play behavior in the year-old infant: Early sex differences. *Child Development, 40,* 21–31.

GOLDEN, M. (1964). Some effects of combining psychological tests on clinical inferences. *Journal of Consulting Psychology, 28,* 440–446.

GOLDFRIED, M. R., & GOLDFRIED, A. P. (1980). Cognitive change methods. In F. H. Kanfer & A. P. Goldstein (Eds.), *Helping people change: A textbook of methods (2nd ed.).* Elmsford, N.Y.: Pergamon Press.

GOLDFRIED, M. R., & SOBOCINSKI, D. (1975). Effect of irrational beliefs on emotional arousal. *Journal of Consulting and Clinical Psychology, 43,* 504–510.

GOLDMAN, R., JAFFA, M., & SCHACHTER, S. (1968). Yom Kippur, Air France, dormitory food, and the eating behavior of obese and normal persons. *Journal of Personality and Social Psychology, 10,* 117–123.

GOLDSMITH, H. H. (1983). Genetic influences on personality from infancy to adulthood. *Child Development, 54(2),* 331–355.

GOLDSMITH, H. H., & CAMPOS, J. J. (1982). Genetic influences on individual differences in emotionality. *Infant Behavior and Development, 5,* 99 (Abstract).

GORDON, J. E., & SMITH, E. (1965). Children's aggression, parental attitudes, and the effects of an affiliation-arousing story. *Journal of Personality and Social Psychology, 1,* 654–659.

GORMLY, J., & EDELBERG, W. (1974). Validation in personality trait attribution. *American Psychologist, 29,* 189–193.

GOTTESMAN, I. I. (1963). Heritability of personality. *Psychological Monographs, 77,* 1–21.

GOTTESMAN, I. I. (1966). Genetic variance in adaptive personality traits. *Journal of Child Psychology and Psychiatry, 7,* 199–208.

GOTTESMAN, I. I., & SHIELDS, J. (1969). Schizophrenia in twins: Sixteen years consecutive admissions to a psychiatric clinic. In M. Manosevitz, G. Lindzey, & D. D. Thiessen (Eds.), *Behavioral genetics: Method and research* (pp. 677–691). New York: Appleton.

GOUGH, H. G. (1957). *Manual, California Psychological Inventory.* Palo Alto, Calif.: Consulting Psychologists Press.

GOUGH, H. G., HALL, R. E., & HARRIS, W. B. (1963). Admissions procedures as forecasters of performance in medical education. *Journal of Medical Education, 38,* 983–998.

GOUGH, H. G., & HALL, W. B. (1975). An attempt to predict graduation from medical school. *Journal of Medical Education, 50,* 940–950.

GOVE, F. L., AREND, R. A., & SROUFE, L. A. (1979). *Competence in preschool and kindergarten predicted from infancy.* Paper presented at the Meeting of the Society for Research in Child Development, San Francisco.

GREEN, R. A., & MURRAY, E. J. (1975). Expression of feeling and cognitive reinterpretation in the reduction of hostile aggression. *Journal of Consulting and Clinical Psychology, 43,* 375–383.

GREENWALD, A. G. (1980). The totalitarian ego: Fabrication and revision of personal history. *American Psychologist, 7,* 603–618.

GRINKER, R. R., & SPIEGEL, J. P. (1945). *Men under stress.* Philadelphia: Blakiston.

GROSSBERG, J. M. (1964). Behavior therapy: A review. *Psychological Bulletin, 62,* 73–88.

GRÜNBAUM, A. (1984). *The foundations of psychoanalysis.* Berkeley: University of California Press.

GUILFORD, J. P. (1959). *Personality.* New York: McGraw-Hill.

GUILFORD, J. P. (1967). *The nature of human intelligence.* New York: McGraw-Hill.

GUR, R. C., & SACKEIM, H. A. (1979). Self-deception: A concept in search of a phenomenon. *Journal of Personality and Social Psychology, 37,* 147–169.

GUTHRIE, E. R. (1935). *The psychology of learning.* New York: Harper & Brothers.

HALVERSON, C. (1971a). Longitudinal relations between newborn tactile threshold, preschool barrier behaviors, and early school-age imagination and verbal development. *Newborn and preschooler: Organization of behavior and relations between period.* SRCD Monograph, Vol. 36.

HALVERSON, C. (1971b). *Relation of preschool verbal communication to later verbal intelligence, social maturity, and distribution of play bouts.* Paper presented at the meeting of the American Psychological Association.

HAMPSON, J. L. (1965). Determinants of psychosexual orientation. In F. A. Beach (Ed.), *Sex and behavior.* New York: Wiley.

HANER, C. F. & BROWN, P. A. (1955). Clarification of the instigation to action concept in the frustration-aggression hypothesis. *Journal of Abnormal and Social Psychology, 51,* 204–206.

HARACKIEWICZ, J. M., MANDERLINK, G., & SANSONE, C. (1984). Rewarding pinball wizardry: Effects of evaluation and cue value on intrinsic motivation. *Journal of Personality and Social Psychology, 47(2),* 287–300.

HARRÉ, R., & SECORD, P. F. (1973). *The explanation of social behavior.* Oxford: Basil Blackwell.

HARRINGTON, D. M., & ANDERSEN, S. M. (1981). Creativity, masculinity, femininity, and three models of androgyny. *Journal of Personality and Social Psychology, 41,* 744–757.

HARRIS, A. H., GILLIAM, W. J., FINDLEY, J. D., & BRADY, J. B. (1973). Instrumental conditioning of large-magnitude, daily, 12-hour blood pressure elevations in the baboon. *Science, 182,* 175–177.

HARRIS, D. B. (1959). Sex differences in the life problems and interests of adolescents, 1935 and 1957. *Child Development, 30,* 453–459.

HARRIS, F. R., JOHNSTON, M. K., KELLEY, S. C., & WOLF, M. M. (1964). Effects of positive social reinforcement on regressed crawling of a nursery school child. *Journal of Educational Psychology, 55,* 35–41.

HARTER, S. (1983). Developmental perspectives on the self-system. In P. H. Mussen (Ed.), *Handbook of Child Psychology, Vol. 4* (E. M. Hetherington, Ed.). New York: Wiley.

HARTIG, M., & KANFER, F. H. (1973). The role of verbal self-instructions in children's resistance to temptation. *Journal of Personality and Social Psychology, 25,* 259–267.

Hartmann, H., Kris, E., & Loewenstein, R. M. (1947). Comments on the formation of psychic structure. In A. Freud et al. (Eds.), *The psychoanalytic study of the child, Vol. 2* (pp. 11–38). New York: International Universities Press.

Hartup, W. W., & Zook, E. A. (1960). Sex role preferences in three- and four-year-old children. *Journal of Consulting Psychology, 24,* 420–426.

Hase, H. D., & Goldberg, L. R. (1967). Comparative validity of different strategies of constructing personality inventory scales. *Psychological Bulletin, 67,* 231–248.

Hashim, S. A., & Van Itallie, T. B. (1965). Studies on normal and obese subjects with a monitored food dispensing device. *Annals of the New York Academy of Sciences, 131,* 654–661.

Hathaway, S. R., & McKinley, J. C. (1942). A multiphasic personality schedule. (Minnesota): III. The measurement of symptomatic depression. *Journal of Psychology, 14,* 73–84.

Hathaway, S. R., & McKinley, J. C. (1943). *MMPI Manual.* New York: Psychological Corporation.

Hawkins, R. P., Peterson, R. F., Schweid, E., & Bijou, S. W. (1966). Behavior therapy in the home: Amelioration of problem parent-child relations with the parent in a therapeutic role. *Journal of Experimental Child Psychology, 4,* 99–107.

Heathers, G. (1953). Emotional dependence and independence in a physical threat situation. *Child Development, 24,* 169–179.

Hebb, D. O. (1972). *Textbook of psychology (3rd ed.).* Philadelphia: Saunders.

Heckhausen, H. (1969). Achievement motive research: Current problems and some contributions towards a general theory of motivation. In W. J. Arnold (Ed.), *Nebraska Symposium on Motivation* (pp. 103–174). Lincoln: Nebraska University Press.

Heider, F. (1958). *The psychology of interpersonal relations.* New York: Wiley.

Heider, F., & Simmel, M. (1944). An experimental study of apparent behavior. *American Journal of Psychology, 57,* 243–259.

Hernstein, R. J., & Wilson, J. Q. (1985). *Crime and human nature.* New York: Simon & Schuster.

Heston, L. (1970). The genetics of schizophrenia and schizoid disease. *Science, 167,* 249–256.

Hilgard, E. R. (1973). The domain of hypnosis, with some comments on alternative paradigms. *American Psychologist, 28,* 972–982.

Hilgard, E. R., & Hilgard, J. R. (1975). *Hypnosis in the relief of pain.* Los Altos, Calif.: Kaufman.

Hoffman, M. L. (1975). Altruistic behavior and the parent-child relationship. *Journal of Personality and Social Psychology, 31,* 837–943.

Holland, J. L., & Richards, J. M., Jr. (1965). Academic and nonacademic accomplishment: Correlated or uncorrelated? *Journal of Educational Psychology, 56,* 165–174.

Holmes, D. S. (1974). Investigations of repression: Differential recall of material experimentally or naturally associated with ego threat. *Psychological Bulletin, 81,* 632–653.

Holmes, D. S., & Houston, K. B. (1974). Effectiveness of situation redefinition and affective isolation in coping with stress. *Journal of Personality and Social Psychology, 29,* 212–218.

Holmes, D. S., & Schallow, J. R. (1969). Reduced recall after ego threat: Repression or response competition? *Journal of Personality and Social Psychology, 13,* 145–152.

Holmes, T. H., & Masuda, M. (1974). Life change and illness susceptibility. In B. S. Dohrenwend & B. P. Dohrenwend (Eds.), *Stressful life events: Their nature and effects.* New York: Wiley.

Holmes, T. H., & Rahe, R. H. (1967). The social readjustment rating scale. *Journal of Psychosomatic Research, 11,* 213–218.

Holton, R. B. (1961). Amplitude of an instrumental response following the withholding of reward. *Child Development, 32,* 107–116.

Holtzman, W. H., Thorpe, J. S., Swartz, J. D., & Herron, E. W. (1961). *Inkblot perception and personality: Holtzman inkblot technique.* Austin: University of Texas Press.

References

539

HOLTZMAN, W. H., & SELLS, S. B. (1954). Prediction of flying success by clinical analysis of test protocols. *Journal of Abnormal and Social Psychology, 49,* 485–490.

HONZIK, M. P. (1972). Intellectual abilities at age 40 years in relation to the early family environment. In F. J. Monks, W. W. Hartup, & J. deWit (Eds.), *Determinants of behavioral development.* New York: Academic Press.

HORNER, M. S. (1969). Fail: Bright women. *Psychology Today.*

HORNER, M. S. (1972). Toward an understanding of achievement related conflicts in women. *Journal of Social Issues, 28,* 157–176.

HOVLAND, C. I., & JANIS, I. L. (Eds.). (1959). *Personality and persuasibility, Vol. 2. Yale studies in attitude and communication.* New Haven: Yale University Press.

HOWARD, K. I. (1962). The convergent and discriminant validation of ipsative ratings from three projective instruments. *Journal of Clinical Psychology, 18,* 183–188.

HOWES, D. H., & SOLOMON, R. L. (1951). Visual duration threshold as a function of word-probability. *Journal of Experimental Psychology, 41,* 401–410.

IRWIN, O. C., & CHEN, H. P. (1946). Development of speech during infancy: Curve of phonemic types. *Journal of Experimental Psychology, 36,* 431–436.

ISCOE, I., WILLIAMS, M., & HARVEY, J. (1964). Age, intelligence, and sex as variables in the conformity behavior of Negro and white children. *Child Development, 35,* 451–460.

ISEN, A. M. (1970). Success, failure, and reactions to others: The warm glow of success. *Journal of Personality and Social Psychology,* 294–301.

ISEN, A. M., HORN, N., & ROSENHAN, D. (1973). Effects of success and failure on children's generosity. *Journal of Personality and Social Psychology, 27,* 239–247.

ISEN, A. M., & LEVIN, P. F. (1972). The effect of feeling good on helping: Cookies and kindness. Unpublished manuscript, Franklin and Marshall College, Lancaster, Pa.

ISEN, A. M., SHALKER, T. E., CLARK, M., & KARP, L. (1978). Affect, accessibility of material in memory, and behavior: A cognitive loop? *Journal of Personality and Social Psychology, 36,* 1–12.

JACCARD, J. J. (1974). Predicting social behavior from personality traits. *Journal of Research in Personality, 7,* 358–367.

JACKLIN, C. N., & MISCHEL, H. N. (1973). As the twig is bent: Sex role stereotyping in early readers. *The School Psychology Digest,* 30–38.

JACKSON, D. N. (1976). *Jackson personality inventory manual.* Port Huron, Mich.: Research Psychology Press.

JACKSON, D. N. (1982). Some preconditions for valid person perception. In M. P. Zanna, E. T. Higgins, & C. P. Herman (Eds.), *Consistency in social behavior: The Ontario symposium, Vol. 2* (pp. 49–101). Hillsdale, N.J.: Erlbaum.

JACKSON, D. N., CHAN, D. W., & STRICKER, L. J. (1979). Implicit personality theory: Is it illusory? *Journal of Personality, 47,* 1–10.

JACKSON, D. N., & PAUNONEN, S. V. (1980). Personality structure and assessment. In M. R. Rosenzweig & L. W. Porter (Eds.), *Annual review of psychology, Vol. 31.* Palo Alto, Calif.: Annual Reviews, Inc.

JAMES, W. (1890). *The principles of psychology, Vol. 1.* New York: Holt.

JANIS, I. L. (1971). *Stress and frustration.* New York: Harcourt.

JENKINS, J. J. (1974). Remember that old theory of memory? Well, forget it! *American Psychologist, 29,* 785–795.

JENSEN, A. R. (1969). How much can we boost IQ and scholastic achievement? *Harvard Educational Review, 39,* 1–123.

JENSEN, A. R. (1980). *Bias in mental testing.* New York: The Free Press.

JERSILD, A. (1931). Memory for the pleasant as compared with the unpleasant. *Journal of Experimental Psychology, 14,* 284–288.

JOHNSON, W. G. (1974). Effect of cue prominence and subject weight on human food-directed performance. *Journal of Personality and Social Psychology, 29,* 843–848.

JONES, A. (1966). Information deprivation in humans. In B. A. Maher (Ed.), *Progress in experimental personality research, Vol. 3* (pp. 241–307). New York: Academic Press.

JONES, E. E. (1964). *Ingratiation: A social psychological analysis.* New York: Appleton.

JONES, E. E., & DAVIS, K. E. (1965). From acts to dispositions: The attribution process in person perception. In L. Berkowitz (Ed.), *Advances in experimental social psychology, Vol. 2.* New York: Academic Press.

JONES, E. E., & NISBETT, R. E. (1971). The actor and the observer: Divergent perceptions of the causes of behavior. In E. E. Jones, et al. (Eds.), *Attribution: Perceiving the causes of behavior.* Morristown, N.J.: General Learning Press.

JONES, W., CHERNOVERTZ, M. E., & HANSSON, R. O. (1978). The enigma of androgyny: Differential implications for males and females? *Journal of Consulting and Clinical Psychology, 46,* 298–313.

JOURARD, S. M. (1967). Experimenter-subject dialogue: A paradigm for a humanistic science of psychology. In J. Bugental (Ed.), *Challenges of humanistic psychology* (pp. 109–116). New York: McGraw-Hill.

JOURARD, S. M. (1974). *Healthy personality: An approach from the viewpoint of humanistic psychology.* New York: Macmillan.

JUNG, C. G. (1963). *Memories, dreams, reflections.* New York: Pantheon.

JUNG, C. G. (1964). *Man and his symbols.* Garden City, N.Y.: Doubleday.

KAGAN, J. (1964). The acquisition and significance of sex typing and sex role identity. In M. Hoffman & L. Hoffman (Eds.), *Review of child development research, Vol. 1.* New York: Russell Sage.

KAGAN, J., HOSKEN, B., & WATSON, S. (1961). The child's symbolic conceptualization of the parents. *Child Development, 32,* 625–636.

KAGAN, J., & MOSS, H. A. (1962). *Birth to maturity: A study in psychological development.* New York: Wiley.

KAHNEMAN, D., & TVERSKY, A. (1973). On the psychology of prediction. *Psychological Review, 80,* 237–251.

KAHNEMAN, D., & TVERSKY, A. (1984). Choices, values, and frames. *American Psychologist, 39,* 341–350.

KALLMAN, F. J. (1953). *Heredity in health and mental disorder.* New York: Norton.

KAMIN, L. J. (1974). *The science and politics of IQ.* Potomac, Md.: Erlbaum.

KANFER, F. H. (1980). Self-management methods. In F. H. Kanfer & A. P. Goldstein (Eds.), *Helping people change: A textbook of methods (2nd ed.).* Elmsford, N.Y.: Pergamon Press.

KANFER, F. H., & KAROLY, P. (1972). Self control: A behavioristic excursion into the lion's den. *Behavior Therapy, 3,* 398–416.

KANFER, F. H., & MARSTON, A. R. (1963a). Determinants of self-reinforcement in human learning. *Journal of Experimental Psychology, 66,* 245–254.

KANFER, F. H., & MARSTON, A. R. (1963b). Conditioning of self-reinforcing responses: An analogue to self-confidence training. *Psychological Reports, 13,* 63–70.

KANFER, F. H., & PHILLIPS, J. S. (1970). *Learning foundations of behavior therapy.* New York: Wiley.

KANFER, F. H., & SEIDNER, M. L. (1973). Self-control: Factors enhancing tolerance of noxious stimulation. *Journal of Personality and Social Psychology, 25,* 381–389.

KANFER, F. H., & ZICH, J. (1974). Self-control training: The effects of external control on children's resistance to temptation. *Developmental Psychology, 10,* 108–115.

KAROLY, P. (1980). Operant methods. In F. H. Kanfer & A. P. Goldstein (Eds.), *Helping people change: A textbook of methods (2nd ed.).* Elmsford, N.Y.: Pergamon Press.

KAZDIN, A. E. (1974). Effects of covert modeling and model reinforcement on assertive behavior. *Journal of Abnormal Psychology, 83,* 240–252.

KAZDIN, A. E. (1975). Covert modeling, imagery assessment, and assertive behavior. *Journal of Consulting and Clinical Psychology, 43,* 716–724.

KAZDIN, A. E., & WILSON, G. T. (1978). *Evaluation of behavior therapy: Issues, evidence and research strategies.* Cambridge, Mass.: Ballinger.

KELLEY, H. H. (1973). The processes of casual attribution. *American Psychologist, 28,* 107–128.

KELLY, E. L. (1955). Consistency of the adult personality. *American Psychologist, 10,* 659–681.

KELLY, E. L., & FISKE, D. W. (1951). *The prediction of performance in clinical psychology.* Ann Arbor: University of Michigan Press.

KELLY, G. A. (1951). *The psychology of personal constructs, Vols. 1 & 2.* New York: Norton.

KELLY, G. A. (1958). Man's construction of his alternatives. In G. Lindzey (Ed.), *Assessment of human motives* (pp. 33–64). New York: Holt, Rinehart and Winston.

KETY, S. S. (1979). Disorders of the human brain. *Scientific American, 241,* 202–218.

KETY, S. S., ROSTENTHAL, D., WENDER, P. H., SCHULSINGER, F., & JACOBSON, B. (1975). Mental illness in the biological and adoptive familes of adopted individuals who have become schizophrenics. In R. R. Fieve, D. Rosenthal, & H. Brill (Eds.), *Genetic research in psychiatry.* Baltimore: Johns Hopkins University Press.

KIESLER, D. J. (1966). Some myths of psychotherapy research and the search for a paradigm. *Psychological Bulletin, 65,* 110–136.

KIHLSTROM, J. F. (1980). On personality and memory. In N. Cantor & J. F. Kihlstrom (Eds.), *Personality, cognition, and social interaction.* Hillsdale, N.J.: Erlbaum.

KIHLSTROM, J. F., & CANTOR, N. (1984). Mental representations of the self. In L. Berkowitz (Ed.), *Advances in experimental social psychology, Vol. 17. Theorizing in social psychology: Special topics* (pp. 2–40). New York: Academic Press.

KIM, M. P., & ROSENBERG, S. (1980). Comparison of two-structured models of implicit personality theory. *Journal of Personality and Social Psychology, 38,* 375–389.

KLAUSMEIER, H. J., & WIERSMA, W. (1964). Relationship of sex, grade level, and locale to performance of high IQ students on divergent thinking tests. *Journal of Educational Psychology, 55,* 114–119.

KLAUSMEIER, H. J., & WIERSMA, W. (1965). The effects of IQ level and sex on divergent thinking of seventh grade pupils of low, average, and high IQ. *Journal of Educational Research, 58,* 300–302.

KLEIN, D. F., GITTELMAN, R., QUITKIN, F., & RIFKIN, A. (1980). *Diagnosis and drug treatment of psychiatric disorders: Adults and children (2nd ed.).* Baltimore: Williams & Wilkins.

KLINGER, E. (1977). The nature of fantasy and its clinical uses. *Psychotherapy: Theory, research and practice, 14,* 223–231.

KLINGER, E., GREGOIRE, K. C., & BARTA, S. G. (1973). Physiological correlates of mental activity: Eye movements, Alpha, and heart rate during imagining, suppression, concentration, search, and choice. *Psychophysiology, 10,* 471–477.

KOBASA, S. C. (1979). Stressful life events, personality, and health: An inquiry into hardiness. *Journal of Personality and Social Psychology, 37,* 1–11.

KOBASA, S. C., MADDI, S. R., & KAHN, S. (1982). Hardiness and health: A prospective study. *Journal of Personality and Social Psychology, 42,* 168–177.

KOGAN, N., & WALLACH, M. A. (1964). *Risk Taking: A Study in cognition and personality.* New York: Holt, Rinehart and Winston.

KOHLBERG, L.A. (1966). Cognitive-developmental analysis of children's sex-role concepts and attitudes. In E. E. Maccoby (Ed.), *The development of sex differences* (pp. 82–173). Stanford, Calif.: Stanford University Press.

KOHLBERG, L. (1969). Stage and sequence: The cognitive-developmental approach to socialization. In D. A. Goslin (Ed.), *Handbook of socialization theory and research* (pp. 347–480). Chicago: Rand McNally.

KOPP, C. G. (1982). Antecedents of self-regulation: A developmental perspective. *Developmental Psychology, 18,* 199–214.

KORIAT, A., MELKMAN, R., AVERILL, J. R., & LAZARUS, R. S. (1972). The self-control of emotional reactions to a stressful film. *Journal of Personality, 40,* 601–619.

KOSTLAN, A. (1954). A method for the empirical study of psychodiagnosis, *Journal of Consulting Psychology, 18,* 83–88.

KRANE, R. V., & WAGNER, A. R. (1975). Taste aversion learning with a delayed shock US: Implications for the "generality of the laws of learning." *Journal of Comparative and Physiological Psychology, 88,* 882–889.

KRANTZ, D. S., GRUNBERG, N. B., & BAUM, A. (1985). Health Psychology. In M. R. Rosenzweig, & L. W. Porter, *Annual Review of Psychology* (pp. 349–384). Palo Alto, Calif.: Annual Reviews Inc.

KRASNER, L., & ULLMANN, L. F. (1973). *Behavior influence and personality: The social matrix of human action.* New York: Holt, Rinehart and Winston.

KRECH, K., CRUTCHFIELD, R., & BALLACHEY, E. (1962). *Individual in society.* New York: McGraw-Hill.

KREMERS, J. (1960). *Scientific psychology and naive psychology.* Groningen, Netherlands: Nordhoff.

KRUMBOLTZ, J. D., MITCHELL, A. M., & JONES, G. B. (1976). A social learning theory of career selection. *The Counseling Psychologist. 6,* 71–81.

KURLAND, S. H. (1954). The lack of generality in defense mechanisms as indicated in auditory perception. *Journal of Abnormal and Social Psychology, 49,* 173–177.

KURTINES, W., & GREIF, E. B. (1974). The development of moral thought: Review and evaluation of Kohlberg's approach. *Psychological Bulletin, 81,* 453–470.

LaBARRE, W. (1947). The cultural bases of emotions and gestures. *Journal of Personality, 16,* 49–68.

LAING, R. D. (1965). *The divided self.* Middlesex, England: Penguin.

LAKIN, M. (1972). *Experiential groups: The uses of interpersonal encounter, psychotherapy groups, and sensitivity training.* Morristown, N.J.: General Learning Press.

LANDFIELD, A. W., STERN, M., & FJELD, S. (1961). Social conceptual processes and change in students undergoing psychotherapy. *Psychological reports, 8,* 63–68.

LANDMAN, J. T., & DAWES, R. M. (1982). Psychotherapy outcome. *American Psychologist, 37,* 504–516.

LANG, P. J., & LAZOVIK, A. D. (1963). Experimental desensitization of a phobia. *Journal of Abnormal and Social Psychology, 66,* 519–525.

LANGER, E. J. (1977). The psychology of chance. *Journal for the Theory of Social Behavior, 7,* 185–207.

LANGER, E. J. (1978). Rethinking the role of thought in social interaction. In J. H. Harvey, W. J. Ickes, & R. F. Kidd (Eds.), *New directions in attribution research, Vol. 2.* Hillsdale, N.J.: Erlbaum.

LANGER, E. J., JANIS, I. L., & WOLFER, J.A. (1975). Reduction of psychological stress in surgical patients. Unpublished Manuscript, Yale University.

LAO, R. C. (1970). Internal-external control and competent and innovative behavior among Negro college students. *Journal of Personality and Social Psychology, 14,* 263–270.

LATANÉ, B., & DARLEY, J. M. (1968). Group inhibition of bystander intervention in emergencies. *Journal of Personality and Social Psychology, 10,* 215–221.

LATANÉ, B., & RODIN, J. (1969). A lady in distress: Inhibiting effects of friends and strangers on bystander intervention. *Journal of Experimental Social Psychology, 5,* 189–202.

LAZARUS, A. A. (1961). Group therapy of phobic disorders by systematic desensitization. *Journal of Abnormal and Social Psychology, 63,* 504–510.

LAZARUS, A. A. (1963). The treatment of chronic frigidity by systematic desensitization. *Journal of Nervous and Mental Diseases, 136,* 272–278.

LAZARUS, R. S. (1974). Cognitive and coping processes in emotion. In B. Weiner (Ed.), *Cognitive views of human motivations.* New York: Academic Press.

LAZARUS, R. S. (1976). *Patterns of Adjustment.* New York: McGraw-Hill.

LAZARUS, R. S. (1981). The stress and coping paradigm. In C. Eisdorfer, D. Cohen, A. Kleinman, & P. Maxim (Eds.), *Models for clinical psychology* (pp. 177–214). New York: Spectrum Medical and Scientific Books.

LAZARUS, R. S., & ALFERT, E. (1964). The short circuiting of threat by experimentally altering cognitive appraisal. *Journal of Abnormal and Social Psychology, 69,* 195–205.

LAZARUS, R. S., ERIKSEN, C. W., & FONDA, C. P. (1950/1951). Personality dynamics and auditory perceptual recognition. *Journal of Personality, 19,* 471–482.

LAZARUS, R. S., & FOLKMAN, S. (1984). *Stress, appraisal and coping.* New York: Springer.

LAZARUS, R. S., & LONGO, N. (1953). The consistency of psychological defense against threat. *Journal of Abnormal and Social Psychology, 48,* 495–499.

LAZARUS, R. S., & MCCLEARY, R. A. (1951). Autonomic discrimination without awareness: A study of subception. *Psychological Review, 58,* 113–122.

LAZARUS, R. S., YOUSEM, H., & ARENBERG, D. (1953). Hunger and perception. *Journal of Personality, 21,* 213–328.

LEARY, T. (1957). *Interpersonal diagnosis of personality.* New York: Ronald Press.

LEARY, T., LITWIN, G. H., & METZNER, R. (1963). Reactions to psilocybin administered in a supportive environment. *Journal of Nervous and Mental Diseases, 137,* 561–573.

LEE, L. C. (1965). Concept utilization in preschool children. *Child Development, 36,* 221–227.

LEFCOURT, H. M. (1966). Internal versus external control of reinforcement: A review. *Psychological Bulletin, 65,* 206–220.

LEFCOURT, H. M. (1972). Recent developments in the study of locus of control. In B. A. Maher (Ed.), *Progress in experimental personality research, Vol. 6.* New York: Academic Press.

LEFCOURT, H. M. (1980). The construction and development of the Multidimensional-Multiattributional Causality Scales. In H. M. Lefcourt (Ed.), *Advances and innovations in locus of control research.* New York: Academic Press.

LEPPER, M. R., GREENE, D., & NISBETT, R. E. (1973). Undermining children's intrinsic interest with extrinsic reward: A test of the "overjustification" hypothesis. *Journal of Personality and Social Psychology, 28,* 129–137.

LEPPER, M. R., SAGOTSKY, G., & MAILER, J. (1975). Generalization and persistence of effects of exposure to self-reinforcement models. *Child Development, 46,* 618–630.

LEVENTHAL, H. (1984). A perceptual-motor theory of emotion. In L. Berkowitz (Ed.), *Advances in experimental social psychology, Vol. 17. Theorizing in social psychology: Special topics* (pp. 118–173). New York: Academic Press.

LEVENTHAL, H., JACOBS, R. L., & KUDIRKA, N. Z. (1964). Authoritarianism, ideology, and political candidate choice. *Journal of Abnormal and Social Psychology, 69,* 539–549.

LEVINE, R., CHEIN, I., & MURPHY, G. (1942). The relation of the intensity of a need to the amount of perceptual distortion: A preliminary report. *Journal of Psychology, 13,* 283–292.

LEVINGER, G., & BREEDLOVE, J. (1966). Interpersonal attraction and agreement: A study of marriage partners. *Journal of Personality and Social Psychology, 3,* 367–372.

LEWIN, K. (1935). *A dynamic theory of personality.* New York: McGraw-Hill.

LEWIN, K. (1936). *Principles of topological psychology.* New York: McGraw-Hill.

LEWIN, K. (1951). *Field theory in social science; selected theoretical papers,* D. Cartwright (Ed.), New York: Harper & Row.

References

LEWINSOHN, P. M. (1975). The behavioral study and treatment of depression. In M. Hersen (Ed.), *Progress in behavior modification* (pp. 19–63). New York: Academic Press.

LEWIS, M. (1969). Infants' responses to facial stimuli during the first year of life. *Developmental Psychology, 1,* 75–86.

LIEBERMAN, M. A., YALOM, I. D., & MILES, M. B. (1973). *Encounter groups: First facts.* New York: Basic Books.

LIEBERT, R. M. (1972). Television and social learning: Some relationships between viewing violence and behaving aggressively. In J. P. Murray, E. A. Rubinstein, & G. A. Comstock (Eds.), *Television and social behavior, Vol. 2. Television and social learning* (pp. 1–34). Washington, D.C.: GPO.

LIEBERT, R. M., & ALLEN, K. M. (1967). The effects of rule structure and reward magnitude on the acquisition and adoption of self-reward criteria. Unpublished manuscript, Vanderbilt University, Nashville, Tenn.

LIEBERT, R. M., & BARON, R. A. (1972). Some immediate effects of televised violence on children's behavior. *Developmental Psychology, 6,* 469–475.

LIEF, H. I., & FOX, R. S. (1963). Training for "detached concern" in medical students. In H. I. Lief, V. F. Lief, & N. R. Lief (Eds.), *The psychological basis of medical practice* (pp. 12–35). New York: Harper.

LITTLE, K. B., & SHNEIDMAN, E. S. (1959). Congruencies among interpretations of psychological test and anamnestic data. *Psychological Monographs, 73,* No. 6 (Whole No. 476).

LOCKSLEY, A., & COLTEN, M. E. (1979). Psychological androgyny: A case of mistaken identity? *Journal of Personality and Social Psychology, 37,* 1017–1031.

LOEHLIN, J. C. (1968). *Computer models of personality.* New York: Random House.

LOEHLIN, J. C., LINDZEY, G., & SPUHLER, J. N. (1975). *Race differences in intelligence.* San Francisco: Freeman.

LOEHLIN, J. C. & NICHOLS, R. C. (1976). *Heredity, environment and personality: A study of 850 sets of twins.* Austin, Texas: University of Texas.

LOEVINGER, J. (1957). Objective tests as instruments of psychological theory. *Psychological Reports Monographs,* No. 9. Southern University Press.

LOPICOLO, J., & LOBITZ, W. C. (1972). The role of masturbation in the treatment of orgasmic dysfunction. *Archives of Sexual Behavior, 2,* 163–171.

LORENZ, K. Z. (1966). *On aggression.* New York: Harcourt.

LOTT, A. J., & LOTT, B. E. (1968). A learning theory approach to interpersonal attitudes. In A. G. Greenwald, T. C. Brock, & T. M. Ostrom (Eds.), *Psychological foundations of attitudes.* New York: Academic Press.

LOVAAS, O. I., BERBERICH, J. P., PERLOFF, B. F., & SCHAEFFER, B. (1966). Acquisition of imitative speech by schizophrenic children. *Science, 151,* 705–707.

LOVAAS, O. I., FREITAG, G., GOLD, V. J., & KASSORLA, I. C. (1965a). Experimental studies in childhood schizophrenia: I. Analysis of self-destructive behavior. *Journal of Experimental Child Psychology, 2,* 67–84.

LOVAAS, O. I., FREITAG, G., GOLD, V. J., & KASSORLA, I. C. (1965b). Recording apparatus for observation of behaviors of children in free play settings. *Journal of Experimental Child Psychology, 2,* 108–120.

LOVAAS, O. I., FREITAG, L., NELSON, K., & WHALEN, C. (1967). The establishment of imitation and its use for the development of complex behavior in schizophrenic children. *Behavior Research and Therapy, 5,* 171–181.

LUBORSKY, L., & SPENCE, D. P. (1978). Quantitative research on psychoanalytic therapy. In S. L. Garfield & A. E. Bergin (Eds.) *Handbook of psychotherapy and behavior change: An empirical analysis (2nd ed.).* New York: Wiley.

LUFT, J. (1951). Differences in prediction based on hearing versus reading verbatim clinical interviews. *Journal of Consulting Psychology, 15,* 115–119.

References

LYKKEN, D. T. (1982). Research with twins: The concept of emergencies. *The Society for Psychophysiological Research, 19,* 361–371.

McCALL, R. B. (1977). Childhood IQ's as predictors of adult educational and occupational status. *Science, 197,* 482–483.

McCARDEL, J. B., & MURRAY, E. J. (1974). Nonspecific factors in weekend encounter groups. *Journal of Consulting and Clinical Psychology, 42,* 337–345.

McCLELLAND, D. C. (1951). *Personality.* New York: Holt, Rinehart and Winston.

McCLELLAND, D. C. (1961). *The achieving society.* New York: Van Nostrand.

McCLELLAND, D. C. (1966). Longitudinal trends in the relation of thought to action. *Journal of Consulting Psychology, 30,* 479–483.

McCLELLAND, D. C. (1985). How motives, skills and values determine what people do. *American Psychologist, 40,* 812–825.

McCLELLAND, D. C., & ATKINSON, J. W. (1948). The projective expression of needs: I. The effects of different intensities of the hunger drive on perception. *Journal of Psychology, 25,* 205–222.

McCLELLAND, D. C., ATKINSON, J. W., CLARK, R. A., & LOWELL, E. L. (1953). *The achievement motive.* New York: Appleton.

McFALL, R. M., & MARSTON, A. (1970). An experimental investigation of behavior rehearsal in assertive training. *Journal of Abnormal Psychology, 76,* 295–303.

McFALL, R. M., & TWENTYMAN, C. T. (1973). Four experiments on the relative contributions of rehearsal, modeling, and coaching on assertive training. *Journal of Abnormal Psychology, 81,* 199–218.

McGINNIES, E. (1949). Emotionality and perceptual defense. *Psychological Review, 56,* 244–251.

McGLASHIN, T. H., EVANS, F. J., & ORNE, M. T. (1969). The nature of hypnotic analgesic and placebo response to experimental pain. *Psychosomatic Medicine, 31,* 227–246.

McKENNA, F. P. (1984). Measures of field dependence: Cognitive style or cognitive ability? *Journal of Personality and Social Psychology, 47,* 593–603.

McNEMAR, Q. (1942). *The revision of the Stanford-Binet Scale: An analysis of the standardization data.* Boston: Houghton Mifflin.

MACCOBY, E. E. (1966). Sex differences in intellectual functioning. In E. E. Maccoby (Ed.), *The development of sex differences* (pp. 25–55). Stanford, Calif., Stanford University Press.

MACCOBY, E. E. (1980). *Social development: Psychological growth and the parent-child relationship.* New York: Harcourt Brace Jovanovich.

MACCOBY, E. E., & JACKLIN, C. N. (1974a). What we know and don't know about sex differences. *Psychology Today,* December, 109–112.

MACCOBY, E. E., & JACKLIN, C. N. (1974b). *The psychology of sex differences.* Stanford, Calif.: Stanford University Press.

MACFARLANE, J. W. & TUDDENHAM, R. D. (1951). Problems in the validation of projective techniques. In H. H. Anderson and G. L. Anderson (Eds.), *Projective techniques* (pp. 26–54). New York: Prentice-Hall.

MADISON, P. (1960). *Freud's concept of repression and defense: Its theoretical and observational language.* Minneapolis: University of Minnesota Press.

MAGNUSSON, D. (Ed.). (1980). *The situation: An interactional perspective.* Hillsdale, N.J.: Erlbaum.

MAGNUSSON, D., & ALLEN, V. L. (Eds.) (1983). *Human development: An interactional perspective.* New York: Academic Press.

MAGNUSSON, D., & EKEHAMMAR, B. (1973). An analysis of situational dimensions: A replication. *Multivariate Behavioral Research, 8,* 331–339.

MAGNUSSON, D., & ENDLER, N. S. (1977). Interactional psychology: Present status and future prospects. In D. Magnusson & N. S. Endler (Eds.), *Personality at the crossroads: Current issues in interactional psychology.* Hillsdale, N.J.: Erlbaum.

MAHER, B. A. (1966). *Principles of psychotherapy: An experimental approach.* New York: McGraw-Hill.

MAHONEY, M. J. (1974). *Cognition and behavior modification.* Cambridge, Mass.: Ballinger.

MAHONEY, M. J., & MAHONEY, K. (1976). *Weight control as a personal science.* New York: Norton.

MAHONEY, M. J., MOURA, N. G. M., & WADE, T. C. (1973). The relative efficacy of self-reward, self-punishment, and self-monitoring techniques for weight loss. *Journal of Consulting and Clinical Psychology, 40,* 404–407.

MALLICK, S. K., & McCANDLESS, B. R.. (1966). A study of catharsis of aggression. *Journal of Personality and Social Psychology, 4,* 591–596.

MALMO, R. B. (1957). Anxiety and behavioral arousal. *Psychological Review, 64,* 276–287.

MALMO, R. B. (1959). Activation: A neuropsychological dimension. *Psychological Review, 66,* 367–386.

MANDLER, G. (1962). Emotion. In E. Galanter (Ed.), *New directions in psychology I* (pp. 267–343). New York: Holt, Rinehart and Winston.

MANDLER, G. (1964). The interruption of behavior. In D. Levin (Ed.), *Nebraska symposium on motivation* (pp. 163–219). Lincoln: University of Nebraska Press.

MANDLER, G. (1975). *Mind and emotion.* New York: Wiley.

MANDLER, G., & WATSON, D. L. (1966). Anxiety and the interruption of behavior. In C. D. Spielberger (Ed.), *Anxiety and behavior* (pp. 263–288). New York: Academic Press.

MANN, R. D. (1959). A review of the relationships between personality and performance in small groups. *Psychological Bulletin, 56,* 241–270.

MANZ, W., & LUECK, H. (1968). Influence of wearing glasses on personality ratings: Cross-cultural validation of an old experiment. *Perceptual and Motor Skills, 27,* 704.

MARKS, I. M., & GELDER, M. G. (1967). Transvestism and fetishism: Clinical and psychological changes during faradic aversion. *British Journal of Psychiatry, 113,* 711–729.

MARKS, J., STAUFFACHER, J. C., & LYLE, C. (1963). Predicting outcome in schizophrenia. *Journal of Abnormal and Social Psychology, 66,* 117–127.

MARKS, P. A. & SEEMAN, W. (1963). Actuarial description of abnormal personality. Baltimore: Williams & Wilkins.

MARKUS, H. (1977). Self-schemata and processing information about the self. *Journal of Personality and Social Psychology, 35,* 63–78.

MARKUS, H., & SMITH, J. (1981). Influence of self-schema on the perception of others. In N. Cantor & J. F. Kihlstrom (Eds.), *Personality, cognition and social interaction* (pp. 233–262). Hillsdale, N.J.: Erlbaum.

MARSDEN, G. (1971). Content analysis studies of psychotherapy: 1954 through 1968. In A. E. Bergin & S. L. Garfield (Eds.), *Handbook of psychotherapy and behavior change.* New York: Wiley.

MARSHALL, G. D., & ZIMBARDO, P. G. (1979). Affective consequences of inadequately explained physiological arousal. *Journal of Personality and Social Psychology, 37,* 970–888.

MASLACH, C. (1979). Negative emotional biasing of unexplained arousal. *Journal of Personality and Social Psychology, 37,* 953–969.

MASLACH, C., MARSHALL, G., & ZIMBARDO, P. G. (1972). Hypnotic control of peripheral skin temperature: A case report. *Psychophysiology, 9,* 600–605.

MASLING, J. M. (1959). The effects of warm and cold interaction on the administration and scoring of an intelligence test. *Journal of Consulting Psychology, 23,* 336–341.

MASLING, J. M. (1960). The influence of situational and interpersonal variables in projective testing. *Psychological Bulletin, 57,* 65–85.

MASLOW, A. H. (1965). Some basic propositions of a growth and self-actuatization psychology. In G. Lindzey & C. Hall (Eds.), *Theories of personality: Primary sources and research* (pp. 307–316). New York: Wiley.

MASLOW, A. H. (1968). *Toward a psychology of being (2nd ed.).* New York: Van Nostrand.

References

MASLOW, A. H. (1971). *The farther reaches of human nature.* New York: Viking.

MASTERS, J. C., & MOKROS, J. R. (1974). Self-reinforcement processes in children. In H. Reese (Ed.), *Advances in child development and behavior, Vol. 9.* New York: Academic Press.

MASTERS, W. H., & JOHNSON, V. (1970). *Human sexual inadequacy.* Boston: Little, Brown.

MATAS, W. H., AREND, R. A., & SROUFE, L. A. (1978). Continuity of adaptation in the second year: The relationship between quality of attachment and later competence. *Child Development, 49,* 547–556.

MATHEWS, K. A. (1984). Assessment of type A, anger, and hostility in epidemiological studies of cardiovascular disease. In A. Ostfeld, & E. Eaker (Eds.), *Measuring psychosocial variables in epidemiological studies of cardiovascular disease.* Bethesda, Maryland: National Institute of Health.

MAY, R. (1950). *The meaning of anxiety.* New York: Ronald.

MAY, R. (1961). Existential psychology. In R. May (Ed.), *Existential psychology* (pp. 11–51). New York: Random House.

MEEHL, P. E. (1945). The dynamics of "structured" personality tests. *Journal of Clinical Psychology, 1,* 296–303.

MEEHL, P. E. (1954). *Clinical versus statistical prediction.* Minneapolis: University of Minnesota Press.

MEICHENBAUM, D. H. (1974). *Cognitive-behavior modification.* Morristown, N.J.: General Learning Press.

MEICHENBAUM, D. H. (1977). *Cognitive-behavior modification.* New York: Plenum Press.

MEICHENBAUM, D. H., & CAMERON, R. (1974). The clinical potential of modifying what clients say to themselves. In M. J. Mahoney & C. E. Thoresen (Eds.), *Self-control: Power to the person.* Monterey, Calif.: Brooks-Cole.

MEICHENBAUM, D. H. & GOODMAN, J. (1971). Training impulsive children to talk to themselves: A means of developing self-control. *Journal of Abnormal Psychology, 77,* 115–126.

MEICHENBAUM, D. H., & SMART, I. (1971). Use of direct expectancy to modify academic performance and attitudes of college students. *Journal of Counseling Psychology, 18,* 531–535.

MELTZER, H. (1930). The present status of experimental studies of the relation of feeling to memory. *Psychological Review, 37,* 124–139.

MERLUZZI, T. V., GLASS, C. R., & GENEST, M. (Eds.). (1981). *Cognitive assessment.* New York: Guilford Press.

MICHOTTE, A. (1954). *La perception de la causalité (2nd ed.).* Louvain: Publications universitaires de Louvain.

MILGRAM, S. (1965). Some conditions of obedience and disobedience to authority. *Human Relations, 18,* 57–76.

MILGRAM, S. (1974). *Obedience to authority.* New York: Harper & Row.

MILLER, G. A. (1956). The magical number seven, plus or minus two: Some limits on capacity for processing information. *Psychological Review, 63,* 81–97.

MILLER, G. A., GALANTER, E., & PRIBRAM, K. H. (1960). *Plans and the structure of behavior.* New York: Holt, Rinehart and Winston.

MILLER, N. E. (1948). Theory and experiment relating psychoanalytic displacement to stimulus response generalization. *Journal of Abnormal and Social Psychology, 43,* 155–178.

MILLER, N. E. (1959). Liberalization of basic S-R concepts: Extensions to conflict behavior, motivation, and social learning. In S. Koch (Ed.), *Psychology: a study of a science, Vol. 2* (pp. 196–292). New York: McGraw-Hill.

MILLER, N. E. (1974). Applications of learning and biofeedback to psychiatry and medicine. In A. M. Freedman, H. I. Kaplan, & B. J. Sadock (Eds.), *Comprehensive textbook of psychiatry (2nd ed.).* Baltimore: Williams & Wilkins.

MILLER, S. M. (1979). Coping with impending stress: Physiological and cognitive correlates of choice. *Psychophysiology, 16,* 572–581.

MILLER, S. M. (1980). When is a little information a dangerous thing? Coping with stressful events by monitoring versus blunting. In S. Levine & H. Ursin (Eds.), *Coping and health: Proceedings of a NATO Conference.* New York: Plenum Press.

MILLER, S. M. (1981). Predictability and human stress: Towards a clarification of evidence and theory. In L. Berkowitz (Ed.), *Advances in experimental social psychology, Vol. 14.* New York: Academic Press.

MILLER, S. M., & GREEN, M. L. (1985). Coping with threat and frustration: Origins, nature and development. In M. Lewis, and C. Soarni (Eds.), *Socialization of Emotions, Vol. 5.* New York: Plenum Press.

MILLER, S. M., & MANGAN, C. E. (1983). The interacting effects of information and coping style in adapting to gynecologic stress: Should the doctor tell all? *Journal of Personality and Social Psychology, 45,* 223–236.

MILSTEIN, R. M. (1980). Responsiveness in newborn infants of overweight and normal weight parents. *Appetite, 1,* 65–74.

MINUCHIN, P. (1965). Sex-role concepts and sex typing in childhood as a function of school and home environments. *Child Development, 36,* 1033–1048.

MINUCHIN, S., ROSEMAN, B. L., & BAKER, L. (1978). *Psychosomatic families: Anorexia nervosa in context.* Cambridge, Mass.: Harvard University Press.

MIRELS, H. L. (1976). Implicit personality theory and inferential illusions. *Journal of Personality, 44,* 467–487.

MISCHEL, H. N. (1974). Sex bias in the evaluation of professional achievements. *Journal of Educational Psychology, 66,* 157–166.

MISCHEL, T. (1964). Personal constructs, rules, and the logic of clinical activity. *Psychological Review, 71,* 180–192.

MISCHEL, W. (1965). Predicting the success of Peace Corps Volunteers in Nigeria. *Journal of Personality and Social Psychology, 1,* 510–517.

MISCHEL, W. (1966). Theory and research on the antecedents of self-imposed delay of reward. In B. A. Maher (Ed.), *Progress in experimental personality research, Vol. 3* (pp. 85–132). New York: Academic Press.

MISCHEL, W. (1968). *Personality and assessment.* New York: Wiley.

MISCHEL, W. (1969). Continuity and change in personality. *American Psychologist, 24,* 1012–1018.

MISCHEL, W. (1970). Sex typing and socialization. In P. H. Mussen (Ed.), *Carmichael's manual of child psychology (rev. ed.).* New York: Wiley.

MISCHEL, W. (1972). Direct versus indirect personality assessment: Evidence and implications. *Journal of Consulting and Clinical Psychology, 38,* 319–324.

MISCHEL, W. (1973). Toward a cognitive social learning reconceptualization of personality. *Psychological Review, 80,* 252–283.

MISCHEL, W. (1974). Processes in delay of gratification. In L. Berkowitz (Ed.), *Advances in experimental social psychology, Vol. 7.* New York: Academic Press.

MISCHEL, W. (1977). The interaction of person and situation. In D. Magnusson & N. S. Endler (Eds.), *Personality at the crossroads: Current issues in interactional psychology.* Hillsdale, N.J.: Erlbaum.

MISCHEL, W. (1979). On the interface of cognition and personality. American Psychologist, 34, 740–754.

MISCHEL, W. (1980). Personality and cognition: Something borrowed, something new? In N. Cantor & J. Kihlstrom (Eds.), *Personality, cognition, and social interaction.* Hillsdale, N.J.: Erlbaum.

MISCHEL, W. (1981). Metacognition and the rules of delay. In J. H. Flavell & L. Ross (Eds.), *Social cognitive development: Frontiers and possible futures.* New York: Cambridge University Press.

MISCHEL, W. (1983). Delay of gratification as process and as person variable in development. In D. Magnusson and V. P. Allen (Eds.), *Interactions in Human Development* (pp. 149–165). New York: Academic Press.

MISCHEL, W. (1984). Convergences and challenges in the search for consistency. *American Psychologist, 39,* 351–364.

MISCHEL, W., & BAKER, N. (1975). Cognitive transformations of reward objects through instructions. *Journal of Personality and Social Psychology, 31,* 254–261.

MISCHEL, W., COATES, B., & RASKOFF, A. (1968). Effects of success and failure on self-gratification. *Journal of Personality and Social Psychology, 10,* 381–390.

MISCHEL, W., EBBESEN, E. B. (1970). Attention in delay of gratification. *Journal of Personality and Social Psychology, 16,* 239–337.

MISCHEL, W., EBBESEN, E. B., & ZEISS, A. R. (1972). Cognitive and attentional mechanisms in delay of gratification. *Journal of Personality and Social Psychology, 21,* 204–218.

MISCHEL, W., EBBESSEN, E. B., & ZEISS, A. R. (1973). Selective attention to the self: Situational and dispositional determinants. *Journal of Personality and Social Psychology, 27,* 129–142.

MISCHEL, W., EBBESEN, E. B., & ZEISS, A. R. (1976). Determinants of selective memory about the self. *Journal of Consulting and Clinical Psychology, 44,* 92–103.

MISCHEL, W., JEFFERY, K. M., & PATTERSON, C. J. (1974). The layman's use of trait and behavioral information to predict behavior. *Journal of Research in Personality, 8,* 231–242.

MISCHEL, W., & LIEBERT, R. M. (1966). Effects of discrepancies between observed and imposed reward criteria on their acquisition and transmission. *Journal of Personaltiy and Social Psychology, 3,* 45–53.

MISCHEL, W., & MISCHEL, H. N. (1976). A cognitive social learning approach to morality and self-regulation. In T. Lickona (Ed.), *Moral development and behavior: Theory, research, and social issues.* New York: Holt, Rinehart and Winston.

MISCHEL, W., & MISCHEL, H. N. (1983). Development of children's knowledge of self-control strategies. *Child Development, 54,* 603–619.

MISCHEL, W., & MOORE, B. (1980). The role of ideation in voluntary delay for symbolically presented rewards. *Cognitive Therapy and Research, 4,* 211–221.

MISCHEL, W., & PEAKE, P. K. (1982). In search of consistency: Measure for measure. In M. P. Zanna, E. T. Higgins, & C. P. Herman (Eds.), *Consistency in social behavior: The Ontario Symposium, Vol. 2.* Hillsdale, N.J.: Erlbaum.

MISCHEL, W., & PEAKE, P. K. (1983). Some facets of consistency: Replies to Epstein, Funder, and Bem. *Psychological Review, 90,* 394–402.

MISCHEL, W., & Schopler, J. (1959). Authoritarianism and reactions to "sputniks." *Journal of Abnormal and Social Psychology, 59,* 142–145.

MISCHEL, W., & STAUB, E. (1965). Effects of expectancy on working and waiting for larger rewards. *Journal of Personality and Social Psychology, 2,* 625–633.

MISCHEL, W., & WRIGHT, J. (1982). The influence of affect on cognitive social learning person variables. *Journal of Personality and Social Psychology, 43,* 901–914.

MISCHEL, W., ZEISS, R., & ZEISS, A. R. (1974). Internal-external control and persistence: Validation and implications of the Stanford Preschool Internal-External Scale. *Journal of Personality and Social Psychology, 29,* 265–278.

MONAHAN, L., KUHN, D., & SHAVER, P. (1974). Intrapsychic versus cultural explanations of the "fear of success" motive. *Journal of Personality and Social Psychology, 29,* 60–64.

MONEY, J. (1965a). Influence of hormones on sexual behavior. *Annual Review of Medicine, 16,* 67–82.

MONEY, J. (1965b). Psychosexual differentiation. In J. Money (Ed.), *Sex research, new developments.* New York: Holt, Rinehart and Winston.

MOORE, B., MISCHEL, W., & ZEISS, A. R. (1976). Comparative effects of the reward stimulus and its cognitive representation in voluntary delay. *Journal of Personality and Social Psychology, 34,* 419–424.

MOOS, R. H. (1968). Situational analysis of a therapeutic community milieu. *Journal of Abnormal Psychology, 73,* 49–61.

MOOS, R. H. (1973). Conceptualizations of human environments. *American Psychologist, 28,* 652–665.

MOOS, R. H. (1974). Systems for the assessment and classification of human environments. In R. H. Moos, & P. M. Insel (Eds.), *Issues in social ecology.* Palo Alto, Calif.: National Press Books.

MOOS, R. H. (1976). *Human adaptation: Coping with life crises.* Lexington, Mass.: Heath.

MOOS, R. H., & INSEL, P. M. (Eds.) (1974). *Issues in social ecology.* Palo Alto, Calif.: National Press books.

MORGAN, A. H. (1973). The heritability of hypnotic susceptibility in twins. *Journal of Abnormal Psychology, 82,* 55–61.

MORGAN, A. H., JOHNSON, D. L., & HILGARD, E. R. (1974). The stability of hypnotic susceptibility: A longitudinal study. *International Journal of Clinical and Experimental Hypnosis, 22,* 249–257.

MORRIS, J. (1975). Fear reduction methods. In F. H. Kanfer & A. P. Goldstein (Eds.), *Helping people change* (pp. 229–271). Elmsford, N.Y.: Pergamon Press.

MORSE, W. H., & KELLEHER, R. T. (1966). Schedules using noxious stimuli I. Multiple fixed-ratio and fixed-interval termination of schedule complexes. *Journal of the Experimental Analysis of Behavior, 9,* 267–290.

MOWRER, O. H., & ULLMANN, A. D. (1945). Time as a determinant in integrative learning. *Psychological Review, 52,* 61–90.

MULAIK, S. A. (1964). Are personality factors raters' conceptual factors? *Journal of Consulting Psychology, 28,* 506–511.

MURPHY, J. M. (1976). Psychiatric labeling in cross-cultural perspective. *Science, 191,* 1019–1028.

MURRAY, E. J. (1959). Conflict and repression during sleep deprivation. *Journal of Abnormal and Social Psychology, 59,* 95–101.

MURRAY, E. J., AULD, F., JR., & WHITE, A. M. (1954). A psychotherapy case showing progress but no decrease in the discomfort-relief quotient. *Journal of Consulting Psychology, 18,* 349–353.

MURRAY, H. A., BARRETT, W. G., & HOMBURGER, E. (1938). *Explorations in personality.* New York: Oxford University Press.

MURRAY, J. (1973). Television and violence: Implications of the surgeon general's research program. *American Psychologist, 28,* 472–478.

MURRAY, J. P., RUBINSTEIN, E. A., & COMSTOCK, G. A. (Eds.) (1972). *Television and social behavior, Vol. II. Television and social learning* (pp. 1–34). Washington, D.C.: Government Printing Office.

MURSTEIN, B. I. (1963). *Theory and research in projective techniques.* New York: Wiley.

MUSSEN, P. H. (1961). Some antecedents and consequents of masculine sex-typing in adolescent boys. *Psychological Monographs, 75,* No. 2 (Whole No. 506).

MUSSEN, P. H. (1962). Long-term consequents of masculinity of interests in adolescence. *Journal of Consulting Psychology, 26,* 435–440.

MUSSEN, P. H., & NAYLOR, H. K. (1954). The relationship between overt and fantasy aggression. *Journal of Abnormal and Social Psychology, 49,* 235–240.

NIMH (National Institute of Mental Health). (1975). *Research in the service of mental health.* (Rep. of the Research Task Force of the NIMH; DHEW Publication No. 75-236.) Washington, D.C.: Author.

NEISSER, U. (1967). *Cognitive psychology.* New York: Appleton.

NEISSER, U. (1974). Review of "Visual information processing." *Science, 183,* 402-403.

NILSON, D. C., NILSON, L. B., OLSON, R. S., & McALLISTER, B. H. (1981). The planning environment report for the Southern California Earthquake Safety Advisory Board. Redlands, Calif.: The Social Research Advisory and Policy Research Center.

NISBETT, R. E. (1968). Taste, deprivation, and weight determinants of eating behavior. *Journal of Personality and Social Psychology, 10,* 107-116.

NISBETT, R. E. (1972). Hunger, obesity, and the ventromedial hypothalamus, *Psychological Reveiw, 79,* 433-453.

NISBETT, R. E., & BORGIDA, E. (1975). Attribution and the psychology of prediction. *Journal of Personality and Social Psychology, 32,* 932-943.

NISBETT, R. E., BORGIDA, E., CRANDALL, R., & REED, H. (1976). Popular induction: Information is not necessarily informative. In J. S. Carroll & J. W. Payne (Eds.), *Cognition and social behavior.* Hillsdale, N.J.: Erlbaum.

NISBETT, R. E., & ROSS, L. D. (1980). *Human inference: Strategies and shortcomings of social judgment.* Century Psychology Series. Englewood Cliffs, N.J.: Prentice-Hall.

NISBETT, R. E., & WILSON, T. D. (1977). Telling more than we can know: Verbal reports on mental processes. *Psychological Review, 84,* 231-259.

NORMAN, W. T. (1961). Development of self-report tests to measure personality factors identified from peer nominations. *USAF ASK Technical Note,* No. 61-44.

NORMAN, W. T. (1963). Toward an adequate taxonomy of personality attributes: Replicated factor structure in peer nomination personality ratings. *Journal of Abnormal and Social Psychology, 66,* 574-583.

NORMAN, W. T. (1966). Convergent and discriminant validation of personality factor measurements. Unpublished manuscript, University of Michigan.

NORMAN, W. T. (1969). To see ourselves as others see us!. Relations among self-perceptions, peer-perceptions, and expected peer-perceptions of personality attributes. *Multivariate Behavioral Research, 4,* 417-443.

OFFICE OF STRATEGIC SERVICES ASSESSMENT STAFF. (1948). *Assessment of men.* New York: Holt, Rinehart and Winston.

O'LEARY, K. D., & KENT, R. N. (1973). Behavior modification for social action: Research tactics and problems. In L. Hamerlynck, et al. (Eds.), *Critical issues in research and practice.* New York: Research Press.

OLWEUS, D. (1977). Aggression and peer acceptance in adolescent boys: Two short-term longitudinal studies of ratings. *Child Development, 48,* 1301-1313.

OPLER, M. K. (1967). Cultural induction of stress. In M. H. Appley & R. Trumbull (Eds.), *Psychological stress* (pp. 209-241). New York: Appleton.

ORNE, M. T. (1972). On the stimulating subject as a quasi-control group in hypnosis research: Why, why, and how. In E. Fromm and R. E. Shor (Eds.), *Hypnosis: Research developments and perspectives.* Chicago: Aldine-Atherton.

ORNSTEIN, R. E. (1972). *The psychology of consciousness.* San Francisco: Freeman.

ORNSTEIN, R. E., & NARANJO, C. (1971). *On the psychology of meditation.* New York: Viking.

OSGOOD, C. E., SUCI, G. J., & TANNENBAUM, P. H. (1957). *The measurement of meaning.* Urbana, Ill.: The University of Illinois Press.

OSKAMP, S. (1965). Overconfidence in case-study judgments. *Journal of Consulting Psychology, 29,* 261-265.

OVERALL, J. (1964). Note on the scientific status of factors. *Psychological Bulletin, 61,* 270-276.

References

552

PAGANO, R. R., ROSE, R. M., STIVERS, R. M., & WARRENBURG, S. (1976). Sleep during transcendental mediation. *Science, 191,* 308–309.

PAHNKE, W. N., & RICHARDS, W. A. (1972). Implications of LSD and experimental mysticism. In C. Tart (Ed.), *Altered states of consciousness.* New York: Anchor.

PASSINI, F. T., & NORMAN, W. T. (1966). A universal conception of personality structure? *Journal of Personality and Social Psychology, 4,* 44–49.

PASTORE, N. (1952). The role of arbitrariness in the frustration-agression hypothesis. *Journal of Abnormal and Social Psychology, 47,* 728–731.

PATTERSON, C. J., & MISCHEL, W. (1976). Effects of temptation-inhibiting and task-facilitating plans on self-control. *Journal of Personality and Social Psychology, 33,* 209–217.

PATTERSON, G. R. (1976). The aggressive child: Victim and architect of a coercive system. In L. A. Hamerlynck, L. C. Handy, & E. J. Mash (eds.), *Behavior modification and families: 1. Theory and research.* New York: Brunner/Mazel.

PATTERSON, G. R., & COBB, J. A. (1971). Stimulus control for classes of noxious behaviors. In J. F. Knutson (Ed.), *The control of aggression: Implications from basic research.* Chicago: Aldine.

PAUL, G. L. (1966). *Insight vs. desensitization in psychotherapy.* Stanford: Stanford University.

PAUL, G. L. (1967). Insight versus desensitization in psychotherapy two years after termination. *Journal of Consulting Psychology, 31,* 333–348.

PAUL, G. L., & SHANNON, D. T. (1966). Treatment of anxiety through systematic desensitization in therapy groups. *Journal of Abnormal Psychology, 71,* 124–135.

PEDERSON, F. A. (1958). Consistency data on the role construct repertory test. Unpublished manuscript, Ohio State University, Columbus.

PEDHAZUR, E. J., & TETENBAUM, T. J. (1979). Bem Sex Role Inventory: A theoretical and methodological critique. *Journal of Personality and Social Psychology, 37,* 996–1016.

PERLMUTER, L. C., & MONTY, R. A. (Eds.) (1979). *Choice and perceived control.* Hillsdale, N.J.: Erlbaum.

PERLS, F. S. (1969). *Gestalt therapy verbatim.* Lafayette, Calif.: Real People Press.

PETERSON, D. R. (1965). Scope and generality of verbally defined personality factors. *Psychological Review, 72,* 48–59.

PETERSON, D. R. (1968). *The clinical study of social behavior.* New York: Appleton.

PHARES, E. J. (1973). *Locus of control: A Personality determinant of behavior.* Morristown, N.J.: General Learning Press.

PHARES, E. J. (1976). *Locus of control in personality.* Morristown, N.J.: General Learning Press.

PHARES, E. J. (1978). Locus of control. In H. London & J. E. Exner, Jr. (Eds.), *Dimensions of personality.* New York: Wiley.

PHARES, E. J., RITCHIE, E. D., & DAVIS, W. L. (1968). Internal-external control and reaction to threat. *Journal of Personality and Social Psychology, 10,* 402–405.

PHILLIPS, J. S., & KANFER, F. H. (1969). The viability and vicissitudes of behavior therapy. *International Psychiatry Clinics, 6,* 75–131.

PIAGET, J. (1932). *The moral judgment of the child.* London: Kegan Paul.

PLOMIN, R., & FOCH, T. T. (1980). A twin study of objectively assessed personality in childhood. *Journal of Personality and Social Psychology, 39,* 680–688.

POSTMAN, L., & BROWN, D. R. (1952). The perceptual consequences of success and failure. *Journal of Abnormal and Social Psychology, 47,* 213–221.

POWELL, G. E. (1973). Negative and positive mental practice in motor skill acquisition. *Perceptual and Motor Skills, 37,* 312–313.

PRENTICE, N. M. (1972). The influence of live and symbolic modeling on promoting moral judgment of adolescent delinquents. *Journal of Abnormal Psychology, 80,* 157–161.

PRICE, R. H. (1974). The taxonomic classification of behaviors and situations and the problem of behavior-environment congruence. *Human Relations, 27* (6), 567–585.

References

553

PRICE, R. H., & BOUFFARD, D. L. (1974). Behavioral appropriateness and situational constraint as dimensions of social behavior. *Journal of Personality and Social Psychology, 30,* 579–586.

PROSHANSKY, H. M. (1976). Environmental psychology and the real word. *American Psychologist, 31,* 303–310.

PROSHANSKY, H. M., ITTELSON, W. H., & RIVLIN, L. G. (Eds.). (1970). *Environmental psychology.* New York: Holt, Rinehart and Winston.

RABKIN, J. G., & STRUENING, E. L. (1976). Life events, stress, and illness. *Science, 194,* 1013–1020.

RACHLIN, H. (1973). Self-control. Unpublished manuscript, State University of New York, Stony Brook.

RACHMAN, S. (1967). Systematic desensitization. *Psychological Bulletin, 67,* 93–103.

RACHMAN, S., & HODGESON, R. J. (1980). *Obsessions and Compulsions.* Englewood Cliffs, N.J.: Prentice-Hall.

RACHMAN, S., & WILSON, G. T. (1980). *The effects of psychological therapy.* Oxford, England: Pergamon Press.

RAPAPORT, D. (1951). The autonomy of the ego. *Bulletin of the Menninger Clinic, 15,* 113–123.

RAPAPORT, D. (1967). On the psychoanalytic theory of thinking. In M. M. Gill (Ed.), *The collected papers of David Rapaport.* New York: Basic Books.

RAUSH, H. L. (1965). Interaction sequences. *Journal of Personality and Social Psychology, 2,* 487–499.

RAUSH, H. L., BARRY, W. A., HERTEL, R. K. & SWAIN, M. A. (1974). *Communication conflict and marriage.* San Francisco: Jossey-Bass.

RAYMOND, M. S. (1956). Case of fetishism treated by aversion therapy. *British Medical Journal, 2,* 854–857.

RECORD, R. G., MCKEOWN, T., & EDWARDS, J. H. (1970). An investigation of the difference in measured intelligence between twins and single births. *Annals of the Human Genetic Society, 84,* 11–20.

REDD, W. H., PORTERFIELD, A. L., & ANDERSON, B. L. (1978). *Behavior modification: Behavioral approaches to human problems.* New York: Random House.

REECE, M. M. (1954). The effect of shock on recognition thresholds. *Journal of Abnormal and Social Psychology, 49,* 165–172.

REKERS, G. A., & LOVAAS, O. I. (1974). Behavioral treatment of deviant sex-role behaviors in a male child. *Journal of Applied Behavior Analysis, 7,* 173–190.

RIMM, D. C., & MASTERS, J. C. (1974). *Behavior therapy: Techniques and empirical findings.* New York: Academic Press.

ROBBINS, L. N. (1972). Dissecting the "broken home" as a predictor of deviance. Paper presented at the National Institute of Mental Health conference on developmental aspects of self-regulation, La Jolla, Calif., February.

RODIN, J. (1981). Current status of the internal-external hypothesis of obesity: What went wrong? *American Psychologist, 36,* 361–372.

RODIN, J., & LANGER, E. J. (1977). Long-term effect of control-relevant intervention. *Journal of Personality and Social Psychology, 35,* 897–902.

ROGERS, C. R. (1942). *Counseling and psychotherapy: Newer concepts in practice.* Boston: Houghton Mifflin.

ROGERS, C. R. (1947). Some observations on the organization of personality. *American Psychologist, 2,* 358–368.

ROGERS, C. R. (1951). *Client-centered therapy: Its current practice, implications and theory.* Boston: Houghton Mifflin.

ROGERS, C. R. (1955). Persons or science? A philosophical question. *American Psychologist, 10,* 267–278.

ROGERS, C. R. (1959). A theory of therapy, personality and interpersonal relationships, as developed in the client-centered framework. In S. Koch (Ed.), *Psychology: A study of a science, Vol. 3* (pp. 184–526). New York: McGraw-Hill.

ROGERS, C. R. (1963). The actualizing tendency in relation to "motives" and to consciousness. In M. R. Jones (Ed.), *Nebraska symposium on motivation* (pp. 1–24). Lincoln: University of Nebraska Press.

ROGERS, C. R. (1970). *Carl Rogers on encounter groups.* New York: Harper & Row.

ROGERS, C. R. (1974). In retrospect: Forty-six years. *American Psychologist, 29,* 115–123.

ROGERS, C. R. (1980). *A way of being.* Boston: Houghton Mifflin.

ROGERS, C. R., & DYMOND, R. F. (Eds.). (1954). *Psychotherapy and personality change, co-ordinated studies in the client-centered approach.* Chicago: University of Chicago Press.

ROGERS, T. B. (1977). Self-reference in memory: Recognition of personality items. *Journal of Research in Personality, 11,* 295–305.

ROGERS, T. B., KUIPER, N. A., & KIRKER, W. S. (1977). Self-reference and the encoding of personal information. *Journal of Personality and Social Psychology, 35,* 677–688.

ROMER, D., & REVELLE, W. (1984). Personality traits: Fact or Fiction? A critique of the Shweder and D'Andrade systematic distortion hypothesis. *Journal of Personality and Social Psychology, 47,* 1028–1042.

ROSCH, E. (1975). Cognitive reference points. *Cognitive Psychology, 1,* 532–547.

ROSCH, E., MERVIS, C., GRAY, W., JOHNSON, D., & BOYCE-BRAEM, P. (1976). Basic objects in natural categories. *Cognitive Psychology, 8,* 382–439.

ROSEN, A. C. (1954). Change in perceptual threshold as a protective function of the organism. *Journal of Personality, 23,* 182–195.

ROSENHAN, D. L. (1973). On being sane in insane places. *Science, 179,* 250–258.

ROSENTHAL, D. (1971). *Genetics of psychopathology.* New York: McGraw-Hill.

ROSENZWEIG, S., & MASON, G. (1934). An experimental study of memory in relation to the theory of repression. *British Journal of Psychology, 24,* 247–265.

ROSS, L. D. (1977). The intuitive psychologist and his shortcomings: Distortions in the attribution process. In. L. Berkowitz (Ed.), *Advances in experimental social psychology, Vol. 10.* New York: Academic Press.

ROTHBART, M. L., & MACCOBY, E. E. (1966). Parents' differential reactions to sons and daughters. *Journal of Personality and Social Psychology, 4,* 237–243.

ROTTER, J. B. (1954). *Social learning and clinical psychology.* Englewood Cliffs, N.J.: Prentice-Hall.

ROTTER, J. B. (1966). Generalized expectancies for internal versus external control of reinforcement. *Psychological Monographs, 80* (Whole No. 609).

ROTTER, J. B. (1972). Beliefs, social attitudes, and behavior: A social learning analysis. In J. B. Rotter, J. E. Chance, & E. J. Phares (Eds.), *Applications of a social learning theory of personality.* New York: Holt, Rinehart and Winston.

ROTTER, J. B., CHANCE, J. E., & PHARES, E. J. (Eds.). (1972). *Applications of a social learning theory of personality.* New York: Holt, Rinehart and Winston.

ROTTER, J. B. (1975). Some problems and misconceptions related to the construct of internal versus external control of reinforcement. *Journal of Consulting and Clinical Psychology, 43,* 56–67.

ROYCE, J. E. (1973). Does person or self imply dualism? *American Psychologist, 28,* 833–866.

RUBIN, I. J. (1967). The reduction of prejudice through laboratory training. *Journal of Applied Behavioral Science, 3,* 29–50.

RUBIN, I. J. (1968). Analyzing Detroit's riot: The causes and responses. *The Reporter,* Feb. 22, 34–35.

RUEBUSH, B. E. (1963). In H. A. Stevenson, et al. (Eds.), *Child psychology. The sixty-second yearbook of the National Society for the Study of Education* (pp. 460–516). Chicago: University of Chicago Press.

References

RUSHTON, P. J., FULKER, D. W., NEALE, N. C., NIAS, D. K. B., & EYSENCK, H. J. (1986, in press). Aggression and altruism: The heritability of individual differences. *Journal of Personality and Social Psychology.*

RUSSELL, P. C., & BRANDSMA, J. M. (1974). A theoretical and empirical integration of the rational-emotive and classical conditioning theories. *Journal of Consulting and Clinical Psychology, 42,* 389–397.

RYCHLAK, J. F. (1981). *Introduction to personality and psychotherapy (2nd ed.).* Boston: Houghton Mifflin.

SAMPSON, E. E., & HANCOCK, T. (1967). An examination of the relationship between ordinal position, personality, and conformity: An extension, replication, and partial verification. *Journal of Personality and Social Psychology, 5,* 398–407.

SARASON, I. G. (1961). The effects of anxiety and threat on the solution of a difficult task. *Journal of Abnormal and Social Psychology, 62,* 165–168.

SARASON, I. G. (1966). *Personality: An objective approach.* New York: Wiley.

SARASON, I. G. (1978). The Test Anxiety Scale: Concept and research. In C. D. Spielberger & I. G. Sarason (Eds.), *Stress and anxiety, Vol. 5.* Washington, D.C.: Hemisphere.

SARASON, I. G. (1979). *Life stress, self-preoccupation, and social supports.* Presidential address, Western Psychological Association.

SARASON, I. G., SMITH, R. E., & DIENER, E. (1975). Personality research: Components of variance attributable to the person and the situation. *Journal of Personality and Social Psychology, 32,* 199–204.

SARASON, S. B., DAVIDSON, K. S., LIGHTHALL, F. F., WAITE, R. R., & RUEBUSH, B. K. (1960). *Anxiety in elementary school children.* New York: Wiley.

SARBIN, T. R., & COE, W. C. (1972). *Hypnosis: A social psychological analysis of influence communication.* New York: Holt.

SARTRE, J. P. (1956). Existentialism. In W. Kaufmann (Ed.), *Existentialism from Dostoevsky to Sartre* (pp. 222–311). New York: Meridian.

SARTRE, J. P. (1965). *Existentialism and humanism* (tr. by Mairet). London: Methuen.

SATIR, V. (1967). *Conjoint family therapy.* Palo Alto, Calif.: Science and Behavior Books.

SCARR, S. (1985). Constructing psychology: making facts and fables for our times. *American Psychologist, 40,* 499–512.

SCARR, S., PAKSTIS, A. J., KATZ, S. H., & BARKER, W. B. (1977). The absence of relationship between degree of white ancestry and intellectual skills within a black population. *Human Genetics, 857,* 1–18.

SCARR-SALAPATEK, S. (1971). Race, social class and IQ. *Science, 174,* 1285–1295.

SCHACHT, T., & NATHAN, P. E. (1977). But is it good for the psychologists? Appraisal and status of DSM-III. *American Psychologist, 32,* 1017–1025.

SCHACHTER, S. (1964). The interaction of cognitive and physiological determinants of emotional state. In L. Berkowitz (Ed.), *Advances in experimental social psychology, Vol. 1* (pp. 49–80). New York: Academic Press.

SCHACHTER, S., GOLDMAN, R., & GORDON, A. (1968). Effects of fear, food deprivation and obesity on eating. *Journal of Personality and Social Psychology, 10,* 91–97.

SCHACHTER, S., & GROSS, L. P. (1968). Manipulated time and eating behavior. *Journal of Personality and Social Psychology, 10,* 98–106.

SCHACHTER, S., & RODIN, J. (1974). *Obese humans and rats.* Potomac, Md.: Erlbaum.

SCHACHTER, S., & SINGER, J. E. (1962). Cognitive, social and physiological determinants of emotional state. *Psychological Review, 69,* 379–399.

SCHACHTER, S., & SINGER, J. E. (1979). Comments on the Maslach and Marshall-Zimbardo experiments. *Journal of Personality and Social Psychology, 37,* 989–995.

SCHANK, R., & ABELSON, R. P. (1977). *Scripts, plans, goals, and understanding.* Hillsdale, N.J.: Erlbaum.

Scheier, M. F. & Carver, C. S. (1980). Individual differences in self-concept and self-process. In D. M. Wegner & R. R. Vallacher (Eds.), *The self in social psychology*. New York: Oxford University Press.

Schneider, D. J. (1973). Implicit personality theory: A review. *Psychological Bulletin, 73,* 294–309.

Schneider, D. J., Hastorf, A. H., & Ellsworth, P. C. (1979). *Person perception (2nd ed.).* Reading, Mass.: Addison-Wesley.

Schutte, N. S., Kenrick, D. T., & Sadalla, E. K. (1985). The search for predictable settings: Situational prototypes, constraints, and behavioral variation. *Journal of Personality and Social Psychology, 49,* 121–128.

Schutz, W. C. (1967). *Joy: Expanding human awareness.* New York: Grove.

Schwartz, G. E. (1973). Biofeedback as therapy. *American Psychologist, 28,* 666–673.

Scott, W. A., & Johnson, R. C. (1972). Comparative validities of direct and indirect personality tests. *Journal of Consulting and Clinical Psychology, 38,* 301–318.

Sears, R. R. (1936). Functional abnormalities of memory with special reference to amnesia. *Psychological Bulletin, 33,* 229–274.

Sears, R. R. (1943). Survey of objective studies of psychoanalytic concepts. *Social Science Research Council Bulletin,* No. 51.

Sears, R. R. (1944). Experimental analyses of psychoanalytic phenomena. In J. McV. Hunt (Ed.), *Personality and the behavior disorders, Vol. 1* (pp. 306–332). New York: Ronald.

Sears, R. R. (1963). Dependency motivation. In M. R. Jones (Ed.), *Nebraska symposium on motivation* (pp. 25–64). Lincoln: University of Nebraska Press.

Sears, R. R. (1965). Development of gender role. In F. A. Beach (Ed.), *Sex and behavior* (pp. 133–163). New York: Wiley.

Sears, R. R., Maccoby, E. E., & Levin, H. (1957). *Patterns of child rearing.* New York: Row.

Sechrest, L., Gallimore, R., & Hersch, P. D. (1967). Feedback and accuracy of clinical prediction. *Journal of Consulting Psychology, 31,* 1–11.

Seligman, M. E. P. (1971). Phobias and preparedness. *Behavior Therapy, 2,* 307–320.

Seligman, M. E. P. (1975). *Helplessness—On depression, development, and death.* San Francisco: Freeman.

Seligman, M. E. P. (1978). Comment and integration. *Journal of Abnormal Psychology, 87,* 165–179.

Seligman, M. E. P., Abramson, L. Y., Semmel, A., & von Baeyer, C. (1979). Depressive attributional style. *Journal of Abnormal Psychology, 88,* 242–247.

Seligman, M. E. P., & Hager, J. L. (1972). *Biological boundaries of learning.* New York: Appleton.

Shaffer, H. R., & Emerson, P. E. (1964). The development of social attachment in infancy. *Monograph of The Society for Research in Child Development, 29,* No. 3.

Shure, G. H., & Rogers, M. S. (1965). Note of caution on the factor analysis of the MMPI. *Psychological Bulletin, 63,* 14–18.

Shweder, R. A. (1975). How relevant is an individual difference theory of personality? *Journal of Personality, 43,* 455–485.

Silverman, L. H. (1976). Psychoanalytic theory: The reports of my death are greatly exaggerated. *American Psychologist, 31,* 621–637.

Singer, J. L. (1955). Delayed gratification and ego development: Implications for clinical and experimental research. *Journal of Consulting Psychology, 19,* 259–266.

Singer, J. L. (1974). Daydreaming and the stream of thought. *American Scientist, 2,* 417–425.

Singer, J. L. (1981). Research implications of projective methods. In A. I. Rabin (Ed.), *Assessment with projective techniques.* New York: Springer.

Singer, J. L., & Antrobus, J. S. (1972). Dimensions of day-dreaming: A factor analysis of imaginal processes and personality scales. In P. Sheehan (Ed.), *The adaptive function of imagery.* New York: Academic Press.

SKEELS, H. M. (1966). Adult status of children with contrasting early life experiences. *Monographs of the Society for Research in Child Development, 31,* No. 3.

SKINNER, B. F. (1953). *Science and human behavior.* New York: Macmillan, 1953.

SKINNER, B. F. (1955). Freedom and the control of men. *American Scholar, 25,* 47–65.

SKINNER, B. F. (1964). Behaviorism at fifty. In T. W. Wann (Ed.), *Behaviorism and phenomenology* (pp. 79–108). Chicago: University of Chicago Press.

SKINNER, B. F. (1971). *Beyond freedom and dignity.* New York: Knopf.

SKINNER, B. F. (1974). *About behaviorism.* New York: Knopf.

SKOLNICK, A. (1966). Motivational imagery and behavior over twenty years. *Journal of Consulting Psychology, 30,* 463–478.

SLOANE, R. B., STAPLES, F. R., CRISTOL, A. H., YORKSTON, N. J., & WHIPPLE, K. (1975). *Psychotherapy vs. behavior therapy.* Cambridge, Mass.: Harvard University Press.

SMITH, E. R., & MILLER, F. D. (1978). Limits on perception of cognitive processes: A reply to Nisbett and Wilson. *Psychological Review, 85,* 355–362.

SMITH, M. B. (1950). The phenomenological approach in personality theory: Some critical remarks. *Journal of Abnormal and Social Psychology, 45,* 516–522.

SMITH, M. L., & GLASS, G. V. (1977). Meta-analysis of psychotherapy outcome studies. *American Psychologist, 32,* 752–760.

SMITH, M. L., GLASS, G. V., & MILLER, T. I. (1980). *The benefits of psychotherapy.* Baltimore: Johns Hopkins University Press.

SNYDER, M. (1979). Self-monitoring processes. In L. Berkowitz (Ed.), *Advances in experimental social psychology, Vol. 12.* New York: Academic Press.

SNYDER, M., & SWANN, W. (1978). Behavioral confirmation in social interaction: From social perception to social reality. *Journal of Experimental Social Psychology, 14,* 148–162.

SNYDER, M., TANKE, E. D., & BERSCHEID, E. (1977). Social perception and interpersonal behavior: On the self-fulfilling nature of social stereotypes. *Journal of Personality and Social Psychology, 35,* 656–666.

SNYDER, M., & URANOWITZ, S. (1978). Reconstructing the past: Some cognitive consequences of person perception. *Journal of Personality and Social Psychology, 36,* 941–950.

SNYDER, S. H., BANERJEE, S. P., YAMOMURA, H. I., & GREENBERG, D. (1974). Drugs, neurotransmitters, and schizophrenia. *Science, 184,* 1243–1253.

SOSKIN, W. F. (1954). Bias in postdiction from projective tests. *Journal of Abnormal and Social Psychology, 49,* 69–74.

SOSKIN, W. F. (1959). Influence of four types of data on diagnostic conceptualization in psychological testing. *Journal of Abnormal and Social Psychology, 58,* 69–78.

SPENCE, K. W., & SPENCE, J. T. (1964). Relation of eyelid conditioning to manifest anxiety, extraversion and rigidity. *Journal of Abnormal and Social Psychology, 68,* 144–149.

SPIELBERGER, C. D. (1962). The effects of manifest anxiety on the academic achievement of college students. *Mental Hygiene, 46,* 420–426.

SPIELBERGER, C. D. (1966). The effects of anxiety on complex learning and academic achievement. In C. D. Spielberger (Ed.), *Anxiety and behavior* (pp. 361–398). New York: Academic Press.

SPIELBERGER, C. D., & DENIKE, L. D. (1966). Descriptive behaviorism versus cognitive theory in verbal operant conditioning. *Psychological Review, 73,* 306–326.

SPIVACK, G., LEVINE, M., & SPRIGLE, H. (1959). Intelligence test performance and the delay function of the ego. *Journal of Consulting Psychology, 23,* 428–431.

SROUFE, L. A. (1977). *Knowing and enjoying your baby.* Englewood Cliffs, N.J.: Prentice-Hall.

STAATS, C. K., & STAATS, A. W. (1957). Meaning established by classical conditioning. *Journal of Experimental Psychology, 54,* 74–80.

References

STAUB, E. (1978). *Positive social behavior and morality, Vol. 1*. New York: Academic Press.

STAUB, E., TURSKY, B., & SCHWARTZ, G. E. (1971). Self-control and predictability: Their effects on reactions to aversive stimulation. *Journal of Personality and Social Psychology, 18,* 157–162.

STELMACHERS, Z. T., & McHUGH, R. B. (1964). Contribution of stereotyped and individualized information to predictive accuracy. *Journal of Consulting Psychology, 28,* 243–242.

STEPHENSON, W. (1953). *The study of behavior*. Chicago: University of Chicago Press.

STERNBERG, R. J. (Ed.). (1982). *Handbook of human intelligence*. New York: Cambridge University Press.

STEUER, F. B., APPLEFIELD, J. M., & SMITH, R. (1971). Televised aggression and the interpersonal aggression of preschool children. *Journal of Experimental Child Psychology, 11,* 442–447.

STOKOLS, D. (1978). Environmental psychology. *Annual Review of Psychology, 29,* 253–295.

STONE, L. J., & HOKANSON, J. E., (1969). Arousal reduction via self-punitive behavior. *Journal of Personality and Social Psychology, 12,* 72–79.

STRUPP, H. H. (1980). Success and failure in time-limited psychotherapy: A systematic comparison of two cases: Comparison one. *Archives of General Psychiatry, 37,* 595–603.

STUART, R. B. (1967). Behavioral control over eating. *Behavior Research and Therapy, 5,* 357–365.

STUART, R. B. (1971). A three-dimensional program for the treatment of obesity. *Behavior Research and Therapy, 9,* 177–186.

STUMPHAUZER, J. S. (1972). Increased delay of gratification in young prison inmates through imitation of high delay peer models, *Journal of Personality and Social Psychology, 21,* 10–17.

STUNKARD, A. I., & KOCH, C. (1964). The interpretation of gastric motility: Apparent bias in the report of hunger by obese persons. *Archives of General Psychology, 11,* 74–82.

SZASZ, T. S. (1960). The myth of mental illness. *American Psychologist, 15,* 113–118.

SZASZ, T. S. (1970). *The manufacture of madness*. New York: Dell.

TAFT, R. (1955). The ability to judge people. *Psychological Bulletin, 52,* 1–28.

TANKARD, J. (1970). Effects of eye position on person perception. *Perceptual and Motor Skills, 31,* 883–893.

TART, C. (1970). Increases in hypnotizability resulting from a prolonged program for enhancing personal growth. *Journal of Abnormal Psychology, 75,* 260–266.

TAYLOR, J. A. (1953). A personality scale of manifest anxiety. *Journal of Abnormal and Social Psychology, 48,* 285–290.

TAYLOR, S. E., & METTEE, D. R. (1971). When similarity breeds contempt. *Journal of Personality and Social Psychology, 20,* 75–81.

TAYLOR, S. P., & EPSTEIN, S. (1967). Aggression as a function of the interaction of the sex of the aggressor and the sex of the victim. *Journal of Personality, 35,* 474–486.

TERMAN, L. M., & MERRILL, M. A. (1960). Stanford-Binet intelligence scale: Manual for the third revision, form L-M. Boston: Houghton Mifflin.

TESTA, T. J. (1974). Causal relationships and the acquisition of avoidance responses. *Psychological Review, 81,* 491–505.

THIBAUT, J., & RIECKEN, H. (1955). Authoritarianism, status, and the communication of aggression. *Human Relations, 8,* 95–120.

THOMAS A., & CHESS, S. (1977). Temperament and development. New York: Brunner/Mazel.

THORESEN, C., & MAHONEY, M. J. (1974). Self-control. New York: Holt, Rinehart and Winston.

THURSTONE, L. L. (1938). Primary mental abilities. *Psychometric Monographs,* No. 1. Chicago: University of Chicago Press.

TITUS, H. E., & HOLLANDER, E. P. (1957). The California F scale in psychological research: 1950–1955. *Psychological Bulletin, 54,* 47–64.

TOUHEY, J. (1974). Effects of additional women professionals on ratings of occupational prestige and desirability. *Journal of Personality and Social Psychology, 29,* 86–89.

References

Tourangeau, R., & Ellsworth, P. C. (1978). *The role of facial response in the experience of emotion.* Unpublished manuscript, Yale University.

Truax, C. B., & Mitchell, K. M. (1971). Research on certain therapist interpersonal skills in relation to process and outcome. In A. E. Bergin & S. I. Garfield (Eds.), *Handbook of psychotherapy and behavior change* (pp. 299–344). New York: Wiley.

Tsujimoto, R. N. (1978). Memory bias toward normative and novel trait prototypes. *Journal of Personality and Social Psychology, 36,* 1391–1401.

Tudor, T. G., & Holmes, D. S. (1973). Differential recall of successes and failures: Its relationship to defensiveness, achievement motivation, and anxiety. *Journal of Research in Personality, 7,* 208–224.

Tupes, C., & Christal, R. E. (1958). Stability of personality trait rating factors obtained under diverse conditions. *USAF WADC Technical Note,* No. 58–61.

Tupes, E. C., & Christal, R. E. (1961). Recurrent personality factors based on trait ratings. *USAF ASD Technical Report,* No. 61–67.

Tversky, A. (1977). Features of similarity. *Psychological Review, 84,* 327–352.

Tversky, A., & Kahneman, D. (1974). Judgment under uncertainty: Heuristics and biases. *Science, 185,* 1124–1131.

Tyler, L. E. (1956). *The psychology of human differences.* New York: Appleton.

Ullmann, L. F., & Krasner, L. (1967). *A psychological approach to abnormal behavior.* Englewood Cliffs, N.J.: Prentice-Hall.

Ulrich, R. E., Stachnik, T. J., & Stainton, N. R. (1963). Student acceptance of generalized personality interpretations. *Psychological Reports, 13,* 831–834.

Vaillant, G. E. (1977). *Adaptation to life.* Boston: Little, Brown.

Vanderberg, S. G. (1971). What do we know today about the inheritance of intelligence and how do we know it? In R. Cancro (Ed.), *Intelligence: Genetic and environmental influences* (pp. 182–218). New York: Grune & Stratton.

Venn, J. R., & Short, J. G. (1973). Vicarious classical conditioning of emotional responses in nursery school children. *Journal of Personality and Social Psychology, 28(2),* 249–255.

Vernon, P. E. (1964). *Personality assessment: A critical survey.* New York: Wiley.

Von Wright, G. H. (1963). *The varieties of goodness.* London: Routledge.

Wachtel, P. L. (1973). Psychodynamics, behavior therapy, and the implacable experimenter: An inquiry into the consistency of personality. *Journal of Abnormal Psychology, 82,* 323–334.

Wachtel, P. L. (1977). *Psychoanalysis and behavior therapy: Toward an integration.* New York: Basic Books.

Wade, T. C., & Baker, T. B. (1977). Opinions and use of psychological tests: A survey of clinical psychologists. *American Psychologist, 32,* 874–882.

Wahler, R. G., Winkel, G. H., Peterson, R. F., & Morrison, D. C. (1965). Mothers as behavior therapists for their own children. *Behavior Research and Therapy, 3,* 113–124.

Wallach, M. A. (1962). Commentary: Active-analytical vs. passive-global cognitive functioning. In S. Messick & J. Ross (Eds.), *Measurement in personality and cognition* (pp. 199–215). New York: Wiley.

Wallach, M. A., & Wing, C. W., Jr. (1969). *The talented student.* New York: Holt.

Walster, E. (1965). The effect of self-esteem on romantic liking. *Journal of Experimental Social Psychology, 1,* 184–197.

Walster, E., Aronson, V., Abrahams, D., & Rottman, L. (1966). Importance of physical attractiveness in dating behavior. *Journal of Personality and Social Psychology, 4,* 508–516.

Walters, G. C., & Grusec, J. E. (1977). *Punishment.* San Francisco: Freeman.

Walters, R. H., & Parke, R. D. (1967). The influence of punishment and related disciplinary techniques on the social behavior of children: Theory and empirical findings. In B. A. Maher (Ed.), *Progress in experimental personality research, Vol. 4* (pp. 179–228). New York: Academic Press.

References

WANDERSMAN, A., POPPEN, P. J., & RICKS, D. F. (1976). *Humanism and behaviorism: Dialogue and growth*. Oxford, England: Pergamon Press.

WATSON, J. B., & RAYNER, R. (1920). Conditioned emotional reaction. *Journal of Experimental Psychology, 3,* 1–14.

WATSON, R. I. (1959). Historical review of objective personality testing: The search for objectivity. In B. M. Bass & I. A. Berg (Eds.), *Objective approaches to personality assessment* (pp. 1–23). Princeton: Van Nostrand.

WEIDNER, G., & MATTHEWS, K. A. (1978). Reported physical symptoms elicited by unpredictable events and the type A coronary-prone behavior pattern. *Journal of Personality and Social Psychology, 36,* 1213–1220.

WEIGEL, R. H., & NEWMAN, S. L. (1976). Increasing attitude-behavior correspondence by broadening the scope of the behavioral measure. *Journal of Personality and Social Psychology, 33,* 793–802.

WEINER, B. (1965). Need achievement and the resumption of incompleted tasks. *Journal of Personality and Social Psychology, 1,* 165–168.

WEINER, B. (1972). *Theories of motivation: From mechanism to cognition*. Chicago: Markham.

WEINER, B. (1974). *An attributional interpretation of expectancy value theory*. Paper presented at the AAAS Meetings, San Francisco.

WEIR, M. W. (1965). Children's behavior in a two-choice task as a function of patterned reinforcement following forced-choice trials. *Journal of Experimental Child Psychology, 2,* 85–91.

WEISS, J. M. (1971a). Effects of coping behavior in different warning signal conditions on stress pathology in rats. *Journal of Comparative and Physiological Psychology, 77,* 1–13.

WEISS, J. M. (1971b). Effects of punishing the coping response (conflict) on stress pathology in rats. *Journal of Comparative and Physiological Psychology, 77,* 14–21.

WEISS, T., & ENGEL, B. T. (1971). Operant conditioning of heart rate in patients with premature ventricular contractions. *Psychosomatic Medicine, 33,* 301–321.

WEITZENHOFFER, A. M., & HILGARD, E. R. (1959). *Stanford Hypnotic Susceptibility Scale*. Palo Alto, Calif.: Consulting Psychologists Press.

WHITE, B. L. (1967). An experimental approach to the effects of experience on early human behavior. In J. P. Hill (Ed.), *Minnesota symposia on child psychology, Vol. 1* (pp. 201–226). Minneapolis: University of Minnesota Press.

WHITE, B. L., & HELD, R. (1966). Plasticity of sensorimotor development in the human infant. In J. F. Rosenblith & W. Allinsmith (Eds.), *The causes of behavior II* (pp. 60–70). Boston: Allyn & Bacon.

WHITE, B. L., KABAN, B., SHAPIRO, B., & ATTANUCCI, J. (1976). Competence and experience. In I. C. Uzgiris & F. Weizman (Eds.), *The structuring of experience*. New York: Plenum.

WHITE, R. W. (1952). *Lives in progress*. New York: Dryden.

WHITE, R. W. (1959). Motivation reconsidered: The concept of competence. *Psychological Review, 66,* 297–333.

WHITE, R. W. (1964). *The abnormal personality*. New York: Ronald.

WHITE, R. W. (1972). *The enterprise of living*. New York: Holt.

WHITING, J. W. M., & Whiting, B. (1966). Personal communication on a current research project, 1962, Reported in R. Oetzel. Annotated bibliography in E. E. Maccoby (Ed.), *The development of sex differences*. Stanford, Calif.: Stanford University Press.

WHITING, J. W. M., & WHITING, B. (1969). The behavior of children in six cultures. Unpublished manuscript, Harvard University.

WICKLUND, R. A., & FREY, D. (1980). Self-awareness theory: When the self makes a difference. In D. M. Wegner & R. R. Vallacher (Eds.), *The self in social psychology*. New York: Oxford University Press.

WIGGINS, J. S. (1973). *Personality and prediction: Principles of personality assessment*. Reading, Mass.: Addison-Wesley.

References

WIGGINS, J. S. (1979). A psychological taxonomy of trait-descriptive terms: The interpersonal domain. *Journal of Personality and Social Psychology, 37,* 395–412.

WIGGINS, J. S. (1980). Circumplex models of interpersonal behavior in personality and social psychology. *The Review of Personality and Social Psychology.*

WILEY, R. C. (1979). *The self concept, Vol. 2: Theory and research on selected topics.* Lincoln: University of Nebraska Press.

WILSON, G. T., & O'LEARY, K. D.. (1980). *Principles of behavior therapy.* Englewood Cliffs, N.J.: Prentice-Hall.

WILSON, W. R. (1979). Feeling more than we can know: Exposure effects without learning. *Journal of Personality and Social Psychology, 37,* 811–821.

WINDER, C. L., & WIGGINS J. S. (1964). Social reputation and social behavior: A further validation of the peer nomination inventory. *Journal of Abnormal and Social Psychology, 68,* 681–685.

WISSLER, C. (1901). The correlation of mental and physical tests. *Psychological Review Monograph Supplement, 3,* No. 16.

WITKIN, H. A. (1965). Psychological differentiation and forms of pathology. *Journal of Abnormal Psychology, 70,* 317–336.

WITKIN, H. A., DYK, R. B., FATERSON, H. F., GOODENOUGH, D. R., & KARP, S. A. (1962). *Psychological differentiation.* New York: Wiley.

WITTGENSTEIN, L. (1953). *Philosophical investigations.* New York: MacMillan.

WOLF, R. (1966). The measurement of environments. In A. Anastasi (Ed.), *Testing problems in perspective* (pp. 491–503). Washington, D.C.: American Council on Education.

WOLFF, P. (1966). Unpublished paper presented at the Tavistock Conference on Determinants of Infant Behavior, London, September, 1965. Cited in D.A. Hamburg & D.T. Lunde, Sex hormones in the development of sex differences in human behavior. In E. E. Maccoby (Ed.), *The development of sex differences* (pp. 1–24). Stanford, Calif.: Stanford University Press.

WOLPE, J. (1958). *Psychotherapy by reciprocal inhibition.* Stanford, Calif.: Stanford University Press.

WOLPE, J. (1963). Behavior therapy in complex neurotic states. *British Journal of Psychiatry, 110,* 28–34.

WOLPE, J., & LANG, P. J. (1964). A fear survey schedule for use in behavior therapy. *Behavior Research Therapy, 2,* 27–30.

WOLPE, J., & LAZARUS, A. A. (1966). Behavior therapy techniques: A guide to the treatment of neuroses. Elmsford, N.Y.: Pergamon Press.

WOLPE, J., & RACHMAN, S. (1960). Psychoanalytic evidence: A critique based on Freud's case of Little Hans. *Journal of Nervous and Mental Diseases, 31,* 134–147.

WORTMAN, C. B., & BREHM, J. W. (1975). Responses to uncontrollable outcomes. In L. Berkowitz (Ed.), *Advances in experimental social psychology, Vol. 8* (pp. 278–336). New York: Academic Press.

WORTMAN, C. B., COSTANZO, P. R., & WITT, T. R. (1973). Effect of anticipated performance on the attributions of causality to self and others. *Journal of Personality and Social Psychology, 27,* 372–381.

WRIGHT, J. (1983). Structure and perception of behavioral consistency. Unpublished doctoral dissertation, Department of Psychology, Stanford University, Calif.

YATES, B. T. (1985). *Self-management: Science and art of helping yourself.* California: Wadsworth.

YATES, B. T., & MISCHEL, W. (1979). Young children's preferred attentional strategies for delaying gratification. *Journal of Personality and Social Psychology, 37,* 286–300.

ZAJONC, R. B. (1980). Feeling and thinking: Preferences need no inferences. *American Psychologist, 35(2),* 151–175.

ZAJONC, R. B., MARKUS, H., & MARKUS, G. B. (1979). The birth order puzzle. *Journal of Personality and Social Psychology, 37,* 1325–1341.

ZELLER, A. (1950). An experimental analogue of repression. I. Historical summary. *Psychological Bulletin, 47,* 39–51.

ZIMBARDO, P. G. (1969). The human choice: Individuation, reason, and order versus deindividuation, impulse, and chaos. In W. J. Arnold and D. Levine (Eds.), *Nebraska symposium on motivation* (pp. 237–307). Lincoln: University of Nebraska Press.

ZIMMERMAN, B. J., & ROSENTHAL, T. L. (1974). Observational learning of rule-governed behavior by children. *Psychological Bulletin, 81,* 29–42.

ZIV, A., KRUGLANSKI, A. W., & SHULMAN, S. (1974). Children's psychological reactions to wartime stress. *Journal of Personality and Social Psychology, 30,* 24–30.

ZUBIN, J., ERON, L. D., & SCHUMER, F. (1965). *An experimental approach to projective techniques.* New York: Wiley.

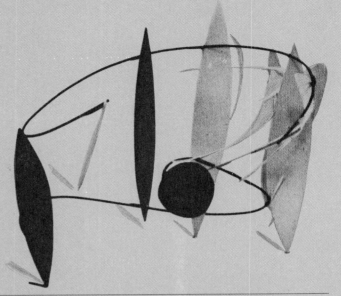

INDEXES

Author Index

Kanfer, F. H., 337, 367, 370, 376, 414, 425, 436
Karoly, P., 352, 414
Karp, L., 100, 264
Karp, S. A., 446
Kassorla, I. C., 318, 330
Katz, S. H., 143
Kaye, C., 454
Kazdin, A. E., 83, 344, 348, 370–371, 434
Kelleher, R. T., 286
Kelley, H. H., 122, 241–242
Kelley, S. C., 284
Kelly, E. L., 78, 172, 216–217
Kelly, G. A., 199, 205–209, 223–224, 227, 241, 359, 377
Keniston, K., 487
Kenny, D. A., 244
Kent, R. N., 359
Kety, S. S., 178, 180, 335
Keyes, M., 183
Kidder, J. D., 325, 352
Kiesler, D. J., 83
Kihlstrom, J. F., 101, 266
Kim, M. P., 222
Kirker, W. S., 249
Klaiber, E. L., 447
Klausmeier, H. J., 445
Klein, D. F., 185
Kleitman, N., 30
Klerman, G., 185
Klinger, E., 32, 62
Kobasa, S. C., 408
Kobayashi, Y., 447
Koch, C., 429
Kogan, N., 152
Kohlberg, L., 178, 449, 485–487, 489
Kopp, C. G., 414, 418, 425, 428, 436
Koriat, A., 410
Kostlan, A., 76
Krane, R. V., 307
Krantz, D. S., 359, 361
Krasner, L., 87, 332–333, 337, 354, 375
Krech, K., 77
Kremers, J., 75
Kris, E., 53
Kruglanski, A. W., 398
Krumboltz, J. D., 8
Kuethe, J. L., 104
Kuhn, D., 458–459
Kuiper, N. A., 249
Kupers, C. J., 426–427
Kurdirka, N. Z., 156
Kurland, S. H., 105
Kurtines, W., 489

LaBarre, W., 258
Laing, R. D., 85, 255
Lakin, M., 238
Lamberth, J., 331
Landfield, A. W., 224
Landman, J. T., 83
Lang, P. J., 321, 347, 371
Langer, E. J., 101, 243, 253, 393, 425, 494–495
Lao, R. C., 170, 393
Latané, B., 482–484
Lazarus, A. A., 319, 321, 342
Lazarus, R. S., 96, 104, 108, 264, 408, 410
Lazovik, A. D., 321, 347, 371
Leary, T., 133, 209–210
Lee, L. C., 445
Lefcourt, H. M., 169, 170
Lepper, M. R., 353
Leventhal, H., 156, 263
Levin, H., 451
Levin, P. F., 264
Levine, M., 169
Levine, R., 96
Levinger, G., 469
Levinson, D. J., 156
Levitt, E. E., 103
Lewin, K., 196–199, 389, 390
Lewinsohn, P. M., 394–395
Lewis, M., 448–449
Lieberman, M. A., 233
Liebert, R. M., 294, 296, 427–428, 480
Lief, H. I., 410
Lighthall, F. F., 403
Lindzey, G., 143
Little, B. R., 177, 309
Little, K. B., 76
Litwin, G. H., 210
Lobitz, W. C., 359
Locksley, A., 462
Loehlin, J. C., 143, 181–182
Loevinger, J., 131, 173
Loewenstein, R. M., 53
Longo, N., 104
LoPicolo, J., 359
Lorenz, K. Z., 474
Lovaas, O. I., 318, 330, 351–352, 359
Lowell, E. L., 65, 67, 274
Luborsky, L., 83, 93
Lueck, H., 243
Luft, J., 75
Lykken, D. T., 184
Lyle, C., 219
Lott, A. J., 279
Lott, B. E., 279

McAlister, A. L., 362
McAllister, B. H., 411, 500
McCall, R. B., 147
McCandless, B. R., 391
McCardel, J. B., 233
McCleary, R. A., 96
McClelland, D. C., 4, 65, 67, 69, 70, 77, 96, 274
McDonald, F. J., 486
McFall, R. M., 349, 359
McGaugh, J. L., 366
McGinnies, E., 94, 95
McGlashin, T. H., 103
McGowan, B. K., 306
McHugh, R. B., 78
McKay, G., 411
McKenna, F. P., 79
McKeown, T., 144
McKinley, J. C., 153
McNemar, Q., 445
Maccoby, E. E., 443, 445–446, 448, 451–452, 454–455
Maccoby, N., 362
MacFarlane, J. W., 66
MacKinnon, C., 487
Maddi, S. R., 408
Madison, P., 99
Magnusson, D., 135, 162, 175–176, 199, 493, 495
Maher, B. A., 178, 397
Mahoney, K., 356–357
Mahoney, M. J., 356–357, 363, 367, 434–436
Mallick, S. K., 391
Malmo, R. B., 324, 396
Manderlink, G., 353
Mandler, G., 236, 385, 388, 396
Mangan, C. E., 105, 107
Mann, R. D., 159
Manz, W., 243
Marks, I. M., 349
Marks, J., 219
Marks, P. A., 155
Markus, G. B., 143
Markus, H., 143, 214, 249
Marsden, G., 221
Marshall, G. D., 101, 102, 263
Marston, A. R., 349
Martin, B., 169
Maslach, C., 101, 102, 263
Masling, J. M., 151, 172
Maslow, A. H., 199, 210–211, 228
Mason, G., 92
Masters, J. C., 356, 426, 435
Masters, W. H., 12, 359–360
Masuda, M., 408

Subject Index

Dehumanization, 480–482
Delay of gratification,
  and cognitive transformation, 422
  correlates of, 423–425
  defined, 414
  in development, 423
  effects of models on, 416–418
  and expectations, 416
  experimental paradigm, 177, 415–416
  necessity of, 414–415
  psychoanalytic view of, 418
  and self-distraction, 421
  summary of research, 422–423
  use in classifying situations, 177
  and waiting behavior, 418–422
Depression,
  Beck's approach to, 364
  characteristics of, 394
  and frustration, 394
  as insufficient reinforcement, 394-396
  treatment of, 395–396
Desensitization,
  efficacy of, 344
  procedure, 341–343
  and symptom substitution, 340
  in the treatment of asthma, 343
  use of biofeedback in, 343
  use of relaxation in, 343
  uses of, 343–344
Deviance,
  behavioral approach to, 331
  disease models of, 332
  and legal rights, 335–336
  and mental illness, 334–335
  phenomenological approach to, 227–238
  as problematic behavior, 335
  see also Adaptation
Diffusion of responsibility, 480–482, 484
Disease models,
  criticisms of, 332–333
  of deviance, 332
  hazards of, 334
Dreams,
  activity during, 31
  daydreaming, 32
  Freudian dream symbols, 38
  Freud's interpretation of, 62
  post-Freudian research, 30–32
  REM and NREM sleep, 30
  use in psychoanalysis, 81
  usefulness in psychodynamic assessment, 62–63

  see also Psychoanalytic treatment; Psychodynamic assessment

Ego, 32–33
  see also Ego-control; Ego-resiliency
Ego-control, 168–169
Ego-resiliency, 168–169, 425
Ego psychology,
  see Neo-Freudian psychoanalytic developments
Emotion,
  and causal attribution, 264
  and cognition, 260
  cross-cultural expression of, 260
  defined, 256
  effects on performance, 403–404
  and frustration, 386–387
  impact on behavior of, 264
  measurement of, 324
  physiological responses to, 256–257
  theories of, 257
Emotionality,
  individual differences in, 13–14
  and self-actualization, 209–210
Encoding strategies,
  as a person variable, 309
Encounter groups,
  aim of, 232
  described, 231–232
  effects of, 232–233, 234
  theoretical bases of, 232
  and the unconscious, 237–238
Environmental psychology,
  defined, 493
Environments,
  classification of, 493, 494
  constraints on behavior by, 499–500
  impact of, 493–494
  interaction of person and, 495
  and social behavior "scripts", 494–495
  see also Situation
Existential theories,
  see Phenomenological theories
Existentialism, 200, 209
Expectancies,
  and aggression, 475, 478
  in behavior prediction, 293
  and happiness, 387
  measurement of, 321
  as a person variable, 309–310
  types of, 310
  and subjective values, 293
Experimentation,
  control group, 16
  defined, 15

illustrated, 16–17
independent and dependent variables, 15–16
random assignment, 17
use of statistics in, 18
Extraversion-introversion, 47
  as personality type, 118
  as trait dimension, 126–127, 129

Factor analysis,
  defined, 159
  problems with, 160
Family therapy, 85–87
Field theories,
  assumptions of, 196
  and Lewin's life space, 198
Free association,
  defined, 62
  Jungian view of, 47–48
  use in psychoanalysis, 81–82
  usefulness in psychodynamic assessment, 62–63
  see also Psychodynamic assessment
Freudian theory,
  see Psychodynamic theory
Frustration,
  and aggression, 388–389
  defined, 384–385
  and depression, 394
  diverse effects of, 389
  and emotional arousal, 386–387
  and helplessness, 391–392
  methods of coping with, 390
  and persistence, 388
  and self-distraction, 421
Frustration-aggression hypothesis, 388–389
Functional analyses,
  case examples, 328–329
  defined, 327–329
  of self-destructive behavior, 330
  Skinner's approach to, 276–277
Functional autonomy, 196

Genetics,
  disorders, 179
  effects on intelligence, 179
  and individual differences, 181
  and personality traits, 178
  and schizophrenia, 180–181
  versus environment, in studies of twins, 181–182
Gestalt psychology, 197–198
Global assessment,
  defined, 73
  use of situational testing in, 72–73

Obesity,
  and biology, 432–434
  and cues for eating, 429, 432
  and weight control, 434–436
Observational (cognitive) learning,
  acquisition vs. performance in, 297
  of assertive behavior, 347–349
  basic processes of, 299–300
  described, 295–296
  in the development of fear, 300
  effects on delay of gratification, 416–
    418
  in fear modification, 344–347
  and modeling of aggression, 479–480
  products of, 299–300
  role of expectations in, 297–298
Oedipal conflict, 43–44
Operant conditioning,
  and discrimination, 284–285
  examples of, 283
  and generalization, 284
  mechanics of, 282–283
  reinforcement in, 282–284
  see also Behavior change;
    Reinforcement
Orality,
  in the infant, 42

Perceptual defense,
  defined, 94
  research strategies, 94
  problems in research on, 94–95
  see also Cognitive avoidance;
    Repression-sensitization continuum
Personal Construct Theory, 206
Personal constructs,
  and adaptation, 208
  behavioral referents for, 207, 227
  case of Gary W., 224, 224–226
  as a cause of behavior, 213
  defined, 206
  and individual as scientist, 207
  and Kelly's Rep Test, 223
  and psychotherapy, 208
  and role-playing, 208
  see also Constructive alternativism
Personality,
  behavioral conception of, 373
  biological bases of, 178
  constructivist view of, 504
  defined, 4
  development of, in psychodynamic
    theory, 41–43
  dynamics in Lewinian theory, 199

as a field of study, 5–6
  influence of genes on, 180–183
  Jung's conception of, 48
  overview of major approaches to, 503
  resistance to a science of, 10–11
  of situations, 176
Personality assessment,
  see Behavioral assessment;
    Phenomenological assessment;
    Psychodynamic assessment; Trait
    assessment
Phenomenological assessment,
  accuracy of self-report in, 218–219
  case of Gary W., 217–218
  use of interviews in, 220–222
  see also Semantic differential; Role
    Construct Repertory (Rep) Test
Phenomenological theories,
  basic assumptions of, 194–195
  common themes, 212–213
  comparison to behavior theories, 376–
    377
  criticism of behaviorism by, 288–289
  evolution of, 267
  and existentialism, 199–200, 209,
    212–213
  overview, 268
  sources of, 195
  strengths and weaknesses, 266
  and the unconscious, 235–237
  see also Existentialism; Field theories;
    Personal Construct Theory; Self
    theories
Preparedness (biological),
  alternative explanations of, 307
  defined, 306–307
  effect on learning, 305
  and humans, 307
Projective techniques,
  and ambiguous stimuli, 65–66
  consistency in scoring and
    interpretation, 67
  rationale for, in psychodynamic
    assessment, 66–67
  and situational testing, 71–73
  see also Dreams; Free association;
    Rorschach; Thematic Apperception
    Test
Prototypes,
  and trait theory, 134
Psychoanalytic theory,
  see Psychodynamic theory
Psychoanalytic treatment,
  criticisms of, 83–85
  and the "good" patient, 84–85

nature of insight in, 83
  resistance in, 81–82
  therapeutic goal, 82
  transference in, 82
  use of free association and dreams,
    81
  value of, 83–84
Psychodynamic assessment,
  case of Gary W., 59–62
  case of Pearson Brack, 318
  and clinical intuition, 62
  use of a diagnostic council in, 71–72
  use of situational tests in, 72–73
  use of projective techniques in, 67–
    71
  see also Clinical judgment; Global
    assessment
Psychodynamic theory,
  and anxiety, 34–35
  and conflict, 34, 80–81
  defense mechanisms in, 35, 89–90
  and expanding consciousness, 209–
    210
  fixation in, 43
  "Freudian slips" and "mistakes",
    39–40, 91
  and the healthy personality, 80
  identification in, 43–44
  image of the person in, 44–45
  libido, 36–37
  motivational determinism in, 41
  and the origin of neuroses, 39
  origins of, 27–29
  overview, 110
  personality development in, 41–43
  psychic structure, 29–32
  psychosexual stages in, 41–43
  regression in, 43
  sex and aggression in, 29–30
  strengths and weaknesses, 109–110
  see also Repression; Unconscious
Psychometric assessment,
  see Trait assessment
Psychometric testing,
  ethical concerns in, 163
  and intelligence, 158–159
  and moderator variables, 152
  objectivity in, 150–151
  origins of, 138
  and overlapping measures, 157–
    158
  scoring, 148–149
  use of correlations in, 151–152
  use of self-report in, 147, 149–150,
    153

and childhood socialization, 452–453

correlates of, 455–456

defined, 447

during development, 454–455

and moderator variables, 454–455

role of consistency strivings in, 449–450

and social learning, 450–451

and social structure, 452–453

stability of, 456

and "unconscious ideologies", 456–457

see also Androgyny; Sex differences

Sexual preference,
  influences on, 440

Situation (psychological environment),
  in behavioral assessment, 318–319

  and behavior prediction, 176

  and competence, 497

  constraints on behavior, 499–500

  in interaction with person, 175

  in Lewin's life space, 198–199

  a personality of, 177

  powerful and weak, 497

  specific effects of, 495–496

  see also Environments

Social cognition, 241

Social inference,
  impact of base-rate data on, 246

Social interaction,
  and competence, 468–469

  and physical attraction, 467–468

  as a reciprocal influence process, 500–501

  reciprocity in, 470

  and similarity, 469–470

Social learning assessment,
  focus of, 302–303

  see Behavioral assessment

Social learning theories,
  and adaptive performance, 310

  and behavioral specificity, 302

  and complex behavior patterns, 304

  and deviance, 337

  expectancies and values in, 293

  and morality, 488–489

  overview of, 377–378

  role of stimulus in, 303–304

  and "scripted" behavior, 494–495

  and sex-typing, 450–451

  strengths and weaknesses, 374, 375–377

  view of person in, 304

see also Behavior theories; Behavioral assessment; Observational learning

Stereotypes,
  cognitive economics and, 245

  and expectations, 246–247

  and implicit personality theories, 244

  and retrospective distortions, 247–248

  and trait assessment, 161–162

  use in personality assessment, 75

Stimulus,
  ambiguity in psychodynamic assessment, 58

  role of, in social learning theories, 303–304

Stimulus control,
  described, 353

  in treatment of insomnia, 353–354

  and weight control, 435

Stress,
  cognitive appraisal of, 408

  measurement of, 408, 409

  methods of coping with, 409, 410–411, 425

  and physical illness, 408

  sources of, 384

  see also Frustration

Subconscious information processing, 100–101

  and hypnosis, 101

Subjective values,
  as person variable, 311

Subliminal perception,
  described, 96

  research on, 96–97

Superego, 33

Suppression,
  defined, 90

  and repression, 90–91

Thematic Apperception Test (TAT),
  illustrated, 65

  and need for achievement, 67–71

  rationale and scoring, 65

  use in psychodynamic assessment, 63–65

Therapeutic communities, 354–356

Trait assessment,
  case of Gary W., 152–153

  and individual behavior prediction, 173–174

  and intelligence, 158–159

  overview, 189

  and personal revelations, 164

and personality-rating semantics, 161–162

and stereotypes, 161

strengths and weaknesses, 187–188

use of factor analysis in, 159–160

use of self-report in, 147, 149–150

see also California *F* Scale; Factor analysis; Psychometric testing

Traits,
  Allport's conception of, 122–124

  basic dimensions of, 131–133, 161

  biological bases of, 178

  Catell's conception of, 124–126

  consistency of, 120, 171–173

  as construct of perceiver, 161–162, 244

  defined, 121

  as dependent upon person and situation, 175

  as explanations of behavior, 121–122

  generality and stability of, 128

  and prototypes, 134–135

  stability over time of, 171–173

  as summaries of "act trends", 135

  utility of, 174–176

  see also Ego-control; Ego-resiliency

Transcendental meditation, 233

  see also Meditation

Type A behavior,
  characteristics of, 120

  correlates of, 120

Unconscious,
  as a force in human learning, 98

  and awareness, 98

  conflict in, 80–81

  and encounter groups, 237–238

  function of, 90

  in Jungian psychology, 47–48

  "Mistakes" in psychodynamic theory, 39–40, 91

  and phenomenological theory, 235–236

  and subliminal perception, 96

  see also Hypnosis; Projective techniques; Repression

Validity,
  defined, 165

  types of, 165–166

Vicarious conditioning,
  defined, 300

  in the development of fear, 300

  see also Observational learning

Unmasking The Face (Reprint Edition) Paul Ekman and Wallace V. Friesen, Consulting Psychologists Press, 1984. P. 263, Six Flags Great Adventure, Jackson, New Jersey.

Chapter 11: pp. 275 and 276, The Bettmann Archive, New York. P. 279, Erika Stone/Peter Arnold, New York. P. 282, Helena Frost, New York. P. 285, Rick Smolan/Stock, Boston.

Chapter 12: p. 294, courtesy Albert Bandura, Stanford University Psychology Department, California. P. 296, Alan Carey/The Image Works, Woodstock, New York. P. 298, courtesy Albert Bandura, Stanford University Psychology Department, California. P. 308. Samuel Teicher, Hewlett, New York. P. 309, Rick Smolan/Stock, Boston.

Chapter 13: p. 334, Burke Uzzle/Woodfin Camp, New York.

Chapter 14: p. 346, courtesy Albert Bandura, Stanford University Psychology Department. P. 352, Photos by Allan Grant, Los Angeles. P. 370, Rick Smolan/Stock, Boston.

Chapter 15: p. 388, Sepp Seitz/Woodfin Camp, New York. P. 392, Bill Stanton, New York.

Chapter 17: p. 450, Yan Lukas/Photo Researchers, New York. P. 457, A. T. & T. Historical Archives, New York.

Chapter 18: pp. 476 and 477, copyright © 1965 Stanley Milgram. From the film *Obedience* distributed by the New York University Film Library, New York. Courtesy Alexandra Milgram, New York. P. 481, courtesy Professor Philip G. Zimbardo, Stanford University, California. P. 483, Paul Sequeira/Rapho/Photo Researchers, New York.